CONTENTS

FOURTH EDITION

COGNITIVE PSYCHOLOGY

Robert L. Solso

University of Nevada, Reno

ALLYN AND BACON
Boston • London • Toronto • Sydney • Tokyo • Singapore

The book is dedicated to my mother, Elizabeth Pressly Solso, who taught me to love life, and to the memory of my father, F. I. Solso, who taught me to love knowledge.

Copyright © 1995, 1991, 1988, 1979 by Allyn & Bacon
A Simon & Schuster Company
Needham Heights, MA 02194

Executive Editor: Laura Pearson
Editorial Assistant: Jennifer Normandin
Production Administrator: Marjorie Payne
Editorial-Production Service: Chestnut Hill Enterprises, Inc.
Text Designer: The Book Company
Cover Administrator: Linda Dickinson
Cover Designer: Susan Slovinsky
Composition/Prepress Buyer: Linda Cox
Manufacturing Buyer: Megan Cochran

Credits appear on page 577, which constitutes an extension of the copyright page.

Library of Congress Cataloging-in-Publication Data
Solso, Robert L.
   Cognitive psychology / Robert L. Solso.—4th ed.
     p.   cm.
   Includes bibliographical references and indexes.
   ISBN 0-205-15831-5
    1. Cognition.   2. Cognitive psychology.   I. Title.
BF311.S653   1995
153—dc20   94-36865
                                               CIP

Printed in the United States of America
10 9 8 7 6 5 4 3 2 1   99   98   97   96   95   94

SECTION III MEMORY

SECTION IV MNEMONICS, EXPERTS, AND IMAGERY

PREFACE

To the Student

During the history of cognitive psychology, much has been learned about the way people perceive and process information. These developments are due to the dedicated efforts of numerous cognitive psychologists aided by an improved technology. This combination has yielded a rich harvest of knowledge about perception, memory, neurocognition, thinking, and information processing—indeed, all of human cognition.

Among the important recent findings in cognition is the connection between the thinking mind and its corresponding neurophysiological activities. Reflecting the importance of brain studies, the United States Congress passed a resolution designating the 1990s as the Decade of the Brain. As we are about to leave this remarkable century of advancements in all areas of science and enter perhaps an even more exciting one, I hope to have caught the spirit of these lively times by reporting accurately and in a stimulating way the current findings and theories in cognition.

Cognitive psychology, along with other scientific endeavors, is the result of the effort of individual scholars. Throughout this book I have introduced you to some of these important figures by including their photographs.

I hope the contents of this book will let you know where we cognitive psychologists have been; report accurately the best ideas, theories, and experiments; and prepare you to comprehend future developments.

Some students may choose to follow a career in a branch of the cognitive sciences. If the contents of this book stimulate you to work toward continuing the job we have started, the labor will have been entirely rewarded.

Finally, I am interested in what you think about the book and would welcome your reactions and comments.

To the Professor

It has been twenty-five years since the first edition of *Cognitive Psychology* by Solso was published. Writing the first edition was particularly challenging because I had no example to follow, except the now classic book of the same title by Ulric Neisser, which was published in 1967, and the hundreds of articles and symposia papers that were unsystematically strewn about my office and home. I did have the good fortune to sit in on Ed Smith's class on cognition at Stanford University; his taxonomy is still used (although, somewhat modified) in the present book and in many others. Now, there are a score or more textbooks on this theme and many more that discuss topics as far ranging as cognition and the law, cognition and psychotherapy, cognition and society, and cognition and education, to name but a few. Since those early days of the "cognitive revolution," the sphere of influence of those interested in this topic has expanded greatly, far exceeding what I envisioned a quarter of a century ago. However, it is my impression that the major topics that formed the discipline during that time are still viable today, although the emphasis has shifted over the past twenty-five years.

In this edition I have tried to retain the best features of the previous editions while adding important new material and changing the emphasis of the book to reflect recent changes. In particular, I have retained the comprehensive nature of the book. There is a risk in writing a comprehensive text in that students may feel overwhelmed with the immense amount of material to cover in a single course. My advice: You do not have to cover the whole book in a single term. More will be said on that a little later.

With the field undergoing significant change and development during the past decade, it has become increasingly difficult to cover all areas of cognition reasonably. I have emphasized mainstream studies and ideas and have eliminated some of the more offbeat aspects of the field. Although there is a need for specialized books that are written from a specific point of view, I trust that many will welcome a comprehensive book on cognitive psychology, a task which only a few writers have attempted.

Those of you who have used *Cognitive Psychology* for the past few years will be pleased to find that for material that presents contradictory findings, an exposition is given, followed by a summary of the results in which certain conclusions are made. This summary was first used in the third edition and is in response to the needs many of you have expressed to me. Also, I have maintained an active laboratory in which some of the ideas expressed in this book are further tested by my students and me. We have occasionally referred to this work for the purpose of both clarifying a principle and letting the reader know that cognitive psychology is an active, ongoing science. It is hoped that such studies will lead some to continue the search for more complete answers to some of the questions raised.

As with the third edition, most chapters begin with a brief review of the historical antecedents of the topic presented; however, in some chapters this review has been shortened to make room for current information. Since the field of cognitive psychology changes so rapidly, I believe it is important for readers to know something of the history of a topic so that they may understand new information within the context of past events.

In addition to adding new references to each chapter and removing some out-of-date studies, this edition emphasizes the following things:

- There is a significant addition of new physiological information and related topics, including recent findings in neurocognitive imaging technology. The inclusion of these topics is in response to the rapidly changing nature of cognitive psychology and important new discoveries in the field of brain science and neurocognition.

- The organization of the chapters and sections follows an information-processing sequence that starts with the perception of signals by the sensory/brain system to higher order processes such as memory, language, and thinking. The present edition contains six sections that follow the above organizational schema. I believe the addition of sections reflects the increasingly diverse nature of the field.

- Attention has been given to neurally inspired models of connectionism and parallel distributed processing (PDP). Although these matters are concentrated in a few places (Chapters 1, 2, and 8), they also are distributed throughout the book.

- Each chapter has a section called Critical Thinking in which the reader is encouraged to analyze or contemplate the immediate subject matter. I have found that these sections, and others you might invent, are a good means to stimulate discussion in class. Students tend to think more deeply about issues and probably retain the knowledge better when topics are discussed. Class discussion also provides an opportunity for students to practice and improve their analytic skills.

- This edition is more colorful than previous ones. The second color has been added, not to make the book more glitzy (although it does that too) but to enliven the pages, to make ideas appear more distinct, and to enhance the visualization of figures and tables. The result is a book that is more appealing and, ultimately, more instructive. I hope you find the use of a second color pleasing and helpful in your effort to offer an interesting and informative class on cognitive psychology.

- Finally, there are photographs of many cognitive scientists in this edition. Since cognitive psychology is largely the invention of cognitive psychologists, it seems only fitting that these inventors be recognized. The selection of photographs was largely a matter of judgment and availability. Some important figures do not appear due to their personal desire for anonymity, the unavailability of appropriate photographs, or space limitations. I am deeply indebted to those who did respond to my request for photographs and to others who allowed me to use my own candid photographs. Thank you all.

In writing a comprehensive book on cognitive psychology, it is my intention to present a work that would be attractive to many professors who prefer to select their favorite topics for coverage in a one-term class. It may be possible to cover all sixteen chapters in one course, but most professors have told me that they select certain chapters and not others. (In my own class I cover all but one or two chapters, although an enterprising graduate student of mine covered the entire book in one five-week summer session!) I have written the text so that some chapters may be dropped without losing the continuity of the book. Following are several suggested models:

1. A brief general introduction to cognition—Chapters 1, 3, 4, 6, 7, 11, 12, 14, and 15.
2. A neuro-cognitive system—Chapters 1, 2, 3, 5, 6, 7, 8, 11, 13, and 16.
3. An applied approach—Chapters 1, 3, 4, 5, 6, 7, 8, 9, 10, 13, 14, 15, and 16.

4. A thinking-problem-solving emphasis—Chapters 1, 4, 5, 7, 8, 10, 13, 14, 15, and 16.

5. A Memory Course—Chapters 1, 2, 3, 6, 7, 8, 9, 10, 11, 12, 13, and 14.

6. A Cognitive-Developmental Course—Chapters 1, 4, 5, 6, 7, 8, 9, 10, 11, 12, 13, 14, and 15.

These models of chapters are only basic suggestions to which chapters of your own liking and/or specialty may be added or other melds created.

Many people have contributed to this book, and it is a pleasure for me to recognize them here. Many of you, faithful users over the years, have expressed your opinions of the book to me in person or by letter. Your continued use is most deeply appreciated, and your comments have been most important. Also, the students who have written or given me feedback in several ways have helped me keep in contact with the most important group—namely, the people to whom the book is directed. Many researchers have kept me informed on their latest discoveries, and to you I am particularly obliged. In numerous instances many of you have sent me preprints and reprints of your important work from sources that would otherwise be practically impossible to find. The manuscript for the third edition was professionally reviewed by A. Bancroft, Indiana University; Cheryl Arnold, Hendrix College; Dr. Christian McGlasson, St. Cloud State University; Paul Jose, Loyola University of Chicago; Jonathan Golding, University of Kentucky; Gary Raney, University of Massachusetts/Amherst; Scott W. Brown, University of Southern Maine; Tom Hewett, Drexel University; John W. Webster, Towson State University; Michael A. Bokoros, Central Connecticut State University; Marilyn L. Turner, Wichita State University; and Gerald Gillespie, Kansas Wesleyan University. These reviewers, plus the reviewers from previous editions, have helped keep me on track, and to each I express my thanks and gratitude. The editor from Allyn and Bacon was Laura Pearson, and her assistant was Jennifer Normandin. They provided expert advice and support throughout this project and are gratefully acknowledged here. Myrna Breskin of Chestnut Hill Enterprises provided exemplary assistance in the production of this book, the contents of which are immeasurably enhanced by her extraordinary skill and patience. Finally, my graduate assistant, Alan Rees, from the University of Nevada, Reno deserves special acknowledgment for his reading and critical analysis of the entire third and fourth editions. To all, I humbly acknowledge your invaluable assistance and express my heartfelt thanks.

Introduction

Thanks to the development of new logical tools, the diverse deployments of the computer, the application of the scientific method to human psychological processes and cultural practices, our deeper and more rigorous understanding of the nature of language, and the many discoveries about the organization and operation of the nervous system, we have attained a more sophisticated grasp on the issues put forth originally by Plato, Descartes, Kant, and Darwin.

Howard Gardner

WHAT IS COGNITIVE PSYCHOLOGY?

When you read and think about this question, you are engaging in cognition. Cognitive psychology deals with the perception of information (you read the question), it deals with understanding (you comprehended the question), it deals with thought (you asked yourself whether you knew the answer), and it deals with the formulation and production of an answer (you may have said, "Cognitive psychology is the study of thinking."). Cognition touches all parts of the perceptual, memory, and thinking processes and is a prominent characteristic of all people.

Cognitive psychology is the scientific study of the thinking mind and is concerned with:

- How we attend to and gain information about the world
- How that information is stored in memory by the brain
- How that knowledge is used to solve problems, to think, and to formulate language

Cognitive psychology involves the total range of psychological processes—from sensation to perception, neuroscience, pattern recognition, attention, consciousness, learning, memory, concept formation, thinking, imaging, remembering, language, intelligence, emotions, and developmental processes—and cuts across all the diverse fields of behavior. The course we have charted—the scientific study of the thinking mind—is both ambitious and exciting. Because the scope is great, the range of studies will be diverse, and because the topic deals with viewing the human mind from a new perspective, your views of the intellectual nature of humankind may be changed profoundly.

This chapter is labeled "Introduction"; however, in a sense the entire book is an introduction to cognitive psychology. This chapter offers a general picture of cognitive psychology, reviews its history, and describes theories of how knowledge is represented in the human mind.

Before we consider the technical aspects of cognitive psychology, it maybe useful to gain some perspective on the assumptions we humans make in processing information. To illustrate the way we interpret information, consider, for example, a common event: a motorist asking a police officer for directions. Although the cognitive processes involved seem simple, they are not.

Motorist: Say, I'm new in this town; can you tell me how to get to Robbie Robotland?

Police Officer: Well, did you want the video games or computers, because they have two different stores.

M: Oh. Well . . .

P: I guess it doesn't make any difference because they're across the street from each other.

M: I'm looking for a thinking program—you know, something that simulates problem solving.

P: Well, they've got that in computers.

M: In computers?

P: Yes, in the software area. So . . . do you know where the coliseum is?

M: Is that the building with the kind of cone shape or is that the one that . . .

P: No, but you know where that is—that's the Expo site; remember, they had the Expo in 1988.

M: Oh yes, I know where the Expo is.

P: OK, that's the Expo site. Well, it's kind of hard to get there from there, but if you go down from where you are now, if you go down this street one stoplight and then to the flagpole, turn right one block to another light, and then make a left, go over the train tracks past the lake to the next stoplight near the old mill . . . Do you know where the old mill is?

M: Is that the street on the bridge that says "one-way street" up to the old mill?

P: No, it's two-way.

M: Oh, it must be the other bridge. OK, I know which street . . .

P: You can tell it by the large sign that says "Once you have lost a jewel you can never replace it." Something like that. It's an ad for a night deposit box. I call it the bozo box because it's the Bozwell Bank. Anyway, you'll go by the old mill—that's where La Strada's restaurant is, in the Eldorado—and you turn left—no, right—then one block turn left and that's Virginia. On Virginia Street you can't miss it. It's on the right-hand side of the street.

M: You're kidding. I'm staying in a motel on Virginia Street.

P: Yeh?

M: I was going the wrong direction. Here I am in the other end of town. Two blocks from my motel room! I could've walked there.

P: What motel are you in?

M: The Oxford Motel.

P: Oh, the Oxford?

M: Well, its not "primo," but they have a pretty good library.

P: Huh?

The episode described took less than two minutes, yet the amount of information perceived and analyzed by the two people is staggering.

How might a psychologist view the process? One way is in simple stimulus-response (S-R) terms, for example, a flagpole (stimulus) and a right turn (response). Some psychologists, especially those representing a traditional behavioristic approach to psychology, feel that the entire sequence of events can be adequately described (albeit in a much more detailed way) in these S-R terms. Although this position has certain appeal in its simplicity, it cannot adequately describe the cognitive systems involved in the exchange. To do so thoroughly, it is necessary to define and analyze specific components and then to integrate them into a large cognitive model. It is from just such a standpoint that cognitive psychologists examine the complex phenomena of human behavior.

Using the example on page 3, how might a cognitive psychologist view the process? He or she begins by making certain assumptions about the cognitive characteristics possessed by the motorist and the police officer. In the left column of Table 1.1 are the assumptions made; in the right column are the topics in cognitive psychology that deal with the assumptions.

INFORMATION-PROCESSING MODEL

These assumptions are then integrated into a larger system, or cognitive model. One model commonly embraced by cognitive psychologists is an information-processing model.

An information-processing model assumes that cognition can be analyzed into a series of stages. At each stage certain unique operations are performed on incoming information. The eventual response (for example, saying, "Oh yes, I know where the Expo is") is assumed to be the outcome of this series of stages and operations (for example, perception, coding of information, recall of information from memory, concept formation, judgment, and language production). Each stage receives information from preceding stages and then performs its unique function. Since all components of the

TABLE 1.1

Assumptions About Cognitive Characteristics

Assumption	Topic in Cognitive Psychology
Ability to detect and interpret sensory stimuli (e.g., visual and auditory)	Detection of sensory signals and neuroscience
Tendency to focus on certain sensory stimuli and to disregard others	Attention
Detailed knowledge of the physical characteristics of the environment	Knowledge
Ability to abstract certain parts of the event and integrate those parts into a well-structured schema that gives meaning to the total episode	Pattern recognition
Ability to extract meaning from letters and words	Reading and information processing
Capacity to retain immediate events and to integrate those events into an ongoing sequence	Short-term memory
Ability to form an image of a "cognitive map"	Mental imagery
Understanding on the part of each person of the role of the other	Thinking
Ability to use "memory tricks" to aid in recall of information	Mnemonics and memory
Tendency to store linguistic information in a general form	Abstraction of linguistic ideas
Ability to solve a problem	Problem solving
General ability to act in a meaningful way	Human intelligence
Inference that the directions can accurately be translated into a complex motor response (driving an automobile)	Language/motor behavior
Ability to recall quickly from long-term memory specific information that is immediately applicable to the present situation	Long-term memory
Ability to translate visual events into spoken language	Language processing
Knowledge that objects have a specific name	Semantic memory
Inability to perform perfectly	Forgetting and interference

information-processing model are in some way related to each other, it is difficult to identify an initial stage, but for convenience we can think of the sequence as starting with incoming stimuli.

These stimuli—the environmental cues in our example—are not directly represented in the police officer's brain but are transformed into neurological structures and meaningful symbols, what some cognitive psychologists have labeled "internal representations." On the most fundamental level, light (or sound) energy emanating from the perceived stimulus is transduced (converted) to neural energy, which in turn is processed through the above-mentioned hypothetical stages to form the internal repre-

Critical Thinking: Cognition

Cognition in Everyday Life

Throughout this book small sections on critical thinking about cognition will appear. In these parts you will be asked to use the knowledge of the current chapter in a critical thinking demonstration.

The next time you visit a supermarket or a mall, pause for a few moments and observe the various examples of cognitive psychology which surround you. Pay particular attention to: (1) the use of forms and colors to gain attention, (2) your own reaction to environmental cues (e.g., where do your eyes focus and how long do you look at an object or person), (3) the use of memory in understanding language, context, and the interpretation of the sights and sounds of your environment. Jot down your impressions of these matters and read them over in about a week. What principles discussed in this chapter apply?

sentation of the perceived object. This internal representation is understood by the police officer and, when combined with other contextual information, provides the basis for his answer to the question posed by the motorist.

Two important questions raised by the information-processing model are the subject of considerable debate among cognitive psychologists: First, what are the stages through which information is processed? Second, in what form is information represented in the human mind? Although there are no easy answers to these questions, a major portion of this book deals with both issues, and it will be useful to keep these questions in mind. One way cognitive psychologists have attempted to answer them is by incorporating into their research the techniques and theories of specific psychological disciplines, of which several are described here.

THE DOMAIN OF COGNITIVE PSYCHOLOGY

Modern cognitive psychology freely draws theories and techniques from twelve principal areas of research (see Figure 1.1): cognitive neuroscience, perception, pattern recognition, attention and consciousness, memory, representation of knowledge, imagery, language, developmental psychology, thinking and concept formation, human intelligence, and artificial intelligence. Each area is covered in its own chapter.

Cognitive Neuroscience

Only within the past few years have cognitive psychologists and cognitive neuroscientists (brain scientists) formed a close working relationship. Thus far, this union has produced some of the most provocative developments in the study of our mental character. Cognitive psychologists are seeking neurological explanations for their findings, and

FIGURE 1.1

Principal research areas of cognitive psychology.

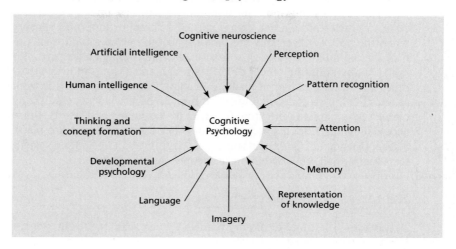

neuroscientists are turning to cognitive psychologists to explain observations made in their laboratories. In the earlier example of the befuddled motorist and the police officer, every part of the cognitive process—from sensation to memory to driving—is supported by basic electrochemical processes taking place in the brain and nervous system.

Perception

The branch of psychology directly involved with the detection and interpretation of sensory stimuli is perception. From experiments in perception, we have a good understanding of the sensitivity of the human organism to sensory signals and—more important to cognitive psychology—of the way we interpret sensory signals.

The police officer's description of the street scene is essentially dependent upon his ability to "see" the pertinent environmental cues. "Seeing," however, is not a simple matter. The sensory stimuli (in this case, largely visual) must be of a certain magnitude to be perceived. That is, if the motorist is to execute the described maneuvers, the cues must be of a certain strength. In addition, the scene is an ever-changing one. As the motorist's location changes, new cues emerge. Several cues become more important than others in the perceptual process. Signposts are distinguishable by their color, location, shape, and so on. Many of these images are in constant flux, and to translate the directions into performance the motorist must make a rapid adjustment in behavior.

The experimental study of perception has helped identify many of the parts of this process, some of which are discussed in Chapter 3. However, the study of perception alone does not adequately account for the expected performance; other cognitive systems are involved, including pattern recognition, attention, consciousness, and memory.

Pattern Recognition

Environmental stimuli rarely are perceived as single sensory events; they usually are perceived as part of a more meaningful pattern. The things we sense—see, hear, feel, taste, or smell—are almost always part of a complex pattern of sensory stimuli. Thus, when the police officer tells the motorist to "go over the train tracks past the lake . . . near the old mill," he is using words to describe complex objects (train tracks, lake, old mill). At one point the officer describes a sign and assumes the driver to be literate. But think about the problem of reading. Reading is a complex effort in which the reader is required to form a meaningful pattern from an otherwise meaningless array of lines and curves. By organizing the stimuli that make up letters and words, the reader may then access meaning from his or her memory. The entire process takes place in a fraction of a second, and considering all the neuroanatomical and cognitive systems involved, this feat—performed daily by billions of people—is wondrous.

Attention and Consciousness

Attention. The number of environmental cues available to the police officer and motorist is overwhelming. If the motorist attended to all or even a sizable number of them, he would never find the computer store. Although we are information-gathering creatures, it is evident that under normal circumstances we are also highly selective in the amount and type of information to which we attend. Our capacity to process information seems to be limited to two levels—sensory and cognitive. If too many sensory cues are imposed upon us at any given time, we can become overloaded; if we try to process too many events in memory, we also can become overloaded. The consequences of this may be a breakdown in performance.

In our example, the police officer—intuitively inferring that if he overloaded the system, performance would suffer—disregarded many cues the motorist undoubtedly would perceive. Despite the officers precaution, if the cartoon shown on page 3 displays an accurate representation of the motorist's cognitive map, he is hopelessly confused.

Consciousness. *Consciousness* is defined as "the current awareness of external or internal circumstances." Although it is a word "worn smooth by a million tongues (Miller, 1962), it is certainly one of the slipperiest concepts to define operationally. Rejected as being "unscientific" by the behaviorists, the word *consciousness* and the concept it represents simply will not fade away. For most people, consciousness is very real. When you glance at your watch and it reads "10:42 (P.M.)," you are conscious, or aware, of that external signal, much as the motorist was conscious of the directions given by the police officer and what those directions meant. However, your reading of the time also brings up another conscious thought, one that was initially activated by reading the time but is from "inside." That conscious thought might be, "It's getting late; I'd better finish this chapter and go to bed"—just as the motorist may have thought, "I hope this cop knows where Robbie Robotland is and tells me without giving me a hassle. Oh, where is my car registration. Is my insurance up to date? Act calm. I remember where the bridge is. I can 'see' the flagpole." All of these conscious thoughts may have flashed through the person's mind in a few seconds. *Consciousness,* the term that will not go away, has gained new respectability recently and now is a concept studied seriously in modern cognitive psychology.

Memory

Could the police officer describe the scene without memory? Certainly not, anymore than he could function without perception. In fact, memory and perception work together. In the example, two types of memory contribute to the officer's answer. The first type retains information for a limited time, long enough for him to carry on a conversation. This memory system seems to hold information for only a brief period, when new information displaces it. The entire exchange would have taken only about 120 seconds, and it is unlikely that all the details were permanently retained by either the police officer or the motorist. However, these details were stored in memory long enough for both of them to keep track of the sequence of elements making up the dialogue,[1] and some of the information may have found its way into their permanent memory. This first memory stage is called short-term memory (STM) or, in this case, a specialized form of memory called working memory.

On the other hand, a great amount of the answer is drawn from the police officer's long-term memory (LTM). Most obvious is his knowledge of the language. He didn't refer to the lake as a kumquat, or the Expo site as a rubber tire, or a street as a basketball; he drew words from his LTM and more or less used them correctly. There are additional cues that indicate LTM is involved in his description: ". . . Remember they had the Expo in 1988." In a fleeting second, he was able to recall information about an event of years before. That information did not come from an immediate perceptual experience; it was stored along with a vast number of other facts in his LTM.

The information available to the police officer came from his perception, STM, and LTM. In addition, we can infer that he was a thinking person, that the information was conceptualized in a scheme that "made sense."

Imagery

To answer the motorist's question, the police officer formed a mental image of the environment. This mental image was in the form of a cognitive map, a type of internal representation of the juxtaposed buildings, streets, street signs, stoplights, and so on. From the cognitive map he was able to draw out the significant cues, order them in a meaningful sequence, and transform those images into language that, we hope, would allow the motorist to construct a similar cognitive map. That re-formed cognitive map would then provide the motorist with a reasonable picture of the city, which could be transformed later into the act of driving an automobile along a certain route. Although the

---

[1]For example, the police officer had to retain briefly that the motorist was looking for "Robbie Robotland," that he knew the location of Expo, even (at least until he finished asking, "What motel are you in?") that the motorist was staying at a motel. Similarly, in the case of the motorist, he had to retain briefly that there were two Robotlands (to be able to reply that he wanted the one selling a thinking program); that the officer had asked if he knew the Expo site; that he had to pass the old mill; and so on.

experimental study of mental imagery is relatively new to psychology, some significant research has recently been reported; it is discussed in Chapter 10.

Representation of Knowledge

Fundamental to all human cognition is the representation of knowledge: how information, derived from sensory experiences, is symbolized and combined with the things stored in the brain. If we are to take literally the thought bubbles over the police officer and the lost motorist in the cartoon on page 3, the two had considerably different cognitive representations. One of the problems we have in communicating with each other is that the world is never identically represented. What you see, hear, smell, taste, or feel is not the same as what I experience and represent in memory; and what I experience and store in memory is not identical to your experience. In spite of these inherent dissimilarities between representations of knowledge, most humans do experience and depict experiences in similar enough ways to get along well in the world. Cognitive psychologists are especially interested in the topic of internal representations of knowledge, and a large part of this book deals with this topic in one form or another. The history of knowledge representations is reviewed later in this chapter.

Language

To answer the motorist's question successfully, the police officer had to have extensive knowledge of the language. That knowledge involves more than knowing the proper names for the landmarks. Equally importantly, it involves knowing the syntax (the customary arrangement and relationships of the words) of the language. The sequence of words, although it might not satisfy a fussy English professor, does communicate. In nearly every sentence uttered by the police officer, the essential grammatical rules are observed. The officer didn't say, "Got well that computers in they've"; he did say, "Well, they've got that in computers." We all can understand what he meant. In addition to finding the appropriate word in his lexicon and forming grammatically correct sentences, the officer had to coordinate the complicated motor reactions necessary to articulate the message. Also, communication between people is much more than what they say or write. Most obvious is the use of gestures, or body language, to communicate, and it is likely that both motorist and police officer pantomimed much of their meaning as they played out their verbal fugue. Finally, we may appreciate the richness and complexity of the connotative features of language. Reconsider this brief exchange at the end of the conversation: P: What motel are you in? M: The Oxford Motel. P: Oh, the Oxford? M: Well, its not "primo,". . . . Something about the intonation of the police officer's rejoinder, "Oh, the Oxford." was a signal read by the motorist as "Why are you staying in such a crummy dump?" Language and communication are far more than words.

Developmental Psychology

This is another important area of cognitive psychology that has been intensely studied. Recent experiments and theories in developmental cognitive psychology have greatly expanded our understanding of how cognitive structures develop. In the case of the example we have been studying, we can only infer that the speakers share developmental experiences that allow them (more or less) to understand each other. Chapter 13 deals with cognitive development.

Thinking and Concept Formation

Throughout this episode the police officer and the motorist exhibited an ability to think and to form concepts. When asked how to get to Robbie Robotland, the officer replied, after some intermediate steps, "Do you know where the coliseum is?" indicating that if the motorist knew this landmark, he could easily be directed to Robbie Robotland. When he didn't, the officer developed another plan for answering the question. Furthermore, the officer's use of some words (such as "train tracks," "old mill," "La Strada's restaurant") indicates that he had formed concepts that were similar to the concepts shared by the motorist. Later in the conversation, the police officer seemed baffled when the motorist told him that the Oxford Motel had "a pretty good library." Motels and libraries generally are incongruous, and knowing this, the officer, as you might have done, asked, "What kind of motel is that?"

Human Intelligence

The police officer and the motorist each made certain assumptions about the intelligence of the other. These assumptions included (but were not restricted to) the ability to understand a common language, to follow instructions, to convert verbal descriptions into actions, and to behave according to the rules of their culture. In Chapter 15 some recent cognitive theories of human intelligence are considered in detail.

Artificial Intelligence

The motorist is interested in finding "a thinking program," presumably for his personal computer. A program of this sort might emulate human cognition in a problem-solving task. To write a program that simulates thought, it is necessary to understand at least the fundamental attributes of human thought. This is a primary task of cognitive psychology. The specialty within computer science called artificial intelligence (AI) has had a major influence on the development of cognitive science, especially since the design of programs requires knowledge of how we process information. A related and fascinating topic (dealt with in detail in Chapter 16) addresses whether a "perfect robot" can simulate human behavior. Imagine, for example, a superrobot that has mastered all the perceptual, memory, thinking, and language abilities of humans. How would it answer the motorist's question? If the robot were identical to a human, the results would be identical, but consider the difficulty of developing a program that would make an error, as the police officer did ("you turn left"), and then, realizing its error, correct it ("no, right").

ANTECEDENTS OF MODERN COGNITIVE PSYCHOLOGY

As we have learned, a great portion of cognitive psychology deals with how knowledge is represented in the mind. The lively issue of representational knowledge—what some cognitive psychologists call internal representation or codes—has probably evoked the same fundamental questions over centuries: How is knowledge acquired, stored, transformed, and used? What is *consciousness* and where do conscious ideas originate? What is the nature of perception and memory? What is thought? How do these abilities develop? These questions reflect the essential issue of representational knowledge—how ideas, events, and things are stored and schematized in the mind.

In pursuing this topic, we trace the impressions of many scholars as they approach the question of how events outside the human subject are given internal action. A principal theme—one that spans many centuries of thought—is the structure of knowledge and the transformation, or processing, of knowledge.

The Representation of Knowledge: The Early Period

The fascination with knowledge can be traced to the earliest writings. Early theories were concerned with the seat of thought and memory. Ancient Egyptian hieroglyphics suggest that their authors believed that knowledge was localized in the heart—a view shared by the early Greek philosopher Aristotle but not by Plato, who held that the brain was the locus of knowledge.

Cognition, conation, and affect.

The traditional view of the mind was that it had three aspects: cognition, the actions of the intellect; conation, the actions of the "will"; and affect, the actions of the emotions. The idea that minds were composed of intellect, purpose, and emotions seems not at all unrealistic in today's world. (See Figure 1.2.)

FIGURE 1.2

The traditional view of the human head having three aspects.

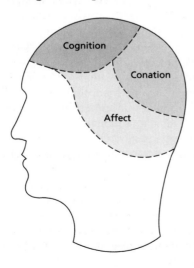

What the mind consisted of was considered by the Greek philosophers within the context of what we now identify as structure and process. Use of the terms *structure* and *process* did not really begin until the seventeenth century, and from that time on the focus of interest has shifted continually from one to the other.

The importance of these terms necessitates a brief digression from the historical review to define them more fully. *Structure*, as it relates to the organization or makeup of the cognitive system, is largely metaphorical, that is, the structures postulated are representative of the organization of mental entities, not literal descriptions of them. For example, the structure of memory is conceptualized by some theorists to consist of short-term and long-term memory, represented by the metaphor of two "storage boxes." Other such metaphors that we will deal with include "boxes in the head," "trees," "libraries," "levels of processing," "propositions," "abstractions," and "schemata."

As cognitive psychologists have combined efforts with brain scientists, many of the once hypothetical structures have become less conjectural and more demonstrable. Indeed, recent experiments have revealed the existence of neurological structures that correspond to some of the symbolic structures hypothesized by psychologists for years. These exciting findings are presented in following chapters.

The term *process* refers to systems of operations or functions that in some way analyze, transform, or change mental events. *Process* is active; *structure* is relatively static. Process will be encountered throughout this book in relation to memory coding, forgetting, thinking, concept formation, and so on.

Although modern psychologists still tend to emphasize either structure or process, there is an increased awareness that a definitive psychology of thought embraces both working together. The dichotomy and interaction are something like the structure of a bee's honeycomb and the processes that operate within it. The structure or architecture of the honeycomb is formed by the bees and is generally fixed (for example, its size, shape, position, and capacity), while the activity or processes (such as the gathering of nectar, its transformation into honey, and the storage of honey) are constantly in flux although acting in conjunction with the structure. Much of the current excitement in cognitive psychology is generated by the discovery of new structures and the processes associated with them and by the recognition that both structure and process contribute to our understanding of the cognitive nature of the human mind.

Structure and process work together in the processing of information, each partially the consequence of the other. Some structures are formed as information is processed, and processes are somewhat governed by structure. Because structures and processes work together, it is sometimes difficult to separate their functions in analytic cognitive psychology. In the final analysis, processes and structure must be integrated into a total cognitive system.

The Representation of Knowledge: The Middle Period

Renaissance philosophers and theologians seemed generally satisfied that knowledge was located in the brain. Some even went so far as to render its structure and locus graphically (see Figure 1.3). In the figure, knowledge is shown as acquired not only through the physical senses (*mundus sensibilis*—touch, taste, smell, vision, and hearing) but also from divine sources (*mundus intellectualis*—*Deus*). During the eighteenth

FIGURE 1.3

Seventeenth-century view of the structure and workings of the mind.

century, when philosophic psychology was brought to the point where scientific psychology could assume a role, the British empiricists—George Berkeley, David Hume, and, later, James Mill and his son John Stuart Mill—suggested that internal representation is of three types: (1) direct sensory events (*esse est percipi,* or "perception is reality"); (2) faint copies of percepts, or those that are stored in memory; and (3) transformation of these faint copies, as in associated thought. Hume, writing in 1748, said of the capacity for internal representation: "To form monsters, and join incongruous shapes and appearances, costs the imagination no more trouble than to conceive the most natural and familiar objects." This notion of internal representation and transformation postulates that internal representations are formed according to definable rules, and that such formation and transformation takes time and effort—assumptions underlying much of modern cognitive psychology. (The latter assumption is the basis of much current research in cognitive psychology. Subjects' reaction times are taken as a measure of the time and effort required to perform internal representations and transformations.) Also, recent findings in cognitive neurosciences have located anatomical structures related to specific psychological processes.

During the nineteenth century, psychologists started to break away from philosophy to form a discipline based on empirical results rather than on speculation. Conspicuous as a factor in this emergence was the activity of the early psychologists—Gustav Fechner, Franz Brentano, Hermann Helmholtz, Wilhelm Wundt, G. E. Müller, Oswald Külpe, Hermann Ebbinghaus, Sir Francis Galton, Edward Titchener, and William James.

By the last half of the nineteenth century, theories of the representations of knowledge were clearly dichotomous: there were those, led by Wundt in Germany and Titchener in the United States, that emphasized the structure of mental representation; and those, led by Brentano[2] in Austria, that emphasized the processes or acts. Brentano considered internal representations to be static entities of little value in psychology. He took the study of cognitive acts of comparing, judging, and feeling to be the proper subjects of psychology. The rival theories dealt with many of the same issues discussed two thousand years before by Plato and Aristotle. However, unlike the case with previous philosophic speculation, both theories were subjected to testing by experimentation.

About the same time in America, James critically analyzed the new psychology that was developing in Germany. He established the first psychological laboratory in America,[3] wrote the definitive work in psychology in 1890 (*Principles of Psychology*), and developed a well-reasoned model of the mind. James considered the subject matter of psychology to be our experience of external objects. Perhaps James's most direct link with modern cognitive psychology is in his view of memory, in which both structure and process play an important role. (Those ideas and their modern counterparts are discussed in Chapter 6.) F. C. Donders and James Cattell, contemporaries of James, were performing experiments using the perception of brief visual displays as a means of determining the time required for mental operations. Their reports frequently described experiments that dealt with topics we would now call cognitive psychology. The technique, subject matter, procedures, and even the interpretation of results of these early scientists seem to have anticipated the emergence of the discipline a half-century later.

The Representation of Knowledge: Early Twentieth Century

The representation of knowledge, as we have used this term, took a radical turn with the advent of twentieth-century behaviorism and Gestalt psychology. The behaviorist views of internal representation were cast in a framework of stimulus-response (S-R) psychology, and Gestalt theorists built elaborate conceptualizations of internal representation within the context of isomorphism—one-to-one relationship between representation and reality.

Psychological studies of mental processes as conceptualized in the late nineteenth century suddenly became unfashionable, displaced by behaviorism. Studies of internal mental operations and structures—such as attention, consciousness, memory, and thinking—were laid to rest and remained so for about fifty years. To the behaviorists, internal states were subsumed under the label of "intervening variables," which were de-

---

[2]See Boring, A *History of Experimental Psychology* (1950), for a more complete history.
[3]Both James and Wundt established laboratories in 1875.

© 1974 by Sidney Harris - *American Scientist* magazine.

fined as hypothetical constructs presumed to represent processes that mediated the effects of stimuli on responses and were neglected in favor of making observations on behavior (the things that animals did that could be observed) rather than on the mental processes that were the underpinning of behavior.

In 1932, some years before the cognitive revolution swept across psychology, learning psychologist Edward Tolman from the University of California at Berkeley published *Purposive Behavior in Animals and Man.* In this seminal work, Tolman observed that what rats learn in a maze is the lay of the land rather than simply a series of S-R connections. Tolman, conducting a series of ingenious experiments in which a rat was trained to find food by following a single roundabout pathway, found that, when given the opportunity to go directly to the food, the animal took it. It went directly to the place where the food was rather than follow the original pathway. The animal, according to Tolman's interpretation, gradually developed a "picture" of his environment that was

A major disagreement between behaviorists and cognitive psychologists concerns the nature of cognitive processes and "internal determinants" of behavior. For the behaviorist, cognitive processes such as thinking and sensing are behavioral; they are the things people do. For the cognitive psychologist, cognitive processes are the bases of behavior; they are essential to the study of the intellectual nature of the species, which is fundamental to our understanding of behavior.

later used to find the goal. This picture was called a cognitive map. The rats in Tolman's experiments exhibited their possession of a cognitive map by reaching a goal (the food) from a number of different starting points. This "internal map" was, in effect, the way information about their environment was represented. It would be unwarranted to suggest that Tolman's research directly affected modern cognitive psychologists, but his postulate about cognitive maps in animals did anticipate the contemporary preoccupation with how knowledge is represented in a cognitive structure.

Also in 1932 Sir Frederick Bartlett from Cambridge University wrote *Remembering*, in which he rejected the then popular view that memory and forgetting can be studied by means of nonsense syllables, as had been advocated by Ebbinghaus in Germany during the previous century and which was a popular topic in experimental psychology throughout the middle of the twentieth century. In the study of human memory, Bartlett argued, the use of rich and meaningful material under naturalistic conditions would yield far more significant conclusions. To study human memory, Bartlett had subjects read a story and then try to recall as much of the story as they could. He found that an important aspect of remembering a story was the subject's attitude toward the story. In Bartlett's words, "The recall is then a construction made largely on the basis of this attitude, and its general effect is that of a justification of the attitude." In effect, what you remember about a story is based on the overall impression created by the story, or the theme of the story. Recall of specific facts then tends to corroborate the principal theme. Bartlett introduced the concept of schema as a unifying theme that describes the essence of an experience. Schema theory plays a central role in modern theories of memory.

The fecund ideas of Tolman in America and Bartlett in England ran contrary to the intellectual zeitgeist of the 1930s, which was centered in other accounts of animal and

Edward C. Tolman (1886–1959).
Developed the concept of cognitive map.
Photograph courtesy of Archives of the
History of American Psychology,
University of Akron, Akron, Ohio 44303.

human behavior. Nevertheless, in retrospect, it is possible to appreciate the visionary nature of their work and how much it influenced the thinking of future cognitive psychologists.

The Reemergence of Cognitive Psychology

In the 1950s interest again began to focus on attention, memory, pattern recognition, images, semantic organization, language processes, thinking, and even consciousness (the most dogmatically eschewed concept), as well as other "cognitive" topics once considered outside the boundary of experimental psychology (vis-à-vis behaviorism). New journals and professional groups were founded as psychologists began more and more to turn to cognitive psychology. As cognitive psychology became established with even greater clarity, it was plain that this was a brand of psychology different from that in vogue during the 1930s and 1940s. Among the most important forces accounting for this neocognitive revolution were the following:

- *The "failure" of behaviorism.* Behaviorism, which generally studied overt responses to stimuli, failed to account for the diversity of human behavior, as in the case of language (see the earlier analysis of the conversation between the police officer and motorist). Furthermore, there were some topics ignored by the behaviorists that seemed to be profoundly related to human psychology. These included memory, attention, consciousness, thinking, and imagery. It was apparent that internal mental processes were very real parts of psychology and required investigation. Many psychologists thought that these internal processes could be operationally defined and incorporated within a general study of the mind.

- *The emergence of communication theory.* Communication theory prompted experiments in signal detection, attention, cybernetics, and information theory—areas of significance to cognitive psychology.

- *Modern linguistics.* New ways of viewing language and grammatical structure became incorporated into attitudes concerning cognition (see above).

- *Memory research.* Research in verbal learning and semantic organization provided a sturdy empirical base for theories of memory, which led to the development of models of memory systems and the appearance of testable models of other cognitive processes.

- *Computer science and other technological advances.* Computer science, and especially a subdivision of it—artificial intelligence—caused reexamination of basic postulates of problem solving, memory processing and storage, as well as of language processing and acquisition. Research capabilities were greatly expanded by new experimental devices.

- *Cognitive development.* Psychologists interested in development psychology discovered an orderly unfolding of abilities with maturation. Notable among developmental psychologists during this period was Jean Piaget, who described how children develop an appreciation for concepts from infancy to adolescence. Such progress of abilities seems to be natural.

Cognitive Psychology—The Beginnings

During the late summer of 1956, a symposium on information theory was held on the campus of MIT. Many of the leading figures in communication theory were in attendance and listened to talks by Noam Chomsky, Jerome Bruner, Allen Newell and Herbert Simon, and George Miller, among others. The meeting had an indelible effect on many of its participants, and the general feeling was that something new was being created that significantly changed the way psychological processes could be conceptualized. Reflecting on the meeting several years later, George Miller (1979) wrote:

I went away from the Symposium with a strong conviction, more intuitive than rational, that human experimental psychology, theoretical linguistics, and computer simulation of cognitive processes were all pieces of a larger whole, and that the future would see progressive elaboration and coordination of their shared concerns. . . . I have been working toward a cognitive science for about twenty years, beginning before I knew what to call it. (p. 9)

So profound were the changes in American psychology during the last half of the twentieth century that it has been called the cognitive revolution.

From the earliest concepts of representational knowledge to recent research, knowledge has been thought to rely heavily on sensory inputs. That theme runs from the Greek philosophers, through Renaissance scholars, to contemporary cognitive psychologists. But are internal representations of the world identical to the physical properties of the world? Evidence is increasing that many internal representations of reality are not the same as the external reality—that is, they are not isomorphic. Tolman's work with laboratory animals and Bartlett's work with human subjects suggest that information from the senses is stored as an abstract representation. Furthermore, studies of neurology clearly show that stimuli from the outside world are sensed and stored as in a neurochemical code.

A somewhat more analytic approach to the topic of cognitive mapping and internal representation of information has been taken by Norman and Rumelhart (1975). In one experiment they asked residents of college housing to sketch floor plans of their apartments. As expected, the students were able to identify the prominent architectural features—the location of rooms, major utilities, and appliances. There were, however, omissions and errors. For example, many drew a balcony flush with the exterior of the building, although in fact it extended beyond. From the errors made in reconstructing the floor plan, we can learn a great deal about the subject's internal representation of information. Norman and Rumelhart conclude:

> The memory representation is not simply an accurate rendition of real life, but in fact is a combination of information, inference, and reconstruction from knowledge about buildings and the world in general. It is important to note that when the mistake was pointed out, all the students were surprised at what they had drawn.

An important principle of cognitive psychology is introduced by these examples. The most evident is that our representation of the world is not necessarily identical to the actual nature of the world. The representation of information is, of course, related to the stimulation received through our sensory apparatus, but it is also modified. This modification of information seems to be related to our past experiences, which have resulted in a rich and complex network of knowledge. Thus, incoming information is abstracted (and to some degree distorted) and stored within the subject's memory system. Such a notion does not deny that some sensory events are directly analogous to their internal representations, but it does suggest that the storage of sensory stimuli may be (and frequently is) subject to abstraction and modification as a function of a subject's rich and complex web of previously structured knowledge.

CONCEPTUAL SCIENCE AND COGNITIVE PSYCHOLOGY

Two ideas that are used frequently throughout this book are the notions of conceptual science and cognitive models. Although related, they differ in the sense that conceptual science is a very general concept, while cognitive models refer to a specific class of conceptual science.

From observation of objects and events, both experimentally controlled and in nature, scientists develop concepts in order to:

Organize observations
Make observations meaningful
Relate the elements deriving from their observations
Develop hypotheses
Direct subsequent observations
Predict unobserved events
Communicate with others

Cognitive models are specialized forms of scientific concepts and have the same purposes. Although they have been variously defined, we will define a cognitive model as a metaphor, based on observations and on inferences, that describes the detection, storage, and use of information.

Scientists may find a useful metaphor that elegantly structures their concepts, but then new research may prove the model wrong, requiring its revision or abandonment. Sometimes the model may be so useful as a framework for research that, even though not perfect, it is maintained. For example, although cognitive psychologists have conceptualized the previously mentioned two types of memory, short-term and long-term, some evidence exists that suggests that dichotomy misrepresents the reality of memory systems. Nevertheless, the metaphor is still useful to conceptualizing cognitive processes for analytic purposes. When models lose their vitality as analytical or descriptive tools, they are abandoned. In the next section, both conceptual science and cognitive models are more thoroughly discussed.

One way to mark the development of science is by the concepts that emerge through experimentation and observation. The scientist does not change nature (except in a limited sense), but observation of nature does change the way a scientist conceptualizes it. In turn, our conceptualization of nature directs our observations! Cognitive models, as well as other models of conceptual science, are the consequence of observations and, to some degree, the determinant of observations. The issue is related to the above mentioned one of how knowledge is represented by the human observer. As we learned, many times the internal representation of information does not coincide perfectly with external reality. Our internal representation of percepts may distort reality. One means of bringing the external reality into clearer focus is use of the scientific method, as well as precise instrumentation. In effect, there is a constant effort to transcribe the observation of nature into cognitive structures that are accurate representations of nature and, at the same time, compatible with the observer's sense of reason and comprehension. The numerous concepts discussed in this book—from visual perception, to memory structure, to semantic memory—are all based on this logic.

The logic of conceptual science can be illustrated by consideration of developments in the physical sciences. For example, it is generally acknowledged that matter is composed of elements whose existence is independent of direct human observation. The way elements are classified, however, greatly influences the way scientists perceive the physical world. One classification scheme divided the "elements" of the world into the categories *earth, air, fire, and water.* When this rudimentary taxonomy of alchemy gave way to more critical observation, elements—such as oxygen, carbon, hydrogen, sodium, and gold—were "discovered," and it became possible to study the characteristics of elements as they combined with each other. Hundreds of diverse laws about the combining properties of the elements were discovered. Because elements seemed to combine in an orderly fashion, some thought that the elements could be arranged in a pattern that would make the scattered laws of atomic chemistry meaningful. One scientist who thought this was Dmitri Mendeleev, a young Russian who wrote the name and atomic weight of all the elements then known on a series of cards—one element to a card. By arranging and rearranging the cards time and again, he finally hit on a meaningful pattern, now well known as the periodic table of elements.

Mendeleev's procedure is an apt example of how natural information is structured by the mind so that it both accurately portrays nature and is understandable. It is important to understand that the periodic arrangement of the elements is subject to different interpretations. Mendeleev's interpretation may not be the only one possible, or even the best (and there may not even *be* a natural order) but the order suggested does help us to understand one part of the physical universe and seems compatible with the "real" nature.

Conceptual cognitive psychology has much in common with Mendeleev's structuring of elements. The raw observation of how knowledge is acquired, stored, and used lacks formal structure. Like physical scientists, cognitive scientists seek out schemes that will be intellectually compatible and scientifically valid.

Cognitive Models

As we have said, conceptual science, including cognitive psychology, is metaphorical in character. Models of nature, including cognitive models, are abstract organizational ideas derived from inferences based on observations. The structure of the elements *may* be classified into a periodic table, as Mendeleev suggested, but it is important to realize that the classification scheme is a metaphor. Asserting that conceptual science is metaphorical does not reduce its utility. Indeed, one of the purposes of building models is to make observations more comprehensible. Other needs are served by conceptual science; it provides researchers with a structure within which specific hypotheses can be tested, and it enables them to predict events on the basis of the model. These functions were elegantly served by the periodic table. On the basis of the arrangements of elements in it, scientists, rather than performing the endless helter-skelter experiments involving chemical combinations, could accurately hypothesize chemical combination and displacement laws. Furthermore, elements not yet discovered could be predicted and their characteristics inferred, even though no direct physical proof of their properties existed. As you approach cognitive models, keep in mind the analogy of Mendeleev's model, since cognitive models, like those in the physical sciences, are based on inferential logic and are useful in our understanding of cognitive psychology.

In summary, a model is based on inferences drawn from observations. Its purpose is to provide an understandable representation of the character of the observation and, in developing hypotheses, aid in making predictions. We now consider a few models in cognitive psychology.

We begin our discussion of cognitive models on an austere level, dividing the cognitive process into only three components: the detection of stimuli, the storage and transformation of stimuli, and the production of responses.

$$\text{Detection of stimuli} \quad \rightarrow \quad \text{Storage, transformation of stimuli} \quad \rightarrow \quad \text{Production of responses}$$

This sequential processing model, close to the S-R model mentioned earlier, was frequently used in some form in the early conceptualizations of psychological processes. Even though the model seems to express the basic stages of cognitive psychology, it offers so little detail that it does little to enhance our understanding of the processes. It is equally inadequate in its capacity to inspire hypotheses or predict behavior. This primitive model is roughly analogous to early conceptualization of the universe as being composed of earth, air, fire, and water. The taxonomy does represent one way to view the phenomena, but it belies their complexity.

One of the first and most frequently cited cognitive models dealt with memory. In 1890 James expanded the concept of memory to include primary memory and secondary memory. Primary memory was hypothesized to deal with immediate events, and secondary memory with permanent, "indestructible" vestiges of experience. The model was as follows:

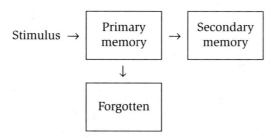

A later revision of the model by Waugh and Norman (1965) satisfied many of the demands for an acceptable model. It is comprehensible and it is a source of hypothesis and prediction; however, it, too, is overly simplistic. Can *all* human memory processes and storage systems be accurately described by this model? Hardly, and it was inevitable that more complex models would evolve.

A modified and expanded model of the Waugh and Norman model is shown in Figure 1.4. Notice that a new storage system and several new routines have been added. However, even this model is incomplete and needs to be expanded.

During the emergence of cognitive psychology, model making became a favorite pastime of psychologists, and some of their creations are truly wonderful. The common solution to the problem of too simple models is to add another box, another routine, another storage system, another component to be tested and analyzed. Such creative effort seems justified in light of what we presently know about the vastness of the human cognitive system.

By now you may have concluded that model making in cognitive psychology is as out of control as was the sorcerer's apprentice. That conclusion is not entirely justified, for the task is so vast—analysis of how information is detected, represented, and transformed as knowledge, and how knowledge is used—that, were we to confine our conceptual metaphors to simplistic models, we would fail to elucidate the involved and comprehensive domain of cognitive psychology.

These models have one element in common: they are based on a sequence of events. A stimulus is presented, we detect it through the sensory system, we store and transform it in memory, and we react to it. Models of human cognition bear some similarities to the sequential steps involved in computer processing; indeed, the patterning of human information processing was constructed along the lines of a computer metaphor.

F I G U R E   1 . 4

Modified Waugh and Norman cognitive model. Adapted from Waugh and Norman (1965)

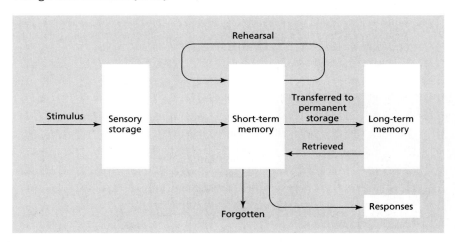

The Computer Metaphor and Human Cognition

Although Pascal, Descartes, and others dreamt of computing machines centuries ago, it was not until the development of high-speed digital computers about fifty years ago that practical machines were invented. These machines gained enormous acceptance and are presently used in virtually every aspect of modern life. Curiously, they also have had an impact on the way humans view their own minds, in addition to being an important tool for scientists interested in the study of cognition. Originally, such devices were thought to be wonderful number crunchers capable of performing a multitude of complex mathematical operations in a fraction of the time required by humans. However, it was quickly discovered that they could perform functions that resembled human problem solving. This discovery hinted that the long-awaited intelligent robot might be just around the corner, and perhaps, ominously, Aldous Huxley's brave new world might be more of a reality than originally feared. (For further discussion of thinking machines, refer to the final chapter of this book.)

In 1955 Herbert Simon, a professor at the Carnegie Institute of Technology (now Carnegie Mellon University) in Pittsburgh, is said to have announced to his class, "Over Christmas, Allen Newell and I invented a thinking machine." Shortly after that announcement, Simon and Newell's computer (dubbed "Johniac" after John von Neumann [4]) was capable of working out a proof of a mathematical theorem. The real breakthrough, however, was conceptual rather than computational. Simon and Newell had shown not only that a computer was capable of simulating one limited aspect of human thought but also that computers and their multifarious internal networks could provide a model of the way humans think. Although Simon and Newell pursued topics of problem solving at a more general level, and not a theory of neural or electronic mechanisms for information processing, the idea that computers could model human cognition greatly excited psychologists. A new metaphor had been born.

The logic of the new metaphor was "Give me a dozen healthy computers, with their own special programs, and I will produce the thinking of a doctor, lawyer, merchant, and even beggarman and thief." In effect, if computer programs could operate according

---

[4] John von Neumann was a mathematician who authored the notion that it was possible to store a program within a computer's internal memory, thus avoiding reprogramming each time a procedure was to be performed. See Chapter 16 for more details.

Allen Newell (left) 1927–1992 and Herbert Simon. Pioneers in the field of artificial intelligence and "thinking machines."

to the same rules and procedures as the human mind, then they should be able to perform functions indistinguishable from those performed by humans. Computers could do things that appear to be intelligent, thus the label "artificial intelligence" or "AI." The marriage between cognitive psychologists and computer scientists seemed destined for utter bliss. Psychologists could provide the rules and procedures we follow when we perceive, store information in memory, and think, while computer scientists could write programs that would mimic these functions. However, the honeymoon was less than euphoric. Unfortunately, what computers do well (perform high-speed mathematical functions and abide by rule-governed logic) humans do poorly, relatively speaking. And what humans do well (form generalizations, make inferences, understand complex patterns, and have emotions) computers do stupidly, or not at all. For example, if I ask you to find the square root of 2.19 by hand, it will likely take several minutes; a computer can solve the problem in milliseconds. However, if I ask you if you know Karen Wood, who lives on Ridgecrest, who goes to the Presbyterian Church, and is studying for a master's degree in cellular biology, you might say, "Yes, I know who you're talking about, but her name is Carol West and she lives on Crestview and she's working on a Ph.D. in physiology." Computers just can't do that . . . yet.

However, the marriage is not over, and a second generation of cognitive-computer scientists are working toward building computers that look something like a brain. These are complete with layers of interconnected electronic surrogate neurons, whose organizational "hardware" mimics the "wetware" of the brain, and they contain programs that mimic the functions of organic neural networks. These new computers are sometimes called neural networks and act more like humans than the earlier versions. They are able to make generalizations and understand complex visual patterns, are slow at math, and make witless mistakes. They still do not have emotions but are nevertheless a mark of success.

The computer analogy has lurked in the background of cognitive psychology for most of its brief history. Occasionally the analogy got mixed up: computers were not modeled after the way humans thought, but rather people began to think that the brain was really a very complex computer. We now know that there are fundamental differences between the internal workings of computers and the internal workings of the brain. Nevertheless, the computer metaphor continues to have a profound and generally positive impact on the development of cognitive psychology.

Cognitive Science

Three powerful areas of scientific development—computer science, neuroscience, and cognitive psychology—converge to create a new science called *cognitive science*. The boundaries among these disciplines are sometimes hard to distinguish: some cognitive psychologists may be closer to neuroscience, others to computer science. One thing is clear, however: the science of human cognition is undergoing a radical transformation due to major changes in computer technology and brain science. Our subject is cognitive psychology, but we will make full use of recent discoveries in neuroscience and computer science that illuminate the cognitive properties of the human species.

As with most emerging sciences, new models appear frequently. Some stand the test of empirical research; others do not. Recently, one model has received an unusual amount of attention. This model is known by several interchangeable labels, including "parallel distributed processing" (PDP), "connectionism," and "neuronetwork systems." The main features of this model are described next and in Chapter 2.

Neuroscience and Cognitive Psychology

During the early stages of cognitive psychology, little attention was given to physiological psychology or neuroanatomy. It was quite enough to establish a new way of conceptualizing the mind and, besides, the information-processing model and computer metaphor seemed adequate. Moreover, students of neurophysiology and related areas seemed to be absorbed with microscopic structures bearing little resemblance to broad cognitive topics such as thinking, perception, and memory.

Much of the early information on the brain and its functions resulted from head traumas incurred during wars and accidents. For example, during World War I, neurosurgeons treating victims of shrapnel wounds to the brain learned a great deal about the specialized functions of that organ (for example, which areas were associated with vision, speech, hearing, and so on) as well as the general functions. The central issue neurologists struggled with was whether the brain was a holistic organ, with operations distributed throughout its infrastructure, or whether activities were localized and tied to specific regions. For example, did learning a specific act take place in a localized area of the brain, or was learning distributed throughout many parts of the brain? Among the most prominent of the scientists who wrestled with these issues was Karl Lashley (1929). In his experiments, Lashley destroyed specific parts of the brains of rats who had learned to run a maze. He showed that performance declined according to the total *amount* of the brain destroyed but was not related to the *location* of the lesions (see Chapter 2 for more on Lashley's work).

Recently, progress has been made in the field of neuroscience, which comprises both the structural aspects of the brain and its peripheral components, as well as the functional aspects. In the 1960s researchers found structural elements that would later have a direct impact on cognitive psychology. Some of these discoveries were made at the Johns Hopkins School of Medicine by Vernon Mountcastle, whose work dealt with the *cerebral cortex*—the top layer of the brain, thought to be involved in higher mental functions. Mountcastle (1979) discovered that connections among the cells of the cortex, or *neurons,* are many times more numerous than had been thought. (Neurons are the basic cells of the nervous system that conduct neural information.) Perhaps most intriguing was the discovery that the system of neural connections appeared to be distributed in a parallel array in addition to serial pathways. The network of parallel neural connections seems to range over a large territory, with functions occurring at the same time in several locations. This type of processing is in contrast to serial or sequential processing, in which one nerve impulse is passed on to another nerve, and then on to another. Mountcastle writes, "These connective subsets are distributed systems, each composed of modular elements in several or many brain regions, connected in both parallel and serial arrays. They form the neuronal pathways for distributed and parallel processing within the brain" (cited in Restak, 1988, p. 22). The way the brain functions, according to this view, is that processing networks are distributed throughout the cortex rather than localized. Thus, there is no "master homunculus" guiding the activities of neural processing, or "ghost neuron" concealed in the background to oversee action. Localized parts of the brain associated with vision, speech, motor actions, and so on are specialized only in the sense that they receive inputs and make outputs associated with those functions.

Additionally, some studies have found that many functions are actually distributed throughout the brain.

Thus, a psychological function, such as retrieving something from memory, is *distributed* throughout the brain and accomplished through parallel routines at several sites.

These discoveries seemed to offer a solution to one of the toughest problems faced by the young science of cognition: how relatively slow neurotransmission can produce such diverse and fast cognition. Consider this example: A skilled pianist is given an intricate piece of music to play, and she does so with dazzling dexterity. If the "neuromachinery" operated in a sequential way—an impulse from one neuron jumping to another and then on to another—by the time the pianist would be able to respond to one note, it would be well past the time she should respond to another. Cognitive psychologists study just such phenomena and have discovered that the interstroke interval (ISI), the time elapsed between the playing of one note and the playing of a second, is about 50 milliseconds.[5] Compensating for the sluggish neurosystem with which we are all endowed, we process information (such as notes on a page that are to be translated into finger movements) in several different subsystems, all acting more or less at the same time. The simultaneous processing of information in several subsystems suggests a parallel processing of information: both cognitive psychologists and neuroscientists recognize this and have incorporated the notion of parallel processing into their models of psychology and neurology.

Parallel Distributed Processing (PDP) and Cognitive Psychology

Many people have been associated with this model of human cognition, but David Rumelhart and James McClelland have done the most to formalize the theory (see especially their two-volume *Parallel Distributed Processing*, 1986). There are many components to the theory; this section addresses only the basic ones.

Essentially, the model is neurally inspired, concerned with the kind of processing mechanism that is the human mind. Is it a type of von Neumann computer—a John-iac—in which information is processed in sequential steps? Alternatively, might the human mind process information in a massively distributed, mutually interactive parallel system in which various activities are carried out simultaneously through excitation and/or inhibition of neural cells? PDPers opt for the latter explanation. "These [PDP] models assume that information processing takes place through the interactions of a large number of simple processing elements called units, each sending excitatory and inhibitory signals to other units" (McClelland, Rumelhart, & Hinton, 1986, p. 10). These

---

[5]One millisecond (msec.) equals 1/1000 second. Fifty milliseconds equal 1/20 second, or about the time of an eye blink.

**David Rumelhart (left)
and James McClelland.
Formalized the neurally
inspired PDP model.**

units may stand for possible guesses about letters in a string of words or notes on a score. In other situations, the units may stand for possible goals and actions, such as reading a particular letter or playing a specific note. Proponents suggest that the PDP models are concerned with the description of the internal structure of larger units of cognitive activity, such as reading, perceiving, processing sentences, and so on. The theory is comparable to atomic theory in physics; the basic units correspond to subatomic particles, which may document the internal structures of atoms that form the constituents of larger units of chemical structure. By studying the basic units, we may better understand the properties of larger units of psychological activity.

One of the appeals of the PDP model is that it is tied to neuroanatomical functioning. It has been reasonably well established that human thought takes place in the brain, which consists of tens of billions of interconnected neurons. These relatively simple neurons, which interact with hundreds of thousands of other neurons, are basic to the complex processing of information. While most human brains are capable of involved thought, the nature of neural transmission places constraints on the speed with which processing can take place. PDP modelers consider this factor in their theory and have developed an explanation as to how complex processes, such as the visual identification of a common object, can take place in a short period of time. As an example of the types of constraints imposed by the brain on the processing of information, consider the speed with which neural transmission takes place. Neural transmission is a relatively sluggish, noisy affair (to use computer argot), with some neurons requiring 3 milliseconds to fire.[6] If neural activities, which logically underlie all cognitive functions, require a relatively long period of time to function, then what processing mechanism would allow us to make complex decisions in a brief period of time?

Let's illustrate the point made above. Suppose you are shopping in a supermarket, actively thinking about the ingredients you must select to make a Greek salad, and out of the corner of your eye you see and recognize your professor of cognitive psychology. How long does the recognition process take? Not long at all. Experiments conducted under well-controlled laboratory conditions show that from the onset of a complex visual stimulus until the recognition and response to that stimulus, about 300 millisec-

---

[6]The time required to close a circuit in a computer is approximately 1 million times faster and is measured in nanoseconds. A nanosecond is one-billionth of a second.

onds elapse—less than one-third of a second! How is that possible, given the slothful speed of neurotransmission? The answer suggests that the brain processes visual information, as well as other stimuli, by means of massive parallelism.

The brain does not store memory in any single neuron or probably even in any local set; but it does store memory in an entire ensemble of neurons distributed throughout several parts of the brain. If two neurons are simultaneously activated, the bond between them is strengthened. On the other hand, if one is activated and another inhibited, the bond is weakened. Memory in such a system, then, is in the pattern of activated and inhibited networks distributed throughout the system rather than located in a specific subsystem. One theory of PDP views memory and retrieval of information from memory in a model that is similar to the way neural networks work.

Thus far, PDP models seem consistent with the basic structure and processing of the brain, but that alone is not sufficient reason to accept PDP as a psychological theory. Its importance as a psychological theory will ultimately be tested by observations that will either confirm or deny the validity of the model. At this time the model is creating new excitement among its advocates, who are working toward cognitive theories based on massive parallel processing. More is reported on PDP in other parts of this book.

Summary

The purpose of this chapter is to set the stage for the rest of the book by introducing you to cognitive psychology. Many important and varied aspects of cognitive psychology are discussed in this chapter. Some of the main features include the following:

1 Cognitive psychology is concerned with how we acquire, transform, represent, store, and retrieve knowledge, and with how that knowledge directs what we attend to and how we respond.

2 One commonly adopted model is the information-processing model, which assumes that information is processed through a series of stages, each of which performs a unique function.

3 Two questions raised by the information-processing model are:
(a) What are the stages through which information is processed?
(b) In what form is knowledge represented?

4 Cognitive psychology uses research and theoretical approaches from major areas of psychology, including neuroscience, perception, pattern perception, attention and consciousness, memory, representation of knowledge, imagery, language, developmental psychology, thinking and concept formation, human intelligence, and artificial intelligence.

5 Historical antecedents of modern cognitive psychology include Greek philosophy; eighteenth-century empiricism; nineteenth-century structuralism; and the neocognitive revolution influenced by modern developments in communication theory, linguistics, memory research, and computer technology.

6 The main theme of the cognitive revolution is that internal processes are *the* subject matter of psychology. This is in contrast with behaviorism which proposes that response or behavior is the true subject matter of psychology.

7 Conceptual science is a useful metaphor devised by humans to help comprehend "reality." Psychologists devise conceptual models in cognitive psychology with the aim of developing a system that reflects the nature of human perception, thought, and understanding of the world.

8 Cognitive models are based on observations that describe the structure and processes of cognition. Model building can make observations more comprehensible.

9 The information-processing model has dominated cognitive psychology, but other models, occurring in computer science and in neuroscience, have been combined with cognitive psychology to form cognitive science.

10 Parallel distributed processing (PDP) is a model of cognition in which information is thought to be processed in a way similar to neurological networks. Those networks suggest that neural processing occurs simultaneously, in different regions, with simple connections being either strengthened or weakened.

Key Words

cognitive map	PDP
cognitive model	perception
cognitive neuroscience	process
conceptual science	representation of knowledge
information-processing model	schema
internal representation	structure
isomorphism	

Recommended Readings

Howard Gardner has written a lively history of cognitive science in *The Mind's New Science*, which is highly recommended, as is Zenon Pylyshyn's *Computation and Cognition: Toward a Foundation for Cognitive Science.* Karl Pribram, a neurophysiologist, has a thoughtful article in *American Psychologist* entitled "The Cognitive Revolution and Mind/Brain Issues." Posner (ed.), *Foundations of Cognitive Science*, and Neisser, *Cognition and Reality: Principles and Implications of Cognitive Psychology*, will serve to introduce several issues in cognitive psychology. The first few chapters of Klatzky, *Human Memory: Structures and Processes*, may be helpful, as well as portions of Anderson and Bower, *Human Associative Memory.* As an introduction to the philosophy of science, Kuhn, *The Structure of Scientific Revolutions*, is recommended. A collection of outstanding papers in cognitive science has been assembled by Collins and Smith in *Readings in Cognitive Science: A Perspective from Psychology and Artificial Intelligence.* The best source to gain a perspective on American psychology, including the emergence of cognitive psychology, is Ernest Hilgard's *Psychology in America: A Historical Survey.* A good account of the schism between behaviorism and cognitive psychology can be found in the lively book by Bernard Baars, *The Cognitive Revolution in Psychology.* Finally, for detailed information on parallel distributed processing, see the two-volume work by Rumelhart and McClelland, *Parallel Distributed Processing: Explorations in the Microstructure of Cognition.*

Neurocognition

Neuroscience and cognitive science share the goal of trying to understand how the mind-brain works. In the past, discoveries at the neuronal level and explanations at the cognitive level were so distant that each often seemed of merely academic significance to the other . . . However, there is now a gathering conviction among scientists that the time is right for a fruitful convergence of research from hitherto isolated fields.

Patricia S. Churchland and Terrence J. Sejnowski

EXPLORING AND MAPPING THE BRAIN—AN INTRODUCTION

A little over 500 years ago Columbus "discovered" America, and the hottest scientific theme of that time was the charting of the seas and the new world. Today, scientists are exploring an even more fundamental territory, one that is far more intimate—the world of the human brain. While the geography of the Western hemisphere is vast in size and complex in climate, the brain is small in size and its gelatinous mass weighs only about three pounds. However, its intricate network of neurons comprises *the* most complicated system known. While the gross geography of the human brain has been known for a very long time (it is likely that ancient people saw far more human brains than we do), the specific geography and functions of the brain are only beginning to yield their secrets. This exploration of the new world has been aided by imaging technology that allows us to see through the solid wall of the skull. Like the ancient mariner who charted dangerous seas, safe lagoons, and "widowmaker" reefs, cartographers of the mind are mapping areas in which visual processing, semantic analysis, auditory interpretation, and a myriad of other cognitive functions take place. This chapter is a logbook of some of the geography, maps, and processes of the brain.

Much of the recent excitement in cognitive psychology is due to new developments in a discipline that combines cognitive psychology and neuroscience, a specialty called *neurocognition*. Before discussing the details of neurocognition, briefly consider the larger question of how neurocognition fits into the mind-body dichotomy contemplated by scientists and philosophers for centuries and recently reexamined by cognitive neuroscientists equipped with a dazzling mélange of scientific instruments.

The brain is the last and greatest frontier . . . the most complex thing we have yet discovered in our universe.

James Watson

MIND-BODY ISSUES

Remarkably, we humans occupy two worlds at the same time.

The first is the physical world of things that exist in time and space. These things have physical properties that follow physical laws, such as the laws of gravity, which govern falling bodies; the laws of centrifugal force, which control the action of rotating objects; or the neurological laws, which regulate the transmission of an impulse from one neuron to another (neurotransmission).

The second world is populated by memories, ideas, thoughts, images, and so on. These are also governed by laws, although sometimes finding them is more difficult than finding those that govern the physical world.

Because, traditionally, we have set out to find rules in the two worlds using different techniques, many philosophers and scientists have thought that these worlds are fundamentally different. This dichotomous conclusion is based on the assumption that one world is focused on the physical universe, or body, as it applies to people, while the other is centered on the mental universe, or mind. The separation of mind from body is intuitively logical, or self-evident, but the interaction between the worlds is equally self-evident. Your mental inability to concentrate on a test may be related to the massive physical harm you inflicted on your body at last night's toga party.

Some philosophers of science argue that the only real world is the world of the mind and that the physical world is an illusion. Conversely, some argue that the only real world is the physical world and that the mind is ultimately a function of the brain. A frequent criticism of the latter position is that it robs humanity of its lofty, idealistic spirit. One basic problem the mind-body dualists have is trying to figure out how the mind is connected to the body and vice versa. There are various ideas about the connection.

The following is a simplified interpretation of the mind-body issue. When we talk of *mind*, we are talking about the things that are done by the brain; for example, thinking, holding things in memory, perceiving, judging, as well as being in love, feeling pain, plotting schemes to rule the world, composing music, and making jokes. The mind, in this sense, comprises the processes carried out by the brain.

The brain has physical properties (discussed in some detail later in this chapter) that are in a constant state of flux. The brain never rests totally but is always teeming with electrochemical activity. However, the general architecture; the network of neu-

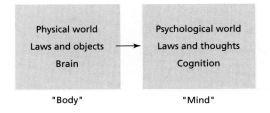

Memory and Cerebral Blood Flow—An Example

Endel Tulving,[1] an eminent cognitive psychologist, has applied recent techniques in brain science to portray different types of regional cerebral blood flow (rCBF) that were associated with different types of memory. Although previous researchers had been working in the direction of combining up-to-date techniques in neuroscience with cognitive experiments, Tulving's graphic representation of specific types of brain functions with hypothetical memory processes was a harbinger of the direction cognitive psychology and brain science were taking.

Brain scientists have been measuring cerebral blood flow as an indication of neural activity (and its corresponding metabolic requirements) for some time. The technique involves injecting a radioactive tracer into the bloodstream of a fully conscious subject. This tracer has a half-life of only 30 seconds, and the procedure is safe. Blood flow is detected by a cluster of 254 extracranial detectors, which circle the subject's head. Each detector scans an area of approximately 1 square centimeter. Each tiny cell is assigned a color that corresponds to the rate of blood activity and can be portrayed in a computer-generated visual mosaic. Even a novice can see the differences in rCBF in the photographic displays. Some areas are active, some inactive, and others are in between. (See the illustrations on the inside front cover.)

Tulving's procedure was simple, though he used complex instruments. Subjects were asked to think about different topics while undergoing rCBF scanning. Some topics were related to episodic,[2] or temporally dated, episodes, such as personally experienced events (for example, a holiday or seeing a movie). Others were related to semantic experiences such as general or world knowledge, which the subject may have acquired by reading books. The result of this experiment showed reasonably consistent patterns of blood flow (and hence neural activity) associated with both episodic and semantic thinking.

To understand the magnitude of this discovery (and others of a similar nature conducted in other laboratories throughout the world), consider the purpose of most experiments and observations in cognitive psychology and neuroscience. For the most part, cognitive psychologists have been interested in developing major models of the mind, which are validated by behavioral observations and describe accurately the important details of our mental life. Neuroscientists,[3] on the other hand, have been interested in understanding the basic structure of the nervous system, including the brain and its normal and pathological functions. Both sciences attempt to understand how the mind-brain works. Experiments such as Tulving's tend to authenticate the contribution of both sciences. Cognitive psychologists have found a physical basis for some of their theories (for example, different types of memories), and neuroscientists have successfully related their observations of cerebral brain flow to a major model of cognition.

---

[1]See Tulving, 1989a, 1989b, 1994; and Tulving, et al., 1994, for further investigations.

[2]The terms *episodic* and *semantic* are technical terms used to describe types of memory. See Chapter 6 for a more complete description.

[3]Neuroscientists are scientists who study neuroscience, or the branch of science that encompasses the study of neuroanatomy, neurophysiology, brain functions, and related psychological and computer models.

rons; the location of major landmarks on the cortex; the areas of the brain that are related to functions such as sensory feelings, motor control, vision, and so on are generally stable and change little. What takes place in the brain—the brain processes—changes more readily. Minds tend to be more dynamic than brains. We can change our thoughts rapidly and without much obvious structural (architectural) change in the brain, even though the pattern of electrochemical transmissions may be extremely changeable. Our conscious thoughts may shift swiftly from the ridiculous to the sublime, from inner space to outer space, and from sacred to profane in less time than it takes to read this sentence. The physical changes in neural activity cause changes in the mind. However, even though minds tend to be dynamic, they also have their consistencies; our general mode of thinking, our attitudes toward religion, our aspirations, our view of the family, and so on are reasonably stable. This chapter is about both mind and brain and about how cognitive psychology and neuroscience have, after centuries of deliberation, for the first time in the intellectual history of our species, through impressive scientific imaging technology, shed some light on the topic.

Our recent, and unusual, attention to the brain and cognition is based on a fundamental tenet: All cognition is the result of neurological activity. That means that pattern recognition, reading, attention, memory, imagery, consciousness, thinking, and the use of language as well as all other forms of cognition are a reflection of the activity of neurons, mostly those that are concentrated in the brain's cerebral cortex. Additionally, since the things we do—speak, solve problems, operate machines, and so on—are based on cognition, then all behavior is likewise predicated on neural activity.

NEUROCOGNITION

Out of neuroscience and cognitive psychology, a new science has been fashioned called *neurocognition* (or sometimes *neuropsychology*), defined as "the study of the relationships between neuroscience and cognitive psychology, especially those theories of the mind dealing with memory, sensation and perception, problem solving, language processing, motor functions, and cognition." Because of the efforts of neuropsychologists, hypothetical constructs such as memory types and language processing are no longer so conjectural but seem to have specific neurophysiological correlates. Furthermore, microscopic structures of the brain, when viewed as neuronetworks, seem to be related to larger components of human cognition, such as memory, perception, problem solving, and the like.

Perhaps another generation will view such gross demonstrations of cortical neural activity, which correspond to equally gross categories of thinking, as a primitive attempt to use knowledge from two previously disparate sciences to understand the central mechanisms of human cognition. Nevertheless, this early work will be remembered as a turning point in both cognitive psychology and neuroscience, and the exciting part for contemporary students of cognition is that they will witness and, in some cases, create a new science of the mind. It's a wonderful time to be alive!

Cognitive Psychology and Neuroscience

There are several reasons contemporary psychologists are using information and techniques from neuroscience in their pursuit of cognition. These include:

- The need to find physical evidence for theoretical structures of the mind. The search for the properties of the human mind stretches back to the beginning of history, if not before, but has been constantly frustrated because of the tenuous nature of the supporting evidence. The development of sophisticated equipment has made it possible to materially prove the existence of certain hypothetical structures and thus validate some theories of language, perception, form identification, cognition, motor function, and memory. See Tulving (1989a, 1989b) for an example.

- The need on the part of neuroscientists to relate their findings to more comprehensive models of the brain and behavior. Even if it were possible to identify every minute detail of neurofunctions, this would tell us little about the network and systems properties that are essential to the understanding of cognitive effects.

- The clinical goal to find correlates between brain pathology and behavior. For generations neurologists have been concerned with the way in which brain traumas, lesions, infarctions, thromboses, and tumors affect behavior and with the procedures that might alleviate related symptoms. These concerns require a better understanding of human functioning and psychology. Conversely, psychologists interested in the psychological treatment of organically impaired patients require better understanding of the physical causes of such behavior.

- The increased involvement of neurological functions in models of the mind. Specifically, cognitive psychologists interested in parallel distributed processing (PDP) (also called connectionism or neuronetwork systems) are interested in finding psychological models consistent with neurological structures and functions.

- The work of computer scientists who are attempting to simulate human cognition and intelligence by developing computers that behave in a way that is similar to the human brain. These approaches to brain and computer are sometimes called neuronet architectures. They include the subspecialty of perceptrons,[1] which is the simulation of neuralnets in computer architecture. Such developments of computer architecture and function require detailed understanding of brain architecture and function.

- The development of techniques that allow scientists to peer into the human brain and that reveal structures and processes never before seen. These include positron emission tomography (PET or PETT) scans, computerized axial tomography (CAT or CT) scans, magnetic resonance imaging (MRI), electroencephalography (EEG), scalp recordings of evoked potentials, and blood flow measures. These largely noninvasive tools are possible because of advances in computer technology and brain scanning techniques.

---

[1]The word *perceptron* was first used in 1957 by a Cornell Aeronautical Laboratory scientist, Frank Rosenblatt, who built one of the first neuralnets. In 1968 Minsky and Papert published a book entitled *Perceptrons.*

> Evolution has encased the brain in a rock-hard vault of bone, wrapped it in layers of tough membrane, and cushioned it in a viscous bath of cerebral spinal fluid. These protective shields pose particularly difficult challenges for scientists who would like to observe human brain activity directly.
>
> *Gordon Bower*

The alliance between neuroscience and cognitive psychology is characterized by the use of models of inquiry from both disciplines to examine human thinking, perception, and cognition. From the domain of neuroscience comes the study of neurology (the system of neuroconnections in the brain and their functions). From the domain of cognitive psychology comes the study of hypothetical structures such as memory, perception, and cognition. In neurocognition both domains are represented. Of special interest is the interaction between these two domains. For example, scientists interested in neurocognition might ask, "What is the relationship between memory and neurology?"

Because neuroscience has become increasingly important in the study of cognitive psychology, an introduction to some of the elementary aspects of human neurology follows.

THE NERVOUS SYSTEM

The central nervous system consists of the spinal cord and brain. Our discussion focuses on the brain, with particular attention to the structures and processes that bear on neurally inspired cognitive models.

"Brain"

The earliest written reference to the brain is found in Egyptian hieroglyphs written during the seventeenth century B.C. The hieroglyphic character for brain is shown here as *'ys*. According to the eminent Egyptologist James Breasted, it has been found eight times in ancient writings. In one source, known as "The Edwin Smith Surgical Papyrus," found in 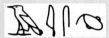 the rare-book room of the New York Academy of Medicine, the author describes the symptoms, diagnoses, and prognoses of two patients with head wounds. The early Egyptians knew that injuries to one side of the brain caused an affliction in the opposite side of the body.

The basic building block of the nervous system is the neuron, a specialized cell that transmits neural information throughout the nervous system. The human brain is densely packed with neurons. Some estimates place the number at more than 100 billion (about the number of stars in the Milky Way), each of which is capable of receiving and passing nerve impulses to sometimes thousands of other neurons and is more complex than any other known system, terrestrial or extraterrestrial. Each cubic inch of the human cerebral cortex contains about ten thousand miles of nerve fibers, which connect the cells together (Blakemore, 1977). Figure 2.1 presents a view of the tangled mass of neurons in the brain of a rabbit. This photomicrograph of the stained cells of its cortex shows only about 2 percent of all cells in the photograph. Compare this photograph with the diagram of a neuron (see Figure 2.2), and try to locate the dendrites and axons. At any given time, many of the cortical neurons are active, and it is thought that cognitive functions such as perceiving, thinking, awareness, and memory are carried out by

FIGURE 2.1

Photograph of an enlarged view of the visual cortex of a rabbit. Only about 2 percent of all cells are shown. Photo by Hendrik Van der Loos, in Blakemore (1977).

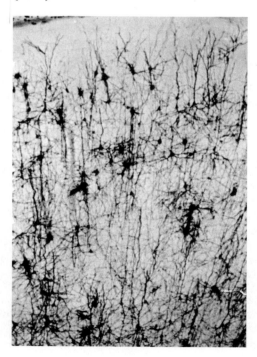

FIGURE 2.2

Drawing of a neuron.

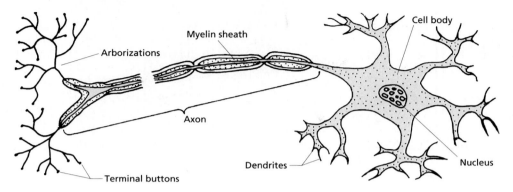

the simultaneous firing of neurons located throughout this complex neural network. It is difficult to imagine the vast number of neurons that are simultaneously activated and the intricate infrastructure that supports the system. Therein lies a paradox: because the brain is so complex, it may never fully understand itself!

The Neuron

There are perhaps as many as a thousand different types of neurons (see Kandel, Schwartz, & Jessell, 1991), each of which carries out specialized functions in a variety of locations (see Figure 2.2). The main morphological regions of the neuron include:

1. The dendrites, which gather neural impulses from other neurons. Dendrites are highly arborized, suggesting the branches and twigs of a tree.
2. The cell body, in which nutrients and waste products are filtered in and out through the permeable cell wall.
3. The axon, a long, tubular transmitting pathway in which signals from the cell body are passed along to other cells by means of junctures known as synapses. Axons in the brain may be tiny or may reach up to 1 meter or more in length. Large axons are surrounded by a fatty substance called the myelin sheath, which acts as a type of insulation for the neuron.
4. The presynaptic terminals, or buttons, found at the ends of the fine branches at the terminus of the axon. They are near the receptive surface of other neurons at a juncture, or synapse, and transmit information to other neurons.

At the synapse the axon terminal on one side releases a chemical, which acts on the membrane of the dendrite of another neuron. This chemical neurotransmitter changes the polarity, or electrical potential, of the receiving dendrite. A neurotransmitter is like a switch that can be turned on or off (hence the compelling similarity between neural

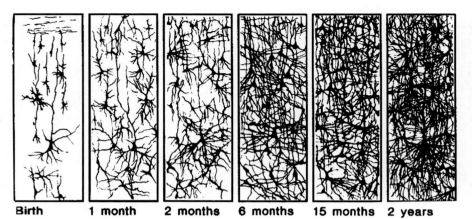

Birth   1 month   2 months   6 months   15 months   2 years

Neural Networks from Birth to 2 Years of Age

A human baby has almost all of its neurons at birth. However, the connections among neurons continue to grow, reaching astronomical numbers: a small sample is shown in the illustration at left.

functions and the dichotomous nature of computer switches). One class of neurotransmitter has an inhibitory effect, which tends to make the next neuron less likely to fire. Another class has an excitatory effect, which makes the next neuron more likely to fire. Recently, as many as thirty different neurotransmitters have been identified. Some seem to perform ordinary functions, such as maintaining the physical integrity of the cells; others, such as acetylcholine, seem to be related to learning and memory.

At birth, not all synaptic connections are complete, nor are all neurons completely myelinated; however, most neurons are present. In adulthood all synapses are grown in completely, and all appropriate cells are myelinated. In adults synapses do not propagate. In adults the average cell body and dendrite have the capacity to receive about one thousand synapses from other neurons, and the average axon has the capacity to send synapses to about one thousand other neurons.

The speed with which impulses move along the axon is related to size. In the smallest axon, neurotransmission creeps along at about 0.5 meter per second (about 1 mile per hour), while in the largest axons the rate is 120 meters per second (about 270 miles per hour). (These speeds are many thousands of times slower than transmission and switching speeds in a computer.) The brain is always alive with electrochemical activity, and an excited neuron may fire as often as one thousand times per second. The more times a neuron fires, the more effect it will have on the cells to which it synapses. These firings can be observed by means of electroencephalography (EEG) recordings, which

When an axon of cell A is near enough to excite cell B . . . some growth or metabolic change takes place in both cells such that A's efficiency, as one of the cells firing B, is increased.

Donald O. Hebb

Donald O. Hebb (1904–1985). Early researcher in neurocognition whose seminal ideas are frequently used in connectionistic models.

measure the electrical activities of regions of the brain, or by single-cell recordings of activities in individual neurons of animals. In some instances (for example, the perception of a particular visual pattern), it is possible to detect single-cell firings and translate them into auditory signals. The sound is reminiscent of a distant machine gun firing rapid volleys.

Human knowledge is not localized in any single neuron. It is believed that human cognition takes place in the large patterns of neural activity that are distributed throughout the brain, function in parallel, and operate by means of excitatory or inhibitory connections, or "switches." A number of different theories, including the influential theory of Donald Hebb (1949), have been proposed that address the issue of the connection strengths between units. In a simplified version of a connectionist model, when unit A and unit B are simultaneously excited, the strength of the connection between them increases. When units are not mutually excited, the connection between them weakens. It is no coincidence that the basic assumptions underlying PDP models are similar to these neural models.

The Brain: From Compartmentalization to Mass Action

For centuries the brain has been a puzzle. It is less so now because of the tenacious work of numerous researchers over several decades, but it still has its secrets.

Early scholars believed that the brain had nothing to do with thought and perception. Aristotle, for one, ascribed such functions to the heart. Much later, the pseudoscience of phrenology held that character, personality, perception, intelligence, and so on were exactly localized in the brain (see Figure 2.3). Phrenologists believed that personal character, aptitude, and emotions could be measured by examining the bumps on the outer surface of the skull. This view received early scientific support from neurologists, who discovered that some brain functions were related to specific areas.

As we learned in the first chapter, the focus of research in brain science for more than a century has been to find specific brain regions that correspond to specific behaviors. Important findings were made that confirmed the notion of compartmentalization; that is, some functions, such as motor activities, language processing, and sensing, are

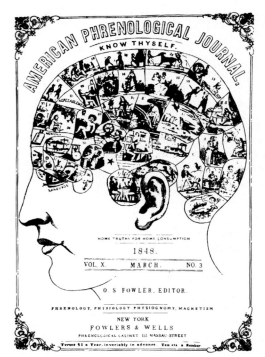

FIGURE 2.3

Phrenological map of the brain.

each associated with a specific area of the brain. The theory of compartmentalization reached its zenith among the phrenologists, who claimed to locate in the brain such attributes as generosity, mother love, secretiveness, combativeness, and even Republicanism. However, one French neurologist, Pierre Flourens, considered this a lot of nonsense. In his investigations, he excised portions of the human brain and examined the effect of the surgery on behavior. He concluded that motor and sensory functions are not a matter of simple localization in specific regions, as suggested by other researchers, but that these functions are also distributed in other parts of the brain. Traumas or injuries to the brain seemed to affect all higher functions equally, a position later called the aggregate field theory.

Compartmentalization is contrasted with the view that the brain operates as a holistic organ, with cognitive processes distributed throughout. There is a compromise view, which seems consistent with the best knowledge in the field. It holds that some mental attributes are localizable to specific regions, or constellations of regions, within the brain. These include control of motor responses, sensory terminals, vision, and some language processing. However, many functions—especially higher-order cognitive processes such as memory, perception, thinking, and problem solving—are divided into subfunctions, which are distributed throughout the brain. We will trace the development of this argument, beginning with an overview of the brain and its functions.

Early phrenological mechanical measuring device.

The Anatomy of the Brain

The anatomy of one hemisphere of the brain is shown in Figure 2.4. The brain is divided into two similar structures, the right and left cerebral hemispheres. The hemispheres are covered by the cerebral cortex, a thin, gray, moist material densely packed with the cell bodies of neurons and short unmyelinated axons. The cerebral cortex is only about 1.5 to 5 millimeters (1/4 inch) thick (Crick & Asanuma, 1986). Because it is deeply convoluted, the surface area of the cortex is greater than it appears. The ridges between the folds are called gyri (singular, gyrus), and the grooves are called sulci (singular, sulcus). Deep and prominent sulci are called fissures. If the cortex were spread out, it would measure about 324 square inches, or about three times the amount seen on the surface. The convoluted cortex, with its characteristic walnut appearance, makes it possible to increase its surface area without increasing the size of the skull, a clever biological solution that enables the human animal to retain its mobility and thus survive, unencumbered by a monstrous cranium. It is within the cerebral cortex that human thought, sensation, language processes, and other cognitive functions take place.

The brain processes information contralaterally. That is, sensory information from the spinal cord (for example, the sense of touch) that enters the left side of the body crosses over and is initially processed in the right hemisphere. Also, the motor areas of each hemisphere control movements of the opposite side of the body.

FIGURE 2.4

Schematic drawing of the major sections of the human brain.

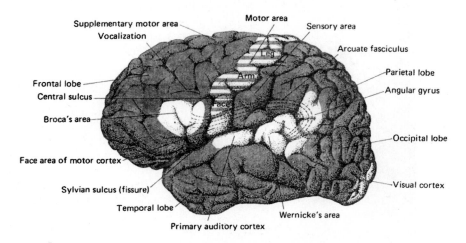

The surface of each hemisphere is divided into four major sections, some of which are marked off by major convolutions or fissures. These four areas are the frontal, temporal, parietal, and occipital lobes. Although each lobe is associated with specific functions, it is likely that many functions are distributed throughout the brain.

Early knowledge about the specialized functions of the brain can be traced to the last century. Especially important is the work of the French neurologist Pierre Paul Broca, who studied aphasia, a language disorder in which the patient has difficulty speaking. This disorder is commonly found in stroke victims. Postmortem examination of aphasics' brains revealed lesions in the area now called Broca's area (see Figure 2.5). In 1876 the young German neurologist Karl Wernicke described a new type of aphasia, which was characterized by the inability to comprehend rather than the inability to speak.

Wernicke agreed with earlier scholars that certain mental functions are localized but that these are, for the most part, concerned with simple perceptual and motor activities. Complex intellectual processes such as thinking, memory, and understanding result from the interactions among perceptual and motor areas. Support for this position came around the turn of the century, when the Spanish physiologist Santiago Ramón y Cajal showed that the nervous system is made up of discrete elements, or neurons.

What had been a mosaic concept of the mind (conceptually not far removed from the phrenological view, without the bump readings) was now a connectionist concept: complex cognitive functions take place and can be understood in terms of the network of links among neurons. Furthermore, Wernicke suggested that some functions are processed in parallel in different parts of the brain. Wernicke's hypothesis about the brain and its functions proved to be important to modern cognitive psychologists.

Redundant processing of information, as suggested by the parallel processing theory, might appear wasteful and contrary to the view that animal systems are efficient to the point of parsimony. However, it is arguable that involved biological systems are usually redundant. Certainly this is true in the case of reproduction, where many times more eggs are produced than are fertilized and, among many species, many times more offspring are spawned than grow to maturity. Redundancy in nature is likely to play a central role in survival and adaptability. Perhaps redundant and parallel processing of neural information by humans increases our chances for survival and procreation. Thinking, and the science of cognition we now enjoy, are the serendipitous by-products of these primary functions.

The theories of Flourens, Broca, and Wernicke on the relationship between the brain and behavior were expanded by the American psychologist Karl Lashley of Harvard University. Lashley, however, was not concerned with aphasia in humans but with the locus of learning in rats. In his influential book *Brain Mechanisms and Intelligence* (1929), Lashley expressed his interest in brain injuries and behavior, with the aim of shedding light on the issue of localization versus generalization of functions. To study such phenomena, he examined lesions in the brains of rats to determine their effects on the animals' ability to master a complex maze. Small areas of damage to a rat's brain did not have much effect on maze performance. Since no specific area seemed tied directly to learning, Lashley concluded that learning was not confined to specific neurons. Lashley developed a theory called mass action, in which the importance of individual neurons is minimized and memories seem to be distributed throughout the brain. Lashley (1950) concluded that "There are no special cells reserved for special memories." The importance of his ideas lies in their suggestion that the brain operates in a holistic rather than compartmentalized manner. (About the same time, Alexander Luria was developing similar ideas in the Soviet Union.)

Recent studies of memory and blood activity (which is thought to reflect neural activity) suggest that some memory functions may be associated with certain areas of the brain, but perhaps not to the precise degree suggested by earlier data (see Penfield, 1959, for example).[2] We now believe that the brain contains areas associated with specific functions (such as, motor reactions) but that the complete processing of this class of information also engages other parts of the brain. Other functions (such as, thinking) seem to be widely distributed throughout the brain.

---

[2]This is not to suggest that Penfield's observations are erroneous, but that they are difficult to replicate.

Karl Lashley **(1890–1958). Founded the principle of mass action. APA president, 1929. Photo courtesy of Harvard University Archives.**

Space restrictions require that we examine only a sample of the existing experimental and clinical studies of brain structure and processes. Nonetheless, some general conclusions and their implications are in order:

- Many mental functions seem to be localized to specific regions or constellations in the brain, such as motor regions and sensory terminals. However, in addition to the regional concentration of these functions, further processing appears to take place in different sites.
- Many higher-order mental functions (such as thinking, learning, and memory, among others) seem to be redundantly processed. Neural processing of this class of information is redundant in the sense that it is distributed throughout the brain and processed in parallel at many locations.
- Damage to the brain does not always lead to a diminution of functions. This may be because the intact connections can take over the original function or the intact connections can be rearranged in a way that allows them to accomplish the primary task. In general, however, performance diminishes correspondingly to the amount of tissue destroyed.

Consider a model of neural processing that is consistent with the existing clinical, experimental, and psychological knowledge. This model of neural processing proposes that neurons process information in a serial way, somewhat analogous to the von Neumann computer mentioned earlier.

In this model (see Figure 2.5A), information from one neuron is passed to another neuron, then to another neuron, and so forth. Although this model may be consistent

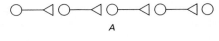

A

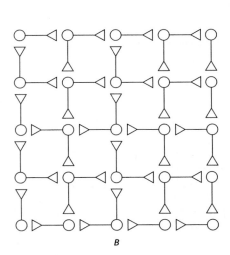

B

FIGURE 2.5

A. A cellular connection model in which neurons are connected in series. B. A cellular connection model in which chains of neurons are connected in series and in parallel. When a neural link is broken, the system typically does not fail completely because of the possibility of parallel processing.

with some of the experimental evidence, it seems too simple to account for some findings, especially the work of Lashley, which would suggest that a break in the link does not (altogether) interfere with the process. Another possibility is that the processing of complex, higher-order, intellectual tasks is accomplished through a series of functional links in a parallel network (see Figure 2.6B). In this model, information is processed in parallel as well as in series. Thus, if part of the pathways is destroyed, the system does not necessarily break down completely, but it allows alternative pathways to take over some functions. The latter theory seems to be more consistent with the data and has influenced current thinking in cognitive psychology.

Many recent models of the brain have been made possible because of technical developments in the field of neuroscience, which have allowed a clearer view of the physical structures and internal workings of the human organism. Following is a brief review of those developments that have had an impact on cognitive psychology.

NEUROPHYSIOLOGICAL SENSING TECHNIQUES

A few years ago, neurologists had only a few tools and techniques to use in the direct observation and exploration of the human brain. These included excising of tissue, electrical probes, EEG recordings, and postmortem examinations. Psychologists, on the other hand, invented a whole arsenal of techniques in which the mind revealed itself, such as the momentary presentation of stimuli and measuring of reaction time. Recently, however, new instruments have been invented that have profoundly accelerated our understanding of the brain and, for our purposes, spun off a new breed of scientist that is part neurologist and part cognitive psychologist. The new technology was originally developed for the diagnosis of brain disorders, but it has now become a valuable research tool. These methods have already led to important new discoveries in the study of human cognition and promise to be an integral part of the future of cognitive science.

Many of these new techniques scan the brain in one way or another, with apparatuses similar to those shown in Figure 2.6A. In such procedures a patient is placed in the center of the scanning instrument similar to the one shown in Figure 2.6A, which records impressions from within the cranium or other parts of the body. The scan produces a cross-sectional image of the brain or other body part. The impression is first enhanced by a computer, then color coded, and finally displayed on a video terminal. Photographs and/or hard copies of the display are often made.

The microscope and telescope opened vast domains of unexpected scientific discovery. Now that new imaging methods can visualize the brain systems used for normal and pathological thought, a similar opportunity may be available for human cognition.

Michael I. Posner

FIGURE 2.6

Brain scanning techniques. All cognitive activities—from reading this text, to feeling anxious over a test, to listening to a lecture on modern architecture—are accompanied by an increased demand for energy within localized areas of the brain. These demands are met by increased blood flow and glucose supply. By monitoring oxygen, glucose, and blood flow, it is possible to identify the areas of increased metabolism and hence determine which areas of the brain are most active. A. Overall procedure for obtaining brain scans with a video display. B. CAT scan procedure in which low-intensity X-ray beams scan the brain. C. PET scan procedure, in which radioactive tracers are detected by peripheral sensors. These techniques have been useful in medical diagnosis and in studies of neurocognition.

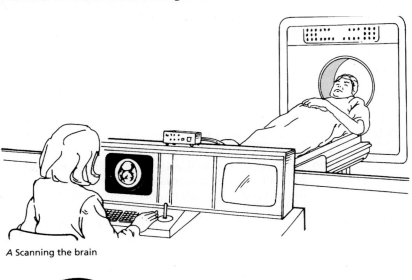

A Scanning the brain

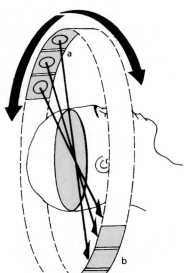

B CAT scan procedure

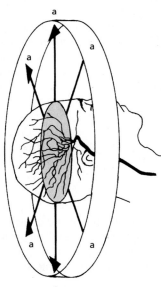

C PET scan procedure

Two types of brain scans are in general use: the computerized axial tomography (CAT or CT) scan and the positron emission transaxial tomography (PET or PETT) scan[3] discussed below. Other techniques include magnetic resonance imaging (MRI).

MRI and EPI

In the MRI technique the body is surrounded with very powerful electromagnets that align the nuclei of hydrogen atoms found in water. From these measures, it is possible to infer varying densities of hydrogen atoms and their interaction with surrounding tissues. Since hydrogen reflects water content, it is possible to use the MRI for diagnostic and research purposes. One of the main drawbacks of the technique, up until recently, has been the time it takes to form images using MRI technology. Because it required long exposure time, the technique was acceptable for viewing static biological structures. However, it was nearly useless for rapidly changing functions, those associated with cognition. It is now possible to apply high-performance data acquisition techniques that make it possible to capture an image in as little as 30 milliseconds, which is brief enough to record fast-acting cognitive functions. Also, the new methods, called echo-planar MRI (EPI), are capable of high-resolution images of functional activity in the brain. It is likely that further developments in the next few years will make EPI a practical tool for discrete visualization of brain structures and processes conducted in real time. For more detailed information, see Schneider, Noll, & Cohen, 1993; and Cohen, Rosen, & Brady, 1992.

CAT Scans

The CAT scanner works by means of an X-ray machine that rotates around the skull, bombarding it with thin, fan-shaped X-ray beams (see Figure 2.6B). The beams are recorded on sensitive detectors on the opposite side of their source. This procedure is different from a conventional X-ray examination, which gives only one view of the body part. Also, with conventional X rays, large molecules (such as calcium in the skull) absorb the rays and partially occlude the organs behind them. The CAT scan rotates the X-ray beam 180 degrees, resulting in numerous "pictures" of the same organ and producing an internal cross section, or "slice," of the body part. This graphic cross section, called a tomogram (literally, "section writing"), has become critical in medical diagnosis. By displaying local blood flow and metabolic activities associated with pathology, tomography has led to more accurate diagnoses. In cognitive psychology, CAT scans have been used to display cognitive structures. An even more sophisticated version of the CAT technique, the dynamic spatial reconstructor (DSR), shows internal structures in three dimensions. One advantage of CAT is the ubiquity of machines. As of the mid 1990s, more than 10,000 scanners were in use in American hospitals. Also, recent technology has helped solve one of the problems with this technique. The temporal resolution, or shutter speed, had been about 1 second, with the result that dynamic processes (even the heart beat) appeared blurred. Now, an ultrafast CAT has been developed that speeds up processing so that previously blurred images are now clear.

---

[3]Sometimes also called SPECT, for single-photon emission computed tomography.

CAT scans of tomorrow.

PET Scans

PET scans (Fig. 2.7) differ from CAT scans in that they use detectors to measure radioactive particles in the bloodstream. Active parts of the brain require greater blood flow, hence more radioactive tracers amass in operative areas. These tracers emit rays, which can be converted into visual maps. The application of PET scans to cognitive neuropsychology has been particularly useful. At Lund University in Sweden, research scientists Jarl Risberg and David Ingvar (see Lassen, Ingvar, & Skinhoj, 1979),[4] working in collaboration with Steve Petersen, Michael Posner, Marcus Raichle, and Endel Tulving, have pioneered the use of PET scans in cognitive psychology (see Posner, et al., 1988). PET technology has provided some very interesting results (some of which is presented in this book), but the widespread research application is handicapped because of very high costs and because the time for images to be recorded is long (at present about 20 seconds).

The early PET studies measuring regional cerebral blood flow were based on the inhalation of 133xenon, which was used as the tracer substance. Risberg and Ingvar have successfully used 195mgold, administered intravenously. With this tracing material, high-resolution "maps" can be made in a very few seconds (Risberg, 1987, 1989; and Tulving 1989a, 1989b), thus giving the researcher considerable latitude in collecting cognitive data.

[4]See also *Scientific American*, September 1992, a special issue on "Mind and the Brain," and *Newsweek*, April 20, 1992, for readable accounts of brain function, blood flow, and imaging techniques.

Functional MRI   **PET**

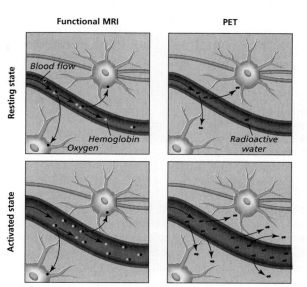

Resting state

Blood flow

Hemoglobin
Oxygen

Radioactive
water

Activated state

F I G U R E   2 . 7

**Blood flow to the brain
provides the signals detected
by functional MRI and PET.
When resting neurons (top)
become active (bottom),
blood flow to them increases.
MRI (left) detects changes in
oxygen levels, which rise in
the nearby blood vessels
when they are at rest. PET
(right) relies on the increased
delivery of injected
radioactive water, which
diffuses out of the vessels to
reach all parts of the brain.**
Scientific American, **April
1994, Raichle.**

Of particular interest to cognitive psychologists is the use of cortical blood-flow patterns in memory research.[5] For the past few years, Tulving has been developing a theory of memory that posits two unique types: episodic and semantic, or memory for personal events and memory for general knowledge, respectively. In one experiment (Tulving, 1989a), the subject was asked to think silently about an episodic (personal) event and then to think about something general. The research was conducted with a high-resolution Cortexplorer 256-HR system, which was developed by Risberg. For the tracer, a small amount of radioactive gold with a half-life of only 30 seconds was injected into the subject's bloodstream. Blood flow was monitored by measuring the number of tracers approximately 7 or 8 seconds after injection of the radioactive gold. The number of tracers in each area was measured by a battery of 254 extracranial gamma-ray detectors that snugly encircled the subject's head. Each detector scanned an area of approximately 1 square centimeter and produced a colored, two-dimensional map of the brain, which consisted of 3,000 pixels. Several measurements were made over a period of 2.4 seconds, and, with the assistance of appropriate computer transformations, they were made visible. The results of one subject's rCBF are shown in color on the inside front cover (top).

These photographs require some study to understand them, but initially we can see general differences in the patterns of blood flow, namely, neural activity, associated with different regions of the brain. Basically, it appears that episodic (personal) retrieval is accompanied by greater activation of the anterior portion of the cerebral cortex, and

---

[5]Although in several subsequent chapters memory research is discussed in detail, at this time we will consider a few topics in memory specifically related to brain tomography

Steven Petersen, **along with his colleagues at Washington University (St. Louis), has done pioneering work with PET and cognitive processes.**

semantic (general) retrieval is accompanied by greater activation of the posterior regions. Although these data are so fresh that further work is needed before definitive theoretical statements can be made, it seems safe to conclude that episodic and semantic memory systems involve different brain processes and that each has its own location. This in turn suggests that we may have multiple memory systems. Such observations are also consistent with pathological studies of lesions and subsequent loss of episodic memory (see Milner, Petrides, & Smith, 1985; and Schacter, 1987, for details).

In another attempt to find a direct correlation between cognitive processes and brain activity, Michael Posner, Steven Petersen, and their associates at the McDonnell Center for Higher Brain Functions at Washington University have conducted a series of significant experiments dealing with the processing of words by the normal, healthy brain. Using PET scanners, Petersen, Fox, Posner, Mintun, and Raichle (1988) injected short-lived radioactive isotopes in subjects to trace blood flow in the brain. There were four stages in one experiment in this group: (1) a resting stage, (2) the appearance of a single word on a screen, (3) the reading of the word aloud, and (4) the production of a use for each word. Each of these stages produced its own visual "signature" ; see the color illustration on the inside cover (bottom). (Datum from "hearing" is from another experiment.)

In this experiment, when a subject looked at a word on a screen, the occipital region of the cortex was activated; when hearing a word, the central part of the cortex was activated; when speaking a word, motor regions were activated; and when asked to produce related words (for example, if the word *cake* appeared, the subject was to produce

Elementary operations, defined on the basis of information processing analyses of task performance, are located in different regions of the brain. Because many such elementary operations are involved in any cognitive task, a set of distributed functional areas must be orchestrated in the performance of even simple cognitive tasks.

Petersen & Fiez

COMPUTER PETS

By means of PET images, researchers at the University of California (Irvine) have been looking inside the brain of computer game specialists and novices. In the PET images shown here collected by Richard Haier, we see the brain activities of a novice player on the left and those of an experienced player playing the same game on the right. The greater number of "hot spots" in the novice's brain suggest a much greater level of activity, as might be exhibited in someone who is learning a cognitive task, in this case, playing a computer game. The experienced player, on the other hand, burns less energy during the task, which suggests a greater efficiency (or at least a lesser demand for cerebral nutrition) in neural activity required for a well-learned task.

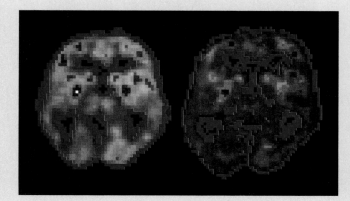

PET images depict levels of activity in the brains of two people playing a computer game. With blue and grey indicating high levels of activity, the scans reveal that an experienced player (right) burns significantly less energy than a novice (left). Learning, then, seems to be a function not of greater effort but of increased neuronal efficiency. Indeed, players who score high on standard IQ tests show the most precipitous drop in mental exertion while learning the game.

a verb that went with the word, such as *eat*), the associative region produced the greatest amount of activity, but other general activity throughout the cortex was also observed.

Even thought PET technology is still in its infancy, it will likely be refined in the future. In addition, other technologies will likely emerge. Even at this stage, the early results have already had a significant impact on cognitive psychology and related sciences. For example, the question of the localization of brain functions so widely touted by the phrenologists may have some credibility, although I hasten to add that the techniques and general theory of phrenology are *not* about to gain scientific respectability! Nor is the notion that many of the brain's functions require the cooperative integration of widely distributed areas in doubt. However, what does seem to be true, given the impressive initial studies, is that there is a surprising number of region-specific activities

EEG AND "SHADOWS OF THOUGHT"

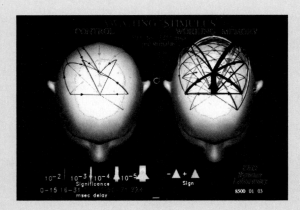

Recently Alan Gevins and his colleagues of the EEG Systems Laboratory in San Francisco have developed a "super" EEG system, called Mental Activity Network Scanner (MAN-SCAN), which can record as many as 250 images of cerebral activity per second. EEG recordings are also lighting fast—as fast as one-thousandth of a second, which is a real advantage over other imaging techniques that, in some instances, require many seconds to capture an image. For many years conventional EEG recordings have been used to record the minute electrical signals originating in the brain. Studies of traditional EEG recordings led to the discovery of low-amplitude beta waves, which were associated with alertness and attentiveness, and slower, larger alpha waves, which were associated with tranquility and relaxation. In MANSCAN a soft helmet with 124 electrodes is placed on the subject's head, and computers track the shifting centers of electrical activities. The tiny electrical impulses detected by the electrodes are plotted on a high-resolution MRI map of the brain, giving a dynamic impression of, as Gevins calls it, "shadows of thought." In the figure shown here, brain scans of five people are shown (see Gevins & Cutillo, 1993). In the left figure, subjects are waiting for a single number to appear. In the right figure, subjects must remember two digits while waiting for a third to occur. As shown, in the more complex task much greater communication between different areas of brain takes place as contrasted with the relatively simple EEG activity associated with the simple task. It may be, that keeping something in mind while monitoring other events requires diverse mental operations.

involved in complex cognitive tasks, such as specific types of language processing and attention matters. For example, it has been found that when we pay attention to real words, such as the text you are reading, specific posterior brain areas are activated. Nonsense words, however, do not activate these centers. Additionally, specific frontal and temporal areas of the brain are activated when subjects are asked to indicate the use of a noun (for example, hammer-pound) or its classification into a category (hammer-tool). (See McCarthy et al., 1993; Petersen et al., 1990; Petersen & Fiez, 1993; Posner, 1992, and Posner & Raichle et al., 1994.)

The above studies make use of recent advances in the neurosciences that tell us something about cognition, thought, and memory as well as the nature of the brain and its functions. We now turn our attention to the topic of the specialization of cerebral hemispheres.

A TALE OF TWO HEMISPHERES

If you removed the cranium from any person, you would see a brain with two plainly visible parts, each about the size of a fist, known as the right and left hemispheres of the cerebral cortex. Even though they appear identical, the two parts of the cortex differ widely in function. This difference in humans has been known for centuries, and it has also been observed in most mammals and in many vertebrates.

The purpose of contralaterality is still not completely understood but has contributed to the theory that the two hemispheres carry out distinctively different functions. There has been a profusion of scientific (see Kandel, Schwartz, & Jessell, 1991; Kupferman, 1981; and Sperry, 1982) and popular (see Ornstein, 1972) ideas about the functions of the hemispheres. (One even proposes that Eastern mysticism and Western rationalism are associated with the right and left hemispheres, respectively.)

Clinical evidence for contralaterality was first recorded by the ancient Egyptians, but the scientific confirmation of opposing functions emerged during the last century, when brain surgeons noted that tumors and excisions in the left hemisphere produced different effects from similar pathology in the right hemisphere. Left-hemisphere damage resulted in language impairment, while patients with damage to the right hemisphere were observed to have difficulties dressing themselves. Further indications of functional asymmetry appeared in the 1950s, when physicians treating patients with severe epilepsy cut the corpus callosum—the massive bundle of nerves that connects the two hemispheres (see Bogen & Vogel, 1962). By severing the connective tissue between the two main structures of the brain (a procedure called cerebral commissurotomy) surgeons hoped to confine the effects of an epileptic seizure to one hemisphere. Apparently, this worked. (Such radical surgery is not commonly done today.)

"Split-Brain" Research. Also in the 1950s, Roger Sperry at the California Institute of Technology conducted research on animals concerning the effect of the so-called split-brain procedure. The main thrust of this work was to determine the different functions associated with each hemisphere. Of particular interest was the finding by Myers and Sperry (1953) that cats that had undergone this procedure behaved as if they had two

Critical Thinking: Eye Movements and Hemispheric Processing

Try this little experiment. Ask a friend to answer this question: "What does it mean when we say, 'Facts are the abridgment of knowledge.'" Did your friend's eyes move to the right? Now ask, "Image your home and count the number of windows." Did the eyes look to the left? In general, especially among right-handed people, activation of left-hemisphere functions—those associated with language processing—are accompanied with right-body activities or right-sided orientations, while right-hemisphere functions—those associated with visual and/or spacial tasks—are accompanied with left-body activities.

Roger Sperry (1924–1994), Nobel
Laureate, introduced split-brain
research, which opened a new area
of research with far-reaching
implications regarding the brain.

brains, each of which was capable of attending to, learning, and remembering information independent of the other.

Sperry and his colleagues, notably Michael Gazzaniga, had an opportunity to study human patients who had undergone commissurotomies. In one study (Gazzaniga, Bogen, & Sperry, 1965), they observed that a patient who was given a common object, such as a coin or comb, in his right hand could identify it verbally, since information from the right side crosses over to the left hemisphere, where language processing is centralized. However, if given a common object in the left hand, the patient could not describe it verbally; he could point to it, but only with his left hand.

The studies conducted by this group and others indicated that, indeed, the left hemisphere is associated with special functions such as language, conceptualization, analysis, and classification. The right hemisphere is associated with integration of information over time, as in art and music; spatial processing; recognition of faces and shapes; and such mundane tasks as knowing our way around a city or getting dressed. These findings tend to support the argument for localization of functions. However, subsequent work indicated that the right hemisphere was capable of more linguistic processing, especially written language, than was initially believed. In addition, younger patients exhibited well-developed capacities in both hemispheres (Gazzaniga, 1983). Overall, these observations suggest that there is considerable plasticity in the developing human brain and that functions are not as clearly separated as they once were believed to be but rather are shared by various regions and hemispheres.

Much of the current work in the field of hemisphere specialization has dealt with visual perception, which has a unique system of processing contralateral information. Consider the visual system's anatomy in relation to the hemispheres (see Figure 2.8).

As shown, the processing of visual information follows the crossover principle, at least partly. Light information (for example, the light's reflecting off the text you are now reading) is picked up initially by the receptor neurons in the eyes. The system of nerve pathways from each eye to the brain is more complicated than that of other sensory systems. About half the nerve fibers from each eye follow the principle of contralaterality, but the remaining half do not; that is, they terminate on the same side as detected. Consider the left eye as shown in Figure 2.8. Information detected by the right side of its retina (the light-sensing membrane at the back of the eye, shaded gray) is con-

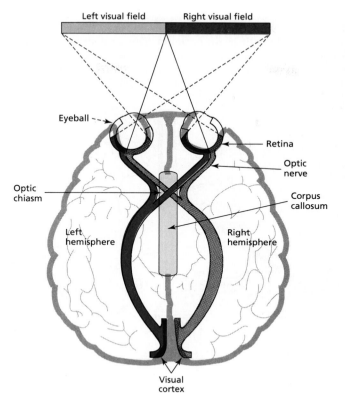

Left visual field   Right visual field

Eyeball

Optic
chiasm

Left
hemisphere

Retina

Optic
nerve

Corpus
callosum

Right
hemisphere

Visual
cortex

FIGURE 2.8

Schematic drawing of
the neural pathways
between the retinas and
the right and left
cerebral hemispheres.
Note that some of the
nerve fibers from each
eye cross over to the
opposite hemisphere at
the optic chiasm and
some do not.

nected to the right hemisphere, and information detected by the left side of its retina is connected to the left hemisphere. The same type of routing holds for the right eye.

If the corpus callosum is cut, as in the split-brain procedure, then information detected by, say, the right retina of the right eye would be "trapped" in the right hemisphere, since the corpus callosum is the conduit between the hemispheres. Likewise, information detected by the left retina of the left eye would be limited to the left hemisphere. Experiments in this area have produced fascinating results. If a split-brain subject is blindfolded, given a common object (such as a ball or a pair of scissors) in one hand, and then asked to retrieve that object by touch alone, the subject can do it, but only with the same hand that initially touched the object. If asked to retrieve the object with the opposite hand, the results show that the subject can do so with accuracy no greater than chance.

In a similar line of inquiry, a subject gazes at a particular point. It is then possible to present a visual stimulus that has been positioned so as to be detected by either the right or left side of the retina. Figure 2.9 illustrates the apparatus used in these types of

FIGURE 2.9

Apparatus used to study split-brain patients. The subject looks at a fixed point on a screen. A picture or word is momentarily presented on the screen, so that one hemisphere can process it. The subject is then asked to pick up the object, which is out of sight.

studies. In a typical experiment, a commissurotomized patient receives a stimulus, such as a picture or word, to the right or left of the fixation point so that the information is recorded in either the right or left hemisphere. If a picture (for example, a pair of scissors) is flashed momentarily to the left of the subject's fixation point (to be recorded and processed in the right hemisphere) and then the subject is asked to select the object by sight or touch, he or she can do so using the left hand, but not the right.

An equally impressive demonstration of the bilateral nature of the hemispheres is found in an often-cited article by Levy, Trevarthen, and Sperry (1972). In this experiment, a split-brain patient was asked to look at a fixation point. A "chimeric" face (half man and half woman) was momentarily flashed on the screen in a position that favored the processing of the woman's face in the right hemisphere and the man's face in the left (see Figure 2.10).

The subject did not report anything unusual about the composite, even though each hemisphere perceives a different face. When asked to tell about the face, the subject verbally described a man's features, which supports the concentration of verbal information in the left side of the brain. However, when asked to select the face from an array of photographs, the subject picked the woman's, which supports the concentration of pictorial information in the right side of the brain (see Bradshaw & Nettleton, 1981; and Springer & Deutsch, 1984, for a thorough discussion of cerebral specialization).

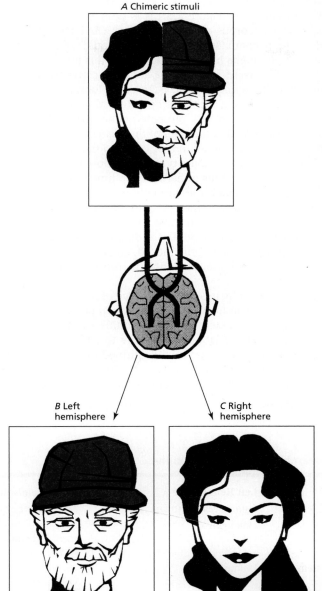

A Chimeric stimuli

B Left hemisphere

C Right hemisphere

Vocal naming

Visual recognition

FIGURE 2.10

Display of chimeric face (A) used with commissurotomized patients. Each hemisphere appears to register separate images: the left (B) records a man's face, the right (C) a woman's. When asked to describe the face, the subject verbally labels it as a man's; but when asked to point out the face among a display of faces, the subject selects the woman's.

Cognitive Studies with Intact Subjects. Because of the curious neural pathways involved in visual processing (see Figure 2.8), it is possible to do lateralization experiments with subjects whose corpus callosum is intact. Obviously, it is far easier to find unimpaired subjects than commissurotomized ones, and, as a consequence, a great number of cognitive experiments have been done with this population. Also, the procedure is relatively straightforward, and the apparatus is conventional. Typically, a subject, screened for handedness and gender, is asked to look at a central viewing point presented on a computer screen or tachistoscope. A word, a color, or some other type of visual information is then momentarily presented either to the right or left of the fixation point. Information presented to the right of the fixation point crosses over to the left hemisphere, and information to the left crosses over to the right hemisphere. The subject is then typically asked to make some type of decision about the visual information (for example, was it a word?), and his or her reaction time is recorded. The rationale behind the design is that if information is normally processed in one or the other hemisphere, then access to that information should be fast; if information is initially processed in the "wrong" hemisphere, it must pass over to the "correct" hemisphere to be processed, an operation that takes time. It should be noted that the amount of time involved in these experiments is very brief indeed, and a difference of 50 milliseconds is considered large. Of course, very precise timing instruments are necessary for this type of research.

Researchers have successfully used the technique of presenting a momentary stimulus to the right or left visual field to evaluate information processing. For an overview of these results, see Table 2.1. It is noted that results in this area are often equivocal due to faulty research design, subject variables, and failure to replicate previous experiments. Nevertheless; in general, these findings have confirmed that words and letters produce left-hemisphere superiorities, while faces and slanted lines produce right-hemisphere superiorities. Other studies have indicated differences in gender (Boles, 1984), in auditory

TABLE 2.1

Summary of Research on Cerebral Functions

Function	Left Hemisphere	Right Hemisphere
Auditory system	Sounds related to language	Music, environmental sounds
Spatial processes	Unknown	Geometry, direction sense, mental rotation of geometric forms
Somatosensory system	Unknown	Tactile recognition, Braille detection
Memory	Verbal memory	Nonverbal memory
Language processing	Speech, reading, writing, arithmetic	Metered prosody
Visual system	Letters, words, surrealistic art	Geometric patterns, faces, realistic art
Movement	Complex voluntary movement	Spatial-pattern movements

processing (Ivry & Lebby, 1993), during sustained visual attention (Whitehead, 1991), in prototype formation (Rees, Kim, & Solso, 1993), and in handedness (Annett, 1982). These studies have also suggested that the type of visual stimuli has differential effects depending on the hemisphere in which the material is processed (Boles, 1987). (See Chiarello, 1988; Kosslyn, Sokolov, & Chien, 1989; Bradshaw & Nettleton, 1981; and Springer & Deutsch, 1981, for overviews of the topic.)

The reason for laterality is less clearly understood than the fact that it does appear consistently, especially in humans. One intriguing hypothesis by Corballis (1989) gives the phenomenon an evolutionary basis: human evolutionary history reveals that right-handedness, tool use, and the development of left-hemispheric mechanisms for language use developed in hominids as long as 2 or 3 million years ago and set the stage for the development of more complex functions. Corballis (1989) writes, "Beginning some 1.5 million years ago with the emergence of the larger brained H. erectus, tool culture became more complex. However, a truly flexible tool culture and the rapid, flexible speech of modern humans may not have developed until later still, perhaps 150,000 years ago, when H. sapiens sapiens emerged in Africa, to subsequently populate the globe" (p. 499). According to Corballis, the evolution of hemisphere specialization may be associated with flexibility of thought and generativity, or the ability to combine elements using rules to create new associations—be they words, sentences, or more complex tools. Generativity may be uniquely human and is associated with the left cerebral hemisphere. Corballis's theory is fascinating, but it should be considered in light of studies done on language processing and tool use by chimpanzees and apes (see Gardner & Gardner, 1969). Further developments in this area are worth watching.

Impressive as they are, these experiments regarding the dissimilar nature of the hemispheres need to be considered in a larger context. Although a sizable number of careful experiments and demonstrations have indicated that some functions are located in specific areas of the cortex, it is likely that cerebral processing is also distributed throughout other places in the brain. Even in the case of hemisphere specialization, the brain seems to operate as a holistic organ. It should be noted that many of the research paradigms reported here involved patients whose corpora callosa have been severed and were designed to demonstrate the bilateral nature of the human brain. In normal humans the connective tissues are intact, and the two hemispheres operate cooperatively with massive "communication" between them.

Cognitive Psychology and Brain Science

In an effort to understand the human mind better, cognitive psychologists have become more interested in the organ of the mind—the brain. Their interest in the brain sciences has been matched by that of brain scientists looking to cognitive psychology to provide models of human information processing. We have seen that specialization as well as diversity of functions can be found in the human brain. The nervous system appears to be a massive parallel processing system, which is thought to be necessary for the rapid, complex, and creative processing of information.

Discoveries from brain science have had a direct impact on cognitive psychology and computer science. Theories of information processing have embodied knowledge from neuroscience. An example of this is the recent interest in neurally inspired PDP models. In the field of computer science, we see renewed interest in the modeling of computers, not only to perform humanoid functions but also to mimic neuronetworks in their architecture.

Summary

1   The mind-body issue has been debated for centuries. The term *mind* refers to the functions of the body, specifically the brain.

2   Using studies of regional cerebral blood flow (rCBF), Tulving found specific regions of the brain that are active during episodic memory processes and other regions active during semantic memory processing.

3   Neurocognition is the scientific study of the relationships between cognitive psychology and neuroscience. Several reasons exist for the alliance between psychology and neuroscience. These include the need to find physical evidence for theoretical properties of the mind; the need among neuroscientists to find more comprehensive models of brain and behavior; the need to find relationships between brain pathology and behavior; the increased use of neurally inspired models of cognitive science; the increased use of computers to model neurological functions; and the invention of techniques that enhance the ability to depict brain structures more clearly.

4   The basic building block of the nervous system is the neuron, whose principal parts are the dendrites, cell body, axon, and synaptic juncture where neurotransmission takes place.

5   Neurologists have long debated whether the functions of the brain could be localized. The conclusion is that some gross functions are localized (for example, speech) but that functions are generally distributed throughout the brain.

6   Recently, brain scientists have developed techniques that allow high-resolution graphic depictions of brain activity. These techniques include MRI, PET, and CAT scans as well as other imaging procedures.

7   Split-brain and cognitive research has indicated that processing of information in the right hemisphere differs from that in the left hemisphere.

Key Words

aggregate field theory	mass action
cerebral commissurotomy	myelin sheath
cerebral cortex	neurocognition
cerebral hemispheres	neurotransmitters
compartmentalization	perceptrons
connectionism	phrenology
contralaterality	presynaptic terminals
corpus callosum	retina
electroencephalography (EEG)	sulci
fissures	synapse
gyri	tomogram

Recommended Readings

The field of neurocognition is relatively recent, and some of the best references are to be found in current issues of journals. Germane periodicals include *Science, Brain and Behavioral Sciences, Cortex, Journal of Neurophysiology, Psychobiology, Nature, Brain, and Brain and Cognition,* among others. Corballis's article "Laterality and Human Evolution" appears in *Psychological Review* (1989).

Some books of interest are Restak, *The Mind;* Blakemore, *Mechanics of the Mind;* Ornstein, *The Psychology of Consciousness;* and Benson and Zaidel, eds., *The Dual Brain: Hemispheric Specialization in Humans.* More specialized, but highly recommended, are Kandel, Schwartz, and Jessell, *Principles of Neural Science* (3rd edition); Thompson, *The Brain: A Neuroscience Primer* (2nd edition); and Squire and Butters, eds., *Neuropsychology of Memory.*

Perception of Sensory Signals

T HIS CHAPTER DEALS WITH how human observers gather information about their environment and with some of the initial stages through which that information is processed. We begin our examination of human cognition with the detection of sensory signals, because it is the initial step in the processing of information and because its elements, being relatively concrete and tangible, are somewhat more easily comprehended than others. We see, hear, smell, taste, and feel the phenomena of the world as the first link in a chain of events that subsequently involves coding information; storing information; transforming information; thinking; and, finally, reacting to information that in turn leads to new sensory cues that may initiate the cycle again. As shown in Figure 3.1, physical energy that falls within the limited range of human detection stimulates the sensory system, is transduced (converted to neural energy), is briefly held in a sensory storage, is subjected to further processing by the central nervous system (CNS) and coded, and may be passed on to memory systems for processing, the results of which can initiate responses that become part of the stimulus field for further processing. (A large portion of the remainder of this book deals with the very complex and abstract processing of information that takes place in the memory systems.)

It is useful to keep in mind that the flowchart shown in Figure 3.1 (and others used throughout the book) is a representation—in this case, of the hypothetical stages through which information is processed. It is certainly not the case that the brain is arranged more or less as shown in the illustration; but this model and the many more to

FIGURE 3.1

The stages of information processing showing external phenomena and internal processes and structures.

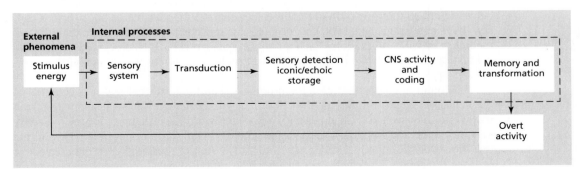

follow have value as visual conceptualizations of the various stages of information processing postulated in cognitive psychology. What is new in cognitive psychology is the capability to see the activation of the brain as information is being processed. These new techniques, mentioned in the previous chapter, suggest that the hypothetical stages shown in this figure are analogous to actual physiological processes. With these recent viewing techniques, the dream of scientists throughout the twentieth century to observe the locus of brain activities associated with cognitive processes is rapidly becoming a reality. Some of these recent findings and trends are shown in this chapter and in later chapters on memory and higher-order cognition.

Cognitive psychologists are interested in the perceptual process for several reasons: (1) It is presumed that higher-order cognitive phenomena (for example, thinking, memory, and semantic organization) are a consequence of events outside the organism. (Hence, the study of the identification of sensory signals may provide clues as to how these higher-order phenomena develop.) (2) There is evidence that the observer's detection of sensory signals is influenced by his or her past intellectual history and needs. (3) If information is stored in memory in an abstract form, then knowledge of the "real" nature of sensory experiences can help in determining the extent and form of the abstraction (in terms of its departure from the "real").

This chapter is organized around three aspects of the perceptual phenomenon: (1) the sensory perception of stimuli per se, (2) perceptual span, and (3) perceptual stages.

SENSATION AND PERCEPTION

We know through our senses. Our knowledge of the world is initially sensory in nature; stimuli above a certain level of intensity activate sensory receptors. What we make of these sensations is largely a matter of our knowledge of the world.

The term *sensation* refers to the initial detection of energy from the physical world and is studied, in detail, by specialists in psychophysics, that branch of experimental psychology that deals with the relationship between the physical world and its detection through the sensory system. The study of sensation generally deals with the structure and processes of the sensory mechanism (the ear, the eye, and so on) and the stimuli that affect those mechanisms.

The term *perception*, on the other hand, involves higher-order cognition in the interpretation of sensory information. *Sensation* refers to the initial detection of stimuli; *perception* to an interpretation of the things we sense. When we read a book, hear a concert, have a massage, smell cologne, or taste caviar, we experience far more than the immediate sensory stimulation. Each of these sensory events is processed within the context of our knowledge of the world; our previous experiences give meaning to simple sensory experiences.

The point of contact between the inner world and the external reality is centered in the sensory system. Studies of the relationship between the physical changes of the world and the psychological experience associated with these changes occupy the activities of a large and important group in psychology. Our study of psychophysics in this text, however, is limited to only a few topics. The first of these topics is the concept of sensory thresholds, in which we consider how much physical energy is necessary for conscious-psychological detection to occur. The next topic is a contemporary approach to sensory thresholds called signal detection theory. The final topic in this chapter deals with how much information can be perceived in a brief period.

Illusions

The dichotomy between sensory experiences and the perceived interpretation of those experiences has occupied a central position in perceptual research and continues to intrigue many cognitive psychologists. One line of research uses measurement of the physical and psychological quality of the same sensory stimuli. Sometimes the two measures of reality, the "real" and the perceived, do not match, as in the case of perceptual illusion. A well-known example used in perceptual research is the Müller-Lyer illusion (see Figure 3.2), in which two equal segments of a line seem unequal. Although there are at least twelve theories as to the cause of this illusion (Boring 1942), it is probably partly influenced by our past experiences, which have taught us to expect that certain shapes are far away and others close. On the other hand, some argue that this illusion (and many more like it) reflects deep-seated invariant structures of the brain. A more involved type of illusion is that in the drawing by M. C. Escher shown in Figure 3.3. Here the visual cues of proximity and distance and of the behavior of running water do not appear consistent with each other.

Previous Knowledge

The relationship between perception and previous knowledge of the world is manifested not only in simple geometric illusions but also in the interpretation of scientific data. Figure 3.4A shows post holes found in an archaeological dig. If your knowledge of the tribe in question led you to the hypothesis that their huts had been rectangular, you would tend to "see," or interpret, the post hole data as shown in Figure 3.4B. Conversely, other hypotheses might lead you to interpret the pattern of post holes differently, as in Figure 3.4C. A useful exercise would be to hypothesize that the huts were triangular and to attempt an outline along those lines, selecting "relevant" and "irrelevant" post holes.

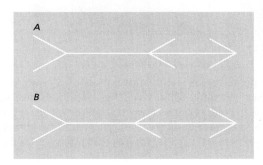

FIGURE 3.2

The Müller-Lyer illusion. The line segments in A are of equal length; those in B, which appear equal, are actually unequal.

FIGURE 3.3

"Waterfall" by M. C. Escher. M. C. Escher Heirs, c/o Cordon Art, Baarn, Holland.

So, the way you and I perceive the basic information of the world seems to be greatly influenced by our past learning—otherwise these curious lines on this page, called letters, would not be perceived as parts of words and the words would be devoid of meaning. We learn what visual (and auditory, tactical, gustatory, and olfactory) signals mean. Our brain is rich with associative structures that interpret the basic stimulus energy of the natural world.

FIGURE 3.4

Plans of huts hypothesized from the positions of post holes found in an archaeological dig. A: pattern of holes (black shapes). B and C: hypothetical plans of huts.

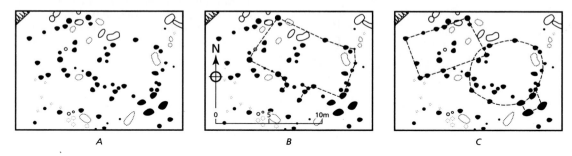

Sensory-Brain Predisposition

There is another side to the sensory and perceptual process that is supported by studies of the physical makeup of the sensory system and the brain. The physiological rudiments of the sensory system, which is commonly thought to be composed of the receptors and connecting neurons of the five senses (hearing, sight, touch, taste, and smell), have been known for several centuries. For example, in the early part of the seventeenth century, the philosopher Descartes did experiments on the eye of an ox. These experiments revealed some of the basic processes of vision (see Figure 3.5).

Each of these senses has, to a greater or lesser degree, yielded its secrets through the effort of physiologists, physicians, and physiological psychologists throughout the past 150 years. Knowledge about the brain and its role in perception, on the other hand, has been slow to develop, partly because of its inaccessibility. Direct observation of the workings of the brain typically involved the removal of a portion of its hard calcified case, which had evolved over millennia for the very purpose of keeping the brain from harm's way, or the postmortem scrutiny of brains by physicians interested in finding the neurological basis for symptoms. These studies indicated some gross features, such as the well-known contralaterality of the brain in which cerebral damage to one hemisphere resulted in a deficiency in the opposite side of the body. Other, traumatic episodes, such as getting rapped on the back of the head in the region called the occipital lobe, result in "seeing stars." We "see" bright flashes, and yet the eye does not detect such things. It appears that by stimulating the occipital cortex directly, something like vision is actuated in that part of the brain. Brain scientists have recently been able to observe the sensory, perceptual, and cognitive processes of the brain without removing the skull or clobbering people in the cranium. These techniques involve both behavioral data, such as reaction time experiments, or imaging technology, as discussed in the previous chapter (PET, CAT, MRI, and the like). Now, for the first time in the science of the mind, it is really possible to see the workings of the brain as it perceives information about the world and how those perceptions are routed through the labyrinth of the brain.

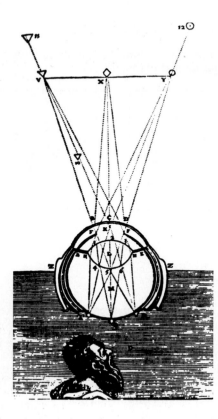

FIGURE 3.5

Descartes's diagram of an eye. In *La Dioptrique* (1637) Descartes showed the result of an experiment with an ox eye from which the outer back surface had been removed and replaced with paper showing tiny inverted images.

There is another side to the story of sensory signals, and that is the theoretical and evolutionary side. Some of these thoughts pose the question: What is the rationale of our sensory, perceptual, and cognitive system as a reflection of the world. The windows of the mind, the human sensory system, emerged with the physical changes that occurred in our evolving planet. Very simple organisms developed specialized cells that reacted to light, and, over millions of years, those cells became more and more specific in operation until, in time, something like an eye emerged (see Figure 3.6). With the evolution of the eye, the brain also emerged. After all, it's nice to see the world, but even nicer to understand what it means! The eye (and other sensory organs) are as stupid as

Mind and world . . . have evolved together, and in consequence are something of a mutual fit.

William James

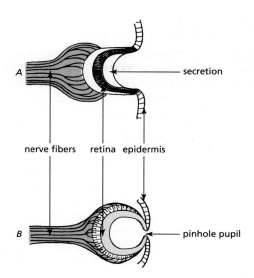

secretion

nerve fibers retina epidermis

pinhole pupil

FIGURE 3.6

The eye pit of a limpet is shown in A, and the pinhole eye of a nautilus showing rudimentary receptions and nerve fibers is shown in B.

the brain is wise, but one without the other is like the beauty of a rose to a statue. Conversely, a wise brain without sensory input is devoid of essential knowledge of the world. Sensations of the world and what they mean are as much a function of the biologically fixed mechanisms as they are of the past history of the observer.

Some contemporary scholars, such as Roger Shepard, have been searching for the perceptual-cognitive universals of the world (see Shepard 1992, 1994, and 1995). The way our genes shape an individual's perceptual and cognitive capacities are explored in answer to the age-old question, "How is the physical world seen by the human brain and eye?" The quest is an ancient one going back at least to Greek philosophers. However, aided by modern technology, we may be getting closer to finding some of the invariant structures of the eye and brain that distort in unique ways our entire knowledge of the universe. Alas, we cannot lay out all of the details of these theories, but to the curious, you will find a plethora of new sources on the topic.

Our view of the perceptual process, then, is that the detection and interpretation of reality is determined by the stimulus energy sensed, by the structural composition of our sensory systems and brain, and by the knowledge we had prior to a particular experience. A large portion of cognitive research is concerned with the question of how the sensory systems and brain distort sensory information. It now seems that the things stored in our memory are frequently abstract representations of reality. The key to the processing of sensory information and its cognitive interpretation seems to be the abstraction of information. At the sensory level, information is very specific, whereas on the interpretation level, information is commonly abstract. Our view of the world is determined by the integration of what we know (in an abstract sense) with what we sense (in a specific sense). Throughout this book (especially in the discussion of semantic memory), we expand this notion. Now, however, we turn to another aspect of how sensory information is perceived.

Threshold

The belief that one had a conscious experience when stimulus energy was transduced to the brain gave rise to numerous psychophysical experiments on thresholds. It was thought that when the amount of energy available exceeded a certain level (the threshold), it excited sensory neurons or "passed through," much as one might pass through a doorway. Energy inadequate to excite neural activity was said to be below the threshold, or subliminal; energy adequate to excite activity was said to be above the threshold, or supraliminal. The concept of thresholds from the point of view of signal detection theory is more complex, as we shall see later in this chapter.

When we consider the theme of thresholds in psychology, inevitably we run across an interesting topic with practical applications: the subject of subliminal messages. At the turn of the century, Knight Dunlap (1900) investigated subliminal perception[1] by showing two lines of equal length to subjects and asking them to identify which line was longer. In some conditions, a very faint shadow of the distorting "wings" of the Müller-Lyer illusion (see Figure 3.2) was projected, producing the illusion of one line's being longer than another. These "subliminal" stimuli did indeed create an illusion that caused subjects to misjudge the length of the lines. Prophetically, others had difficulty

---

[1]The term *subliminal perception* has worked its way into common American usage, but, like many technical terms used colloquially, the meaning is distorted. *Subliminal perception* is an oxymoron: if a signal is below the limen (threshold), it is imperceptible. The common (and now technical) use of the term suggests that *subliminal perception* is the unconscious perception of weak, or disguised, superliminal stimuli.

Everything We Know Is Wrong

It is useful to think of the various elements of the sensory system as channels that are open to external reality. Only the sensations that are detected by our receptors are available for higher-level processing and, because the system is limited in its receptivity, our knowledge is necessarily restricted. It is likely that we overemphasize the importance of the features of our physical universe that we can detect, while underemphasizing the importance of those we do not perceive or that require special filters to facilitate their transduction. Consider the change in your view of "reality" if your eyes could "see" infrared radiation but could not "see" the normally visible part of the spectrum. Would our day and night schedules be the same? What would be the effect on history, on marketing, on fashions, on philosophy—indeed, on the whole of society? Most importantly, consider the effect on how we conceptualize reality. Because we apprehend reality through such limited (hence distorting) channels, we are forced to conclude that everything we know is wrong. However, within the limits of our sensory apparatus, we are able to rough out a descriptive system of how we process the immense amount of information that we can detect, being mindful that the reality of our immediate world is many times more bustling than that sensed.

reproducing these findings (see Manro & Washburn, 1908), and to this day the field is replete with contradictory findings.

Many have heard of the apocryphal use of subliminal advertising popularized by Norman Cousins (1957), in which the words *Eat Popcorn* and *Drink Coke* were flashed on a movie screen so briefly that most people did not report seeing them. Reportedly, sales of popcorn and Coca = Cola rose. So insidious were such revolutions that the Federal Communications Commission (FCC, 1957) ruled that subliminal advertising is deceptive and inconsistent with the obligations of a licensee.

In spite of the potential commercial value of subliminal advertising, the results of many experiments and campaigns have been inconclusive and sometimes contradictory (see Holender, 1986; and Pratkanis & Greenwald, 1988). Some of the popular books in the field even border on the absurd. One way to interpret the field is to consider it as part of the important area of priming, in which the data tend to be more reliable. We consider this issue in a later section. Now, consider the psychophysical problem of establishing thresholds, or limens.

The relationship between the energy of stimulus and the resulting psychological sensation is not clear-cut. A typical relationship between probability of detection and strength of stimulus is shown in Figure 3.7. If sensory thresholds were absolute and discrete, however, and if our measurement techniques were perfect, we would routinely expect functions to be like those shown in Figure 3.8.

Our human subject in this world of perfect sensory detection, when exposed to a specific energy of sound or light, of taste, of pressure, or of other stimuli would constantly report his or her sensation. However, it appears that sensory judgments are based not only on the nature of the physical stimuli but also on the subject's decision processes, which, in turn, are based on a complex array of cognitive mechanisms. Raw energy of above-threshold value is judged by the subject as to whether it provides a stimulus strong enough to produce a positive response. That subjective evaluation is intimately related to the immediate psychological consequences as well as to the subject's experience in dealing with similar events. Not only are human beings prone to have

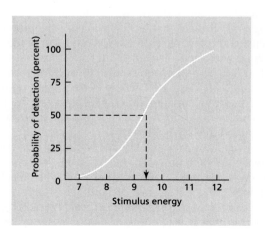

FIGURE 3.7

Typical relationships between strength of stimulus and probability of detection.

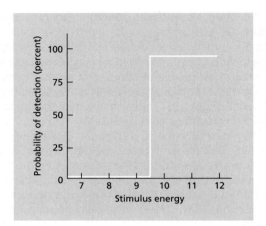

FIGURE 3.8

The ideal relationship between strength of stimulus and probability of detection.

their sensations influenced by higher-order cognitive mechanisms (memory, meaning, thought), but the stimulus or signal may also have ambiguous characteristics that distort its detection and interpretation. For example, even under highly controlled laboratory conditions, all noise (extraneous stimuli) may not be eliminated. An analogy might be made with the noise that is generated by highly sensitive laboratory instruments. A powerful amplifier capable of detecting the faintest of signals and magnifying them may itself generate extraneous sound that can be confused with a subject's response.

SIGNAL DETECTION THEORY

The introduction of signal detection theory in the mid-1950s significantly altered the way in which sensory thresholds were conceptualized. At that time, experimental psychologists were clearly influenced by behaviorism, which held, among other things, that psychology should study only behavior, or overt responses that could be directly observed and measured. Central to the behavioristic approach was the concept of stimulus-response (S-R) psychology, which held that all behavior can be viewed in terms of responses to stimuli. The science of psychology, therefore, was one of identifying stimuli and the responses associated with them, as well as the processes that were hypothesized to intervene between S and R. The approach seemed to work quite well, especially in establishing sensory thresholds (as described above), verbal learning research, animal studies, and other major topics of the day. Gradually, however, the psychological community came to the realization that human behavior was an enormously complex event that could not be understood in simple S-R terms.

Among the forces that changed the way the human organism was conceptualized were advances in signal detection, which provided the much needed basis for postulating the links between the stimulus energy of our external world, its detection, and the internal representation that was the consequence of both the stimulus and previous knowledge. Signal detection theory had its origin in electrical engineering and statistical-decision theory. During World War II, engineers developed a theory of signal detection that was applied to the detection of aircraft by radar equipment. The similarity between radar signal detection equipment and human signal detection capabilities was noted by Tanner and Swets (1954) in a seminal report. The paper was concerned with the human subject's behavior in detecting light signals in a light background and as such dealt with the general topic of sensory thresholds. The part of the theory that was to have the greatest impact on psychology was the implication that human decisions about the presence or absence of a stimulus are influenced not only by signal strength but also by the nature of the task and the subject's knowledge of the results. Later investigators demonstrated that the probability of detecting a signal could be manipulated by providing such things as a payoff for a correct identification, or "hit," of a signal.

To illustrate the complexities of sensory detection, consider the plight of a lonely radar observer on a distant Alaskan outpost. The observer's task is to peer vigilantly into a radarscope several hours a day watching for something that hopefully will never be seen: a flight of enemy aircraft. If an enemy flight does appear, recognition of the signal may be critical to the lives of millions of people. If the observer's judgment is in error, that mistake may lead to interception of nothing but a flight of birds. Two types of stimuli can appear on the radarscope: evidence of aircraft or "noise"—the "extraneous stimuli" referred to in the previous section.[2] If noise is reported as a plane, the observer is guilty of a false alarm; if a plane is reported as noise, the observer is guilty of a "miss"—a serious dereliction. Only two other conditions are possible: one is a "hit" and the other is a correct rejection so that planes are reported as planes and noise is reported as noise. Table 3.1 shows these relationships.

---

[2]The terms *signal* and *noise* are borrowed from electronic communications, within which context *signal* refers to a regularly fluctuating electrical impulse and *noise* refers to any disturbance that obscures or reduces the quality of a signal. Psychologists have generally adopted these definitions but have modified the definition of *signal* to mean the stimulus the subject is asked to identify, while *noise* is the context of stimulation in which a signal may appear. Noise may be produced internally, as in the case of random neural activity, or externally, as in the case of background stimuli.

T A B L E   3 . 1

The Stimulus-Response Outcome Matrix for the Observer Responding Either "Yes" or "No" on Each Trial of a Detection Experiment

		Subject's Response Alternatives	
		"Yes, signal is present"	"No, signal is absent"
Stimulus Alternative	**Signal + Noise**	HIT A positive response when the signal is present	MISS A negative response when the signal is present
	Noise	FALSE ALARM A positive response when *no* signal is present	CORRECT REJECTION A negative response when *no* signal is present

From this basic model, we are beginning to understand human thresholds in complex experiences requiring a decision on the basis of ambiguous and/or hard-to-detect stimuli. In addition to the magnitude of the stimulus, two other factors affect the detection decision: observer expectancy that the signal (in our example, the airplane) will or will not appear, and whether reward or punishment can be expected to result from the decision.

The expectancy factor may develop as a result of the subject's instructions in the task ("Keep your eyes peeled; there's trouble in the Near East") or of prior knowledge ("At this time of year, a great number of geese migrate south" or "I saw some birds a few hours ago; there must be some more").

In the laboratory, the effect of both factors on signal detection can be manipulated and measured, the second less easily. If the radar technician's decision is a miss or a false alarm, the result may be tragic or costly. In the laboratory we can measure the effect of anticipatory reward or punishment on signal detection by manipulating the payoff contingency. For example, we may ask our subject to identify a cue in the visual field that will appear randomly in half the trials. If the right answer is given when the stimulus is actually present (or absent), we pay the subject five cents; if the subject misses or makes false-positive ("false alarm") identification, we subtract five cents. A payoff matrix for this plan would be symmetrical, as shown in Figure 3.9A. If we change the payoff rules so that twenty-five cents is paid for a hit while the payoff schedule for the other sections is unchanged (Figure 3.9B), we can expect an increase in "cue present" responses. Conversely, if we pay twenty-five cents for responding no when the cue is not present while the payoff schedule for the other decisions is unchanged (Figure 3.9C), then we would expect more "cue absent" responses.

Observer's Criterion and the Concept of Threshold

Another factor in signal detection is the strength of the signal. A powerful or unambiguous signal is more readily identified than a weak or ambiguous one. This factor is not

FIGURE 3.9

Payoff matrix for three schedules of reward.

		Decision				Decision				Decision	
		Cue present	No cue			Cue present	No cue			Cue present	No cue
Stimulus	Cue present	+5¢	−5¢	Stimulus	Cue present	+25¢	−5¢	Stimulus	Cue present	+5¢	−5¢
	No cue	−5¢	+5¢		No cue	−5¢	+5¢		No cue	−5¢	+25¢
		A				*B*				*C*	

Iran Jet Tragedy Probe Blames U.S. Ship Crew

Radar Data Reportedly Was Misread

A military investigation of the shooting down of an Iranian civilian airliner last month found that crew error arising from the psychological stress of being in combat for the first time was responsible for the disaster, Defense Department officials familiar with the inquiry said yesterday. . . .

The investigation found that in the stress of battle, radar operators on the Vincennes mistakenly convinced themselves that the aircraft they had spotted taking off from the airport in Bandar Abbas, Iran, was hostile and intended to attack the Vincennes.

With the perceived threat fast approaching, they wrongly interpreted what they saw on their radar screens in a way that reinforced this preconceived notion. . . .

The ship was also on high alert as the result of intelligence warnings that the Iranians might attempt terrorist attacks against Americans over the Fourth of July.

Source: New York Times, August 3, 1988.

---

uncommon to our social life. Suppose you are at a social gathering, and you notice someone of the opposite sex making frequent eye contact with you from across the room. How do you interpret that signal? Is it a stimulus to further social contact? Should you go to that person and introduce yourself? What determines your behavior? According to the principles of signal detection theory, you would probably react in light of your previous knowledge (and in this case, needs), the probable payoff (or punitiveness), and the interpreted strength of the "come hither" look. These forces can be identified and studied more clearly within the confines of the experimental laboratory, and, although the setting may not be as romantic as in the social situation, the experimental variables are likely to be more easily specified and unambiguously controlled.

In addition to its importance as a methodological tool in many fields of psychology, signal detection theory has far-reaching implications for the perspective it offers on the phenomenon of information processing. In brief, that perspective is that our perception of reality is directly influenced by our internal state as well as by extrinsic stimuli. No longer can the position be defended that our perceptual detection mechanisms are energized only by sensory cues falling on "mindless" creatures. Instead, it is far more realistic to view the detection of stimuli as a combination of forces, some of which originate within our cognitive domain. Signal detection theory, and its later psychological adaptation, provided modern psychologists with a link between the earlier analytic findings of psychophysics and the cognitive systems hypothesized to explain the detection of sensory events, which had eluded empirical testing. The development of cognitive science was also facilitated by other theories in information processing.

Another important issue in the development of cognitive psychology dealt with the amount and kind of information human subjects can process. We now turn to this issue.

PERCEPTUAL SPAN

How much can we experience at a brief exposure? This long-asked question is concerned with the phenomenon called perceptual span, an early component in the processing of information. We know that the world is teeming with stimuli, a huge number of which are within the range of sensory detection. How many of these sensations are available for further processing?

Much of the confusion in considering human perceptual span resulted from the failure to discriminate between two hypothetical structures—preperceptual sensory store and short-term memory. The following often-cited early reference to the problem by William Hamilton (1859/1954) makes no distinction between the two storage systems.

> How many several objects can the mind simultaneously survey, not with vivacity, but with absolute confusion? I find this problem stated and differently answered, by different philosophers, and apparently without a knowledge of each other. By Charles Bonnet the mind is allowed to have a distinct notion of six objects at once; by Abraham Tucker the number is limited to four; while Destutt-Tracy again amplifies it to six. The opinion of the first and last of these philosophers, appears to me correct. You can easily experiment for yourselves, but you must beware of grouping the objects into classes. If you throw a handful of marbles on the floor, you will find it difficult to view at once more than six, or seven at most, without confusion; but if you group them into twos, or threes, or fives, you can comprehend as many groups as you can units; because the mind considers these groups only as units.

If we have time to count the marbles, we will be nearly perfect each time, but, as Hamilton suggests, we apparently have a sensory store that is capable of quick decisions based on brief exposure to events. Common knowledge confirms this notion. If we close our eyes, we continue to "see" the world; if a piece of music ceases, we still "hear" it; if we remove our hand from a textured surface, we still "feel" it. Each of these sensory memories fades rapidly, however, and most are soon forgotten. What are the boundaries of these transitory impressions? How long do they last? How much can be perceived in how short a time?

The first experiment investigating perceptual span dealt with vision, not only because vision is an important sense but also because it is somewhat easier to exercise experimental control over visual than over other stimuli (touch or taste, for example). Visual studies also had a practical side in that they were related to the rapidly developing research in reading. (Many early studies of the perceptual span were concerned with the amount of information that could be apprehended in a brief period.) Javal (1878) had observed that reading was not done by smoothly scanning a line of text but was a matter of jumping from one fixation point to another. Reading, or the gathering in of textual material, took place at the fixation points, not during the jumps, or saccadic movement (Cattell, 1886a, 1886b; and Erdmann & Dodge, 1898). These early studies indicated that the most information that could be gathered during a single exposure was about four or five letters of unconnected matter.

It is important to our discussion of iconic memory (see the following section) to recognize that the conclusions of these early reading studies were based on what subjects reported seeing. This failed to take into consideration the possibility that the perceptual persistence was greater than four or five letters, but that the subject was conscious of—

that is, recalled having perceived—only four or five. One explanation of this phenomenon of capacity greater than recall is that at least two stages are called into play in the
reporting of stimuli: (1) the perceptual span and (2) the recall of immediate impressions. Until a series of critical experiments proved it wrong, however, the immutable
"fact" remained for sixty years that on average about 4.5 letters constituted the perceptual span in reading.

These critical experiments had two major effects on cognitive psychology. First, our
understanding of the capacity of the perceptual span was significantly changed; second,
the processing of information came to be viewed as taking place in successive stages,
each of which operated by different principles. This latter result was to strengthen the
"boxes in the head" metaphor as a way of representing hypothetical cognitive structures. We will encounter this metaphor in later chapters.

Now consider the current state of knowledge about momentarily presented visual
stimuli.

ICONIC STORAGE

Neisser (1967) called the persistence of visual impressions and their brief availability for
further processing a stage or condition known as iconic memory. There is some question as to whether the term *memory* is properly applied to these sensory phenomena.
Memory to many (if not most) cognitive psychologists suggests coding and storage of information in which higher-order cognitive processes are used. Although iconic memory
does involve some storage, recent findings suggest that it seems to be independent of
higher-order processes such as attention.

Many researchers have found that incoming information is accurately represented
in iconic memory but disappears quickly if not passed on for further processing. The
question arose whether, while making a verbal report—that is, "reading" visual information out of a rapidly fading sensory register—the subject loses some information. If
this were the case, then the amount of information thought to be contained in the perceptual span was actually only the amount of information that could be reported before
it faded away—in other words, a joint function of iconic fading and the time required to
report the visual information.

Sperling (1960) suspected that the earlier technique, in which subjects were asked
to report as many items as they could remember, is actually a test of what subjects remember of what they saw, which may be different from what they initially perceived.
The icon, or visual impression, may contain more than we can remember. To overcome
the problem, Sperling developed a partial-report technique (see Figure 3.10) in which for
50 milliseconds a subject was presented with an array of letters such as the following:

R	G	C
L	X	N
S	B	J

If subjects try to recall as much as they can of the nine letters presented, the
chances are they will recall four or five. Immediately following the display of each row

FIGURE 3.10

Recall in relation to delay of cue. Bar at left indicates when and how long letters were flashed; bar at right, immediate memory for this material. Adapted from Sperling (1960).

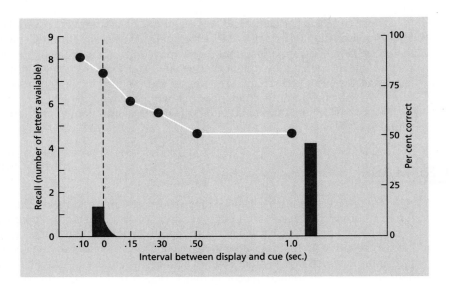

of letters, however, Sperling presented one of three tones—a high-, medium-, or low-pitched one. (Thus, in the example above, *RGC* might have been cued by a high tone, *LXN* by a medium-pitched tone, and so on.) The tones served to cue the subject to recall the first, second, and third row of letters, respectively. The result was that each line was recalled correctly nearly 100 percent of the time. Since the subject did not know in advance which of the three rows would be cued for recall, we can infer that all nine letters were equally available for recall; therefore, the sensory store must hold at least nine items. Another feature of Sperling's work was that it varied the time between the display of the letters and the presentation of the tone, making it possible to gauge the length of iconic storage. If the tone was delayed more than 1 second, recall dropped to the level expected in full-report examinations (see Figure 3.10).

Effect of Delay of Cue

To estimate the decay properties of this very brief store of information, studies have been done in which one interval between the letter display and the onset of the cue (a tone or a bar marker) was varied. The effect on recall indicated duration of the icon to be about 250 milliseconds (1–4 seconds).[3]

There is evidence that independently presented meaningless patterns can be combined in iconic memory to produce a meaningful pattern. In an experiment by Eriksen and Collins (1967), subjects were presented with two clusters of dots (see Figures 3.11A and B) that, when superimposed (see Figure 3.11C), produced the trigram *VOH*. The interval between presentation of the first and second patterns varied between 0 and 500 milliseconds. Success in identification of the trigram indicated the duration of iconic memory. Accurate identification declined gradually with time and then fell off sharply when the interval was more than 100 milliseconds. The results are generally consistent with those of Sperling.

Capacity

It appears that iconic storage is capable of briefly holding visual information in its original form with considerable detail. Some suggest that the capacity is nearly limitless (within the confines of the neural capacity of the retina). Iconic storage also appears to be a rather primitive type of memory in which information is not transformed or associated with other information.

From sensory storage experiments (Sperling, 1960, 1963, 1967), we can estimate the icon's capacity to be at least nine letters. Two factors limit our ability to determine iconic maximum capacity. The first is related to the role of cueing in iconic recall. It is possible to extend the visual display used in the Sperling experiment cited earlier to a 4×4 (as Sperling himself tried) or 5×5 array of letters and then cue recall with one of four or five tones. However, the cueing conditions in such an extended display must be more complex than those of the three-tone experiment discussed earlier and, presumably, more complex cognitive steps are required of the subject. One of those steps

---

[3]This is about the same time as that of the above mentioned fixation period in reading, and some have speculated that during reading subjects briefly record visual information—words and letters—and move on to further images only after the image is recorded.

FIGURE 3.11

Dot patterns used in testing duration of iconic-memory superimposition. Patterns A and B produce C, in which letters *VOH* are recognizable. From Eriksen and Collins (1967).

A   *B*   *C*

involves interpreting the cue and then searching the rapidly fading icon for its counterpart. More complex cues take more time to decode, and during that time the icon may fade, thus distorting the resultant impression of maximum storage capacity. A second factor limiting our ability to assess maximum iconic capacity is the fact that the retrieval of one item can have a detrimental effect on the retrieval of subsequent items. Tulving and Arbuckle (1963) have called this output interference, although similar phenomena have long been known by other names.

We can, then, make some conclusions about the nature of iconic memory. It is transitory, lasting only a few hundred milliseconds; it is accurate (some report it to be of photographic clarity); it has the capacity to summate information; it seems independent of subject control; and its storage capacity is at least nine items, and very likely far greater.[4]

Icons and Iconoclasts

Few theories in cognitive psychology have enjoyed such immediate success and long-term popularity as the iconic "discovery" by Sperling in 1960. However, some cognitive psychologists have questioned the ecological importance of the concept. For example, Haber (1983) argues that "the notion of an icon as a brief storage of information persisting after stimulus termination cannot possibly be useful in any typical visual information-processing task except reading in a lightning storm." Basically, the argument against the icon is that normal human perception does not involve brief fixations and that our heads and eyes are rarely motionless. Haber does not deny that considerable data exist on what he labels "visual persistence," but he does assert that normal vision is not made up of discrete flashes.

The anti-iconoclasts (see Coltheart, 1983; and G. R. Loftus, 1983) argue that the existence of the icon is undeniable and that it is created during the first tens of milliseconds of fixation upon which perception of the icon, not the stimulus itself, takes place.

ECHOIC STORAGE

If we "see" after the external physical stimulation has passed, can we "hear" after sound has passed? Apparently so. Neisser (1967) has dubbed the sensory memory for audition "echoic memory."[5] Echoic storage is similar to iconic storage in the sense that the raw sensory information is held in it with true fidelity (in order that the pertinent features can be extracted and further analyzed) for a very short time. As in the icon, which allows us an additional time to view fleeting stimuli, echoic storage allows us ad-

---

[4]The parameters of iconic memory and interpretation of experimental results within the framework of iconic memory remain a lively topic in contemporary cognitive psychology. For a discussion of these topics, see Holding (1975a, 1975b) and Coltheart (1975). For possible retinal characteristics in iconic memory, see Sakitt (1976) and Sakitt & Long (1979).

[5]The term has stuck despite the fact that it now appears that Neisser may have actually included other systems in his original description. Some researchers (for example, Baddeley, 1976; and Massaro, 1972) have used the term *preperceptual auditory memory* for the auditory equivalent of iconic memory, and, for later stages of auditory processing, the term *short-term auditory memory*.

ditional time to hear an auditory message. If we consider the complex process of understanding common speech, the utility of echoic storage becomes obvious. Auditory impulses that make up speech are spread over time. Information contained in any small fraction of speech, music, or other sound is meaningless unless placed within the context of other sounds. Echoic storage, by briefly preserving auditory information, provides us with immediate contextual cues for comprehension of auditory information.

Although a complete description of short-term memory is presented in Chapter 7, it is important that a distinction be made between it and echoic storage. Storage time in echoic storage is very short (between 250 milliseconds and 4 seconds); in STM it is relatively long (10–30 seconds). Auditory information is held accurately in both systems, but probably less faithfully in STM. Both have limited capacity while providing us with necessary contextual cues for understanding.

Several ingenious experiments have demonstrated the characteristics of echoic storage. Following the lead of Sperling (1960) and Averback and Coriell (1961), experimenters developed techniques whereby postcue signals allowed the subject to report only a portion of complex auditory stimuli. As with the vision studies, the technique provided information on the size and duration of the storage.

Stereophonic and quadraphonic equipment were used to generate a matrix of signals that would parallel those of the visual experiments of Sperling and others. One of the first demonstrations of echoic memory came from Moray, Bates, and Barnett (1965) in their paper "Experiments on the Four-Eared Man." The subject (with only two ears) was placed in the center of four loudspeakers or fitted with quadraphonic earphones that permitted four messages to be presented simultaneously—much as they might at a party or if the subject were in the center of a Beethoven string quartet. In each of these examples, a subject can attend to one voice (or signal) or another. In Moray's experiment, the message was one to four letters of the alphabet presented simultaneously through two, three, or all four channels. As in the early visual experiments, the subject was asked to repeat as many letters as possible. In the partial-report portion of the experiment, four lights, corresponding in position to the sources of the sound, could be illuminated to cue the subject as to the channels from which he or she should recall the letters. The lights were presented 1 second after the letters. Results, indicating that recall for partial report of auditory cues was superior to that for whole reports, were interpreted as supporting the notion that auditory information was briefly held in echoic storage.

An even closer analogy to the Sperling partial-report technique is found in an experiment by Darwin, Turvey, and Crowder (1972). Through stereophonic headphones, subjects were presented a matrix of auditory information (comparable to the visual display described earlier) consisting of three triplets of mixed random digits and letters. What the subject heard was three short lists of three items each, such as the following:

Left Ear	Both Ears	Right Ear
B	8	F
2	6	R
L	U	10

The time for the presentation of all items was 1 second. Thus, a subject would hear, simultaneously, "B" and "8" in the left ear, and "F" and "8" in the right. The subjective

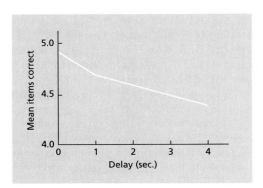

FIGURE 3.12

Recall in relation to delay of auditory cue. Adapted from Darwin, Turvey, and Crowder (1972).

experience is that right- and left-ear messages can be localized as emanating from their source, and the "middle message" (which usually emanates from a signal present in both ears simultaneously) appears to come from inside the head. This technique, similar to the three visual rows used by Sperling, in effect created a "three-eared man." Recall was measured either by means of the whole-report or partial-report techniques. A visual cue (a bar) was projected onto the left, middle, or right portion of a screen in front of the subjects. As with the visual studies, delaying the cue made it possible to trace the decay of memory. Darwin and his fellow researchers delayed the visual recall cue by 0, 1, 2, and 4 seconds; the corresponding amounts recalled are shown in Figure 3.12. Apparently echoic storage lasts up to 4 seconds but is most vivid during the first second after auditory stimulation.

We have reviewed two of the sense modalities through which information is detected: vision and hearing. Unfortunately, not enough data have been collected on taste, olfaction, or touch to allow us to make a definitive case for or against an early perceptual memory store for these senses corresponding to the iconic and echoic storage of vision and audition. Some evidence has been presented that suggests our tactile sense involves a somewhat analogous early store (Bliss et al., 1966).

FUNCTION OF SENSORY STORES

The seminal work on vision and audition has given the field of cognitive psychology important constructs that help explain the information-processing chain of events. What is the overall purpose of these brief and vivid sensory impressions of external reality? How do they fit into the larger reality of cognitive psychology?

Remarkably little attention has been directed toward integrating theories of sensory information into the larger scheme of human events. One speculation concerning iconic and echoic storage (and other possible, analogous systems) is that the extraction of information from the external, physical world follows a law of parsimony. Given the astronomical amount of sensory information that continuously excites our nervous system and the limited ability of higher-order cognitive systems to process information, only a small fraction of sensory cues can be selected for further processing.

This consideration seems to apply to vision and audition: It seems appropriate, even necessary, for the sensory system to hold information momentarily so further processing of pertinent items may take place. In reading, for example, an accurate impression of letters and words may be necessary for comprehension, and in listening it is likely that everything from understanding conversations to music is contingent on the exact recording of auditory signals.

It seems that a delicate balance exists between selecting the appropriate information for further processing and rejecting the inappropriate information. Temporary, vivid, and accurate storage of sensory information, as exists in echoic and iconic storage, seems to provide us with a mechanism by which we can select only the pertinent information for further processing. By preserving the complete sensory impression for a brief period, we can scan the immediate events, picking out those stimuli that are most salient and fitting them into the tangled matrix of human memory. When all works properly, no more or no less information is coded, transformed, or stored than is necessary for humans to carry on a normal existence. The speculation of Edwin Boring (1946) a long time ago seems compatible with this notion: "The purpose of perception is economy of thinking. It picks out and establishes what is permanent and therefore important to the organism for its survival and welfare."

Iconic storage, echoic storage and storage of other sensory information allow us the opportunity to extract only the information to be subjected to further processing. The very limitations of the human nervous system prohibit the recording and processing of all, or even a sizable fraction, of the bits of information available from our brief sensory store.

Our capacity for complex processing of visual stimuli may be understood in terms of sensory storage; the ability to read may well be based on iconic storage that allows us to extract cogent features from the visual field while discarding those extraneous stimuli that are unimportant. Similarly, our capacity to understand speech may well be based on echoic storage that allows us to hold auditory cues briefly in the presence of new ones so that abstractions can be made on the basis of phonetic context.

The development of short-term sensory stores, and other stores less clearly defined, may have been an essential component in evolution. Their function as survival mechanisms is purely speculative, but it is plausible that they allow us to perceive "everything" and yet attend to only the essential components of our percepts, making for the most economical system evolved. Sensory storage gives us the time to extract critical features for further processing and action.

Research efforts into sensory storage continue to go forward, with some researchers looking at the complexities of information transfer within these stores (for example, information transfer in iconic systems). Yet other promising research has attempted to find a neurological basis for echoic storage by means of EEG recordings and rCBF observations. (See especially the Finnish work by Mäntysalo & Näätänen, 1987; and Näätänen, 1987.) These new studies bear watching since with newer technology our capacity to image the structural components of cognition may make more visible the components of perception and thought.

Summary

1   Cognitive psychologists are interested in perception because cognition is presumed to be a consequence of external events, sensory detection is influenced by previous experiences, and knowledge about sensory experience may tell us how information is abstracted at the cognitive level.

2   Sensation refers to the relationship between the physical world and its detection through the sensory system while perception involves higher-order cognition in the interpretation of sensory signals.

3   Illusions occur when one's perception of reality is different from "reality." Illusions are often caused by expectations based on past experiences.

4   The perceptual process consists of the detection and interpretation of reality as determined by the stimulus sensed, the structure of the sensory system and brain, and previous knowledge.

5   Sensory thresholds are not absolute but are determined by both signal strength and the observer's decision processes.

6   Signal detection theory, from engineering and statistical-decision theory, has changed the way sensory thresholds are conceived and studied by psychologists. Factors found to influence thresholds are signal magnitude, nature of the task, observer expectancy, reward or punishment consequences, and the observer's criterion.

7   Studies of perceptual span concern the basic question of how much we can experience from a brief exposure.

8   Reporting stimuli perceived from a brief presentation is a dual-stage process: (1) the perception or actual sensory registration, and (2) the recall or ability to report what was registered before it fades. Partial-report techniques address the problem of confounding sensory capacity with recall ability.

9   Iconic storage holds visual input and appears to be independent of subject control factors (for example, attention). Capacity is estimated to be at least nine items with a duration of approximately 250 milliseconds.

10 Echoic storage holds auditory input with a duration of about 4 seconds.

11 Iconic and echoic storage may allow us to select relevant information for further processing, thus providing one type of solution to the problem of capacity limitations inherent in the information-processing system.

Key Words

echoic memory	sensation
iconic memory	signal
noise	signal detection theory
output interference	subliminal
perception	supraliminal
observer's criterion	threshold

Recommended Readings

Among the best introductions to many of the topics in this chapter are Massaro, *Experimental Psychology and Information Processing;* Klatzky, *Human Memory: Structures and Processes;* Baddeley, *The Psychology of Memory;* and Posner (ed.) *Foundations of Cognitive Science.*

Recent issues of *Perception and Psychophysics, Cognitive Psychology, American Journal of Psychology, Journal of Experimental Psychology: Human Perception and Performance,* and *Memory and Cognition* frequently carry reports on the subjects discussed in this chapter.

Pattern Recognition

IN THE PRECEDING CHAPTER on the detection of sensory signals, we saw how difficult it is to isolate sensory signals and to study the way we initially process them without, at the same time, resorting to a discussion of higher-order cognitive processes. In this chapter we turn our attention to pattern recognition. A pattern, in the present context, refers to a complex composition of sensory stimuli that the human observer may recognize as being a member of a class of objects. Thus, when I look at my friend's face, hear a Bach cantata, or taste sweet-and-sour pork, I am able to recognize each of these percepts as something previously experienced. The question is, what cognitive mechanisms need to be inferred to describe the process by which these complex patterns are recognized? Do I first see my friend's nose, eyes, lips, chin, ears, and hair and then put all these features together, or do I first see her whole face and then recognize her nose, eyes, lips, chin, ears, and hair?

In our discussion of the detection of sensory stimuli, we emphasized the perception of rather simple stimuli whose detection was based largely on the nature and strength of the stimuli. The processing of this information was data driven rather than conceptually driven. Data-driven processing is initiated by the arrival of sensory data, while conceptually driven processing of information starts with the human subject's forming a concept or an expectation of what information is likely to be encountered. It is likely that the human observer goes about the day-to-day perception of information by means of both data-driven and conceptually driven processes. Recognition of patterns is determined jointly by the information available to the senses and the knowledge stored in memory.

This chapter provides a bridge between the detection of simple sensory signals, which tend to be data driven, and the perception of complex patterns, which tend to be conceptually driven. In this chapter our discussion of pattern recognition concentrates on the early, somewhat uncomplicated processing of visual patterns that engage so-called higher-order processes only when necessary. Because cognitive systems are interrelated, on occasion we have to include in our discussion topics that are discussed in detail in later chapters.

The ability to recognize familiar patterns of sensory information is a spectacular human and animal attribute. This attribute allows us to recognize an old friend in a sea of faces, to identify an entire musical theme from a few notes, to read words, to enjoy the taste of a vintage wine, or to appreciate the smell of a rose. In our everyday life, we all use pattern recognition and may be deceived into thinking that the process is simple. How, for example, do you recognize your grandmother? Do you do it by means of "a grandmother template" that no other grandmother will fit? Do you have a grandmother prototype that epitomizes your grandmother but will still allow you to recognize her when she has her glasses on, or even when she has her hair done differently? ("Why, Gramma, I scarcely recognized you.") Alternatively, do you perform a hasty scan of her features and check each item against a master feature list for "my grandmother"? Although our discussion deals exclusively with visual pattern recognition, other forms of patterns—auditory, tactile, and so on—also affect our behavior. These have been less frequently investigated than visual pattern recognition, and this chapter reflects that disparity. As we shall see, even everyday pattern recognition involves a complex interac-

Form Perception

At this moment two American spacecraft called *Voyager* are hurtling through space on their way to the stars. These space vehicles are extraordinary in that attached to each is a gold-coated phonograph record, which, when decoded by creatures from some distant civilization, will tell about our planet and culture. Each record has about 90 minutes of music, sounds from the earth, greetings in 60 languages, and 118 "photographs" of people and planet. What, if anything, might intelligent inhabitants from a distant civilization make of this information? More important for human cognitive psychologists, what assumptions about human perception and information processing are embodied in this task?

Photographs 61 and 62 have been reproduced to illustrate the assumptions we make about human and alien perception of complex forms. In photograph 62, a Bushman hunter and (presumably) his son are hunting a small, horned, four-legged animal. Most humans easily discern that the animal is larger than the absolute size in the photograph. In photograph 61, scientists created a silhouette of the three principal forms in the photograph along with measurements of the animal and the boy. It was anticipated that an alien would be able to use these measures to understand the concept of depth perception, which we humans take for granted. However, when we consider the probable unique evolutionary history of earthlings and other creatures, it is unlikely that even these cues would be sufficient for complete and immediate understanding. We humans bring to form perception a myriad of cognitive and physiological attributes that produce a singular impression that, as far as we know, is special among intelligent beings.

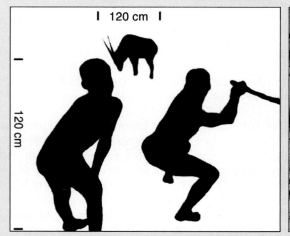

Diagram by Jon Lomberg. From Murmurs of Earth: *The Voyager Interstellar Record*, by Carl Sagan, F. D. Drake, Ann Drugen, I. Ferris, Jon Lomberg, and L. S. Sagan. Random House, Inc. N. R. Farbman, *Life Magazine*, Time, Inc., in Sagan et al.

tion between sensation, perception, STM, LTM, and a cognitive search for identification of stimuli.

As complex as the process of object recognition is, it is also performed more or less accurately within a fraction of a second. From both laboratory studies and common knowledge, we know several things about pattern recognition. These include the human capacity to:

Principle	Example
• Recognize familiar patterns promptly and with a high degree of accuracy.	• We easily recognize the faces of our friends, the interior of our house, and street signs.
• Operate on unfamiliar objects.	• Even though we have never seen an unusual shape (an unusual *A*, for example), our visual-perceptual system may analyze it.
• Accurately perceive objects that are placed or rotated at different angles.	• We recognize a coffee cup, even though it may be placed upside down.
• Identify objects partly hidden from view, occluded, or in some other way "noisy."	• We infer that hidden parts of objects exist, as in the case of the lower torso and legs of TV reporters.
• Perform pattern recognition quickly, with subjective ease, and with automaticity.	• We move through a world in which shapes and objects are constantly changing, and yet we process this information swiftly and without undo effort.

VISUAL PATTERN RECOGNITION

What, then, are the cognitive processes we must postulate to account for our ability to classify and understand visual patterns? The question has been approached from several theoretical positions; each of the following is considered in this chapter:

Gestalt Theory. Pattern recognition is based on the perception of the whole pattern of stimuli. Parts of the entire configuration derive their meaning from their membership in the whole.

Bottom-Up and Top-Down Processing. Pattern recognition is initiated by the parts of the pattern (bottom-up) that, when summed, lead to the recognition of the whole pattern; alternatively, recognition of the whole leads to recognition of the components (top-down).

Template Matching. Pattern recognition occurs when a match is made between sensory stimuli and a corresponding internal mental form.

Feature Analysis. Pattern recognition occurs after incoming stimuli have been analyzed according to their simple features (similar to bottom-up processing).

Prototype Theory. Pattern recognition occurs when a match is made between a perceived pattern and an abstracted or idealized mental pattern.

Form Perception. Pattern perception is examined from various theoretical positions.

Pattern Recognition among Experts. Pattern recognition among specialists in a variety of fields is examined.

It should be recognized that each of these viewpoints may share some theoretical features with other viewpoints; the distinctions provide an organizational scheme for our following discussion.

Vision

In Chapter 2, we discussed the basic anatomy of the eye. Vision, the act of sensing electromagnetic waves, is made possible because of the eye's unique structure, which is precisely aligned to detect photopic energy. Light rays enter the eye through the cornea and lens, which focus an image on the retina. The recognition of a pattern, whether a simple two-dimensional black-and-white form or a complex three-dimensional colored form, is always represented on the retina as a two-dimensional[1] form. From these two-dimensional representations on the retina, higher-order perception—including the illusion of three-dimensionality—is made possible when the impulses are passed along to the visual cortex and, when combined with existing knowledge, lead to the recognition of, say, our grandmother when we see her. The magic that has surrounded the visual process for centuries is, at last, giving way to scientific understanding.

The visual system is the most complex of all sensory systems. The human eye has about 7 million cones, which are sensitive to well-illuminated stimuli, and 125 million rods, which are sensitive to poorly illuminated stimuli. This distribution of rods and cones in the retina is not even. Cones are concentrated in the fovea, and rods are spread away from the fovea. Despite the uneven distribution of sensory neurons in the eye, many models of visual perception, especially those built on a computer metaphor, conceptualize the visual system as a type of matrix that can be described geometrically as conforming to an x and y grid. In addition to the number of sensory cells and their geographic location, another factor in understanding visual perception is the intensity of stimuli, or how bright an object is, and what influence that has on sensation. It has been discovered that bright objects and dark objects are similarly represented.

Several ongoing projects are attempting to emulate human vision using computers, which have been built on the information just presented. At this time it is impossible to build an artificial eye with millions of sensors. What has been built is a television "eye" with a 512×512 array (which has 262,144 pixels, or "picture elements") that crudely simulates the human eye. The pixels can be turned on or off, and light intensity can be further simulated by computer programs. Identifying visual boundaries of real objects has also been successfully simulated (see Marr, 1982, for details). We shall return to computer vision in Chapter 16, but now we will turn our attention to models of human visual information processing.

GESTALT THEORY

Some patterns of stimuli seem to be classified the same way by many people. For example, if shown this pattern of visual stimuli,

---

[1]The image that falls on the retina occurs over a period of time, which some might consider another dimension.

most people would recognize it and label it a square. The way we organize and classify visual stimuli was studied by Gestalt psychologists during the early part of the twentieth century. Pattern organization to these early Gestalt psychologists involved all stimuli working together to produce an impression that went beyond the sum total of all sensations. Wertheimer (1923) captures the essential principles of Gestalt psychology in the following passage:

> I stand at the window and see a house, trees, sky. Now on theoretical grounds I could try to count and say: "here they are . . . 327 brightnesses and hues." Do I have "327"? No, I see sky, house, trees; and no one can really have these "327" as such. Furthermore, if in this strange calculation the house should have, say, 120 and the trees 90 and the sky 117, I have in any event this combination, this segregation, and not, say, 127 and 100 and 100; or 150 and 177. I see it in this particular combination, this particular segregation; and the sort of combination or segregation in which I see it is not simply up to my choice: it is almost impossible for me to see it in any desired combination that I may happen to choose. When I succeed in seeing some unusual combination, what a strange process it is. What surprise results, when, after looking at it a long time, after many attempts, I discover—under the influence of a very unrealistic set—that over there parts of the window frame make an N with a smooth branch . . .

Some patterns of stimuli, according to Wertheimer, tend to be naturally (or "spontaneously") organized. For example, in all likelihood your impression of the following is of a series of eight dots.

● ● ● ● ● ● ● ●

If the dots form the pattern,

●● ●● ●● ●●

you tend to see four sets of two-dot patterns, and it is quite difficult to rearrange the pattern mentally so you see the first dot alone, the second and third dots together, the fourth and fifth dots together, the sixth and seventh dots together, and the eighth dot alone. The same eight dots arranged as follows:

will tend to be seen as a square, a circle, and an abstract form, respectively.

Consider also the way the eye "naturally" organizes the direction in which the triangles are pointed[2] in Figure 4.1. Look at this figure for several seconds, and you will see the orientation shift from one direction to another and yet another. One explanation of this change is that the mind's eye is constantly searching for alternate perceptual organization. In this instance, the stimuli that impinge on the retina are identical, but the interpretation is different. Although the reorganization may occur spontaneously, it can

---

[2]For much more detailed analysis see Palmer, 1989.

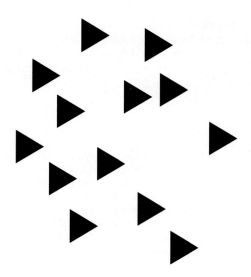

F I G U R E   4 . 1

Look at this display of triangles. In which direction do they point? Look again. Does the direction change? Can you control the direction?

also be voluntarily controlled. Such demonstrations show the influence of higher-order mental processes on visual perception.

The influence of past memories on form perception can also be seen in Figure 4.2. Examine the two figures briefly. What do you see? In Figure 4.2A, people generally see a stable two-dimensional object, and in Figure 4.2B an unstable three-dimensional one. However, if you look closely, you will see that both figures are identical except that they are misaligned by 45 degrees. Why do we have this radically different perception of two nearly identical patterns? One reason is that through past experience we see boxes positioned in the orientation shown in Figure 4.2B. This reminds us of a box that has three dimensions. The form in Figure 4.2A is unboxlike. At best, it would be an odd orientation for a box. We do not easily see the dimensionality associated with a box, but we do see a symmetrical two-dimensional object that appears to be two squares held up by a frame. This powerful illusion may be particularly compelling for people growing up in Western civilization; but would the illusion hold for people who might not come into contact with boxes or angular forms in their everyday lives? Probably not. (See Deregowski, 1980, for further discussion.)

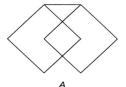

A   B

F I G U R E   4 . 2

Effect of orientation on perception. Which of these forms appears to be three-dimensional?

Common Grouping and the Real World

Graphic designers have known the powerful influence that Gestalt principles have on conveying a message. Consider the example below of common grouping.

Here the background shading exerts a powerful influence over the message being read. It is likely that common regions help organize the text.

A conspicuous assumption of the early Gestalt psychologists—especially Kohler (1947)—was that spontaneous organization of pattern was a natural function of the stimulus itself and only minimally related to the past experience of the subject. Although the controversy about the source of "natural organization" continues, a considerable number of experimental reports (some based on cross-cultural observation) support the notion that "natural organization" of patterns is directly tied to the perceptual history of the human subject.

Study of pattern recognition by cognitive psychologists has extended the work of the early Gestalt psychologists. Some recent cognitive psychologists have concentrated on the "internal" structures and processes that are associated with complex pattern recognition rather than emphasizing the characteristics of simple stimuli. Following are some of these models and the patterns on which they are based.

CANONIC PERSPECTIVES

One extension of the ideas expressed by the Gestaltists can be seen in the work with canonic perspectives. Canonic perspectives are views that best represent an object or are the images that first come to mind when you recall a form. If I ask you to think of a common object, say, a typewriter, the image that comes to mind is likely to be the canonic perspective. Research in this area is important, since it combines findings from Gestalt psychology with prototype formation, a topic that is covered in some detail later in this chapter.

If your canonic perspective of a typewriter is the same as mine, you conjured up a view of a typewriter that is generally from the front, rotated to the left a few degrees, and viewed from a slightly elevated position. You did not "see" it from directly above, from the back, with a large book occluding part of it, or from the perspective of a tiny ant crawling over the levers and keys. However, each of these perspectives is possible. (Much more is reported on visual imagery in Chapter 10.)

One theoretical explanation of the generality of canonic perspectives is that, through common experience with objects, we develop permanent memories of the most representational view of an object and of a view that discloses the greatest amount of information about it. Thus, studies of canonic perspectives tell us something about form perception, but they tell us much more about human information processing, prototype formation (or the typicality of objects as represented in memory), and economy of thinking.

Experimental data have supported these conclusions. Palmer, Rosch, and Chase (1981) photographed a series of common objects from different perspectives (see Figure 4.3). Subjects rated the perspectives for typicality and familiarity. In a second part of the experiment, subjects were shown the photographs of the horse and other objects (for example, a camera, a car, a piano, or so on) that had been similarly evaluated and were asked to name the objects as rapidly as they could. Not surprisingly, the canonic views were identified most quickly, with reaction times increasing as a function of the rated distance away from canonicality. It should also be noted that the visual system still operates with a reasonable degree of efficiency, even when evaluating less than "perfect" figures.

The reason reaction times are generally longer for less canonic pictures is probably due to several reasons: (1) Fewer parts of the object may be discernible. Look at the back view in Figure 4.3. How much of the horse can you see by looking at its rear? Not much. (And who knows whose name you might come up with if presented with this perspective.) (2) The best (canonic) view (figure in the upper left) is one that is most commonly experienced. We "see" typewriters, chairs, cars, telephones, and horses from one orientation more than others, and therefore that view is more familiar to us. (3) The canonic view is an idealized, or best, view of the object. Through endless impressions of the world, we form a mental picture of a class of objects in which the epitome of the class is represented in memory. When I ask you to imagine a typewriter, it is likely that your impression is one of a garden-variety typewriter, not one of an unconventional model with a weird shape. The same principle works for recalling dogs, horses, sports cars, and birds. This view is consistent with theories of prototype formation, which are discussed shortly.

FIGURE 4.3

Twelve perspective views of a horse used in Palmer, Rosch, and Chase experiment (1981) with mean "goodness" ratings.

BEST (1.60)   SIDE (1.84)   FRONT-SIDE (2.12)   FRONT-SIDE-TOP (2.80)

SIDE-TOP (3.48)   FRONT (3.72)   BACK-SIDE (4.12)   BACK-SIDE-TOP (4.29)

FRONT-TOP (4.80)   BACK-TOP (5.56)   BACK (5.68)   TOP (6.36)

BOTTOM-UP VERSUS TOP-DOWN PROCESSING

How do we recognize a pattern? Do we identify a dog because we have first recognized its furry coat, its four legs, its eyes, ears, and so on, or do we recognize these parts because we have first identified a dog? This problem—whether the recognition process is initiated by the parts of the pattern, which serve as the basis for the recognition of the whole (bottom-up), or whether it is primarily initiated by a hypothesis about the whole, which leads to its identification and subsequent recognition of the components (top-down)—is called the parsing paradox. (The terms *bottom-up* and *top-down* are borrowed from computer language.)

Some theorists (for example, Palmer, 1975a) have suggested that under most circumstances, the interpretation of parts and wholes takes place in top-down and bottom-up directions simultaneously. As an example of the interactions of part-to-whole and whole-to-part strategies, Palmer cites the recognition of parts of a face with context and

Critical Thinking: Pattern Recognition

Pattern Recognition

Look at the figures below. Which two are alike? How did you come to that conclusion? What factors entered into your decision? See discussions of template matching, priming, and feature analysis for additional thoughts.

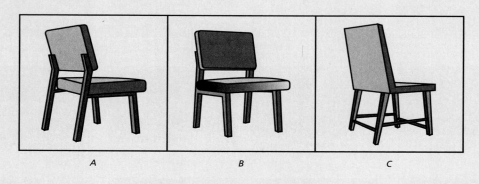

A   B   C

without context. As shown in Figure 4.4, the parts of a face that can easily be recognized in context are somewhat ambiguous when seen alone, although recognizable when more detail or information is supplied.

We expect to see certain objects in various contexts, for example, a stethoscope in a physician's office, silverware in a kitchen, a typewriter in an office, and a hydrant in a street scene. It is likely that this world knowledge is what facilitates identification of objects in familiar contexts and hinders identification of objects in inappropriate ones. Several investigations of this "context effect" by Biederman and his associates (Biederman, 1972; Biederman, Glass, & Stacy, 1973; also see the section entitled "Geon Theory" later in this chapter) have shown that, when subjects search for objects in real-world scenes (for example, objects in a campus scene or street scene), recognition, accuracy, and time required to identify objects are related to the appropriateness of the objects' location in the scene.

From these and similar studies on word and letter identification in context, it is clear that the perception of objects is greatly influenced by the subject's expectation as determined by context.

TEMPLATE MATCHING

One idea of how the brain recognizes shapes and patterns is called template matching. A template in our context of human pattern recognition refers to an internal construct that, when matched by sensory stimuli, leads to the recognition of an object. This idea of pattern recognition holds that a great number of templates have been created by our

F I G U R E   4 . 4

Facial features recognizable in the context of a whole face in profile (A) are less recognizable out of context (B) differentiated more fully and realistically (C) the features are more recognizable. From Palmer (1975a).

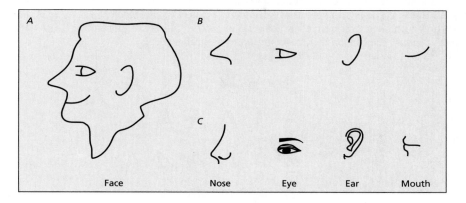

| Face | Nose | Eye | Ear | Mouth |

life experience, each template being associated with a meaning. Thus, the visual identification of a shape—say, a geometric form—would occur as follows: The light energy emanating from the form falls on the retina and is transduced to neural energy, which is transmitted to the brain. A search is made among existing templates. If a template is found that matches the neural pattern, then the subject recognizes it. After a match between the object and its template is made, further processing and interpretation of the object may occur.

Template matching, as a theory of pattern recognition, has some strength as well as some weakness. On the positive side, it seems apparent that to recognize a shape, a letter, or some visual forms, some contact with a comparable internal form is necessary. On some level of abstraction, the things in the external reality need to be recognized as matching a memory in the long-term memory. On the negative side, a literal interpretation of the template matching theory meets with some difficulty. For example, if recognition is possible only when a 1:1 match is found between the external object and its internal representation, then an object with even slight misalignment between itself and the template would not be recognized. Such a rigorous interpretation of the theory would imply that countless millions of templates need to be formed to correspond to each of the varied geometric forms we see and recognize.

The ease with which we identify visual patterns in our daily life may lead us to think that the process is simple, but if we try to duplicate pattern recognition by some artificial means, we find success elusive. Take, for example, the recognition of a letter and the development of word recognition. Although it may take several years to become a skilled reader, once we have learned to identify the orthographic configuration that makes up a word, we can immediately recognize that word in various contexts, pronounce it, and recall its meaning. How would you simulate the initial process of letter

The Remarkable Versatility of Human Form Perception

S hown here are a diverse lot of letters which you easily recognize as variations of the letter *A*. However, it is unlikely that you have seen and formed a precise memory for all of these versions. We can do this task, and many other similar pattern recognition tasks, because we have formed an impression of various class of objects, such as an *A*, and are able to apply that information to a wide class of similar forms.

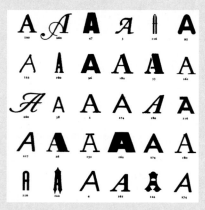

recognition in a machine or computer? One way would be to have each of the twenty-six letters stored in a computer memory. Then, each time a letter was scanned by an optical device, the perceived visual configuration would key the memory (template) associated with that letter. Thus the word *CARD* would be analyzed as C-A-R-D, with *C* fitted into the slot in memory corresponding to the configuration *C*. *A* would find a match in the *A* slot; and so on. "Voilà!" our computer may exclaim, "I'm reading letters." However, what if we ask it to recognize the letters in *card*? There are no lowercase configurations in its memory. The solution is simple, you might assert: increase the memory to include lowercase letters. However, how would our computer read (as we can) the letters in ᒐᐯꓤᗡ or *Card* or *C ARD* or ᗡᔓA◖ ? Of course, the process of reading involves a much more complex process than simple letter identification. The technique used by computers (of matching specific letter configurations against specific configurations in its memory) is called template matching, and it works something as a key in a lock does. A key's configuration of ridges and slots needs to correspond exactly to a lock's configuration if it is to release the lock. In template matching, if the visual configuration corresponds to a compatible memory representation, information, in terms of pattern recognition, is released. In the preceding example of the computer, the method of template matching to recognize various anomalies in the word *CARD* encountered difficulties, much as a bent key might in releasing a lock.

Template Matching in Computers

Template matching is the basis of many coding systems that are part of everyday living. For example, nearly all banks in the United States use a system of identifying accounts by groupings of special digits (the ABA number) printed at the bottom of checks,

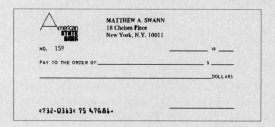

and many markets use similar codes printed on packages for speeding the checkout process and maintaining inventory. (The bar code identifies the item for which the computer supplies the price, which is then entered on the cash register tape.) Both types of codes are read by means of template matching. An ABA number has distinctive features that make it possible for a computer to distinguish between the letters, and a bar code is read on the basis of the position, width, and spacing of the lines. Codes are converted by the scanner into electrical impulses, which constitute the patterns of signals that are transmitted to the computer. The computer identifies the pattern by matching it with an analogue (template) that is in its memory.

Thus, template matching is a simple pattern recognition procedure based on fitting the exact configuration of sensory information to a corresponding configuration in the brain and, despite its restricted capacity, has some useful conceptual and practical applications. We deal with the conceptual issues raised by template matching later; the practical applications are numerous.

For human pattern recognition, then, a strict interpretation of the model would mean that millions of separate templates need to be formed, each corresponding to a specific visual pattern. If we were to store that many templates, our cerebrum would be so bulky we would need a wheelbarrow to cart it; the feat seems to be neurologically impossible. Even if it were possible, gaining access in memory to untold millions of templates would require a time-consuming search that our rapid recognition of numerous patterns suggests does not exist. Finally, our ability to recognize unfamiliar shapes and forms (for example, a novel letter *A*) also makes the process unlikely.

Geon Theory

An alternative to an unyielding template model, which requires countless millions of forms to match the everyday sights of the world, is a theory that posits that the human

Irving Biederman **has advanced our understanding of object recognition through innovative experiments and theories, especially geon theory.**

information processing system has a limited number of simple geometric "primatives" that may be applied to complex shapes. One theory, which also bears some resemblance to feature analysis (discussed later in the chapter), was developed by Irving Biederman of the University of Southern California and adopts such an idea. Biederman's concept of form perception is based on the concept of the geon, which stands for "geometrical ions." It proposes that all complex forms are composed of geons. For example, a cup is composed of two geons: a cylinder (for the container portion) and a ellipse (for the handle). (See Figure 4.5 for examples of geons and objects.) Geon theory, as espoused by Biederman (see Biederman, 1985, 1987, 1990; Biederman & Cooper, 1991; Biederman and Gerhardstein, 1993; and Cooper and Biederman, 1993) proposes that the recognition of an object, such as a telephone, a suitcase, or even more complex forms, consists of recognition by components (RBC) in which simple forms are found in complex forms.

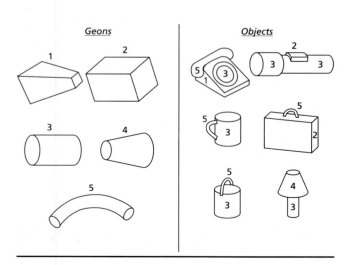

FIGURE 4.5

Geons and objects. Objects are represented as configurations of geons, which are simple visual volumes. From Biederman (1990).

Geons and Art?

Pablo Picasso, the great abstract painter, was influenced by Paul Cézanne, the great impressionist painter. Cézanne wrote a letter to Picasso advising him to examine the nature of "cones, cylinders, and spheres" as he believed that complex paintings should be organized around these "basic" forms. Picasso took the advice seriously and experimented with assembling a painting with these basic forms, which eventually led to cubistic renditions.

Geons are 24 distinct forms and, like the letters of the alphabet, make up a type of system that when combined fabricates more complex forms, much as the words on this page are composed of letters. The number of different forms that can be generated by combining primitive shapes is astronomical. For example, three geons arranged in all possible combinations yield a total of 1.4 billion three-geon objects! However, we use only a fraction of the total possible number of complex forms. Biederman estimates that we use only about 30,000, of which we have names for only 3,000.

One test of geon theory is in the use of degraded forms, as shown in Figure 4.6. Which of these figures (A or B) is easier to identify?

In the illustration, 65 percent of the contour has been removed from a common object. In the cup on the left (A), the lines from the middles of the segments were removed, which still allows the viewer to see how the basic segments are related. In the cup on the right (B), the deleted lines are from the vertices, which include critical corners that relate segments one to another. Biederman presented objects of this type to subjects for 100 milliseconds. He found that when the connecting lines were removed (A), a correct identification was made about 70 percent of the time; when the vertices were deleted (B), the number of correct identifications was about 50 percent. Thus, consistent with a theory that holds that object identification is grounded on seeing basic forms, by removing critical relational information, the object was harder to see than when such information was provided.

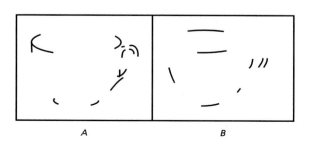

A   B

FIGURE 4.6

Sixty-five percent of the contour has been removed from a cup, centered at either midsegments (A) or vertices (B). From I. Biederman, "Human Image Understanding: Recent Research and a Theory" in *Computer Vision, Graphics and Image Processing,* 1985, 32, 29-73. Copyright 1985 by Academic Press. Reprinted by permission.

Priming Technique

In other experiments involving object classification tasks, Biederman and others used a priming technique in which a stimulus is briefly presented (a prime) and then, after a delay, a second stimulus is presented and a subject is asked to make some judgment regarding the second stimulus, such as, "Is the second stimulus the 'same' as the first?" The technique has been used by cognitive psychologists for several generations, and a type of simple priming (cueing subjects to make a response) can be found in the early history of experimental psychology, dating back to the nineteenth century. With the advent of the modern tachistoscope (a device that allows the brief presentation of stimuli and measures response time), computers, and, most recently, brain imaging technology, priming experiments have become increasingly popular. The rational behind priming experiments, especially those designed to test semantic effects, is that by activating one item which may be related to another item, the acceptability of the second item is enhanced. This effect is called the *semantic priming effect* and is discussed in some detail in Chapter 12. If, for example, you see a bright-red square patch, you will recognize the word *"BLOOD"* faster than if you saw no stimulus or if you saw a bright-green square patch (see Solso & Short, 1979). (Martians may transpose these tendencies, but here we are confining our observations to earthly creatures.)

A second type of effect called the *object priming effect* is similar to semantic priming. Typically there are two stages. The first stage consists of the presentation of an object, say a line drawing of an airplane, followed by an interval that may be as brief as 100 milliseconds or as long as months. In the second stage, a second object, similar to the original but commonly changed, rotated, elaborated, or degraded in some way (for example, some of the contours may be left out), is presented and the subject's accuracy and (sometimes) reaction time is measured. In some instances, the reverse procedure is used, that is, the subject sees a degraded form and then is asked to identify a completed object. Control subjects get the same treatment but without the presentation of the first item. (See Tulving & Schacter, 1990, for further details.)

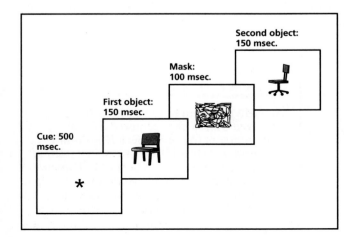

Cue: 500 msec.

First object: 150 msec.

Mask: 100 msec.

Second object: 150 msec.

FIGURE 4.7

Sequence of events on a 0° orientation difference, "different" trial with familiar objects in the same-different task. Only if the two exemplars of the chair were the same, whatever the orientation in depth, were the subjects to respond "same." (The designation of orientation on different trials was arbitrary.)

Complementary Image 2

**Same Name,
Different Exemplar**

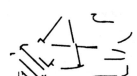

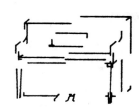

FIGURE 4.8

Example of prime and object used in Biederman and Cooper (1991).

Consider the typical priming experiment shown in Figure 4.7 in which a subject is given a cue followed by a stimulus, a mask (to suppress after-image effects), and a second stimulus. In a large number of experiments using visual material, priming of an object with a similar form measurably enhances perception of a form. The use of priming techniques raises an important issue for cognitive psychology; that is, the presentation of the prime, or initial stimulus, seems to activate a whole range of response tendencies of which the observer is not conscious. This nonconscious activation is called *implicit memory* as contrasted with *explicit memory,* which involves the conscious recall of previous experiences. In the example shown in Figure 4.7, it is unlikely that anyone consciously thought about the second type of chair when they saw the first. For this reason, the type of memory being tested is called implicit memory.

An application of the priming technique in which a component theory of object recognition was tested can be found in Biederman and Cooper (1991). To test the recognition of common forms (for example, a piano, a flashlight, or a padlock), subjects were first primed with outline drawings of figures in which parts of the lines were missing. For each of these a corresponding drawing was shown in which the name of the object was the same as the prime, but the type of object differed (for example, the prime was a grand piano, but the object was an upright piano—see Figure 4.8). The results indicated that the priming effect was visual, rather than conceptual. This is consistent with other findings in studies of short-term memory (see discussion of Posner and associates in Chapter 7).

FEATURE ANALYSIS

Another approach to the problem of how we extract information from complex stimuli is feature analysis. This notion holds that pattern perception is a high-order processing of information that is preceded by a step in which complex incoming stimuli are identified according to their simpler features. Thus, according to this approach, before the full-blown pattern of visual information is appreciated, its components are minimally analyzed. On a simple visual level, a word (for example, *ARROW*) is not immediately translated into its definitional or imaginal representation in our memory (for example, "a pointed shaft shot from a bow" or "→"). Neither is it read as "arrow," nor are the individual letters perceived as (A-R-R-O-W), but rather the features, or components, of each character are detected and analyzed. Thus the *A* of *arrow* may be fractured into two diagonal lines (/ \), one horizontal line (—), a pointed head (^), an open bottom (/⌒\), and so on. If the recognition process is based on feature analysis (and there is good evidence to support this), the earliest stages of information processing are more complex than we might first guess.[3]

Two lines of research—neurological and behavioral—have supported the featural-analysis hypothesis. First we will take up experiments by Hubel and Wiesel (1959, 1963a, 1963b)[4] and Hubel (1963) that give direct evidence of the type of information coded in the visual cortex. These researchers inserted small wires, or microelectrodes, in the visual cortex of a lightly anesthetized cat or monkey and then studied the neural activity that resulted as simple patterns of light were projected onto a screen directly in front of the animal's eyes. By recording excitation of single nerve cells and amplifying the resulting electrical impulse, they found that some cells respond only to horizontal forms, while others respond only to vertical ones. In other experiments they found that some cells are sensitive to edges of visual stimuli, some to lines, and still others to right angles. Figure 4.9 shows the amplified brain activity in a cortical cell of a very young (and visually inexperienced) kitten correlated with specific orientations of a light slit (A to E) that was presented on a screen within the vision of the animal. Horizontal bars above each activity recorded indicate periods when light was visible. Hubel (1963b) concluded that the development of these cortical codes of perceptual forms was innate and specific to each cell.

One can now begin to grasp the significance of the great number of cells in the visual cortex. Each cell seems to have its own specific duties; it takes care of one restricted part of the retina, and it responds best to one particular shape of stimulus and to one particular orientation. To look at the problem from the opposite direction. For each stimulus—each area of the retina stimulated, each type of line (edge, slit, or bar), and each orientation of stimulus—there is a particular set of simple cortical cells that will respond. Changing any of the stimulus arrangements will cause a whole new population of cells to respond. The number of populations responding successively as the eye watches a slowly rotating propeller is scarcely imaginable.

The complex and awkward mechanism of breaking patterns into simpler features, then, may be not only within the realm of neurological possibilities but also neurologically necessary. That is, feature analysis may be a stage in informational analysis that must occur before higher-level pattern analysis can take place.

Eye Movements and Pattern Perception

A direct approach to feature analysis is observation of eye movements and eye fixation. This line of research presumes that if you gaze for a relatively long time at a certain fea-

---

[3]To appreciate the complex sensory and perceptual (and motor) apparatus necessary for "simple" perception and reaction, think of what is involved in hitting a tennis ball in flight. In a fraction of a second, we are able to judge its shape, size, speed, color, trajectory, spin, and anticipated location. Our brain must translate all of this information (which is recorded in only two dimensions on the retina) into a motor reaction, which, if successful, allows us to return the ball. In addition to the fact that this takes place in only a flash of time, much of the information is constantly changing (for example, the ball's relative size, speed, and trajectory).

[4]Hubel and Wiesel shared the Nobel prize with Sperry in 1981.

FIGURE 4.9

Responses of a cell in the cortex of a very young kitten to stimulation of
the eye with a light slit. A to E indicate the orientation of the light slit
(heavy bar) relative to the receptive field axis (dashed lines). For example,
in E, the slit was oriented as in A and B but moved rapidly from side to
side. From Hubel and Wiesel (1963).

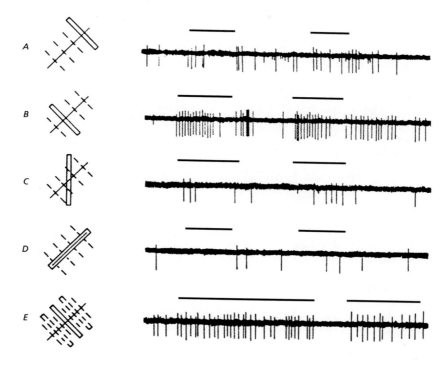

ture in a pattern, you are extracting more information from it than from a feature only
cursorily viewed. This approach has been taken by Mackworth (1965, 1970), and
Yarbus (1967). The results of the fixation experiments by Yarbus, a Russian psychologist, are shown in Figure 4.10. Yarbus suggests that the more information carried by a
feature (for example, the people or relationships in the illustrations shown), the longer
the eyes stay fixed on it. He also concludes that the distribution of fixation points is a
function of the subject's purpose. In one series the subject was asked to make certain
estimates regarding the complex pattern (for example, the material circumstances of the
family, and the ages of the people). Under these circumstances the focus tends to be on
those features most important to the subject's purpose. Thus, the perception of features
within complex patterns seems not only to depend on the nature of the physical stimuli
but also to engage higher-order cognitive processes, such as attention and purpose.

FIGURE 4.10

Records of eye movements of subject examining picture at upper left. Trace 1 was made when subject examined picture at will. Subsequent traces were made after subject was asked to estimate the economic level of the people shown (Trace 2); judge their ages (3); guess what they had been doing before arrival of the "visitor" (4); remember their clothing (5); remember their positions (and those of objects) in the room (6); and estimate how long the "visitor" had not seen the "family" (7). From Yarbus (1967).

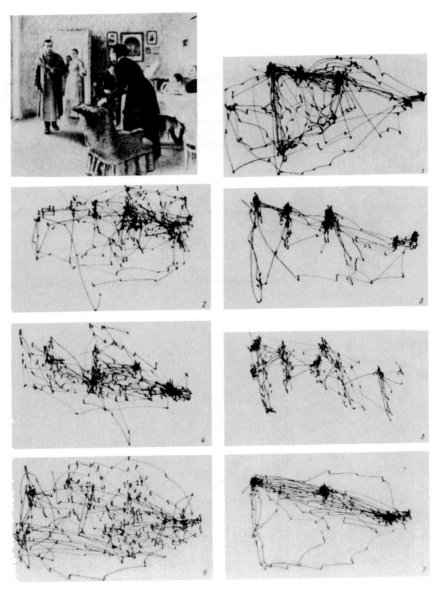

PROTOTYPE MATCHING

An alternative to template matching and feature analysis as a means of recognizing patterns is prototype formation. It seems likely that, rather than form specific templates or even features for the numerous different patterns we are called upon to recognize, some kind of abstraction of patterns is stored in LTMs and that abstraction serves as a prototype. A pattern would then be checked against the prototype and, if a resemblance were found, the pattern would be recognized. The prototypical-matching hypothesis in humans seems to be more compatible with neurological economy and memory search processes than template matching, and it also allows for recognition of patterns that are "unusual" but in some way related to the prototype. In this system, we may, for example, form a prototype of the idealized letter A, against which all other As are evaluated in terms of how closely they fit the model. Where the degree of mismatch is great, as in the case of letters other than A, we recognize the lack of a match and reject the letter as an A; we may then search for a prototype that fits the letter better.

Evidence for prototype matching is all around us, and the hypothesis has a strong intuitive credibility. For example, we recognize a Volkswagen, even though it may be of a different color or shape or have a lot of fancy doodads that are at odds with the idealized model in our head. A prototype in this sense is not only an abstraction of a set of stimuli, but it is also the epitome or the "best" representation of the pattern.[5]

Although the argument seems to favor prototype matching over template matching, you might ask whether an exact match between image and template is necessary or whether templates only serve as an approximation of the image that unlocks the memory. If the latter were the case, however, how could you make the fine distinctions necessary for common visual discrimination? Consider, for example, the close featural similarity of O and Q, and B, P, and R. Although these visual patterns are similar, we seldom confuse them. In effect, then, templates cannot be sloppy, for if they were, we would make many errors in pattern recognition—and we seemingly do not.

As a theory of pattern recognition, then, template matching has utility in computer programs (check-code reading and so on) but, in its rigid form, inadequately accounts for the diversity, accuracy, and economy of human pattern recognition. To sum up, pattern recognition presumes an operation conducted in memory. At the simplest level, it is safe to assert that a pattern is identified by some process that matches sensory information with some trace held in a repository of information.

Abstraction of Visual Information

As we have suggested, template matching may occur at one level of visual recognition, but at another level prototypes may be used. This view holds that a prototype is an abstraction of a set of stimuli that embodies many similar forms of the same pattern. A prototype allows us to recognize a pattern even though it may not be identical (only similar) to the prototype. For example, we recognize a diverse number of As, not because they fit neatly into cerebral slots but because the members of the class A have some common properties.

---

[5]In a civilization in which physical glamour is prized, the prototypes of womanhood and manhood may be the winner of the Miss America Pageant and the male box office star, respectively, and our evaluation of each other may in some way be related to how closely one approximates the prototypical ideal.

The empirical studies seeking evidence concerning prototypes as a means of pattern recognition have largely addressed the questions of how prototypes develop and by what process new exemplars are quickly classified. The question is not new; Bishop Berkeley (cited in Calfee, 1975) worried about it a long time ago:

> In his mind's eye all images of triangles seemed to have rather specific properties. They were equilateral or isosceles or right triangles, and he searched in vain for a mental image of the "universal triangle." Although it is easy to define verbally what we mean by a triangle, it is not clear what the "perfect" triangle looks like. We see lots of different kinds of triangles; from this variety what do we create in our mind as the basis for recognizing a triangle? (p. 222)

Berkeley's speculative odyssey for the "perfect" triangle spanned several centuries and was finally empirically studied, in what has itself become a prototypical experiment, by Posner, Goldsmith, and Welton (1967). They searched for the prototype of a triangle (and other forms) and then measured subjects' reaction to other forms that were something like the prototypical one. In the first part of their experiment, they developed a series of prototypes (see Figure 4.11) formed by placing nine dots in a 30 × 30 matrix (standard, 20-squares-per-inch graph paper). These formed either a triangle, a letter, or a random arrangement. Four distortions of each of these original forms, which served as prototypes, were made by shifting dots from their original positions. (Figure 4.11 also shows the distortions of the triangle pattern.) Subjects were shown each of the four distortions one at a time and asked to classify the pattern by prototype. After subjects classified each pattern (by pressing a response button that indicated how they classified the pattern), they were told which of their choices had been correct; the prototype was not presented.

FIGURE 4.11

The four prototypical patterns and four distortions of the triangle pattern used by Posner, Goldsmith, and Welton in their study. Adapted from Posner, Goldsmith, and Welton (1967).

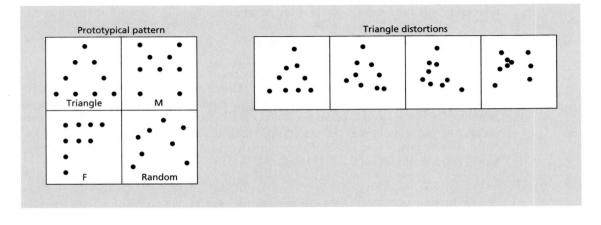

From this first experiment it was evident that the subjects had learned to classify distorted patterns of a specific prototype into a common category, while other patterns, derived from another prototype, were sorted into another common category. The original task was followed with a transfer task, in which subjects were asked to classify a series of patterns into one of the three previous categories. The new sets of patterns were composed of (1) the old distortions, (2) new distortions (based on the original prototypes), and (3) the prototypes themselves. The old distortions were easily correctly classified (with an accuracy level of about 87 percent). More importantly, the prototypes (which the subjects had never seen or classified) were correctly classified about equally well. The new distortions were classified less well than the other two types. Because the prototypes were as accurately classified as the old distortions, it would seem the subjects had actually learned something about the prototypes—even though they had never seen anything but distortions of them.

The remarkable feature of this experiment is that the prototype, or schema, was classified correctly about as frequently as the original learned distortion and more frequently than the new (control) distortion. Posner and his colleagues argue that information about the prototype was abstracted from the stored information (based on the distortion) with a high degree of efficiency. Not only are prototypes abstracted from distorted exemplars, but also the process of pattern learning involves knowledge about variability. The possibility that the correct classification of the prototype was based on the familiarity of the prototype (triangle, *F*, and *M*) in the experience of most people was dealt with in an experiment by Petersen et al. (1973). Their results indicated that prototypes and minimally distorted test patterns of highly meaningful configurations were more easily identified than meaningless prototypes and minimally distorted test patterns. However, where the degree of distortion was great, the opposite was true; that is, the highly meaningful prototype was less often identified than the one with low meaningfulness. Their results are not inconsistent with Posner and his team but tease out the interaction between what Berkeley may have called the "universal triangle" and its distortion. Apparently, we abstract prototypes on the basis of stored information. Well-learned forms do not seem to accommodate as wide a range of distortion as less well-learned forms. Bishop Berkeley's search for the perfect triangle has led to the conclusion that all triangles are equal, but some are more equilateral!

Our search for a prototype and our ability to abstract it, even when we don't directly perceive it, was nicely illustrated in an experiment by Franks and Bransford (1971). They composed a series of 5- × 8-inch cards that contained pairs of colored geometric figures. One card had the prototype, and the remainder had "transformations" of the prototype. The base, or prototype, was a small triangle in a large square on the left and a small diamond in a large circle on the right. The subjects were told to reproduce the figure during a training phase of the experiment, but they were not told that they would be asked to recognize the figure later. The transformations followed rules as noted in the figure: a major permutation would be the switching of the left and right figures; a minor one would be a change in an enclosing and enclosed element; and so on. After subjects had seen only the transformations, which varied in their distance from the prototype, they were given a recognition task that included rating their confidence in their decision. The recognition task included the prototype (not previously seen) and the transformations. Results (see Figure 4.12) were that subjects recognized the prototype with greater probability than the transformations (previously seen) and did so with

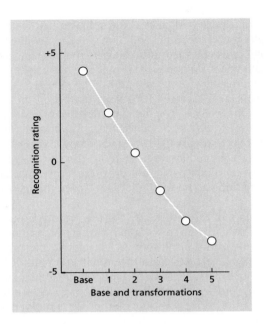

FIGURE 4.12

Subject confidence in recognition of
base and transformations. Adapted
from Franks and Bransford (1971).

a greater degree of confidence. It was also found that the recognition ratings were related to the transformational distance, with the prototype most frequently recognized,
transformations consisting of one permutation next, and so on.

In another example of pattern recognition, based on real-life figures, Reed (1972)
composed faces of remarkably undistinguished characteristics that differed in several re-
spects, such as, eye placement, length of the nose, height of the forehead, and placement of the nose. Each feature was shown in one of three aspects. (The eyes and mouth
have three positions relative to the enclosing line of the face, and the nose has three
lengths.) In a typical problem, subjects were asked to classify these schematic faces (see
Figure 4.13) into one or the other of two rows of faces (see Figure 4.14). Reed found that
his college student subjects abstracted a prototype of each row as a basis for comparison with the exemplars (the three faces in Figure 4.13). The strategy most often em-
ployed was one of abstracting a prototype and comparing the distance of patterns from
each. Reed concluded that "the predominant strategy was to form an abstract image or

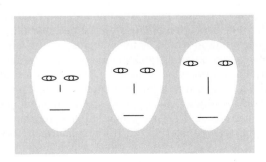

FIGURE 4.13

Schematic faces representing the three
ways in which they could vary in the
Reed experiment. Adapted from Reed
(1972).

FIGURE 4.14

Two rows of faces into one of which subject was to classify faces shown in Figure 4.13. Adapted from Reed (1972).

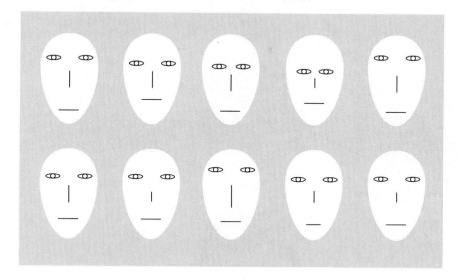

prototype to represent each category and to classify test patterns on the basis of their similarity to the two prototypes" (p. 401).

Pseudomemory

In an experiment of prototype formation that embodied the Franks and Bransford procedure, Solso and McCarthy (1981a) found that subjects falsely recognized the prototype as a previously seen figure with greater confidence than they identified previously seen figures. This phenomenon is called pseudomemory. They hypothesized that a prototype is formed on the basis of frequently experienced features. These features, such as individual lines in a figure or parts of a human face, are stored in memory. A general index of the strength of the memory for features can be determined by the frequency of exposure to the feature. Frequently perceived features are, in general, more likely to be permanently stored in memory than are rarely perceived features. Furthermore, it may be that the rules that govern the relationships between features in a pattern are not as well incorporated in memory as the memory for features themselves. Thus we can conceptualize the process of acquiring knowledge about a pattern as consisting of two stages: acquisition of information about the features of the pattern and acquisition about the relationships between the features. Perhaps the most intriguing part of the puzzle of prototype formation is the evidence that the two stages appear to develop at different rates as we acquire knowledge about a pattern. It is something like a race in which two runners run at different rates. The faster runner is analogous to feature learning, and the slower runner is analogous to learning relationships.

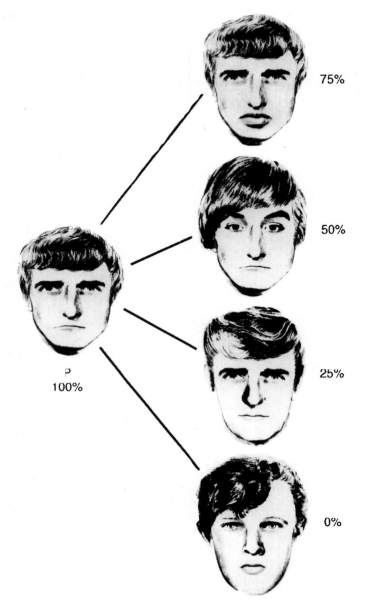

75%

50%

25%

P
100%

0%

FIGURE 4.15

Prototype face and exemplar faces used in Solso and McCarthy (1981a). The 75 percent face has all the same features as the prototype face except the mouth; the 50 percent face has different hair and eyes; the 25 percent face has only the eyes in common; and the 0 percent face has no features in common with the prototype face.

In the Solso and McCarthy experiment, a prototype face was composed from an Identikit, a face-identification device used in police work that consists of a series of plastic templates, each representing a facial characteristic such as hair, eyes, nose, chin, and mouth. From each of the three prototype faces selected, a series of exemplar faces was derived ranging in similarity to the prototype face (see Figure 4.15). Subjects were shown the exemplar faces and then a second set of faces, which contained some of the original faces, some new faces that were scaled in their similarity to the prototype face, and the prototype face. The subjects were asked to judge the faces as being members of the previously seen set or new faces and to rate the confidence of their impression. As

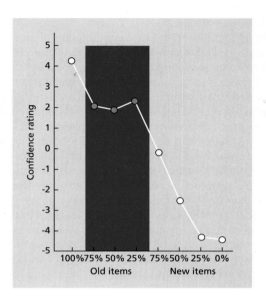

FIGURE 4.16

Confidence ratings for prototype face, old faces, and new faces. From Solso and McCarthy (1981a).

can be seen in Figure 4.16, not only did subjects rate the prototype faces as an old (previously seen) face, but they also gave that face the highest confidence rating (an example of pseudomemory).

From the foregoing we can draw some conclusions about visual prototype formation and use. The previously cited research indicates that we (1) form a prototype on the basis of averaging the characteristics of its exemplars; (2) acquire some specific information about prototypes when we deal only with exemplars; (3) acquire some general information about the common properties of prototypes, with well-known prototypes yielding less generous inclusiveness than less familiar (or recently learned) prototypes; (4) judge exemplars in terms of their transformational proximity to prototypes; and (5) form prototypes on the basis of abstractions from exemplars and then evaluate the relationship between forms of the prototypes on the basis of their distance from the prototype as well as from other individual examples.

Prototype Theory: Central-Tendency versus Attribute-Frequency

From the above mentioned experiments and many other studies, two theoretical models of prototype formation have emerged. In one model, called the central-tendency model, a prototype is conceptualized as representing the average or mean of a set of exemplars. The research of Posner and his colleagues as well as Reed tends to support this model. Posner and Keele (1968), for example, believe that a prototype is represented mathematically by a hypothetical point in multidimensional space at which the means of the distances along all attributes intersect. We can see in the Posner and Reed experiments how subjects form a prototype that is an abstraction of a figure. Thus the prototype is an abstraction stored in memory that represents the central tendency of the category.

The second model, called the attribute-frequency model, suggests that a prototype represents the mode or most frequently experienced combination of attributes. The experiments of Franks and Bransford, Neumann (1977), and Solso and McCarthy support this model. In this model a prototype is synonymous with the "best example" of a set of patterns. A prototype is a pattern that incorporates the most frequently experienced features expressed in a series of exemplars. While the prototype is often unique because it is made up of a unique combination of attributes (think of the unique geometric forms in Frank and Bransford's experiment or the unique face in Solso and McCarthy's experiment), the features themselves have been previously experienced. The features (the geometric components, or face parts) are the building blocks of the prototype. Each time a person looks at a pattern, he or she records both the features in the pattern and the relationship between the features. However, according to the attribute-frequency model, upon the introduction of a prototype (which incorporates many of the previously perceived attributes), an individual believes he or she has previously seen the figure because the attributes have been stored in memory. Since the relationships between the features have been seen fewer times than the features (in most experiments the exemplars are shown only once), knowledge about the relationships of features is less well stored in memory than is the knowledge about features.

FORM PERCEPTION: AN INTEGRATED APPROACH

Up to this point we have considered several hypotheses about pattern recognition in humans. First we considered the human visual system with its enormous capacity—and its limitations. Then we considered some topics in Gestalt psychology, which suggested that visual patterns are "naturally" organized in predictable ways. Next we discussed the topics of top-down and bottom-up processing, and we learned of the importance of contextual cues on form perception. Three models of form perception were discussed: template matching, feature analysis, and prototype formation. In developing the different approaches to form perception, it may appear to the reader that the problem is as confusing as the one facing the seven blind men who are asked to describe an elephant. One grabs hold of the tail and depicts the creature as a great rope; another holds its trunk and portrays it as a serpent; the next feels the elephant's side, which appears to be like a wall; and so on.

Each of our various theories of form perception seems to lay hold of only one aspect of the entire picture without integration. Quite the contrary is true. Each theory is essentially correct, but each also needs support from the others. For example, at a simple level of processing, some type of feature detection operates, as the experiments by Hubel and Wiesel demonstrate. However, a comprehensive view of form perception is more expansive than simple bar identifiers. Conceptually, some type of match between things in memory and things seen, as suggested by the template model, seems reasonable. Nevertheless, this theory also fails to account for the diversity of pattern recognition. Perhaps the geon theory will account for both the diversity and adaptability of the human eye and mind to understand a world filled with complex forms that require rapid and accurate identification. The prototype concept, although well documented, must, at some level, turn to other models to account for the initial stages of perception. Thus, the many theories of form perception are complementary rather than antagonistic. Form perception is a complicated affair, and, at present, no single comprehensive theory has been developed to account for all of its components.

PATTERN RECOGNITION AMONG EXPERTS

Pattern Recognition in Chess

So far our perceptual displays have been simple; even Reed's deadpan faces are stripped of complexity. How are more complex patterns viewed? Chase and Simon (1973a, 1973b) studied this problem by analyzing the complex pattern made by pieces on a chessboard and the way chess masters differed from ordinary players. Intuition may tell us that the cognitive differences between the two are a matter of how many moves ahead the master player can think. The intuition is wrong, at least according to the research of de Groot (1965, 1966), who found that master players and weaker players thought ahead about the same number of moves, considered about the same number of moves, and had a similar search for patterns of moves. It may be that master players even consider fewer alternative moves, while the weaker player wastes time looking at alternatives that are totally inappropriate. What is the difference? One is the master's ability to reconstruct a pattern of chess pieces after viewing if for only a few seconds; the weak player has great difficulty in doing so. The key to this observation is in the nature of the pattern: it must make sense. If the pieces are arranged in a random order, or illogically, then both masters and beginners do equally poorly. Perhaps the masters put together several pieces into chunks, much as you and I would put together letters to form words, and then put the chunks together in a larger meaningful pattern, much as we might form words into sentences. Experienced masters, then, would seem to have greater capacity to reproduce the pattern because they are able to encode the bits and pieces into chess schemata.

Chase and Simon checked this hypothesis using three types of subjects—a master, a Class A player (a very strong player), and a beginner. In one experiment their subjects were asked to reconstruct twenty chess patterns in plain view—half from the middle games and half from end games selected from chess books and magazines (see Figure 4.17). In this task, two chessboards were placed side by side and the subject was to reconstruct on one chessboard the arrangement of chess pieces shown on the other. In a second experiment, subjects scanned a chess pattern for five seconds and then reconstructed it from memory. Chase and Simon found that scanning time was about the same for the master and the Class A player and the beginner, but that the time spent in reconstructing was much less for the master than for the others (Figure 4.18); Figure 4.19 shows the number of pieces correctly placed. Further analysis of these data indicated that the ability to see chunks, or meaningful clusters, of chess pieces made it possible for the better players to gather more information in the given time.

FIGURE 4.17

Example of a chess middle and end game and its randomized counterparts.

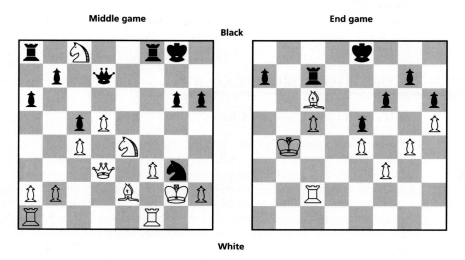

Middle game | End game

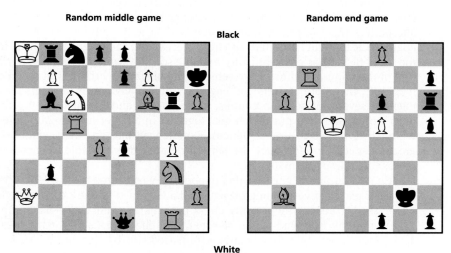

Random middle game | Random end game

The Chase and Simon experiment has significant theoretical implications. Chunks of information held together by abstract relationships may constitute the basis for a theory of pattern syntax. Bits of information without any meaningful context or grouping are hard to encode, be they letters, geometric forms, notes, or chess pieces; however, when fitted into a meaningful structure (such as poetry, architecture, music, an elegant

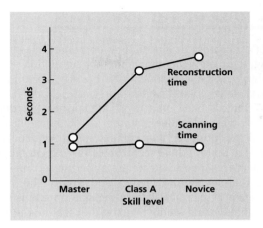

FIGURE 4.18

Scanning and reconstruction times for chess players of three levels of skill. Adapted from Chase and Simon (1973a).

chess defense), they become significant because they are easily abstracted in terms of a common grammar. Modern information theorists have developed pristine models of the mind based on structural levels. We have witnessed the growth of structural grammar in language (discussed further in Chapter 12), in music, in body responses, in graphic tasks, and in chess problems. A prevalent human attribute, applicable to all sensory forms, may be the tendency to code information into higher-order abstractions of reality into which new information is fitted. The above mentioned experiments on chess perception, and other experiments in which immediate stimuli are abstracted, support this postulate.

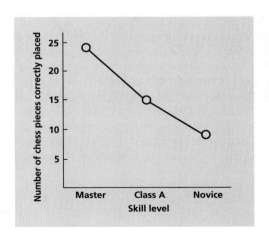

FIGURE 4.19

Distribution of correct placement of chess pieces by players of three levels of skill. Players were shown original pattern for 5 seconds. Adapted from Chase and Simon (1973a).

PATTERN RECOGNITION—THE ROLE OF THE PERCEIVER

We have covered quite a lot of territory in this chapter on pattern recognition: bottom-up and top-down processing; template matching; computer simulation of pattern recognition; feature analysis; physiological components in pattern recognition; prototype matching; cognitive structure; letter identification; and forms, faces, and chess problems. In most of these topics it has been hard to isolate specific functions of pattern recognition without calling on other cognitive systems. Throughout our discussion we have occasionally considered the influence that context and redundancy have on pattern recognition and learned that both of these factors bear directly on the recognition of sensory stimuli. These topics are covered in greater detail in the section on language in Chapter 12 as they relate to the perception of letters and words. The one system that seems to crop up time and again is memory. Pattern recognition seems to involve several lower-order systems, such as visual storage, analysis of features, synthesis of features, and prototypical matching. However, pattern recognition in humans also involves LTM. In our natural environment the world is filled with sensory stimuli, which, when organized and classified, create a recognition of a pattern. The stimuli themselves are empty of meaning, existing in their primitive form whether or not we perceive them. They do become meaningful when analyzed into higher-order patterns. Look and listen to your immediate environment. What do you see and hear? What do you smell, taste, or feel? Certainly you do not perceive raw, vacuous stimuli (even though we are confident that these stimuli are exciting our sensory system), but you do sense things that mean something to you. The bell in the distance, the tree outside a window, the series of letters on this page, and the smell of fresh bread, are all examples of stimuli that, when recognized by the brain, take on a fuller meaning than the physical structures that they excite. That meaning is provided by our memory for these events, which casts immediate experiences in a larger realm of reality. The meaning of sensory stimuli is provided by the perceiver.

In one of the adventures of Sherlock Holmes, the eminent detective is able to portray accurately the life and style of a certain character through a series of brilliant deductions based on a few clues, which are, in effect, cues to memory and association. The cues, which were equally available to his companion, Dr. Watson, were coded and structured in Holmes's mind in such a way that the deductions seemed "elementary" to him, but not to Watson. After Holmes explains what the cues mean, he reproaches his companion by saying, "You 'see' but you do not 'observe!'" All normal humans "see," but the ability to abstract the things we see into meaningful patterns is, to a large extent, a function of the previous structure and knowledge of past experiences.

In Chapter 12 on language, we discuss the perception and human analysis of letters and words within an information-processing context. In that chapter we shall see, as we have in this one, that our experiences, as they are represented in memory, play a major role in what and how we see.

Summary

1   The ability to identify and process visual patterns has been approached from several theoretical positions: Gestalt psychology, bottom-up versus top-down processing, template matching, feature analysis, and prototype recognition.

2 Gestalt psychologists proposed the perception of visual patterns to be organized according to the principles of proximity, similarity, and spontaneous organization.

3 Pattern recognition may be initiated by the parts of the pattern, which are then summed (bottom-up processing), or as a hypothesis held by the perceiver, which leads to recognition of the whole and subsequent recognition of the components (top-down processing).

4 Experimental work indicates that object perception is greatly influenced by contextually derived hypotheses.

5 Template matching holds that pattern recognition occurs when an exact match is made between sensory stimuli and a corresponding internal form. This position has conceptual and practical utility, but it is unlikely as an explanation for many complex cognitive processes, such as our ability to interpret unfamiliar shapes and forms correctly.

6 Feature analysis asserts that pattern recognition occurs only after stimuli have been analyzed according to their simple components. Data from neurological and behavioral experiments lend support to this hypothesis.

7 Prototype formation asserts that pattern perception occurs as a result of abstractions of stimuli, which are stored in memory and serve as idealized forms against which patterns are evaluated. Two models proposed by prototype theory are the central-tendency model, which states that a prototype presents the mean or an average of a set of exemplars, and the attribute-frequency model, which states that a prototype represents the mode or a summation of the most frequently experienced attributes.

8 Visual pattern recognition in humans involves visual analysis of input stimuli and long-term memory storage.

Key Words

attribute-frequency model
bottom-up processing
canonic perspective
central-tendency model
conceptually driven processing
feature
feature analysis
geon
Gestalt psychology
pattern

pattern recognition
priming
priming effect
prototype
prototype recognition
pseudomemory
similarity
template matching
top-down processing

Recommended Readings

Most of the readings recommended for Chapter 3 are relevant to this chapter. Other sources include Reed, *Psychological Processes in Pattern Recognition;* Lindsay and Norman, *Human Information Processing;* Murch, *Visual and Auditory Perception;* and McBurney and Collings, *Introduction to Sensation/Perception.* Rock's book *The Logic of Perception* is an excellent addition to the field.

Attention

The problem of understanding the nature of attention seemed intractable only a few years ago, but developments in neuroimaging and cognitive psychology now allow us to provide specific anatomical and cognitive details about the attention system of the human brain.

Michael I. Posner

M ORE THAN A HUNDRED years ago, William James wrote that "everyone knows what attention is." He explained that

> It is the taking possession by the mind, in clear and vivid form, of one out of what seem several simultaneously possible objects or trains of thought. Focalization, concentration of consciousness are of its essence. It implies withdrawal from some things in order to deal effectively with others. (1890, pp. 403–404)

It is improbable, of course, that he meant that we know all there is to know about attention. We did not in 1890, and we do not now. However, through a number of carefully designed experiments on attention, it has been possible to define the issues involved, and several models have emerged that present an overall perspective on the issue. This chapter is primarily about the emergence of attention as a component of cognitive psychology and includes the exciting new developments in neurocognition. It is divided into four parts: common experiences with attention, models of attention and descriptions of the major issues of the field, a discussion of the issues and models, and the neurocognition of attention.

We shall use this general definition of *attention:* "the concentration of mental effort on sensory or mental events." Research on attention seems to cover five major aspects of the topic: processing capacity and selective attention, level of arousal, control of attention, consciousness, and cognitive neuroscience.

Many of the contemporary ideas of attention are based on the premise that there are available to the human observer a myriad of cues that surround us at any given moment. Our neurological capacity is too limited to sense all of the millions of external stimuli, but, even were these stimuli detected, the brain would be unable to process all of them; our information-processing capacity is too limited. Our sensory system, like other kinds of communication conduits, functions quite well if the amount of information being processed is within its capability; it fails when it is overloaded.

The modern era of attention was introduced in 1958 by the late Donald Broadbent, a British psychologist, who wrote in an influential book, *Perception and Communication*, that attention was the result of a limited-capacity information-processing system.[1] The essential notion of Broadbent's theory was that the world is made up of many more sensations than can be handled by the perceptual and cognitive capabilities of the human observer. Therefore, in order to cope with the flood of available information, humans selectively attend to only some of the cues and tune out much of the rest. Broad-

[1]The impact of this work was not limited to the topic of attention but had a profound effect on the emergence of cognitive psychology as a whole.

Donald Broadbent. (1926–1992)
**Opened up the field of attention
and information processing.**

bent's theory is discussed in some detail later in this chapter. For now, the rudiments of
the model of processing can be conceptualized as a "pipeline" theory. Information, say,
in the form of a human voice, enters a channel, or pipeline, and is passed along in serial
order from one storage/processing system to another: from a sensory store, to a
short-term storage system, and then on to a long-term storage. The original theory has
been altered slightly (those refinements are addressed later in this chapter), but the essential
architecture of the system remains.

It was long thought that we can attend to one cue only at the expense of another. If
we attempt to understand simultaneous messages, especially of the same kind, some
sacrifice must be made in accuracy. For example, we may be able to attend to the highway
while we drive a car (a highly practiced habit) and even listen to the radio at the
same time, but it is difficult to attend simultaneously to more than one cue of the same
modality—such as two auditory cues or two visual cues. It is even difficult to operate at
peak performance when we are confronted with two conceptual tasks as in the case of
mentally dividing a dinner check for seven people and being asked the time. Such a situation
might produce the answer, "Each of you owes 7:27 P.M., and it's $12.54 plus tip."

Our everyday experience tells us that we attend to some environmental cues more
than others and that the attended cues are normally passed along for further processing,
while unattended cues may not be. Which are attended to and which are not seem to
stem from some control we exercise over the situation (such as looking at the instant replay
to see whether the football player stepped out of bounds) and from our long-term
experience (such as reading a technical report to find a special fact). In either situation,

Within the last few weeks, I know a professor who applied skincream, which was packaged in a tube almost identical to toothpaste, to his toothbrush and started brushing his teeth before realizing the error; measured water in a coffee pot, placed the pot on the coffee maker, turned it on, and, after seeing that nothing was happening, realized he had failed to pour the water into the coffee maker's tank; and while lecturing on kinetic art (and thinking about an experiment with dancers) used the term "kinesthetic art." Most people do stupid things like this every day and when they realize what they have done, feel embarrassed.

As an exercise in critical thinking about attention, keep track of your own absentminded behavior for several days (or if you choose, the witless remarks and actions of others, such as your cognitive psychology professor) and then organize them into types and actions. It is likely that you will find most of the errors are due to automatic processing (your brain is on "automatic pilot") and/or you are attending to something else ("head in the clouds"). People who study such things find that people commonly repeat actions, use the wrong word, will substitute items, or forget an important ingredient of some action.

the attention mechanism focuses on certain stimuli in preference to others, although not all of the "extraneous" stimuli are necessarily excluded entirely from attention; they may be monitored or toned down. This is particularly evident with auditory cues, as at a party where we may attend to one voice while being somewhat mindful of other, surrounding ones. Most of us have had the experience of having our attention drift from the voice of our conversation partner to that of someone imparting a choice bit of gossip in another conversation. It is easy to tune in on the voice recounting the gossip while we attempt to conceal our inattention to our conversation partner's pedestrian account of a trip to Barcelona. Of course, we may embarrass ourselves with some absentminded rejoinder such as "Have you ever been to Europe?"

Another case might be that of watching a performance of Molière's *Le Malade Imaginaire,* at the point at which two characters (the hypochondriac and his doctor) begin talking at the same time. You may try to hear all, find it only confusing, and so tune in to one, continuing to hear, but not understanding, the other. In the sense that we are regularly bombarded with a profusion of sensory signals and are called upon to make choices as to which are to be processed, all of one's waking existence is comparable to this example.

Five issues of attention can be identified in these examples:

1. Processing capacity and selectiveness
2. Control
3. Automatic processing
4. Neurocognition
5. Consciousness

Examples of Competing Stimuli

In the discussion of signal detection in Chapter 3, we learned that our capacity to react to a signal is related in part to how "clean" it is, that is, how free of competing information or "noise" it is. You may have become aware of the phenomenon if you have driven in parts of Canada, where major highway signs are printed in both English and French.

If you attend to only one cue—say, the English—you can barrel through intricate intersections without a hint of trouble; however, if you puzzle over the compound stimulus, switching attention from one to the other, travel can be hazardous.

To use the play as an example, you attend to only a minor portion of the activity on the stage. You are apt to attend selectively, focusing on some cues (such as the person who is speaking) more than others. One reason you attend selectively is because your ability to process information is restricted by "channel capacity." Second, you have some control over which features you choose to attend. For example, while two characters may be talking simultaneously, you can exercise some control over the one to which you will listen. Third, your perception of events is related to your automatic processing of material. Fourth, recent investigations into the neurocognitive basis of attention have suggested that the attention system of the human brain is separate from other systems of the brain, such as the data processing systems. These recent discoveries have implications for cognitive theories of attention as well as serve as a bridge between neuroscience and cognitive psychology, which is discussed later. Finally, those things that you attend to are part of your conscious experience. These five issues occupy stage center in the research on attention. We now consider each.

PROCESSING CAPACITY AND SELECTIVE ATTENTION

The fact that we selectively attend to only a portion of all cues available is evident from various common experiences, such as those described earlier. The reason for this is often attributed to inadequate channel capacity, our inability to process all sensory cues simultaneously. This notion suggests that somewhere in the processing of information a bottleneck exists, part of which is due to neurological limitations. It is analogous to shining a flashlight in a darkened room to illuminate the things in which we are interested, keeping the other items in the dark. In Chapter 2 we described foveal vision, in which the clear perception of objects is limited to a narrow visual angle. With respect to the amount of information we respond to and remember, however, there appears to be a constraint in cognitive power in addition to these sensory limitations. Thus, we carefully aim the attentional flashlight, process that that we attend to, and disregard (or moderate) the other ambient information.

Several models have been suggested that describe the location and function of this bottleneck in the processing of information. One of these models (see Figure 5.1A), associated with Broadbent, presumes that the bottleneck is at or just prior to the stage of perceptual analysis. A bottleneck positioned at this location means that some unattended information is not passed on for further perceptual analysis. In another model (see Figure 5.1B), associated with Deutsch and Deutsch, the bottleneck is located at or just prior to response selection. This model suggests that all information is subjected to some perceptual analysis, but only a portion is responded to. In the case of our Molière example, Model A (sometimes called the early filter model) would predict that the message from the unattended voice would not be decoded in perceptual analysis; in effect it would not be heard. According to Model B, both voices would be heard but the response would only be to one. In a later section these theories are discussed more thoroughly. Research on selective attention and channel capacity has dealt with both auditory and visual signals.

Auditory Signals

The information-processing approach to attention largely grew out of auditory research, but since that time visual as well as semantic research has emerged. Early research by Cherry (1953) led to the development of an experimental procedure called *shadowing,* now a standard method of studying auditory attention. In shadowing, a subject is asked to repeat a spoken message as it is presented. The task is not difficult if the rate of speech is slow, but if the speaker talks rapidly, the subject cannot repeat all the infor-

F I G U R E 5 . 1

General models of selective attention. Adapted from Kahneman (1973).

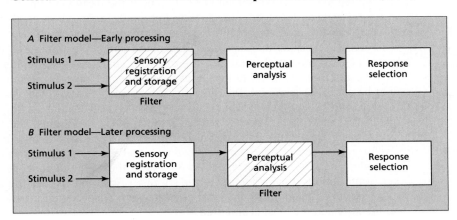

mation that comes in. Most of us have tried this, perhaps in a game. Cherry's experiments, however, had an added feature: two auditory messages were simultaneously presented—one to be shadowed and the other ignored. These messages were sometimes presented through a headphone or over loudspeakers placed at different locations. Cherry (1966) observed:

> The remarkable thing is that over very wide ranges of texts [the subject] is successful, though finds great difficulty. Because the same speaker reads both messages, no clues are provided by different qualities of voice, which may help in real-life cocktail party conversation. Again, since the messages are recorded and heard through headphones, all binaural directivity aids are removed. (p. 280)

Despite the ability of subjects to shadow, Cherry found that they remembered little of the shadowed message. Perhaps most of the processing of information was done in a temporary memory, so there could be no permanent storage and understanding of the message. The unattended messages were even (understandably) more poorly remembered. When the message was speech, the subjects did report that they recognized it as speech, but a change from English to German in the unattended speech was not noticed. The ability to focus on one message and reduce processing from other information seems to be an important human attribute; it allows us to process a limited amount of information without overloading the capacity for information processing.

What can we conclude from Cherry's observation? Since many of the major cues (for example, visual ones) were eliminated in his experiments, the subject must have tuned in to other cues, and these cues are thought to be related to the regularities of our language. In the course of our lifetime, we gather an immense amount of knowledge about phonetics, letter combinations, syntax, phrase structure, sound patterns, clichés, and grammar. Language can be understood when presented in one ear even when another auditory signal is presented in the other ear because we are capable of attending to contextural cues and immediately checking them with our knowledge of the language. Anomalous messages (those that don't conform to the normal grammatical and lexical structure) are required to have powerful signal characteristics before being admitted. Highly familiar messages are processed more easily. Of greater theoretical importance is the fate of the "forgotten" message. How much, if any, information sinks in from unattended channels? Remember our chap at the party who blurted out the inappropriate rejoinder "Have you ever been to Europe?" He must have heard something in his "deaf" ear that prompted him to ask that inappropriate question.

In at least one experiment (Moray, 1959), information piped into the "deaf" ear was not retained by subjects listening to the opposite channel, even though some words were repeated as many as thirty-five times. Even when Moray told his subjects that they would be asked for some information from the rejected channel, they were able to report very little. Moray then took a significant step: he prefaced the message in the unattended channel with the subject's name. Under those conditions, the message was admitted more frequently. (Isn't this also true at a party? Someone on the other side of the room says, "And I understand Randy's wife had sex with . . . " At that moment all the Randys and lovers of Randy's wife, who until then were completely engrossed in other conversations, turn a live ear to the speaker.) However, the need to attend to one message is apparently strong, and, with the exception of special information, little other than the attended message is admitted.

Can we speculate as to what type of a cognitive system(s) will account for these findings? There is no evidence to suggest that the ears are not being equally stimulated on the sensory level. Nor is there any evidence that one of the messages does not reach the auditory cortex. There is, however, some evidence that different parts of the cortex are involved in attention, while other parts are involved in information processing (Posner, 1988), a topic addressed later in this chapter.

Visual Signals

There are some similarities between attentional variables in vision and hearing. Most people are able to recall some visual information from an unattended source, even when they consciously try to attend to only one message. We may focus our attention on one source, but we are more or less aware of other events that are going on at the same time.

In an experiment on visual attention, Neisser (1969) demonstrated what he called *selective reading*, in which subjects read the lines of one color in a text whose lines were of alternative colors. If the subject selectively attends to only one color and if that precludes processing of information printed in the other color, then the information in the other color ought not to be processed. That is, for the most part, what happened. Even repeated words in the unattended visual channel were not recognized, but highly conscious material (such as the subject's name) presented in the "unattended" channel was often noticed. (Note the similarities between this experiment and Moray's auditory experiment.)

Another experiment on selective viewing was conducted by Neisser and Becklen (1975). For their experiment, two different events were separately videotaped (see Figure 5.2) The first involved a game, played in front of a blackboard, in which one player tries to slap another's hands. (Neisser and Becklen were the actors in the skit.) The second event showed three men throwing a basketball to one another while they moved about a room. The two scenes were superimposed (see Figure 5.2C), and the subjects were asked to follow the action in only one, indicating which they were watching by

F I G U R E   5 . 2

Outline drawings of frames from two films used in experiment in "selective looking." A is from the "handgame" film; B, from the basketball film; and C is the two superimposed. From Neisser and Becklen (1975).

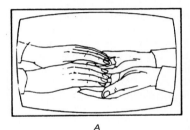

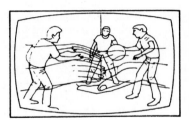

A   B   C

Ulric Neisser. Made significant contributions to many topics in cognitive psychology and whose 1967 book, *Cognitive Psychology*, did much to define the field.

pressing a button when something significant happened in the attended episode. The subjects seemed to follow one of the visual episodes without difficulty; they rarely noticed unusual events in the other episode. It was very difficult to keep track of both episodes. Several reasons may be given for these results. First, the unattended episode must have been seen peripherally a good deal of the time, which, because of the poorer quality of peripheral vision, would exclude some of the cues in the unattended episode. Another interpretation is made by Neisser and Becklen:

> Event perception may be so organized that when a particular structured flow of information is being followed, or a particular representation constructed, the perceiver cannot follow or construct an unrelated one. The results of . . . selective listening studies suggest that this is true, at least for certain levels of complexity and certain stages of learning. (p. 493)

Selective Attention

*R*ead the message in **this type** *starting with* the word **Among.** *Somewhere* **Among** *hidden* **the** *in* **most** *the* **spectacular** *Rocky Mountains* **cognitive** *near* **abilities** *Central City,* **is** *Colorado,* **the** *an* **ability** *old* **to** *miner* **select** *hid* **one** *a* **message** *box* **from** *of* **another.** *gold.* **We** *Although* **do** *several* **this** *hundred* **by** *people* **focusing** *have* **our** *looked* **attention** *for* **on** *it,* **certain** *they* **cues** *have* **such** *not* **as** *found* **type** *it.* **style.** *If* **When** *you* **we** *walk* **focus** *300 paces* **our** *due* **attention** *west* **on** *and* **certain** *600 paces* **stimuli** *northwest* **the** *of* **message** *the* **in** *"Glory Hole"* **other** *Saloon* **stimuli** *and* **is** *dig* **not** *3 feet,* **clearly** *you* **identified.** *will* **However** *find* **some** *enough* **information** *gold* **from** to **the** *go* **unattended** *to* **source** *a* **may** *Tina Turner* **be** *concert* **detected.**

What did you read? Can you tell anything about the message that appeared in **this type?** If so, what words caught your attention and why did they? Several cues helped keep you on the right course; these include the physical nature of the stimuli, the meaning of the sentences, and the syntax. Cues from the unattended message may have distracted you. You may have been distracted by "emotional" words (for example, *gold, "Glory Hole," Saloon, Tina Turner*) or distinctive visual cues (for example, *600, 300*).

MODELS OF SELECTIVE ATTENTION

The Filter Model: Broadbent

The first complete theory of attention was developed in Great Britain by Broadbent (1958). Called a *filter model,* the theory, related to what has been called the single-channel theory, is based on the idea that information processing is restricted by channel capacity, as originally expressed in the information-processing theory of Shannon and Weaver (1949).

Broadbent argues that messages traveling along a specific nerve can differ either according to which of the nerve fibers they stimulate or according to the number of nerve impulses they produce. (Neuropsychological studies have disclosed that high-frequency signals and low-frequency signals are carried to different fibers.) Thus, in the case of several nerve fibers firing at the same time, several sensory messages may arrive at the brain simultaneously. In Broadbent's model (see Figure 5.3), these would be processed through a number of parallel sensory channels. (These channels were assumed to have distinct neural codes and could be selected on the basis of that code. For example, a high-pitched signal and a low-pitched signal presented simultaneously could be distinguished on the basis of their physical characteristics even though both would reach the brain simultaneously.) Further processing of information would then occur only after

FIGURE 5.3

Information-flow diagram that accommodates views of various recent theories. Included are elements of Broadbent's theory that are not dealt with in the text. Adapted from Broadbent (1958).

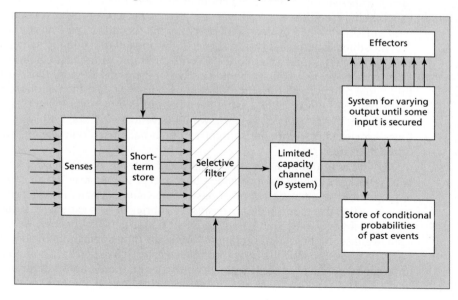

the signal was attended to and passed on through a selective filter into a limited-capacity channel. In Figure 5.3 we can see that more information can enter the system than can be processed by the limited-capacity channel. Broadbent postulated that, in order to avoid an overload in this system, the selective filter could be switched to any of the sensory channels.

Intuitively, the filter theory seems valid. It is obvious that we have a limited information-processing capacity. To make some meaning out of what we hear, the brain may attend to one class of impulses (based on physical characteristics), much as a crossover filter in high-fidelity audio equipment is capable of detecting messages (electrical impulses) of one frequency level or another and sending each such message on to its respective speaker for more processing. When the situation calls for it, we can switch our attention to another channel. However, if selection is on the basis of the physical qualities of signals, as Broadbent originally thought, then switching attention should be unrelated to the content of the message.

In an early experiment, Broadbent (1954) used the dichotic listening technique to test his theory. Subjects were presented with three digits in one ear and, at the same time, three different digits in the other ear. Thus a subject might hear:

Right Ear   4, 9, 3
Left ear   6, 2, 7

In one condition, subjects were asked to recall the digits by ear of presentation (for example, 493 and 627). In another condition, subjects were asked to recall the digits in the sequence in which they appeared. Since two digits at a time were presented, the subjects could recall either member of the pair first but had to report both before continuing through the sequence. Thus, in this condition, the subject could report the digits in this manner: 4, 6, 2, 9, 3, 7.

Given the amount of information to be recalled (six items) and the rate of presentation (two per second), Broadbent could expect about 95 percent recall accuracy. In both experimental conditions, recall was less than expected. In the first condition, subjects were correct about 65 percent of the time; in the second, 20 percent of the time.

Broadbent interpreted the difference to be a result of having to switch attention between the sources more often in the second condition. In the first condition, where subjects were asked to recall all the items from one ear and then all those from the other, they could attend to all the stimuli from one "channel" and then all those from the second (the latter, presumably, having been held briefly in some memory system). In the second condition, however, subjects would have to switch their attention at least three times—for example, from left to right ear, then back from right to left, and once more from left to right.

It is easy to think of the selection process in terms of perception; however, Broadbent (1981) and others have extended the concept to memory. We all carry within us a large number of representations of past events—for example, knowledge of dozens of friends, schedules of forthcoming events, memories of past experiences, thoughts about family members, and so on. At any moment in our personal history, we can recall only a small subset of these representations, while the others remain in the background waiting to be used. Broadbent's connection between selective perception and memory raises important theoretical as well as practical issues but, more important for our current discussion, reminds us that selective perception is not confined to a narrow range of phenomena—it touches almost every other cognitive system.

The results of an experiment by a couple of Oxford undergraduates, Gray and Wedderburn (1960), raised questions about Broadbent's filter model. They presented to alternate ears the syllables composing a word (in sequence) and random digits, so that when a syllable was "heard" by one ear, a digit was "heard" by the other. For example:

Left Ear	Right Ear
OB	6
2	JEC
TIVE	9

If Broadbent's filter theory (based on the physical nature of auditory signals) was correct, the subjects, when asked to repeat what they had "heard" in one channel, should have spewed out gibberish—for example "ob-two-tive" or "six-jec-nine." They didn't; they said (in the case of our example), "objective," thereby showing their capacity to switch rapidly from channel to channel.

In a second experiment (sometimes called the "Dear Aunt Jane" or "What the hell" task), Gray and Wedderburn used the same procedure but presented phrases (such as "Mice eat cheese," "What the hell," or "Dear Aunt Jane") instead of syllables. For example:

Left Ear	Right Ear
Dear	3
5	Aunt
Jane	4

As in the experiment with syllables and digits, the subjects tended to "hear," in this example, "Dear Aunt Jane"; thus, they apparently grouped the message segments by meaning. In Gray and Wedderburn's words, ". . . subjects were acting intelligently in the situation."

It can be argued that these investigators were using a biased test, that such a task as trying to make sense out of broken words and phrases naturally caused their subjects to flip-flop the channel selector in a way that is not normally done when attending to information.

Other researchers challenged the single-channel theory on the basis of results from galvanic skin response (GSR) experiments. In these experiments certain words presented in the attended ear were followed by an electrical shock. Re-presentation of the word produced a change in GSR. Following conditioning of the GSR, the subjects were asked to shadow a message. The conditioned word was presented occasionally in the unattended channel. Some found that change in GSR was produced when this occurred. In one experiment (von Wright, Anderson & Stenman, 1975), the change in GSR resulted in presentation not only of the conditioned word, but also of synonyms and homophones of it. These results suggest that "unattended" signals are not only detected but also semantically processed. However, Wardlaw and Kroll (1976) failed to replicate some of these findings (by Corteen and Wood, 1972) and questioned the robustness of the effect. Forster and Govier (1978) not only replicated the findings but also demonstrated an even more robust effect of the degree to which semantically similar words

Attention, Consciousness, and Subliminal Perception

Many theories of attention engage two controversial issues: (1) the issue of consciousness and (2) subliminal perception, or the effect of stimuli that are clearly strong enough to be above the physiological limen but are not conscious. As we have seen in the text, contemporary models of attention focus on where the selection of information takes place. Inherent in many of these theories is the notion that people are not aware of signals in the early part of the processing of information but, after some type of decision or selection, pass some of the signals on for further processing.

Largely stimulated by the work of Sigmund Freud, psychologists for more than a century have been interested in the dichotomy between the conscious part of the mind and the unconscious part. One problem in accepting Freud's characterization of the dichotomous mind (especially by the behaviorists) is that such theoretical matter lacked objective sub-

stance. Nevertheless, experiments by cognitive psychologists as well as case studies from psychoanalysts have supported the dichotomous view of the mind.

The question of being able to perceive signals that are below the threshold is problematic for many research psychologists, who regard this as voodoo psychology. How can we "hear" without hearing? Yet studies of attention clearly show that it is possible to retain information that has been neglected. The topic of subliminal perception is closely related to the priming effect, in which the display of a word, for example, facilitates the recognition of an associate to that word without any conscious awareness of the process. Furthermore, several studies (Underwood, 1976, 1977; and Philpott & Wilding, 1979) have shown that subliminal stimuli may have an effect on the recognition of subsequent stimuli. Therefore, some effect of the subliminal stimuli is observed.

could produce a positive GSR. As in the Corteen and Wood experiment, they conditioned a GSR to a word (for example, *SHIPS*) by pairing it with a small electrical shock. Then, in a shadowing experiment, subjects were instructed to attend to one channel. In the unattended channel, the original word (*SHIPS*) was presented; in another condition, a synonym was presented (*BOATS*); and in a third condition, an acoustically similar word was presented (*SHIMS*). In all three conditions (the original word, its synonym, and its homonym) GSR recordings were observed.

A more substantial test of the filter theory was made by Anne Treisman and her colleagues; her work is described next.

The Attenuation Model: Treisman

Among the most obvious problems of the filter model is the detection of sensitive information (such as the subject's name) through an unattended channel. Moray (1959) did such an experiment and found that subjects noticed their own names from the unattended channel about one-third of the time. We also know from common experience that we can monitor a second message while attending to another. A parent in church

Anne Treisman. **Developed an attenuation model of attention.**

may be engrossed in a sermon heard over a background of caterwauling in the nursery. The teaching is clearly understood, and the wails, cries, and screams of the children bother not our serene parishioner. However, let the faintest whisper be emitted by the listener's child, and that signal is heard as clearly as Gabriel's trumpet. In fairness to Broadbent, his original theory postulated that the selection filter does occasionally admit one or two highly "probable" (likely to occur, given the context) words through the unattended channel.

It was time for a new, or at least modified, model of attention. Treisman presented one.

To explain the fact that subjects could sometimes hear their own names through the unattended channel, Moray suggested that some kind of analysis must occur before the filter. Treisman, arguing against that, suggested that in the subject's "dictionary" (or store of words) some words have lower thresholds for activation. Thus important words or sounds, such as one's own name or the distinctive cry of one's child, are activated more easily than less important signals. Her elegant model retains much of the architecture of Broadbent's model while accounting for the empirical results obtained by Moray.

It may be recalled that, in Broadbent's model, one channel is switched off when attention is directed to the other channel. Most noteworthy of Treisman's work is her experiment in which subjects were asked to attend to a message in one ear, while the linguistic meaning shifted from one ear to the other. For example, the message "There is a house understand the word" was presented in the right ear while "Knowledge of on a hill" was presented in the left. We tend to follow the meaning rather than attend to the message from one ear, even when told to report the message received in that one ear. Thus the subjects reported hearing: "There is a house on a hill." In one experiment Treisman (1964a) had French-English bilingual subjects shadow a passage from Orwell's *England, Your England*. In one ear the voice spoke in English; in the other, French. Unknown to the subjects, the passages were the same but slightly offset in time. As the offset was gradually reduced, many subjects noticed that the two messages were the same in meaning. It would appear that the "unattended" voice was not cut off from their knowledge of the second language.

Treisman's data and those of other researchers seemed at odds with the filter model. Some cerebral "executive," before it analyzed signal characteristics, had to make a decision to do so. Obviously, some initial screening of information must take place. According to Treisman, the first of these screens evaluates the signal on the basis of gross physical characteristics, and more sophisticated screens then evaluate the signal in terms of meaning (see Figure 5.4).

FIGURE 5.4

Selective listening, assuming A (a limit to perceptual capacity) and B (a limit to response capacity). Adapted from Treisman and Geffen (1967).

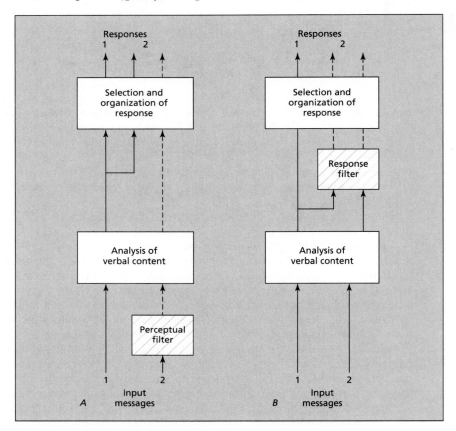

The initial screening takes place by means of an attenuator, or perceptual filter—a device that regulates the volume of the message and that intercedes between the signal and its verbal processing. Treisman's model suggests that "irrelevant messages" are heard with a dull, not deaf, ear.

How well does Treisman's attenuation model work? It is certainly a logical explanation of how we can hear something without attending to it and how we attend to meaning rather than to the physical characteristics of the message alone. However, the problem of how decisions are made remains, even if in an attenuated form. Does a simple attenuator have the capacity to analyze the intricate features of a message and check them with some master control to see whether they should or should not pass through?

Furthermore, can it do all this in the twinkle of an eye necessary to keep pace with the ongoing panorama of auditory events? These questions have sparked debate as to exactly what attributes Treisman ascribed to the attenuator. She clarified her position in a letter to the author. With regard to the attenuator, Treisman (1986) wrote:

> My suggestion was that the attenuator treats *all* [emphasis mine] unattended messages alike, regardless of their content. The effects of probability, relevance, importance, etc., are all determined within the speech recognition system, exactly as they are for the attended message if it arrives with a low signal-to-noise ratio. . . . The only difference between unattended and attended messages is that the unattended message has its overall signal-to-noise ratio reduced by the selective filter, and therefore fails to excite lexical entries for any of its content except a few words or phrases with unusually low detection thresholds. The attenuator selects only on the basis of general physical properties such as location or voice quality.

Visual Attention.   Thus far we have concentrated on the auditory aspects of attention, but all sensory experiences (visual, auditory, olfactory, gustatory, and tactical)[2] are governed by rules of attention. Vision, color, and form perception have received the greatest amount of analysis (see Chapter 4 on form perception) outside of audition. For a look at visual attention, consider the stimuli in the upper part of Figure 5.5. Here, you can "see" the cluster of +s in a field of large Ls.

In experiments of this type, Treisman and her associates and Julesz and his associates have found that when visual elements are distinctive, as they are in Figure 5.5, the boundaries jump out to the viewer within 50 milliseconds. Now, look at Figure 5.5B. Here you can "see" the Ts (outlined for emphasis) with some effort, although they certainly do not jump out of the context as the +s do. Yet, the compositional elements are identical (that is, a + is made up of two lines at right angles to each other, as is a *T*). Because the visual system "sees" the Ts to be similar to the background and the +s to be dissimilar, the two tasks require different amounts of attentional effort to process. Both Treisman and Julesz hypothesize that two different processes in visual attention are operating. In the first stage (see Figure 5.6), there is an initial, *preattentive process* (a kind of master map of an image) that scans the field and rapidly detects the main features of objects, such things as size, color, orientation, and movement, if any. Then, according to Treisman, different properties of the object are encoded in specific *feature maps,* which are located in different parts of the cortex.

Since the appearance of Broadbent's original notion of attention in the 1950s, which not only influenced a whole generation of researchers including Treisman but also was important in the development of a limited-capacity model of information processing, a dozen or more theories have been put forth, all of which modify and/or attack some of his basic notions. Unfortunately, some have portrayed Broadbent's theory as an either/or theory, in which information is processed either in one channel or in another. That char-

---

[2]Shift your attention from the visual reading of this text to another modality, say touch, and focus on the pressures felt on your left foot by your shoe. Think about it. Now, try to center your attention on each of the other senses, and spotlight the experiences associated with each sensation.

FIGURE 5.5

It is possible to "see" the rectangular cluster of +s in these figures, but more difficult to "see" the Ts. The first stage of attention seems to be a preattentive scanning, which surveys the general field and yields basic information, such as seeing the +s. Seeing the Ts requires focal attention.

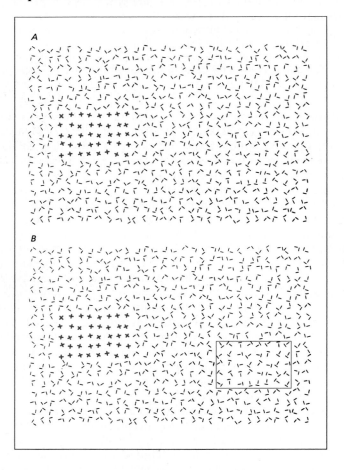

acterization is wrong. What Broadbent (1958) wrote was "Once again we cannot say simply 'a man cannot listen to two things at once.' On the contrary, he receives *some* information even from the rejected ear: but there is a limit to the amount, and details of the stimulus on the rejected ear are not recorded" (p. 23) (emphasis added). No single theory of attention has replaced the original one, although much of the research has helped clarify specific issues involved in human attention.

FIGURE 5.6

A model of the stages of visual perception and attention. Initially, some basic properties of a visual scene (color, orientation, size, and distance) are encoded in separate, parallel pathways that generate feature maps. These maps are integrated into a master map. Focused attention then draws on the information from the master map to analyze in detail the features associated in a selected region of the image. From Treisman (1988).

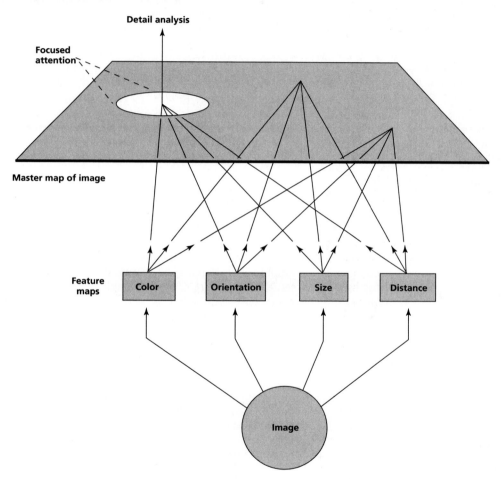

Recent research in attention has focused on several important issues including (1) the role of "automatic processing" and attention, (2) consciousness, (3) the internal neurological mechanisms that are related to the psychology of attention, and (4) selective attention and the processing of complex information by experts. We consider the first three of these topics in this chapter and the fourth topic in Chapter 9.

Critical Thinking: Can You Rub Your Belly and Tap Your Head Simultaneously?

With one finger tap out the rhythm to a well-known song, such as "Happy Birthday to You." Wasn't that easy? Now, with a finger on the other hand, tap out "Jingle Bells" (or some other well-known song.) That too is easy. Now, tap out both songs simultaneously. Can you do it? Why not? With a great deal of practice, you may be able to do this successfully. If you can, it is likely that you learned to do it by tapping out one tune so well that you could do it on "automatic pilot" (see Automatic Processing) while attending consciously to the other. Accomplished piano players do similar tasks with practice. It is likely that the simultaneous processing of such acts is regulated by a motor timer in the cerebellum—that large structure in the very hind part of the brain resembling a cauliflower—but other parts of the brain are also involved.

AUTOMATIC PROCESSING

Work by LaBerge and Samuels (1974) and LaBerge (1975, 1976) has utilized both the concept of allocation of attention and automatic processing in accounting for the effects of attention. As we have seen throughout this chapter, the human subject is frequently (if not always) confronted by myriad stimuli while at the same time participating in several activities. For example, as we drive a car, we may look simultaneously at a map, scratch, shuffle our feet, eat a hamburger, put on sunglasses, and so on. In terms of allocation of effort, however, we are directing more attention to driving than to other activities, even though some attention is given to the other activities. It appears that highly practiced activities become automatic and thereby require less attention to perform than do new or slightly practiced activities. This relationship between automatic processing and attention has been described by LaBerge (1975):

> For example, imagine learning the name of a completely unfamiliar letter. This is much like learning the name that goes with the face of a person recently met. When presented again with the visual stimulus one recalls a time-and-place episode which subsequently produces the appropriate response. With further practice, the name emerges almost at the same time as the episode. This "short-circuiting" is represented by the formation of a direct line between the visual and name codes. The process still requires attention . . . and the episodic code is used now more as a check on accuracy than as the mediator of the association. As more and more practice accumulates, the direct link becomes automatic (Mandler, 1954). . . . At this point the presentation of the stimulus evokes the name without any contribution by the Attention Centre. Indeed, in such cases, we often observe that we cannot prevent the name from "popping into our head."

LaBerge's concept may help account for quite a lot of human activity under stressful conditions. Norman (1976) has provided us with an apt example. Suppose that a diver is entangled in his or her scuba apparatus while beneath the surface. To survive, the diver needs to release the equipment and gradually float to the surface. Norman points out: "Practicing the release of one's weight belt over and over again while diving in a swimming pool seems a pointless exercise to the student. But if that task can be made so automatic that it requires little or no conscious effort, then on the day that the diver needs to act under stress, the task may get performed successfully in spite of the buildup of panic" (p. 66). For automaticity of processing to occur, there must be a free flow of information from memory to the subject's control of actions.

The automatic processing of information was given much needed structure by Posner and Snyder (1974, 1975), who describe three characteristics of an automatic process:

- An automatic process occurs without intention. In the case of the Stroop Test (a test involving words, such as *RED* or *GREEN*, that are printed in different colors in which subjects are to name the color), people normally experience conflict between the two tasks and frequently read the words when asked to name the colors. Reading, a more powerful automatic process, takes some precedence over color naming and occurs without the intention of the subjects. Likewise, in priming experiments the effect operates independent of intention or conscious purpose on the part of the subject. For example, it is easier to recognize the word *NURSE* after seeing the word *DOCTOR*.

- Automatic processes are concealed from consciousness. As pointed out in the previous example, priming effects are mostly unconscious. We do not "think" about automatic processes, which suggests the third characteristic:

- Automatic processes consume few (or no) conscious resources. We can read words or tie a knot in our shoelaces without giving these activities a thought. They take place automatically and without effort.

The importance of studies of automaticity may be that they tell us something of the complex cognitive activity that seems to occur outside of conscious experience. Furthermore, skills such as typing, scuba diving, playing the violin, driving a car, playing tennis, and even using the language correctly and making social judgments about other people are likely to be well-practiced ones that for the most part, run automatically. Skillful performance in these matters may free consciousness to attend to the more demanding and changing onslaught of activities that require attention. The topic of automaticity engages the most enigmatic of topics in psychology: consciousness, a topic with which the chapter ends.

THE NEUROCOGNITION OF ATTENTION

As we learned in previous chapters, neurocognition represents a new direction in cognitive psychology. Stimulated by important discoveries in neurology and computer sciences, neurocognition has spread to nearly every region of cognitive psychology, including attention. While it is easy to think of the neurocognitive study of attention as the opening of a new frontier, some former studies have influenced our thinking.

Activation and Habituation

Some of these studies have dealt with the neurophysiology of the brain, especially the *reticular activating formation*. This is a complex region located in the midbrain and connected to most areas of the cortex. It contains many groups of neurons, which are involved in the activation or arousal of other parts of the brain. Other studies have focused on habituation, the research procedure in which a stimulus is presented repeatedly until the subject no longer reacts to it (thus, the subject habituates to the stimulus). More recent developments have attempted to identify specific parts of the cortex associated with attention.

Even before Broadbent proposed his influential theory of attention, another line of physiological research had led to the discovery of the importance of the reticular activating formation (RAF). This formation is sometimes called the arousal system, since it is related to attention and orienting reflexes, for example, the type of reaction a dog might have upon hearing a bell.[3] It appears that this system is involved in many of the activities associated with arousal, which is related to the more general topic of attention.

When a subject is confronted with a novel stimulus that grabs his or her attention, more than simple orienting reflexes can be observed. There is an actual increase in sensory sensitivity: the pupils of the eyes dilate; the EEG reading shows an arousal pattern; there is a pause and then a decrease in the respiration rate; the blood vessels of the limbs constrict, while those in the brain dilate (perhaps an ancient stratagem to enhance survival when doing battle). Scientists became interested in the neurological considerations of attention partly because of studies of the increase in blood flow to the brain under elevated arousal states.

Attention and the Human Brain

The connection between attention and the human brain was originally investigated by correlating attentional deficits with brain traumas. This early work was largely confined to neuropathology. For example, a lesion or stroke in one part of the brain might be associated with a type of attentional deficit. Unfortunately, pathological observations were commonly based on gross insults (strokes and gunshot wounds know no boundaries) and thus the specific locus of the brain involved in specific kinds of attention problems remained veiled. There was an additional problem in that specific pathological observations were frequently based on postmortem examinations, which allow for, to say the least, minimal interaction between the subject and observer. Pathological studies did, however, suggest that attention was partly tied to a specific cortical region. Recently, researchers interested in attention and the brain have engaged techniques, developed in both cognitive psychology and brain science, which significantly expand our understanding of this relationship. Furthermore, there is an impressive catalog of techniques to draw upon in both disciplines that do not require the subject to die, to suffer a massive stroke, to take a bullet in the head, or to surrender to a surgical procedure in order for observations to be made.

The focus of these recent efforts has generally been in two areas:

1. There is the search for correlates between the geography of the brain and attentional processes (Corbetta et al., 1991; Mountcastle, 1978; Pardo, Fox, & Raichle,

---

[3]Pavlov observed the orienting reflex when his dogs were confronted by a novel stimulus; they pricked up their ears and turned toward the stimulus.

Michael I. Posner. **Did seminal work in attention, memory, and neurocognition, which has opened up new areas of cognitive psychology.**

1991; Posner, 1988, 1992; [especially] Posner & Petersen, 1990; and Whitehead, 1991). These studies have made use of the full range of cognitive techniques discussed in this chapter (for example, dichotic listening, shadowing, divided attention, lexical decision tasks, shape and color discrimination, and priming) and remote sensing devices used in neurological studies (for example, MRI and PET scans) as well as traditional reaction-time experiments.

2. Techniques developed in the cognitive laboratory are used as diagnostic tests or in the investigation of pharmacological agents that supposedly act selectively in the attentional process (Tinklenberg & Taylor, 1984). Following is a brief discussion of some conclusions.

Consider the matter of finding correlates between brain anatomy and attention. There appear to be anatomically separate systems of the brain that deal with attention and other systems, such as the data processing systems, that perform operations on specific inputs even when attention is directed elsewhere (Posner, 1992). In one sense, the attention system is similar to other systems (the motor and sensory systems, for example) in that it interacts with many other parts of the brain but maintains its own identity. Evidence for this conclusion can be found in patients with brain damage who demonstrate attentional problems but not processing deficits (or vice versa).

Attention and PET. Current research on attention has used brain imaging technology (mainly PET), and although it is impossible to report all of the recent studies (or even a reasonable cross section, so vast is the new data in this field), it is possible to give a glimpse of some work being done in this important area of neurocognitive research by some of its foremost scientists. The basic methodological technique for PET investigations is discussed in Chapter 2. Although an explanation of the technique is not repeated here, it is important to remember that this is a procedure in which blood flow rates in the brain are evaluated by means of radioactive tracers. As the brain metabolizes nourishment through use, more blood is called for. These actions are monitored by means of radioactive sensors and transposed by a computer into a geographic map of the cortex in which "hot spots," regions of concentrated blood flow, are identified.

FIGURE 5.7

The areas of the cerebral cortex of the human brain involved in attention are shown. Attentional networks are shown by solid colored shapes on the lateral (outside) and medial (cross-section) surfaces of the right and left hemispheres. It appears that the parietal lobes are involved in the attentional network (see solid colored square); the right frontal lobes are related to vigilance; and the diamonds are part of the anterior attention network. The oval and circle are word processing systems, which are related to visual word form (ellipse) and semantic associates (circle).

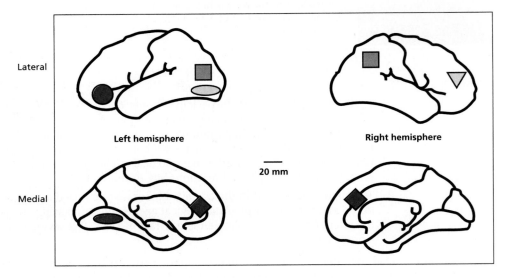

Lateral

Left hemisphere

Right hemisphere

20 mm

Medial

Typical of these experiments is the work of Peterson and his colleagues (Petersen et al., 1990) in which subjects were shown words, nonwords that resembled words, and consonant strings. As shown in Figure 5.7, the areas activated for words and regular nonwords (but not consonant strings) were the ones shown with an open ellipse (left figures). Curiously, patients who suffer nonfatal lesions to these areas frequently are unable to read words but may read letter by letter. For example, shown the word *Opera*, these patients cannot read it but can say the letters one by one, and, by so doing, the string is (probably) represented into an auditory code. Other areas of the brain take over the functioning, and these patients can say what the word is. Additional studies of the brain by means of PET show other areas involved in specific types of attention, as shown in Figure 5.7. Each of these designated areas of the brain is involved in selective attention in different ways, and to thoroughly understand the nature of the brain in attention, it is necessary to consider the topic of awareness and consciousness (see the next section). The current state of knowledge of the cortex's role in awareness and attention is that the attentional system produces the contents of awareness in the same way as other parts of brain, such as the visual system, and organizes the way other sensations are processed, such as how the visual world is perceived.

CONSCIOUSNESS: RESPECTABLE, USEFUL, AND NECESSARY

We continue our discussion of attention by considering consciousness, an idea that is both ancient and modern. The topic of consciousness has been hotly debated among prophets, philosophers, playwrights, psychoanalysts, and psychologists for a long time. William James (1890) equated consciousness with a selecting agency that chooses one thing from many stimuli, the chosen stimulus being emphasized and accentuated while other events are suppressed. The beginning of scientific psychology in the last century was dominated by the study of consciousness and the method of introspection. While some of the pioneers of psychology (such as Wundt and Titchener) subscribed to a single-minded notion of consciousness, others (such as Helmholtz and Freud) suggested that unconscious processes had a profound effect on human behavior and conscious thoughts. With the advent of a psychology bent on developing cause-and-effect laws of behavior, however, the topic lost its attractions.

Recently, however, there have been two important developments in the study of consciousness. First, several theorists have begun to reexamine the topic from the perspective of contemporary cognitive psychology and, especially, human memory and attention. Second, the study of consciousness has been greatly enhanced through studies of neurocognition assisted by brain imaging technology.

Consciousness is defined as "awareness of events or stimuli in the environment as well as awareness of cognitive phenomena such as memories, thoughts, and bodily sensations." As with so many topics central to the study of our intellectual life, the study of consciousness was banished from experimental psychology by behaviorists during the first part of this century and labeled "epiphenomenal."[4] Recent efforts of several cognitive psychologists[5] have restored the study of consciousness to the status of "respectable, useful, and necessary" (Mandler, 1975a).

Perhaps because the topic does not lend itself to easy analytic measures, experimental psychologists have not attacked the problem of consciousness with the same boldness exhibited with other problems, for example, the study of auditory attention. Also, there has been a dearth of theoretical models to guide research in the field.

[4]The reader interested in this history is directed to Ernest Hilgard's chapter "Consciousness in Contemporary Psychology" in the 1980 *Annual Review of Psychology.*

[5]See Hilgard, 1980; Kihlstrom, 1987; Miller, 1980; Posner, 1989; Tulving, 1985b; and G. Underwood, 1982.

> **Perhaps the last frontier of science—its ultimate challenge—is to understand the biological basis of consciousness and the mental processes by which we perceive, act, learn, and remember.**
>
> *Kandel, Schwartz, & Jessell, 1991, (p. 3).*

Explicit and Implicit Memory

The experimental study of consciousness has taken several forms (we mentioned priming experiments earlier), including studies of explicit and implicit memory. *Explicit memory* refers to the conscious recall of information, the type of memory you might use when answering a question on an examination. *Implicit memory,* on the other hand, is more germane to our discussion of consciousness since it refers to memory that is divulged through a performance change that is related to some previous experience, such as in the case of priming experiments discussed earlier in this chapter. In many cases, implicit memory is revealed when previous information facilitates task performance and *does not require conscious recall of those experiences.* When I ask you to recall the name of Woody Allen's ex-wife, you actively and consciously search your memory to find the name *Mia Farrow,* which is an example of explicit memory. If I show you a badly degraded figure (so degraded and so brief that you have no idea what it is) for a very brief period of time and then show you the whole figure and ask to identify it, your reaction time and accuracy will be measurably enhanced over a similar experiment in which the degraded prime is not shown. Yet, your conscious awareness of the influence of the prime is likely to be absent.

There is a long history of studies of implicit memory, including speculation by Freud on unconscious memories and memory without awareness (see Jacoby & Witherspoon, 1982), but one fundamental problem still remains: Does the demonstrable presence of implicit and explicit memory depend on a single underlying cognitive system or on multiple systems? While the question is unanswered, it is important to grasp that much of the current research on consciousness is framed in the context of these two memory systems. Theoretical models of consciousness among cognitive psychologists are relatively sparse.

Theoretical model building of consciousness is easy to find among fringe type mystics, but credible cognitive psychologists have been generally mute on the topic. An exception is Tulving, who suggests that three varieties of consciousness can be isolated in the human: autonoetic, noetic, and anoetic. Each of these varieties is associated with three types of memory: episodic, semantic, and procedural, respectively. Although a detailed discussion of the memory types appears in Chapter 7, an outline of the essential components follows.

Episodic memory involves the remembering of personally experienced events. Semantic memory has to do with representable knowledge about the world. Procedural memory deals with how things are done—acquisition, retention, and utilization of skills. Tulving postulates that each of these systems is characterized by its own kind of consciousness.

The relationship between memory systems and consciousness is summarized in Table 5.1. The most sophisticated form of consciousness is autonoetic, or "self-knowing," consciousness, which is associated with episodic memory. This form of consciousness is necessary for the remembering of personally experienced events. Someone using autonoetic consciousness may recall a personal event that is thought to be a fact about his or her past life. This form of consciousness, which is related to episodic memory, is distinguished from noetic and anoetic consciousness, which deal with perceiving, thinking, imagining, or dreaming. In noetic, or "knowing," consciousness, the person may be aware of objects and events and their relationships even in the absence of those

T A B L E   5 . 1

**The Relationship Between Memory Systems
and Varieties of Consciousness**

Memory System		Consciousness
Episodic	$\longleftrightarrow$	Autonoetic
$\downarrow$		$\downarrow$
Semantic	$\longleftrightarrow$	Noetic
$\downarrow$		$\downarrow$
Procedural	$\longleftrightarrow$	Anoetic

From Tulving (1985b).

objects and events. In this sense it is a symbolic form of consciousness. Anoetic consciousness is sometimes called "nonknowing," since it is temporally bound to the current situation. This form of consciousness allows the person to register environmental cues and respond behaviorally to the present environment.

Tulving's distinction between types of consciousness, together with his correlation of each type with a kind of memory, seems to be an important step in removing studies of consciousness from the murky metaphysical speculation of a previous generation and placing the topic squarely in the center of contemporary memory and cognitive psychology. The fate of this avant-garde idea bears close watching. An area of investigation that has caught the attention of many people is the field of brain research, especially as it relates consciousness to attention (see previous section) and to hemispheric specialization, a topic we now consider.

Consciousness: Hemispheric Specialization

As long ago as 1869, the French physician Paul Broca (for whom a region of the brain related to speech production is named) discovered that the rule of body symmetry did not seem to apply to brain functioning. Patients with brain damage in the left cerebral hemisphere were associated with slow and labored speech patterns, but similar damage in the right hemisphere did not produce speech difficulties. Recent studies by Roger Sperry and his colleagues (see Sperry, 1968, 1974) present further evidence of the asymmetrical functioning of the brain. As we learned in Chapter 2, these studies are called split-brain research and have been conducted on patients whose corpus callosum has been severed.

The implication of this research for studies of consciousness is that two types of consciousness, one for language awareness and processing in the left hemisphere and one for spatial functions in the right hemisphere, may be operating. Robert Ornstein has argued that the development of one half of the brain over the other may account for some of the fundamental intellectual differences among individuals. Some people exhibit unusual verbal ability, while others are better at mechanical and spatial relations. Could such differences be attributed to right-brain or left-brain dominance? Ornstein also suggests that Western cultures tend to emphasize logical thinking, reading, and verbal processing of information, generally associated with the left hemisphere, while other cultures, especially Eastern ones, emphasize a different form of consciousness that is based on intuition and insight which may be centered in the left hemisphere.

One way we can think of consciousness is to distinguish between material of which we are immediately aware and material that is at a more obscure level.

Levels of Consciousness

It appears that each of the five senses is susceptible to various levels of consciousness. Pay attention to the sense of touch. Before reading the previous sentence (and hence directing your attention to the sense of sight), you probably were unaware of the weight of your clothes, the pressure of your glasses on your forehead and temples, the restriction of your toes by shoes, or the feeling of weight on your buttocks. Yet, when your attention is directed toward each of these sensations, you become consciously aware of it. Here, the link between attention and consciousness is apparent. We can direct our attention, and hence our consciousness, but, in everyday life, we experience various levels of consciousness for each sense. Sometimes our concentration on a single thought is so great that all other thoughts and sensations are excluded. We become lost in thought. Most of our psychic energy seems to be devoted to a single entity. At other, more relaxed periods, it seems that our attention is much more diffuse and many sensations capture our attention.

Internal phenomena, such as memories, also seem to be susceptible to several levels of consciousness. As you read this section, your conscious mind may be directed primarily to the ideas of consciousness, but it is likely that other thoughts and memories intrude on the message contained in this section. Sometimes these thoughts become so strong that you may read several paragraphs without comprehending a thing.

The issue of the depth of memories and consciousness has had a stormy history in psychology, from E. B. Titchener's belief that the subject matter of psychology should be the study of consciousness, to John Watson's (1913) dictum that "the time seems to have come when psychology must discard all references to consciousness," to Sigmund Freud's belief that topics of consciousness and unconsciousness are central to understanding normal and abnormal personalities.

Memories that can be called into consciousness rather easily (such as the name of a close friend) are described as being at the *preconscious state*. When recalling information from the preconscious state, we bring it into the conscious state.

Other memories are less accessible. These memories and thoughts are called *unconscious ideas,* most of which are thought by Freud and his followers to be unavailable. They believe most unconscious ideas have been repressed because they represent a threat to some aspect of our personality.

It seems appropriate to discuss consciousness in the context of attention, since it shares the common dimension of limited processing capacity. The previous discussion would suggest that we can attend to and/or process only a limited amount of information at a time, and it is generally recognized (although empirical data on this subject are hard to find) that we can be conscious of only one thing at a time.

George Mandler (1974) has argued that the limited capacity of short-term memory, immediate memory span, limitations in judgment tasks, and so on can usefully be ascribed to the limited capacity of conscious content. There exist only a few serious theoretical discussions of consciousness within an information-processing framework. One is by Shallice (1972), who argues that rehearsal of information in memory and selective attention seem to imply a conscious process. He further argues that consciousness serves a dual purpose: to select what action system will be dominant and to set a goal for the action system.

In closing this chapter on the topic of attention and consciousness, it is important to reemphasize that both topics are fundamentally related. It is likely that our recent information about the localization of attentional networks in the brain by means of advanced imaging technology will be correlated with subjective awareness of events and thoughts. These relationships will, undoubtedly, become clarified in the near future with increased popularity of techniques and innovative cognitive experiments. These are exciting times. We now know details of topics generations of scholars thought impossible to investigate and others forbade.

Summary

1   Attention is the concentration of mental effort on sensory or mental events. Many contemporary ideas about attention are based on the premise that an information-processing system's capacity to handle the flow of input is determined by the limitations of that system.

2   Research on attention covers five major aspects: processing capacity and selectiveness, control of attention, automatic processing, the neurocognition of attention, and consciousness.

3   Capacity limits and selective attention imply a structural bottleneck in information processing. Two models propose different locations for this bottleneck. One model locates it at or just prior to perceptual analysis (Broadbent); another model asserts that all information is analyzed and the bottleneck is located at or just prior to response selection (Deutsch and Deutsch).

4   The attenuation model of selective attention proposes a perceptual filter, located between signal and verbal analyses, which screens input by selectively regulating the "volume" of the message. Stimuli are assumed to have different activation thresholds, a provision that explains how we can hear without attending.

5   Recent work in neurocognition has studied attention from the perspective of activation and habituation and has sought correlates between parts of the brain and attentional mechanisms.

6   Consciousness is the awareness of internal and external information.

7   Explicit memory refers to conscious recall of information while implicit memory is indicated through performance changes related to previous experience which, in many cases, does not require conscious recall of those experiences.

8 Distinct levels of consciousness are associated with different memory systems; autonoetic, noetic, and anoetic levels of consciousness correspond respectively to episodic, semantic, and procedural memory systems.

9 Results of split-brain research suggest two types of consciousness—one for language functions associated with the left hemisphere and one for spatial relations associated with the right hemisphere.

10 Consciousness can be divided into: (1) the conscious, (2) the preconscious, and (3) the unconscious.

Key Words

anoetic consciousness	implicit memory
attention	noetic consciousness
automatic processing	preattentive process
autonoetic consciousness	preconscious state
channel capacity	priming
consciousness	shadowing
explicit memory	subliminal perception
feature maps	unconscious state
habituation	

Recommended Readings

Historically, Broadbent's *Perception and Communication* is an important work and still makes interesting reading. Also recommended are two books by Neisser, *Cognitive Psychology* (the first "modern" book in the field) and *Cognition and Reality: Principles and Implications of Cognitive Psychology.* A slightly more specialized treatment of attention can be found in Norman, *Memory and Attention;* Kahneman, *Attention and Effort;* Mandler, *Mind and Emotion;* and Klatzky's *Memory and Awareness.* Gregory's *The Oxford Companion to the Mind* is an intellectual tour de force to be enjoyed by anyone interested in ideas, cognition, and attention. Highly recommended papers include Kihlstrom's article "The Cognitive Unconscious" in *Science;* Cowan's article in *Psychological Bulletin;* Posner and Petersen's chapter on "The Attention System of the Human Brain" in the *Annual Review of Neuroscience;* Pashler's "Doing Two Things at the Same Time" in *American Scientist;* and, for a touch of automaticity and PDP, Cohen, Servan-Schreiber, and McClelland's article (1992). Robert Ornstein's book, *The Evolution of Consciousness: The Origins of the Way we Think,* is both amusing and informative, and Baars's *A Cognitive Theory of Consciousness* is thoughtful and provocative.

MEMORY:
Theories and
Neurocognition

O F THE GREAT PROBLEMS facing cognitive psychologists, none is more enigmatic than the nature of the brain's memory structure. Cramped within a calcified vessel, weighing only about 1 1/2 kilograms, is an astonishing memory device. The human brain is the executive of our life, guiding our actions; it is the terminus of sensations, from which knowledge is fashioned; it is the repository of memory, from which meaning is derived; and it is the heart of our emotions, giving life feeling. However, of all the frontiers that have yielded to exploration and civilization, understanding the seat of knowledge is only beginning. But what a beginning! We have learned more about memory in the past several decades than in all the time before, and current studies of the neurological basis of memory, aided by powerful new techniques, are reshaping our views of this fascinating topic.

The study of human memory easily lends itself to the dichotomy mentioned in Chapter 1: structure and process. Many cognitive psychologists embrace a structural notion of memory that is itself dualistic, postulating a short-term memory (STM) and a long-term memory (LTM). This view, which is compatible with an information-processing model, has enjoyed great popularity. In recent years some challenging ideas about the nature of human memory have caused many cognitive psychologists to question the validity of a dualistic model of memory. Those theorists whose interest lies in the structural aspects of memory are concerned with developing a description of the characteristics of the stages (or boxes in terms of a diagram) through which information presumably flows.

The processing of information has also received the careful attention of memory theorists. Processing in the present context refers to the "fate" of perceived information: how it is coded, transformed, associated, stored, rehearsed, recalled, and forgotten. In effect, processing is what takes place in the boxes of a diagram.

"Software" and "Hardware." The scientific study of human memory is currently approached from two positions. One group emphasizes the structural-processing components of memory, using conventional psychological means (such as presenting some type of information and measuring the accuracy of subsequent recall). Another group is interested in the neurological basis of memory, sometimes using brain imaging technology and sometimes investigating memory changes with the use of specialized types of pathology (such as might occur with patients who have experienced a brain lesion in a specific part of the brain) or through the administration of pharmacological agents that affect neurotransmission. Metaphorically, we can think of the first group as the "software" group in the sense that its members are pursuing the way memory works, sometimes in everyday life, and the second group the "hardware" group in the sense that its members are investigating the network of neurons and their interconnections that are associated with memory processes.

EARLY STUDIES

It is unlikely that Herman Ebbinghaus, who lived in Germany and who wrote the first scientific account of memory experiments (*On Memory*, 1885), could have foreseen the impact his work would have throughout the history of the study of learning and memory. Consider the circumstances that prevailed during his time. Even though everyone "knew" what memory was and philosophers had speculated about its purpose for years, no systematic formulation of memory structure had been tested, no sophisticated analytic apparatus was available, and no database of previous experimentation existed. Thus his exploration of the unknown properties of memory was undertaken with little information and few tested apparatus to guide him. He did have a hunch that sensations, feelings, and ideas that had at one time been conscious remained hidden somewhere in memory. His view of the contents of memory and its accessibility is eloquently expressed in the following passage, in which he speaks of once-conscious sensations, feelings, and ideas.

> Although the inwardly-turned look may no longer be able to find them, nevertheless they have not been utterly destroyed and annulled, but in a certain manner they continue to exist, stored up, so to speak, in the memory. We cannot, of course, directly observe their present existence, but it is revealed by the effects which come to our knowledge with a certainty like that with which we infer the existence of the stars below the horizon. . . .

The zeitgeist in which Ebbinghaus worked deemed that learning and memory could be understood by looking at formed ideas and then working backward to find their source. Ebbinghaus reversed the procedure; he studied how memory developed and, by so doing, was able to bring under scientific control the variables that were previously inseparable from the memory. Equipped with the most improbable of candles, the nonsense syllable, he ventured into the darkness of inaccessible memory. Although he shed little light on that subject, Ebbinghaus did emerge with a method to study learning that is still used. His search for the answer to the question of how memory is formed required that he develop a task that was unknown to his experimental subject. Since Ebbinghaus was not only the chief theorist and experimenter but also his own subject, he faced the problem of finding something to teach himself that he didn't already know,

Herman Ebbinghaus (1850–1909).
The first to present systematic studies of memory and forgetting. Wrote *On Memory* in 1885.

hence his use of nonsense syllables—nonword, three-letter consonant-vowel-consonant sequences. The nonmemorable terms *ZAT, BOK,* and *QUJ* were born to be forgotten and so they were. Ebbinghaus tenaciously rehearsed list after list of nonsense syllables and then tried to recall them after 20 minutes, 1 hour, 8–9 hours, 1 day, 2 days, 6 days, and 31 days. Figure 6.1 shows just how much he forgot. Included in his experimental studies of memory were the effects of list length on learning time, the effects of practice on learning, and the learning and memory of serially ordered items. This technique of serial learning had its origin with Ebbinghaus and became a standard technique that was used for years. Serial learning acquired prominence recently not only as a learning procedure (as originally proposed by Ebbinghaus) but also as a method of distinguishing short-term memory from long-term memory. Unfortunately, Ebbinghaus himself never discovered his "stars below the horizon." It is likely that he would be pleased with the type of research being done in today's laboratories. There are even some answers to the questions he raised more than a hundred years ago as to how sensation, feelings, and ideas, once conscious but now inaccessible, can be recalled.

Although Ebbinghaus's search for the hidden stars of memory was not entirely successful, it did not dissuade Harvard's William James from continuing the search for the structure of memory. James's work was to have a direct influence on information-processing theories and modern memory theories.

Shortly after Ebbinghaus wrote *On Memory,* James published his two-volume classic *Principles of Psychology* (1890). James takes note of Ebbinghaus's heroic series of daily reading of nonsense syllables and lauds his exact measurement of memory. In a metaphorical style that is similar to Ebbinghaus's, James adds his own speculation as to lost thoughts:

> [The task] which lies before us deals with the way in which we paint the remote past, as it were, upon a canvas in our memory, and yet we often imagine that we have direct visions of its depths. The stream of thought flows on; but most of its segments fall into the bottomless abyss of oblivion. Of some, no memory survives the instant of their passage. Of others, it is confined to a few moments, hours, or days. Others, again, leave vestiges which are indestructible, and by means of which they may be recalled as long as life endures. Can we explain these differences?

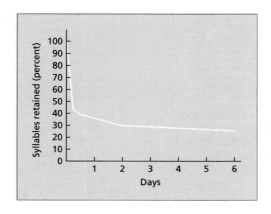

FIGURE 6.1

Ebbinghaus's forgetting curve for nonsense syllables.

William James (1842–1910).
Philosopher, physician, psychologist
whose dual-memory concept served as
the basis of modern theories of memory.
Author of *Principles of Psychology,* 1890.

James thought that we can. The ongoing panorama of conscious experience is too transitory to be considered memory. For James, recollection from memory requires effort and should be distinguished from the recovery of something from direct conscious experience. He distinguished between the immediate memory, which he called *primary,* and the indirect memory, which he called *secondary.* James based much of his depiction of the structure of memory on introspection, and he viewed secondary memory as the dark repository of information once experienced but no longer easily accessible. There is a remarkable parallel between the two states of consciousness—primary and secondary memory—that he postulated and an idea that was about to boil over in Vienna and spread throughout the world. Few people had heard of Sigmund Freud in 1890, and his concept of the unconscious mind was still in the formative stage and two decades away from being fashionable.[1]

According to James, primary memory, closely related but not identical to what is now called short-term memory, never left consciousness and gave a faithful rendition of events just perceived. Secondary memory, or permanent memory, was conceptualized as paths, etched in the brain tissue of subjects but with wide individual differences. "As he stated, some minds are like wax under a seal—no impression, however disconnected with others, is wiped out. Others, like jelly, vibrate to every touch, but under usual conditions retain no permanent mark" (1890). Thus, memory was dualistic in character: permanent and transitory. However, little scientific evidence was presented, other than the unreliable data from introspection, to distinguish operationally between the two systems. That happened about seventy-five years later, when the relationship between primary memory and secondary memory was described by Waugh and Norman (1965), as shown in Figure 6.2. (This is considered later in this chapter.) In their model, a verbal item enters primary memory and then may be held there by rehearsal or may be forgotten. With rehearsal, the item may enter secondary memory and become part of the permanent memory of the subject.

The early theories of Ebbinghaus and James about the deep structure of memory were laid to rest for a long time, while their influence in other areas of psychology proved to be more palatable to the analytic and functional psychology that was rapidly emerging in the United States. It was not until the recent emergence of cognitive psychology and neurocognition that these early psychologists were recognized for their adventuresome exploration of the structural properties of memory. Another venture is

---

[1]James did not cite Freud in his two-volume work, *Principles of Psychology,* published in 1890.

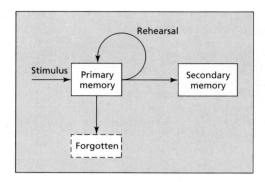

FIGURE 6.2

Model of primary and secondary memory systems. Adapted from Waugh and Norman (1965).

currently underway in America and other countries that may turn out to be the most exciting of all our journeys into the human mind—the neurocognition search for memory.

THE NEUROCOGNITION OF MEMORY

The current studies into the neurocognition of memory are straightforward in content. They involve the plotting of functions on the topography of the brain, the routing of memory traces, and the identification of the neural changes in the brain associated with memory formation and change. Many of the techniques used in these studies have been discussed earlier and, in general, include the use of brain imaging technology (for example, PET scans, MRI, and EEG recordings), electrical probes of the brain (for example, use of minute electrical stimulation for the prompting of memories), the use of chemicals and drugs that affect neurotransmission at the synapse (for example, the use of pharmaceutical agents in the treatment or study of memory enhancement or reduction), and the study of pathological types presenting unusual memory deficits (for example, see the boxed material entitled "Case Study: Specific Memory Loss").

Case Study: Specific Memory Loss

A few years ago a patient identified as CW, who was a music producer for the BBC, was stricken by a rare form of encephalitis, a condition in which the brain becomes inflamed. In his case, the result was a memory deficit in which his memory span lasted only a few seconds. His memory for common events, such as what he just ate for lunch, a song he had just sung, and so on vanished soon after the event. In the words of his wife, he "is trapped forever in the groove of a scratched record." Yet, remarkably, he can remember the words to songs, he can conduct a choir, and his musical ability seems unaffected. It appears that some parts of the brain store facts (names, images, and events) and others store procedures (such as how to do things).

In the case of the mapping of the areas of the brain associated with specific memories and memory functions, three sites seem to be directly involved, although it should be emphasized that memory functions are distributed throughout the brain. As shown in Figure 6.3, these sites are the cortex, the outer surface of the brain thought to be involved in higher-order cognition such as thinking, problem solving, and remembering; the cerebellum, the cauliflower-looking structure at the base of the brain involved in the regulation of motor functions and motor memory; and the hippocampus, an S-shaped structure deep inside both cerebral hemispheres that is believed to process new information and route it to parts of the cortex for permanent storage. (It is likely that the hippocampus was damaged in CW's case, since past memories were intact but new memories were difficult to form.) Studies of the brain now suggest that two types of memories, *procedural memory* and *declarative memory*, are associated with these major structures. Procedural memory deals with motor skills, such as handwriting, typing skill, and (probably) our ability to ride a bicycle; it resides principally in the cerebellum. Declarative memory consists of information and knowledge of the world, such as the name of a favorite aunt, the location of the nearest pizza parlor, and the meaning of words, plus a vast lot of other information; it is stored in the cerebral cortex.

Through the use of exciting new techniques, the structural architecture of the human brain is becoming better known. Of even greater interest to cognitive psychologists are discoveries of the functional properties of the brain; their interrelationships; and their relationship to memory, perception, emotions, language, and other cognitive attributes. As a result of these discoveries, psychologists have hypothesized that two types of memory exist: short-term and long-term memories. A wealth of psychological data supports such a notion, but now it appears that additional physiological evidence exists based on the structural and processing characteristics of the brain.

Also, it is becoming evident that sensory information is routed to the cortex soon after it is experienced. There, temporary links are formed among neurons and persist only briefly, but long enough for uncomplicated actions to take place, such as remem-

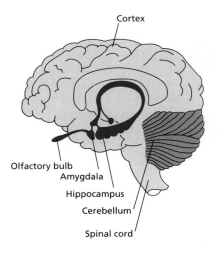

Cortex

Olfactory bulb
Amygdala
Hippocampus
Cerebellum
Spinal cord

FIGURE 6.3

The hippocampus below the two main cerebral hemispheres appears to process and route incoming information that is stored in the cortex and cerebellum.

Memory Mapping with PET

Until recently, attempts to identify brain regions participating in human memory were limited by lack of experimental techniques; case studies of brain-damaged patients provided the principal means of neuroanatomical investigation in humans. The development of noninvasive functional brain-imaging techniques such as PET makes possible unprecedented advances in understanding the neuroanatomical basis of memory and other cognitive processes.

Adina L. Roskins (1994)

bering a telephone number long enough to dial. In order for these impressions to become permanent a process called *long-term potentiation* (LTP) must occur. This is the tendency of nerve cells that have been exposed to a rapidly repeated stimulus to enhance their response tendencies for an extended period of time. LTP has been observed at hippocampal synapses in mammals. One theory suggests that the dendrites stimulated in this way sprout new growth, which facilitates long-term memories. Long-term declarative memories are thought to begin as the cerebral cortex sends information to the hippocampus, a process that strengthens the memory by rapidly and repeatedly exciting the neural circuit in the cortex. The strengthening of long-term memory may be achieved through voluntary actions, such as repeating a telephone number over and over again, or, in some instances, through involuntary actions, such as might occur in the case of a traumatic or emotional experience. For example, we may vividly recall the details of an automobile accident without conscious rehearsal of the event.

In summary, although much yet remains to be learned about the neurobiology of memory, some things are established. Physical events from the external world, such as light and sound energy, are detected by the sensory system, transduced to nerve impulses, and transmitted to the brain. From there they are initially analyzed and simultaneously routed to other centers, including the hippocampus area where, among other functions, their emotional content is assessed. This trace (sometimes called *engram*) is further rerouted to the cortex and other locations where neurochemicals are activated, sometimes leading to the formation of permanent memory traces so that when the same or similar sensory impression is perceived, the memory trace may be activated. With this basic understanding of the neurocognitive structure of memory, we now turn to the traditional psychological studies and theories of memory.

TWO MEMORY STORES

William James's dualistic concept of memory made good sense from an introspective standpoint. It also seems valid from the standpoint of the structural and processing features of the brain. Consider the details of the preceding paragraph. Unless you are blessed (cursed?) with a photographic memory, it is not likely that you can remember all of the specific details in that paragraph. Nevertheless, at the time you read it, it was accurately represented in your consciousness. Some facts remain and will be available for recall in the future. Your common sense tells you that two types of memory exist— one brief and one long.

Evidence for two memory states also comes from physiological studies. Performance by animals in learning trials is poorer when the trials are followed immediately by electroconvulsive shock (ECS). That this is the case (while earlier learning is unaffected) suggests that transfer from a transitory memory to a permanent memory may be interfered with (Weiskrantz, 1966). Persons who suffer from amnesia caused by a head trauma frequently indicate no recall of the few seconds preceding the trauma. This condition, called short retrograde amnesia, is distinguished from the loss of memory for longer events, called long retrograde amnesia. For those who suffer from the latter condition, immediate events are completely lost, while the events preceding the trauma by minutes and hours are frequently retained. In addition, a large number of lesion, PET, and trauma studies support the dualist theory of memory (see above and later sections).

Actually, recall directly after trauma seems unaffected. The results of a study by Lynch and Yarnell (1973) support this. These researchers interviewed football players who had received head traumas. The interviews, after a brief neurological examination, were conducted within 30 seconds after the injury. The players were also interviewed 3 to 5 minutes after and (as the situation permitted) every 5 to 20 minutes thereafter. (Uninjured players served as controls.) In the interviews immediately after the trauma, subjects accurately recalled the circumstances. For example, "[I was hit] from the front while I was blocking on the punt." However, 5 minutes later they were unable to recall any of the details of the play. For example, "I don't remember what happened. I don't remember what play it was or what I was doing. It was something about a punt." It seems that the details of occurrences just prior to an amnesia-inducing event are stored temporarily in memory but are not passed on to (or consolidated in) permanent memory.

Finally, there is a large body of behavioral evidence—from the earliest experiments on memory to the most recent reports in the psychological literature—that supports a dualistic theory. If Ebbinghaus had pursued serial free recall of items, he might have found those elusive stars that he sensed existed but that remained below the perceptual horizon for so long. When a person learns a series of items and then recalls them without attempting to keep them in order, the "primacy" and "recency" functions emerge. That is, very recent items seem to be readily recalled (recency effects); earlier items are more poorly recalled; and earliest items, again, more readily recalled (primacy). Such data are consistent with a dual-memory concept. The characteristic U-shaped curve of free recall of serial items is shown in Figure 6.4. In this curve we can see that the most recent events are most likely to be recalled, the first items are next most likely, and the middle items are least likely to be recalled. Remember asking what kind of ice cream was available when you were a child? It is likely you selected the last flavor named or the first.

Primacy and recency effects had been known for a long time, and their incorporation into a two-process theory of memory seemed a logical step. In such a scheme, information gathered by our sensory system is rapidly transferred to a primary-memory

FIGURE 6.4

Free recall in a serial task.

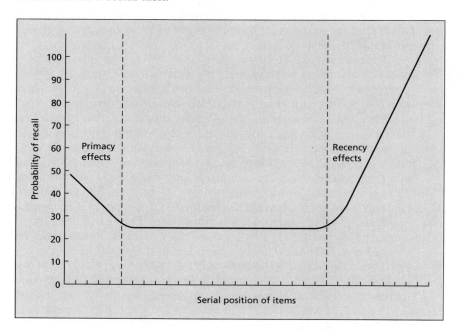

store and is either replaced by other incoming information or held there by rehearsal. With a lot of other information coming in, as in serial learning, information held in the short-term store is bumped out by new information. In a free-recall procedure, the items that occurred immediately prior to the free recall (presumably held in short-term memory) are easily remembered (they haven't been bumped out), while a few items deposited in secondary memory are available, but less so. The serial position curve fits well into a dual-memory theory, but how can we account for the primacy effects? It is thought that, because the early items are held longer, they receive more rehearsal, which enhances their availability in a free-recall procedure.

If we assume two memory stores, then it appears that, during free recall, subjects spew out those items they have just experienced, that is, those in short-term memory. We can trace the storage capacity of STM by identifying the point at which the recent curve begins to emerge. The number of items in that span is rarely larger than eight, so memory dualists conclude that two stores exist, with STM having a capacity of less than eight items.

The issue of whether memory is based on one or on two stores remains open to debate. Powerful arguments are voiced by both sides, and closure of the issue must await further research.

MEMORY IN THE LARGER COGNITIVE DOMAIN

As we learned in Chapter 3, the amount of information that can be detected by our sensory system (even with its limited sensitivity) is enormous. Much of the information is uninteresting to us or simply outstrips our capacity to handle it. Only a little information is processed to the level of our STM, and, with appropriate processing, some of this may eventually be held in LTM.

Sensory (iconic, and so forth) memory stores nothing, unless you count the few hundred milliseconds of neural activity; short-term memory is capable of holding some information; and long-term memory is nearly limitless in its storage capacity. The longevity of memory within these three hypothetical structures mirrors their storage capabilities. Some characteristics of these hypothetical components are outlined in Table 6.1, which should be taken as a general guide to storage systems.

The development of a cognitive system involves a great deal of guesswork. Even though the systems depicted in this section are the consequence of many painstaking experiments, they still represent an inferential jump from what can be observed to the nature of the underlying structures. Many cognitive scientists are unwilling to make the jump from data to hypothetical constructs; many others who are willing have drawn different conclusions from the data (and hence envision different structures).

T A B L E   6 . 1

Characteristics of Components of Cognitive Storage Systems

Storage Structure	Processes				Cause of Failure to Recall
	Code*	Capacity	Duration	Retrieval	
Sensory "store"	Sensory features	12–20 items† to huge	250 msec.–4 sec.	Complete, given proper cueing	Masking or decay
Short-term memory	Acoustic, visual, semantic, sensory features identified and named	7 ± 2 items	About 12 sec.; longer with rehearsal	Complete, with each item being retrieved every 35 msec.	Displacement, interference, decay
Long-term memory	Semantic, visual knowledge; abstractions; meaningful images	Enormous, virtually unlimited	Indefinite	Specific and general information available, given proper cueing	Interference, organic dysfunctioning, inappropriate cues

*How information is represented
† Estimated

Critical Thinking: Attention and Memory

"You'll never learn anything if you don't pay attention!" admonished my third-grade teacher—more than once. While it is possible to learn things without conscious attention, a phenomenon called incidental learning, it is true that learning and memory are enhanced if we pay attention to matters.

In our everyday life, we are constantly being bombarded with stimuli, usually in the form of advertising and new headlines, that demand our attention and frequently create a need in us to buy. It is almost as if advertisers and newspaper editors equate attention with memory and, in order to attract our attention, present outlandish, paradoxical, or incongruous themes. Take a few minutes each day for a week to record these provocative events. Consider some of the issues raised in the previous chapter regarding attention and its influence on memory.

MODELS OF MEMORY

This section reviews a few of the more viable memory theories.

Waugh and Norman

The first modern behavioral model to travel down memory lane, and one whose concept of primary memory has served as a departure point for most modern theories, was developed by Waugh and Norman (1965). The theory is dualistic; primary memory (PM), a short-term storage system, is conceptualized as being independent of secondary memory (SM), a longer-term storage system. Waugh and Norman borrowed freely from William James's dichotomy of primary and secondary memory and illustrated their theory by means of the model shown in Figure 6.2, which encouraged the memory metaphor of boxes in the head that soon proliferated in the literature of cognitive psychology.

What Waugh and Norman did that James never attempted was to quantify properties of primary memory. This short-term storage system was taken to have very limited capacity, so that loss of information from it was postulated to occur not as a simple function of time but (once the storage capacity was exhausted) by displacement of old items by new ones. PM could be conceptualized as a storage compartment much like a vertical file, in which information is stored in a slot or, if all the slots are filled, displaces an item occupying one of the slots.

Waugh and Norman traced the fate of items in PM by using lists of sixteen digits, that were read to subjects at the rate of one digit per second or four digits per second. The sixteenth (or "probe") digit was a repeated digit, one that had appeared in either the third, fifth, seventh, ninth, tenth, eleventh, twelfth, thirteen, or fourteenth position. The probe digit, accompanied by a tone, was the cue for the subject to recall the item that followed the probe digit the first time it occurred. A typical series of digits might be

7 9 5 1 2 9 3 8 0 4 6 3 7 6 0 2 (tone)

The correct recall in this case would be *9* (the digit following the first presentation of *2*). In this instance, ten items intervene between the initial presentation and the probe. Since subjects did not know which digit would be cued, they could not focus their attention on any one digit and rehearse it. The purpose of presenting digits every second or quarter second was to determine whether forgetting was a function of decay (presumed to be due to time) or interference in PM. If forgetting was a function of decay, then less recall could be expected with the slower rate (one digit per second); if forgetting was a function of interference in PM, then no difference in recall could be expected according to the presentation rate. The same amount of information is presented at both presentation rates, which, by Waugh and Norman's logic, allows the same time for decay to occur. It might be argued that even at one item per second, subjects would allow extra experimental information to enter their PM, but later experimentation (Norman, 1966a) in which presentation rates varied from one to ten digits (for a given period), yielded data consistent with a rate of forgetting expected from the original model. As can be seen in Figure 6.5, the rate of forgetting for the two presentation rates is similar. Interference seems to be a greater factor than decay in forgetting in PM.

Waugh and Norman's system makes good sense. PM holds verbal information and is available for verbatim recall; this is true in our ordinary conversation. We can recall that last part of a sentence we have just heard with complete accuracy, even if we were

F I G U R E   6 . 5

Results of a probe-digit experiment. Adapted from Waugh and Norman (1965).

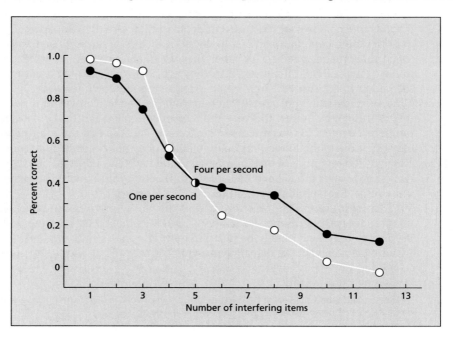

barely paying attention to what was said. However, to recall the same information some-time later is impossible unless we rehearse it, which makes it available through SM.

The model has gone through some transformation since it was introduced, and crit-ics have attacked it on the basis of not adequately accounting for the apparent com-plexity of short-term memory. Nevertheless, it has served as a model of the mind from which other models were developed.

Atkinson and Shiffrin

The proliferation of the boxes-in-the-head explanation of human memory was well under way when Atkinson and Shiffrin (1968) reported their system,[2] the framework of which was based on the notion that memory structures are fixed and control processes variable. They share the dualist concept of memory described by Waugh and Norman but postulate far more subsystems within STM and LTM. It is as if Waugh and Norman proposed the elements of earth, air, fire, and water, and Atkinson and Shiffrin proposed the elements found in the periodic table—the latter notion being more complex, dy-namic, comprehensive, and better able to explain a wider variety of phenomena. Atkin-son and Shiffrin noted that a simplistic notion of memory was not powerful enough to handle the complexities of attention, comparison, retrieval control, transfer from STM to LTM, imagery, coding sensory memory, and so on. The only solution was to divide and conquer, that is, to conceptualize memory properties and to develop empirical rules for differentiating them.

In their model, memory has three stores: (1) the sensory register, (2) the short-term store (STS), and (3) the long-term store (LTS). A stimulus is immediately registered within the appropriate sensory dimension and is either lost or passed on for future pro-cessing. A subcomponent of the sensory register is the visual system, which corre-sponds to iconic storage discussed in detail in Chapter 3. Its properties are well defined; it is rich in information and fast to decay. Although when Atkinson and Shiffrin devel-oped their model systems for other sensory modalities were less clearly known than today (they still hold many secrets), they provided space for them in their model in an-ticipation that future research would disclose the unknown features.

Atkinson and Shiffrin make an important distinction between the concepts of mem-ory and memory stores; they use the term *memory* to refer to the data being retained, while *store* refers to the structural component that contains the information. Simply in-dicating how long an item has been retained does not necessarily reveal where it is lo-cated in the structure of memory. Thus, in their system, information can be admitted to LTS shortly after it has been presented, while other information can be held for several minutes in STS and never enter LTS.

The short-term store was regarded as the working system, in which entering infor-mation decays and disappears rapidly (but not as rapidly as from the sensory register). Information in the STS may be in a different form than it was originally (for example, a word presented visually may be represented aurally in the short-term store).

---

[2]Atkinson and Shiffrin developed the rudiments of their theory in 1965, when they described mathemat-ical models for memory and learning in a technical report.

Information contained in the third system, the long-term store, was envisioned as relatively permanent, even though it might be inaccessible because of the interference of incoming information. The function of the LTS was to monitor stimuli in the sensory register (controlling those stimuli that enter the STS) and to provide storage space for information from the STS.

Information processing from one store to another is largely controlled by the subject. Information briefly held in the sensory register is scanned by the subject, and selected information is introduced into the STS. Transfer of information from the STS was regarded as capable of taking place so long as it was held there. Atkinson and Shiffrin postulated that information might enter the long-term store directly from the sensory register.

Central to the Atkinson-Shiffrin theory is this concept of subjects' exercising some control over information flow in and out of STS, and it is the separation of structure and control that most clearly distinguishes the Atkinson-Shiffrin model from other theories of memory. Control of memory systems may take many forms, but the most obvious is the conscious or unconscious control of the short-term buffer. It is within this space that subjects may exercise the greatest control. They may fill the buffer with many items, which may leave little "room" for work (or processing), or they may shift their attention to new items and thus eliminate old ones from the buffer by nonrehearsal. Another control process important in the model is coding, by which incoming information is categorized according to information from the long-term store. The use of mnemonic devices, such as imagery, is an example of this process.

Atkinson and Shiffrin's model is not intended to be a closed system; it provides a general but necessarily incomplete memory model. In a later publication, Shiffrin and Atkinson (1969) expand the nature of control processes (see Figure 6.6) that subjects can call into play at their discretion. Which specific control factors are activated depends on the nature of the task and the immediate instructions. This master executive of the system serves a role similar to that of a computer program, which governs the flow of information from one store to another, with each store performing its unique treatment of the information. In this model, incoming stimuli pass from receptors to the sensory register, a very short-lived—several hundred milliseconds (remember the icon?)—store. If not rehearsed, information that has been transmitted to the STS will decay and be lost in about 30 seconds. With rehearsal, control processes can maintain information in the STS for long periods of time. Some information in the STS is transferred to the LTS, which is the permanent repository of knowledge. Information in LTS is organized in locations that are determined by the components of the memory itself.

We can now look back on the two dualistic theories with the wisdom that frequently comes with time and experimentation. The earlier model of Waugh and Norman gave us the gross anatomy of memory, and the later model of Atkinson and Shiffrin gave us the concept of a human memory system that keeps track of incoming information and exercises some control over its limited information-processing capacity.

Level of Recall (LOR)

In a report (not widely known in the West) by P. I. Zinchenko (1962, 1981), a Russian psychologist, the matter of how a subject interacts with the material to be learned and

FIGURE 6.6

Model of memory system with control process expanded. Solid arrows indicate paths of information transfer; dashed arrows are connections permitting comparison with information arrays as well as potential paths for signals that activate transfer, rehearsal mechanisms, and so forth. Long-term store is postulated to be permanent; short-term store, no more than 30 seconds (without rehearsal); and the sensory register, a few hundred milliseconds. Adapted from Shiffrin and Atkinson (1969).

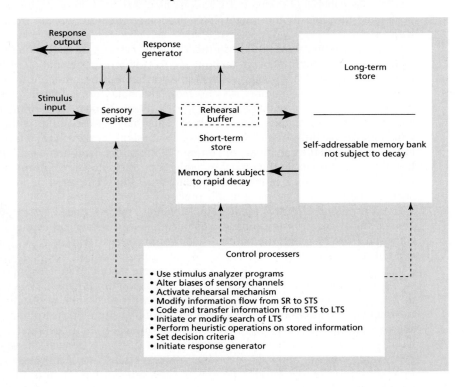

committed to memory was introduced. The basic notion was that words encoded by deep means would be retained in incidental memory better than if encoded by other superficial means. Thus the memorability of words was profoundly influenced by the goal of the subject at the time the material was presented. Different goals were thought to activate different systems of connections because subjects have different orientations toward the material.

The thesis was tested in an experiment in which subjects were given ten series of four words. The first word was to be connected to one of the other words, but the instructions varied for each of three groups. An example of a series is *HOUSE—WINDOW—BUILDING—FISH*. In the first condition the subjects were asked to identify the word whose meaning was different from the first word (*HOUSE—FISH*). In a second

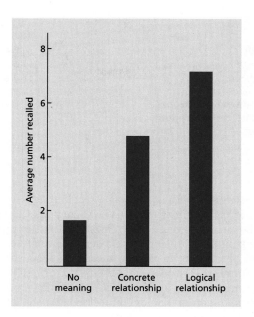

FIGURE 6.7

Recall of words under three different instructions. Data from Zinchenko (1962, 1981).

condition subjects were asked to make a concrete connection between the first word and one of the other words (*HOUSE—WINDOW*). In the third condition the subjects were asked to make a "logical" connection between the first word and one of the other three words (*HOUSE—BUILDING*). Zinchenko thought that by altering the instructions the subjects would not only have different goals toward the material but also be required to examine each item for meaning. After a brief interrupting task, the subjects were asked to recall the items. The data are shown in Figure 6.7. In the condition in which subjects formed logical connections between the first word and another word, recall of the target word occurred with greater frequency than the other conditions. Recall of the concrete relationship words was greater than the no-meaning condition.

Thus the level of recall (LOR), as Zinchenko called it, is determined by the goal of an action. In the experiment cited, we can see that when subjects were given a learning set, or instructions to process material at different levels (to use contemporary jargon), recall of the material was affected greatly. Because the original paper was published in Russian and not widely distributed, it has not been incorporated into the larger framework of memory models. Nevertheless, as we shall see, the experiment presented by Zinchenko and the theoretical importance to the concept of levels of processing, which has had a profound influence on cognitive psychology, has important consequences for our conceptualization of human memory.

Level of Processing (LOP): Craik

It is likely that progress in the early stages of scientific development is made more by reaction and counterreaction than by the discovery of great immutable truths. Craik and

**Fergus Craik. Challenged traditional
ideas of memory with the concept of
levels of processing.**

Lockhart's (1972) level-of-processing (LOP) model, as a reaction against the boxes-in-the-head scheme of memory, is consistent with that view. They take the position that data can be better described by a concept of memory based on levels of processing. The general idea is that incoming stimuli are subjected to a series of analyses starting with shallow sensory analysis and proceeding to deeper, more complex, abstract, and semantic analyses. Whether a stimulus is processed at a shallow or deep stage depends on the nature of the stimulus and the time available for processing. An item processed at a deep level is less likely to be forgotten than one processed at a shallow level. At the earliest level, incoming stimuli are subjected to sensory and featural analyses; at a deeper level, the item may be recognized by means of pattern recognition and extraction of meaning; at a still deeper level, it may engage the subject's long-term associations. With deeper processing a greater degree of semantic or cognitive analysis is undertaken. Consider word recognition, for example. At the preliminary stages, the visual configuration may be analyzed according to such physical or sensory features as lines and angles. Later stages are concerned with matching the stimuli with stored information—for example, recognition that one of the letters corresponds to the pattern identified as *A*. At the highest level, the recognized pattern "may trigger associations, images or stories on the basis of the subject's past experience with the word" (Craik & Lockhart, 1972, p. 675).

The significant issue, in Craik and Lockhart's view, is that we are capable of perceiving at meaningful levels *before* we analyze information at a more primitive level. Thus, levels of processing are more a "spread" of processing, with highly familiar, meaningful stimuli more likely to be processed at a deeper level than less meaningful stimuli.

That we can perceive at a deeper level before analyzing at a shallow level casts grave doubts on the original levels-of-processing formulation. Perhaps we are dealing simply with different types of processing, with the types not following any constant sequence. If all types are equally accessible to the incoming stimulus, then the notion of levels could be replaced by a system that drops the notion of levels or depth but retains some of Craik and Lockhart's ideas about rehearsal and about the formation of memory traces. A model that is closer to their original idea but that avoids the box notion is shown in Figure 6.8. This figure depicts the memory activation involved in proofreading a passage as contrasted with that involved in reading the same passage for the gist of the material. Proofreading, that is, looking at the surface of the passage, involves elaborate shallow processing and minimal semantic processing. Reading for gist, that is, trying to get the essential points, involves minimal shallow processing, or "maintenance

FIGURE 6.8

Memory activation in two kinds of reading. Figure based on drawing kindly supplied by F. I. M. Craik.

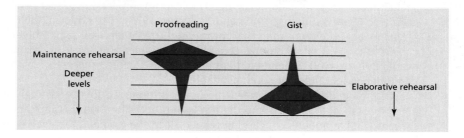

rehearsal" (held in memory without elaboration), but elaborate semantic processing.[3] As a result of some studies (Craik & Watkins, 1973; and Lockhart, Craik, & Jacoby, 1975), the idea that stimuli are always processed through an unvarying sequence of stages was abandoned, while the general principle that some sensory processing must precede semantic analysis was retained.

Levels of Processing versus Information Processing

Information-processing models of memory have generally stressed structural components (for example, sensory store, STM, and LTM) dealing with processing (for example, attention, coding, rehearsal, transformation of information, and forgetting) as operations that are tied (sometimes uniquely) to the structural components. However, another approach is to postulate process and then to formulate a memory system in terms of these operations. Craik and Lockhart have taken just such a position, and their implicit criticism of the information-processing model (along with Neisser, 1976) suggests that it is falling on hard times.

Where information-processing models of memory stress the sequence of stages through which information is moved and processed, this alternate viewpoint argues that

---

[3]Another example of this latter kind of memory activity would be a typist who concentrates on responding to letter sequences but has very little understanding of the material being typed. A third example is one that will also serve as an introduction to an experiment by Craik and Watkins. I asked the members of a seminar group studying cognitive psychology to recall as many of their elementary-school teachers as they could. They did remarkably well. Then I asked them to try for the earliest article of clothing they could recall wearing, and everyone recalled some favorite garment. Finally I asked them to recall all the articles of clothing they had ever owned. Some of the procedures were quite ingenious, including complex organization matrices—for example, dress clothes; sportswear; sloppy clothes; clothes by age, color, function; and so on. Even though some aggressively pursued this task for several weeks, all agreed that they could not retrieve the memory for all clothes, despite the fact that they had undoubtedly been highly familiar with each article of clothing. The ability to recall some things from memory (teachers' names, favorite clothing) and not others (all clothing) may represent the level of processing to which certain objects are subject; "special" objects may be more deeply processed than mundane ones. (An alternate explanation might be that the students' memory of the other clothing was affected by interference.)

memory traces are formed as a by-product of perceptual processing. Thus, the durability of memory is conceptualized as a function of the depth of processing. Information that is not given full attention and is analyzed only to a shallow level is soon forgotten; information that is deeply processed—attended to, fully analyzed, and enriched by associations or images—is long lasting. The levels-of-processing model is not free of criticism (see Craik & Tulving, 1975; and Baddeley, 1978). The criticism includes that (1) it seems to say little more than that meaningful events are well remembered, a mundane conclusion; (2) it is vague and generally untestable; and (3) it is circular in that any events that are well remembered are designated "deeply processed," with no objective and independent index of depth available.

One clear difference between the boxes-in-the-head theory (Waugh and Norman, and Atkinson and Shiffrin) and the levels-of-processing theory (Craik and Lockhart) is their respective notions concerning rehearsal. In the former, rehearsal, or repetition, of information in STM serves the function of transferring it to a longer-lasting memory store; in the latter, rehearsal is conceptualized as either maintaining information at one level of analysis or elaborating information by processing it to a deeper level. The first type, maintenance rehearsal, will not lead to better retention.

Craik and Tulving (1975) tested the idea that words that are deeply processed should be recalled better than those that are less so. They did this by having subjects simply rate words as to their structural, phonemic, or semantic aspects. Typical of questions used are the following:

Structural: Is the word in capital letters?

Phonemic: Does the word rhyme with *WEIGHT*?

Semantic: Would the word fit the sentence
"He met a _____ in the street."?

Craik and Tulving measured both the time to make a decision and recognition of the rated words. (In another experiment, recall was also measured.) The data obtained (Figure 6.9) are interpreted as showing that (1) deeper processing takes longer to accomplish and (2) recognition of encoded words increases as a function of the level to which they are processed, with those words engaging semantic aspects better recognized than those engaging only the phonological or structural aspects. Using slightly different tasks, D'Agostino, O'Neill, and Paivio (1977); Klein and Saltz (1976); and Schulman (1974) obtained similar results.

The previous studies support the idea that memory is a function of how initial information is first encoded; semantically encoded information is better recalled that perceptually encoded information. Adopting a neurocognitive perspective on this topic (some philosophers refer to this perspective as "biological reductionism"), one searches for the anatomic substrata of the strong memory effect associated with levels of processing. Fortunately, just such an investigation has been done by Kapur, Craik, Tulving, Wilson, Hoyle, and Brown (in press) using PET imaging technology with exhilarating results. The task used in the experiment conducted by Kapur and his colleagues was similar to the studies mentioned above. In one condition subjects were asked simply to detect the presence or absence of a letter in a word (for example, Does the word contain the letter a?), and in another condition different subjects studied each word and were asked whether it represented something that was living or nonliving. In the first condi-

FIGURE 6.9

Initial decision latency and recognition performance for words as a function of the initial task. From Craik and Tulving (1975).

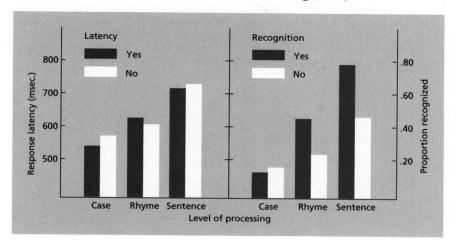

tion, the processing was considered to be shallow; in the second, deep. Behavioral responses (yes or no) to these questions were recorded by means of clicking a computer mouse, but the momentous data was the activation of specific brain areas as recorded by PET images using ^{15}O-labeled water which were gathered during the performance of these two tasks. The behavioral data indicated that subjects had substantially better recognition memory for the words processed at the deep level (living or nonliving thing) than for words processed at the shallow level (*a* or no *a*). The results of the PET images are shown in Figure 6.10.

Here the differences between the two groups showed a significant increase in cerebral activation in the left inferior prefrontal cortex during the semantic deep task as compared with the perceptual shallow task. In the present study it appears that the left prefrontal region, which was associated with enhanced memory performance, may be the locus of this type of memory storage. The complete understanding of memory process, of course, must consider cognitive processes, neural activity, and memory performance integrated into an overall theory of memory.

Self-Reference Effect (SRE)

New light was shed on the levels-of-processing concept when Rogers, Kuiper, and Kirker (1977) showed that self-reference is a powerful method variable. Using a method similar to that of Craik and Tulving (1975), they asked subjects to evaluate a list of forty adjectives on one of four tasks hypothesized to vary in depth, or semantic richness.

FIGURE 6.10

The regions of the brain which show increased cerebral blood flow
in deep processing (living and nonliving) condition. The upper-left
figure is a side view, with the frontal areas to the right and occipital
lobe to the left. The upper-right figure is a vertical cross section. The
grid and numbers represent standard coordinate spaces. VPC is a
vertical line through the posterior commissure, and VAC is a vertical
line through the anterior commissure.

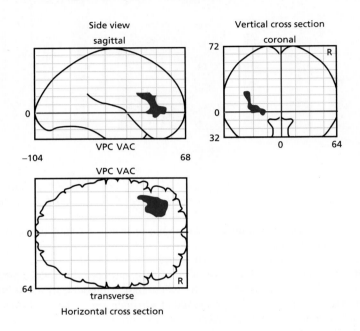

Included were structural, phonemic, semantic, and self-reference tasks. Typical cue
questions were as follows:

        Structural task: Big letters? (Adjective presented in the same size type as rest
                      of question or twice the size.)

        Phonemic task: Rhymes with? (Word did or did not rhyme with presented ad-
                      jective.)

        Semantic task: Means same as? (Word was or was not synonymous with pre-
                      sented adjective.)

    Self-reference task: Describes you?

As in the Craik and Tulving study, it was assumed that words more deeply coded
during rating should be recalled better than those words with shallow coding. After the
subjects rated the words, they were asked to free-recall as many of the words they had
rated as possible. Recall was poorest for words rated structurally and ascended through

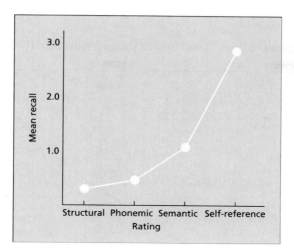

FIGURE 6.11

Mean recall for both yes and no ratings as a function of rating tasks. Data from Rogers, Kuiper, and Kirker (1977).

those phonemically rated and semantically rated. Self-reference words were recalled best. Figure 6.11 shows the recall data from the study by Rogers and his colleagues. From these data, it is clear that words rated on a self-reference task lead to greater recall, which suggests that self-rating functions are a powerful coding device.

Whether or not these self-rating memories are stored in different parts of the brain remains a question.

Rehearsal and LOP. Craik and Watkins (1973) devised a clever experiment to test the prediction of the boxes-in-the-head theory (that STM rehearsal leads to longer-lasting memory) versus levels-of-processing theory (that deep processing rather than STM rehearsal[4] leads to more permanent memory). They had subjects hold certain words in STM for varying lengths of time. Presumably, an item held in STM longer would be rehearsed more than an item briefly held. Subjects were presented a series of words and told to remember the last word that started with a certain letter, say *G*. The list contained several G-words, and each time a new one appeared, the subject would then abandon the preceding G-word. By varying the number of words intervening between G-words, Craik and Watkins could gauge the amount of rehearsal to which each G-word had been subjected. A list might be: *daughter, oil, rifle, garden, grain, table, football, anchor, giraffe. . . .* Here, rehearsal units (in terms of intervening items) would be, for *garden*, 0, and for *grain*, 3.

After they saw the lists, the subjects were unexpectedly asked to recall as many words as they could. The results are shown in Figure 6.12. Recall of an item that had had many intervening items should have been enhanced, according to the boxes-in-the-head theory; however, if rehearsal was simply maintaining the item without elaborating

---

[4]*Rehearsal* is used in this context to mean maintenance of information, not elaboration of information.

FIGURE 6.12

STM as a function of storage time. Data from Craik and Watkins (1973).

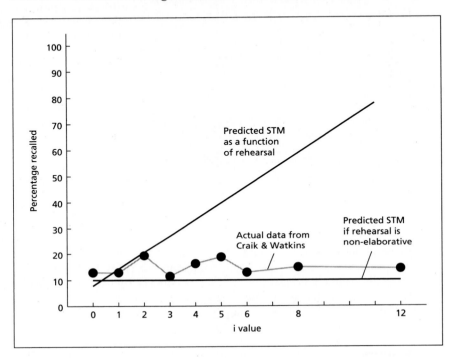

it, then the amount of rehearsal should have had little effect on recall. Thus, if short-term recall is a function of rehearsal, the results should have approximated the diagonal line in Figure 6.12; if short-term recall is unaffected by maintenance rehearsal without elaboration, then the results should have approximated the straight horizontal line. Craik and Watkins's data (the white line) clearly support the latter prediction: maintenance rehearsal does not improve memory. This conclusion is in distinct opposition to the dualistic theory of memory, which suggests that rehearsal has the effect of transferring information from a short-term store, or rehearsal buffer, to a longer-term store.

Thus it appears that the dualist theory has boxed itself in; the data presented by Craik and Watkins seem to indicate a serious flaw in the theory, while offering an alternative one that better accounts for the data. Or does it? In the original theory, Craik and Lockhart contend that the depth-of-processing notion involves the necessary and inevitable series of stages. Although they emphasize that material may be processed at different levels, the orderly sequence of processing of the boxes model would also seem capable of accommodating different depths of processing by the addition of several minor subroutines. In a later paper, Craik and his colleagues (Lockhart, Craik, & Jacoby, 1975; and Craik & Jacoby, 1975) abandon the view that a series of stages is necessary and inevitable, but they remain somewhat obscure as to what it is that is actually being processed and how it is being done.

Episodic and Semantic Memory: Tulving

Tulving (1972, 1983, 1986, 1989a, 1989b) classified memory into two types: episodic and semantic. Tulving's classification is important. While it is commonly assumed that a single memory state exists in LTM, Tulving distinguishes two forms as a means of orienting research and theoretical development.

Episodic memory "receives and stores information about temporally dated episodes or events, and . . . relations among those events." Thus memories of a particular experience (for example, seeing the ocean, getting kissed for the first time, going to a good Chinese restaurant in San Francisco) constitute episodic memory events. These events are always stored in terms of "autographical reference." Episodic memory is quite susceptible to change and loss, but it is important in forming the basis of recognizing events (for example, people and places) encountered in the past. These memories lack much of the formal structure that we impose on other information, notably that stored in semantic memory.

Semantic memory is the memory of words, concepts, rules, and abstract ideas and is necessary for the use of language. In Tulving's words:

> It is a mental thesaurus, organized knowledge a person possesses about words and other verbal symbols, their meaning and referents, about relations among them, and about rules, formulas, and algorithms for the manipulation of these symbols, concepts, and relations. Semantic memory does not register perceptible properties of inputs, but rather cognitive referents of input signals.

When we use the word *blue,* we probably do not refer to a specific episode in our memory in which this word was used, but rather to the general meaning of the word. In our daily life we frequently retrieve information from semantic memory that is used in conversation, in solving problems, and in reading a book. Our capacity to process diverse information in rapid succession is attributable to a highly effective retrieval process and well-organized information in semantic memory.

Semantic memory and episodic memory differ not only in their contents but also in their susceptibility to forgetting. The information in episodic memory is lost rapidly as

Endel Tulving. **Hypothesized two types of memory, episodic and semantic, and demonstrated different cortical activity associated with each.**

new information is constantly coming in. The retrieval process itself is part of the flow of information into episodic memory. For example, asked to multiply 37 × 3 (which calls on information in semantic memory) or to recall what you ate for breakfast (which calls on information in episodic memory), you must first enter those retrieval questions (as "events") in your episodic memory. You may also record in episodic memory that you multiplied 37 × 3 and that you recalled what you had for breakfast. Episodic memory gets a constant workout (and changes as a consequence of it), while semantic memory is activated less often and remains relatively stable over time.

Tulving's recent hypothesis about memory systems is a stimulating challenge to traditional information-processing models. In a paper entitled "How Many Memory Systems Are There?" (1985a), he depicts memory as consisting of a number of systems, each of which serves a different purpose and operates with different principles. The combination of systems and principles makes up what we call memory. Let's consider the details of this challenging hypothesis.

One Memory System or Multiple Memory Systems. As we have seen in this chapter, the number of systems of memory necessary to account for observations in the field of memory ranges from one to many. Tulving suggests five reasons that we should consider multiple memory systems:

1. So far no profound generalizations can be made about memory as a whole.

2. Memory is believed to develop through a long evolutionary history, a process that is characterized by uneven growth. Human memory, as a natural phenomenon, is thought also to reflect such evolutionary quirks.

3. Studies of brain functioning have shown that different brain mechanisms exist for different types of environmental excitation.

4. Most of our assumptions about mental processes are wrong and will be replaced by better theories.

5. Profoundly different learning and memory processes (for example, making motor adaptation to distorting lenses versus remembering the funeral of a close friend) are beyond the ken of a single unitary theory of memory. (1985a, p. 197)

Memory Systems

The (memory) theory holds that episodic and semantic memory are two of the five major human memory systems for which reasonably adequate evidence is now available. The other three systems are procedural, perceptual representation, and short-term memory. Although each system serves particular functions that other systems cannot serve . . . several systems usually interact in the performance of tasks in everyday life as well as in the memory laboratory.

Endel Tulving (1993)

According to Tulving, the system of memory that best accounts for the complexity and adaptability of the human creature is a three-part classification system: procedural, semantic, and episodic memory. (The latter two components have been described previously.)

These three systems are thought to be monohierarchical in that the lowest system, procedural memory, contains the next system, semantic memory, as its single entity, while semantic memory contains episodic memory as its single specialized subsystem. Although each of the higher systems depends on and is supported by the lower system(s), each system has unique capabilities.

Procedural memory, the lowest form of memory, retains connections between stimuli and responses and is comparable to what Oakley (1981) referred to as associative memory. Semantic memory has the additional capability of representing internal events that are not present, while episodic memory allows the additional capability of acquiring and retaining knowledge of personally experienced events.

The Case of K. C.: Episodic Memory Impaired

In the fall of 1980, a thirty-year-old man, identified in the literature as "K. C.," suffered a serious motorcycle accident while returning from work to his home in Toronto. This unfortunate accident has provided psychology with a vivid example of the organic nature of episodic and semantic memory. As a result of the accident, K. C. knows many things but cannot remember anything.

Episodic memory stores information about personal experiences and allows us to travel back in personal time. If you try to recall what movie you saw last night, you are tapping episodic memory.

Semantic memory enables us to assimilate knowledge and information in a general sense. When you think about something you know, such as the influence of economic conditions on political candidates or how to play chess, you are using semantic memory.

K. C. seems to have semantic memory but not episodic memory. He knows, for example, that his family has a summer cottage and where it is located. He can even point out its location on a map. He knows that he spends some weekends there but cannot remember a single occasion when he was at the cottage or a single event that happened there. He knows how to play chess but cannot recall having played chess before with anyone. He knows he has a car and knows its make and year, but he cannot remember a single trip he took in it. Equally deficient is his ability to conjure up images about his future. Alas, K. C. seems to be frozen in a cognitive world that knows no past and anticipates no future.

K. C. can play chess, but he cannot remember playing anyone.

Supporting evidence for semantic and episodic memory has been dramatically demonstrated by Tulving (see the discussion in Chapter 2; Tulving 1989a, 1989b; and Tulving et al., 1994), who has presented physical documentation for memory systems. Two types of studies have been reported. In one Tulving describes the case of a man known as "K. C.," who suffered brain damage from a motorcycle accident (see the boxed material entitled "The Case of K. C.: Episodic Memory Impaired"). The regions of the brain most severely injured included the left frontal-parietal and right parietal-occipital areas. K. C. remains densely amnesic, but the type of amnesia is remarkable. He has difficulty remembering normal, everyday, conscious experiences. He cannot bring back to conscious awareness "a single thing that he has ever done or experienced" (1989a). However, he is not mentally retarded, he is able to carry on what appears to be a normal conversation, he can read and write, he can recognize familiar objects and photographs, and he is aware of what he has done for a minute or two after he has done it. Apparently, K. C.'s accident caused serious damage to the part of the brain necessary for the functioning of episodic memory and, to a much lesser extent, the semantic system.

The second type of study indicates the cortical locus of semantic and episodic memory by measuring regional cerebral blood flow (rCBF). Because the technique and findings were discussed in Chapter 2 and briefly at the beginning of this chapter, they are not repeated here, except in summary. By measuring the flow of blood in the cortex (which is interpreted as an indication of localized neural activity) with a modified PET scanning procedure, it was possible to create a cortical map of the brain during different memory operations. When a subject engaged in semantic memory activities, specific regions of the brain "lit up," while episodic activities led to the activation of other areas of the cortex.

HERA model. Further physiological evidence for episodic memory and a model of hemispheric differences has recently been put forth by Tulving and his colleagues (see Tulving et al., 1994). Data from PET studies suggest that the encoding and retrieval of semantic memory may take place in different parts of the brain. According to the model, the left and right prefrontal lobes are part of an extensive network of neurons that support episodic remembering, which takes place in the prefrontal part of the cortex. The model is called *HERA*, which stands for "hemispheric encoding/retrieval asymmetry," and maintains that the frontal lobes are involved in episodic memory, a well-accepted conclusion as suggested by clinical and neuropsychological studies of brain-injured patients and by PET studies. Recent PET studies, however, suggest that the two prefrontal areas (the right and left) play different roles in episodic memory. The left prefrontal cortical regions seem to be more involved in retrieval of information from semantic memory and in simultaneously encoding novel aspects of the retrieved information into semantic memory. The right prefrontal cortical regions seem to be more involved in episodic memory retrieval.

The conclusions of these observations (from the study of K. C. and the measurement of rCBF) offer tangible grounds for the organic basis of hypothetical cognitive systems. Specifically, episodic and semantic memory systems now appear to be related to definite cortical activities. In addition to finding a nexus between memory theory and physiological structures, these observations give us a glimpse of the direction future research in the field of memory is likely to take.

A Connectionist (PDP) Model of Memory: Rumelhart and McClelland

The approach to memory espoused by Tulving in the preceding section found direct correlates between neural activities and types of memory. The connectionist (or PDP) model, developed by Rumelhart and McClelland (1986) and others, is also neurally inspired but attempts to describe memory from the even finer-grained analysis of processing units, which resemble neurons. Furthermore, since Tulving's model is derived from observations of brain activities, the connectionist model is based on the development of laws that govern the representation of knowledge in memory. One additional feature of the PDP model of memory is that it is not just a model of memory; it is also a model for action and the representation of knowledge. The rudiments of the PDP model are discussed in Chapter 1.

A fundamental assumption of the PDP model is that mental processes take place through a system of highly interconnected units, which take on activation values and communicate with other units. Units are simple processing elements that stand for possible hypotheses about the nature of things, such as, letters in a display, the rules that govern syntax, and goals or actions (for example, the goal of typing a letter on a keyboard or playing a note on the piano). Units can be compared to atoms, in that both are building blocks for more complex structures and combine with others of their kind to form larger networks. A neuron in the brain is a type of unit that combines with other neurons in a parallel processing mode to form larger systems.

Units are organized into modules, much as atoms are organized into molecules. Figure 6.13 shows a simple information-processing module. In this highly oversimplified representation of a module (in fact, the number of units per module would range

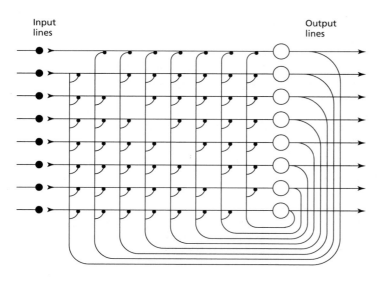

Input lines   Output lines

FIGURE 6.13

A simplified version of a processing module, which contains eight processing units. Each unit is connected to all other units, as indicated by the branches of the output lines that circle back onto the input lines leading into each unit. Adapted from McClelland and Rumelhart (1985).

from thousands to millions), each unit receives information from other modules (left) through the input lines and, after processing, passes information to other modules through the output lines (right).

In this model, information is received, permeated throughout the model, and leaves traces behind when it has passed through. These traces change in the strength (sometimes called weight) of the connections between individual units in the model. A memory trace, such as a friend's name, may be distributed over many different connections. The storage of information (for example, a friend's name) is thought to be content addressable—that is, we can access the information in memory on the basis of its attributes. You can recall your friend's name if I show you a picture of him, tell you where he lives, or describe what he does. All of these attributes may be used to access the name in memory. Of course, some cues are better than others.

Even though the theory is abstract, it touches real-life activities. To continue with the example of your friend's name, suppose I ask, "What is the name of the man you play tennis with?" Such an inquiry gives at least two content-addressable cues: man and tennis partner. If you play tennis with only one man (and you know his name), then the answer should be easy. If you have many partners who are men, then the answer may be impossible. Additional information (for example, the man with the beard, the left-handed player, the guy with red tennis shorts, the dude with the rocketlike serve, the chap with the Boston terrier, and so forth) may easily focus the search. You can imagine how very narrow the search would be if all of these attributes were associated with only one person: the man you play tennis with has a beard, is left-handed, wears red tennis shorts, has a hot serve, and has a terrier. In real life, each of these attributes may be associated with more than one person. You may know several people who have a hot serve or have a beard. If that is the case, it is possible to recall names other than the intended one. However, if the categories are specific and mutually exclusive, retrieval is likely to be accurate. How can a PDP modular concept of memory keep these interfering components from running into each other?

According to this model, information is represented in memory in terms of numerous connections with other units. If an attribute is part of a number of different memories and is activated (for example, What was your friend's name . . . ?), then it will tend to excite all the memories in which the attribute is a part. One way interfering components are kept from overrunning the system is to conceptualize the relationship between units as being subject to inhibitory laws. Thus, when we identify the person you play tennis with as a man, in theory we inhibit all searches for people who are women. When we add that he has a Boston terrier, then we do not search for the names of people with whom you do not play tennis and who do not own a Boston terrier.

Jets and Sharks. Memory systems of the sort just described have been studied by McClelland (1981) and McClelland and Rumelhart (1985), who illustrate how this system of content-addressable memory would work in a PDP model. In Table 6.2 are the names of several nefarious (and hypothetical) characters who live in a bad neighborhood (also make-believe). A subset of the units that represent this information is shown in Figure 6.14.

T A B L E 6 . 2

Attributes of Members Belonging to Two Gangs, the Jets and the Sharks

Name	Gang	Age	Education	Marital Status	Occupation
Art	Jets	40s	J.H.	Sing.	Pusher
Al	Jets	30s	J.H.	Mar.	Burglar
Sam	Jets	20s	Col.	Sing.	Bookie
Clyde	Jets	40s	J.H.	Sing.	Bookie
Mike	Jets	30s	J.H.	Sing.	Bookie
Jim	Jets	20s	J.H.	Div.	Burglar
Greg	Jets	20s	H.S.	Mar.	Pusher
John	Jets	20s	J.H.	Mar.	Burglar
Doug	Jets	30s	H.S.	Sing.	Bookie
Lance	Jets	20s	J.H.	Mar.	Burglar
George	Jets	20s	J.H.	Div.	Burglar
Pete	Jets	20s	H.S.	Sing.	Bookie
Fred	Jets	20s	H.S.	Sing.	Pusher
Gene	Jets	20s	Col.	Sing.	Pusher
Ralph	Jets	30s	J.H.	Sing.	Pusher
Phil	Sharks	30s	Col.	Mar.	Pusher
Ike	Sharks	30s	J.H.	Sing.	Bookie
Nick	Sharks	30s	H.S.	Sing.	Pusher
Don	Sharks	30s	Col.	Mar.	Burglar
Ned	Sharks	30s	Col.	Mar.	Bookie
Karl	Sharks	40s	H.S.	Mar.	Bookie
Ken	Sharks	20s	H.S.	Sing.	Burglar
Earl	Sharks	40s	H.S.	Mar.	Burglar
Rick	Sharks	30s	H.S.	Div.	Burglar
Ol	Sharks	30s	Col.	Mar.	Pusher
Neal	Sharks	30s	H.S.	Sing.	Bookie
Dave	Sharks	30s	H.S.	Div.	Pusher

From McClelland (1981).

In this figure, the groupings on the periphery enclose mutually exclusive information. (For example, Art cannot also be Rick.) All of the characters' attributes are connected in a mutually excitatory network. If the network is well practiced, that is, if the connections between units are established, then we can retrieve the properties of a given individual.

FIGURE 6.14

A sample of the units and connections needed to represent the characters in Table 6.2. Bidirectional arrows indicate that the units are mutually excitatory. Units within each cloud are mutually exclusive (that is, one cannot belong to the Jets and the Sharks). From McClelland (1981).

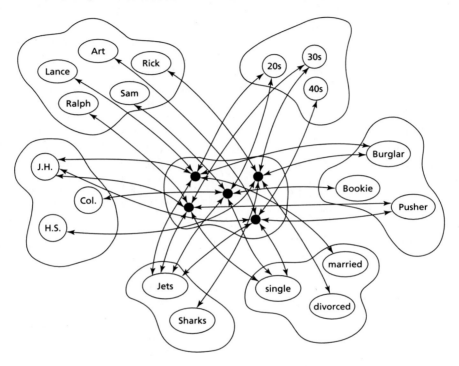

Suppose you want to retrieve the attributes of Ralph. By probing the system with Ralph (there is only one Ralph in the system), you can recall that he is a Jet, in his thirties, attended junior high school, is single, and is a drug pusher. In effect, we have recalled a representation of Ralph. In other words, Ralph is what he is. However, if we access the system from another angle and with less than complete information, we would end up with ambiguous results. For example, if we search for a person who is a Jet, is in his thirties, attended junior high school, and is single, we retrieve two names—Ralph and Mike. In this example, more information would be needed to be specific. (Police investigations are conducted with a similar network of inclusiveness and exclusiveness.)

One of the qualities of the connectionist model of memory is that it can account for complex learning, the type of memory operations we encounter in everyday life. These operations might involve the learning of a category or prototype formation (see Chapter

5). These processes are far more involved than the learning of nonsense syllables, as originally done by Ebbinghaus and reported in the beginning of this chapter.

A Boy and His Dog. Consider the following example of prototype learning, suggested by McClelland and Rumelhart (1986). A small boy sees many different dogs, each only once and each with a different name. All the dogs have slightly different features but can be considered a variation of the prototype dog, the epitome of "dogness." Just as in the case of Solso and McCarthy's prototype face, which was formed through experience with exemplar faces, the boy forms a memory for a prototypical dog on the basis of experience with exemplar dogs. As in the case of faces, the boy is likely to recognize the prototype dog as a dog, even if he has never seen it. Of course, the boy is not likely to remember the names of each of the individual dogs, though the most recently seen dog may still be in memory. The rationale offered by the connectionist model for prototype formation is somewhat similar to the example presented for the members of the Jets and the Sharks. In the case of the boy and his (prototype) dog, the connectionist model assumes that each time the boy sees a dog, a visual pattern of activation is produced over several of the units in the module. In contrast, the name of the dog produces a reduced pattern of activation. The combined activation of all exemplar dogs sums to the prototype dog, which may be the stable memory representation. Thus, the model, more detailed than presented here, seems to account for this form of memory quite nicely.

The connectionist model of memory has won many disciples in the past few years. The reason for its popularity is due in part to its elegant mathematical models, its relationship to neural networks, and its flexibility in accounting for diverse forms of memories.

Summary

1   The first detailed scientific account of memory experiments was done by Herman Ebbinghaus.

2   William James's early distinction between primary and secondary memory was a forerunner of modern dualistic memory theories.

3   Modern brain imaging technology (for example, PET) has been useful in identifying specific brain structures associated with memories.

4   The neurocognition of memory shows that the cerebral cortex, the cerebellum, and the hippocampus are all involved in memory storage and processing.

5   Evidence for the existence of two memory stores is provided by physiological (for example, ECS), clinical (for example, amnesia), and behavioral (for example, free-recall) studies.

6   The first modern dualistic memory model was developed by Waugh and Norman, who also provided evidence suggesting that forgetting in STM is influenced more by interference than by decay.

7   Atkinson and Shiffrin proposed an information-processing model of memory that assumes fixed memory structures, each having a number of subsystems, and variable control processes with activation determined by the demand characteristics of the task.

8   The levels-of-processing theory holds that memory is a by-product of analyses performed on incoming stimuli, with memory trace durability a function of the complexity or depth of those analyses.

9   Analysis of PET data indicates that the left prefrontal area of the brain is involved in deeper processing.

10   Information-processing models and the levels-of-processing position differ with respect to the importance of structure and process and to the nature of rehearsal. Information-processing theories generally emphasize structure and maintenance rehearsal, whereas the levels-of-processing position stresses processing and elaborative rehearsal.

11   Tulving emphasizes memory as a multiple system involving both systems and principles and proposes a three-part classification that includes procedural, semantic, and episodic memories. Recent observations have suggested that semantic and episodic memories are associated with localized cerebral activity.

12   The PDP model of memory postulates processing units that bear some resemblance to neurons. Mental processes, including memory, take place through a system of interconnecting units.

Key Words

decay
declarative memory
dualistic memory theory
engram
episodic memory
HERA (hemispheric encoding/retrieval asymmetry)
levels of processing
long-term memory (LTM)

long-term potentiation (LTP)
nonsense syllable
primary memory
procedural memory
secondary memory
semantic memory
short-term memory (STM)

Recommended Readings

A popular book by Baddeley called *Your Memory: A User's Guide* is a good place to begin your reading. Historically interesting is the first book on memory by Ebbinghaus (1885), which has been translated from German to English and is available as a paperback. A classic in psychology is William James's, *Principles of Psychology*, also recently reprinted; it is recommended not only because of its historical significance but also because some of James's speculations have become an integral part of the contemporary literature in cognitive psychology.

Several texts that give an excellent overview of memory are Baddeley, *The Psychology of Memory*; Klatzky, *Human Memory: Structures and Processes*; Adams, *Learning and Memory*; and D. Norman, *Memory and Attention*.

Most authoritative for particular models of memory are the original sources. These are generally more technical than the summary presented in this chapter, but they are understandable with some effort. Suggested are Waugh and Norman's article in, *Psychological Review*; Atkinson and Shiffrin in Spence and Spence, eds., *The Psychology of Learning and Motiva-*

tion: Advances in Research and Theory; Craik and Lockhart's article in *Journal of Verbal Learning and Verbal Behavior;* Tulving in Tulving and Donaldson, eds., *Organization of Memory;* and Tulving's article in *The Behavioral and Brain Sciences. Varieties of Memory and Consciousness: Essays in Honor of Endel Tulving,* edited by Roediger and Craik, and *Current Issues in Cognitive Processes: The Tulane Flowerree Symposium on Cognition,* edited by Izawa, are recommended.

Some current studies on the neurocognition of memory are particularly suggested, including Petersen et al. in *Nature;* Petersen et al. in *Science;* and most of the *Proceedings of the National Academy of Sciences,* Volume 91, 1994, which is largely devoted to the work of Tulving and his associates.

MEMORY: Structures and Processes

B OTH TRADITIONAL AND CONTEMPORARY theories of memory were discussed in Chapter 6. These theories have provided us with a rich conceptual basis for organizing the many empirical results of experimental psychologists. In this chapter we discuss some of the data collected by researchers trying to solve the problems of memory structures and processes. To retain the traditional concept of two memory stores, the chapter is divided into two sections—short-term memory and long-term memory. This organization is based on the assumption that the processing of information is first treated in a short-term store. This store, or short-term memory, does not operate independently of permanent memory but is constantly in contact with the knowledge that is stored there. Also, information and knowledge stored in a long-term store are constantly in contact with new incoming information that alters and enriches its content.

SHORT-TERM MEMORY

Between the receptors (which gather countless thousands of stimuli from our environment) and the expansive repository of information and knowledge (long-term memory, or LTM) is the hypothesized structure called short-term memory (STM). Tiny in capacity but huge in importance, it seems more clearly than any other memory system to be where we first process the stimuli originating from the environment. Its minimal storage capacity is matched by limited processing capacity, and some think that there is a constant trade-off between storage capacity and processing capabilities. According to Klatzky (1975), items in STM can be stored and worked on much as a carpenter might do so on his workbench: the space available may be used for work or storage, so that allocation for one reduces the space for the other. The Klatzky metaphor is useful, but it is also a simplification of a highly complex and clouded concept. At present we think that STM serves as a transitory store that can hold a limited amount of information and that can transform and use the information in the production of responses.

Our earlier discussion of James's primary memory and Ebbinghaus's forgetting curve set the stage for a remarkably simple yet highly significant discovery. In 1959 Lloyd Peterson and Margaret Intons-Peterson demonstrated that our capacity to store information in a temporary memory bank is severely limited and susceptible to gross forgetting if we do not have the opportunity to rehearse the information.[1] Their experiment represented a turning point in our experimental conceptualization of short-term retention and, along with other seminal experiments, books, and studies, helped launch what was to become the cognitive revolution. Their experiment was an important one. Prior to this time the distinction between STM and LTM had been made on the bases of

---

[1]A similar discovery was made by J. Brown (1958) working in England; hence the designation "Brown-Peterson technique."

Lloyd Peterson **and**
Margaret Intons-Peterson.
**Discovered the duration
of short-term memory.**

neurological structures (see Hebb, 1949) and psychological concepts (see James, 1890). The concept of short-term retention did not occupy a central position in the psychology of that time and had not been supported by behavioral data. Furthermore, the results of memory experiments led many theorists to embrace the notion that forgetting (or, more specifically, the failure to recall information from memory) was based on interference rather than on decay or the lack of opportunity to consolidate experienced events. Thus, the stage was set for some hard evidence that a memory system (which we now call STM) was affected by some mechanism other than interference alone.

In the experiment done by the Petersons, subjects were read a three-letter cluster and asked to recall it after varying periods. During these periods (between hearing the letters and attempting to recall), subjects counted backward by threes from a three-digit number presented immediately after the three-letter cluster, as here:

Experimenter says: CHJ/506

  Subject responds: 506, 503, 500, 497, 494, and so on

Thus, the time between representation of the letters and recall was filled with the subtraction task, which prevented rehearsal of the letter sequence. The dramatic effects are noted in Figure 7.1, which shows that recall seriously eroded in the absence of rehearsal.

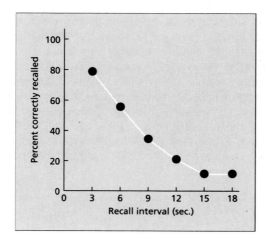

FIGURE 7.1

Recall as a function of recall interval where rehearsal was prevented. Adapted from Peterson and Peterson (1959).

Does Short-Term Memory Exist?

The answer to this question must surely be yes, and in two senses:

Memory in the short term. *First of all, people must be able to retain information over brief intervals of time. This is beyond argument as a general proposition. . . .*

Hebb's dual-trace theory . . . *Hebb proposed that if the original activity continues for some*

period . . . structural changes at the synaptic contacts among cells could carry the memory thereafter. These structural changes would correspond to long-term memory, many thought, and the earlier continued activity—reverberation—might be identified with short-term memory.

Robert G. Crowder (1993)

These results suggested that some memory system could store information, but that if the information was not rehearsed, it dropped out of memory. These findings implied that there was a transitory memory (STM) that had characteristics quite unlike the permanent repository of information (LTM); hundreds of experiments have given us a good picture of its characteristics. In this chapter we review some of these distinguishing features of STM and how that structure fits into an overall information-processing theory, touching occasionally on some of the controversy that still surrounds STM.

The reasons supporting the arguments for two memory stores (stated in Chapter 6) can be summarized as follows: (1) casual introspection suggests that some things are remembered for a short time and others for a long time; (2) physiological studies indicate that short-term functions can be interrupted, while long-term functions seem to remain intact; and (3) psychological experiments suggest that the retrieval of some information in memory is characteristic of a short-term function while retrieval of other information is characteristic of a long-term function, for example, primacy and recency data.

Despite the widespread acceptance of the reality of STM as a separate and distinct psychological construct, some have explained data from experiments supporting STM in terms of a single memory store and within the context of levels of processing. Yet, compelling data from neurocognition attests to the reality of a short-term memory store—one that momentarily holds and processes sensory impressions.

Neurocognition and STM

The neurophysiological findings from the mid-1950s until the present time suggest that a separate memory store could be located structurally within the human brain. The original studies appeared about the same time as the famous Peterson and Peterson psychological experiment reported earlier in this chapter, but they dealt with clinical patients who experienced some form of physical trauma or brain lesion. The most famous case was that of H. M. It was presented by Brenda Milner (1966), a researcher in Canada, where much celebrated work in neurocognition developed.[2] The patient complained of

---

[2]Craik, Hebb, Milner, Moscovitch, Penfield, Roberts, Sergent, Tulving and many others did their principal work in Canada.

severe epilepsy and, following a medical workup, a bilateral surgical excision (of the medial temporal region) was done to relieve him of the symptoms. The procedure removed parts of the temporal lobe, including the hippocampus. Although the patient's epilepsy was improved, he became profoundly amnesic and could not seem to store new information in LTM; his STM was unimpaired. He could recall a series of numbers momentarily presented but could not retain similar information over long periods of time. His long-term memories formed before the operation were normal, and he even performed well on standard IQ tests, yet he could not learn the names or faces of people he saw regularly. He could converse normally with Milner when she visited him but not recall her previous visits. H. M.'s STM seemed intact, but his ability to form new LTMs was wanting. Because the lesions took place in the temporal lobe and hippocampus, it is apparent that these sites contain important memory structures. Specifically, it seems that the hippocampus is an interim depository for long-term memory in which early experienced information is processed and then transferred to the cerebral cortex for more permanent storage. Then Milner made a startling discovery that changed the way STM and LTM was conceptualized. Patients, such as H. M., with temporal lobe lesions can learn implicit types of tasks that involve perceptual and motor skills. Furthermore, these patients can retain the memory of these tasks for long periods of time. H. M., for example, could learn to draw an image in a mirror and retain that skill over time (see Figure 7.2A).

As shown in Figure 7.2B, H. M.'s learning improved over trials, but he had no knowledge of performing the task. Thus, his procedural memory seemed to function normally, but his ability to learn new information was deficit.

There is also the case of K. F., studied by Elizabeth Warrington and Tom Shallice (1969), who performed oppositely; he had great difficulty learning a series of digits (he could recall only one digit reliably), but his LTM and his ability to learn new material for a long period of time seemed to be intact. This brief sample, augmented by research on dozens of other physically damaged patients (see Kandel, Schwartz, & Jessell, 1991; Martin, 1993; Pinel, 1993; Shallice & Vallar, 1990; and Squire, 1987, for further information), suggests that there are anatomical structures involved in two types of memory. The larger question, however, concerns the storage and processing of information. That part of the puzzle is still largely unknown.

Capacity of STM

The amount of information stored in STM is small compared with the vast amount stored in LTM. The earliest recorded evidence of the limited capacity of STM (or "immediate" memory) seems to have come from Sir William Hamilton, a nineteenth-century philosopher, who is said to have observed: "If you throw a handful of marbles on the floor, you will find it difficult to view at once more than six, or seven at the most, without confusion" (cited by Miller, 1956b). Whether Hamilton actually did this experiment is unknown, but a similar one was done in 1887 by Jacobs (cited in Miller, 1956a), who read aloud a sequence of numbers, in no particular order, and asked his listeners to write down immediately as many as they could recall. The maximum amount of numbers recalled was about seven. Using dots, beans, nonsense syllables, numbers, words, and letters, experiments of this type have been conducted throughout this century with consistent results: immediate memory seems to be limited to about seven units.

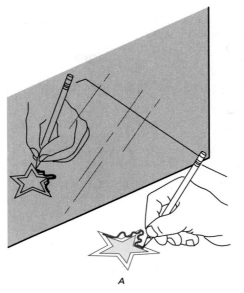

A

FIGURE 7.2

A. In this test, the subject's task is to trace between the two outlines of the star while viewing his or her hand in a mirror. The reversing effect of the mirror makes this a difficult task initially. Crossing a line constitutes an error.

B. H. M. shows clear improvement in motor tasks on the star test, which is a procedural memory. From Blakemore (1977).

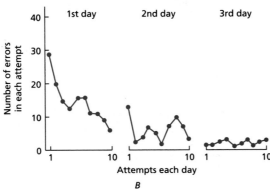

B

STM and Chunking. That STM holds seven units regardless of the type of data involved seems paradoxical. Obviously a string of words has greater information content than a string of letters. For example, chances are that, presented the string *T, V, K, A, M, Q, B, R, J, L, E, W,* you could recall about seven letters, and presented the string *towel, music, boss, target, salad, church, money, helium, sugar, parrot, music, chicken,* you would again recall about seven items (depending on the rate of presentation). However, by inspecting the amount of information recall (at least in terms of letters), it is obvious that more information is recalled in the latter condition than in the former. Miller (1956b) offered an explanation as to how items are coded in STM. He postulated a model of memory in which seven units of information could be held. Individual letters represented individual pieces of information, and, as such, each letter would fill a slot.

Sir William Hamilton pondered the capacity of STM as early as the 1800s.

The letters that composed a word, however, were "chunked" into one word unit, so that each of these word units also occupied one slot in STM. Thus the increased capacity (in terms of numbers of letters) of STM was achieved through the coding of letter sequences into word units. So, even though our immediate memory capacity seems to be limited to seven units of information, chunking (or coding single units into larger units) greatly expands our capacity. For Miller, this kind of linguistic recoding seemed to be "the very lifeblood of the thought process." At the very least, chunking is important be-

George Miller. **His book *Language and Communication* (1951) shaped the direction of psycholinguistics and cognitive psychology. APA president, 1969.**

cause it offers an explanation of how so much information is processed through STM, which, if restricted to seven units, would pose a bottleneck in the information-processing sequence.

STM, LTM, and Chunking. The capability of STM to handle a vast amount of information, then, is facilitated by our ability to chunk information. However, chunking cannot occur until some information in LTM is activated. Our extensive knowledge can impose a structure on seemingly unrelated material once a match occurs between the incoming items and their LTM representation.

The link between LTM and chunking was nicely illustrated in an experiment by Bower and Springston (1970), in which subjects were read a letter sequence and asked to recall the letters. In one condition (A) the experimenters read the letters so that they formed no well-known group (hence, not in LTM); in another condition (B) they read the letters so that they formed well-known groups. Note the following example:

Condition A   FB . . . IPH . . . DTW . . . AIB . . . M

Condition B   FBI . . . PHD . . . TWA . . . IBM

There can be little doubt that the letters read in the second condition (B), which were more readily recalled, are clustered along the lines of abbreviations well known to most college students. In effect, the pause after FBI, PHD, and so on allows subjects to "look it up" in their mental lexicon and thereby encode the letters in a chunk, much as you are now forming word chunks out of the letters on this page. The capacity of STM, then, may be limited to seven units, but the density of information in a unit can vary enormously.

The Coding of Information in STM

Auditory Code. One of the best ways of discriminating between two things is to subject both to the same experimental condition and evaluate the results. If the things react differently, then a case can be made that the things are different. A botanist's fern is a case in point. If a newly discovered fern reacts to sunlight and soil conditions in a way that is different from another fern, then we may logically infer that the two ferns are functionally different. A similar logic has been used in the classification of memory stores. STM seems to operate by means of an auditory code, even if the information is detected by a nonauditory code such as a visual one. Although recent evidence suggests some overlap in codes, the predominant coding of information in STM seems to be auditory.

Consider this everyday experience. An information operator gives you a telephone number, say, 969-1391. Presumably that number must be retained in STM until you can complete the call. How do you keep it alive? Chances are (if you don't write it down) that you repeat it to yourself or aloud, "969-1391, 969-1391," and so on. This practice is one of maintaining an auditory representation of the digits in STM. Thus from the standpoint of common sense, we hold information in STM by auditory rehearsal. You may argue, however, that the source of the information (the operator's voice) was auditory, which biased the nature of STM storage. In fact, the same auditory rehearsal is likely to occur even if you find the number in a directory, which is a visual stimulus. In whatever manner the information may be represented, storage in STM seems to be auditory.

Because science is suspicious of commonsense answers, differences in storage properties as a means of distinguishing between STM and LTM have been examined extensively in the laboratory. Some important results are summarized in the next sections.

In an often cited experiment, R. Conrad (1963, 1964) found that STM errors were made on the basis of auditory rather than visual characteristics. Conrad's experiment had two stages. In the first he measured the recall of errors made on a set of letters that were visually presented; in the second he measured the errors made by subjects to whom the same set of letters was read over a background of white noise. Each set in the first stage consisted of six letters. Some were letters that sounded alike, for example, *C, V; M, N; S, F.* Each of the six letters was displayed for 0.75 second. The subjects were to recall the order of the items. The results indicated that even though the letters were visually presented, the errors were made on the basis of their sound. For example, *B* was frequently recalled as *P, V* as *P,* and *S* as *X.*

Further evidence of the acoustic nature of STM was demonstrated by Conrad (1970), who studied the auditory confusion of congenitally deaf students. The results indicated that the confusion errors of deaf subjects could be classified into two rather distinct categories—those that showed acoustic intrusions and those that did not. On the basis of interviews with the teachers of the deaf students, Conrad rated the students on how well they spoke. The good speakers were the students who experienced acoustic intrusions; the poorer speakers tended to make different types of errors. It is reasonable to assume that some deaf people transform visual symbols into a code that is functionally similar to a phonemic code during the STM experiences and that the result of that process may be acoustic errors. Thus STM seems to extend even to a population whose sensory capabilities restrict auditory processing.

Although there seems to be a strong case for the acoustic nature of STM, there are some challenging alternative theories, which we take up in the next section.

Visual Code. We have seen that many experiments have validated the conclusion that storage of information in STM takes the form of acoustic coding. A number of recent experiments, however, seriously question the inferences that STM codes information only by means of an auditory code. Some evidence suggests that STM may also code information by means of a visual code, while others suggest that STM may code information by means of a semantic code.

Posner and his associates (Posner, 1969; Posner et al., 1969; and Posner & Keele, 1967) suggest that, at least part of the time, information is coded visually in STM. In their experiment, subjects were shown two letters, the second to the right of and simultaneously with, or a brief time after, the first. Subjects were to indicate, by pressing a button (and, thereby, recording their reaction time), whether the two letters were the same. The second letter was identical to the first in name and form (AA), or the same in name but different in form (Aa), or different (AB or Ab); and it appeared simultaneously with, or 0.5, 1, or 2 seconds after, the first. (Table 7.1 shows the format of the experiment.)

Reaction time in the second condition (Aa) was longer than in the first (AA). One explanation for the difference is that identical letters are judged on the basis of their physical (or visual) characteristics, while letters having the same name but different vi-

TABLE 7.1

Reaction Time Format Used by Posner and Keele (1967)

Condition	Exemplar Letters*	Correct Response
Visual and name match	A A	Same
Name match	A a	Same
Visual and name mismatch	A B	Different
Visual and name mismatch	A b	Different

*Interval of presentation: 0–2 sec.

sual characteristics are compared in terms of their verbal characteristics; the latter process, it is hypothesized, takes more time. As far as our discussion of codes in STM is concerned, the important conclusion is that apparently the AA match was made at least partly on the basis of a physical (or visual) code. This advantage (as shown in Figure 7.3) lasts only a brief period.

FIGURE 7.3

Reaction time as a function of interval for visual and name matches in mixed lists and for visual matches in pure lists. The two experiments were highly similar, except that in Experiment 2 intervals between stimuli were longer. Adapted from Posner et al. (1969) and Boies, Posner, and Taylor (1968).

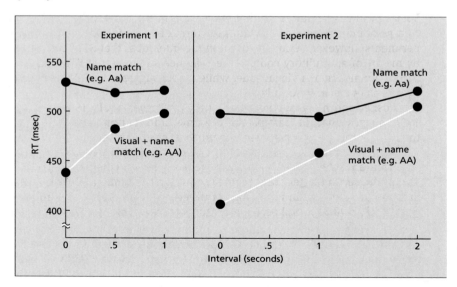

Having established that visual codes can exist in STM (in addition to auditory codes), Posner set out to describe the steps involved. To test a hypothesis that coding of some information in STM is first visual and then based on the name, Posner et al. (1969) and Boies, Posner, and Taylor (1968) used the reaction-time model shown in Figure 7.3. As may be recalled, one of the intervals of presentation of letter pairs was zero. The rationale for this was that coding involves visual aspects first, then the reaction time for physically (visually) identical stimuli simultaneously presented should be very brief. If name coding occurred slightly after visual coding, then the reaction time for name-identical (but not physically identical) stimuli simultaneously presented should be relatively long. As shown in Figure 7.3, during the very early part of STM processing the identical code takes much less time than the name code, but that effect disappears after about 1 or 2 seconds when the name code takes over. Recently, however, Boles (1994) has raised questions about these experiments presenting data that show that phonemic representations of letters plays a small, if any, role in the early processing of letters.

The extent to which information is processed in STM was demonstrated in an experiment by Solso and Short (1979) that was procedurally similar to the reaction-time experiments presented above. We hypothesized that shortly after information is perceived, it is simultaneously coded in different systems. Solso and Short used physical colors (green, blue, red, yellow, brown, and purple) because these stimuli seem particularly rich in their ability to be coded. The research was predicated on the assumption that colors are represented in short-term memory in at least three distinctive codes. One code is physical (for example, the color *red*), another is the name of the color (for example, *red*), and the third is conceptual (for example, an associate of the color *red*, such as *blood*). Subjects in this experiment were asked to respond by pressing a key if the color presented "matched" (physically, by name, or by associate) a color, a name of a color, or an associate of the color. The color, name, and associate were presented simultaneously with the color or delayed 500 or 1,500 milliseconds.

The average reaction times are presented in Figure 7.4. As might be expected, the reaction time for a color-color match was faster than between a color and its name or between a color and its associate when there was no delay between the presentation of stimuli. As the delay between the stimuli increased, however, the differences between the reaction times decreased. In the color-color matching condition, the reaction times were actually greater when the delay between the two stimuli was increased from 500 milliseconds to 1,500 milliseconds (see Figure 7.4). From these data it seems that the emergence of a color code occurs prior to the name code or associate code. However, after about 500 milliseconds a name code begins to emerge, and after about 1,500 milliseconds an associate code emerges.

These experiments (Posner et al., and Solso & Short) suggest that the processing of information in a short-term store is achieved through a type of parallel processing of stimuli (a model is shown in Figure 7.5 for colors). It seems that things perceived (colors, for example) initially are passed on from the sensory system to be simultaneously coded in memory. In the case of colors and letters, the first code to reach a level of operable strength (strong enough to be measured reliably) is a physical code—color-color or A-A, for example. This code seems to reach full strength in the first 500 milliseconds after the stimulus has been detected and perhaps decays slightly. A name code is initiated in parallel and reaches full strength after about 500 milliseconds. An associate

FIGURE 7.6

Experimental procedure for release-from-PI studies.

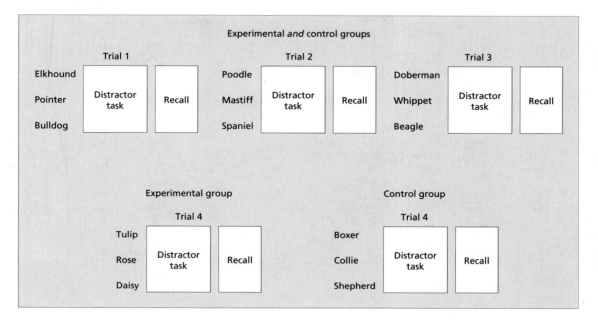

would probably have continued after the shift to the new set of words at Trial 4. Wickens's experiments include a wide variety of categories (for example, professions, meats, flowers, vegetables, words and numbers, taxonomic, sense impression, and masculine and feminine), all with similar results.

Some have criticized Wickens's experiments on several counts. First, for proactive interference effects to take place, the subject's LTM should be engaged in a direct way. Knowledge of dogs, for example, is necessary for canine PI to develop, and the subject, in these experiments, would have to be cognizant of the concept of "dogness" to be released from it. This first criticism is a kind of "straw man." No one has suggested that STM and LTM operate in a vacuum. There is a constant interplay between the two hypothetical memory stores, and most theorists acknowledge the interaction between LTM and STM. All memory operations, it seems, are guided and influenced by long-term memory and goals, including the processing of information in STM. The second criticism is more problematic. In a typical release-from-PI experiment, subjects are given several groups of information (such as the three sets of dogs in the previous example) before the "releasing" set is presented. The time spanned by this procedure may take up to several minutes, which may be outside the range of STM. PI, its buildup, and its release may all be LTM processes, which, although interesting, tell us little about the nature of semantic processing in STM.

FIGURE 7.7

Results from typical release-from-PI experiments. From Wickens (1973).

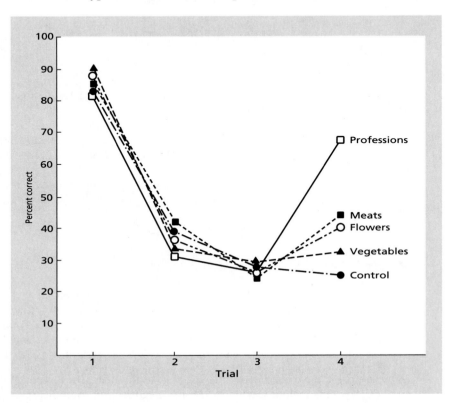

However, other research has presented convincing evidence that semantic processing does occur in STM. One study by Solso, Heck, and Mearns (1987, 1993) not only
demonstrates semantic processing in STM but also serves as an introduction to the
Sternberg paradigm, which is discussed in detail in the next section. For our present
purposes, it is enough to know that the Sternberg paradigm is a technique used to measure the means used to access information in STM.

Consider this problem. Suppose the following words are individually presented to
you at the rate of 1.2 seconds each.

SPHERE

MOON

PLANET

GLOBE

Then suppose you are given the following words, individually presented, and asked whether or not they were members of the original set.

MOON

STEEL

EARTH

How would you predict the performance of subjects in identifying the second set of words as being members of the previous set? If you guessed that subjects correctly identify *MOON* as a previously seen word and correctly reject *STEEL,* you are right. What about *EARTH?* This word is clearly not a member of the original set, yet subjects frequently "false alarmed" on this word. They misidentified it as a member of the original set. The basis of this misidentification is related to the semantic relationship that *EARTH* has with the members of the original set. Most important for our present discussion of STM and semantic codes is the fact that the entire process takes place in about 12 seconds, well within the parameters of STM. In addition to showing the semantic nature of STM, these data suggest that a form of abstraction, or prototype learning, can occur in STM.

Retrieval of Information from STM

In this section, we deal with how stored information is retrieved.

The modern era of information processing was significantly influenced by an experimental technique developed by Saul Sternberg (1966, 1967, 1969), whose name it bears. This technique involves a serial scanning task in which the subject is shown a series of items such as numbers, each for 1.2 seconds. It is presumed that these items become recorded in the subject's STM. The entire series constitutes a memory set. After the subject is satisfied that the items are available in his or her memory, the subject pushes a button and is immediately presented with a probe digit that may or may not be the same as a digit in his or her immediate memory set. The subject's task is simply to signal whether the digit is among the items in the memory set. Each new trial contains a different memory set. The experimenter may vary the size of the memory set from one to six items, which is well within the immediate memory span of subjects. Few errors are made, and the principal data are the times between the presentation of the probe and the subject's response. The Sternberg paradigm is presented in Figure 7.8.

Reaction time should reflect the time it takes to search through the memory set and may serve as a basis for delineating STM structure and laws of retrieval of information from the structure. We are not surprised that the larger the memory set, the greater the reaction time; more information in STM requires more time to access. Two other findings, however, are surprising. One is that the reaction times changed uniformly according to the number of items in a set (see Figure 7.9). Each new item in the memory set seemed to require a fixed amount of processing time, and that amount of time was cumulative with other processing times. In one experiment (Sternberg, 1966), the amount of time required to process additional memory set items was about 38 milliseconds per item.

FIGURE 7.8

The Sternberg paradigm.

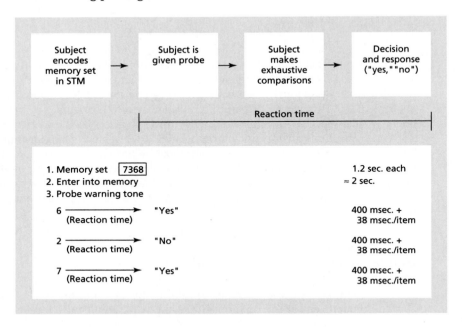

The second surprise has a far-reaching impact on views of how we recover information from STM. The reaction-time characteristics were nearly identical for items that were in the memory set and those that were not. It would seem obvious, however, that if *7*, the first item in the memory set of Figure 7.8, is also the probe item and if we process STM information in order, then we ought to be able to respond more rapidly than if *8* is the probe item. In the latter case we would have to scan the entire set—not just the first item—to make a decision. If the probe item is *8*, serial scanning time of the set for a match should be equal to the time required to determine that there is no match (because *8* is preceded by all the other digits in the string). Since the position of the matching items was distributed in each of the positions, we can assume that the average position would be in the middle of the set. Thus, if subjects used a serial search of their STM, finding probed items that were in the set would take (on the average) half the time needed to probe items not in it. (Probing the latter would require a search of the complete set.) Hence, the slope of a curve of reaction time versus set size should be twice as steep for probes not in the set.

Similar results have been observed over a wide range of stimulus material, including letters, words, colors, faces, and phonemes, with the slope of the reaction function sometimes more steep or less steep, but the relationship between the yes and no responses remaining invariant. Composition of the test group has little influence on the

FIGURE 7.9

Reaction time as a function of number of items in a series. Adapted from Sternberg (1969).

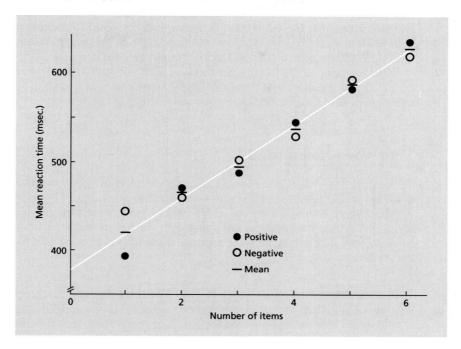

main results. They hold for children, schizophrenics, college students, alcoholics, and subjects stoned on marijuana. (Although the last have a reaction-time curve higher, not steeper than normal, leading one wag to comment that marijuana does not make you steeper, only higher.)

These remarkable demonstrations of search characteristics in STM suggest that, given the constraints of the paradigm, the search seems to be exhaustive rather than self-terminating.

LONG-TERM MEMORY

If we "live" in our short-term memory, then the repository of knowledge that gives meaning to our immediate existence resides in the long-term memory. Our ability to deal with the tiny slice of sensory events that constitutes the present in the ongoing continuum of time seems to be the main function of our transitory STM, while our ability to deal with the past and to use that information to understand the present is the function of our LTM. In one sense, our LTM allows us to live in two worlds simultaneously (the past and the present) and, by so doing, allows us to understand the ceaseless flood of immediate experience.

LTM's most distinguishing feature is its diversity—of codes, abstraction of information, structure, capacity, and permanence; other memory stores we have discussed are relatively limited in these features. Thus our discussion of LTM begins as we contrast it with sensory memory and STM, two memory systems that store information for a very brief time and do not abstract and store it in an involved structure.

The capacity of LTM seems limitless, and its duration virtually endless. To understand this, we consider first the neurological aspects of LTM, then the types of information held in LTM, and finally its general architecture or organization.

Neurocognition and LTM

For centuries scientists have known that the brain is involved in memory; without a brain we would be senseless, mindless, and without memory. The tricky part is to determine where memories reside and how the brain stores information in long-term memory—simple questions to the most complicated phenomena known to humans. Nevertheless, determined researchers have made impressive discoveries regarding both questions.

Having One's Cake and Eating It Too. The answer to the first question about the location of memories is that memories are "located"[3] in specialized areas *and* throughout the brain. For example, recent PET investigations show that the frontal area of the brain is involved in the deep processing of information, such as determining whether a word is of a living or nonliving thing (see the work of Kapur et al., 1994; and Tulving et al., 1994), which would suggest that that type of memory operation is highly specialized. However, other regions of the brain are also involved, only to a less specialized degree, and, this principle of specialization and generalization seems to apply to other types of memory operations and storage systems (see Zola-Morgan & Squire, 1990).

Some brain regions seem to be essential in the formation of memories. These regions include the hippocampus and the adjacent cortex and thalamus, as indicated through study of clinical patients who suffer damage from these areas. However, the hippocampus itself does not provide permanent long-term memories; if it did, then H. M. (discussed in the first part of this chapter) would not have had old LTM. Many permanent long-term memories seem to be stored (and processed) in the cerebral cor-

---

[3]The use of the word *located* tends to muddy the issue. Memories are not like black socks, which may appear on one's feet, or behind the dryer, or neatly folded in a dresser drawer. Memores are organic and involve neurological connections between a myriad of neurons. Location, in this sense, is as meaningless as trying to find the wind . . . it is found in some places more than others, but it is distributed throughout the planet.

tex. It is well established that sensory information is passed along to specific brain regions. Information from the eyes and ears, for example, is passed to the visual cortex and auditory cortex, respectively. It is likely that long-term memories for these types of sensory experiences are also stored in or near these sites. However, and this is one of the many complicating issues in brain science, sensory experiences are cerebrally multifarious. When you read the words in the preceding sentence, the information from your eyes is processed in the visual cortex (no doubt about it), but when you consider the meaning of the word *multifarious,* you use other parts of the brain, perhaps even to the point of subvocalizing or actually saying the word and thereby activating regions associated with auditory memories.

How the Brain Works—Simple and Sweet. How the brain stores information in LTM is the second difficult simple question. Even though the brain is the universe's most complicated thing, some answers are beginning to emerge from the neurocognitive laboratory. One explanation of how long-term memories are formed is based on the early pioneering work done by Donald Hebb, whom we have encountered several times in this book. The simplified version of his notion of long-term memory is that information in short-term memory is converted in LTM if it remains in STM long enough. This because in STM a *reverberating circuit* of neural activity takes place in the brain, with a self-exciting loop of neurons. If the circuit remains active for a period (a type of self-stimulation), then some chemical and/or structural change occurs and the memory is permanently stored. From the cognitive literature, we know that merely holding information in STM does not assure its permanence (see, for example, the research of Craik and Watkins, discussed in the previous chapter). However, if information is combined with other, existing, meaningful memories, then long-term memorability is enhanced.

The next section is called "Sugarcoated Golden Memories." You will find it has nothing to do with endearing memories experienced by old geezers (as you might initially think) but is a subtle mnemonic for glucose, a sugar, that has been shown to be related to enhanced learning. That fact is now more likely to persist in your memory because it has been variously associated with other well-entrenched, and perhaps even emotional, memories. What is *golden* a mnemonic for?

Sugarcoated Golden Memories. Some experiences are remembered better than others. Exciting, ego-involving, or even traumatic experiences seem to stick in memory better than complicated political theories, for example. Animal studies have indicated that when an exciting event occurs, the adrenal medulla increases its secretion into the blood stream of epinephrine (adrenaline), which has now been demonstrated to enhance consolidation of a memory (McGaugh, 1990). It is likely that epinephrine does not directly stimulate the brain's synapses (there is the matter of crossing the blood-brain barrier), but it converts stored glycogen to glucose (a sugar), thereby raising the blood level of glucose, which nourishes the brain. Some experimental research supports the notion that directly injecting glucose after learning enhances future memory of the event (Gold, 1987; and Hall & Gold, 1990). This *petit tour* of the neurocognition of LTM is in itself only a sweet sample of the burgeoning literature on the topic. Surely, new developments will be reported on this exciting topic in the near future and bear watching.

LTM: Storage and Structure

Codes. In our discussion of STM, we saw that information is stored acoustically, visually, and semantically, but the type of code used is sometimes questioned. We have no comparable difficulty in describing the coding mechanisms in LTM, although there is some disagreement about their relative importance. In LTM, information is clearly coded acoustically, visually, and semantically. The multidimensional coding of information in LTM can be easily illustrated. For example, a black-and-white bird sometimes perches outside my window. I know it's a western magpie when it makes a sound like one, or when I see it, or when I read about a western magpie and I associate that information with other semantic information about birds—feathered creatures, wildlife, and so on.[4] In addition to the common knowledge about acoustical, visual, and semantic codes operating in LTM, an impressive number of research articles has validated its complex coding system. In general, we can think of LTM as the repository of all things in memory that are not currently being used but are potentially retrievable. A very general list suggested by Bower (1975) of some of the classes of information contained in LTM includes the following:

- Our spatial model of the world surrounding us—symbolic structures corresponding to images of our house, city, country, and planet and information about where significant objects are located in that cognitive map.
- Our knowledge of physical laws, cosmology, and of the properties of objects and things.
- Our beliefs about people, about ourselves, and about how to behave in various social situations.
- Our values and the social goals that we seek.
- Our motor skills for driving, bicycling, shooting pool, and so on. Our problem-solving skills for various domains. Our plans for how to achieve various things.
- Our perceptual skills in understanding language or interpreting paintings or music. (From Bower, 1975, p. 56)

Despite the diversity, emphasis in the literature has been on the semantic code in LTM, and this emphasis is reflected in this book.

Organization. Perhaps the most pervasive assumption about LTM is that information in it is organized in some orderly way. This assumption is so widely accepted that researchers rarely ask whether information in LTM is organized. The question more often asked is how information in LTM is organized. A moment of introspection is enough to validate the assumption. If you are asked to recall what you were doing on a certain day—say, July 7, 1990—how do you go about finding an answer? Chances are you search for some easily identifiable information that is related to and near that time and work backward or forward to July 7. It is likely that the events on that day are somehow

---

[4]I have never tasted, smelled, or felt a western magpie, but if I had I would also probably be able to recognize one by these sensations. Gustatory, olfactory, and tactile codes seem to operate in LTM, although precious little research has been done with them.

related to and organized with other information. Perhaps a birthday, other anniversary, or a particular national holiday was near that date. You might try to remember what you did during the summer of 1990 or to locate the day of the week on which the date fell. You might remember that on the last day of June you paid your rent. The information you settle on, then, provides a cue for finding what you were doing on July 7. On the other hand, imagine how you might answer the question if your memory was not systematically organized. You might randomly sample information from your LTM in something of this manner: Bank of Chicago, 3.14, LS/MFT, however, Lake Tahoe 361-2849, ESP, Kunta Kinte, Mars, and so on. Of course, this is a silly lot of information, but it is equally silly to imagine an unorganized LTM. The fanciful representation of LTM suggests that within it items are linked in a way similar to that of an intricate telephone network. Retrieval of specific information occurs by means of entering the network, which is capable of calling up other related information until the desired information is contacted. The network of interrelated and associated information is far more complex than can be depicted. In any case, the way we recall common information suggests that LTM is organized.

There is a growing body of knowledge that suggests specific information is recorded within a well-structured and highly practical network. This concept implies that new information entering LTM does not require synthesis of a new network (which would defeat the utility of organization, as each event would require its own system), with an endless number of minor organization schemes the result. Instead, new information is recorded within existing organizations. Much of the research in semantic organization, which is described in Chapter 8, shows that the network can be remarkably sparse.

Capacity and Duration. It is hard to imagine the volume and duration of information contained in LTM, but we can make some reasonable estimates of these characteristics. Even the most obscure information is readily available to us. For example, I can remember and "see" the exact spot I dropped my hunting knife in the creek, the license number of my dad's car, the precise details of a bracelet I gave to a girlfriend, the location of an oil can tucked away in a remote corner of a garage cabinet, and yet none of these events has been in my consciousness for at least thirty years! Even in an era when the information capacity of electronic computers is prodigious, the capacity of the human brain for storing detailed information over long periods (and in so small a space) remains unequaled.

How can we remember so much? One revealing answer to that question is suggested in the way college students tried to remember the names of their fourth-grade teacher. It is plausible that each student had plenty of opportunity to encode the teacher's name, although most admitted that they had not thought of him or her in years. Some of their introspections about the retrieval process follow:

Student K. S.

1. Remember what school I went to. What year did I change to Lowell School? Second or third grade?
2. Location of classroom
3. Visualize teacher—tall and thin
4. Same teacher as third grade
5. Miss Bell?
6. She was friendly with my sixth- and seventh-grade teacher.

7. If I entered Lowell School in the third grade, then the classroom was on the East end. If this was my second classroom in Lowell School, it was on the West end.
8. Yes, Miss Bell.

Student J. C.

1. First thing I thought of was a nun or lay teacher: nun—sister.
2. Second thing I thought of was a most common name that nuns have, almost a surname—Sister Mary.
3. Third thing I thought about was all the grief I had with that nun in fourth grade.
4. Fourth thing I remembered is that her name began with an A, then I remembered Al, then I thought of Alvira—Sister Mary Alvira.
5. Wrong last name, remembered a province in Canada—Sister Mary Alberta.

From these examples and other more rigidly controlled experiments, we can gain some appreciation of the multitude of memory traces we easily store over a long period. Of course, we cannot remember all events of the past as if they happened only yester-

Flashbulb Memories

In the course of a lifetime, several events occur that are so startling that they and the surrounding circumstances become a vivid part of one's permanent memory. For example, people who were alive on December 7, 1941, can recall, even today, learning of the bombing of Pearl Harbor. The news of President Kennedy's assassination on November 22, 1963, is remembered clearly by those who lived through this period. Few will forget the tragic destruction of the *Challenger* spacecraft as seen on live television in January 1986.

During the autumn of 1983, I was living in Moscow as an exchange scientist with the Academy of Sciences. Upon returning to my room late one evening and tuning in "The Voice of America," I was shocked to learn that the Soviets had shot from the sky a Korean airliner, resulting in heavy loss of lives. Several months after the episode, I wrote the following recollection:

A flashbulb memory had occurred in me, and all the immediate events were imprinted on my permanent memory and would remain vivid for years. . . . Even incidental memories were indelibly impressed in memory. In this case, I can remember the exact position of my portable Sony shortwave receiver on the table, the color of the chair I was sitting on (red), and the number of lights turned on (two), etc. Also, the events immediately prior to and following the experience are clear in my memory. I can still "see" the fellow travelers who accompanied me on the brief bus ride from the Palace Theater to the Academy of Sciences Hotel. I can "hear" the voice of the old druzhinniki who kept guard at the hotel entrance as he asked me for the umpteenth time to "produce your pass." I even remember what I was thinking and about my own status as a visitor in the Soviet Union.

This special type of memory is called "flashbulb memory" by Brown and Kulik (1977), who use the term to suggest that a surprising event of short duration fixes in memory, with photographic clarity, the details of the event and the context in which the event was perceived. Another feature of flashbulb memories is that they seem to be personally important. For example, in my own case I was concerned about possible American reprisal against the Soviets and their counterreaction. Brown and Kulik suggest that flashbulb memories are created at the moment the event oc-

day. That loss of recall may be attributed to interference (the intervention of information that blocks the recall of old memory traces) or decay (the weakening of a memory trace through disuse).

Very Long-Term Memory (VLTM)

Some interesting data have been gathered on the fate of very long-term memories (VLTM), or memories more than three-months old.

High School Classmates. A landmark of VLTM research is that of Bahrick, Bahrick, and Wittlinger (1975). In their ambitious effort to trace the longevity of memory, they tested 392 high school graduates for memory of names and portraits of classmates selected from old yearbooks. The nine retention intervals tested ranged in length from 3.3 months to almost 48 years! The sample (almost 50 subjects in each of the 9 groups) was

curs, and they attribute the phenomenon to the activation of a "Now Print" command that permanently fixes the event. Ulric Neisser (1982) contends that some memories become "flashbulb memories" primarily through the significance attached to them after the event has occurred—later that day, the next morning, and in subsequent months and years.

A few years ago, David Rubin of Duke University had students rate events that might be considered "flashbulb." The results were as follows:

Cues	Percent*
A car accident you were in or witnessed	85
When you first met your roommate at Duke	82
The night of your high school graduation	81
The night of your senior prom (if you went or not)	78
An early romantic experience	77
A time you had to speak in front of an audience	72
When you got your admissions letter from Duke	65

Cues	Percent*
Your first date—the moment you met him/her	57
President Reagan was shot in Washington	52
The night President Nixon resigned	41
The first time you flew in an airplane	40
The moment you opened your SAT scores	33
Your 17th birthday	30
The day of the first space shuttle flight	24
The last time you ate a holiday dinner at home	23
Your first class at Duke	21
You heard that President Sadat of Egypt was shot	21
When you heard that the Pope had been shot	21
The first time your parents left you alone for some time	19
Your 13th birthday	12

*Percent of Duke students in memory experiment who reported [that] events on experimenter's list were of "flashbulb" quality.

From Rubin (1985)

huge, and an involved testing procedure was developed. First, subjects were asked to free-recall or list the names of all the members of their graduating class whom they could remember. Then, a picture recognition task was given in which photographs were selected from the subject's yearbook and presented in random order for identification along with some other photographs. A third task was to identify names similarly (name recognition). The fourth and fifth tasks were to match pictures with names and names with pictures, respectively. Finally, a picture-cuing task was given in which the subject was to recall the name of one classmate from his or her picture.

The overall results are portrayed in Figure 7.10. It is noteworthy that the recognition level for the faces of former classmates was astonishingly high (about 90 percent over 34 years), while name recognition and name matching declined after 15 years. The sharp decline in recognition and recall data after about 35 years of stability may reflect some degenerative process of advancing age. The ability to match names with faces and picture recognition remains the same over a very long period, about 90 percent from 3.3 months to 34 years. The data gathered by Bahrick and his colleagues confirm the notion that VLTM does, indeed, last for a very long term, and the invariance of recognition memory over such a long time is surprising. The results suggest that recognition memory for distant events is affected by the degree of initial encoding and the distribution of rehearsal. In the above example, the initial learning of facts about classmates was very thorough, taking place, in most instances, over years. Also, throughout the years intervening between graduation and the experiment, the subjects may have had occasion to think about "the good ol' days," attend class reunions, or in some way reminisce about a distant but precious face.

VLTM for Spanish—Evidence for Permastore? How long will your memory for a foreign language last? In another ambitious study done by Bahrick (1984; also see Bahrick & Phelps, 1987), the maintenance of Spanish over a span of 50 years was examined. The subjects in this massive study were 773 people who had learned Spanish in high school. They provided such data as the amount of original training, their grades, and how often they had used the language after study. Tests of reading comprehension and recall and recognition tests for vocabulary, grammar, and idioms were given. In general, Bahrick found that the more thoroughly Spanish had been learned, the better the performance on the subsequent test—a finding that should surprise no one. However, the degree of very long-term retention is, if not surprising, gratifying to all who plan to live a long life. Knowledge of Spanish, in general, declined most sharply during the first 3 years and then seemed to reach a stable state, for about another 30 years. Some drop-off of knowledge, especially in reading comprehension, was noted after about 25 years. However, much of the originally learned knowledge was still usable after 50 years! This "permanent" memory was called *permastore,* and it would seem that knowledge of Spanish, and presumably other foreign languages, remains reasonably viable for a very long time.

VLTM and Cognitive Psychology. Assuming you are reading this book for a course in cognitive psychology, perhaps you have asked yourself, "How much of this information will stay in my LTM?" An answer to that question can be found in an article by Conway, Cohen, and Stanhope (1991) called " On the Very Long-Term Retention of

FIGURE 7.10

Adjusted mean retention scores for subjects tested in six categories. Adapted from Bahrick, Bahrick, and Wittlinger (1975).

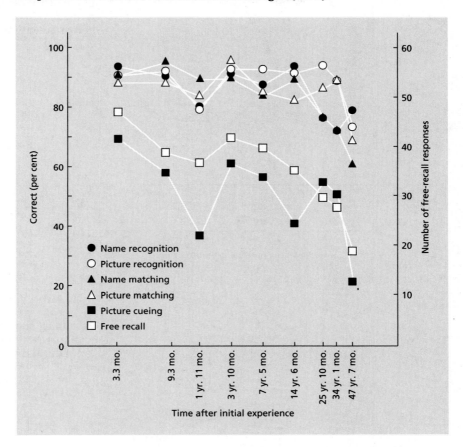

Knowledge Acquired Through Formal Education: Twelve Years of Cognitive Psychology." The experimenters sampled a large number of students (N = 373) who had completed a course in cognitive psychology as long ago as 12 years. The former students were asked to complete a memory test designed to assess their retention of material learned a long time ago. The test consisted of memory for proper names of researchers and concepts. The results are shown in Figure 7.11.

Retention of names showed a slightly more rapid decline than the recall and recognition of concepts, a finding consistent with what many professors of cognitive psychol-

F I G U R E   7 . 1 1

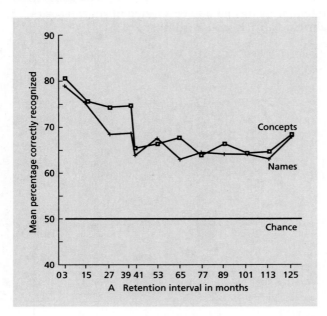

A. Mean percentages of correctly recognized names and concepts across retention intervals.

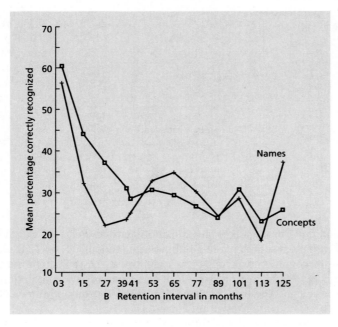

B. Mean percentages of correctly recalled names and concepts across retention intervals.

ogy (and I suspect other subjects) see in much shorter retention intervals. As shown in Figure 7.11A, the recognition of both names and concepts follow the same trend. In Figure 7.11B we see a much sharper initial decline in the recall of names and concepts. An interesting, if not altogether expected, finding was a high relationship between grades and VLTM scores. It pays to study or, an alternative hypothesis, it pays to have a good memory.

These data are consistent with the landmark experiments of Bahrick and his colleagues in the sense that VLTM for information, be it old class chums or STM/LTM dichotomy, declines rapidly at first and then levels off and remains at a sustained level, above chance, for many years. The finding that concepts are retained longer than names needs some interpretation. It is likely that new names, with which the student is (presumably) poorly motivated to commit to LTM (what value is it to know, in the long run, that Bahrick, Bahrick, and Wittlinger collected important data on VLTM), would be variously associated with other memories of the principle of VLTM, namely, that people tend to forget rapidly at first and then not much. Ebbinghaus, a name (like his nonsense syllables) likely to be forgotten, continues to be right. Finally, one has to suspect that the emphasis placed on names versus concepts by individual professors, and perhaps even the emphasis placed on these things in the text used, might influence the results, although, I hasten to add, that the results are entirely consistent with previous studies of VLTM and support the main conclusions found by others.

You might ask how professors do at remembering the names of their students, a type of tables-reversed question from the research that was just reviewed. In one study Seamon and Travis (1993) tested for both name free recall and portrait-cued recall. Name recall declined sharply after one semester and face recognition declined after two semesters, while name recognition remained perfect. Consistent with Bahrick's findings and with those of Conway and his colleagues, these results suggest that name recall may be dependent on contextual cues which are, understandably, diminished over time.

Memory for Pictures. A remarkable demonstration of the ability to recognize pictures over a very long time was given by Shepard (1967). From a large number of highly memorable pictures (for example, advertisements in magazines), he selected 612. The pictures were projected one at a time onto a screen at a rate set by the subject. After the subject viewed the 612 individual pictures, a recognition test was given in which 68 of the 612 were shown paired with one new picture each. The subjects were to indicate which of each pair was the picture they had previously viewed. The immediate-recognition task yielded a very high percentage of "hits," 96.7 percent. Two hours later, in the part of the experiment particularly germane to our discussion of VLTM, the subjects were again asked to judge another set of old/new pairs of photographs. This time 99.7 percent of the pictures that had already been seen were recognized. Subjects were subsequently given recognition memory tasks of the same sort after 3 days, 7 days, and 120 days. As can be seen in Figure 7.12, subjects were able to recognize the already viewed pictures very well, even after a week. Similar results have been reported by Nickerson (1965, 1968) and Standing (1973) using 10,000 pictures. Standing, Conezio, and Haber (1970) presented 2,560 color slides to subjects and found that recognition ranged from 97 percent to about 63 percent over a year. Somewhat more interesting is the decline in recognition scores after about 4 months. Did memory for the picture fade, or did other images intervene and confuse the subjects? The data gathered after 3 days and 7 days

FIGURE 7.12

Results of Shepard's recognition test. Adapted from Shepard (1967).

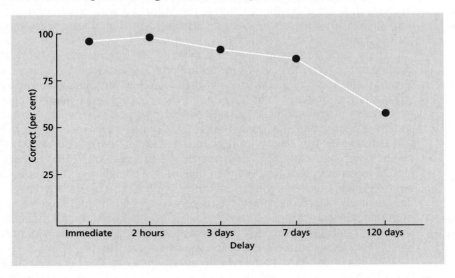

would suggest that the memory for pictures was encoded in the subjects' LTM and that the decline of recognition memory after 4 months would appear to be a function of the intervention of confusing images. In the next section we consider the effects of loss of information, or the inability to recall information from memory.

Autobiographical Memories

Autobiographical memories are memories of an individual's past history. Although personal memories have always been a topic of interest among nonspecialists, they also have been the subject of several interesting psychological studies. One reason these types of memories are interesting is that they are about the individual and his or her unique history. The person—you, your friend, or anyone—is the focus of autobiographical memories. The individual is the expert, since no one knows his or her life better. These memories also can tell us quite a lot about an individual's personality and concept of self.

The contents of personal memory do not comprise an even collection of sensory impressions. Our LTM does not record information unintelligently, but rather it is highly selective in choosing its contents. We remember close relatives, the look of our first car, the first time we had sex, school colors, the name of our hometown, heroes, bullies, and villains, a few cute things our children did, the floor plan of our home, and mother's good china. Contrary to our best intentions, we do not "remember this night forever," or "never forget you," or "think about you every day." We forget a lot of things, and sometimes those things that are very dear to us at the moment fade rapidly. Others remain forever. The contents of one's personal memory are not unlike the contents of one's attic. It is more a selective collection of important and odd memories than an indiscriminate stowing of all sensory impressions in our cerebral warehouse.

Autobiographical memories, if not perfect, are generally quite good. Objective data on this topic are hard to come by (after all, who can contest a personal memory?), but some researchers (for example, Field, 1981) have interviewed various members of the same family, the "facts" of whose personal history could be validated by other members of the family. Such recollections as "I'm sure I had tonsillitis on July 3, as it was just before the Fourth of July and I had to miss the parade on Main Street" can be verified by checking with other family members and consulting medical records. Validating studies show a correlation of about $+0.88$ between family members when asked factual questions. A much lower correlation of about $+0.43$ is reported for emotions and attitudes (Field, 1981). Of course, we all know families in which the correlation between family members' attitudes is negative.

Vintage Memories

Throughout our lifetime we gather countless impressions of our world and carefully store many as treasured memories. Elderly people seem to have an especially rich store of preserved impressions and, like discovering a flower pressed between the pages of a cherished book, once vivid impressions can be recovered from the pages of memory. In talking with elderly people, it is almost as if they draw a book from memory, open it, and begin to recount its contents; then they turn to another section, tell of its contents, and, finally, carefully return the book to its original place so that it can be found again.

A short time ago I asked members of my cognitive psychology class to visit with elderly neighbors or relatives to record some very long-term memories. The following is a brief sample of one of the papers:

"I was born in 1885. . . . My mother died when I was 8 years old so I lived back and forth with relatives and went sometimes to school in the city of Kahoka, Mo., which consisted of about 5 rooms and sometimes to the country school named Star, which was only 1 room where more than one grade was taught. Star School

had windows all around looking out on the trees, a blackboard at the front and a little porch and cloakroom where you entered. . . . For entertainment we had the county fair, exhibiting all the local products. There were rides such as the Ferris wheel and merry-go-round, and pony rides. They sold ice cream cones and had lemonade stands. These items sold for 5 cents each. . . . I remember my Uncle John taking me to these events as well as one time when he took me to a show which featured hypnosis. . . . When we were sick they would give us a spoonful of Ayres sarsaparilla, a patent medicine bought at the drug store. . . . I hope this information will help you with your school project, and that you'll come and see me soon. Your Great-grandmother Menke." (Thanks to Scott Menke. May 24, 1987).

Notice that Great-grandmother Menke recounted "important" events from her childhood that were important to her: pony rides, ice cream cones, and lemonade stands. She also had a strong visual memory as evidenced by her accurate recall of the floor plan of her early school.

Diary Studies of Autobiographical Memory. Fortunately, some enterprising psychologists have undertaken the herculean task of keeping a record of their daily activities and then sampling their memories of these activities. One of these studies by Linton (1982; also see Wagenaar, 1986) concentrated on the recollection of episodic experiences over a 6-year period. Each day she wrote on cards a brief description of at least two events that happened on that day. Every month she selected two cards at random; she then tried to recall the events written on the cards and fix the date of the events. She also rated the memory for its saliency, or importance, and for emotionality, both at the time of recall and at the time of writing the card. Linton's results (see Figure 7.13) contained a few surprises. The rate of forgetting was linear, not curvilinear, as many forgetting curves from the time of Ebbinghaus onward have been. From this, we can infer the significant conclusion that memory for everyday, episodic events over a long period of time becomes gradually less available and that the ability to retrieve these items deteriorates at a steady rate. Linton noted two types of forgetting. One was associated with events repeated over time, such as attending committee meetings. In memory, meetings merged with other meetings. A second type of forgetting was associated with events that she simply forgot. One surprise was the failure to find a strong relationship between the rated importance and emotionality of a memory and its recallability. This finding is contrary to "common knowledge" and some other studies, but it is consistent with the "I'll never forget this night" pledge and the subsequent inability to recall the night.

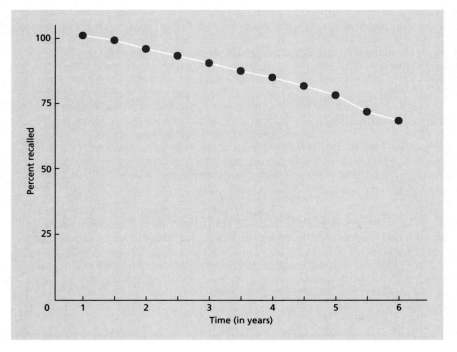

FIGURE 7.13

Percent of items forgotten during six years. From Linton (1982).

Another technique used to access the contents of one's bag of memories is to recall thematic life events. In another ambitious study, Sehulster (1989) tried to recall information about opera performances at the Metropolitan Opera spanning 25 years. Sehulster, the lucky patron of the Met for more than a quarter of a century, attempted to free-recall the details about the dates and casting of 284 performances. Validation of Sehulster's memory was done by checking the programs. Unlike the Linton self-study, Sehulster found primacy and recency effects; that is, opera performances seen toward the first and last part of the 25-year span were recalled better than those in the middle. Sehulster also found that the importance (or intensity) of the opera also contributed significantly to its recallability. Significant performances were, understandably, better recalled than pedestrian ones. Nevertheless, some performances stuck out in Sehulster's memory. Finally, the more times Sehulster rehearsed the information, for example, listened to records of those operas he attended, the greater the likelihood of recall.

Thus far, our review of personal memories has concentrated on individual accounts of private experiences. These matters have also been studied from the perspective of group data. In a series of studies, David Rubin of Duke University has shown that people remember some periods of their lives better than others and that for most people the recall of past times is remarkably similar. Rubin (1987; and Rubin, Wetzler & Nebes, 1986) found, for example, that people who reach their middle years (50s and beyond) tend to remember more episodes from their youth and early adult years than from more recent years (see Figure 7.14).

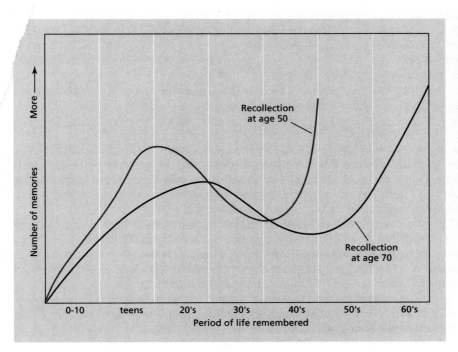

FIGURE 7.14

Memory tends to be selective for events as well as for periods. Especially interesting is the tendency of the middle years to be less recallable. By the age of 70, people remember more from their 20s, while those in their 50s recall more from their teens. From Rubin (1987).

"It seems to be that reminiscence flows more freely about the period in life that comes to define you: the time of your first date, marriage, job, child," Rubin explains. Our relative inability to remember events that happened between the ages of 40 and 55 may not be due to the dullness of those years but to the increased stability and routine nature of life during that period. In the sameness of life, one memory becomes merged with another and thus becomes less memorable. The period that seems inaccessible is before the age of 4. While some psychoanalysts may contend that childhood repression of sexual desires accounts for this amnesia, another, more cognitive view is that these memories were not well integrated into a larger concept of personal history.

Forgetting

The remarkable memory feats of the old graduates and Spanish students mentioned in the previous section may cause you to think that nothing is lost from LTM. (That illusion may last only until your next examination.) Forgetting, or the loss of the ability to recall information once available, rather than memory per se has dominated traditional research in LTM.

Decay Theory. If information is not used or rehearsed, forgetting may occur with time. In a nutshell, that is the point of view of the theorists who subscribe to the decay theory of forgetting. All memory involves a change in the central nervous system, and it is believed that information processing leaves a trace—some change in the actual tissue of the neuroanatomy—that, with disuse, may fade much as a once distinct pathway will grow faint if unused. Impressions that were once vivid (for example, my phone number of ten years ago) seem nearly to have dissolved through disuse. These abandoned traces suffer not from lack of encoding or even retrieval cues but from neglect. Decay theory is intuitively appealing. It makes sense to think of something that is not used as losing its strength over time.

One basic objection to the decay theory is that it does not adequately explain the influence of activities that intervene between the original learning and later recall. Forgetting may be greatly affected by subsequent events, which may block (or, in some instances, assist) the recall of old memories. In an early experiment, Jenkins and Dallenbach (1924) had two groups of subjects learn a ten-item list of nonsense syllables—one late at night and the other early in the morning. In addition to being tested immediately after learning, the night subjects were awakened after 1, 2, 4, or 8 hours and tested for recall. The day subjects reported back to the laboratory at the same time intervals as the night subjects but carried on their normal daily activities. As shown in Figure 7.15, recall declined with time in both instances; however, the important finding for decay theory lies in the difference between the results for those who slept after memorization and those who remained awake. If decay is a natural result of disuse alone, as one would anticipate would occur over time, then we would expect subjects in both groups to forget the same amount. They didn't. Under conditions that allowed for greater interference (the waking condition), greater forgetting occurred. Thus, the experiment of Jenkins and Dallenbach suggests that forgetting is much more related to the forces of interference than simply decay over time.

FIGURE 7.15

Average recall of nonsense syllables by subjects after interval of sleep and after interval of waking. Adapted from Jenkins and Dallenbach (1924).

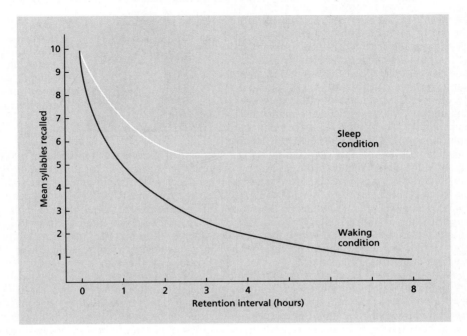

Although some data suggest that neurological breakdown occurs with age and disease, no data exist that would lead us to conclude that the principal reason we fail to retrieve information from LTM is neurological decay. Nevertheless, current neurological research may produce important correlates for memory research.

Interference. Interference not only lends itself to closer experimental control than other forgetting models, but it is also directly in the mainstream of the strong current of associationism, which has dominated research in human memory and learning for nearly a century. The tradition holds that associative bonds are formed between specific stimuli and specific responses and that these associative connections are held in memory so long as other competing information does not interfere with them. For example, if you learn that Fact A is associated with Fact B, the associative relationship could be represented as A-B, or a paired associate. The ability to recall B as a response to A may be interfered with if new information is presented.

How well does interference theory hold up under experimental testing? Studies of interference theory easily lend themselves to laboratory testing, and two principal paradigms for the investigation of interference have emerged: retroactive inhibition (RI) and

The "Permanence" of Memory

The scene is a courtroom. After the star witness has taken an oath to "tell the truth, the whole truth and nothing but the truth," she gives a graphic account of a grisly murder and, at the proper dramatic moment, is asked, "Is that person who raised the ten-pound sledgehammer high over his head and plunged it deeply into the fragile skull of the defenseless and recently departed Ms. Abernathy in the courtroom?" "Yes, he is." "And would you point him out?" "It's him! The shabby-looking character sitting at the defendant's table." Strong stuff, but such galvanizing testimony is not confined to soap operas. Similar scenes are played out frequently in actual American courts. The effect of an eyewitness's testimony in persuading a jury of the guilt or innocence of a defendant is usually overwhelming. However, until recently, the credibility of eyewitness testimony was unchallenged.

Several years ago Elizabeth Loftus from the University of Washington presented some evidence of her own that indicated human memory was not as permanent as first thought. In one of her experiments, college students were asked to view a videotape of an automobile and then answer a series of questions based on what they had seen. Half the subjects were asked, "How fast was the white sports car going while traveling along the country road?" The other half was asked, "How fast was the white sports car going when it passed the barn while traveling along the country road?" Notice that in the second condition *barn* was introduced in the question, although the film contained no barn. One week later the subjects were asked whether they had seen a barn in the videotape. In the second condition 17 percent of the subjects reported seeing a barn, which of course did not exist in the film, as contrasted with only 3 percent in the first condition.

In a related experiment Loftus, Miller, and Burns (1978) showed subjects a series of slides

Elizabeth Loftus. Her work on malleability of memory has been frequently applied to eyewitness identification cases.

in which a sports car stopped at an intersection and then turned and hit a pedestrian. Half the students saw a slide with a yield sign at the corner; the other half saw a slide with a stop sign. In subsequent questioning, opposite information regarding the critical yield and stop signs was introduced. That is, for some of the students who saw the stop sign, new information calling the sign a yield sign was introduced, and for some the yield sign was called a stop sign. Later, subjects were asked to select from a pair of slides which one they recognized as being part of the original set. Of the group of subjects who had not been given the misleading information, 75 percent selected the correct slide; for those who had been given incorrect information, the correct slide was chosen only 41 percent of the time. What has happened to the original memory? Loftus (1983) offers a coexistence hypothesis that suggests that the introduction of new material does not alter previous memories but makes them less accessible.

Loftus has demonstrated that it is possible to create something as huge as a barn and as important as a yield sign instead of a stop sign (or stop sign instead of a yield sign) for some subjects. It seems unlikely that one could mistake a flyswatter for a ten-pound sledgehammer involved in a brutal and savage act of carnage, but such eyewitness accounts have been questioned increasingly due to the important work of Loftus.

proactive inhibition (PI). RI refers to the inhibitory effect new material has on old material; PI refers to the inhibitory effect old material has on new material. The two paradigms and their respective experimental conditions are illustrated in Figure 7.16. Each of these paradigms allows the researcher a great deal of latitude to delve into the nature of forgetting, with minute attention to the fate of previous and intervening associations. We have all experienced trying to recall a new telephone number only to be confused by the memory of an old one (PI), or trying to recall an old number and being confused by a new one (RI).

One resolution to the dilemma of past learning's interfering with new learning postulates two types of LTM systems. In our discussion of memory models, we touched on one such point of view by Tulving. His distinction between semantic and episodic memory may provide the answer to why interference is so widely demonstrated in the laboratory, while in everyday life new information has little deleterious effect on past knowledge. The previous research on the effects of interference is largely based on human subjects' learning word (or nonsense syllable) lists, which, according to Tulving, takes place in the subject's episodic memory. Episodic memory, it may be remembered, holds temporally coded information, while semantic memory holds information about the use of language—words, meaning, referents, and rules. In laboratory study of the effects of interference in verbal learning, the subject is likely to be asked to learn to associate two verbal units, say, *WOJ-BELL*. The response word *BELL* is actually not

FIGURE 7.16

Paradigm for testing of retroactive and proactive inhibition.

	Task 1	Task 2	Interval	Test
Retroactive inhibition				
Experimental group	Learn list A	Learn list B	Retention interval	Recall list A
Control group	Learn list A		Retention interval	Recall list A
Proactive inhibition				
Experimental group	Learn list A	Learn list B	Retention interval	Recall list B
Control group		Learn list B	Retention interval	Recall list B

"learned" in the laboratory (the subject knows its definition), but it is part of the subject's semantic memory. What is learned is that *BELL* is a response to *WOJ*, events that are dependent on the specific laboratory episode. That relationship is, therefore, stored in episodic memory, according to Tulving's viewpoint. Furthermore, if traditional psychological experiments on verbal learning are largely studying episodic memory, then the laws of interference are also largely based on episodic functions and not (at least generally) validated in semantic memory. It is likely that episodic memory is very susceptible to interference, through the enormous traffic of information in and out of it, while semantic memory may remain relatively isolated from this flow of information and its effects. To illustrate this argument, consider the contents of semantic memory. We have stored the rules of English grammar, the multiplication table, that January is the first month of the year, that Oklahoma is shaped like a sauce pan, that it is proper to say "sorry" when you spill tea on someone, that honey tastes sweet, and so on. No amount of new information is going to cause me to forget any of that information; interference probably has very little to do with the recall of these facts. In summary, two different memory systems seem to be operating in LTM—one episodic, which is susceptible to interference effects, and the other semantic, which is not.

Cue-Dependent Forgetting. Thus far we have examined the principles of forgetting as they are conceptualized from a traditional associationistic standpoint. Another consideration, growing out of information processing, is that we fail to recall something not because it has decayed or that it has been obstructed but because the cueing conditions are too remote from the thing we are trying to recall. This is not so much a notion of forgetting, which implies that memory is lost, as it is one that presumes that unretrieved memories are alive and well and situated in an associative web where they wait for the proper stimulation to release them. This explanation of forgetting, called cue-dependent forgetting by Tulving (1974), has roots in the well-accepted theory that all learning takes place within a context and that we encode information in relation to its immediate perceptual environment. Forgetting, or, more specifically, the failure to recall something from memory, is a failure of the retrieval cues to match the encoded nature of items in memory. There are common examples, such as the student who fails to give the correct answer on an examination and laments, "I knew the answer, but I didn't know what you wanted." Retrieval cues and encoding cues, in this instance, are incongruent. My general instruction, "Name your fourth-grade teacher," fails to prompt a quick reply because it lacks, as retrieval cues, properties present during the original learning occasion. The introspective protocols given earlier in this chapter reveal a search process that, in large part, reflects self-generated cues specific to the immediate environment of the original learning (for example, the school I went to, location of the classroom, visualization of the teacher—tall and thin, and so on).

Cue-dependent forgetting, an intuitively appealing theory, was empirically tested by Tulving and Pearlstone (1966). They gave subjects a list of nouns organized according to categories. (For example, *bomb* and *cannon* would be under *Weapons.*) Half the subjects were given a list of the original category names (cues), but all were instructed to learn the exemplars, not the categories. Subjects were then asked to recall all the words they could. The results are shown in Figure 7.17. As can be seen, the presence of the category cues had a very significant influence on the number of words retrieved from

FIGURE 7.17

Average number of words recalled with and without category cues. Adapted from Tulving and Pearlstone (1966).

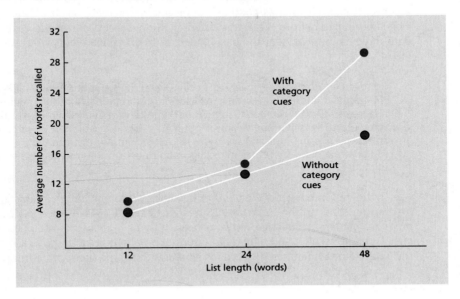

memory, especially in the case of the longer lists of 48 words. Even more convincing support for cue-dependent forgetting (or cue-dependent recall) can be found in Tulving and Psotka (1971). Here subjects viewed lists of 24 words, each of which consisted of 6 categories of 4 words each. One list was as follows:

hut	captain	zinc
cottage	corporal	copper
tent	sergeant	aluminum
hotel	colonel	bronze
cliff	ant	drill
river	wasp	saw
hill	beetle	chisel
volcano	mosquito	nail

It was clear to the subjects in this experiment that the words were grouped by categories. After three presentations of each list, a free-recall task was given. Groups were given 1, 2, 3, 4, or 5 lists. After 10 minutes of neutral activity, subjects were given the names of all the categories (for example, types of buildings, earth formations) and then asked to recall all words.

The results (see Figure 7.18) show that noncued recall drops off sharply as a function of the number of interpolated lists—an entirely expected result in light of what we know of the properties of RI. Of far greater significance (and somewhat surprising) is the performance curve for cued recall. Those data indicate that when a subject is given a category cue, recall is as good as the original immediate recall ("original learning"). The sharp decrement in recall attributed to RI does not occur in the cued recall. These data force us to reconsider the basic tenets of interference theory. According to Tulving (1974):

> Retroactive interference observed in the overall noncued recall test reflects changes in the retrieval information, rather than loss of information from the memory traces. The changes in the informational content of the retrieval environment are brought about by interpolated learning and recall of other lists. The presentation of category names restores the missing information to the learner's cognitive environment . . . thereby making possible recovery of the information laid down in the memory store at the time of initial learning.

In view of Tulving's evidence that ties retrieval to encoding circumstances, the following question arises: How closely related to recall cues must encoding cues be in order to operate as effective retrieval cues? Tulving's answer is that "specific retrieval cues facilitate recall if and only if the information about them and about their relation to the TBR [to be remembered] words is stored at the same time as the information about

FIGURE 7.18

Recall from a list of 24 words in 3 successive tests: original learning, cued recall, and noncued recall. Adapted from Tulving and Psotka (1971).

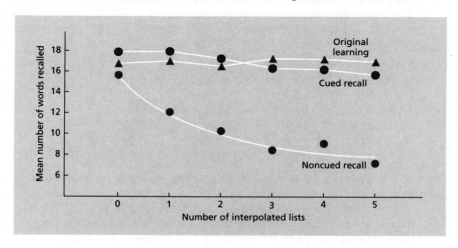

the membership of the TBR words in a given list"[5] (Tulving & Osler, 1968, p. 599). There can be little doubt that this principle, called the encoding specificity principle (another ESP), means that a retrieval cue can be effective only if encoded at the time of study. This bold principle seems disparate with research that has demonstrated that recognition memory (recognizing an item that has been learned, as in selecting the answer in a multiple-choice test or identifying the face of a friend) is under some circumstances better than recall memory (retrieval of a learned item, as in response to a question such as, "Where is Buckingham Palace?") We can well appreciate this when we try to think of the names of famous characters whose initials are C. C. (See below.) One argument for the superiority of recognition memory is the fact that recall involves recognition. If you roam through LTM in search of a fact (say, someone's name), you must not only search for the name but also be able to recognize it once it is found.

[5]Victor Borge, the pianist-humorist, stands this idea on its ear: "I learned to speak Japanese. I learned by having the tape machine under the pillow while I slept, and it really worked. The trouble is I can only speak it when I'm asleep."

Some famous C. C.s: Calvin Coolidge, Charlie Chaplin, Chubby Checker, Charlie Chan, Carol Channing, Coco Chanel, Christopher Columbus, Carlos Castaneda, Christopher Cross, Charles Carroll, Carol Cole, Cassius Clay, Claudette Colbert . . .

Summary

1   Short-term memory capacity is limited to about seven items, but the density or amount of information per item can be increased by chunking (for example, regrouping letters into words).

2   Patients with lesions to the temporal lobe of the hippocampus show that these structures are involved in the storage of long-term memories.

3   Chunking procedures in short-term memory require accessing information from long-term memory.

4   Coding of information in short-term memory involves at least visual, acoustic, and semantic codes. Evidence suggests visual coding occurs before acoustic and semantic coding.

5   High-speed short-term memory retrieval appears to operate by means of an exhaustive rather than a self-terminating process.

6   Memories seem to be stored locally and generally.

7   The neurocognitive view of long-term memory storage suggests that activation of neural circuits which results in an electro-chemical change and structural change in neural circuitry.

8   Coding in long-term memory is presumably multidimensional and most likely involves a semantic code as well as codes based on all sensory modalities. The literature has primarily emphasized semantic coding.

9   Capacity and duration of long-term memory are practically limitless.

10   Forgetting is the inability to recall information that was once available. The principal explanations of forgetting are decay, interference, and lack of proper cuing.

11   Memory decay proposes that forgetting occurs because of disuse of previously learned information.

12   Interference theory views forgetting as the result of events that intervene between original learning and later recall. The two paradigms most often used in studies of interference are retroactive inhibition (new material that interferes with old learning) and proactive inhibition (old material that interferes with new learning).

13   Cue-dependent forgetting proposes that recall failure does not necessarily mean that memories are lost but may merely be inaccessible due to an incongruence between encoding and retrieval cues.

Key Words

autobiographical memories	LTM
Brown-Peterson technique	permastore
chunking cue-dependent forgetting	proactive inhibition (PI)
codes in STM	probe item
encoding specificity principle	retroactive inhibition (RI)
flashbulb memory	reverberating circuit
forgetting	Sternberg paradigm
H.M.	STM

Recommended Readings

Among the most readable of recent books that contain lively discussions of STM are Klatzky, *Human Memory: Structures and Processes*; Baddeley, *The Psychology of Memory*; Lindsay and Norman, *Human Information Processing*; and Norman, *Memory and Attention* (1st or 2nd ed.).

On a more advanced level are Tulving's chapter "Episodic and Semantic Memory" in his *Organization of Memory: Quo Vadis?*; and Kennedy and Wilkes, eds., *Studies in Long Term Memory*.

Neisser's *Memory Observed* and Tulving's *Elements of Episodic Memory* are also recommended highly. Klatzky's book *Memory and Awareness* is a highly readable account of memory research from an information-processing perspective. *Practical Aspects of Memory,* by Gruneberg, Morris, and Sykes, has some interesting chapters. Cohen has written a fascinating memory book called *Memory in the Real World,* which is recommended.

See also *Memory & Cognition,* Vol. 21, 1993, which is largely devoted to the topic of short-term memory.

The Representation of Knowledge

T HIS CHAPTER IS ABOUT the representation of knowledge, which is to some the most important concept in cognitive psychology. Some even go so far as to contend that "Science is organized knowledge" (Spencer, 1864/1881). Before discussing knowledge— also a favorite theme of philosophers, theologians, and poets—it is necessary to understand how this often clouded term is used by psychologists. By *knowledge* we mean "the storage and organization of information in memory." Information, as we saw in previous chapters, is derived from the senses, but it is not the same as knowledge. Knowledge is organized information; it is part of a system or network of structured information. We focus on the representation of semantic information, since it continues to be the dominant theme in this area. In addition, several avant-garde topics that promise to change the way we think about how knowledge is represented and stored in memory are introduced. These topics include neurocognition and connectionism. Consider first the traditional use of words as a means to understand knowledge.

The traditional tools that have been used to elucidate human knowledge are lexical units—words, nonsense syllables, and parts of words. From Ebbinghaus through the most recent journal article, words (words alone, words together, parts of words, words visually presented, unusual words, common words, words in sentences, words that go together, words that are different) have enjoyed great popularity among cognitive psychologists.

Why this fascination with words? One reason is that the degree of verbal development in human beings far exceeds that of other species; hence, that attribute serves as a phylogenetic demarcation. Some estimates (Baddeley, 1990) place the number of words a person knows the meaning of at 20,000 to 40,000 and recognition memory many times that number. Another reason, most important for cognitive psychology, is that semantic structure allows us to identify what is stored in the mind and how the stored thing is related to other entities in the mind. Of course, for the cognitive psychologist, words per se are as uninteresting to study as are the bleeps on the oscilloscope. Words derive their vitality not from some intrinsic worth but from the concepts and relationships that they reflect and that make the facts and structures of knowledge come alive with meaning. By studying the ways words seem to be represented in memory, we can learn something about three components of the representation of knowledge: the content, structure, and process involved.

SEMANTIC ORGANIZATION

Semantic organization is normally conceptualized as a grouping or clustering of elements that are alike in meaning—for example, Reagan, Clinton, Bush, Nixon, Carter, Kennedy (presidents); Clinton, Carter, Kennedy (Democratic presidents); and Reagan,

Critical Thinking: The Extent of Semantic Knowledge

Read the following sentence: "Last summer Charlee saw Mona Lisa at the Louvre." How confident are you that.

1. Mona and Charlee had coffee at a sidewalk cafe on the Left Bank?
2. Mona smiled at Charlee?
3. Charlee had dinner in Paris?
4. Charlee carried French currency?
5. Charlee's IQ is more than 100?
6. Charlee is a male?

From this brief, uncomplicated sentence, a profusion of information is inferred, and it is likely that your inferences (as exhibited in your answers to the above questions) are very similar to those of other people.

Today, listen carefully to a simple sentence expressed by another person, and analyze it in terms of the way the words are stored in memory. What model of semantic memory would fit your observations?

Nixon, Bush (Republican presidents). More complex semantic models deal with the relationship of concepts to one another (for example, Clinton was a governer, Clinton is a Democrat, Clinton has a nose).

ASSOCIATIONIST APPROACH: DEVELOPMENT

Early in the history of psychology, words seemed to lend themselves easily to use in the dominant experimental paradigm, which was based on associating a stimulus with a response. Words could be used not only in paired-associate learning to test the rapidly emerging concepts of learning as a function of the frequency of associations but also as independent variables that had a separate character of their own. Lexical units (words, nonsense syllables, and parts of words) could be varied in terms of similarity, meaningfulness, context, orthography, and other dimensions, and they provided the early verbal-learning investigators with a well-stocked analytic arsenal with which to attack the problem.

Almost neglected in the flurry of research on lexical units was the larger picture of how the human mind transformed these verbal units into an organized structural network. Ironcially, as we have observed in other portions of this book, the genesis of the idea of organizational structure in memory can be traced to a much earlier period. Four years after William James published his classic work, *Principles of Psychology*, Kirkpatrick (1894) wrote: "A complete act of memory requires that impressions shall be retained, recalled, and recognized as familiar and as *belonging* with certain other impressions" [italics added] (p. 602). The technique Kirkpatrick used, which is now used to verify the way people organize verbal material, was to allow subjects to free-recall a list of words in any sequence they chose. This technique, so common in today's cognitive laboratory, attracted a few early disciples,[1] but interest in free-recall research as a means of studying memory soon died out and was dormant until the 1950s. The reason was explained by Kausler (1974). "The near suspension of research with the free-recall method is a testimony to the persuasive and long-standing clout exercised by Ebbinghaus on the verbal learning community" (pp. 332–333). This prodigious "clout" and the development of behaviorism (a doctrine inimical to consciousness-based views) lasted half a century, until the necessity to develop techniques that would disclose the way the mind organizes and imposes a structure on the information we perceive forced a return to Kirkpatrick's free-recall technique.

Organizational Variables: Bower

The contemporary period in the study of organizational factors in memory was influenced by a series of papers by Gordon Bower and his associates (Bower, 1970a, 1970b; Lesgold and Bower, 1970; and Bower et al., 1969). In the tradition of Bousfield but in the context of modern cognitive theory, Bower used organizational factors in both traditional and contemporary ways. As in past research, Bower attempted to demonstrate the influence of structural organization on free recall. Bower believes that organization of semantic entities in memory has a much more powerful influence on memory and recall than has been previously demonstrated. In one experiment (Bower et al., 1969), Bower's group looked at the potent influence on recall of organizational variables by constructing several conceptual hierarchies. An example of a conceptual hierarchy for the word *minerals* is shown in Figure 8.1.

These and many more experiments provided a bridge between an austere view of humankind's intellectual functions and one that envisioned a network of associations connected to other associations, and to other associations, and so on.

[1]See Kausler's (1974) excellent historical review.

Gordon Bower. **Made significant discoveries in memory, mnemonics, mathematical psychology, and language processing.**

FIGURE 8.1

A conceptual hierarchy of words for the word *minerals*. Adapted from Bower et al. (1969).

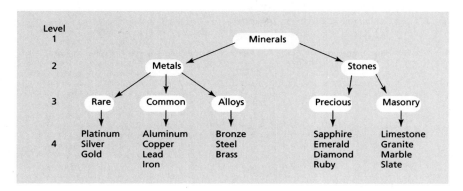

SEMANTIC MEMORY: COGNITIVE MODELS

The views of semantic organization described in the previous section were dominated by associationism, the doctrine that there are functional relationships between psychological phenomena. In recent times, the approach to semantic memory has shifted from the associationistic viewpoint to a cognitive viewpoint, which assumes that detailed cognitive structures represent the way semantic information is organized in memory. In the following section, some of these cognitive models are reviewed.

Set-Theoretical Model

In a set-theoretical model of memory, semantic concepts are represented by sets of elements, or collections of information. In this model, unlike the case with the clustering concepts, a word that encompasses a concept may be represented in LTM not only by the exemplars of the concept but also by its attributes. Thus, the concept *birds* may include the names of types of birds—canary, robin, hawk, wren, and so on—as well as the attributes of the concept—sings, flies, has feathers. In a set-theoretical model, memory consists of numerous sets of attributes—or, rather, of constellations of events, attributes, and associations represented by each lexical entity—and retrieval involves verification, that is, a search through two or more sets of information to find overlapping exemplars.

In its simplest form, verification of propositions (for example, "a robin is a bird") is done by comparing only the attributes of one set *(bird)* with the attributes of another set *(robin)*. The degree of overlap of attributes (see Figure 8.2) forms the basis for a de-

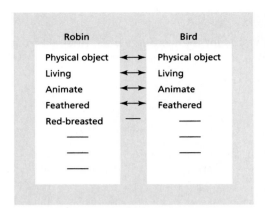

FIGURE 8.2

Attributes of two sets (*bird* and *robin*) with high degree of overlap.

cision about the validity of the proposition. As the distance between the sets becomes greater, the reaction time in making a decision should increase, a notion consistent with the research assumption inherent in some network models.

Two types of logical relationships between semantic categories are examined in this model: the universal affirmative (UA) and the particular affirmative (PA). In the UA case, all members of one category are subsumed in another category, which is represented as "All S are P" (for example, "All canaries are birds"); in the PA case, only a portion of the members of one category make up the member of another category—which is represented as "Some S are P" (for example, "Some animals are birds"). The validity of the statements is determined by the set relationships of the semantic categories. The set relationships, or commonality, is gauged by the number of exemplars the two propositions share. For example, the proposition "Some females are writers" could be represented as "Some S are P," where S represents "female" and P represents "writers":

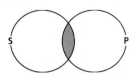

(You may recognize this figure as a Venn diagram, used to illustrate propositional statements.) The degree of validity of the logical assertion "All S are P (UA) and some S are P" is contingent on the amount of overlap (shaded area), or the exemplars they have in common.

To understand the model better, consider a typical experimental procedure. A subject is seated before a screen in which a sentence of the type "All coins are pennies" or "Some coins are pennies" appears. The subject indicates whether the statement is true or false. Statements of the "Some coins are pennies" type (PA) require less reaction time than those of the "All coins are pennies" type (UA). (One might reason that verification of the sentence "Some pennies are coins" would require a search of our memory only until a single instance of a penny's being a coin is found. That is, we would not need to consider *all* pennies.)

The Representation of Knowledge

The five models of representational knowledge may be summarized as follows:

Clustering Model

Concepts tend to be organized in clusters. Free recall of "unrelated" words indicates that categorically similar words—for example, camel, donkey, horse; John, Bob, Tom; cabbage, lettuce, spinach—are recalled together. (Notably the work of Bousfield and Bower.)

Set-Theoretical Model

Concepts are represented in memory as sets, or collections of information. The set can include instances of a category (for example, the category *bird* can include the instances of robins, wrens, eagles, and so on) and also attributes, or properties, of a category (for example, *bird* is characterized by wings, feathers, flight, and so on). (Notably the work of Meyer.)

Semantic Feature-Comparison Model

Concepts are represented in the memory as a set of semantic features. Two distinctive features are associated with an item's meaning:

(1) defining features, which are essential components, and (2) characteristic features. (Notably the work of E. Smith and Rosch.)

Network Model

Knowledge exists in memory as independent units connected in a network. The storage of words is tied to a complex network of relationships; for example, *bird* and *robin* are stored in terms of the relationship between them, that is, a robin is a bird. Specific models include (1) teachable language comprehender (TLC) by Collins and Quillian and (2) human associative memory (HAM) by Anderson and Bower and ACT* (adaptive control of thought) by Anderson.

Neurocognitive Model

Knowledge is represented in the organization of neuronetworks. Studies of pathological types, such as amnesic patients, have been done (Squire). Knowledge is in the connections between units (Rumelhart and McClelland).

Semantic Feature-Comparison Model

The semantic feature-comparison model of Smith, Shoben, and Rips (1974) and Rips, Shoben, and Smith (1973) grew out of an attempt to resolve inconsistent predictions of the other models. The feature-comparison model shares a set-theoretical structure with the set-theoretical model but differs in several important assumptions. The first assumption is that "the meaning of a word is not an unanalyzable unit but rather can be represented as a set of semantic features" (Smith, Shoben, & Rips, 1974). A broad set of features related to any word varies along a continuum from very important to trivial. A robin, for example, may be described according to these features: has wings, is a biped, has a red breast, perches in trees, likes worms, is untamed, is a harbinger of spring. Some of these are critical defining features (wings, legs, red breast), while others are only characteristic features (perches in trees, likes to eat worms, is untamed, and is a harbinger of spring). Smith and his colleagues propose that the meaning of a lexical unit can be represented by features that are essential, or defining, aspects of the word (defining features) and other features that are only accidental, or characteristic, aspects (characteristic features).

Take the example "A bat is a bird." Although one defining feature of birds is that they have wings, strictly speaking a bat is not a bird. However, a bat does fly, has wings, and looks something like a bird. Loosely speaking, a bat is a bird. Such terms as *technically speaking, loosely speaking,* or *appear to be* are all examples of linguistic hedges, which we commonly use to expand conceptual representations. As is shown in Table 8.1, a "true statement" would be identified on the basis of both defining and characteristic features; a "technically speaking" statement, on the basis of defining but not characteristic features; and a "loosely speaking" statement, on the basis of characteristic but not defining features. (Smith et al., 1974). Validation of a proposition (such as "A robin is a bird"), within the context of two types of features, is based more on the important (defining) features than on the less important (characteristic) features.

The first stage of validation of the statement involves a comparison of both the defining and characteristic features of the two lexical categories (*robin* and *bird*). If there is considerable overlap, then the sentence is validated. If there is no (or only tangential) overlap, then the sentence is judged to be invalid. If there is some overlap, a second-level search is activated in which specific comparisons are made between the two lexical units on the basis of their shared defining features.

Rosch has done research based on the logic that some members are more typical of a category than others. For example, a knife and rifle are typical weapons, while a cannon and club are less so, and a fist and chain are even less weaponlike. Rosch thought that because objects vary in typicality of their categories, the tendency might be to form prototype categories. Consider the category of birds. Most people would agree that a

TABLE 8.1

Examples of Linguistic Hedges

Hedge	Statement	Features Represented by Predicate Noun	
		Defining	*Characteristic*
(A true statement)	A robin is a bird.	+	+
	A sparrow is a bird.	+	+
	A parakeet is a bird.	+	+
Technically speaking	A chicken is a bird.	+	–
	A duck is a bird.	+	–
	A goose is a bird.	+	–
Loosely speaking	A bat is a bird.	–	+
	A butterfly is a bird.	–	+
	A moth is a bird.	–	+

robin is a good example of a bird but that an ostrich and chicken are not so good. When we use the word *bird*, we generally mean something close to the prototype bird or, in this case, something like a robin. In order to test the notion, Rosch (1977) presented subjects with sentences that contained the names of categories (for example, *birds* and *fruit*). Some of the sentences might be:

I saw a bird fly south.

Birds eat worms.

There is a bird in a tree.

I heard a bird chirping on my windowsill.

Rosch then replaced the category name with a member of the category (for example, *bird* was replaced by *robin, eagle, ostrich,* and *chicken*) and asked subjects to rate how sensible the sentences were. In each sentence *robin* was taken to make good sense, and *eagle, ostrich,* and *chicken* less sense. It seems plausible that the typical member of the category is similar to the prototype of the category.

The feature-comparison model seems to account for some of the unresolved issues of the set-theoretical model, but at the same time it has its own shortcomings. Collins and Loftus (1975) have criticized using defining features as if they have absolute properties. No single feature is absolutely necessary to define something (for example, try to define, in legal terms, a "blue" movie by using a single critical feature). A canary is still a bird even if it is blue, or has no wings, or can't fly—that is, no single feature makes a canary. Subjects seem to have difficulty in judging whether a feature is defining or characterizing.

In spite of the unresolved conflict between the set-theoretical model and the feature-comparison model, both models enhance our understanding of semantic memory in several important ways. First, they provide specific information about the multiple dimensions of semantic memory. Second, they use semantically categorized information as a starting point for an overall theory of semantic memory that embraces the vast network of memory functions. Third, because these models involve complex memory operations, they touch on the larger issue of the nature of our representation of knowledge, a principal part of which is the matter of the storage of semantic symbols and the laws that govern their recall.

Network Models

Collins and Quillian. The best known of the early network models, proposed by Allen Collins and Ross Quillian, grew out of an earlier conceptualization of memory organization that was based on a computer program (Quillian, 1968, 1969). The model depicted each word in a configuration of other words in memory, the meaning of any word being represented in relationship to other words (see Figure 8.3). In this example, the information stored with *canary* is "a yellow bird that can sing." *Canary* is a member of the category, or superset, *bird* (as indicated by the arrow from *canary* to *bird*) and has the properties of "can sing" and "is yellow" (arrows from *canary* to these properties). At a higher node, the general properties about birds are nested together ("has wings," "can fly," and "has feathers"), information that need not be stored with each separate kind of

FIGURE 8.3

Hypothetical memory structure for a three-level hierarchy. Adapted from Collins and Quillian (1969).

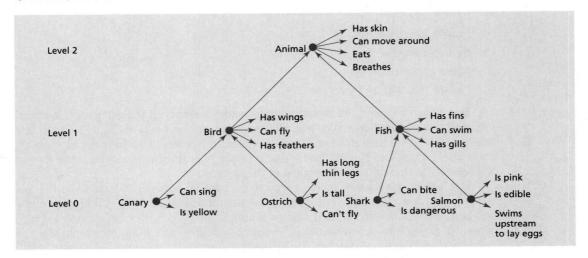

bird. Correspondingly, information about fish (for example, "can swim"[2]) is stored in another wing of the structure. The proposition "A canary can fly" is validated by retrieval of the information that (1) a canary is a member of the superset of birds and (2) a bird has the property "can fly." This system of semantic memory, by means of single rather than redundant entry of elements, minimized the space required for information storage. A model of this sort is considered to be an economical one in computer storage design.

An appealing feature of the Collins and Quillian model is that it makes explicit the means by which information is retrieved from semantic memory. To search our memory for validation of a specific proposition (for example, "A shark can move around"), we must first determine that a shark is a fish, a fish is an animal, and an animal has the property "can move around." This is a rather circuitous route. Another assumption of the model is that all this intrastructural travel takes time. Appropriately, Collins and Quillian tested the model by having subjects judge the truth or falsity of a sentence. The principal dependent variable is the time it takes to validate this; the independent variable is the proximity of items in semantic memory.

Collins and Quillian's model suggests that semantic memory consists of a vast network of concepts, which are composed of units and properties and are linked by a series of associationistic bonds. In spite of the fact that the model has been criticized on spe-

[2]As any Jerome Kern fan knows, "Fish gotta swim, birds gotta fly. . . ."

Clyde the Elephant: What Do You Know?

Consider a common happening of telling a story, in this example, a story of Clyde the Elephant. Already you know far more about Clyde than is explicitly told in those few words. You know, with a fair degree of certainty, that Clyde is gray, has a few scraggly hairs and four legs, and could not be taken for a ride in your Volkswagen. You have knowledge about Clyde, and you haven't even met him. Of course, you really don't know these facts about Clyde. In fact, you know very little in the sense of scientific validation of information. However, you know quite a lot about elephants, and since Clyde is represented as a member of that class, you can make many logical deductions about his character. Assume that knowledge is represented in a type of a descriptive hierarchy in which ideas are stored in terms of IS-A relationships (see the figure shown here).

In this system it is possible to see that an elephant is a (IS-A in the argot of knowledge modelers) mammal, a mammal is an animal, an animal is a physical object, and so on. One objection to this view of the organization of knowledge is that it requires many steps to an-

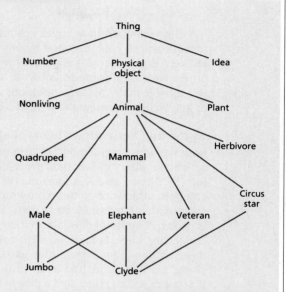

The organization of knowledge in an IS-A hierarchy. From Fehlman (1989).

swer questions about Clyde (for example, "Is Clyde pulled down by gravity?").

cific attributes, such as that the associationistic strength varies within the network (for example, the subordinate category of wrestling is less easily identified as a sport than baseball) or that some association violates the cognitive economy of the system, it argues for modification of the system, not abandonment of it. Furthermore, in its modifications, the model has provided an effective springboard to subsequent models.

As we have seen, the organization of knowledge in memory has been approached from several vantage points. One is to account for the rapidity with which we answer questions such as those in the list shown here:

Where is Moose Jaw?

Does a fish have eyes?

What is the square root of 50?

Which prime minister was known for the rose he frequently wore?

What is Beethoven's telephone number?

What is the name of Mick Jagger's daughter?

Why do some women wear high-heeled shoes?

Is an apple a porcupine?

How many of these could you answer, how fast were your answers, and what factors influenced your answers? If your access to knowledge is similar to that of others, it is likely that some of the answers were quickly located, others took more time, while others were impossible to know or ridiculous. (What is remarkable is that most of us can answer many of these questions, as well as many others, so quickly.) What model of knowledge representation might account for these differences?

Spreading Activation Theory: Collins and Loftus (1975). One system, which has become increasingly important (especially among connectionists), is called a spreading activation theory of semantic processing, developed by Allan Collins and Elizabeth Loftus (1975); see also J. Anderson, 1983b. The model, shown in Figure 8.4, is built on a complex association network in which specific memories are distributed in conceptual space with related concepts that are linked by associations. In Figure 8.4 the concept *red* is shown. The strength of association between concepts is indicated by the length of the connecting lines. Long lines, such as those between *Red* and *Sunrises,* indicate a somewhat remote associate; shorter lines, such as those between *Red* and *Fire,* indicate a closer association. At the heart of many knowledge representation models is the idea that concepts are associated as they are in the Collins and Loftus model. Also, with a bit of imagination, we could conceive a system of neuronetworks that embody some of the features of this model.

In the Collins and Loftus model, there is a spreading activation among concepts, which may account for the results of priming experiments (the effect of making a word or concept more accessible following the presentation of a related word, or prime). For example, if I show you the color *red,* it is likely that you will be able to recognize the word *RED* faster than you would without the prime. Furthermore (see Solso & Short, 1979), if you see the color *red,* recognition of its associate, for example, *"blood,"* is also enhanced. Presumably, even more distal associates would be activated; for example, the spread of activation may extend to associates of associates. In the above example, the color *red* primes *blood;* however, *blood* may prime *plasma,* even though the only relationship between the color *red* and *plasma* is through *blood.*

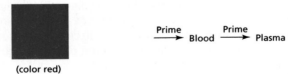

(color red)

In such an extended distributed activation network, an estimate of the capacity for the color *red* to prime *plasma* (through *blood*) is conceptualized as a function of the algebraic summation of all competing associates. Some effort has been directed toward this end (see Kao, 1990, and Kao & Solso, 1988).

Neural Imaging Techniques and Pathway Activation. In addition to the traditional behavioral study of activation pathways, recent studies have taken advantage of

FIGURE 8.4

A spreading activation theory of semantic processing. The ellipses stand for concepts, and the lines are associations. The strength of the relationship between concepts is represented by the length of the line. The assumption that knowledge can be represented as a vastly complex network of associations is a pivotal part of most neuronetwork models of cognition. From Collins and Loftus (1975).

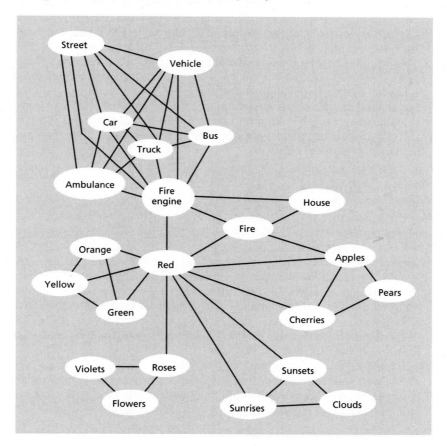

advanced neural imaging technology to show that physical, phonological, and semantic codes of words activate quite separate neural areas (Posner et al., 1988; and Posner & Rothbart, 1989). Posner and his colleagues distinguish between repetition priming, which comes from repeating the same item twice (such as showing a subject the color *red* as a prime for the same color), and semantic priming, which comes from presenting a semantically related prime and its target (such as showing the color *red* followed by *blood*). Behavioral studies have shown that both priming effects yield reliable data and seem to take place automatically, that is, without conscious control or awareness. Are these processes managed by different parts of the brain?

Using positron emission tomography (PET) scans (see Chapter 2 for details), Petersen and his colleagues (1988) evaluated regional blood flow in the cortex as a measure of neural activity associated with different semantic tasks. They found that visual word forms are developed in the ventral occipital lobe, while semantic tasks involve the left-lateralized part of the brain. The word form areas seem to be activated even when the subject is passive, for example, when the subject is told simply to look at the word. The semantic area is activated only when the subject is asked to process the word actively, for example, when the subject is asked to name the word or to classify it silently. These studies suggest that visual word form is automatic and mostly independent of attention, whereas semantic priming—the type of thing done to rough out the gross properties of representational knowledge—seems to work very closely with attentional factors that are both behavioral and, as we now know because of recent discoveries of brain flow, cortical. In addition to verifying the neural basis of cognition, these studies tell us more about the possible relationship between attentional factors and the representation of knowledge.

Propositional Networks

Representation of semantic knowledge in propositional terms is both the oldest and the newest game in town. The notion that complex ideas can be expressed in terms of simple relationships was central to ancient Greek thought, was a fundamental premise of nineteenth-century associationism, and has experienced unusual popularity among contemporary cognitive theorists. A proposition is defined by Anderson (1985) as the "smallest unit of knowledge that can stand as a separate assertion." Propositions are the smallest units that are meaningful. Many theorists subscribe to the concept of propositional representation of knowledge (see Anderson & Bower, 1973; Anderson, 1976, 1983a; Kintsch, 1974; and Norman & Rumelhart, 1975), and yet each interprets the concept somewhat differently.

HAM and the Representation of Knowledge. Anderson and Bower (1973) saw the representation of knowledge within a network of semantic associations called HAM, or human associative memory, as a principal issue in cognitive psychology:

> The most fundamental problem confronting cognitive psychology today is how to represent theoretically the knowledge that a person has: what are the primitive symbols or concepts, how are they related, how are they to be concatenated and constructed into larger knowledge-structures, and how is this "information file" to be accessed, searched, and utilized in solving the mundane problems of daily living. (p. 151)

To find the nexus between the problems of daily living and the representation of knowledge, they use propositions, which are statements or assertions about the nature of the world. A proposition is an abstraction resembling a sentence, a kind of remote structure that ties together ideas or concepts. Propositions are mostly illustrated with semantic examples, but other forms of information, for example, visual representation, can also be depicted in memory by proposition.

John R. Anderson. **Developed
influential theory of associative
memory (HAM, ACT*).**

The purpose of LTM is to record information about the world and provide accessibility to the stored information. In propositional representations, the principal structure for recording information is the subject-predicate construction. Simple declarative sentences illustrate the point:

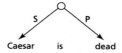

The sentence "Caesar is dead" is represented as having two components, the subject (S) and predicate (P), both sprouting from a "fact node," which represents the idea being asserted.

More involved sentences, such as "Diana married Charles," that contain a subject, a verb, an object (O), and a relation (R) to a modifying clause are represented in HAM the following way:

Many sentences involve context, for example (to borrow from Anderson and Bower), "During the night in the park the hippie touched the debutante."

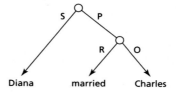

Here, time (T), location (L), and context (C) are added to a fact-idea (F) statement. Branches of the tree structures are joined by conceptual nodes, which are presumed to exist in memory before the encoding of a sentence. Nodes represent ideas and the linear association between ideas; therefore, understanding of a specific fact may be contingent upon the relationship to other conceptual facts.

The basic content is "wired" together in an associative web of more and more complex structures, but all can be broken down to sets of two or fewer items emanating from a single node.

ACT.* HAM was the basic associationistic model developed by Anderson and Bower (1973). A comprehensive model was developed by Anderson called ACT. It eventually gave way to ACT* ("act star"), which stands for "adaptive control of thought" and is the latest in the series of ACT models. We begin our discussion of this influential theory by describing its general framework (see Figure 8.5). Stimuli are encoded into working memory from the outside world, spin around the system, and outputs, in the form of "performances," are manifest in some actions. It is what happens when information "spins around the system" that is interesting.

In this framework there are three types of memories: working, declarative, and productive. These are defined below:

Working memory, a kind of enterprising short-term memory, contains information the system can access currently, including information retrieved from long-term declarative memory. Essentially, working memory refers to active memory, as shown in Figure 8.5. It is central to most of the processes involved.

Declarative memory is the knowledge we possess about the world (for example, knowing that good wine is produced in California and France or being able to recall

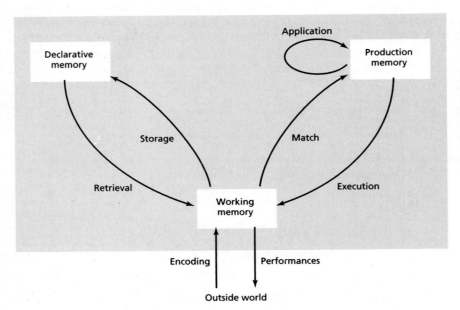

FIGURE 8.5

A general framework for the ACT* production model showing major components and their interlinking processes. From Anderson (1983a).

Declarative Knowledge and Procedural Knowledge

Thus far we have treated "knowledge" as if it pertained only to information about the world and its properties. Philosophers call this declarative knowledge, in the sense that we have knowledge of the validity of declarative sentences. When I ask you about the meaning of the following sentence: "I put my raincoat in the bathtub because it was wet," you know, that is, you have knowledge—that *it* in the sentence refers to *raincoat,* not *bathtub.* The reason you know what *it* refers to is that you have extensive knowledge about wet raincoats, bathtubs, human behavior, and perhaps certain people who don't want wet raincoats on their immaculate furniture. On the other hand, if you were in a burning building and preparing to make a mad dash for safety through savage flames, *it* might, understandably, refer to *bathtub.* However, traditional epistemology, the branch of philosophy that investigates the nature, origin, and limits of human knowledge, distinguishes between knowing that (*declarative* knowledge) and knowing how (*procedural* knowledge). It seems that some forms of humor are based on "catching" people who have been led to believe one thing and then are surprised by the true intention. One of the best-known examples is from Groucho Marx, who once said, "I shot an elephant in my pajamas. . . . What he was doing in my pajamas, I'll never know!" In the bathtub example, we know *that* it is used for bathing and, occasionally, for drying out raincoats, but we also know *how* to take a bath. That form of knowledge (procedural) is quite different from declarative knowledge. In any comprehensive theory of the representation of knowledge, then, it is important to include both forms of knowledge.

some of the contents of your last cognitive psychology class). It seems that in Anderson's view, episodic and semantic information are included in declarative memory. Declarative representation of knowledge comes into the system in chunks, or cognitive units, comprising such things as propositions (such as, "Beth loves Boris"), strings (such as, "one, two, three"), or even spatial images ("A circle is above the square"). From these basic elements new information is stored in declarative memory by means of working memory. When information is retrieved from declarative memory it resembles the calling up of information from permanent memory as might be stored on a hard disk in a computer and is temporarily held for processing in working memory.

Production memory is the final major component in the system. Production memory is very close to procedural knowledge, which simply refers to the knowledge required to do things, such as tie shoes, do mathematics, or order food in a restaurant. The difference between procedural and declarative knowledge is the difference between knowing how and knowing what. (The concepts of declarative and procedural representations are commonly used ideas in discussions of knowledge, and we expand on these concepts later in the chapter.)

At the foundation of ACT* is the concept of production systems, or the notion that underlying human cognition is a set of conditional-action pairs called productions. At the simplest level, a production is a pair of IF-THEN clauses, where the IF part specifies some condition that must be met for the second part, the THEN part, to be executed.

When a production is applied, its action is placed in working memory. A type of production rule follows:

> IF   *a* is the father of *b* and *b* is the father of *c*,
>
> THEN   *a* is the grandfather of *c*.

This production would function if we substitute names for letters. Thus, if the following propositions were active in working memory—"IF Andrew is the father of Ferdinand and Ferdinand is the father of Robert"—then the inference, "THEN Andrew is the grandfather of Robert," would be possible.

Other slightly more complex forms of productions can be shown in the following addition example:

> 67
> 39
> 72
> ———

In this example the application of a series of subgoals to work through the columns would be:

> IF   the goal is to do an addition problem,
>
> THEN   the subgoal is to interate through the columns of the problem.
>
> IF   the goal is to interate through the columns of an addition problem and the rightmost column has not been processed,
>
> THEN   the subgoal is to interate through the rows of the rightmost column.

and so on. In a similar example, Anderson lists twelve steps involved in a production system. The complexity of steps increases as the problem increases, for example, in the division problem $56 \div 4 = $ ____ .

Knowledge Representation in ACT.* Knowledge representation in ACT* is central to the theory. Anderson proposes a tricode theory of knowledge representation. The three codes include:

- A *temporal string,* which encodes the order of a set of items, for example, "one, two, three, and so on."

- A *spatial image,* which encodes spatial representations, for example, the coding of a square or triangle.

- An *abstract proposition,* which encodes meaning or semantic information, for example, "Bill, John, hit."

The properties of these three representations and the processes involved are shown in Table 8.2.

The first of these codes, the temporal string, records the sequential structure of events. With it, we can recall the sequence of events in our daily experience. For example, we can recall the sequence of events in a movie we recently saw or in a football game. We are less able to fix, in absolute time, the occurrence of these events.

The Properties of the Three Representations

Process	Temporal String	Spatial Image	Abstract Proposition
Encoding process	Preserves temporal sequence	Preserves configural information	Preserves semantic relationships
Storage process	All or none of phrase units	All or none of image units	All or none of propositions
Retrieval process	All or none of phrase units	All or none of image units	All or none of propositions
Match process			
A. Degree of match	End-anchored at the beginning	Functions of distance and configurations	Function of set overlap
B. Salient properties	Ordering of any two elements, next element	Distance, direction, and overlap	Degree of connectivity
Execution: Construction of new structures	Combination of objects into linear strings, insertion	Synthesis of existing images, rotation	Insertion of objects into relational slots, filling in of missing slots

From Anderson (1983a, p. 47)

Spatial representations have seemingly been problematic for Anderson.[3] However, in ACT*, spatial representations are treated as one of the principal ways information is coded. Configural information, the type of information displayed in a figure, a form, or even a letter, is thought to be encoded in memory, but the size of the configuration is less important. Thus, we may encode the letter *Z* in its correct orientation but not its size. We may recognize *Z* half its size or twice its size, but if rotated 90 degrees, it might resemble an *N*.

The encoding of propositional representations is more abstract than the other types of codes, since it is independent of the sequence of the information. The proposition "Bill, John, hit" does not specify who is the hitter and who is the hittee. What is encoded is that the arguments John and Bill are involved in hitting.

The representation of propositional knowledge is similar to our earlier discussion of HAM. Consider how the following sentence would be represented by ACT*: "The tall lawyer believed the men were from Mars" (see Figure 8.6). In this figure, propositional representations involve structure, category, and attribute information. A central node stands for the propositional structure, and the links that emanate from it point to various elements, such as the relationship ("believe"), the object ("man from Mars"), and the agent ("tall lawyer").

[3]In Anderson and Bower (1973) and Anderson (1976), the position taken was that the only type of knowledge representation is propositional.

FIGURE 8.6

ACT*'s proposition encoding of "The tall lawyer believed the men were from Mars." From Anderson (1983).

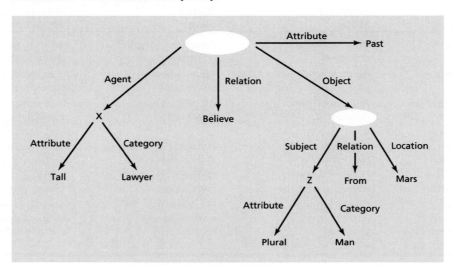

In addition to the general features of ACT* described in this section, Anderson has applied the system to a wide range of other conditions and cognitive tasks, including control of cognition, memory for facts, language acquisition, and spread of activation. These topics, all important, are beyond the space we can give to them here. (There is, however, no prohibition against reading the original sources.)

REPRESENTATION OF KNOWLEDGE—
NEUROCOGNITIVE CONSIDERATIONS

It is self-evident to say that people learn from experience. What is less obvious is that those experiences modify the nervous system and that the ways in which it is modified form the neurological basis for the representation of knowledge. One approach to the neurological basis of memory is through the study of the molecular and cellular biology of individual neurons and their synapses (Squire, 1986). Although such efforts have told us a great deal about the physiology of neurons, they beg the larger question of how these microscopic entities are related to knowledge representation. Recent studies in neurocognition have tried to integrate findings in neurophysiology with theories in cognitive psychology. One direction these studies have taken is to search for the location of memory.

The Search for the Elusive Engram

The controversy surrounding the locus of memory in the brain is presented in Chapter 2. A traditionally important issue is whether memory and knowledge are distributed or localized in the cortex. One element central to this discussion is the search for the elusive *engram* (literally, "a trace," or, in the present context, a collection of neural charges that represent memory). Some areas of the brain are associated with specific functions (such as vision), yet functions such as memory seem to engage various locations, each of which may function simultaneously, or in parallel, with other locations. Recently, Larry Squire (1986) suggested that information storage may be more localized than thought earlier and that memory may be stored as changes in the same neural systems that participate in perception. This hypothesis may seem contrary to the findings of Lashley (see Chapter 2), who concluded that memory is widely distributed throughout the brain. However, Squire argues that Lashley's views are consistent with his own if one considers complex learning (for example, a rat's learning to traverse a maze) as the processing of many types of information (such as visual, spatial, and olfactory) in which each type is separately processed and localized. "Thus, memory is localized in the sense that peculiar brain systems represent specific aspects of each event, and it is distributed in the sense that many neural systems participate in representing a whole event" (Squire, 1986, p. 1613).

What Amnesic Patients Tell Us When They Forget

One way theories of representational knowledge can be investigated neurocognitively is through the study of pathological types. Some studies done with amnesic patients (for example, Baddeley & Warrington, 1970; Milner, 1972; and Squire, 1986) show strong evidence for short-term and long-term memory.

Two types of amnesia have been identified: *retrograde amnesia,* which is the inability to recall information acquired prior to the onset of the disorder, and *anterograde amnesia,* which is the loss of information presented after the onset of the memory disorder. Retrograde amnesia is a disorder of the retrieval of information, while anterograde amnesia is a disorder of encoding information. Both types of amnesia can be temporary or permanent.

Temporary retrograde amnesia may develop when a person experiences head trauma, such as a football player who has "had his bell rung." (See Chapter 7 for a discussion of the football player mentioned in Lynch and Yarnell's study.) Sometimes a "ding" on the head produces retrograde amnesia, in which a few seconds or minutes of the person's life are lost to memory. Another form of temporary retrograde amnesia occurs when a patient undergoes electroconvulsive shock therapy (ECT) or suffers a serious head trauma, such as might occur in a severe automobile accident. In these cases, memories acquired over the previous weeks or even months may become unavailable.

Amnesia can also be permanent. Some causes of permanent amnesia include prolonged use of ECT, severe traumas, stroke, or other cerebral vascular ruptures, such as encephalitis and other diseases. Permanent amnesia can also be brought on by massive consumption of alcohol. One disorder commonly brought about by severe alcoholism is called *Korsakoff's syndrome.* It results in bilateral damage to the diencephalon. Korsakoff patients may be confused and have difficulty moving and seeing. Many times this is brought on by a final alcoholic bash in which the patient "drinks himself blind." If the binge does not end in death, recovery is possible, except for a permanent form of amnesia in which the patient has difficulty learning anything new. Both permanent and temporary forms of amnesia have been studied for clues to the neurological basis of cognition.

Cognitive Tasks and Amnesia. Temporary retrograde amnesic patients (for example, those patients whose memory is temporarily impaired as a result of ECT) can keep a short list of numbers in memory for several minutes with rehearsal but are unable to recall the information after an intervening period of distraction. It seems that temporal information is stored within a brain area unaffected by this form of amnesia, but the capacity for long-term memory may require the operation of other areas that *are* impaired by the disorder.

Another avenue of research has been to use amnesic patients to establish a neurological basis for short-term and long-term memory. In several important early studies (for example, Milner, Corkin, & Teuber, 1968), it was shown that a profoundly amnesic patient, known in the literature as H. M., exhibited considerable learning and retention of perceptual-motor skills. Thus, some complex cognitive ability remained intact in H. M., while other tasks, which required the recall of episodic events, were seriously impaired. (See Chapter 7.)

These seminal studies led other researchers to consider further cognitive tasks to study with amnesic patients, such as memory operations. In one study Cohen and Squire (1980) found that amnesic patients could acquire the skill involved in reading words from a mirror-reversed display, but when questioned later about the task, they could neither remember the words nor the skill they had practiced. (See also the case of K. C. in Chapter 6.)

Similarly, amnesic patients can learn the best solution to a puzzle, such as the well-known "Tower of Hanoi."[4] (See Cohen & Corkin, 1981.) To solve this puzzle, considerable parts of the cognitive system must be intact and operable. Specifically, it requires that both skill learning and the ability to learn procedures be intact; these comprise one type of mental representation. Amnesic patients, on the other hand, are deficient in their memory for facts and episodes, another type of mental representation. Since the root cause of amnesia lies in neurological disorders, we can conclude that underlying neurological structures support two types of cognitive tasks—those involving skill learning and those involving episodic recall.

Could it be that knowledge is represented in the brain in terms of knowing how (as in skill learning) and knowing what (as in episodic recall)? (More is reported on this in the following section on representational and declarative knowledge.)

Finally, some studies have investigated the priming effect, or the effect of a cue on subsequent performance, with amnesic patients. In one investigation by Jacoby and

---

[4]The "Tower of Hanoi" puzzle contains several rings of descending size stacked on top of each other on a peg. There are also two empty pegs. The task is to move the entire series of rings to one of the other pegs, moving only one ring at a time and always placing a smaller ring on a larger one.

Witherspoon (1982), several Korsakoff patients were asked questions such as, "What is an example of a reed instrument?" Later, the subjects were asked to spell *read* and *reed*. Normally, we would expect the spelling to be *read*, a much higher-frequency word, but in this experiment both the amnesic and control subjects spelled the word *reed*, because of the priming of that word in the question. However, when given a recognition test of previously heard words, the Korsakoff patients were unable to recognize the words they had heard. In contrast, the control subjects were able to recognize the words. These results suggest that the process of activation, as exhibited in the priming effect, is unaffected by amnesia, while the ability to recognize a previously heard word is affected. This latter ability may require additional processing of information and cerebral functions. Furthermore, these findings support the notion that an important distinction in the way knowledge is represented may be in terms of the activation of neural pathways and the access of episodic memory.

Knowing **What** *and Knowing* **That**

Our pursuit of the neurocognitive basis of representational knowledge continues with studies of *declarative* and *procedural* (or nondeclarative) knowledge. As previously mentioned, declarative knowledge is explicit and includes facts and episodes, while procedural knowledge is implicit and is accessible through performance. I may know that a bicycle has two wheels, a handlebar, and a frame (declarative knowledge), but I can only demonstrate that I know how to ride it (procedural knowledge) by actually doing so. One way to test for declarative and procedural knowledge is through priming and recognition experiments.

Priming, you may recall, is a test in which a subject is given a cue, usually a word, that is in some way related to the target, usually an associated word. The prime facilitates the recognition of the target. For example, if I give you the word *TABLE* (the prime), your recognition of the word *CHAIR* (the target) is facilitated. Priming is thought to tap procedural knowledge, because the response is implicit and there is a more or less automatic activation of existing pathways. Therefore, if amnesic patients demonstrate positive performance on a priming task, we could conclude that their procedural knowledge would remain intact; if they performed poorly on a word recall task, we could conclude that their declarative knowledge was impaired. Several experiments have confirmed this hypothesis (for example, Shimamura & Squire, 1984.)

A Taxonomy of Memory Structure

Studies have indicated that declarative and nondeclarative knowledge can be isolated by investigating pathological types. However, the question still remains of whether these types of knowledge are only a part of a larger system of the representation of knowledge in memory. If they are, what is the larger system? One approach to this problem is to try to fit the existing information about representational knowledge into a taxonomy, or an organized scheme. An intriguing taxonomy has been suggested by Squire (1986) and Squire et al. (1990) in which declarative and nondeclarative memory are thought to be the two major types of memory (see Figure 8.7).

Larry Squire. **Neurocognitive studies have helped establish important links between cognitive psychology and neuroscience.**

According to Squire, the experimental evidence supports the idea that the brain is organized around fundamentally different information storage systems, as illustrated in Figure 8.7. Declarative knowledge comprises episodic and semantic memories, and nondeclarative knowledge includes skills, priming, dispositions, and other nonassociative types of representations.

One feature of this system is that it accepts both conscious and unconscious memory as serious topics for research. In addition, information can activate both types of knowledge. For example, take the perception of the word CHAIR after seeing the word TABLE. From previous priming studies, we know that the perception of CHAIR is en-

F I G U R E   8 . 7

A tentative taxonomy for the representation of types of memory. Declarative memory contains episodic and semantic memory, while nondeclarative memory includes skills, priming, dispositions, and other types of memories. From Squire et al. (1990).

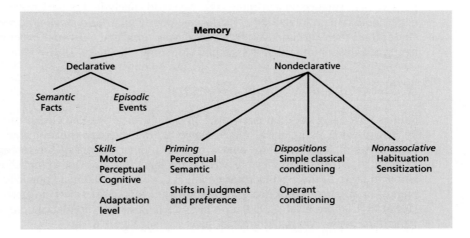

hanced if preceded by TABLE, and that the effect is largely unconscious and procedural. Priming is also likely to engage declarative knowledge in normal subjects. The engagement of declarative knowledge might be to store the word TABLE in episodic memory and have it become part of one's conscious experience. Supporting evidence for the model draws on a wide latitude of studies, including animal studies, the examination of histological sections, human cognitive experiments, and studies of the behavior of amnesic patients.

The importance of the above mentioned experiments and theories seems to lie in two domains. First, they address the issue of the structure of knowledge. As such, they integrate various types of memories in an organized scheme, which accounts for declarative and nondeclarative knowledge and for conscious and unconscious processes. Second, they provide some of the most eloquent examples of the unification of brain science and cognitive psychology, especially as related to the central theme of the organization of knowledge.

CONNECTIONISM AND THE REPRESENTATION OF KNOWLEDGE

Connectionism can be defined as "a theory of the mind that posits a large set of simple units connected in a parallel distributed network, (PDP)." Mental operations, such as memory, perception, thinking, and so on, are considered to be distributed throughout a highly complex neuronetwork, which operates in a parallel manner. The theory is based on the assumption that units excite or inhibit each other throughout the system at the same time or in parallel. This is in contrast with serial processing theories, which suggest that processing between units is done only in sequence. The number of pairs of units involved, even in a simple task such as typing a word, may be considerable. It is within the connections between pairs of units that knowledge is distributed throughout the system. How can knowledge, the most complicated of topics thus far encountered, be expressed in terms of simple excitatory and inhibitory connections between units? In this section we try to answer that question.

In many of the previous models of information representation, knowledge was stored as a static copy of a pattern. The position is similar to the concept of isomorphism discussed in Chapter 1. An object, image, or thought is stored in memory with its attributes and connections with other objects, images, and thoughts. When recognition of an item is called for (for example, "Do you know Clyde the Elephant?"), a match is made between the elements of the question and the information stored in memory. Also, the associates of the elements (for example, that elephants are gray), are activated, although the level of activation appears to be far less than for the central items *Clyde* and *elephant*. Still, the way knowledge is represented is more or less static, and the means used to access knowledge is through matching stored information with a cue.

Knowledge representation in connectionistic models of cognition is quite different from models that store objects, images, and so forth. First, in connectionistic models the patterns themselves are not stored; what is stored is the connection strength between units, which allows these patterns to be re-created.

"The difference between PDP models and conventional models [of knowledge representation] has enormous implications, both for processing and for learning. . . . The representation of knowledge is set up in such a way that the knowledge necessarily influences the course of processing. Using knowledge in processing is no longer a matter of finding the relevant information in memory and bringing it to bear; it is part and parcel of the processing itself" (McClelland, Rumelhart, & Hinton, 1986, p. 32).

Second, connectionistic models approach learning differently. In traditional representational models, the goal of learning is the formation of explicit rules that allow for retrieval of information and generalization of cues. We know that Clyde is an elephant and that, like most other elephants, he is gray and cannot easily fit into your Volkswagen. We know these things because we have learned rules. PDP models only assume that learning consists of the acquisition of connection strengths that allow a network of simple units to act as if they knew the rules. Rules are not learned; connections between simple units are. Even though our behavior seems to be rule governed, it is because of the underlying network of connections in the brain that we make these inferences.

Third, it is important to restate that the PDP model is neurally inspired; however, it is not the same as identifying specific neural pathways. Such a model would be imprac-

Nineteenth-Century Connectionism

Connectionism could conceivably be said to date from the ideas of William James. In his treatise called *Psychology: The Briefer Course* (1892), James described the process as follows:

The manner in which trains of imagery and consideration follow each other through our thinking, the restless flight of one idea before the next, the transitions our minds make between things wide as the poles asunder, transitions which at first sight startle us by their abruptness, but which, when scrutinized closely, often reveal intermediating links of perfect naturalness and propriety—all this magical, imponderable streaming has from time immemorial excited the admiration of all whose attention happened to be caught by its omnipresent mystery. [Therefore we should ascertain] between the thoughts which thus appear to sprout one out of the other, principles of connection. . . .

James also anticipated the rule on reinforced synapses that psychologist Donald Hebb would develop fifty years later. In *Psychology: The Briefer Course* James postulated, "Let us then assume as the basis of all our subsequent reasoning this law: When two elementary brain-processes have been active together or in immediate succession, one of them, on recurring, tends to propagate its excitement into the other."

At the same time, James described a mechanism for association that is uncannily like neural networks. Thought *A*, of a dinner party, is composed of details *a, b, c, d*, and *e*. Thought *B*, of walking home afterward, is similarly composed of details *l, m, n, o*, and *p*. All details connect all other details, "discharging into each other," according to James. As a result, then, "the thought of *A* must awaken that of *B*, because *a, b, c, d*, and *e* will each and all discharge into *l* . . ."; and *l* "vibrates in unison" with *m, n, o*, and *p*.

From Finkbeiner (1988).

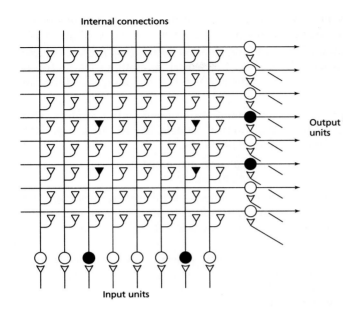

Internal connections

Output units

Input units

FIGURE 8.8

A connectionist association matrix. Input units are on the bottom, and output units are along the right side. The filled circles are active units, and the filled triangles indicate which connections would change so that the input would evoke the output. Learning of associative relationships involves changing the strengths between the input units and the output units. Modified from McClelland as suggested by Schneider (1987).

tical, since the model would be as complex as the brain itself. *Neurally inspired* simply means that the metaphor upon which the model is based is the brain rather than the computer, upon which some previous models have been based (see especially Collins and Quillian). The fact that PDP models are neurally inspired bears directly on the representation of knowledge. All knowledge is located in the connections, as might be the case with the neural connections. In the computer metaphor, knowledge is thought be stored in certain units. When we think of knowledge in the conventional sense, we are likely to think of it as being collected and stored someplace. The difference between these perspectives is considerable. For example, the PDP model suggests that "all knowledge is *implicit* in the structure of the device that carries out the task rather than *explicit* in the states of units themselves" (Rumelhart, Hinton, & McClelland, 1986, p. 75).

To illustrate the notion that all knowledge is in the connections, consider Figure 8.8. In this figure, input units are on the bottom and output units are on the right-hand side. Active units are filled in. Knowledge is stored in the strengths of connections between units, theoretically similar to the way neuronetworks represent information. The strength of the relations between units is simplified here. In the original system, detailed mathematical statements, which specify the strength of the connections, are given.

Summary

1   Semantic organization refers to the way concepts are organized and structured in memory.

2   Two principal viewpoints have dominated studies of semantic organization and differ in their respective focuses. The associationist approach has focused on func-

tional relationships between concepts, and the cognitive approach has focused on mental structures that describe the relationship between meaning and memory.

3   Associationist studies examine semantic organization by studying the form of free recall (for example, what words are recalled together), assuming such protocols provide information about the nature of the organization of concepts and the underlying cognitive structure.

4   Cognitive models organize data from semantic experiments into comprehensive theories of memory and include set-theoretical models, the feature-comparison model, network models, and propositional networks.

5   Set-theoretical models propose that concepts are organized by numerous sets of information, which include categories and attributes.

6   The semantic feature-comparison model assumes a set-theoretical structure but distinguishes attributes either as defining, essential features or as characteristic, descriptive features. Concept validation is presumably based more on defining features.

7   Network models assume that concepts are stored in memory as independent units interrelated by specific and meaningful connections (for example, "A robin is a bird"). Additional assumptions concern memory retrieval by verification of both target and related concepts and the idea that intrastructural movement during retrieval requires time.

8   The spreading activation theory of semantic processing (Collins and Loftus) is based on a complex network in which simple associations (for example, "red" and "fire") are linked together in conceptual space. The theory is instrumental in accounting for priming effects and the facilitating effects of recovering a word or concept from memory when preceded by a related word.

9   Propositional network models propose that memory is organized by a complex associative network of propositional constructions that are the smallest units of meaningful information (for example, "New York is large").

10   ACT* (adaptive control of thought) by Anderson is an associationistic theory of memory in which three types of memories are posited: working memory, declarative representation, and production memory.

11   Recent studies in neurocognition have tried to integrate findings in neurophysiology with theories in cognitive psychology. For example, studies of amnesic patients have proved quite profitable in the never ending search for answers about how the brain works.

12   Two types of knowledge have been identified: declarative knowledge and procedural knowledge. Declarative knowledge is explicit and includes facts; procedural knowledge is implicit and may be sampled through performance. A taxonomy of memory structure in which declarative and nondeclarative memory are integral parts has been developed by Squire.

13   Knowledge is represented in PDP models as connections between units, which is theoretically similar to the way neural networks represent information.

Key Words

ACT*	Korsakoff's syndrome
amnesia	network model
characteristic features	PDP
clustering model	procedural (nondeclarative) knowledge
connectionism	proposition
declarative knowledge	priming
defining features	representational knowledge
ECT	semantic feature-comparison model
engram	set-theoretical model
knowledge	spreading activation theory

Recommended Readings

In addition to those works on memory suggested in previous chapters, there are several good references on semantic memory. The early material on clustering in an associationistic framework is in Kausler, *Psychology of Verbal Learning and Memory*—probably the most authoritative historical review available. For those interested in a psycholinguistic point of view, Edward Smith has a broad, comprehensive review of semantic memory in "Theories of Semantic Memory," which is found in *Handbook of Learning and Cognitive Processes*, edited by Estes. A scholarly approach to semantic memory can be found in Kintsch, *The Representation of Meaning in Memory*, and Miller and Johnson-Laird, *Language and Perception*. Collins and Loftus, "A Spreading Activation Theory of Semantic Processing" in *Psychological Review* gives a current view of their theory.

Network theories are thoroughly discussed in Anderson and Bower, *Human Associative Memory*, a remarkably ambitious book. In *Language, Memory, and Thought*, Anderson gives a detailed account of a revision of HAM called ACT. Also see *The Architecture of Cognition* by Anderson. Another noteworthy book is by Norman and Rumelhart (and the ELINOR [see Chapter 16] research group), *Exploration in Cognition*. A recent book, *Neuroscience and Connectionist Theory*, edited by Gluck and Rumelhart, although technical in places, is highly recommended. Barsalou's book, *Cognitive Psychology*, stresses semantic memory and is especially recommended for those looking for detailed technical and theoretical discussion of these topics.

Mnemonics and Experts

THE PREVIOUS THREE CHAPTERS on memory covered the theoretical and empirical side of the topic. This chapter generally emphasizes a different perspective—the practical, or applied, nature of memory, mainly in relationship to mnemonic techniques and experts, with less emphasis on theoretical considerations. By mnemonics we mean techniques or devices, such as a rhyme or an image, that serve to enhance the storage and the recall of information contained in memory. Two parts of memory are incorporated into this definition: (1) the storage, or coding, of information and (2) the remembering of information that is stored. We shall see that some of the most successful mnemonic techniques assist in both these activities.

We first review some of the common mnemonic techniques, then discuss the intellectual faculties involved in mnemonic activity, and, finally, present some cases of extraordinary memory. The chapter ends with a review of experts, those people who have extraordinary skill in special areas.

People have long been concerned with memory and have long sought means to improve it—and for good reasons. Success, as commonly defined in business, law, medicine, schoolwork, music, and interpersonal relationships, is to a large measure dependent on the ability to recall specific information. Many people have capitalized on our concern for memory by selling memory courses and books that promise to increase memory in a few "easy lessons." We will look at some of these systems later.

MNEMONIC SYSTEMS

There are dozens of devices to aid (or in some cases replace) memory. Speeches are normally delivered from notes; television performers use teleprompters; salesclerks retrieve items from stock with the help of visual indexes; physicians check symptoms in handbooks; and students even compose "crib cards." Early Greek and Roman orators used a technique called the method of loci; religious people have used beads or prayer wheels to facilitate the recitation of formal prayers; generations of Native Americans passed on their rituals and philosophy through memorized stories; and the oral folk history of numerous groups is filled with vivid imagery, which enhances memory.[1]

Method of Loci

Among the best documented of the early mnemonic devices is the method of loci. Cicero, in *De Oratore,* describes the method in a story about Simonides, the Greek poet.

---

[1]The late Alex Haley, author of *Roots,* has indicated that much of the oral history preserved among his ancestors was rich in imagery.

Mnemosyne—Mother of Muses

In Greek mythology, Mnemosyne (from which the word *mnemonic* is derived) was the mother of the nine muses of arts and sciences. Memory was considered the oldest and most revered of all mental skills from which all others are derived. It was believed that if we had no memory, we would have no science, no art, no logic.

Simonides was commissioned to write a lyric poem praising certain Roman noblemen and to recite it at a banquet where many people were assembled. As the story goes, Simonides was called outside after delivering his poem. While he was outside, the building collapsed, killing the celebrants. The catastrophe was so devastating that even relatives could not distinguish one mutilated body from another. Simonides, however, entered the ruin and correctly identified each body on the basis of where it was located in the banquet hall. It is, of course, impossible to authenticate this story, but it does provide us with a clue as to how a mnemonic system based on location could work. Fixing in his memory the names of people in relationship to their location, Simonides was able to recall them.

The method of loci consists of:

- Identification of familiar places sequentially arranged.
- Creation of images of the to-be-recalled (TBR) items that are associated with the places.
- Recall by means of "revisiting" the places, which serves as a cue for the TBR items.

Does the system work? There is abundant casual evidence and some empirical evidence to indicate that it does. Gordon Bower (1970b, 1972) has analyzed the method of loci and illustrated the way this technique might be used to remember a shopping list.

Suppose the shopping list (left column) and loci (right column) are as follows:

hot dogs	driveway
cat food	garage interior
tomatoes	front door
bananas	coat closet shelf
whiskey	kitchen sink

The loci are arranged in a familiar sequence, one easy to imagine moving through. The next step is to create some bizarre imagery in which the items on the shopping list are associated with the loci. Bower illustrates this process in the following way: The first image is a "giant *hot dog* rolling down the *driveway*"; the second, "a *cat* eating noisily in the *garage*"; the third, "ripe *tomatoes* splattering over the *front door*"; the fourth, "bunches of *bananas* swinging from the *closet shelf*"; the fifth, a "bottle of *whiskey* gurgling down the *kitchen sink*"; and, finally, recall of the list activated by mentally touring the familiar places, which cues the items on the list.

Peg Word System

The peg word, or peg list, mnemonic system has several forms, but the basic idea is that one learns a set of words that serve as "pegs" on which items to be memorized are "hung," much as a hat rack has pegs on which hats, scarves, and coats may be hung. In one variation of this basic system, the subject learns a series of rhyming pairs, such as the following:

one is a bun	six is a stick
two is a shoe	seven is a heaven
three is a tree	eight is a gate
four is a door	nine is a line
five is a hive	ten is a hen

After the peg list has been learned, the learner must "hook" a set of items to the pegs. One way this can be done is by imagining an interaction between the peg word and the TBR word. For example, if the first word in a series of TBR words is *elephant*, it can be imagined to interact with *bun* (remember "one is a bun") in some way. If the interaction is bizarre, it seems that the effect is better than if the interaction is commonplace. In this example, you might think of an "elephant burger" in which a great elephant is squeezed into a small hamburger bun. If the next TBR item is *lion*, you might associate it with the peg word *shoe* by imagining a lion's wearing tennis shoes or thinking of enormous "cat's paws" outfitted with shoes. The use of peg word mnemonics in the memorization of a shopping list is illustrated in Figure 9.1.

Key Word Method

A slightly different form of the peg word technique is the key word method, used by Atkinson (1975), Atkinson and Raugh (1975), and Raugh and Atkinson (1975) in second-language instruction. A key word is an "English word that sounds like some part of the foreign word" (Atkinson 1975, p. 821). After subjects associate the spoken foreign word with the key word, they form a mental image of the key word interacting with the English translation. Thus a chain is formed between the foreign word and its English translation, composed of a key word that is acoustically similar to the foreign word and an imaginal relation between the key word and the actual English word. Consider *pato*, the Spanish word for "duck." *Pato* is similar in sound to "pot-o." Using the word *pot* as the key word, we could image a duck with a pot over its head. Alternatively, consider the Russian word *zronok*, which means "bell." *Zronok* sounds something like "zrahn-oak," with emphasis on the last syllable. Using the word *oak* as the key word, we could imagine an oak tree with bells as acorns. Figure 9.2 shows the stages of the process using this example.

How well does this system work? In an experiment by Atkinson and Raugh (1975), subjects learned 120 Russian words (40 words per day over a period of 3 days). Prerecorded Russian words were presented through headphones; for the experimental group, key words and English translations were presented visually and for the control group, only English translations were presented. Three training sessions were given each day.

FIGURE 9.1

Memorization using peg word mnemonics. From G. Bower (1973a).

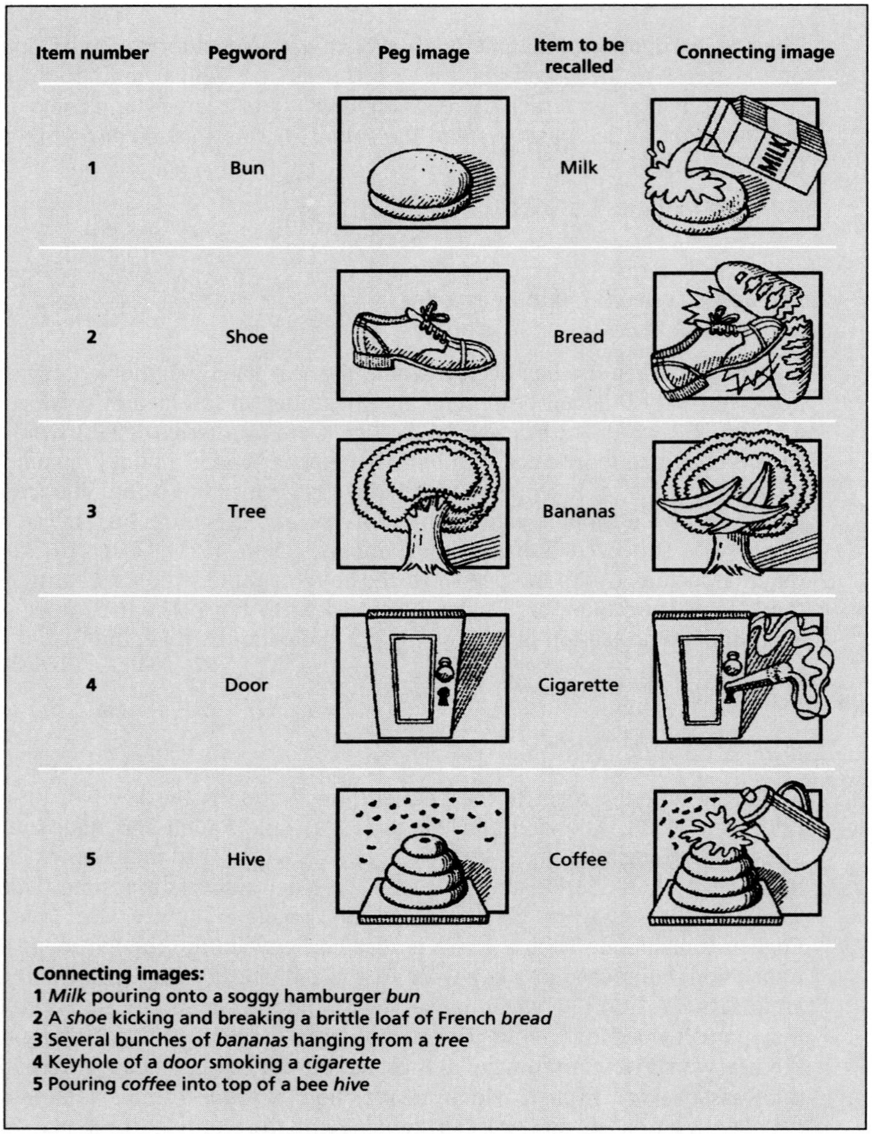

Item number	Pegword	Peg image	Item to be recalled	Connecting image
1	Bun		Milk	
2	Shoe		Bread	
3	Tree		Bananas	
4	Door		Cigarette	
5	Hive		Coffee	

Connecting images:
1 *Milk* pouring onto a soggy hamburger *bun*
2 A *shoe* kicking and breaking a brittle loaf of French *bread*
3 Several bunches of *bananas* hanging from a *tree*
4 Keyhole of a *door* smoking a *cigarette*
5 Pouring *coffee* into top of a bee *hive*

The key word group fared much better than the control group. In fact, subjects in the key word group learned more words in two training sessions than comparable control subjects did in three. Not only did subjects in the key word group initially do better than subjects in the control group, but, in a surprise recall session 6 weeks later, the probability of a correct response was 43% for key word subjects and only 28% for control subjects.

FIGURE 9.2

**Steps in learning the Russian word *zronok* by the key word method.
Adapted from Solso and Johnson (1994).**

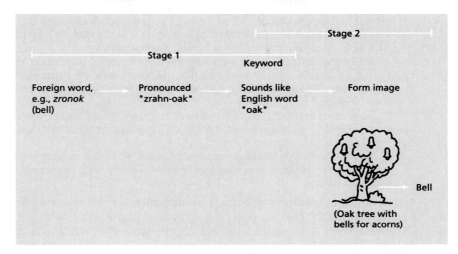

Stage 1

Stage 2

Keyword

Foreign word, e.g., *zronok* (bell) → Pronounced "zrahn-oak" → Sounds like English word "oak" → Form image

Bell

(Oak tree with bells for acorns)

The researchers also found that, in general, it is better to provide the key word rather than have the subject generate it.

Organizational Schemes

There is little doubt that knowledge is structured in a systematic way. As we learned in the previous chapter, the way knowledge is structured is the subject of much controversy, but few challenge the notion that some structure exists. All mnemonic systems are based on the structuring of information so that it is easily memorized and retrieved. The structure may be based on places, time, orthography, sounds, imagery, and so on. Another powerful mnemonic technique is to organize information into semantic categories, which are then used as cues for recall.

Suppose that, in an experiment in word recall, one group of subjects is given 2 minutes in which to learn by rote the following list of words:

bird	hill	web	smoke
boy	home	hand	wool
bread	nail	glass	vegetable
church	nurse	apple	train
feet	queen	hair	carpet
tiger	pepper	grass	star

After the 2 minutes, the subjects are asked to add columns of digits for 4 minutes. They then try to recall the words on the list.

Three other groups are given the same words, the same study time, and the same distractor task (adding digits), but with certain other conditions. The second group is also given a line drawing of the object designated by each word and asked to visualize the objects. The third group is asked to memorize the same words by rereading the following story, into which they are incorporated.

The Fantastic Trip

Instead of being in **church,** where he belonged, the **boy** was hiding on the **hill.** He had bare **feet,** although the **nurse** told him he might step on a **nail.** In his hand was an **apple** on which, from time to time, he sprinkled black **pepper.**

While a spider spun its **web** over his head, he dreamed of running away from **home.** The thread of this thought went like this. He would hide on a **train** until he got to the coast. From there he'd fly to a faraway **star** on a magic **carpet** or by rubbing an enchanted **glass.**

Once there he would marry the **queen,** lie on the **grass,** and never comb his **hair** or eat a **vegetable.** If he got bored, he'd hunt a **tiger** for fun and watch the **smoke** shoot from his gun.

But before the boy could finish the daydream, he began to grow tired. As he started to feed **bread** crumbs to a nearby **bird,** he saw a sheep with soft **wool.** He lay down on it and fell asleep.

And finally, the fourth group is asked to memorize the words as they are semantically organized below. (They are given the additional instruction that they can help themselves remember the categories by recalling the name *B. F. NAPP,* which is made up of the first letters of the category names.)

Body Parts	**Foods**	**Nature**
feet	bread	hill
hand	pepper	grass
hair	apple	smoke
nail	vegetable	star
		web

Animal Life	**Places**	**Processed Things**
boy	church	glass
nurse	home	wool
queen	train	carpet
bird		
tiger		

These categories can be further represented in a "tree structure" as shown in the figure here:

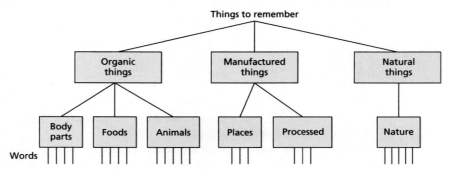

Which mnemonic technique is "best"? Douglas Herrmann (1987) found that some techniques work well for some types of material, while other techniques work well for other types. Specifically, for paired associate learning, imagery mediation worked best; for free-recall learning, the story mnemonic seemed to be superior; while for serial learning, the method of loci worked well. In another assessment of mnemonic techniques, Garcia and Diener (1993) found that when tested over a week the method of loci, peg word, and acrostics proved to be about equal in effectiveness.

One other very important component of mnemonic techniques is their effectiveness in organizing material. However, the effectiveness of mnemonics is also related to other considerations, many of which are addressed in this book.

Recall of Name

According to Lorayne and Lucas (1974), who wrote the popular *The Memory Book,* the learning of a name in association with a face involves three steps. The first, remembering the name, may be done by paying close attention to the way the name is pronounced and then by forming a substitute name or phrase for it.[2] For example, the formidable name *Antesiewicz,* pronounced something like "Ante-sevage," can be remembered as "Auntie-save-itch"; *Caruthers* as a "car with udders"; and *Eberhardt* as "ever hard"; and so on. These substitute names are rich in their imaginal properties. All of us can make up an image of these substitute names, some of them most bizarre.

The second step involves searching for an outstanding feature in the person's face—a high forehead, a beard, unusual glasses, a crooked nose, full cheeks, warts, dimples.

The final stage involves associating a substitute word with an outstanding feature. Thus, if you are introduced to a man whose name is Wally Kelly, whose distinguishing features are a receding hairline and ample belly, the *W* made by his hairline may serve as a cue for Wally, and the belly, a cue for Kelly. Of course, if you forget the code, you may mistakenly call him Walter Stomach.[3] Another example is the hockey player Esposito. The name suggests "expose a toe," which can then be associated with his nose, which may look like an exposed toe. Then there is Tony Bennett, whose name might suggest "bend net," a shape you can associate with the Golden Gate Bridge, which could be further associated with Bennett's rendition of "I Left My Heart in San Francisco."

---

[2]Note the similarities between this technique and the research by Atkinson (1975) and Atkinson and Raugh (1975).

[3]This brings to mind a footnote in Kausler's (1974) *Psychology of Verbal Learning and Memory:*

Strengthening your imagery muscle forms the core of "how to improve your memory" training programs. Long before imagery's present scientific fad, this author matriculated in such a mail-order program. I have forgotten why, having been an early drop out, but I do recall that Lesson 1 consisted of vignettes on the uses, and potential misuses, of bizarre visual images. For example, there was the young man who learned each new body-name association by creating an image of the body that exaggerated a prominent physical feature. The trick was to select a feature that would, in turn, decode verbally into the person's name. The system worked well until he was introduced to a Mrs. Humach. Her most prominent feature was a rather generous stomach. Upon encountering her again several months later, he greeted her with a friendly "Nice to see you again, Mrs. Kelly."

Unless relevant information is attended to (in the cases just mentioned, this refers to the name and the person's physiognomy), even the best mnemonic technique is useless. It seems that the first step in the successful coding of information is focusing our attention on the information we want to hold in our memory. Attention, also an important part of memory for other items (such as dates, words, ideas, and places) is the key initial stage in the memory process. Where it is not exercised, even the best mnemonic technique will fail.

Recall of Words

Nearly everyone has made up a word or phrase in which the initial letter of a word to be recalled is coded. Some of the better-known initial-letter mnemonic devices follow.

The names of the cranial nerves are learned by anatomy students according to this rhyme:

> On Old Olympia's Towering Top
> A Finn and German Vault and Hop

The nerves are olfactory, optic, oculomotor, trochlear, trigeminal, abducens, facial, auditory, glossopharyngeal, vagus, accessory, and hypoglossal. (Of course, going from the *G* in *German* to *glossopharyngeal* is another matter!) Every student of music has probably learned "*Every Good Boy Does Fine*" for the lines and "*FACE*" for the spaces of the musical staff. Some of us learned to spell *arithmetic* and *geography* by learning, respectively, "*A Rat In Tom's House Might Eat Tom's Ice Cream*" and "*George Elliot's Old Grandfather Rode A Pig Home Yesterday.*" The names of the nine muses can be prompted by the phrase "See, see, my Puttee," which can signify the code *CCMPUTTEE*, translatable to Calliope, Clio, Melpomene, Polyhymnia, Urania, Thalia, Terpsichore, Erato, and Euterpe. The acronym *ROY G BIV* is composed of the initial letters of the names of the spectral colors: *r*ed, *o*range, *y*ellow, *g*reen, *b*lue, *i*ndigo, and *v*iolet.

In these examples the mnemonic uses the first letter of the TBR word. It appears that the initial letter carries the greatest amount of information of any letter in a word, which would suggest that words are coded in LTM according to initial letters—as, for example, in the indexing of a dictionary. The second most important letter tends to be the last one (but the rule is frequently violated in the case of words ending in *s*, *d*, and *e*—letters that give little information). Crossword puzzle addicts are likely to be familiar with this phenomenon. If the initial letter is cued by a mnemonic system, it is generally the most salient letter cue possible.

Support for the cuing potential of initial letters has been demonstrated by Solso and Biersdorff (1975). Subjects were asked to recall a list of words. A word that was not recalled was then cued by either its first letter, something associated with the word in common experience, or a word that rhymed with the TBR word. If the subject still failed to recall the word, dual cues were presented, for example, the first letter *and* an associate. The rhyme, letter, and associate cue all aided the subjects in recall, but, most important for our present discussion, if the results due to guessing were compensated for, the initial-letter cue was the best for recall.

Critical Thinking: Expertise and Knowledge

In a recent paper, Bédard and Chi (1993) state that "the studies (of expertise) have shown that a large, organized body of domain knowledge is a prerequisite to expertise." What is knowledge? Before you read further, formulate your own definition of knowledge and relate it to expertise.

Experts in the field of expertise and knowledge believe that knowledge can be classified in terms of its quantity or its structure. Experts have greater quantity of domain-specific knowledge; a fact that is self-evident (an expert in carpentry knows far more about his or her craft than a novice). More important, however, is the way experts *organize* their knowledge. Experts organize knowledge in ways that make it more accessible, functional, and efficient.

The use of mnemonic techniques may increase one's specific knowledge base (a prerequisite for expertise), but the organization of knowledge is also vital.

EXTRAORDINARY MEMORIES

People with unusual or extraordinary memory may be classified as either professional mnemonists, those who consciously apply a mnemonic technique, or spontaneous mnemonists, those whose capacities seem to have developed more or less naturally without conscious effort and without use of a technique, or trick.

Although there are numerous anecdotal accounts of people with phenomenal memories, they are most difficult to authenticate. There are several accounts of such people, however, about whom much is known, and a few of these people have been studied intensively. Accounts of some of these are presented here.

S.: Luria

The most celebrated case of extraordinary memory (and also one of the best documented) is that of S. (S. V. Shereshevskii), whose capabilities were studied by the distinguished Russian psychologist A. R. Luria (1960, 1968). The semiclinical study began in the mid-1920s when S. was working as a newspaper reporter. He changed jobs several times and finally became a professional mnemonist.

S. was able to recall without error a list of words that was increased to 30, to 50, and to 70. Luria reports that "in order to imprint an impression of a table consisting of twenty numbers, S. needed only 35 to 40 seconds, . . . a table of fifty numbers required somewhat more time . . . 2½ to 3 minutes" (Luria, 1968, p. 21). A typical experiment carried out by Luria is described here:

[S.] spent 3 min. examining the table I had drawn on a piece of paper (Table 1), stopping intermittently to go over what he had seen in his mind.

Table 1

6	6	8	0
5	4	3	2
1	6	8	4
7	9	3	5
4	2	3	7
3	8	9	1
1	0	0	2
3	4	5	1
2	7	6	8
1	9	2	6
2	9	6	7
5	5	2	0
X	0	1	X

It took him 40 sec. to reproduce this table (that is, to call off all the numbers in succession). He did this at a rhythmic pace, scarcely pausing between numbers. . . . He read off the numbers which formed the diagonals (the groups of four numbers running zigzag through the chart) in 35 sec, and within 50 sec ran through the numbers that formed the horizontal rows. Altogether he required 1 min, 30 sec to convert all fifty numbers into a single fifty-digit number and read this off.

Several months later when Luria asked S. to recall the list, he did so as accurately as he had on the first occasion. Luria reports:

The only difference in the two performances was that for the later one he needed more time to "revive" the entire situation in which the experiment had originally been carried out: to "see" the room in which he had been sitting; to "hear" my voice; to "reproduce" an image of himself looking at the board. But the actual process of "reading" the table required scarcely any more time than it had earlier. . . .

Luria performed numerous experiments of the same sort with similar results. S. did not seem to forget—even if it involved nonsense material—after days, months, or even years!

Alexander Luria **(1902–1977). Made basic discoveries in neuropsychology and wrote book on S.**

Luria observed that S.'s phenomenal memory was accompanied by extreme synesthesia, a condition in which sensory information from one modality (for example, auditory) evokes a sensation in another modality (for example, visual). Most of us have some synesthetic experience; people tend, for example, to associate high-pitched tones with bright, piercing light, and dark tones with dark, somber colors. Few, however, are as synesthesiac as S., who, when he was mentally "reading" a series of items from memory, would hear noises in the testing area as if they were "puffs of steam" or "splashes," which interfered with his "reading" of the information.

When presented with a tone of 30 cycles per second with an amplitude of 100 decibels, S. reported that he first saw a strip 12–14 centimeters wide and the color of old, tarnished silver; a tone of 50 cycles per second with an amplitude of 100 decibels produced the experience of a brown strip against a dark background that had red, tongue-like edges. The experience was also accompanied by a sense of taste "like that of sweet and sour borscht." At 500 cycles per second and 100 decibels, S. saw a "streak of lightning splitting the heavens in two." The same tone at 74 decibels changed to a dense orange color that "made him feel as though a needle had been thrust into his spine." The same responses were obtained when the tones were repeated.

S. also experienced synesthetic responses to voices, once commenting to Luria, "What a crumbly yellow voice you have." His reactions to certain other voices were more flattering; one he described as "though a flame with fibers protruding from it was advancing toward me," adding, "I got so interested in his voice, I couldn't follow what he was saying."

E: A Case of Photographic Memory

During most courses in cognitive psychology, a student will inevitably ask something like, "What about photographic memory? Aren't there some people who can look at a page and tell you verbatim everything they have seen?" I don't know how my colleagues answer that question, but I usually reply, "If you know of such a person, bring him or her into my lab. Most of us have been looking for someone who has that extraordinary ability for a very long time." It is my experience that stories of people with "photographic memory" are apocryphal. The psychological literature is largely mute on this issue, although the Sunday newspaper supplements and supermarket tabloids are more vocal.

One case of photographic memory is reported by Stromeyer (1970). The subject, Elizabeth, is a very intelligent, skilled artist who teaches at Harvard. She can mentally project an exact image of a picture onto a surface. Her image appears to be an exact copy of the original, and Elizabeth can look at the image and describe it in detail. Psychologists call this *eidetic imagery* (a talent sometimes found in children) rather than the more trendy *photographic memory*. Elizabeth's ability is not restricted to visual images; she can also visualize, say, a poem in a foreign language she had read several years earlier. She can "copy" a line from the top of the poem or bottom equally well by writing as fast as she can, an ability that came in handy in high school examinations.

Is Elizabeth unique? In the two decades since the original report, no other such case has been reported. If there is another Elizabeth out there just waiting to be discovered, please—call home.

These synesthetic components seemed important in S.'s recall process, since they provided a background for each item to be recalled. The process is described by S.:

> . . . I recognize a word not only by the images it evokes but by a whole complex of feelings that image arouses. It's hard to express . . . it's not a matter of vision or hearing but some overall sense I get. Usually I experience a word's taste and weight, and I don't have to make an effort to remember it—the word seems to recall itself. But it's difficult to describe. What I sense is something oily slipping through my hand . . . or I'm aware of a slight tickling in my left hand caused by a mass of tiny, lightweight points. When that happens I simply remember, without having to make the attempt. . . .

There is also evidence to indicate that S. used the method of loci as a mnemonic. When presented with a series of items to be remembered, he would mentally distribute them along a familiar street in Moscow, starting at Pushkin Square and going down Gorky Street, and then recall the items by taking a mental walk along the same street using familiar landmarks as visual cues for retrieving the items. Errors arose from misperception rather than forgetting, sometimes because the item was not "seen," having been "placed" in some dark corner or because it was very small.[4] An egg, for example, might not be recalled because it had been "placed" against a white surface.

S.'s vivid imagery also tended to interfere with his ability to understand prose, and abstract poetry seemed particularly difficult.[5] He reported that, when listening to a voice, each word spoken elicited an image, which sometimes "collided" with others. When he read, he reported a similar type of imaginal interference. For example, the simple sentence "The work got under way normally" caused this reaction: "as for *work*, I see that work is going on . . . but there's that word *normally*. What I see is a big, ruddy-cheeked woman, a *normal* woman . . . then the expression *got under way*. Who? What is all this? You have industry . . . and this normal woman—but how does it all fit together? How much I have to get rid of to get the simple idea out of the thing!"

It appears that in S.'s case, his enormous capacity and the longevity of information are related to a combination of things, including imagery, synesthesia, and mnemonics.

V. P.: Hunt and Love

In 1971 Hunt and Love (1972) discovered a man (V. P.) whose extraordinary memory rivals that of S. The case of V. P. is particularly interesting to cognitive psychologists for two reasons: V. P. demonstrated an unusually expansive memory, and, perhaps more

---

[4]See Kosslyn's work (described in Chapter 10) for a noteworthy discussion of the size of images and the recall of features within the image.

[5]It seems that Shereshevskii sometimes enjoyed demonstrating his unusual ability to students and lay audiences. At one public demonstration the host asked him to memorize a string of numbers. The host went to the blackboard and wrote "36912151821242730333639424548515457." There were a few snickers among the mathematically sophisticated audience as Shereshevskii puzzled over the list for about a half minute. Then he turned away from the blackboard and recited the list perfectly. In the spirit of good fun, the host then told Shereshevskii that most of the people in the audience could do the same because the list was composed of a very simple linear progression of numbers. Shereshevskii was not amused, but the incident further points out the literal nature of his extraordinary memory. I learned this story while teaching at Moscow State University under the auspices of a Fulbright grant.

important, he was systematically examined by a team of contemporary cognitive psychologists who used many of the research techniques discussed in this book.

It is a strange coincidence that V. P. was born in Latvia and spent his early life in a town not far from that of S. By the age of 3½, he could read, and at the age of 5, he had memorized the street map of Riga, a city of 500,000. When he was 10, he memorized 150 poems. After World War II, V. P. lived in displaced-persons camps in Germany until 1950. At the time, because books were in short supply, a great deal of stress was placed on note taking and rote memorization. However, V. P. seems to have had an unusual memory even before this period.

At the time that Hunt and Love observed V. P., he was a store clerk, an avid competition chess player, and sometimes a graduate student. His IQ (Wechsler Adult Intelligence Scale) was 136, with the highest scores obtained on tasks involving memorization and the lowest on mechanical ability. He said of the latter ability that "I even have difficulty putting lead in a pencil."

Hunt and Love had V. P. read Bartlett's (1932) "The War of the Ghosts" twice. After having him count backward by 7s from 253 to 0, they had him recall specific portions of the story after 1 minute, 5 minutes, 30 minutes, and 45 minutes, and the entire story after 1 hour and after 6 weeks. (He was not told he would be expected to recall the story after 6 weeks.) Reproduction of the story after 6 weeks was nearly identical to that after 1 hour, and both performances were superior to the best by ten control subjects.

In a test similar to one by Luria, V. P. was asked to study and recall a list of 48 numbers. He did so perfectly after about 4 minutes of study time and recalled the series with only one transposition error 2 weeks later. Unlike S., V. P. did not seem to rely on unusual visual memory in this task; an example of the mnemonic he used was to store a row of numbers as a date and then ask himself what he had been doing on that date.

The results suggest that V. P.'s LTM was extraordinary. To test his STM, Hunt and Love used the Brown-Peterson paradigm (see Chapter 6). V. P.'s performance and those of twelve control subjects are shown in Figure 9.3. It appears that V. P.'s recall is much better over time than that of the control subjects, which would suggest that he is able to retain meaningless trigrams even in the presence of interfering tasks (which are believed to block rehearsal). V. P. did comment that, because of his knowledge of many languages, he was able to associate the meaningless trigrams in the experiment with a meaningful word. If this is the case, then the Brown-Peterson technique may be a test for his ability to store a meaningful chunk of information (a form of organization) over a brief period of time.

In introspecting on his phenomenal memory, V. P. stressed the importance of "concentration." Hunt and Love comment on this factor:

> In more formal terms, V. P. is much better than most people in creating stimulus codes. There is a conscious effort involved. If he can, V. P. studies the information he is to remember for a longer time than the average person will spend. When we watched him playing blindfolded chess matches, we could see that, although he was acting with considerable flair, he was also working very hard. He would make "casual" jokes while thinking about his next move, but the veins on his forehead were standing out. The fact that he could joke while calculating moves indicates he has an ability that most of us do not have: he can do a number of mental tasks in parallel. This would perhaps account for his phenomenal performance of the Brown-Peterson task. Unlike most subjects, he seems to be able to repeat numbers backwards while processing information in memory.

FIGURE 9.3

Recall by V. P. and twelve control subjects of three-consonant trigrams.
Adapted from Hunt and Love (1972).

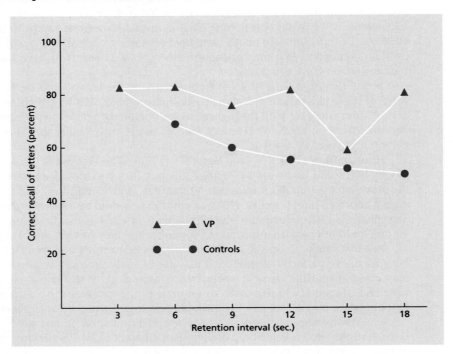

JC: Ericsson and Polson

There is a waiter in Boulder, Colorado, who is able to remember complete dinner orders
for twenty or more people. He is known as JC (John Conrad) in the psychological literature. Ericsson and Polson (1988a, 1988b) have studied JC extensively. In addition to
the intrinsic interest of this case,[6] Ericsson and Polson have analyzed JC experimentally
and within the context of theories of cognitive psychology.

For more than two years, JC has appeared in Ericsson and Polson's laboratory,
which resembles a restaurant, to take orders and recall information from memory. In a
typical experiment, "customers" (actually photographs of faces) are situated around a
table with a stack of cards before them. On the cards are "orders," which have been randomly generated by a computer. The "menu" consists of four categories of food: en-
trées, temperature (for example, rare, medium rare, and so forth), salad dressing, and
starches. Between 3 and 7 items are available within each category (for example, en-

---

[6]When was the last time you had a waiter who could remember your order, even with a note pad? "Now,
let's see, who ordered the chicken fricassee?"

trées included steak Oscar, sirloin brochette, filet mignon, rib eye, barbecue, Boulder steak, and teriyaki). JC would select one customer, take the order (as read by the experimenter), and then continue clockwise around the table until all orders were heard. JC was usually asked to recall the orders soon after they had been taken; but at least once, the experimenters asked him to recall orders taken hours before.

Several inconsistencies exist between the laboratory setting and a real restaurant, most of which the experimenters were aware. One would suspect that JC might do much better with the orders in his home environment, where the cues are richer and give greater latitude for forming associations. Also, cardboard faces, an important retrieval cue, are not the same as warm-blooded bodies. Dinner orders randomly generated by a computer, even with the constraint that each order contain a salad, an entrée, a starch, and cooking instructions, might result in a real mishmash diet. Also, the experimenters did not include a category for wine—a barbaric oversight! Nevertheless, the situation provided an adequate stage for JC to show his acumen. (General psychology students served as control subjects.)

The overall results of these experiments are shown in Figure 9.4. Most apparent is that JC did not forget orders, even when the information load was great—and certainly in excess of the "magical number 7." It may appear that the task is not all that challenging, but it is—amateurs fared poorly with large orders.

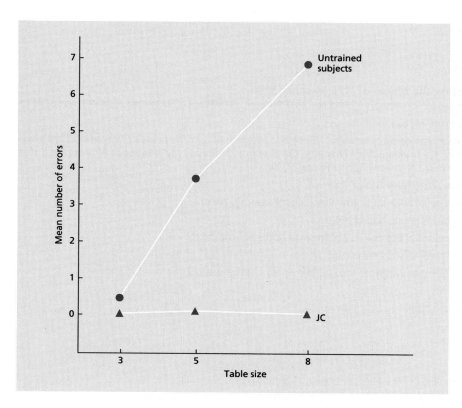

FIGURE 9.4

Average number of errors for JC and untrained subjects as a function of table size. From Ericsson and Polson (1988a).

How did JC perform so well? Essentially, he used an organizational scheme to encode orders. One part of the organization of information was to encode orders in groups of four. After taking the first four orders, he carefully studied and rehearsed them. Then, as if he turned over a new page, he dealt with the next four orders, almost as if he deposited the first set of information from STM to an intermediate-term memory store and then opened a new STM store. JC also encoded the menu information in unique ways. For salad information he used the first letter of each dressing; bleu cheese was *B*, oil and vinegar was *O*, and so on. The degree to which steaks were to be cooked was a type of spatial pattern. For example, if one set of four cooking orders were "rare, medium, medium rare, and rare," the image created would resemble a kind of inverted *V* or, perhaps appropriate to the geography of Colorado, an inverted peak.

In one phase of the experiment, JC was asked to "think aloud" as he took orders from five customers. A portion of that protocol is shown in Table 9.1. Note that throughout the narrative, JC is attending to and speculating about the customer (for example, "Well done and rice seem to fit that guy. Steak Oscar doesn't"). Finally, Ericsson and Polson asked whether JC's ability could generalize to other types of information not related to culinary matters by presenting lists of nonfood-related words. It did, and JC was able to recall these items much better than did the control subjects, although not quite as well as food-related items.

It is difficult to know whether JC is unusually gifted in memory ability. However, it is clear that he has developed a series of mnemonic devices, most of which have been described in this chapter, to enhance the coding and retrieving of information in a mea-

T A B L E   9 . 1

Protocol Data Supporting the Model of JC's Memory Skill

E: *Why don't you start thinking out loud.*

S: *Oh, it is five. I thought it was going to be eight. These five people look like they don't fit together. That's unusual. Out of your real estate magazine. This guy, the first guy, looks like he's way out of place with this group of people, so we'll see how easy his order is. OK. Go.*

E: *Steak Oscar, well done, Thousand Island, rice.*

S: *OK. Well done and rice seem to fit that guy. Steak Oscar doesn't. Next.*

E: *Barbeque, well done, bleu cheese, baked potato.*

S: *That sounds fairly standard. TB is my salad dressing notation and next.*

E: *Filet mignon, medium well, Thousand Island, fries.*

S: *TBT, rice, baker, fries. Temperatures are making an easy pattern. Next.*

E: *Filet Mignon, rare, oil and vinegar, fries.*

S: *TB. What's the salad dressing?*

E: *Thousand Island.*

S: *TBTO. Starch for No. 4?*

E: *Fries.*

S: *Fries, OK. Rice, baker, fries, fries, TBTO. Next . . .*

surable way. That ability seems to be applicable to other, nonspecialized types of memory operations.

Others

Several other cases of extraordinary memory have appeared in the literature. One such is reported by Hunter (1962), who documented the unusual mathematical skill of A. C. Aitken, a professor of mathematics at the University of Edinburgh, Scotland.[7] In 1933 Aitken's memory was tested by presenting him with 25 unrelated words, which he read through twice. Asked to recall the list 27 years later, he began with a few words and then gradually increased the list until all 25 words were correctly recalled. He had also read and memorized a form of "The War of the Ghosts" and recalled it nearly perfectly 27 years later. His memory and retrieval ability were no less spectacular than his numerical ability. On hearing the number *1961*, Aitken immediately recognized it as 37×53, and also $44^2 + 5^2$ and $40^2 + 19^2$.

Another case of extraordinary memory, reported by Coltheart and Glick (1974), is of interest because it deals with iconic memory (see Chapter 3). Their subject, Sue d'Onim[8] (or O.), had the ability to "talk backward"—that is, to pronounce a normally presented word backward.[9] (Thus *major* would be "rojam"; *plastic*, "citsalp"; *peppertree*, "eertreppep.") O.'s iconic memory seemed to be considerably greater than would be expected. Shown a row of 8 letters for 100 milliseconds, she was able to report a mean of 7.44, while control subjects reported about 5. Coltheart (1972b) interprets these results to mean that O. can visually encode information about four times faster than normal.

Unfortunately, far too few cases of extraordinary memory have been reported to make more than superficial generalizations about it. Indeed, one observation we can make about the cases described here is that the memory characteristics of the individuals studied are all somewhat different. S. and V. P. seem to have used some type of mnemonic system whose structure was less rigid than others—in S.'s case, imagery, and in V. P.'s, semantic mediation. JC seems to use an elaborate organizational structure. Aitken's extraordinary memory seems to incorporate some use of images and rhythm but also seems quite different from the others.

EXPERTS AND EXPERTISE

We close this chapter with a discussion of experts, people who have unusual cognitive abilities, and of expertise, the study of exceptional abilities and skills. There are two parts in this section: the first deals with several observations of experts and their development, while the second part deals with the cognitive interpretation of these observations.

---

[7]Some of the following material is from Hunter as reported in Baddeley, *The Psychology of Memory* (1976).

[8]Coltheart's pun for *pseudonym* and probably a takeoff on Freud's famous case study.

[9]An American entertainer called "Dr. Backwards" of several years ago had a nightclub act in which he pronounced and spelled words backward. There is also a current, although obscure, comic who reproduces sounds backward, much as you might hear if you reversed a tape recording.

One thing that distinguishes us from other creatures is our ability to acquire complex skills. All distinctively human activities—such as mathematics, language, chess, computer programming, sculpture—are acquired skills. . . . People become expert at activities for which there was no possibility of anticipation in our evolutionary history, and the essence of the human genius is just this plasticity.

John R. Anderson

Interest in expertise grew out of artificial intelligence (AI) several years ago and the need to find workable computer programs that could simulate the performance of skilled humans.[10] However, the cognitive study of expertise has recently developed a life of its own. These initial computer programs, sometimes called "expert systems," were designed to mimic what a human expert knows. The problem is that much of the knowledge an expert knows is not formalized.[11] Nevertheless, these tricks of the trade can tell us a great deal about the way information is structured in the minds of experts and novices. They also have some practical application, as in medical diagnosis by "thinking computers" that simulate the diagnostic procedures used by skilled physicians. We touched on these topics in Chapter 4, when we examined the way grand master chess players perceive a chess display. These investigations of skilled chess players have provided AI scientists with just the type of information they need to build intelligent chess-playing programs—and the results have been spectacular, with computers now beating all but the very best players in the world. The study of expertise, however, is not confined to serving the needs of AI. It is an interesting and worthy topic for cognitive psychologists to study, both for its theoretical and pragmatic value. After all, if we choose to develop talented students to become experts, we need some idea of what the cognitive dimensions are that separate the expert from the novice.

After reviewing a large number of studies of experts, Glaser and Chi (1988) have identified some of the characteristics of experts, which follow:

1. Experts excel mainly in their own domains. Experts in mental calculations, for example, are not likely to be experts in medical diagnosis and vice versa.

2. Experts perceive large meaningful patterns in their domain. Chess masters, X-ray diagnosticians, and architects are able to "see" more meaningful patterns within their specialty than nonspecialists.

---

[10]Another area intensely studied, especially by the Soviets and the "human potential" movement in America, is the concept of "peak experience," as might be attained by an athlete during competition.

[11]Things you don't learn in medical school (but should!): A pediatrician I knew kept his stethoscope in a warm compartment, thus diminishing the shock of placing a cold metal instrument on a fevered little body. Were his measurements more accurate? It's hard to tell without empirical validation, but I'm sure his tiny patients were more comfortable.

3. Experts are fast. Expert typists, chess players, computer programmers, mathematicians, and so on work within their specialty with greater speed than others.

4. Experts seem to utilize STM and LTM effectively. It seems that experts have superior memories, but perhaps they simply utilize their memories better.

5. Experts see and represent a problem in their domain at a deeper level than novices. When experts are asked to sort and analyze problems, they tend to deal with deep issues rather than superficial ones.

6. Experts spend a great deal of time analyzing a problem qualitatively. They tend to look at a problem from several angles before plunging into its solution.

7. Experts have self-monitoring skills. They seem to be aware of their errors and are able to make in-course corrections.

The investigation of experts has taken two directions. The first is to find exceptionally skilled people and examine their talent. A sample of these studies includes:[12]

Actors (Intons-Peterson & Smyth, 1987, Noice, 1991; Noice & Noice, 1993).
Architecture (Akin, 1982)
Auditing (Bédard, 1989)
Baseball (Chiesi, Spilich, & Voss, 1979)
Bridge (Charness, 1979)
Chess (Chase & Simon, 1973a, 1973b; among children see Chi, 1978)
Dance (Solso et al., 1986; Solso, 1989; Solso & Dollab, 1995)
Exceptional memories (for example, S. [Luria, 1974], V. P. [Hunt & Love, 1972], and JC [Ericsson & Polson, 1988a&b]
"Geniuses" (for example, in music, chess, science: Hayes, 1986)
Go (Reitman, 1976)
Mathematical ability (for example, A. C. Aitken: Hunter, 1962)
Medical diagnosis (Clancey, 1988; Lesgold et al., 1988)
Musicians (Halpern, 1989)
Physics students (Chi, Glaser, & Rees, 1982)
Stockbrokers (Johnson, 1988)
Taking food orders (Ericsson & Polson, 1988a, 1988b)
Typing (Gentner, 1988)

A second method has been to pick an average citizen (the type you might find standing along the sunny side of a barbershop) and train that person in some skill. Both research methods have their strengths, weaknesses, and assumptions. In the first methodology, it is tempting to assume that experts are born, not made, while in the second methodology, the temptation is to assume the opposite. Before becoming entangled in a nature versus nurture squabble, it is safe to conclude that expertise cannot be developed without some inherent capacity, and that expertise rarely erupts spontaneously and without encouragement (for a more detailed analysis of this issue see Ericsson, Krampe, and Tesch-Römer, 1993). We now turn our attention to some of the theoretical issues involved in the study of expertise.

[12]These well-conducted, interesting studies are recommended reading.

The Structure of Knowledge and Expertise

Thus far we have concentrated on a description of expertise. Some of this research has been based on the selection of samples of subjects—some experts, some novices, and some real tyros, as in the case of the three levels of chess plays described in Chapter 4—and on an evaluation of their knowledge and organization expertise. Two features of the expert (as contrasted with the novice) seem to reappear in the literature. The expert has domain-specific, organized knowledge and knows how to use it efficiently and wisely. For example, it is estimated that a chess master has about 50,000 patterns in memory; a good player, about 1000; and a beginner, only a few. However, the storage of passive information on any given topic alone does not constitute expertise. Organization of knowledge is important too.

In one important study of the organization of information, Chi, Feltovich, and Glaser (1981) used a card-sorting task to see how experts and novices classified problems. Each card had a diagram and description of a physics problem. The novices sorted problems on the basis of literal, surface features, such as the "problems deals with blocks on an inclined plane"; the experts tended to sort the problems on the basis of the principles used to solve the problem, such as the conservation of energy. This trait (surface analysis versus analysis of principles) holds for a variety of different specialties including mathematics, computer programming, and genetics. The same results are found in the classification and analysis of real-world phenomena such as pictures of dinosaurs, types of cameras, and electronic circuit diagrams. Experts have greater knowledge than novices and tend to organize their knowledge in terms of general principles rather than in terms of surface features.

Theoretical Analysis of Expertise

Are people who have developed extraordinary cognitive abilities an embarrassment to traditional cognitive theory? Take the issue of STM. We learned in previous chapters that STM was restricted to a limited number of items temporarily stored, yet the multiplication of numbers, such as $4,652 \times 93$, seems to require the storage of more than 7 items and processing that exceeds STM's capacity. Either the experts introduced in this chapter and others have a different memory system than most of us, or they are using existing knowledge, stored in LTM, to expand their working memory capacity.

Chase and Ericsson (1982) have explained extraordinary memory operations in terms of three principles that account for skilled memory and how experts exploit their LTM to perform unusual tasks.

1. *The mnemonic encoding principle (organization).* This principle asserts that experts encode information in terms of a large existing knowledge base. In memorizing a large number of digits, for example, one expert, a long-distance runner, used "good times" for a one-mile run, a marathon, a 3-kilometer run, and so on to remember various chunks of digits. Is his STM capacity larger? It is doubtful. More likely, he is using existing knowledge to chunk new information. (See Bower & Springston, 1970; and the FBI, PHD, IBM, TWA study in Chapter 7.)

2. *The retrieval structure principle (access).* This principle states that experts use their knowledge of a subject (for example, typing, chess, baseball, selection of

stocks) to develop abstract, highly specialized mechanisms for systematically encoding and retrieving meaningful patterns from LTM. This ability allows experts to anticipate the informational needs of a familiar task and to store new information in a format that will facilitate its retrieval.

3. *The speed-up principle (speed).* Practice increases the speed with which experts recognize and encode patterns. In addition, experts are also able to retrieve information from LTM more quickly than novices. If LTM storage and retrieval are facilitated with extensive practice, then the extent to which new information can be processed is seemingly unlimited.

One ingredient almost overlooked in our discussion of experts is practice, the theme of a detailed analysis by Ericsson, Krampe, and Tesch-Römer (1993). It would seem that underlying the development of experts are hours and hours of dedicated practice. The adage "practice makes perfect," although too simplistic to qualify as a scientific principle, is nevertheless of great significance in the nurturing of skill and expertise.[13] Although simple, mindless, brute practice seems counterproductive but distributed, "intelligent" practice is positively related to expertise.

[13]Several years ago the late Bill Chase gave a talk on experts in which he promised to tell the audience what it would take to become a grand master chess player. His answer: "Practice." After the talk, I asked Chase how much practice. "Did I forget to say how much?" he asked quizzically. "Ten thousand hours."

Summary

1 Mnemonics are techniques that facilitate storage, or encoding, and the recall of information in memory.

2 A variety of mnemonic techniques have been devised and involve such strategies as imagery and mediation (for example, method of loci and peg word system), phonemic and orthographic characteristics (for example, word and number recall), phonemic cues and imagery mediation (for example, name recall and key word method), and semantic organization.

3 The success of mnemonics in facilitating memory is attributed to their assistance in organizing information.

4 Studies of individuals with exceptional memories indicate that their abilities involve a variety of mnemonic technique combinations: method of loci, imagery, and modified peg word system; method of loci, imagery, and synesthesia (for example, S.); and semantic mediation (for example, V. P.).

5 Studies of experts show that they excel in their own domain, perceive meaningful patterns, are fast, utilize LTM and STM well, represent a problem at a deep level, analyze a problem qualitatively, and have self-monitoring skills.

6 Some ordinary people have been trained to perform exceptional mathematical computations and remember long strings of numbers. They do so by efficiently utilizing knowledge in LTM.

7 Skilled performance is achieved through organization of material, access to knowledge, speed of encoding patterns, and practice.

Key Words

expert systems	mnemonic encoding principle
key word method	organizational schemes
mediation	peg word system
method of loci	retrieval structure principle
mnemonic	speed-up principle

Recommended Readings

Popular books on mnemonics that are quite good include Cermak, *Improving Your Memory*; Lorayne and Lucas, *The Memory Book*; Yates, *The Art of Memory*; Young and Gibson, *How to Develop an Exceptional Memory*; Hunter, *Memory: Facts and Fallacies*; and Luria, *The Mind of a Mnemonist*. S. B. Smith has recently written a book about mnemonics called *The Great Mental Calculators: The Psychology, Methods, and Lives of Calculating Prodigies, Past and Present*. Also recommended is *Practical Aspects of Memory* by Gruneberg, Morris, and Sykes; J. R. Anderson's *Cognitive Psychology* and *Cognitive Skills and Their Acquisition*; and *Memory: Interdisciplinary Approaches,* edited by Solomon et al. An edited collection by Chi, Glaser, and Farr, *The Nature of Expertise,* is especially recommended. Jean Bédard and Michelene Chi have an article called "Expertise" in *Current Directions in Psychological Science* (1993), which is a good summary of current knowledge and Ericsson, Krampe, and Tesch-Römer have an article in *Psychological Review* (1993) that is one of the best articles on the topic of expert performance and highly recommended.

Mental Imagery

> Mental imagery is remarkably able to substitute for actual perception . . . having been incorporated into our perceptual machinery by eons of evolution in a three-dimensional world.
>
> *Roger N. Shepard*

THE TOPIC OF MENTAL imagery, once almost totally ignored by experimental psychologists, has, within the last few years, elicited intense interest from many and guarded skepticism from others. In this chapter we consider some of the traditional issues concerning this fascinating topic and emphasize recent theories and experiments.

As with some other concepts in cognitive psychology, imagery is what everyone knows it to be (we have all experienced it) and yet its specific cognitive properties are only approximately known. What is a mental image, and what are its properties? How do you "look at" specific features of an image? What is it that you are "seeing" when you look at a mental image? Is the image "real," or is it conjured up from information that is stored in a different modality? Can you differentiate between an imaginary image and one that you have actually experienced? If so, what is different about them? These are some questions that have bemused philosophers for centuries and currently intrigue cognitive psychologists. Recent research has produced some exciting new findings and theories.

Mental imagery is defined in this chapter as "a mental representation of a nonpresent object or event." This general definition allows for inclusion of visual images as well as images formed through other senses. Although the definition is broad, the discussion here is restricted to visual imagery, the area in which almost all the contemporary research has been done.

Imagery research is diverse, spanning topics as far-reaching as theoretical issues, neurocognitive findings, sports psychology, psychotherapy, cartography and cognitive maps, and even synesthesia. These disparate topics have been organized in this chapter in three major sections. First, a discussion of the history of imagery and current theories is developed. Then, recent neurocognitive evidence for the relationship between sensory processing and imagined processing is presented. The chapter ends with a review of the related areas of cognitive maps and synesthesia.

HISTORICAL OVERVIEW

We can identify three ages of mental imagery: the philosophic ("prescientific") period, the measurement period, and the cognitive and neurocognitive period.

During the philosophic period, mental images were taken to be a principal ingredient in the composition of the mind and sometimes were believed to be the elements of thought. The topic was an integral part of the philosophies of classic Greek philosophy, notably Aristotle and Plato, and, more recently, the British Empiricists, notably John Locke, George Berkeley, David Hume, and David Hartley.

The quantitative assessment of mental imagery can be traced to Galton (1880, 1883/1907), who circulated a questionnaire to 100 people in which he asked them to recall their breakfast table and answer several questions about the images they had. The results indicated little about the imaginal process except that some people reported images that were as clear as the original percept, while others reported little recollection of an image. Galton developed a measure of imagery that was related to sex, age, and other individual differences. The testing of imagery drew the interest of several researchers, such as, Titchener (1909) and Betts (1909). Their investigations consisted in having subjects rate their ability to visualize an object such as an apple, the contour of a face, or the sun sinking below the horizon.

Interest in the mental testing of imagery also quickly sank below the horizon with the advent of behaviorism, as exemplified in the views of Watson (1913). The behaviorist manifesto—as Woodworth (1948) called it—denounced introspection, which was a critical part of the above mentioned tests of imagery. Introspection, according to Watson, formed no essential part of psychology. The new science of behavior was committed to the objective observation of overt responses, and terms such as *consciousness, mental states, mind,* and *imagery* should never be used. This rejection of imagery and subjective introspection of mental images as topics worthy of investigation turned many psychologists away from imagery and toward the objective analysis of behavior. As with so many topics in cognitive psychology, research in imagery lay dormant for many years. However, interest in imagery simply would not go away. The subjective experience was profound, and its influence was wide; its dogged pursuit by a few (notably Allan Paivio and Roger Shepard, and later Stephen Kosslyn and Steven Pinker) returned the topic to the mainstream of cognitive research.

Imagery research was reawakened in the late 1960s on two fronts. The first was related to the quantitative assessment of imagery (Sheehan, 1967a, 1967b; and Sheehan & Neisser, 1969) and its use as a therapeutic vehicle. Also related to the assessment of imagery, but with a stronger theoretical bent, was the research of Bugelski (1970) and Paivio (1969). The second contemporary approach to imagery involved incorporation of the concept into a cognitive model in which the internal representation of information was a central element. This view is evident in the research of Anderson (1976); Shepard (1975); Shepard and Metzler (1971); and, more recently, in the neurocognitive studies by Farah (1984, 1988), Kosslyn (1973, 1975, 1980, 1983, 1988), Kosslyn and his colleagues (1993), and Pinker (1980, 1984, 1985). Each of these theorists has studied imagery from a unique point of view.

IMAGERY AND COGNITIVE PSYCHOLOGY

The study of mental imagery engages the broader question of how information is stored and recalled from memory. We could argue that the neurological activity associated with the storage of information is of a specific form. That is, visual information is coded in terms of an internal "picture" that can be reactivated by calling up the picture, as we might in looking at an album. Alternatively, we could argue that visual information is filtered, summarized, and stored as abstract "statements" about the image. Reactivation

Critical Issues: "Seeing" Without Sensing

We see when a visual object is being viewed, but, through the curiosity of visual imagery, we can also "see" when an object is not being viewed. Humans, and perhaps other animals, can "see" with the mind's eye.

Few dispute that all humans, to some degree, subjectively experience visual images; we can all "see" familiar shapes and forms by thinking of their characteristics.* Consider, for example, this problem: How many windows are there in the house in which you live? In all likelihood the way you answer this question is to form a mental image of your home and then mentally count the windows. Likewise, it appears that we are capable of forming mental representations of other sensory experiences in the absence of the physical stimuli. If I were to ask you to imagine a beach scene on a remote tropical island, you might "see" palm trees, seashells, the sun, and people in various activities, but you might also "hear" the ocean, feel the tropical breeze, smell the salt air. Some people seem capable of composing very vivid mental images, while others find this task difficult.

Over the next few hours, keep track of your mental representations, visual and otherwise. Which images are the most real, what is the relationship between these images and "reality," and what purpose do images play in one's mental life?

*Likewise, we can "hear," "taste," "feel," and "smell" sensations by conjuring up their mental image.

---

of the memory then would consist of recalling the abstract code, which in turn would conjure up the subjective image associated with it. Finally, we could argue that some information is stored visually and some in an abstract form, indicating that multiple codes exist in the mind.[1]

For years, the subject of imagery has been surrounded by controversy. The ancient dispute over whether images are directly represented in the mind (when you imagine a living tree, is there a corresponding tree growing in your head?) or whether images are represented allegorically (when you imagine a tree, is the concept of "treeness" and its attributes represented in your brain?) has been debated for years. The first argument is a radical isomorphic view and, in its extreme form, is essentially foolish—a real tree will not grow in your head no matter how vivid your imagery. The second argument seems, at least, more reasonable (see Pinker, 1984, 1985; Finke, 1985; and Kosslyn, 1994, for excellent overviews of these topics).

Real progress has been made in the quest for a better understanding of imagery through inventive research techniques and clear-cut results (for example, see the re-

---

[1]Some theorists argue that behavioral data are not adequate to settle the issue. Anderson (1976) states:

"At best . . . the imagery-versus-propositional controversy will reduce to . . . a question of which gives the more parsimonious account of which phenomena. Given the earlier results, there is no way to prove one is correct and the other wrong. Moreover, even if parsimony could yield a decision between propositional and imagery theories, there would still remain the possibility that there are other, fundamentally different, representations which are as parsimonious as the preferred member of the propositional-imagery pair."

Mental Imagery and Sports

[First, immerse] yourself mentally in the sport's environment. If it's basketball, see the gym, the stands, the three-point line, the basket. In skiing, learn the terrain changes, the texture of the snow, where the run starts and finishes and the line you want to take down the mountain.

The second preliminary step is visual imagery. *Once you have specified and memorized the task, practice producing a vivid image of the situation, one that uses all your senses. A skier I've worked with imagines riding up in the chairlift, looking over his skis at the top of the*

hill, seeing the colors of the trees and the other skiers' bright clothing against the whiteness of the snow and feeling the sensation of his skis gliding over the snow. He brings in feelings as well as visual images, recalling the exhilaration and joy he experiences in making a good turn.

Once the task is clear and the images vivid, it's time to start the mental rehearsal *itself. Close your eyes and experience the physical activity mentally and emotionally. Everything you visualize should look and feel the same as if you were really on the slopes or on the court.*

From May, 1989.

search of Farah, Kosslyn, and Shepard in this chapter). Nevertheless, the subject of imagery remains controversial. Currently the debate is over the question of whether visual imagery is really visual or is governed by general-purpose cognitive processes (as contrasted with specific visual processes) and over knowledge of how the visual system operates. The visual argument holds that mental imagery involves the same representations used in vision, so that when I "see" a tree, specific types of neural processing and representations are activated. When I "image" a tree, the same (or highly similar) processes and representations are activated. The other side of this argument is that the representations used in imagery are not the representations used in real perception. This argument holds that "thinking in pictures" basically involves knowledge best expressed in terms of traditional (that is, propositional or associative) representations of knowledge.

The plan of this chapter is to discuss the research on imagery with the theoretical considerations hovering closely in the background. The information is organized around three central themes:

1. The dual-coding hypothesis, which suggests that there are two codes and two storage systems—one imaginal, the other verbal—and that information may be coded and stored in either or both (principally the work of Paivio).

2. The conceptual-propositional hypothesis, which proposes that visual and verbal information are represented in the form of abstract propositions about objects and their relationships (principally the work of Anderson and Bower as well as Pylyshyn).

3. The functional-equivalency hypothesis, which suggests that imagery and perception are highly similar (principally the work of Shepard and Kosslyn).

In addition, there are those who suggest that information can be both visual and spatial (for example, Farah, 1988). We begin our trek through the imagery literature by exploring the dual-coding hypothesis.

Dual-Coding Hypothesis

The original work of Paivio and his associates on imagery was done in a paired-associate learning context, a research paradigm very much in fashion at the time. The first step Paivio (1965) took was to scale the imagery quality of nouns by having a group of college students rate nouns for their capacity to arouse an image, that is, "a mental picture, or sound, or other sensory picture." A similar procedure was used by Paivio, Yuille, and Madigan (1968), and Table 10.1 contains a sample of their results, including ratings for concreteness, meaningfulness (the number of associates a word elicits), and frequency (of occurrence of a word in common printed text). These results confirm the obvious: that some words are more imaginal (for example, *elephant, orchestra,* and *church*) and others less imaginal (for example, *contact, deed,* and *virtue*).

Studies by Paivio have led to the dual-coding hypothesis, a major theoretical statement as to how information is represented in memory. The hypothesis is based on the inference that there are two coding systems, or two ways information may be represented in memory: a nonverbal imagery process and a verbal symbolic process. The two

T A B L E   1 0 . 1

Imagery Scores and Scores on Related Attributes for a Representative Sample of Nouns

Noun	Mean Score*			Frequency[†] (per million)
	Imagery	*Concreteness*	*Meaningfulness*	
Beggar	6.40	6.25	6.50	29
Church	6.63	6.59	7.52	AA
Context	2.13	2.73	4.44	1
Deed	3.63	4.19	5.32	A
Elephant	6.83	7.00	6.88	35
Profession	3.83	3.65	5.44	28
Salary	4.70	5.23	5.08	A
Tomahawk	6.57	6.87	6.44	3
Virtue	3.33	1.46	4.87	A

*Ratings were on a scale of 1 to 7; the lower the score, the lower its imagery.

[†]"A" words have a frequency of 50–99 per million words; "AA," 100 or more per million words.

From Paivio, Yuille, and Madigan (1968).

codes—imaginal and verbal—may overlap in the processing of information, but greater emphasis is on one or the other. Suppose, for example, that a familiar and easily named picture is coded both imaginally and verbally, but with the verbal code being less available. This may happen because an extra transformation is involved so that, although the verbal code is aroused, it occurs *after* the imaginal code has been activated. On the other hand, while concrete words may be coded both imaginally and verbally, an abstract word is represented by a verbal code only. The availability of coding for different classes of stimuli is shown in Table 10.2.

In general, the imagery code seems more attuned to concrete information than abstract information, while the verbal code seems more attuned to processing abstract information. However, this does not mean that all words equate with "abstract" and all pictures with "concrete." Sometimes visual stimuli—say, a picture of a mountain, a tree, or an arrow—are better represented by imaginal codes than verbal codes, and the verbal stimuli for these concrete objects—that is, the words *mountain, tree, arrow*—may also be better represented by the imaginal codes.

Conceptual-Propositional Hypothesis

Anderson and Bower were critical of the mental-picture metaphor, stating that "it is not scientifically viable to suppose that memories, or other sorts of knowledge, are carried about in a form like an internal photograph, video tape, or tape recording, which we can reactivate and replay in remembering an image" (1973, p. 453). Even though we are capable of a subjective experience of an image, the underlying cognitive component may be of a form much different from imaginal. One reason Anderson and Bower reject the pictures-in-the-head theory is related to a conservation argument, which states that it is useless to postulate storage of full pictures of scenes because such a memory system would require storage and retrieval well beyond the human capability. Some device—a kind of master homunculus—would still be necessary to view and interpret these internal pictures.

TABLE 10.2

Coding Systems Available According to Stimulus

Stimulus	Coding System*	
	Imagery	*Verbal*
Picture	+ + +	+ +
Concrete word	+	+ + +
Abstract word	– –	+ + +

*Number of plus signs indicate relative availability.

From Paivio (1971b).

The conceptual-propositional hypothesis holds that we store interpretations of events, whether verbal or visual, rather than the imaginal components. Anderson and Bower do not deny that it is easier to learn concrete words than abstract words, but they attribute those results to the supposition that concrete concepts are coded by a rich set of predicates that bind concepts together. They state that "the only difference between the internal representation for a linguistic input and a memory image is detail of information" (p. 460). The following is one of their examples:

> Our words spoken to a listener are like the cryptic directions a playwright provides for a play director, from which a competent director is expected to construct an entire setting, an expressive mood, or an action episode in a drama. To illustrate, in the course of reading a story, you might read the sentence "James Bond ran to his car and drove to the casino." As you read, you can concretize that sentence by bringing to bear all sorts of facts and sensory images about running, about getting into cars, about driving, and so forth. These "fill-ins" would be called upon, for example, if you were to be asked simple questions like "Did James Bond sit in a car? Did he start its motor? Did he move the steering wheel?" Such trivial implications seem immediately available from the referential semantics of the verb phrase "drive a car." What the sentence does is merely mention a couple of signposts (source, instrument, goal) along the way in the description of an event sequence; the listener interpolates or fills in all the interstitial events between the mentioned signposts. Of course, at a later time, the listener is hardly able to say exactly what he heard as compared to what he filled in; if he is asked to tell the story "in his own words," he will probably select slightly different descriptions or signposts to mention in reconstructing the salient episodes (pp. 460–461).

Anderson and Bower's conceptual-propositional hypothesis is a theoretically elegant point of view and one that is compatible with their theoretical model. However, the hypothesis has some difficulty accounting for some imaginal processes that seem to require an internal structure that is second-order isomorphic to the physical objective. Data that seem to reflect such processes have been presented by Shepard and his students and are considered in the next section.

Functional-Equivalency Hypothesis

Shepard. Much of the current excitement in the field of mental imagery is due to the demonstration and interpretation of mental rotation by Shepard and his associates. Using visual cues, Shepard studied mental rotation of visual stimuli in memory. In his

Roger Shepard. **Studies of mental rotation led to theories in mental imagery.**

experiments subjects were asked to judge whether a second stimulus, such as the right-hand one in Figure 10.1, was the same (except for rotation) as the original stimulus (at left). In some cases the second pattern was a mirror image of the first and, therefore, not the "same" as the original stimulus, while in other cases the pattern was identical to the original, but rotated. The degree of rotation ranged from 0 degrees to 180 degrees. The dependent variable was the amount of time required to make a judgment. The results of these experiments indicate that the time required to respond was a linear function of the degree of rotation (see Figure 10.2). That is, a small degree of rotation of the second stimulus was quickly judged, while a large degree of rotation required more time. These data suggest that the subject's internal representation of the images required about 1 second for every 50 degrees of rotation. The results of Shepard's experiments have far-reaching importance for cognitive theory, but for our discussion the relationship between the time required and the degree of rotation suggests that the internal process is an orderly function of the amount of transformation required. Thus it appears that a close relationship exists between the time required for a specific mental rotation and the actual degrees of rotation involved. If we consider both rotations on two scales—time required for mental rotation and degrees of rotation—the correspondence is evident.

In addition to the reaction data presented in Shepard's elegant experiments, some researchers have presented neurological evidence for mental rotation. One of these studies by Georgopoulos and his colleagues (1989) is particularly interesting. They examined the electrical activity in the brain of a rhesus monkey as it performed a mental

FIGURE 10.1

Typical visual forms used by Shepard and Metzler. Form at right is left-hand form rotated 90° counterclockwise. Adapted from Shepard and Metzler (1971).

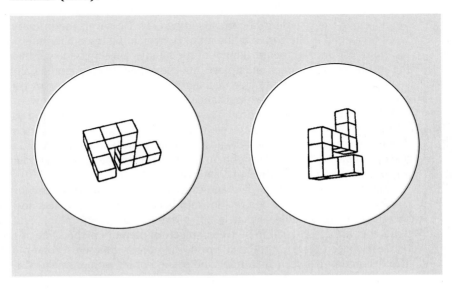

F I G U R E   1 0 . 2

Reaction time as a function of degree of rotation of a form. Adapted from Shepard and Metzler (1971).

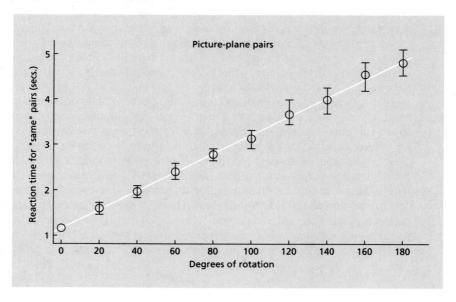

rotation task. The monkey was trained to move a handle on a clocklike apparatus in re-action to the location of a light. When the light appeared in one location, the animal would move the handle in a corresponding way. However, the primary interest lay in what happened in the cortex of the monkey, which the researcher interpreted as mental rotation, just prior to the movement of the handle. During the few milliseconds prior to the response, the animal anticipated the movement. Georgopoulos and his fellow re-searchers measured minute electrical activity in the monkey's motor cortex during this critical period and, with the assistance of computer graphics, showed that individual cells have directional preferences. The cells that responded most frequently during men-tal rotation were those that showed a preference for, say, counterclockwise movement. The results provide direct neurological evidence for mental rotation and suggest that the use of "single cell" recordings of neural activity might be a useful supplement to behav-ioral data in the identification of cognitive operations.

Shepard (1968) and Shepard and Chipman (1970) introduced the term *second-order isomorphism* to represent the relationship between external objects and internal repre-sentations of those objects that is not a one-to-one (isomorphic) kind. This position holds that if the relationship between objects in memory is the same as the relationship between those objects in the real world, then the events are second-order isomorphic. The distinction between first-order and second-order isomorphism is a subtle, but im-

> Although imagery has played a central role in theorizing about the mind since the time of Aristotle, its nature and properties have been surrounded by controversy. Indeed, during the Behaviorist era, its very existence was questioned, and more recently its status as a distinct kind of mental representation has been vigorously debated.
>
> *Stephen M. Kosslyn*

portant, one: objects are not directly or structurally represented in our brains, but the way internal relationships work is very similar to the way external relationships work.

From the research findings of Shepard's group, a strong case seems to develop for the existence of images in the mind that are, if not structurally identical to the real-world object, at least functionally related.

Kosslyn. In a series of inventive experiments, Kosslyn and his associates (Kosslyn, 1973, 1975, 1976a, 1977, 1980, 1981, 1994; Kosslyn & Pomerantz, 1977; and Kosslyn et al. 1993) have investigated imagery from the standpoint of its spatial characteristics and, most recently, with the use of brain imaging technology (to be discussed later). In the main, Kosslyn's research has demonstrated that a mental image is similar to the perception of a real object. Most of his experiments are based on the assumption that an image has spatial properties, which may be scanned, and that it takes more time to scan large distances than short distances. In one experiment (1973), Kosslyn asked subjects to memorize a set of drawings and then to imagine one at a time. At one time they were asked to "focus" on one end of the object they had imagined (for example, if the object was a speedboat, they were asked to "look at" the rear portion). A possible property of the original picture was named, and the subject was asked to decide whether or not it was in the original. The results indicated that longer times were required to make judgments about properties that involved scanning distances. For example, those involving a scan from stern to bow (see Figure 10.3) took longer than those involving one from porthole to bow). Subjects who were asked to keep the whole image in mind showed no differences in the time required to identify properties from different locations. It would appear that mental images can be scanned and that the time required to scan them is similar to that needed to scan real pictures.

Stephen Kosslyn. **Helped develop the field of mental imagery and neurocognition.**

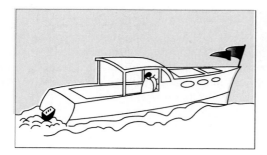

Picture for investigating spatial characteristics of imagery.

If images do share some features of real-object perception (that is, scanning time), are there other features common to percepts and images? Kosslyn, using the fact that small objects are generally seen less clearly than large objects, demonstrated that there are. In one experiment (1975), he had subjects imagine a target animal (for example, a rabbit) next to a small or large creature (for example, a fly or an elephant). A rabbit next to an elephant is reported by most people to be smaller than one of the same size next to a fly (see Figure 10.4). Subjects who were asked to determine the appropriateness of a certain property (for example, ears) to an animal took on the average 211 milliseconds longer to evaluate animals paired with an elephant than those paired with a fly.

To guard against the possibility that such results might derive simply from greater interest in elephants than in flies, Kosslyn tested animals in the context of an elephantine fly and a minuscule elephant. Under these conditions, more time was taken to evaluate the target animal when it was paired with the giant fly than with the tiny elephant.

In yet another experiment, Kosslyn (1975) asked subjects to imagine squares of four different sizes—each six times the area of the next smaller one and each identified by a color name. After the subjects were able to envision the size of the square on the basis of the color, they were given a color and animal name, such as "green bear" or "pink

Typical relationships imagined by subjects in Kosslyn's experiment. Adapted from Kosslyn (1975).

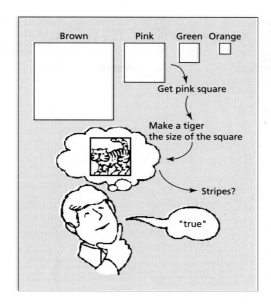

FIGURE 10.5

Process in experiment in which subjects judged appropriateness of a property to an imagined animal paired with boxes of different sizes. Adapted from Kosslyn (1975).

tiger," and asked to summon up an image of the designated animal according to the size of the box linked with the color (see Figure 10.5). After this, a possible property of the animal was presented. The time required to decide if whether the property was a characteristic of the animal was much longer for animals in the small boxes than for those in the larger ones (see Figure 10.6).

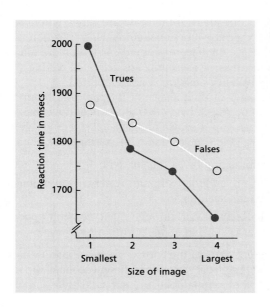

FIGURE 10.6

Times required to determine appropriateness of a property of an animal in experiment depicted in Figure 10.5. Data from Kosslyn (1975).

Taken together, these experiments of Kosslyn and Shepard indicate that visual images seem to reflect internal representations that operate in a way that is analogous to the functioning of the perception of physical objects. On the other hand, not all or even a sizable number of the characteristics of images have been examined.

NEUROCOGNITIVE EVIDENCE

Thus far, our analysis of mental imagery has dealt with studies of the psychology of that phenomenon, and, thus far, we can cautiously conclude that mental imagery and perception of a real stimulus are seductively alike. However, to ascertain the completeness of the analogy of perception to imagery, further validation is required in the form of neurological evidence. Fortunately, a large body of data comes from neurological studies (for example, Gazzaniga & Sperry, 1967; Corballis, 1989; and Milner, 1968). Clinical observations by Luria (1976) and Farah (1988) of neurologically damaged patients show that impairment of the left hemisphere of the brain is associated with disturbances of verbal memory, while right-hemisphere damage is associated with the memory for visual material. These findings tend to support the dual-coding theory of memory: one system for the coding and processing of visual information, another for the coding and processing of verbal information.

The rationale for many experiments dealing with brain activity and imagery is that activation of a cognitive process, such as imagery or verbal thought, is expressed in terms of localized brain activity, which can be measured by regional blood flow (see Chapter 2 for details).

Psychologists have agonized over the question of functional equivalency of images and visual percepts for several decades. The answer may lie within the field of neurocognition. The logic of this quest is simple. If measurements of regional cerebral blood flow (rCBF) indicate that the same areas of the brain are active when we see an object as when we image an object, then the functional-equivalency position is supported (although not definitely established, since regions could carry on more than a single function). Conversely, if different areas of the brain are activated during perception than during imaging, then the equivalency position is not supported.

First, we consider the matter of uniqueness of imagery and brain activity. Strong objective evidence has been reported showing that all parts of the visual cortex are activated when subjects imagine an object or use imagery to solve a problem. Specifically, research by Roland and Friberg (1985) measured rCBF during three cognitive tasks:

1. Mental arithmetic (subtracting by 3s starting with *50*).

2. Memory scanning of an auditory stimulus (mentally jumping every second word in a well-known musical jingle).

3. Visual imagery (visualizing a walk through one's neighborhood, making alternating right and left turns starting at one's front door).

Each task activated different parts of the cortex, but most important for our discussion is the finding that during the visual task, blood flow was most apparent to the posterior regions, which includes the occipital lobe and temporal areas important for higher visual processing and memory. It appears that mental imagery of this sort involves not only visual processing areas but also memory areas.

In a related study, Goldenberg, Podreka, Steiner, Suess, Deeke, and Willmes (1990), using single photon emission computer tomography PET scans to trace brain activity, asked subjects to answer some questions that required visual imagery and some that did not. For example:

"Is the green of pine trees darker than the green of grass?"

"Is the categorical imperative an ancient grammatical form?"

The results indicated that the first type of question produced high levels of blood flow in the occipital regions and in the posterior parietal and temporal visual processing areas, whereas the second nonimagery condition did not.

A detailed and direct test of the hypothesis about perception and imagery has been reported by Kosslyn and his associates (1993) in which an often-used test of imagery was used in a PET study. In this case, a task devised by Podgorny and Shepard (1978) consisted of asking subjects to view a letter (such as the letter *F*) in a grid (the perceptual condition) or to image the letter in an empty grid (the imaginal condition). Then, a mark was presented, and the subjects were to indicate whether the mark fell on or off the letter (see Figure 10.7).

In the original experiment, Podgorny and Shepard found that it took subjects longer to decide whether the marks were close to the letter than farther away. The researchers concluded that it's easier to make an evaluation of inclusiveness and exclusiveness if the mark falls well outside the target. However, the main conclusion of the experiment was that similar results were obtained for the perception group and for the imagery group, which lent support for the functional-equivalency hypothesis.

What Kosslyn and his associates found was somewhat surprising. Although they hypothesized that the visual cortex (the structure located at the posterior portion of the cerebral cortex involved in vision) would be activated during the perceptual task and probably activated during the imaginal task, the PET results clearly showed *greater* activation of the visual cortex during image generation than during perception. It is as if this structure, and perhaps other structures involved in visual processing, had to work harder during image generation than during perception. One possible reason for this finding is that during perception the visual cortex receives detailed visual information from the external world (a kind of bottom-up stimulus) and therefore operates with the object in view, which requires little effort. In contrast, during image generation, the sub-

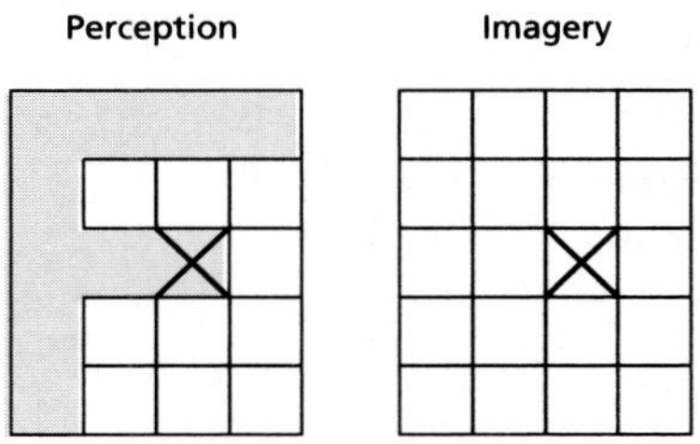

Perception   Imagery

FIGURE 10.7

Example of figure used in the perceptual and imaginal task.

ject must re-create the visual stimulus from memory (a kind of top-down stimulus), which forces it to work harder.

From these studies and many more (see Farah, 1988), several conclusions are appropriate:

1. Studies of brain activity indicate that different areas of the brain are associated with different cognitive tasks.
2. Visual imaginal tasks and vision seem to be situated in similar locations in the brain.
3. Visual imaginal tasks, which require associative knowledge, seem to activate regions of the brain affiliated with memory and vision.
4. Because of their top-down nature, imaginal tasks may require more energy to process than perceptual tasks, which are initially bottom-up tasks.
5. The use of physiological measures of rCBF may resolve some thorny cognitive problems.

One remaining issue has not been addressed in this section. It is the question of whether spatial representations (the type of representations we saw in Shepard's mental rotation experiments) and visual representations (the type of representations dependent on the reconstruction of a visual impression, for example, naming the color of an object such as a football) engage different parts of the brain. In answering this question, we turn to a case study.

In reaction to the argument that the format of mental images is either analogical (positions espoused by those who believe images are functionally equivalent to percepts) or propositional (positions taken by those who reject the idea that images and real perception are highly similar), Martha Farah and her associates (Farah, 1988; and Farah et al., 1993) have looked to the evidence from neurocognition to resolve the issue.

The basic logic of those who have sought neurocognitive explanations of imagery is that by finding specific brain areas associated with imagery and other functions, such as

Martha Farah. **Conducted innovative research in neurocognition, which has identified neurological sites of cognitive processes.**

vision, many of the theoretical questions may be resolved. Specifically, the question of mental images being almost the same thing as vision versus part of a more general system of representing spatial information might be clearly resolved if, for example, it were demonstrated that vision and spatial representation occupied different parts of the brain. Thus, the study of neurophysiology bears directly on cognitive theories of imagery.

As shown, the neurophysiology of imagery has been studied through many of the techniques described in Chapter 2, including CAT scans, EEG recordings, studies of regional cerebral blood flow, neurosurgery, and the study of patients who have experienced some brain trauma. It is the latter case we turn to next.

Farah and her colleagues worked with a brain-damaged patient called L. H., who was a thirty-six-year-old minister working on a second master's degree. When he was 18, he sustained a serious injury to his head in an automobile accident. Subsequent surgery (and CAT scan confirmation) indicated that the parts of the brain that were damaged involved both temporo-occipital regions, the right temporal lobe, and the right inferior frontal lobe, as shown in Figure 10.8. Although L. H. made remarkable recovery and outwardly seemed normal, he was profoundly impaired in visual recognition. For example, he could not reliably recognize his wife or children unless they were wearing distinctive clothes. He also had difficulty recognizing animals, plants, foods, and drawings. Some of the objects L. H. could not recognize are shown in Figure 10.9. He could, nevertheless, make reasonable copies of these figures, even though he did not know their identity. He had good elementary visual capabilities.

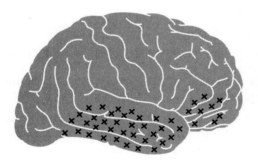
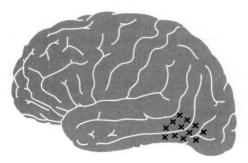

FIGURE 10.8

Areas of damage to L. H.'s brain (in shaded regions). Areas involved include the right temporal lobe and right inferior frontal lobe (upper figure) and the temporo-occipital regions (lower figure). From Farah et al. (1988).

FIGURE 10.9

A. Examples of drawings a brain-damaged patient could not recognize.

B. Patient's reproductions of these figures. From Farah et al. (1988).

A   B

The experimenters in this case were interested in visual and spatial imagery ability vis-à-vis brain injuries. They argued that:

- Spatial representations are not confined to the visual modality (for example, mental rotations, which are considered to be spatial images, not visual images).

- Visual representations are confined to the visual modality (for example, the naming of a color of a common object such as a football).

In the final stage of the experiment, L. H. performed a variety of tasks associated with spatial knowledge and other tasks associated with visual knowledge. Many of the tasks have been described in this chapter.

- *Visual Tasks.* For the visual tasks, animal tails (Does a kangaroo have a long tail?), color identification (What is the color of a football?), size comparison (Which is larger, a popsicle or a pack of cigarettes?), and comparison of state shapes (Which states are most similar in shape?) were presented to L. H. and to a number of control subjects.

- *Spatial Imaginal Tasks.* For the spatial tasks, letter rotation (mental rotation of a letter, similar to form rotation used by Shepard and Metzler), three-dimensional form

FIGURE 10.10

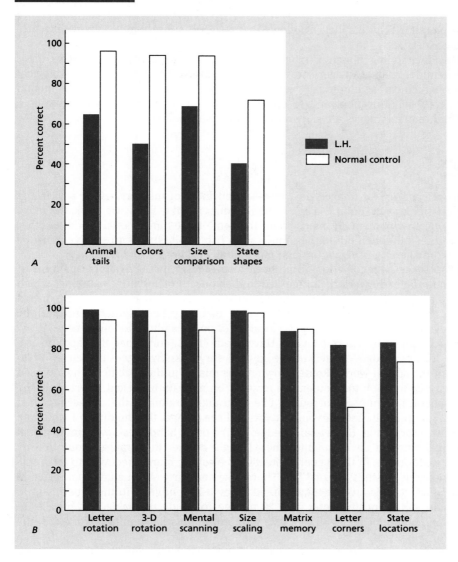

A. Performance of L. H. (dark bars) and normal control subjects (white bars) on four visual imagery tasks. See text for descriptions of tasks.

B. Performance of L. H. (dark bars) and normal control subjects (white bars) on seven spatial imaginal tasks. See text for descriptions of tasks. From Farah (1988).

rotation (see Shepard and Metzler), mental scanning (see Kosslyn), and size scaling (estimates of the same shape of figures regardless of size) were presented to the patient and to control subjects.

The results, shown in Figure 10.10a, clearly show L. H.'s performance on visual tasks as being impaired, presumably due to destruction of specific brain areas; however, these impairments seem to have left intact his ability to perform spatial tasks (see Figure 10.10b). It would appear, therefore, that these two groups of tasks (visual and spatial) tap different types of mental representation that are neurologically distinct. Because they are neurologically distinct, it follows that different subsystems of imaginal representations exist.

Our understanding of mental imagery is enhanced by this study in three ways. First, cognitive entities such as imagery are shown to be governed by underlying neurological functions, which can be empirically measured. Second, cognitive tasks, such as mental rotation, color identification, and so on, are valuable tools in neurological investigations. Third, mental images are shown to be both visual and spatial.

COGNITIVE MAPS

The human capacity for imagery is a powerful attribute of memory, as we saw in the chapter on mnemonics, but it is also essential in our everyday life as we work and move about in our environment. Humans share the same three-dimensional world as other earth creatures (although not in the same way as fish or birds) and, to survive, must be able to use imagery to navigate through our spatial world and avoid harm.

Psychologists have for a long time been interested in the navigational patterns of animals, and the early work of Tolman led to the concept of cognitive mapping, which referred to a general spatial knowledge exhibited by rats in a maze. The distinguished naturalist Von Frisch (1967) published a study of honey bees, which described the means they used in communicating the location of pollen sources to fellow bees.

One experiment by Thorndyke and Hayes-Roth (1982) concluded that humans use two types of knowledge—route knowledge and survey knowledge—in their effort to learn about the spatial world. Route knowledge is related to the specific pathways used to get from one location to another. If a stranger on my campus asked how to find the medical school, I would say something like "You take Virginia to the colosseum; then turn right, go up a hill, and on your left you will see a large, flat building." I would be giving route information. Survey knowledge, on the other hand, deals with more global relationships between environmental cues. I might answer the stranger's question by saying "It's over there, in that general direction." Another, more direct way to form survey knowledge is to study a map. The Thorndyke and Hayes-Roth study took place in the large office complex where they worked. They asked subjects in the experiment to study a map and found that after only 20 minutes of study the subjects were able to judge distances and locations as well as a group of secretaries who had worked in the building for two years.

In a somewhat related study, B. Tversky (1981) and Taylor and Tversky (1992) examined the distortions of memory for geographic locations. In their interesting work, Tversky suggests that distortions occur because people use conceptual strategies to remember geographic information. We have already seen that subjects tend to form prototypes when given simple geometric forms to imagine, and it is likely that even more complex forms of abstracted information are part of the cognitive mapping process of humans.

Following this line of thought, it may be that geographic information is structured in memory in terms of abstract generalizations rather than specific images. Such an argument would avoid the difficult question of how we can store so much information in visual memory, since the storage is condensed into larger units. Your home, for example, is part of a neighborhood, which is part of a city, which is part of a township, which

FIGURE 10.11

Geographical distortion. A. Cognitive map of Reno as east of Los Angeles. B. Actual location of Reno—west of Los Angeles.

is in a region of the state, and so on. When you move from one section to another, say, in your city, the knowledge you use may be in the form of an abstract representation of landmarks rather than a series of discrete visual images. Sometimes these higher structures interfere with decisions made on the local level. For example, if you were asked which city is farther west, Reno or Los Angeles (see Figure 10.11), you would likely answer Los Angeles. (See Stevens and Coupe, 1978). Why? Because we know that Los Angeles is in California and that Reno is in Nevada, which is to the east of California. In this case we are relying on strategic information rather than tactical information, and we are misled.

Mental Maps: Where Am I?

It has long been known that we humans enjoy a geocentric view of the universe. Early scientists, with encouragement from the Church, even placed Earth in the center of the solar system (which required an inelegant theory of planetary motion) before Copernicus jolted us out of the vortex and properly placed Earth as the third planet from the sun. It is common, and understandable, that children regard their home as the center of their universe, surrounded by their neighborhood, city, state, and country. Local egocentric impressions of geography are the result of familiarization and provide emotional comfort. (*Home* is one of the most comforting words in our vocabulary.) Some have suggested that maps, which are basically human impressions of geographic reality, are both a reflection of the objective realities of the world and partly a reflection of the subjective interpretation of these impressions.

Can map drawings provide a window to the mind regarding such matters? There is considerable evidence that expressive forms of representation, such as sketches of maps and other graphic figures,[2] mirror our subjective impression of reality (see the Texan's view of the United States shown here). Most map drawing studies have dealt with systematic distortions and accuracies of regional cognitive maps, such as navigating around a college campus or judging the distance between geographic points. Several studies have considered world-scale cognitive maps. Certainly, ancient maps indicated a degree of unavoidable egocentrism. For example, the ancient Babylonians didn't know what lay past the distant hills. However, now almost all schoolchildren know something of the gross geographic boundaries of the world.

[2]Our colleagues in clinical psychology have subscribed to this idea for a long time, as shown in their use of projective techniques (for example, Draw-a-Person), which are thought to disclose hidden personality traits.

A Texan's view of the United States.

A Texan's veiw of the United States.

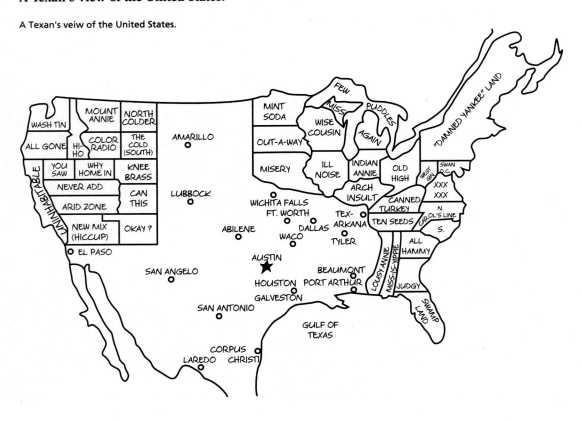

Some years ago a mammoth international study of the image of the world by different nationalities was done to broaden our understanding of cultural differences and to foster world peace. The design was simple. Students in a first-year course in geography from 71 sites in 49 countries were given a blank sheet of paper and asked to sketch a map of the world. The results were fascinating (Saarinen, 1987). Of the nearly 4,000 maps produced, the majority showed a Eurocentric worldview, even if the person who drew the map was from the periphery, as in the case of students from Hong Kong, Singapore, and Thailand. This is probably due to the wide use of Eurocentric maps for more than 500 years. Some American students drew an Americentric map; an example by a student from Chicago (who seems to have some familiarity with Texas and the Caribbean) is shown in Figure 10.12. Australian students tended to sketch Sinocentric maps, with Australia and Asia in the center; several Down Under students drew maps in which not only was Australia centrally located but all other countries were shown in the "lower hemisphere," as shown in Figure 10.13. Maps of this orientation are not common

FIGURE 10.12

View of the world by a student from Chicago.

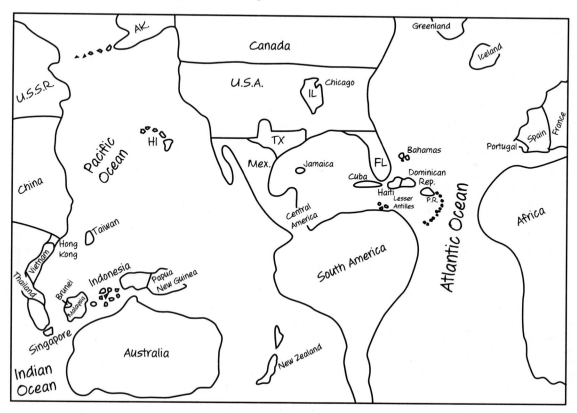

FIGURE 10.13

View of the world by a student from Australia.

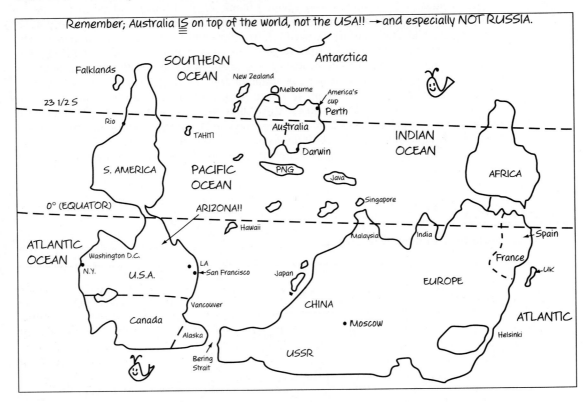

in Australia. One would anticipate that students would draw their own country dispro-portionately larger, but this did not seem to be the case. Prominent countries (the United States and USSR, England, France, and so forth) were on most maps. Africa was gener-ally underrepresented, and its countries seemed less well known. American students did rather poorly on the task, especially in terms of placing countries correctly. Students from Hungary and the Soviet Union produced some of the most detailed maps.

SYNESTHESIA: THE SOUND OF COLORS

Synesthesia is a condition in which sensations from one modality (for example, vision) are experienced in another modality (for example, audition). Thus, an image of an ob-ject may conjure up a sound. In some rare individuals (see the discussion of S. in the previous chapter), the transfer between sensory experiences is extraordinary. It is some-

Literary Metaphors and Synesthesia

The murmur of the gray twilight (Poe)

The sound of coming darkness (Poe)

Sunset hovers like the sound of golden horns (Robinson)

The world lay luminous; every petal and cobweb trembled music (Aiken)

A soft yet glowing light, like lulled music (Shelley)

Music suddenly opened like a luminous book (Aiken)

The notes entered my breast like luminous arrows (Gautier)

Music bright as the soul of light (Swinburne)

The silver needle-note of a fife (Auslander)

The dawn comes up like thunder (Kipling)

From Marks (1987a).

what similar to "cross-talk" in audioengineer's jargon, where signals from one channel are heard in another channel. In many people, the simultaneous experiencing of sensory events is common. Poetry abounds with metaphors of synesthesia (see the box entitled "Literary Metaphors and Synesthesia"), and artists have confirmed the strong relationship between sights and sounds. The Russian abstract artist Kandinsky (1912) wrote that "the sound of colors is so definite that it would be hard to find anyone who would try to express bright yellow in the bass notes, or [a] dark lake in the treble." However, both extraordinary synesthesia and ordinary cross-modal transfer remain somewhat mysterious. There are principles that seem to govern synesthesia and research that supports these principles (Marks, 1987a, 1987b).

Synesthesia tends to be rule governed, not random. For example, there is a positive relationship between increasing the pitch of a sound and increased brightness. (If I cough or sneeze and ask you which is brighter, you are likely to choose the sneeze.)

In one study, Marks (1974) presented to subjects a series of tones varying in pitch. The subjects were asked to match each tone with a series of colors that differed in brightness. As shown in Figure 10.14, there is a substantial positive relationship between pitch and brightness. Marks has extended these correlational observations to reaction-time experiments in which a subject is asked to discriminate two auditory values, say, a high and low pitch, by pressing a reaction-time key. On each trial of the experiment, a dim light or a bright light is also turned on. The relationship between the brightness of the light and the pitch of the tones appears random and (the subject is likely to conclude) irrelevant to the main purpose of the experiment. Nevertheless, as shown in Figure 10.15, there is a reliable relationship between pitch and brightness as measured by reaction time. When the luminance is high (320 cd/m^2), reaction time to high-pitched stimuli is relatively fast, while for low-pitched tones the reaction time is relatively slow.

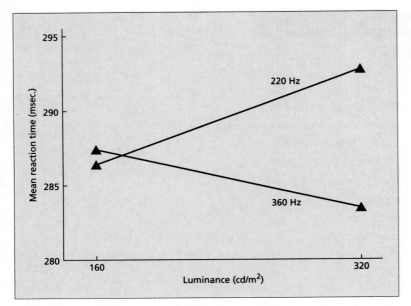

FIGURE 10.14

Ratings of brightness of colors and pitch. From Marks (1974).

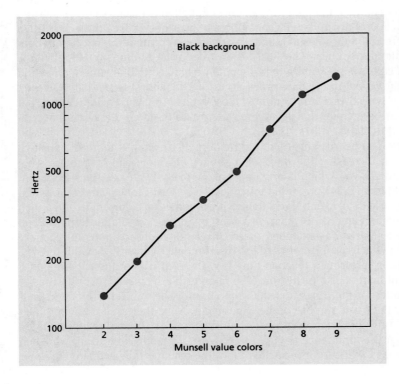

FIGURE 10.15

Mean reaction time for tones of different pitches (Hz) and different brightness (cd/m). From Marks (1974).

In yet another condition, colors and pitches were found to be predictably related. In evaluating the "sound of colors," it appears that yellow and white are bright, red and green intermediate, and black and brown dark. The pitches associated with these colors correspond almost perfectly with high pitches associated with the bright colors and low pitches with the dark colors (Marks, 1987a). Support for these relationships in literary sources is common. Note for example, "She sang with silvery clarity," "The bass produced rich, dark tones, which set the mood for the entire performance of Boris Godunov." Additional experiments confirm these observations.

Our discussion of synesthesia started out with "soft" references (the allegorical character of cross-modal experience—see the box entitled "Literary Metaphors and Synthesia") and ended up with "hard" data (the nearly perfect linear relationship between tones and luminance). Perhaps good science and good art are part of a single reality. However, our concern here is to understand synesthesia in the larger context of cognitive psychology.

There is convincing data to suggest that many people have a type of synesthesia in which images and sounds (as well as other sensory experiences) are entwined. Furthermore, synesthesia can be measured, and from these observations lawful statements can be derived. There is also data that suggest that some people are unusually synesthesiac. These people experience egregious "cross-talk" among sensory experiences (see the discussion of S. in Chapter 9). What mechanisms might account for these observations?

First, consider the physical character of the natural world. Is there any good reason to link sights and sounds? Are bright objects and high-pitched sounds alike physically? Perhaps, but searching for physical explanations may overlook its important psychological character. Second, consider the perceptual and cognitive nature of synesthesia. It may be that our nervous system is structured in a way that "cross-talk" among cortical neurons is a valuable, "prewired" element in the redundant, parallel processing of information in the human brain. In the past, we have had to rely on the mediation of language and reaction-time experiments to find a nexus between sensory experiences. With increased sophistication in the detection of brain activities, it is likely that studies of synesthesia and brain activity will appear shortly and help identify the source and nature of this intriguing issue. Finally, future work in neurocognition, especially recent advancements in imaging technology, will likely demystify many of the intricate problems that currently perplex those who study this curious subject.

Summary

As we noted in the beginning of this section on imagery, early experimental efforts were frustrating. That remains the case. We have presented three viewpoints on imagery—the dual-coding hypothesis, the conceptual-propositional hypothesis, and the functional-equivalency hypothesis. Each viewpoint is both theoretically elegant and intuitively appealing, so the student of imagery is likely to feel frustrated in choosing the "best" model. It seems that information is imaginally coded at some level of processing, while the same information at another level of processing is conceptually coded. Thus the dilemma caused by three appealing hypotheses might be resolved by accepting all three, while acknowledging that the coding of information may span several layers of cognitive processes, each of which transcribes information in its unique way.

1   The study of mental imagery is concerned with the issue of how information is represented in memory.

2   Three distinct theoretical positions can be identified regarding how information is stored in memory. They include the dual-coding hypothesis, the conceptual-propositional hypothesis, and the functional-equivalency hypothesis.

3   The dual-coding hypothesis holds that information can be coded and stored in either or both of two systems: verbal and imaginal. Behavioral and neurological data support this position.

4   The conceptual-propositional hypothesis posits that information is stored in an abstract propositional format that specifies objects, events, and their relationships. This position is theoretically elegant, but it has difficulty accounting for the data indicating imaginal processes that involve a second-order isomorphism (for example, Shepard's work).

5   The functional-equivalency hypothesis holds that imagery and perception are highly similar (principally the work of Shepard and Kosslyn).

6   Two types of representation have been proposed to explain imagery: direct representation and allegorical representation. The latter is generally more widely accepted than the former.

7   It is debated whether visual imagery is in fact visual (specific) or whether it is actually a more general-purpose cognitive process.

8   Neurological evidence has been claimed for mental rotation. Modern research on imagery has been polarized between those who believe that mental images are very much like all other sensory impressions from the physical world and those who believe that objects are represented in terms of the subject's knowledge base. Some view the situation as being a mixture of these two extreme viewpoints.

9   Researchers using measurements of regional cerebral blood flow (rCBF) to study imagery are operating under the assumption that concentrations of blood in the brain correlate with the amount of functioning happening in that part of the brain. The data seem to show that visual processing and sometimes memory areas of the brain are at work when we imagine.

10 People tend to have an egocentric view of the world concerning their mental maps.

11 Synesthesia is a condition in which sensations usually experienced in a single modality are experienced in two modalities. This phenomenon, and those who experience it, have provided for some interesting and informative research. In fact, some very reliable functions have been found in the data.

Key Words

cognitive mapping	mental rotation
conceptual-propositional hypothesis	second-order isomorphism
dual-coding hypothesis	synesthesia
functional-equivalency hypothesis	visual imagery
mental map	

Recommended Readings

Relevant readings on imagery can be found in Paivio, *Imagery and Verbal Processes;* Rock, *Perception;* Anderson and Bower, *Human Associative Memory;* Shepard, "Form, Formation and Transformation of Internal Representations," and Shepard, "The Mental Image," in *American Psychologist.* A definitive account may be found in Pinker, *Visual Cognition.* For a clear description of the "imagery" versus "propositions" argument, Kosslyn and Pomerantz in *Cognitive Psychology* and Pylyshyn in *Psychological Bulletin* and *Psychological Review* are recommended. Also see Kosslyn's *Image and Mind* and his theory in *Psychological Review,* and *Ghosts in the Mind's Machine.* Also, Kosslyn's recent work using PET technology can be found in the *Journal of Cognitive Neuroscience,* and *Science* as well as in a recent book *Image and Brain: The Resolution of the Imagery Debate.* Roger Shepard has a delightful book called *Mind Sights,* which should be read by all those interested in imagery and related topics. The September 1992 issue of *Memory & Cognition* is devoted to mental models and related topics.

LANGUAGE 1: Structure and Abstractions

L ANGUAGE IS CENTRAL NOT only to communication but also to thinking, representation of information, and higher-order cognition. Nearly every general psychology textbook contains a chapter on language, numerous books deal with the psychology of language, the relation between language and brain structures has long been an area of interest, and several dozen journals report current research on the topic. It is now generally agreed that the study of language occupies a central position in contemporary psychology and plays a specifically important role in cognitive psychology and neurocognition.

LANGUAGE: COGNITION AND NEUROLOGY

The study of human language is important to cognitive psychologists for the following reasons:

- Language development among the human species seems to represent a unique form of abstraction, which is a mechanism thought to be basic to cognition. Although other forms of life (bees, birds, dolphins, prairie dogs, and so on) have complex means of communicating and apes seem to use a form of language abstraction,[1] the degree of abstraction is much greater among humans.
- Language processing is important with respect to information processing and storage.
- Many forms of human thinking and problem solving can be conceptualized as processes involving language. Many, if not most, forms of thinking and problem solving are internal, that is, done in the absence of external stimuli. Abstraction into verbal symbols provides one means to think about such events.
- Language is the chief means of human communication, the way in which most forms of information are exchanged.
- Language influences perception, a fundamental aspect of cognition. Some argue that how we perceive the world is affected by the language we use to describe it. On the other hand, language development is at least largely based on our perception of language. So the perceptual-language process becomes one of interdependency;

---

[1]Among the best known and most significant research on language processes among chimpanzees was that conducted by Beatrice and Allen Gardner of the University of Nevada, Reno, who raised a young female chimpanzee named Washoe much as a human child might be fostered. After four years Washoe's vocabulary and "sentence" length were much larger than had previously been thought possible. Additionally, she initiated conversations and did not simply mimic language processes. Also, David Premack has made some remarkable observations of language capabilities in apes, including evidence of syntax, abstraction, accessibility of knowledge, and mnemonic processes. See Premack (1976) for a nontechnical report.

both significantly influence the other. Language from this point of view operates as a window.

- The processing of words, speech, and semantics seems to engage specific cerebral areas and thus provide a meaningful link between neuroanatomical structures and language. In addition, the study of the pathology of the brain has frequently shown manifest changes in language functions, as in the case of aphasia.

For these reasons, language has been extensively studied by cognitive psychologists, *psycholinguists* (specialists who study the relationship between psychology and language), and neuropsychologists, among others.

Neurology. One of the earliest scientific analysis of language involved neurology, and that inquiry continues today. Since ancient times physicians knew that cerebral damage to the brain could affect language functions, but a major breakthrough occurred in 1861 when Paul Broca, a young French surgeon, observed a patient who suffered from paralysis of one side of his body as well as the loss of speech. The patient died and Broca preformed a postmortem examination, which showed a lesion in part of the left frontal lobe—an area that subsequently became known as Broca's area. Subsequent case histories confirmed the original observation that the left frontal area seemed to be involved in speech production, although at first, Broca did not make the association between the left hemisphere and speech. In 1875 Carl Wernicke showed that a lesion in the left temporal lobe, just behind the primary auditory cortex, also affected language processing, but of a different sort than that tied into Broca's area. Where Broca's area seemed to be involved in language production, Wernicke's area (as it was soon to be labeled) was a center of language understanding. Damage to Wernicke's area left patients able to speak but with reduced understanding of spoken or written words; they could speak fluently, but could not really comprehend what was said to them.

Looking back over a century of brain studies and language processing we can confidently conclude that language functions are localized in broadly defined regions that are mostly centered in the left hemisphere. This includes the original sites identified by Broca and Wernicke as well as parts of the (left) associative cortex and temporal cortex. However, since language processing and production is so complicated (consider the vast number of subprocessing activities involved in the simple associative response of seeing the word *RED* and saying "blood"—processes that involve vision, feature and word identification, lexical access, word association, motor activities and speech, and perhaps emotional effects among others), it is likely that other parts of the brain whose

I have been struck with the fact that in my first aphemics the lesion always lay not only in the same part of the brain but also the same side—the left. Since then, from many postmortems, the lesion was always left sided.

Paul Broca (1864)

functions are less than perfectly understood exercise subtle effects. We return to the topic of language and neurology later on in this chapter, but now consider the linguistic side of language.

LINGUISTICS

The study of linguistics is the formal description of the structure of language, including a description of speech sounds, meanings, and grammar.

Language as studied by linguists tends to be competency based (dealing with some ideal potential of the speaker-listener), while psychologists generally view language in terms of performance, or how humans use language. The discipline that incorporates both approaches to the study of language is called psycholinguistics.

Linguistic Hierarchy

Linguists are interested in developing a descriptive framework of language. Their approach is, in one respect, similar to that of a cognitive psychologist interested in developing a model of memory. From our discussion of memory, you may recall that a model of memory involved the content of memory, the structure of memory, and the processes that operate within memory (for example, coding operations, retrieval operations, and transformational operations). Similarly, some linguists are concerned with the development of a model of language—its content, structure, and process. However, unlike memory research, linguistic research postulates a hierarchy that ranges from fundamental components to compound components to very complex components—that is, sound units and meaning units in order of growing complexity. Each level is somewhat dependent on a lower level but may interact with any other level.

The development of a writing system that reflects speech and conveys thought is one of the most significant of humanity's hierarchical creations. In the English language, there are only ten symbols for digits and twenty-six letters, some of which are so redundant or infrequently used that they contribute little to the overall structure of the written language. From these few letters and digits, about forty thousand words in our working vocabulary are constructed, and from these words billions and billions of sentences are created. Well, there may not be as many sentences as there are particles in the universe, but given our insatiable need to communicate with others, we are producing a huge number of original sentences every minute and promise to approach that number someday. When we consider the richness of the human experience generated by so few symbols (from literature such as the Song of Solomon to *Mein Kampf*), the hierarchical coding properties of language are staggering.

Phonemes

The basic unit of spoken language is the phoneme. Phonemes, single speech sounds that are represented by a single symbol, are created by an intricate coordination of lungs, vocal cavities, the larynx, lips, the tongue, and teeth. When all works well, the sound produced is available for rapid perception and understanding by someone familiar with the language being spoken. English uses about forty-five different phonemes, but not equally. Only nine are needed to make up more than half our words, with the most frequently used occurring more than one hundred times more often than the least used. Other languages get by with as few as fifteen phonemes, while some require as many as eighty-five. An analysis of the phonemes of General American English,[2] made by Denes and Pinson (1963), follows:

Vowels

ee as in heat	^ as in ton
I as in hit	*uh* as in the
ε as in head	*εr* as in bird
ae as in had	*oi* as in toil
ah as in father	*au* as in shout
aw as in call	*ei* as in take
U as in put	*ou* as in tone
oo as in cool	*ai* as in might

Consonants

t as in tee	*s* as in see
p as in pea	*sh* as in shell
k as in key	*h* as in he
b as in bee	*v* as in view
d as in dawn	*th* as in then
g as in go	*z* as in zoo
m as in me	*zh* as in garage
n as in no	*l* as in law
ng as in sing	*r* as in red
f as in fee	*y* as in you
θ as in thin	*w* as in we

These few phonemes can be combined in various ways to create thousands of different words that may be phonetically and orthographically similar but occupy distant corners of our semantic reality.

The search for basic phonetic units is similar to the search for distinctive letter features discussed in Chapter 4. Speech sounds that are produced by a coordinated effort of lungs, thorax, tongue, and so on and that include vibration of the vocal cords are classified as *voiced*—for example, *a* or *z*. Speech sounds that do not use vocal cords—such as the *s* in *hiss*—are called *unvoiced* sounds. Among other sounds—voiced or unvoiced—are *fricatives* (produced by restricting the air passage in the mouth), such as *sh, f, v,* and *th,* and *plosives,* or *stops* (produced by interrupting the flow of air for a brief period), such as *t* and *d.*

---

[2]General American is the dialect of English spoken in midwestern and western areas of the United States and influences an increasing number of Americans. Certain phonemes of other regional dialects (such as southern, British, and so on) can be different.

Morphemes

Phonemes are empty; they have no meaning. The smallest unit of meaning in the language is a morpheme. Morphemes may be words, parts of words, prefixes, suffixes, or combinations of these. For example, in the sentence "The old chemist loved joyful sounds," *the* and *old* are free morphemes, which stand alone, while *chemist, joyful,* and *sounds* are the combination of a free morpheme and a bound morpheme. *Chemist* is composed of the morphemes *chem* and *ist; joyful,* of *joy* and *ful;* and *loved,* of *love* and *d.* By combining morphemes, we can generate untold millions of words. In English we

Voiceprints

It seemed inevitable that phonetic analysis would surrender some of its secrets to the relentless probing by electronic means. A spectrographic device has been developed that separates the various frequencies composing a phonetic feature. Auditory signals are transmitted to a series of filters, each of which resonates to a range of specific frequencies in principle like a crossover filter in high-fidelity audio equipment, which separates high-frequency from low-frequency sounds so that they can be routed to the appropriate speaker (woofer or tweeter). Impulses from specific filters are recorded on a moving paper. This permits visual analysis of speech sounds and the production of voiceprints. In the print shown (for the word *said*) the trace in the upper left is of the high-frequency phonemes associated with *s,* while the lower frequencies of *aid* are represented in the other trace (Jakobson, 1972).

It is possible, by use of the spectrograph, to study in minute detail how the acoustic characteristics of the spoken language vary across time. Not only has the recording of "visual speech" allowed researchers to study acoustic characteristics of the spoken language in detail, but it also has a direct practical application in teaching speech to deaf children. Speech development in normal children involves hearing speech, which serves as a model; from the model, a child produces sounds that he or she also hears, and from the

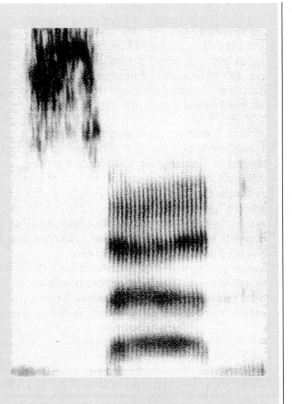

hearing of which corrections can be made. Deaf children lack this feedback loop, but an instantaneous visual feedback system (offered by one spectrograph), even though somewhat crude, may serve as a substitute.

have more than one hundred thousand words formed by morpheme combinations, but even with such a vast number the composition of morphemes is tightly governed by linguistic constraints. One of the linguistic constraints of English is that no more than three consonants may start a syllable; usually it is less than two. Another constraint is that certain letters—for example, *q* and *d* or *j* and *z*—never appear together. These and other constraints on morphological formation, plus the built-in redundancy of our language, act to minimize the number of errors in transmission and decoding.

Syntax

The next level in the linguistic hierarchy is that of syntax, or the rules that govern the combination of morphemes in phrases and sentences. In recent years the principles underlying syntax have been extended to include how information can be transformed from one form to another. This extension began with the proposal, made by Noam Chomsky, of a universal theory of grammar aimed at describing the abstract nature of languages, not just their surface characteristics. The result was not only a theory that changed our conceptualization of linguistics but also one that had a profound effect on psychology, especially psycholinguistics.

The number of different sentences humans can generate is restricted only by time and imagination, both of which are in long supply. In an attempt to understand the structure of language, linguists—those people who study the nature of language—have concentrated their efforts on two aspects: productivity and regularity. *Productivity* refers to the infinite number of sentences, phrases, or utterances that are possible in a language (billions and billions of sentences), and *regularity* refers to the systematic nature of the sentences, phrases, or utterances ("The boy hit the ball" rather than "ball boy The hit the").

Language productivity seems apparent, but the regularity of language is a much more tricky affair. The set of rules that govern the regularity of language is called grammar, and transformational grammar deals with the changes in linguistic forms that may retain the same message. For example:

The cat was chased by the dog.

The dog chased the cat.

Both sentences are correct, convey essentially the same meaning, have similar words, and yet differ somehow in their underlying structure. Apparently, the surface features of a language and the deep structure of a language needed to be separated, and the theories of Chomsky were designed along those lines.

CHOMSKY'S THEORY OF GRAMMAR

The following points are frequently cited as embodying the most important aspects of Chomsky's thesis:

- Language has much underlying uniformity, and the underlying structure is often more closely related to the meaning of a sentence than are the surface characteristics.

- Language is not a closed system but a generative one.

Noam Chomsky. **Changed the way language is viewed with theory of transformational grammar.**

- Within the underlying structures are elements common to all languages, and these may reflect innate organizing principles of cognition. These organizing principles may directly influence the learning and generation of language.

Chomsky directed much criticism toward behaviorism and its basis, S-R learning (including the learning of language), arguing that the development of language cannot be described simply in terms of operant learning principles and that psychological theory must be concerned with underlying processes rather than surface ones. Even though many psychologists dispute Chomsky's criticism, it is generally agreed that it has had far-reaching implications for psychological theory and cognitive research.

Most interest was in three aspects of Chomsky's theory: surface structure, deep structure, and transformational rules. These terms, to be used throughout the following discussion, are generally defined as follows:[3] *surface structure* is "that part of the actual sentence that can be segmented and labeled by conventional parsing"; *deep structure* is "an underlying form that contains much of the information necessary to the meaning"; and *transformational rules* are "those that turn one structure into another structure." Transformational grammar, a revolutionary component of Chomsky's system, details the laws that govern this transformation of one form of linguistic message into another. Consider the sentences: "The jock pursued the sorority girl" and "The sorority girl was pursued by the jock." Both sentences express the same basic idea, which is contained in the deep structure, but the specific form, or surface structure, differs, and transformational rules relate the two.

Transformational Grammar

In another example, the basic meaning of the simple sentence "The short hippopotamus saw the tall giraffe" may also be expressed as "The tall giraffe was seen by the short hippopotamus" or "It was the short hippopotamus who saw the tall giraffe." Our awareness of the true sense of the sentence prevails, despite the semantic rearrangement and, in some instances, alteration of words or morphemes. The integrity of meaning is maintained in deep structure. As another example, try telling a story about some event in your life, such as, going to a concert. After you have told the story, tell it again, but

---

[3]These definitions are simplified versions of those suggested by Chomsky.

Grammatically Correct, Semantically Absurd

Charles Dodgson (later known as Lewis Carroll) gave us many examples of grammatically correct and semantically anomalous language nearly a century ago in *Through the Looking Glass*. A fragment of one of his more neologistically wild specimens is the following:

He took his vorpal sword in hand;
Long time the manxome foe he sought—

So rested he by the Tumtum tree,
And stood a while in thought.
And as in uffish thought he stood
The Jabberwock, with eyes of flame,
Came whiffling through the tulgey wood,
And burbled as it came.

avoid using the same sentences in the retelling. (You probably wouldn't anyway.) Then, under the same constraints, tell it a third time. There seems to be no real end to the ability of varying the means of saying the same thing. The rules underlying this phenomenon are what modern grammarians call transformational grammar. This task, which even children can easily do, is difficult to explain in S-R terms. Speech and language are rarely a passive, repetitive pattern of activity; rather, human language is a productive, generative system. Each sentence we utter is more or less a creative product, which is also more or less easily understood by the listener even though it is novel to both of you. In Chapter 7 and other parts of this book, we have learned how enormous is the capacity of LTM, but even that capacity would be taxed if it had to hold all the sentences we can produce or understand.

One way of explaining our capacity to generate and understand creative sentences is to use the metaphor of a tree, which represents surface structure and deep structure in an orderly fashion. Using this metaphor, the phrase structure of our earlier example "The short hippopotamus saw the tall giraffe" could be diagrammed as follows, with the sentence at the bottom constituting surface structure, and the network above, deep structure:

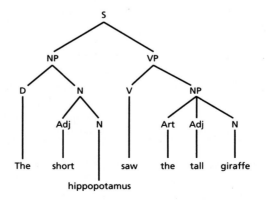

From this simple example, we can identify the fundamental constituents of the sentence, which exist not only on the surface but also on a deeper, abstract level. On the most inclusive level is the sentence (*S*), parsed into the subject and predicate represented as a noun phrase (*NP*) and a verb phrase (*VP*). Contained in the noun phrase (*NP*) are the determiner (*D*) and noun (*N*), which contains an adjective (*Adj*) and a noun (*N*). The verb phrase (*VP*) contains the verb (*V*) and a noun phrase (*NP*) divided into an article (*Art*), adjective (*Adj*), and noun (*N*).

The rules of mathematical transformation seem to offer a basis for representing language in terms in which the specific form may vary while the underlying reality (deep structure) is constant. For example, if $A = B$, then $B = A$; the expression is changed, but the underlying reality is the same. Similarly, $4X = 8$ may be written as $X = 8/4$, and $ab = XY(2X + N)$ may be written as $XY = ab/(2X + N)$. No matter how complex the surface characteristics, the deep structure of underlying reality of the relationship is the same. Transformational grammar uses the same kind of logic; sentences, as mathematical equations, may be rewritten in a variety of forms while maintaining their essential meaning. Thus we can explain our capacity to generate an enormous number of different sentences and several varieties of each sentence not as the result of imitation, which would presume a fantastic memory, but as the result of our innate grasp of certain rules that allow us to form sentences and to transform them into other sentences that express the same meaning. (Chomsky calls this underlying capacity *competence*.) Basic phrase structure rules (using the abbreviations from the tree metaphor just discussed) are as follows:

$$S \rightarrow NP + VP$$
$$NP \rightarrow D + N$$
$$VP \rightarrow Aux \text{ (auxiliary)} + V + NP$$

These rules can be applied to any deep structure to rewrite it in a different and grammatically perfect form while maintaining its true meaning.

The implication of generative grammar is that language analysis should be based on a syntactic level rather than on a phonological or morphological level. It is not that phonological and morphological utterances are unimportant (indeed, they are important) but that a study of linguistics that is limited to only these characteristics fails to account for the variety of linguistic forms that can be rapidly generated and the corresponding ease with which they can be understood. Chomsky illustrates grammatical "correctness" combined with semantic absurdity in the sentence "Colorless green ideas sleep furiously." The grammatical rules for the formation of sentences are limited (again, something does something to something), but the combination of semantic components is limitless. Even in Chomsky's example, if we have an imagination generous enough, the statement is not only grammatically correct but also semantically meaningful.

PSYCHOLINGUISTIC ASPECTS OF LANGUAGE

Innate Properties and Environmental Effects

Among the most controversial aspects of Chomsky's theory is his assertion that the essential components of language are innate and universal rather than, as argued by B. F. Skinner, learned. Thus, reinforcement—a fundamental element of the Skinnerian (behavioral) view—may determine only the morphological aspects of language development. (For example, a child learns to say "apple" when her request for an apple is reinforced by the object.[4])

To return to a question basic to Chomsky's assertions: How does a child generate a perfectly grammatical sentence he or she has never heard? The innate propensity for language, based on deep structure, is offered as the explanation. Chomsky's position does not hold that a particular grammatical system is innate, but it does argue that we have an innate scheme for processing information and forming abstract structures of our language. This may be tied to the biological development of the child. Some evidence suggests that there are biologically determined critical stages for language acquisition, and some studies (Lenneberg, 1964a, 1967, 1969; and Lenneberg, Nichols, & Rosenberger, 1964) have shown a correlation between language and motor development. Lenneberg concluded that "children begin to speak no sooner and no later than when they reach a given stage of physical maturation." His observations on the development of language in children have indicated that the first discriminable characteristic of speech in children's babbling is the intonation contour. The sounds composing the babbling do not seem to have meaning (at least not in the conventional use of that term), but they do have intonations. Later in the development sequence, primitive phonemes appear in children's speech production. Lenneberg (1967) asserts that this latter development is due to maturation, which allows children better control of their vocalization. Prior to the biological development necessary for phonemic formation, only general rhythmic patterns are possible. Speech seems to develop without specific training, as do many motor responses. Some of the maturational stages of speech and language development (and correlative motor development) are shown in Table 11.1.

Although Chomsky produced algorithms that made explicit the series of transformations that account for sentences, Lenneberg suggests that language (and behavior) develop by interaction between the individual and his or her milieu, each shaping the other:

> Maturation may be characterized as a sequence of states. At each state, the growing organism is capable of accepting some specific input; this it breaks down and resynthesizes in such a way that it makes itself develop into a new state. This new state makes the organism sensitive to new and different types of input, whose acceptance transforms it to yet a further state which opens the way to still different input, and so on.
>
> When language acquisition in the child is studied from the point of view of developmental biology, one makes an effort to describe developmental stages together with their tendencies for change and the conditions that bring about that change. I believe that the schema of physical maturation is applicable to the study of language development because children appear to be sensitive to successively different aspects of the language environment. The child first reacts only to intonation patterns. With continued exposure to these patterns as they occur in a given language, mechanisms develop that allow him to process the patterns, and in most instances to reproduce them (although the latter is not a necessary condition for further development). This changes him so

---

[4]A child given a banana after she said "apple" would undoubtedly form the impression that an apple is a long, yellow fruit fed to chimpanzees and children. Would she understand William Tell, apple cider, Snow White's poisoned apple, and apple pie? Would she ask for an apple split, and how would she interpret the apple picked from the Tree of Knowledge?

that he reaches a new state, a new potential for language development. Now he becomes aware of certain articulatory aspects, can process them and possibly also reproduce them, and so on. A similar sequence of acceptance, synthesis, and state of new acceptance can be demonstrated on the level of semantics and syntax.

Several points from our rather lengthy exposition of structural linguistics are important to summarize. From the most general standpoint, we can conceptualize the human brain as a very complex information-processing and storage system. With regard to language, it appears that a great deal of information about language is stored in the form of an abstraction of information (much as we store knowledge of algebra), but we also store specific semantic entities—that is, words. Linguists, especially those subscribing to the ideas of generative grammar, have proposed a description of the abstract character of language and mathematical laws that govern the storage and production of language. Although there is little dispute as to the abstract nature of language, the exact form of abstraction remains debatable.

T A B L E   1 1 . 1

Correlation of Motor and Language Development

Age in years	Motor Milestones	Language Milestones
0.5	Sits using hands for support; exhibits unilateral reaching	Cooing sounds change to babbling by introduction of consonantal sounds
1.0	Stands; walks when held by one hand	Syllabic reduplication; signs of understanding some words; some sounds applied regularly to signify persons or objects, that is, the first words
1.5	Develops prehension and release fully; uses propulsive gait; creeps downstairs backward	Repertoire of 3 to 50 words not joined in phrases; trains of sounds and intonation patterns resembling discourse; good progress in understanding
2.0	Runs (with falls); walks stairs with one foot forward only	More than 50 words; two-word phrases more common; more interest in verbal communication; no more babbling
2.5	Jumps with both feet; stands on one foot for 1 second; builds tower of six cubes	New words every day; utterances of 3 or more words; understanding of almost everything said; still many grammatical deviations
3.0	Tiptoes 3 yards (2.7 meters); walks stairs with alternating feet; jumps 0.9 meter	Vocabulary of some 1,000 words; about 80 percent intelligibility; grammar of utterances closely approximates that of colloquial adult; syntactic mistakes systematic, predictable, and fewer in variety
4.5	Jumps over rope; hops on one foot; walks on line	Language well established; grammatical anomalies restricted either to unusual constructions or to the more literate aspects of discourse

Another viewpoint (not necessarily antagonistic to the first) is that language and biological maturation go hand in hand, each influencing the other. Both of these positions give us a detailed and expansive paradigm in which to frame a cognitive theory of language.

Linguistic-Relativity Hypothesis

Chomsky's emphasis on linguistic universals is an effort to identify linguistic operations that are common to all human languages. As we have seen, it is largely based on deep structure of language and transformations. On the semantic and phonemic level, however, languages are obviously not the same. It is to these surface characteristics that the linguistic-relativity hypothesis is principally relevant.

The idea that our language influences our perception and conceptualization of reality has a very long and somewhat stormy history. The modern version has been associated with Benjamin Lee Whorf (1956) who, through his detailed work in the field, has lent his name to the hypothesis (the Whorfian hypothesis), although an earlier scholar, Edward Sapir, who was Whorf's professor, is credited with the basic hypothesis. (See Sapir, 1958; Mandelbaum, 1958; and Fishman, 1960, for further details.) Whorf concluded that a thing represented by a word is conceived differently by people whose languages differ and that the nature of the language itself is the cause of those different ways of viewing reality. Whorf studied Native American languages and found that clear translation from one language to another was impossible. In one language, he found that no clear distinction is made between nouns and verbs; in another, past, present, and future are ambiguously expressed; and in yet another, there is no distinction between the colors *gray* and *brown*. However, in English, despite the fact that English speakers have no unique physiological apparatus (to enable them, for example, to see the difference between *gray* and *brown*), we have words that make all these distinctions.

Some linguists have examined how language (and specifically lexical units) influences our conception of reality by studying color names. It is acknowledged that our sensory apparatus is sensitive to a wide range of different colors, yet by labeling various colors, our identification of them is affected. Many years ago Gleason (1961) found that while English divides the color spectrum into purple, blue, green, yellow, orange, and red, plus numerous in-between colors, Shona (spoken in parts of Zimbabwe) and Bassa (spoken in Liberia) identify fewer colors and make the divisions at different points, as shown in Figure 11.1.

Of particular interest in this respect is the fact that all normal persons have the same visual apparatus (that is, the same physiological ability to see colors and make color discriminations). Thus, differences in the mental processing of the colors viewed are suspected of being due to the differences among the different language codes. Some research indicates this to be the case. For example, a color that does not fit into the categories delineated by color name (one that is "between" colors) is likely to be remembered as a member of the color it most resembles. Eskimos have many different names for snow (blowing snow, drifting snow, snow you can make igloos from, and so on), which allows them to "see"—to discriminate—many more different types of snow than we who live in a temperate zone can. Similarly, the Hanuos of the Philippine Islands have ninety-two names for various kinds and states of rice. The Whorfian hypothesis suggests that the physical reality is translated, according to some internal representation

FIGURE 11.1

Major divisions of the visible spectrum in three languages. Adapted from R. Brown (1965)

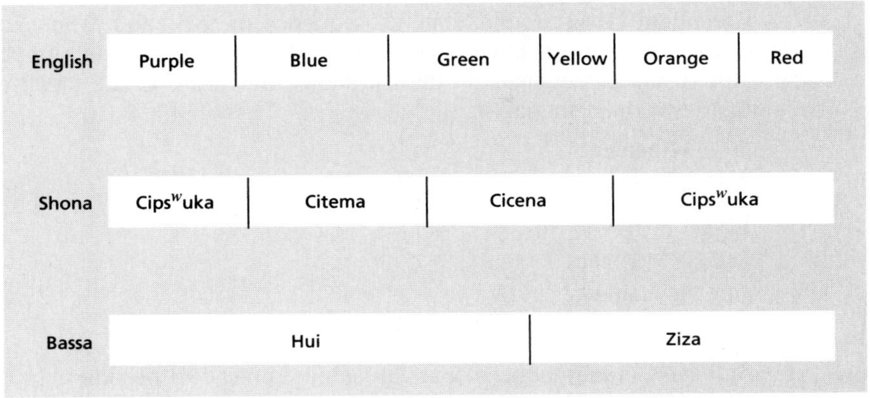

English	Purple	Blue	Green	Yellow	Orange	Red

Shona	Cips^wuka	Citema	Cicena	Cips^wuka

Bassa	Hui	Ziza

of reality, into a perception that is consistent with long-standing cognitive structures. One of the ways information is structured in the brain is apparently related to the specific language codes each of us has developed. These codes differ, as languages differ. This (Whorfian) viewpoint has been strongly opposed by some comparative linguists. Berlin and Kay (1969), for example, examined color names of nearly a hundred languages and concluded that certain basic colors are the same for all languages.

In one experiment they determined the basic color names for twenty languages, and then asked native users of each of the twenty languages to map (that is, to indicate on a series of colors) those they associated with a given color name. Finally, the subjects were asked to mark the color they rated as best or most typical of each color name; this was called the *focal color*. Their results indicate that focal colors were very similar for all groups. These results suggest that there is some basic constraint on the way a subject's experience with colors is coded in language. Thus color names may be more a direct function of perceptual phenomena than a determinant of percepts.

Further evidence in opposition to Whorf's hypothesis has been submitted by Heider (1971, 1972) and Rosch (1973, formerly Heider). She studied New Guinea natives, whose language is Dani. In Dani there are only two color names: *mola*—bright, warm colors—and *mili*—dark, cool colors. By using a recognition test, she found that recognition accuracy was better for focal colors than for nonfocal colors, and yet, if language determines perception, subjects whose language has but two names would predictably experience difficulty in recalling focal as well as nonfocal colors. Thus the case for linguistic determinism (at least of the rigid variety) seems questionable. Anthropologists and psychologists continue to be fascinated by the Whorf hypothesis. Kay and Kempton (1984), writing in *American Anthropologist,* provided a nice review of the empirical research on the hypothesis.

The interplay between culture and words can also be seen in word order. Languages typically have three principal components: subject (*S*), object (*O*), and verb (*V*). Specific languages have their own preference for the sequence of *S, O,* and *V.* In English, for example, the common order is *SVO,* as in the following sentence:

(*S*)   (*V*)   (*O*)
Happy Hans milked the contented cow.

Greenberg (1963) found that the sequence of *S, V,* and *O* in natural languages throughout the world is largely restricted to three preferred orders (reported in Anderson, 1985); the percentages on the list shown here refer to the preferred word orders among the world's languages:

SOV, 44 percent

SVO, 35 percent

VSO, 19 percent

VOS, 2% percent

OVS, 0% percent

OSV, 0% percent

Anderson (1985) noticed that the subject precedes the object in the majority of cases, which is consistent with what we know about cognition. An action is initiated by a subject, which affects an object. It is therefore appropriate that the subject appear early in a sentence. In addition, sentences tend to be built around subjects, and establishing the subject who will likely be the "hero" of the sentence may be an important literary technique. What remains a mystery, and a potentially fruitful area of research, is the question of the equivalence of cognitive experiences of two semantically similar but syntactically dissimilar sentences on comprehension. Perhaps some of the difficult international problems due to "misunderstandings" may in fact be partly due to the different emphasis given to words as a result of the preferred sequencing of words in a given language. I would be happy to see the results of studies in this area.

Consider one more question concerning Whorf's view (that language affects the way we conceive reality, process information, and store things in memory and recall): What is the origin of the lexical units? Why does the Eskimo language have so many names for snow and English have so few? Why do we have so many names for types of automobiles and the Laplanders so few (if any)? One answer is that the more significant an experience is to us, the greater the number of ways it is expressed in the language rather than the other way round—that is, that language determines our percepts. The development of specific language codes, therefore, is dependent on cultural needs; the learning of those codes by members of a language group also involves the learning of significant values of the culture, some of which may be related to survival. The consequence of the development of language codes may further determine what information is coded, transformed, and remembered.

COGNITIVE PSYCHOLOGY AND LANGUAGE: ABSTRACTION OF LINGUISTIC IDEAS

Up to this point we have covered some of the standard subjects in the psychology of language—a sort of nuts-and-bolts review that has drawn more on the collective wisdom of linguists and anthropologists than on cognitive psychologists. In this section our discus-

Sir Frederic Bartlett **(1886–1969).**
Studied language processing and
memory in a natural context.

sion of language focuses on the cognitive analysis of language, and the theme is the search for underlying, abstract cognitive structures of language. The first idea to be discussed is Bartlett's schema theory.

"The War of the Ghosts": Bartlett

Many investigators have concentrated their efforts on psychological processes involving meaningful prose that closely resembles that of real-life language experiences. The best known of the investigations of complex literary material was done by F. C. Bartlett of Cambridge University and reported in his remarkable book *Remembering: A Study in Experimental and Social Psychology* (1932). In this book Bartlett describes several experiments in which brief stories, prose passages, pictures, and Native American picture writings were used to study the remembering (and forgetting) of meaningful material. The procedures were simple. Subjects were given a short story, or other material. They read it and then free-recalled what they could remember after a certain period.[5] In other cases a story would be told to a person, who then retold it to another, who then retold it to another, and so on. By examining the contents of the reproduced version of the stories, it is possible to analyze both the nature of the material coded and the nature of the material forgotten. To illustrate the precise nature of these elements, several subjects' protocols are extensively cited.

Here is the original story:

The War of the Ghosts

One night two young men from Egulac went down to the river to hunt seals, and while they were there it became foggy and calm. Then they heard war-cries, and they thought: "Maybe this is a war-party." They escaped to the shore, and hid behind a log. Now canoes came up, and they heard the noise of paddles, and saw one canoe coming up to them. There were five men in the canoe, and they said:

"What do you think? We wish to take you along. We are going up the river to make war on the people."

[5]The following discussion involves LTM, and it would be useful to integrate this information with the previous discussion of VLTM in Chapter 7.

One of the young men said: "I have no arrows."

"Arrows are in the canoe," they said.

"I will not go along. I might be killed. My relatives do not know where I have gone. But you," he said, turning to the other, "may go with them."

So one of the young men went, but the other returned home. And the warriors went on up the river to a town on the other side of Kalama. The people came down to the water, and they began to fight, and many were killed. But presently the young man heard one of the warriors say: "Quick, let us go home: that Indian has been hit." Now he thought: "Oh, they are ghosts." He did not feel sick, but they said he had been shot.

So the canoes went back to Egulac, and the young man went ashore to his house, and made a fire. And he told everybody and said: "Behold I accompanied the ghosts, and we went to fight. Many of our fellows were killed, and many of those who attacked us were killed. They said I was hit, and I did not feel sick."

He told it all, and then he became quiet. When the sun rose he fell down. Something black came out of his mouth. His face became contorted. The people jumped up and cried.

He was dead.

After about 20 hours, one subject produced this first reproduction:

The War of the Ghosts

Two men from Edulac went fishing. While thus occupied by the river they heard a noise in the distance.

"It sounds like a cry," said one, and presently there appeared some men in canoes who invited them to join the party on their adventure. One of the young men refused to go, on the ground of family ties, but the other offered to go.

"But there are no arrows," he said.

"The arrows are in the boat," was the reply.

He thereupon took his place, while his friend returned home. The party paddled up the river to Kaloma, and began to land on the banks of the river. The enemy came rushing upon them, and some sharp fighting ensued. Presently someone was injured, and the cry was raised that the enemy were ghosts.

The party returned down the stream, and the young man arrived home feeling none the worse for his experience. The next morning at dawn he endeavoured to recount his adventures. While he was talking something black issued from his mouth. Suddenly he uttered a cry and fell down. He friends gathered round him.

But he was dead.

In general, the retold story is shorter, and the style is more informal. Additionally, there are numerous omissions and some transformations. Familiar words replace less familiar words—for example, *boat* for *canoe*, and *fishing* for *hunting seals*.

Eight days later the same subject recalled the following:

The War of the Ghosts

Two young men from Edulac went fishing. While thus engaged they heard a noise in the distance. "That sounds like a war-cry," said one, "there is going to be some fighting." Presently there appeared some warriors who invited them to join an expedition up the river.

One of the young men excused himself on the ground of family ties. "I cannot come," he said, "as I might get killed." So he returned home. The other man, however, joined the party, and they proceeded on canoes up the river. While landing on the banks the enemy appeared and were running down to meet them. Soon someone was wounded, and the party discovered that they were fighting against ghosts. The young man and his companion returned to the boats, and went back to their homes.

The next morning at dawn he was describing his adventures to his friends, who had gathered round him. Suddenly something black issued from his mouth, and he fell down uttering a cry. His friends closed around, but found that he was dead.

This second reproduction is even more abbreviated. The proper name *Kaloma* (*Kalama* in the original) is missing and the excuse "I might get killed" reappears after being missing from the first retelling.

Six months later another subject recalled the following:

> (No title was given.) Four men came down to the water. They were told to get into a boat and to take arms with them. They inquired "What arms?" and were answered "Arms for battle." When they came to the battle-field they heard a great noise and shouting, and a voice said: "The black man is dead." And he was brought to the place where they were, and laid on the ground. And he foamed at the mouth.

In this very short version, all unusual terms, all proper names, and references to supernatural powers have been dropped.

Finally, one subject was asked to recall the story after 2 years and 6 months. He had not seen the original version in that amount of time and, according to his own statement, had not thought of the story. His account follows:

> Some warriors went to wage war against the ghosts. They fought all day and one of their number was wounded.
>
> They returned home in the evening, bearing their sick comrade. As the day drew to a close, he became rapidly worse and the villagers came round him. At sunset he sighed: something black came out of his mouth. He was dead.

Only the barest rudiments of the story remain. Little elaboration of details can be found, and several themes appear that seem to be related to what the subject thought should happen, rather than what actually did happen in the story. For example, in this passage the wounded man finally dies. When? at sunset . . . naturally! It would appear that this theme is part of the popular folk history of our subject; it certainly isn't in the original version. As we learned from the Bransford and Franks studies, it would appear that fragments of information from a variety of sources (the story and general knowledge) combine to fill out the story in the absence of information of the specific facts.

Bartlett (1932) analyzed this type of information in terms of several categories. These include:

- *Omissions.* Specific information seems to drop out. Also, information that is illogical or does not fit into the subject's expectation is not readily recalled.

- *Rationalization.* Occasionally some information is added that would help explain certain incongruous passages.

- *Dominant theme.* Some themes seem to become prominent, and other features are then related to the dominant theme.

- *Transformation of information.* Unfamiliar words are transformed to more familiar ones.

- *Transformation of sequence.* Some events are characterized as appearing earlier in the story, others later.

- *Subject attitude.* The attitude of a subject toward the material determines the degree of recollection.

In making analyses on these bases, Bartlett used the concept of *schema* to account for his results. (His account, written more than half a century ago, appears as fresh as the latest theory.) Schema, in his view, refers to an active organization of past reactions or past experiences. Incoming stimuli all contribute to the buildup of an organized schema. In Bartlett's words:

> There is not the slightest reason, however, to suppose that each set of incoming impulses, each new group of experiences persists as an isolated member of some passive patchwork. They have to be regarded as constituents of living, momentary settings belonging to the organism, or to whatever parts of the organism are concerned in making a response of a given kind, and not as a number of individual events somehow strung together and stored within the organism.

Clearly, Bartlett has anticipated the "abstraction of linguistic ideas" that was empirically tested forty years later by Bransford and Franks, Thorndyke, and Kintsch (which is discussed next) and that has been a recurrent theme in many of the theories of semantic memory mentioned in this book (compare with Rumelhart, Lindsay, & Norman, 1972; Collins & Quillian, 1969; and Neisser, 1976). Some have criticized Bartlett's theory of remembering and schema on the basis that it is too vague and complex to be empirically testable—and with some justification.

Two studies—one less well known by Ballard (1913) who used poetry and a second by Erdelyi and Becker (1974) who used pictures—report improvements in performance (called hypermnesia) over repeated testing rather than a diminished and distorted performance. The difference between the results of Bartlett and Ballard (who was not cited by Bartlett) may be partly due to the type of verbal material used. However, a recent paper by Wheeler and Roediger (1992) suggests that the discrepancy is more likely to be due to the time interval between repeated testing. In general, Wheeler and Roediger found that when the intervals between successive tests are short, improvement occurs; when the intervals are long (as in the Bartlett study), forgetting occurs.

Nevertheless, the contribution of Bartlett is important for three reasons. First, the notion of abstract memory is introduced in his writings. These abstractions form part of the basis for new learning and later for transformation of new information. Second, he

Critical Thinking: Linguistic Abstraction

A convincing body of research indicates that when we read a book, a short story, or a poem, we retain only the essence of the work and not many of the details, which are forgotten, unavailable for recall, or melded with other memories to fabricate a distorted memory. Distorted memory from real-life experiences or from written material may be the result of one's previous knowledge, personal aspirations, or seeing the world in light of one's own belief systems. Try this little experiment: Read a short story, and paraphrase its main points in a few sentences as accurately as possible. Have a friend read the same story without writing the main ideas. Several weeks later, ask your friend to tell you the main ideas in the story. Compare your friend's recollection with your notes. Do the same thing with an abstract poem. What differences do you note between the initial factual description and the subsequent recalled? What might contribute to these differences? Are the differences even greater for an abstract poem?

demonstrated that research with real-life stories was possible and led to useful conclusions. Finally, his work provided an important frame of reference for his own students (Broadbent, Brown, and Conrad) and other scholars (Miller, Neisser, and Rumelhart).

In the time since the introduction of Bartlett's notion that stories are coded and remembered by means of schemata, contemporary researchers have proposed ideas that further add to our understanding of the functional properties of narrative memory. Modern theorists have attempted to quantify some of the basic notions of the abstraction of linguistic ideas. Among the best known of these researchers are Bransford and Franks. We consider their work next.

"Ants Ate the Jelly": Bransford and Franks

It has been asserted that beneath the surface structure of our language is a deep structure that follows systematic rules of transformation. The result of this theory has been the proliferation of hypotheses about other hidden cognitive structures. Among the most intriguing of these are those developed by Bransford and Franks (1971, 1972). One of these (Franks & Bransford, 1971) is reported in Chapter 4. In that experiment, subjects were shown figures that represented transformation of a prototypical figure and were asked to rate the figure as to whether it was a previously seen pattern. In the recognition portion of that experiment, subjects identified, with a high degree of certainty, the prototype that they had never seen. The likely implication is that subjects formed an abstraction, or prototype figure, on the basis of their experience with exemplars. The hypothesis derived from this is that we have a propensity to form abstractions of surface impressions and that these abstractions are the things we store in memory.

Bransford and Franks (1971) also developed a hypothesis concerning the nature of encoding sentences. They composed complex sentences that contained four simple declarative parts, one, two, or three of which could be removed to leave sentences composed, respectively, of three propositions, two propositions, and one proposition. Some of the sentences follow:

Four
The ants in the kitchen ate the sweet jelly which was on the table.

Three
The ants ate the sweet jelly which was on the table.
The ants in the kitchen ate the jelly which was on the table.
The ants in the kitchen ate the sweet jelly.

Two
The ants in the kitchen ate the jelly.
The ants ate the sweet jelly.
The sweet jelly was on the table.
The ants ate the jelly which was on the table.

One
The ants were in the kitchen.
The jelly was on the table.
The jelly was sweet.
The ants ate the jelly.

The experiment consisted of two parts: acquisition of the sentences and a recognition task. During the acquisition part, subjects were read 24 sentences, which consisted of one-, two-, and three-proposition sentences. After each sentence was read, the subjects were engaged in a color-naming task for 4 seconds and then asked a question about the sentence to ensure that the subjects had encoded it. For example, if one of the sentences was "The rock rolled down the mountain," the question might have been "Did what?" After the subjects acquired all 24 sentences, the experimenter read aloud additional sentences—some new and some from the original 24. The new sentences contained different parts of the complex idea that had been presented. In order to form a baseline for recognition, some "noncase" sentences were included. These noncase sentences changed the relationship across idea sets. For example, if a reference sentence was "The rock which rolled down the mountain crushed the tiny hut at the edge of the woods" and another sentence was "The ants ate the sweet jelly which was on the table," a noncase sentence might be "The rock which rolled down the mountain crushed the ants eating jelly in the kitchen." Subjects were asked to indicate which of the sentences (from among the new, original, and noncase sentences read to them) they had heard during the acquisition stage. Regardless of the response, they were then asked to evaluate their confidence in their judgment on a five-point scale (from very low to very high). The findings were that evaluations were essentially the same for old and for new sentences and that subjects' confidence in their recognition corresponded directly to the complexity of the sentence (see Figure 11.2). Thus sentences that seemed to have four propositions received the highest confidence ratings—in the neighborhood of +3.5 (even though no sentences with four propositions were actually presented)—while those containing three propositions were rated lower and so on through the sentence with only one proposition, which received a negative rating. Few were fooled by the noncase sentences, where confidence was around –4. (This control condition was important in that it shows that subjects did not base their confidence on sentence length alone.)

It is likely that subjects expressed greater confidence in having experienced complex sentences because they had abstracted a basic idea from the initial sentences to

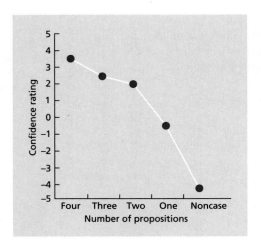

FIGURE 11.2

Confidence in having experienced sentences related to the complexity (number of propositions contained) of the sentence. Adapted from Bransford and Franks (1971).

which they were exposed and stored that abstracted entity rather than simply the sentences themselves in a disconnected series. The implication of these data for a theory of cognition and memory is that human memory for sentences is not merely a transcription of words (like a tape recording) but is the result of a dynamic process in which ideas are abstracted. These abstract ideas are, of course, derived from experience with sentences and form the basis of our impression of new and old sentences. Thus, as Chomsky has attempted to describe a structural linguistics in which language capacity is formulated in abstract principles, Bransford and Franks have attempted to describe how information about ideas expressed in sentences is organized in an idea structure that forms the basis for judging new information.

An important conclusion of the Bransford and Franks experiments is that human subjects do not isolate sentences (presumably in memory) if the sentences are semantically related. Somehow, information from different sentences is combined into an abstracted form, and we tend to remember the abstraction better than the specific form. We have seen throughout this book that modern cognitive psychologists seem preoccupied with the building of structures of mental processing that adequately reflect information processing, memory, and thought. The linguistic components of language suggested by Chomsky's theories seem to represent adequately a form of structural components. The research of Bransford and Franks, on the other hand, seems to give considerable insight into the specific kinds of transformations that are likely to occur in the abstraction of sentences.

Quite a different way to look at linguistic processing is to think of narrative information as being structured in the form of a hierarchy in which the most important ideas are supported by less important statements. From an informal perspective, we seem to think of stories in a hierarchical way. If asked to tell what a book (for example, *Crime and Punishment*) is about, we may try to find a single sentence that embodies its essence. When asked to expand our interpretation of the story, we may discuss the theme, the plot, the setting, and the way it turned out. (See Thorndyke, 1977, for an example.)

From the early theories of Bartlett and sentence and story schemata, we have seen a studious progression and development in the scientific analysis of language abstraction. Both the abstraction of linguistic ideas, as shown in the "ants eating the jelly" study, and in story grammar analysis have supported the general notion that there is a hidden, structural processing of sentences and stories. It is precisely within this hidden structure and its top-down effect that significant progress in understanding of language has taken place within the past few years. Our attention is now directed toward the topic of knowledge and text comprehension. Several new ideas are discussed in the next section, including a comprehensive model of language processing developed by Kintsch. As you study these models, keep in mind the previous research on story abstraction and top-down processing and consider its relationship with these models.

KNOWLEDGE AND COMPREHENSION

We begin with the simple generalization that the greater the knowledge of a reader, the better the comprehension of text. This generalization seems to be valid for readers who have broad knowledge and read colloquial material as well as those who have specialized knowledge and read technical material. One way to account for this generalization is that knowledge can be viewed as an organized collection of information. New information, as might be gathered through reading, can be assimilated more thoroughly when existing cognitive structures and information already exist. Conversely, insufficient knowledge limits comprehension because the reader must develop some structure of knowledge about the material as well as encode the information being read. Comprehension, within this framework, is perceived more as a confirmation of hypotheses about the way the world is thought to be than as a purely original assimilation of new facts. Much, but not all, comprehension is top-down processing. People with specialized knowledge, be it in plumbing, ballet, astrophysics, or motorcar racing, comprehend technical information in their field better than nonspecialists do.[6] Following are several examples of the power of top-down processing.

"Soap Opera" and "Thieves"

Text comprehension and understanding is influenced by situational information or instructions. In one experiment by Owens, Bower, and Black (1979), which illustrates the "soap opera" effect in story recall, subjects were to read a story about a water-skier and the driver of the boat. Half the subjects were introduced to the story by a passage that was designed to persuade the reader to identify with the water-skier, and half by a passage to identify with the driver. The test story was the same for both groups. After the groups read the story, a series of questions was asked. Those positively biased toward the water-skier tended to make errors in his behalf. For example, their reaction to the statement "[the skier] . . . reached for the handle [of the rope tow] but it escaped him" was to blame the failure on the boat driver for not coming close enough. On the other hand, those subjects positively biased toward the driver tended to believe that the skier was not fast enough to grab the handle. The tendency to ascribe guilt to the "other guy" and innocence to "our guy" demonstrates how understanding of textual material can be based on contextual biases.[7]

In yet another frequently cited study, this one by R. Anderson and Pichert (1978), subjects were asked to read a story about the home of a wealthy family from the standpoint of a prospective home buyer or a burglar. Many features about the house and its contents were described, such as its fireplace, musty basement, leaky roof, silverware, coin collection, and television set. The rated importance of these items as well as what was remembered was predictably related to the reader's viewpoints. The would-be thieves seemed to concentrate on the valuable loot, whereas the home buyers focused on the condition of the house. These experiments suggest that understanding or encoding textual material is influenced by contextual information that activates a specific type of schema.

[6]This assumes that all other significant variables (for example, intelligence) are equal.

[7]These findings tend to substantiate the questions raised by Elizabeth Loftus about the reliability of courtroom witnesses.

"Bumper Stickers and the Cops": Kintsch and van Dijk

The model of comprehension espoused by Kintsch and van Dijk is important from the bottom-up and top-down perspective. On the level of reading text material, the model is based on propositions, or abstractions of information, drawn from the text base, while on the level of reader intention, the model posits a goal schema that directs the reader's comprehension of text material.

The model (which is discussed in greater detail in the next section) allows researchers interested in the structure of stories to make precise predictions about the memorability of specific types of information. The technique developed by the authors of the experiment is consistent with modern scientific methodology in psychology as contrasted with the subjective method used earlier in the important work of Bartlett.

For purposes of our discussion, we concentrate on the way student subjects go about storing in memory information acquired from an article called "Bumper Stickers and the Cops." In an experiment done by Kintsch and van Dijk (1978), subjects were asked to read a nontechnical report that was about 1,300 words long. Following the reading of the report, one-third of the subjects were immediately asked to recall and write a summary of it. Another one-third of the subjects were tested after 1 month, and the final one-third after 3 months. The procedure is similar to the one conducted by Bartlett.

All of the recall accounts and summaries were organized into statements that could be identified as:

- Reproductions (statements that accurately reflect the comprehension of the text).

- Reconstructions (statements that are plausible inferences from the main theme aided by the subjects' world knowledge, such as "Beth went to Vancouver by train," might be expanded to include "She went into the station to buy a ticket").

- Metastatements (subjects' comments, opinions, and attitudes on the text).

These components were computer analyzed with specific predictions made by the model. Several important conclusions were made by the authors about text comprehension and memory. As indicated by the data gathered over three different time periods (see Figure 11.3), it appears that subjects lost more and more of the specific details of the report over time but retained the gist of the story with about the same degree of fidelity throughout a 3-month period—a finding consistent with the protocol analysis of Bartlett. Additionally, it seems that the analysis of written material, such as books, stories, and technical reports, is organized in a way that is susceptible to careful empirical study of propositions, which may tell us more about the way text material is organized and how the human mind records and stores in memory written material over time.

This chapter has progressed systematically from very simple linguistic entities (phonemes and morphemes), to syntax and grammar, to psycholinguistic theories, and to the abstraction of linguistic ideas as expressed in the analytic work just presented. One might now wonder whether there are any comprehensive theories of language. Indeed, there are several, but we cannot describe them all. One by Kintsch is particularly significant because it incorporates many bits of wisdom from previous studies and, at the same time, contains a model of the mind. Let's look now at this comprehensive model of language processing.

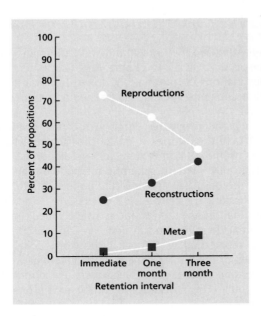

FIGURE 11.3

Proportion of reproductions, reconstructions, and metastatements in the recall protocols for three retention intervals. From Kintsch and van Dijk (1978).

A MODEL OF COMPREHENSION: KINTSCH

In this section we explain the principal components of one influential and extensive model by Kintsch and his coworkers at the University of Colorado (Kintsch 1974, 1979, 1988, 1990a, 1990b; Kintsch & van Dijk, 1978; Kintsch and Vipond, 1979; J. Miller & Kintsch, 1980; and van Dijk & Kintsch, 1983).

This model of comprehension is more than a system that deals with the way textual information is understood. It is a theory that cuts across many topics in cognitive psychology, including memory and comprehension of the written and spoken language.

Walter Kintsch. **Developed influential theories of language comprehension.**

Comprehension is dependent on two disparate sources that are similar to top-down and bottom-up processing, discussed in some detail throughout this book. At the highest level is the goal schema, which decides what material is relevant. At the opposite extreme of the model is the text.

The model is based on the proposition, a term first introduced in our discussion of semantic memory. A proposition is an abstraction, and, as such, it is difficult to define concretely. We can, however, identify some characteristics of propositions: they are abstractions based on observations (such as reading text material or listening to a speaker); they are retained in memory and follow the laws governing memory processes; and, in Kintsch's system, they consist of a predicate and one or more arguments. Predicates correspond to verbs, adjectives, adverbs, or connectives in the words a person reads or hears. This is called the *surface structure*, a term used by several linguists, including Chomsky. Arguments correspond to nouns, noun phrases, or clauses. The model is illustrated with the following little story:

> The Swazi tribe was at war with a neighboring tribe because of a dispute over some cattle. Among the warriors were two unmarried men, Kakra and his younger brother Gum. Kakra was killed in battle.

The first sentence is divided into five groups, as shown in Figure 11.4. In this figure only three of the factors are in working memory. The predicate "was at war with" is considered the most important part of this sentence insofar as comprehension of the story is concerned. The other parts are clustered around it. A significant feature of the model is that the initial processing of text is assumed to take place in STM, which we know has limited capacity. Because of this constraint, only a portion of the propositions is held in memory. With the reading of the second sentence, some of the propositions from the first sentence are still vital in STM (see Figure 11.5). The reader tries to connect the old and new propositions but finds no match between them. Failing to find a match between the propositions in STM, the reader searches LTM for a possible match. This

FIGURE 11.4

Analysis of the first sentence. From Kintsch (1979). Copyright 1979 by Division 15 of the American Psychological Association. Reprinted by permission.

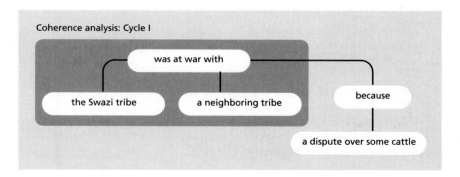

FIGURE 11.5

Analysis of the second sentence. From Kintsch (1979). Copyright 1979 by Division 15 of the American Psychological Association. Reprinted by permission.

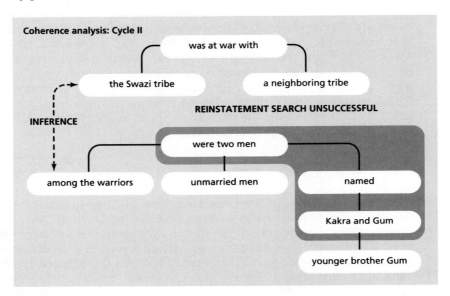

search of LTM is called *reinstatement search* and is one reason that text material may be hard to read. Text material that flows may be easy to read because the reader is able to retain much of the recent material in STM without having to access LTM. In the example, the lack of a match between propositions in the first and second sentence requires the reader to construct a new network for the ideas and to attempt to relate the two sentences (see Figure 11.5). One inference the reader makes is that the two men were members of the Swazi tribe, a reasonable conclusion even though that fact is not stated directly. With the reading of more sentences, the semantic network begins to get more complicated and interrelated. The reading of the sentence "Among the warriors were two unmarried men, Kakra and his younger brother Gum" retains in memory the names of the men, which can easily be related to the information in the last sentence, "Kakra was killed in battle."

Propositional Representation of Text and Reading

One strength of Kintsch's model is that it is possible to make very precise predictions about the effect of certain types of literature on the reading process. Only one sample of the many experiments is reported here.

You'll recall that the model of comprehension holds that the underlying unit of memory for text material is the proposition. Additionally, the model predicts that sentences of greater propositional complexity are more difficult to comprehend than sentences with simple propositional structure, even if the surface complexity of the two sentences is about the same. Kintsch and Keenan (1973) designed an experiment to test this prediction.

Subjects were asked to read ten sentences, all of which had about the same number of words but varied greatly in the number of propositions. Some sentences had as few as four propositions, and others had as many as nine. For example, read the following two sentences:

Romulus, the legendary founder of Rome, took the women of Sabine by force.

Cleopatra's downfall lay in her foolish trust in the fickle political figures of the Roman world.

Which sentence was more difficult to read? If you are like the subjects in Kintsch's and Keenan's experiment, you had more difficulty with the sentence about Cleopatra than the sentence about Romulus. Even though the surface complexity of the two sentences is about the same, they differ markedly in the number of propositions and the macrostructures that are required to interconnect the propositions. A diagram showing the propositions and macrostructures is shown in Figure 11.6.

In the Kintsch and Keenan experiment, subjects were presented with sentences similar to those just discussed by means of slides. The subjects were asked to read each sentence and then to write it. They could then advance the slides and see the next sentence. Of interest was the relationship between propositional complexity and the amount of time subjects required to read the sentence. The authors found an extraordinarily consistent relationship between the number of propositions and the time required

FIGURE 11.6

Number of propositions and macrostructures for two sentences. From Kintsch and Keenan (1973).

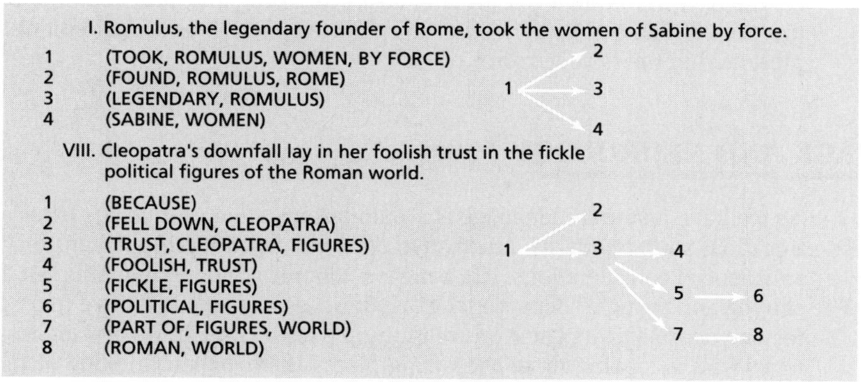

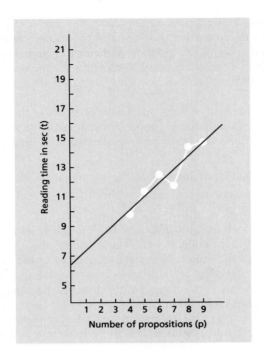

FIGURE 11.7

Reading time as a function of number of propositions per sentence. From Kintsch and Keenan (1973).

to read the sentences; this relationship is shown in Figure 11.7. The time required to read each sentence is predicted by the formula $t = 6.37 + 0.94p$, where t is time and p is the number of propositions. Therefore, a sentence of the length used in Kintsch and Keenan experiment would require about 6 seconds to read and about an additional second for each proposition.

All language and comprehension functions mentioned are mediated by the brain, a fact that has long been known but poorly understood. Recently, however, aided by new technology, the brain's role in language processing and production is beginning to be discovered. Some of these recent developments as well as some traditional concepts are presented in the next section.

LANGUAGE AND NEUROLOGY

As we have just seen, language is a multifarious affair. It involves letter and word identification, sound patterns, associative networks, speech, comprehension, as well as personal-social considerations. It is a means not only of communication but also of problem solving and thought. Because language touches so many cognitive functions, the search for one neurological center or even multiple centers might be as fruitless as the feckless lover who is looking in all the wrong places. Rather than thinking of the neurology of language as localized, it is prudent to consider the neurology of language as consisting of a family of capabilities which have centers, but whose full operation is dependent upon a myriad of centers interacting simultaneously. We have good evidence, for example, that the two centers identified earlier (Broca's area and Wernicke's area) are involved in language production and language comprehension. However, clinical results clearly show that profound aphasia may result if the connecting tissues between these sites is severed.

The study of the neurological basis of language has been investigated by several means, including clinical investigations of brain-damaged patients, electrical stimulation of the brain, psychosurgical procedures, pharmaceutical investigations, and imaging technology. We cannot recount, in detail, findings in all areas, but we can give a sample of research.

Electrical Stimulation. The use of tiny bipolar electrical probes has been used in human and animal experimental work for many decades. Several years ago Penfield (1959) and Penfield and Roberts (1959) stunned the psychological world when they presented verbal protocols of patients undergoing psychosurgery in which low-voltage electrical currents applied to classic language areas, such as Broca's area and Wernicke's area as well as some areas of the motor cortex, interfered with speech production. In one instance, when a probe was placed in the speech zones, the patient (who was awake since the procedure required only local anesthesia) reported, "Oh, I know what it is. That is what you put in your shoes." After the probe was removed, the patient said "foot." (Penfield & Roberts, 1959, p. 123).

More recent experiments using electrical stimulation of the brain by Ojemann (1991) have disclosed some equally interesting data on the brain and language. The technique, which is similar to the one used by Penfield, involves patients who are undergoing a treatment for epilepsy in which a portion of the skull is pealed back exposing the cerebral cortex. One procedure Ojemann used was to show patients a picture and ask that it be named with the probe turned on and with it turned off. As with the Penfield studies, it was possible to map areas of the cortex that were disabled during the task and to eliminate other areas that were not disabled. The results are shown in Figure 11.8 in which the percentage of subjects who showed naming errors is identified in the circled portions. Note that some regions are not affected while in other areas 50 percent to 79 percent of the patients had naming errors while other areas were below 50 percent.

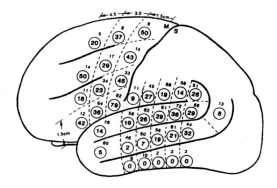

FIGURE 11.8

The results of electrical stimulation of the brain by Ojemann (1991). The small upper number is the number of patients tested, and the circled number is the percentage of patients who showed naming errors when stimulated at that site.

In another task the researcher had patients read a passage such as "The driver will turn at the intersection and then . . ." and complete the sentence. As in the other task, this was done with stimulation and without stimulation to specific areas. In this case the patient sometimes had difficulty reading the sentence, skipped words, or, in some cases, stopped reading completely. In the latter situation, if the probe was moved even slightly (no more than a few millimeters), there was no longer any interference. Thus, it was concluded that in these specific language tasks there were local areas that were critical. Another interesting finding was that the location of sites was highly variable among subjects.

PET Scans and Language. We have reviewed the procedure used in PET scans in Chapters 2 and 8. One advantage of this technology over electrical stimulation is that it is far less intrusive and can be performed on healthy subjects; in contrast, electrical stimulation is usually done as an adjunct experiment during psychosurgery with impaired patients. Several PET studies have been done with words, and the field is developing so rapidly it is likely that many more will be reported in the next few years. Of particular interest is a study by Posner and his colleagues (1988) in which visually presented words caused activation in the occipital lobe while spoken words showed activation in the temporoparietal cortex, a finding entirely consistent with previous neurological studies. These studies are especially revealing when one considers the tasks involved. In one condition, called the semantic task, more complicated processing was examined than was done during the passive viewing of words. In the semantic task, a subject was asked to say the use of a noun. For example, to the noun *hammer*, a subject might say "to pound." Such a task requires not just the passive observation of the word, as in the visual condition, but also access to associative-semantic regions of the brain. Posner and his colleagues found an increased blood flow in the anterior left frontal lobe as shown by the squares in Figure 11.9. While in the auditory condition, subjects were asked to judge whether or not words, such as *pint* and *lint*, and *row* and *though* rhymed, which required phonological analysis of visually presented material. The area activated in this task was the left temporal lobe, which is an area normally associated with auditory processing. These experiments suggest that linguistic processing is modality specific, that is, that semantic processing and auditory processing of visually presented material occur in different sites.

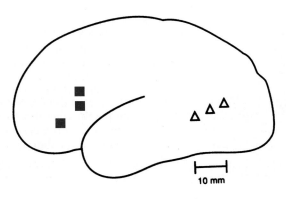

FIGURE 11.9

PET scan data showing areas activated in visual reading. The triangles show areas activated in a passive visual task, while the squares refer to the semantic task. Data from Posner et al. (1988).

10 mm

In this chapter a general overview of language is presented. The next chapter deals with the specific topics of the perception of words and reading. Some recent findings in that domain are also engaging, and we will find that real progress has been made in modern times.

Summary

1 Language is crucial to a wide range of human activities, including communication, thought, perceiving and representing information, higher-order cognition and neurology.

2 Early neurological studies by Broca and Wernicke established centers of the cortex, mostly located in the left cerebral hemisphere, that are involved in speech production and language comprehension.

3 Linguists conceive of language as a hierarchical structure that ranges from simple to increasingly complex components (for example, phonemes, morphemes, and syntax).

4 One feature of recent theories of transformational grammar is that message content of sentences may remain constant despite changes in linguistic form. One thesis (Chomsky) distinguishes between surface and deep structures and argues for the importance of the underlying uniformity of language, the generative nature of language systems, and commonalities in all languages.

5 Three positions regarding language acquisition can be identified: one position (for example, Chomsky) holds that language is an innate, universal propensity; the second position (for example, Skinner) holds that language is learned via reinforcement contingencies; and a third views language development as a function of biological maturation and interactions with the environment.

6 The linguistic-relativity hypothesis proposes that the nature of a language determines how people see and think about reality (language thought), but evidence indicating that perceptual experience is similar to different language speakers makes a strict interpretation of this position questionable.

7 Comprehension in reading is the process of understanding the meaning of written material. Studies of eye fixations indicate that comprehension is influenced by such factors as rare words, the integration of important clauses, and making inferences. Knowledge, either acquired throughout the history of the individual or situational, also affects comprehension.

8 One model of comprehension (Kintsch) suggests that readers understand text material in terms of propositions and goal schemata.

9 Studies of syntactic constructions show cultural differences in preferred word order (for example, subject-verb-object versus verb-subject-object), although the subject precedes the object in the majority of cases.

10 Some functional properties of memory for narrative prose include the following: sentences are stored in memory in combined, not isolated, form; stories, like sentences, can be parsed into their structural components; memory for narrative in-

formation is a function of its structural role; and gist is retained over time, but specific details are forgotten.

11   Studies of the neurology of language suggests that there are specialized areas involved in language processing, but that since language involves so many different subsystems, it is likely that many regions of the brain are engaged simultaneously.

12   The neurology of the brain has been studied by several techniques, including electrical probes and PET scans.

Key Words

bipolar probes	psycholinguistics
Broca's area	schema
comprehension	surface structure
deep structure	syntax
linguistic-relativity hypothesis	transformational grammar
morpheme	Wernicke's area
phoneme	Whorfian hypothesis

Recommended Readings

Excellent older books include R. Brown, *Words and Things,* a general and enjoyable book; Miller, *Language and Communication,* somewhat outdated but a classic; and Cherry, *On Human Communication.*

Original sources on Chomsky's ideas are very specialized, hence difficult for the nonspecialist; more accessible are E. Bach, *Syntactic Theory*; Slobin, *Psycholinguistics*; Kess, *Psycholinguistics: Introductory Perspectives*; and Dale, *Language Development: Structure and Function.* A comprehensive account is H. Clark and E. Clark, *Psychology and Language: An Introduction to Psycholinguistics.*

Also recommended is G. Miller's excellent current book *The Science of Words.* For further treatment of Kintsch's work, read Kintsch and van Dijk in *Psychological Review.* Those interested in the neurology of language are directed to Kolb and Whishaw, *Fundamentals of Human Neuropsychology*; Kandel, Schwartz, and Jessell, *Principles of Neural Science*; and Springer and Deutsch, *Left Brain, Right Brain.*

LANGUAGE 2:
Words and
Reading

T HIS CHAPTER ON WORDS and reading is the second of two chapters on language processing. In the last chapter we discussed the structure of language and its neurological counterparts. In this chapter we review the current theories and research on the detection of letters and the reading of written material.

The detection of letters and reading is of importance to psychologists for two reasons. First, the process represents, in microcosm, an interaction of stimuli and memory that mirrors the human cognitive process, and so understanding the process may be useful in developing models or theories of cognition—of the interplay between the "thing out there" and the "thing in the head." This is particularly true of reading, where a physical stimulus, devoid of any intrinsic value, is given meaning in an abstract memory system. These theories are developed within the context of the letter and word experiments because we know a great deal about both the nature of the stimuli and the experiences subjects bring with them to the perceptual situation. Second, the study of the process involved in letter identification and reading may lead to knowledge that could be used to improve the teaching of reading. The question of what attributes are involved in reading is among the most vexing of educational issues. Some answers to that question may be found by studying the development of reading skills, investigating letter and word identification, and the neurology of reading.

One phase of the inquiry into the process of letter and word identification started out with determining how much we see in a given fixation—a kind of cognitive snapshot—and ended with finding out how the structure of the visual pattern (for example, words) affects its identification. (It was determined that whole words are more easily identified than single letters.)

Toward the end of the nineteenth century, when experimental psychology was emerging in laboratories in Germany, England, and the United States, a French scientist, Émile Javal (1878), discovered that during reading the eye did not sweep across a line of print but moved in a series of small jumps—*saccades*—with momentary fixation occurring between them. James McKeen Cattell (1886a, 1886b) undertook to find how much could be read during a single visual fixation. Using a tachistoscope, he estimated the time it takes to identify such things as forms, colors, letters, and sentences. The results of his experiments conformed to those of the earlier studies of range of attention, but of greater interest for Cattell (and contemporary cognitive psychologists) was the fact that reaction times were related to the subjects' familiarity with the visual material.

By having subjects view a display of letters and words for as little as 10 milliseconds (1/100 seconds), he discovered that the capacity to report letters was not so much a function of the number of letters as it was a function of how close the sequence of letters approached a meaningful sequence—as, for example, in a word. A subject exposed to a display of unconnected letters for 10 milliseconds was able to report three or four letters; if the letters made a word, then up to two words (of three or four letters each);

Critical Issues: Smart Reading

Before reading ahead try to identify the following words: (1) n_t_r_, (2) m_m_r_, (3) p_rs_n_l_t_. Did you find this too difficult?

It has been determined that word perception is influenced by previous experience. We carry around with us some well-established rules of orthography (letter sequence), grammar, semantics, and word associations—all of which assist us in reading as well as everyday living. How much information did you bring to the decoding of this message, and how much was in the stimuli? Our capacity to "see" letters and words is not a passive process, but rather it is an active process in which we search for perceptual objects that already have their representation in memory. If you had difficulty filling in the blanks, consider the following hints: (1) human, (2) long term, (3) traits. Are there other words that could be formed from the letters given above. Why did you not think of them immediately.

and if the words were syntactically related, then the subject could "read" as many as four. Since 10 milliseconds is considerably less than the time required for a saccade,[1] the span of apprehension in the Cattell studies was limited to what might be called (in film-making terms) a single frame of perception. Because the reaction time for familiar words was about the same as it was for unconnected letters and because the span of apprehension for letters in words is greater than for unconnected letters, Cattell concluded that familiar words are read as a whole, or as a total word picture. From this he formulated a concept that has bemused countless hundreds of psychologists and provided the subject matter for volumes of dissertations in the psychology of reading. One of the puzzling dilemmas of this conclusion is the consideration that, to read a whole word, one must somehow perceive its parts and that, if this requires that the parts be examined letter by letter, reaction times should increase accordingly. Cattell attributed the fact that words were more easily identified than disconnected letters to the meaningfulness of the words, but now we know that word identification may be related to other variables. A portion of this chapter is devoted to the reporting of data regarding this problem.

Closely following the early experiments of Cattell was an important discovery by Erdmann and Dodge in 1898. They found that the perception of visual data took place during the fixation period and not during the eye movement and also that subjects could identify a word at a greater distance than they could letters presented individually. The latter finding, and the results of Pillsbury (1897), who demonstrated that "degraded" words (for example, *foyever* for *forever* or *tobxcco* for *tobacco*) are easily read and that in only a few cases (about 22 percent and 14 percent, respectively) could the subject recognize the mutilation, convinced many that the reading of familiar words was tied to the *unity* of the word and not to the recognition of individual letters. Some words seem to be read by experienced readers as whole units rather than letter by letter.

---

[1]A 2-degree saccade takes about 25 milliseconds; a 5-degree saccade, about 35 milliseconds; and a 10-degree saccade, about 45 milliseconds. There is some variation from subject to subject (L. Young, 1963; Rayner, 1978; and Robinson, 1968).

Between the perception of individual letters and total words is the perception of common letter combinations. The language abounds in ubiquitous bigrams (for example, *ie, re, th, st, er, te, of,* and *ar*) and trigrams (for example, *ent, ing, dis, ant, ion, ate, pro,* and many others). Most words, especially long ones, contain very familiar letter combinations, and there is little doubt that our identification of these words is greatly facilitated by that fact.

The first study of familiar letter groups in reading was done in 1917 by Wilkins, who presented subjects with jumbled or artificial elements that, when rearranged, made a familiar phrase. for example:

Elements Exposed	**Phrase as Read**
Washout at Irvington	Washington Irving
Renaistecture Archisance	Renaissance Architecture

She found that subjects to whom the elements in the first column were presented for 50 to 100 milliseconds frequently read them as the common phrase in the second column. (Consider the unhappy fate of a tired driver who comes across the sign "Washout at Irvington" and reads it as "Washington Irving.")

PERCEPTUAL SPAN

Modern cognitive psychologists are as intrigued by the question of perceptual span (how much information can be perceived during a brief presentation) as were their nineteenth-century counterparts. Following are several questions that dominate current thought on letter and word identification. The answers are discussed in this chapter.

- What are the neurological and physical capabilities in letter and word identification?
- What letter and word characteristics affect recognition?
- What normally is the relationship between stimulus and memory factors?
- What are the effects of context and frequency on word recognition?
- What models of cognition need to be developed to describe the process?

First, consider the question of neurological capabilities in the identification of letters or words. Visual acuity is best for images that fall on the part of the retina called the fovea. This small indentation on the back part of the eye is densely packed with photosensitive neurons called *cones* (see Figure 12.1a). Foveal vision encompasses a visual angle of only about 1 to 2 degrees. By fixing your gaze on a single letter of text at a normal viewing distance, you can experience the difference between foveal and peripheral vision. The single letter focused on is very clearly resolved, and some letters on either side may also be seen clearly. However, the letters and words only a few degrees away are quite fuzzy, and letters and words in the periphery are unrecognizable (see Figure 12.1b).

Yet, despite the fact that acuity drops off sharply from the fovea, it appears that identification of some letters and words, especially in the normal course of reading, occurs outside foveal vision. To better understand this seeming paradox, consider recent findings about saccadic eye movement. These rapid eye movements, although often studied in association with the reading process, also occur when a subject views a vi-

FIGURE 12.1

A. Distribution of cones in the retina. Adapted from Woodson (1954). B. Visual acuity in the retina. Shaded area is the "blind spot" (point of attachment of optic nerve). Adapted from Ruch and Patton (1965).

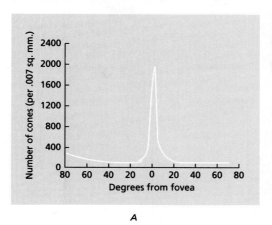
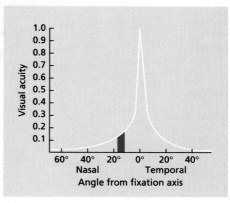

A

B

sual pattern. (See the discussion of Yarbus's work in Chapter 4.) According to Norton and Stark (1971), during reading there are typically 2 or 3 saccades per second, and these occur so fast that they occupy only about 10 percent of the viewing time. A movement of 10 degrees lasts only about 45 milliseconds and, during the movement, vision seems to be impaired, a condition called visual smear (Haber & Hershenson, 1973). It appears, then, that the recognition of letters and words in the nonfoveal field, which frequently occurs in the reading process, must be partly attributed to something other than the physical stimulation of the retina. That "something" is likely to be the human subject's great knowledge of letter and word sequencing as well as his or her understanding of the theme of the text. This is particularly evident among so-called speed readers, whose enormous capacity for processing voluminous information seems to be dependent upon their expectation of the material to follow.

Another way to evaluate visual acuity is through eye-tracking experiments that utilize computers. These experiments have been instrumental in identifying eye movement and eye fixation, which are thought to be tied to the processing of information in reading. These techniques and findings are discussed shortly (see the work of McConkie & Rayner and Just & Carpenter). Yet another technique for evaluating visual acuity has been to use a tachistoscope capable of presenting visual stimuli for a short duration. In these types of experiments, while subjects gaze at a fixation point, a word or phrase is flashed across the screen for a brief time. The subject may be asked to recall distal letters or words. The results of these types of experiments are summarized in Figure 12.2. As shown, the perceptual span generally takes in about two or three words, or about ten to twenty characters.

Given the constraints of the visual system, what can we infer about the process involved in normal text reading? It is likely that textual information that falls on the fovea is clearly detected and passed on to the brain for further processing. During the saccade, little, if any, textual information is being detected or processed. Textual information that

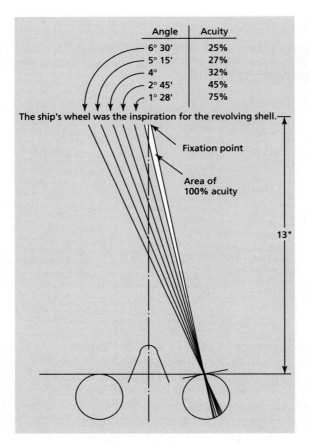

FIGURE 12.2

Visual acuity and perceptual span based on tachistoscopic experiments. From S. Taylor (1965).

is beyond the fovea, in parafovea or in peripheral vision, is poorly resolved neurologically, and yet this seeming sensory handicap does not impede the normal processing of textual material. Some evidence suggests that letters in the poorly resolved parafoveal vision are detected more clearly if they are surrounded by a space. Estes (1977) reconstructed the process involved in normal reading (shown in Figure 12.3).

William K. Estes. **Made significant contributions to many fields of psychology, including learning theory, mathematical psychology, and cognitive psychology. Founding editor of** *Cognitive Science.*

F I G U R E   1 2 . 3

Illustration of fixations and duration (in milliseconds). Also
shown is a hypothetical reconstruction of the information
perceived during fixations of normal text. Notice that at and
near each fixation, letters are clearly perceived, while more
distant letters are poorly perceived with the exception of letters
surrounded by a space. From Estes (1977) and Dearborn (1906).

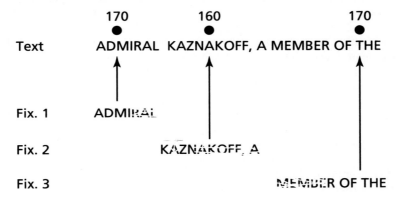

An important task of the verbal processing system, which is to make semantic
sense out of familiar lines and curves, is to fill in the gaps from the information detected
and derive the ultimate meaning intended by the writer. The reading process—from the
moment the eyes focus on textual material, to the derivation of meaning to another saccade—is done in a very brief time period. Later we shall learn of some recent techniques
that have unraveled some of the mysteries of the process.

The study of perceptual span in reading allows examination of the processing of information that is frequently not clearly perceived yet is frequently clearly encoded.
Studies of the reading process seem to reflect the human subject's capability to form hypotheses rapidly about text that requires only the confirmation or denial of his or her expectations rather than the detailed featural analysis of each letter. Some of the research
related to letter and word recognition is presented in the next section.

Tachistoscopic Presentation of Letters and Words

Research on tachistoscopically presented letters and words dates back to the last century. Some of the early studies revealed that more letters could be recognized if they
were presented in a meaningful sequence (for example, words) rather than in a meaningless sequence. More recent research has suggested that letters in words are recognized more clearly than letters alone or in meaningless sequences. These studies have
demonstrated that the number of letters and words a subject can report of briefly presented items is a function of the redundancy of the stimulus.

This technique has several advantages, including the fact that the rapid presentation of the visual information rules out movement of the eyes as a factor and offers con-

trol over the type of material seen. However, as we learned in Chapter 3, subjects may "see" much more than they verbally report.

As was mentioned earlier, Cattell demonstrated that words were more easily recognized than nonwords, while other researchers (Woodworth, 1938) observed that letters are more perceptible if they form a word than if they do not. This effect was called the word apprehension effect (WAE) by Neisser (1967). Reicher (1969) introduced a novel way to study the recognition of letters. In Reicher's technique, which attempted to take into consideration the subject's previous knowledge of letter sequencing (orthography), subjects viewed a display for 35 to 85 milliseconds, the length of exposure depending on individual differences in visual apprehension. As shown in Figure 12.4, the display consisted of either a word, a single letter from the word, or an anagram of the word. Displayed matter was then masked (with Xs), and two-letter alternatives were shown above the position of the letter to be recalled. Subjects were asked which of the two letters they had seen in the display. In the case shown in the figure, the subject was presented *WORD*, with *D* or *K* (each of which—with *WOR*—makes a word) as alternatives in the fourth position. The chance that the subject would choose the right letter (as a function of his or her previous experience with the 4-letter words *WORK* and *WORD*) ought to be nearly even in terms of redundancy theory.[2]

The results of Reicher's experiment indicated that the letters that were part of a word were more frequently identified than those that were part of a nonword letter sequence or than letters presented alone. With Reicher's results, the WAE theory seemed to gain ground. It would appear that the processing of word information makes contact

---

[2]It should be noted that Reicher did not consider the factor of positional frequency or versatility. In the English language, *D* appears in the fourth position of four-letter words nearly twice as often as *K*, and *D* has an overall frequency six times that of *K*.

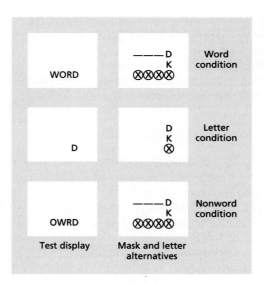

FIGURE 12.4

Visual displays used in Reicher study. From Reicher (1969).

with its representation in memory faster than a single letter (or a letter in an unfamiliar situation) makes contact with its representation. Simply put, the trip between a word and memory takes less time than that between a letter and memory. The implication of these data for the question of how visual information is processed, of course, is significant. In effect, in the visual processing of words, the whole word is perceived, and then letters, and presumably features, are extracted from the basic perceptual unit.

Despite the fact that other researchers found similar results (D. Wheeler, 1970), the exact nature of the word apprehension effect remained in question. M. Thompson and Massaro (1973) pointed out that, in the Reicher task, subjects may have seen only part of the critical letter—just enough to rule out other alternatives. In the example cited above, suppose that a subject saw *WOR* and only a portion of the *D*, say the curved part. Then, when asked to choose between a *D* and a *K*, the subject selects *D* because it contains the curve. Thompson and Massaro examined the influence of featural similarity of the response alternatives. An example of a test item in their experiment is *SLAP*, with the similar-feature task being the choice between *P* and *B* (both of which complete a word) and the distinctive-feature task being the choice between *P* and *M* (both of which also complete a word). Surprisingly, they found *no* effect of similarity on choice alternatives. The possibility arises that when momentarily viewing a word, subjects may synthesize a group of letters that may be compatible with what they have just seen and hold these in working memory until the response alternatives are flashed. Clearly, orthographic information in the subjects' long-term memory influences their decision; for example, it is unlikely that a subject would select *Q* in the fourth position of a four-letter word.[3]

Thompson and Massaro reasoned that if the alternatives (for example, *D* and *K* in the case of *WORD*) were known in advance of the word's being presented, then the subject would have no purpose in synthesizing alternatives; they would already exist in his or her immediate memory. In an experiment to test this hypothesis, Thompson and Massaro found that in the precue condition, the word apprehension effect disappeared and letters presented alone were better detected than letters in words. Other researchers have found essentially the same thing. (See Bjork and Estes, 1973a, 1973b; and Estes, Bjork, & Skarr, 1974.)

Text Processing: Eye Tracking

When we read or view a scene (such as a painting or picture), our eyes make a series of movements, called saccades, and there are periods of time when the eyes stop momentarily, called fixations, which, on average, last about 250 milliseconds, although individual differences both within and between subjects vary considerably. We do this because vision is sharpest in only a very narrow range, about 1 or 2 degrees. The typical saccade is about eight or nine letter spaces and is not affected by the size of the print, assuming it is not too small or too large. About 10 percent to 15 percent of the time we move our eyes back to review textual material; these are called regressions.

As early as 1906 (Dearborn), psychologists were making photographic records of eye movements during reading. Modern eye-tracking systems use videotape recorders

---

[3]However, this might not be the case if the subject is extremely familiar with Near East languages, many of which have words (at least in transliteration) that end in *q*.

and computers to analyze the movement of eyes during reading or when viewing a picture, and since the mid-1970s there has been a resurgence of interest in studies of eye movements applied to reading (see Inhoff & Tousman, 1990; Just & Carpenter, 1987; Raney & Rayner, 1993; Rayner, 1993; and Rayner et al., 1989, for reviews and recent developments) and perception of art (see Solso, 1994).

Some experimental work on the size of perceptual span has used this system. In this work, when a subject fixates on a portion of textual material, changes can be made in other parts of the display. For example, a display could consist of mutilated and normal text to study visual span of text. In these experiments, when the subject fixates on a line, that part of the display fixated on changes to readable text. When the subject makes a saccade, the readable text changes back to mutilated text and a new display of readable print appears near his new fixation point (see Figure 12.5). The span of read-

FIGURE 12.5

Examples of the moving-window paradigm. The first line shows a normal line of text with the fixation location marked by an asterisk. The next two lines show an example of two successive fixations with a window of 17 letter spaces. The remaining lines show examples of other types of experimental conditions. In the asymmetric example, the window extends 3 letters to the left of fixation and 8 to the right; in the similar-letters condition, the letters outside the window are replaced by similar letters rather than Xs; in the no-spaces example, all of the spaces between words are filled in outside the window; in the one-word example, only the fixated word is within the window; and in the two-word example, the fixated word plus the word to the right of fixation is available. From Rayner (1993).

eyes	do	not	move	smoothly *	across	the	page	of	text	Normal
XXXX	XX	XXX	move	smoothly *	acXXXX	XXX	XXXX	XX	XXXX	
										Moving window
XXXX	XX	XXX	XXXX	XXXothly *	across	the	XXXX	XX	XXXX	
XXXX	XX	XXX	XXXX	smoothly *	acXXXX	XXX	XXXX	XX	XXXX	Asymmetric
cqcr	bc	maf	move	smoothly *	acsarr	fbc	qoyc	at	fcvf	Similar- Letters
XXXXXXXXXXXXmove				smoothly *			acXXXXXXXXXXXXXXXXXXXXXX			No-spaces
XXXX	XX	XXX	XXXX	smoothly *	XXXXXX	XXX	XXXX	XX	XXXX	One-Word
XXXX	XX	XXX	XXXX	smoothly *	across	XXX	XXXX	XX	XXXX	Two-Word

able text can be varied. McConkie and Rayner (1973, 1976) and Rayner (1975, 1993) have found that good readers detect letter and word shape information from a limited area of about seventeen to nineteen character spaces from a fixation point (about 5 degrees of visual angle).

Rayner (1975, 1993) has used a similar technique to study how wide the area is from which a reader picks up information about the text. Some (Goodman, 1970) have suggested that, on the basis of the context of information plus partial information from peripheral vision, subjects generate a "hypothesis" as to what will appear next. This means that when reading text, subjects would move their eyes forward to confirm their hypothesis (the more frequent occurrence) or disconfirm their hypothesis (which then requires further processing). A contrary view is expressed by McConkie and Rayner (1973), who assume that subjects use the time during fixation to determine the nature of the text rather than hypothesize what is to follow. However, periphery cues are important in a section of certain information (for example, some features and shapes). When subjects move their fixation point ahead, the perceived pattern is normally consistent with their partial information. Finally, an innovative feature of Rayner's work is the variability of information presented in subjects' peripheral vision. In one experiment Rayner (1975) used a "critical word," which would change to the "word-identical condition" as subjects moved their fixation point toward it (see Figure 12.6 for an example). Thus, in the sentence "The rebels guarded the palace with their guns," the critical word *palace* could change (as the eye moved toward it) to *police*.

Critical Word	Condition
Palace	(W-Ident) Word-identical.
Police	(W-L) Semantically and syntactically acceptable word, some of whose letters are the same as W-Ident.
Pcluce	(N-SL) Nonword, with extreme letters and shape the same as W-Ident.
Pyctce	(N-L) Nonword with altered shape but same initial and end letters.
Qcluec	(N-S) Nonword with end letters reversed.

FIGURE 12.6

An example of the boundary paradigm. The first line shows a line of text prior to a display change with fixation locations marked by asterisks. When the reader's eye movement crosses an invisible boundary (the letter e in *the*), an initially displayed word (*date*) is replaced by the target word (*page*). The change occurs during the saccade so that the reader does not see the change. From Rayner (1993).

eyes	do	not	move	smoothly	across	the	date	of	text	Prechange
*		*		*	*					

eyes	do	not	move	smoothly	across	the	page	of	text	Postchange
							*			

Rayner found that a semantic interpretation (that is, meaning) of a word was made one to six character spaces from the fixation point, but beyond that, at seven to twelve character spaces, subjects were able to pick up only gross visual characteristics, such as word shape and initial and final letters. It appears that information in the near periphery is partially coded, and the extent of the processing is contingent on the distance from the fixation point.

Down-the-Garden-Path Experiments. The method of studying reading by means of eye movements has been used by Carpenter and Dahneman (1981; also see Just & Carpenter, 1987) in whose research brief stories such as follows were read aloud:

> The young man turned his back on the rock concert stage and looked across the resort lake. Tomorrow was the annual one-day fishing contest and fishermen would invade the place. Some of the best bass guitarists in the country would come to this spot.

If you read this passage as most people do, you were lead down the garden path in the first few lines, because when you read the word *bass,* you thought of the fish and pronounced it to rhyme with *mass.* The next word, *guitarists,* disconfirms that interpretation. Eye fixations up to *bass* are normal; however, as may be evident to you, the length of time spent on the word *guitarists* is longer than normal. Additionally, people tend to backtrack and look at the previous word.

The garden-path experiments yield significant insights into the reading process as they relate to the processing of textual material, but the results are even more important in our search for the nature of human information processing and consciousness.

First, these experiments (along with several others) suggest that the early stages of the comprehension of written material may occur during very brief time intervals. Subjects fixed their eyes on *bass* because the meaning of that word, in context, was somehow discordant with the rest of the sentence, and they changed their pattern of reading in a matter of a few hundred milliseconds.

Second, these findings suggest that from the very beginning of the processing of textual material some sophisticated form of comprehension, that is, the derivation of meaning, takes place. It is likely that in reading comprehension is nearly instantaneous with visual perception and need not occur after a trailing, speech-based, short-term memory code. In addition to early and nonspeech-based comprehension, it may be that in reading and other visual experiences we activate a rich chain of associative reactions that are used to understand the thing being perceived.

From the many experiments reviewed in this section, it is clear that the amount of information seen in the perceptual span is rather limited, although the amount of information processed seems to be great. It appears that a portion of the meaning of visual percepts, including letter and word identification, is supplied by readers themselves, a phenomenon that is noted in this and other chapters.

The encoding of a visual symbol involves both the nature of the signal (letter, letter combinations, words) and the expectation of meaning arising from information stored in the long-term memory of each individual. This notion is consistent with signal detection theory (see Chapter 3), according to which the perceiver brings to a perceptual situation various kinds of sensitivity, comparable to the various frequencies of

The Tortured Reading Patterns of Dyslexic People

Dyslexia is a reading deficiency that afflicts otherwise normal people. Some contend that it is constitutional in origin, while others argue it is social and/or psychological. That issue is not resolved. It is clear, however, that many schoolchildren have difficulty in reading, which profoundly affects their lives. The development of eye-tracking apparatus has made possible the measurement of eye fixations of normal and dyslexic people, which may give us insight into this problem. A sample of reading styles for a normal reader (PP) and a dyslexic (Dave) are shown here. The numbers immediately below the dots are the sequence of eye movements, and the larger numbers further below the dots are the fixation times in milliseconds (1000 millisecond = 1 second).

PP
As society has become progressively more complex, psychology has

·	·	·	·	·	·		·	·
1	2	3	4	5	7		8	9
234	310	188	216	242	188		177	159

6
144

Dave
As society has become progressively more complex, psychology has

·	·	·	·	·	·	·	·	·		·	·		·	·
1	2	3	5		6	7	8	9	10		15	12		13	14
311	277	115	412		198	403	266	295	311		193	317		600	312

4
222

11
277

18
206

19
415

PP
assumed an increasingly important role in solving human problems.

·	·	·	·	·	·		·	·	·
11		12	13	15	14		16		18
244		317	229	269	196		277		202

10
206

17
144

Dave
assumed an increasingly important role in solving human problems.

·	·	·	·	·	·		·	·	·		·	·	·
16		21		22	24		25	26	27		28	31	32
369		302		244	310		383	119	487		413	277	366

17
415

20
177

23
288

29
200

33
361

30
117

From Rayner and Pollatsek (1989).

an electronic receiver (for example, a radio), on each of which only certain transmissions can be received.

FAMILIARIZATION: WORD FREQUENCY AND WORD RECOGNITION

The notion has prevailed throughout the history of psychology that familiarization with information (through repeated exposure) influences learning, memory, and perception. Such familiarization is also important in word and letter identification. As we noted, early experiments on reading indicated that subjects' familiarity with written material greatly enhanced their capacity to "see" the word, phrase, or letter combination. How frequently we have seen certain words is relatively easy to measure: simply count the words in a sample of printed matter, and assume that all subjects within a given population (for example, U.S. citizens) are more or less uniformly familiar with them. Such a count (to determine how common a word is in American "English")—was undertaken by E. L. Thorndike in the 1920s and early 1930s and revised in what has now become the familiar Thorndike-Lorge Word Frequency Count (1944). Word frequencies based on about 20 million words gathered from magazines, books, and so on were tabulated into the corpus. A more recent word count was done by Kučera and Francis (1967) and was based on a little more than 1 million words in 15 different categories of matter (for example, newspapers, popular lore, learned and scientific writings, fiction, and so on). Since these simple counts of the frequency of words in the English language, other measures have been made in which more complex indexes of words are an important part. Characteristic of these newer counts is a study done by Rubin and Friendly (1986) in which 925 words (nouns) were evaluated in terms of their recallability. Factors such as availability, goodness, emotionality, pronounceability, and probability of recall in multiple-trial free-recall tasks were evaluated, and it was found that availability, imagery, and emotionality were the best predictors of which words are best recalled. These norms promise to enhance our understanding of the memory process as well as standardize verbal learning material.

The experimental data on word familiarity and word recognition have generally supported the notion that familiarity facilitates recognition. This comes as no surprise; subjective experience tells us that highly familiar words are more easily identified than obscure ones. However, the locus of the effect is of interest to the cognitive psychologist as well as the educator. It may be that familiarity of letter sequences acts as a redundancy factor so that the reader can accurately approximate a word or letter on the basis of well-practiced minimal cues. Thus familiarity with *ing, the, est,* and other frequent letter combinations can cause them to be easily anticipated within word and syntactic contexts. An early study by Howes and Solomon (1951) addressed this issue. They asked subjects to identify words (from the Thorndike-Lorge count) presented for varying amounts of times. Some of the words were common (*country, promise, example*), and some familiar (*testify, swindle, surmise*), and some rare (*titular, pigment, machete*). We can conclude from the results, shown in Figure 12.7, that as the frequency of occurrence of a word increases, there is decline in the time required to "see" (or recognize) it (threshold value), or, conversely, that we require more time to "see" unfamiliar words.

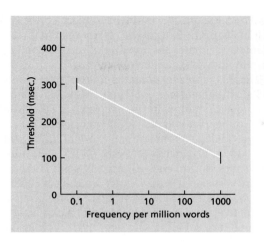

FIGURE 12.7

Threshold values as a function of frequency of occurrence of words in English. Adapted from Howes and Solomon (1951).

CONTEXTUAL EFFECTS

Word Identification

From the material discussed in this chapter, there can be little doubt that redundancy of information is a powerful determinant in the processing of verbal material. There also can be little doubt that the facts support the principle that the human information processor brings to any given perceptual situation an immense amount of information. The perception and processing of information, then, is dependent on the interaction of two classes of variables: the nature of the stimuli and the expectations of the human processor. In human information processing, the greater the expectation, the less the amount of information needed to confirm it, and, conversely, the more the amount of information that is needed to disconfirm it. This hypothesis has been tested in word recognition studies in which subject expectancy was manipulated. One of the first and best of the experiments in this area was conducted by Tulving and Gold (1963), who had subjects read a part of a sentence, very briefly exposed the final word in the sentence, and asked the subjects to identify it. The final word was relevant in one of two conditions and irrelevant in the other. The amount of context varied among one, two, four, and eight words; an example of contexts (in which the final word was *performer*) follows:

The	(performer)
The actress	(performer)
The actress received praise	(performer)
The actress received praise for being an outstanding	(performer)

With the exception of a situation in which the final word is inconsistent with the context, irrelevant-context sentences were similar. The visual threshold was measured by presenting the final word for 10 milliseconds. If the subject "missed," exposure time was increased by 10-millisecond increments until the subject correctly identified the word. The results are shown in Figure 12.8. It can be clearly seen that the amount of relevant information in the context facilitates the rapidity of recognition, while irrelevant information impedes it. Current knowledge of long-term memory strongly suggests that our memory for verbal material is organized along the lines of related information. The results of Tulving and Gold's experiment are consistent with that notion. Specifically, contextual information may serve to "put us in the ballpark" of similar information, so that when a relevant stimulus appears it is more readily perceived.

The results of Tulving and Gold's experiment and those of many others (for example, Fischler & Bloom, 1979, 1985; Stanovich & West, 1979, 1983; and Tanenhaus & Lucas, 1987) have met with some controversy. At issue is what is the active prime in the case of presenting a phrase associated with a target word. One could argue that the entire phrase or sentence that activates related associates[4] is the prime or that certain sensitive words act as the effective stimulus in the spread of associates. In Tulving and Gold's experiment, for example, it may be that the word *actress* alone could prime the word *performer* and that the syntax contributed little to the results. Other experiments have confirmed the effectiveness of single-word primes (see the discussion of lexical decision tasks later in this chapter). The question of what the effective stimulus is in these experiments—the word(s) or the syntax—has been clarified by experiments by Simpson and his colleagues (1989). They partly replicated Tulving and Gold's experiment, except that they added a condition in which the words of the priming phrase were scrambled. Also, they used speed of saying the target word as the dependent variable.

---

[4]The idea that a prime triggers a network of semantic associates is consistent with the model of semantic memory as expressed by Collins and Loftus (1975).

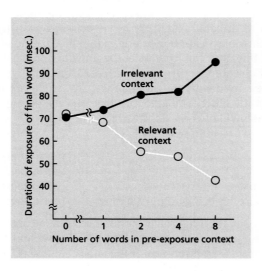

FIGURE 12.8

Visual-duration threshold as a function of length of context for relevant and irrelevant contexts. Adapted from Tulving and Gold (1963).

An example of their task follows:

Normal: John bought four **chairs** to go with his new **table.**

Scrambled: Four with to **chairs** his go John new bought **table.**

Simpson and his group found that the priming effects held up for the first condition but not for the second. Thus, the facilitating effects are not due solely to interlexical spreading activation but depend partly on syntax.

Morton's Logogen

This phenomenon—the relationship of contextual information and word thresholds—is unexplained by the data reported above and similar data reported by other researchers. However, Morton (1969, 1970, 1980, 1981) and A. Jackson and Morton (1984) have provided us with a theoretical model for word recognition that addresses the issue.

Morton's model of word recognition is based on a hypothetical construct called a *logogen,*[5] which he conceptualizes as a device that acts like a kind of adding machine, summing information until, when a certain critical amount is tallied up, a response of the class accumulated becomes available. Each logogen is formed by sensory information—auditory, visual, or contextual. For example, each of these experiences—hearing *table,* reading *table,* or, possibly, free-associating to the word *chair*—would add to the logogen associated with *table.* When a logogen is excited, the subject develops a state of preparedness for a particular type of response. As just illustrated, the response "table" is easily available after having its logogen excited. The strength of the logogen is manifest in the response potential of the word (see Figure 12.9). As the figure shows, responses

[5]From *logos* ("word") and *genus* ("birth" or "origin").

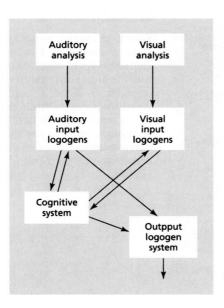

FIGURE 12.9

Flow diagram of modified logogen model. Adapted from Jackson and Morton (1984).

are passed on to an output logogen. According to the logogen model, subjects in Tulving and Gold's experiment required less exposure time to recognize a relevant word in context because the context fed energy into the logogen system, so that when the relevant word appeared, it required less stimulus energy (in terms of exposure duration) to excite the relevant word.

Of particular interest to modern information processing and word recognition theory is the compatibility of the logogen model with signal detection theory. Signal detection theory (see Chapter 3) assumes that sensitivity to stimuli is continuous rather than discrete and that "thresholds" are a matter of a response criterion. Morton has hypothesized that logogens operate as detectors that vary in relation to context and stimulus properties. A logogen's level of excitation (the horizontal axis in Figure 12.10a) is presumed to be normally distributed. The effect of context on the logogen is to raise its mean level of excitation. (The rise is labeled "C" in Figure 12.10b.) A stimulus—for example, a word—also shifts the mean upward (see Figure 12.10c), while multiple cuing (stimulus and context) increases excitability even more (see Figure 12.10d). Finally, word frequency has long-term effects that lower the sensory threshold (see Figure 12.10e). From Morton's figure, one would predict that if stimulus plus context were present and the target (final) word was a high-frequency one, the subject would probably "see" the correct word. Of interest is the fact that it is possible to make quantitative predictions from this model about human performance in a variety of situations. Thus far, data collected and the model's prediction about human performance seem to agree.

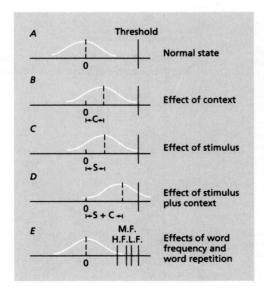

FIGURE 12.10

Effects of certain situations on the state of a logogen. Horizontal axes represent level of excitation. Vertical lines indicate threshold of the logogen. *H. F., M. F.,* and *L. F.* indicate word frequency—high, medium, and low, respectively. When the level of excitation exceeds the threshold, the corresponding word is available as a response. Adapted from Morton (1969).

Interactive Activation Model and Letter and Word Identification: A PDP Perspective

The previous studies have clearly shown that context and familiarization play an important role in the identification of words and letters. Some theories (for example, the logogen model) even give some insight into the complex inner mechanisms underlying such effects. In the model by Morton, each "firing" of a logogen lowers its threshold, thus making identification easier. There are other ways to view this process.

The interactive activation model shares some critical features with the logogen model in that contextual effects facilitate perception. However, it differs in the sense that with frequent use of a word the resting level is activated. Consider the instance of frequently used words—your name, for example. In the logogen model, the threshold for these words is lowered with use. You can recognize your name when said by someone on the other side of a crowded, noisy room (remember the "cocktail party phenomenon"?). In the interactive activation model, frequently used words (such as your name) have acquired a higher resting level of activation, which has the effect of requiring less input to be activated. It is almost as if the neurons involved in the detection of frequent words are already active. Also, because the system works by inhibition, as well as facilitation, between units, frequently experienced words are effective in inhibiting other units. Those subscribing to a connectionist theory (or PDP model) have proposed an even more elaborate internal structure to which we now turn, but keep in mind that the basic processes are the very simple connections between units. Some are strengthened, and some are inhibited.

The connectionistic model, as presented in other parts of this book, is based on excitatory and inhibitory interactions among units (McClelland & Rumelhart, 1981, 1986; and Rumelhart & McClelland, 1982, 1986), which perform in a way analogous to neural functioning in the brain. Although the whole model is complicated, it is based on only a few basic assumptions. Figure 12.11 shows the components of the interactive activation model of letter and word perception. The analysis is based on three levels in which a printed word is first processed by a feature analysis system. The output of that system is passed along to a letter identification level and then to a word level. These three levels of processing may be summarized as follows:

1. *The feature level.* The types of line segments that make up a word (for example, *T* is composed of a vertical — and a horizontal | feature)

2. *The letter level.* Each letter has a unit for each position in a word (for example, *ROSE* would have a unit for *R* in the first position, *O* in the second position, and so on).

3. *The word level.* Each word in the lexicon (personal vocabulary) is represented by a single unit.

In the connectionist model, connections are made among the units within and between levels. Now, consider how the system might handle the actual processing of a single letter (*T*) in the first position of a four-letter word. Figure 12.12 shows the seemingly complicated set of connections. Notice that two different kinds of connections are represented: those with a dot at the terminus and those with an arrow, which represent, re-

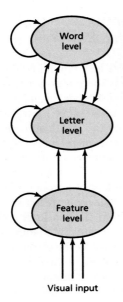

Visual input

FIGURE 12.11

Basic components of interactive activation model of letter and word perception. Excitatory connections are shown by lines and arrows, and inhibitory connections by lines. From McClelland and Rumelhart (1981).

FIGURE 12.12

A set of interactions between units. Excitatory links are shown as an arrow (for example, ⊖ and *T*) and inhibitory links as dots (for example, ⊘ and *T*). In this illustration, the unit for the letter T in the first position of a four-letter word and some of its neighbors are shown at the feature, the letter, and the word levels. From McClelland and Rumelhart (1981). Copyright 1981 by the American Psychological Association. Reprinted by permission.

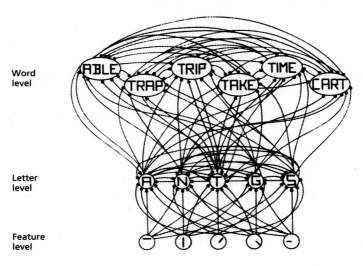

spectively, inhibitory and facilitatory connections. Consistency between levels (facilitatory), as in the case of *T* in the first position being consistent with the words *TRAP*, *TRIP*, and so on, is shown with an arrow, while inconsistency (initiatory) is shown with a dot. At the featural level, the letter *T* is consistent with the feature and the feature is represented by the arrow in the connection between these features and the letter *T.* All other featural connections (in this case) are inhibited, as shown by dots. At the next level, *T* in the first position is consistent with the word *TAKE*, and the units that connect *T* with *TAKE* are excited as are connections between *TRAP*, *TRIP*, and *TIME*. Note that the *T* in *CART* is not excited, since it is not in the first position. Also, the words are mutually exclusive—that is, the "correct" word cannot be *ABLE*, *TRAP*, or any other word, so these words are inhibited (see dots).

Now consider a slightly different case. How does this model handle familiar words that have been partially degraded, as shown in Figure 12.13? In this instance, the letters *W*, *O*, and *R* are completely visible. The fourth letter is ambiguous: it could be either an *R* or a *K*. Before the onset of the display, the activations of the units are at or below zero, but when the display is presented, detectors for the features become active; this is represented with an activity level above zero. Then the feature detectors excite and inhibit

F I G U R E   1 2 . 1 3

The partially occluded word *WORK*, and how an interactive activation model of word recognition might process the display. The letter units are for letters in the fourth position of four-letter words, and the word levels are the activation of appropriate words. From Rumelhart and McClelland (1986).

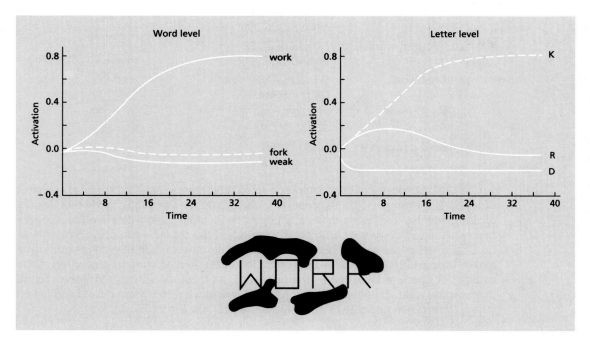

corresponding detectors for letters. For example, the features of the first letter, *W*, are unambiguously activated, which triggers the letter *W* (much as in the case of *T* in the example of the connectionist model just presented). But how does the model handle the partially occluded letter (*R* or *K*)? At the featural and letter levels, it is impossible to decide which of the two letters is probably correct, but the model specifies that the detectors for the other letters—the unambiguously presented letters *W, O,* and *R*—start to activate detectors for words that have these letters in them and also inhibit detectors for words that do not have these letters. There is only one word that matches the context: that word is *WORK,* which becomes more active than any other word.

These examples show how the components of the interactive activation model of letter and word perception work together in reading and figuring out ambiguous displays. Thus far the model has been tested using computer simulation, with impressive results. It is much more detailed than other models and can be empirically tested. It is anticipated that much data will be generated from this model in the next few years.

The next section deals with the effect of context on word recognition from a much different perspective. This approach, which has become very popular because of its reliability and versatility, is called the lexical-decision task (LDT).

Lexical-Decision Task (LDT)

An innovative approach to the problem of contextual effects on word identification has been introduced by Meyer and his associates (Meyer & Schvaneveldt, 1971; and Meyer, Schvaneveldt, & Ruddy, 1972, 1974a, 1974b). They used a lexical-decision task (LDT), a type of priming task, in which the experimenter measured how quickly subjects could tell whether paired strings of letters were words. Typical stimuli were as follows:

Associated words	*BREAD-BUTTER*
	NURSE-DOCTOR
Unassociated words	*NURSE-BUTTER*
	BREAD-DOCTOR
Word-nonword	*WINE-PLAME*
	GLOVE-SOAM
Nonword-word	*PLAME-WINE*
	SOAM-GLOVE
Nonword-nonword	*NART-TRIEF*
	PABLE-REAB

In the procedure a subject looks at two fixation points (see Figure 12.14). A series of letters (for example, NURSE) appears at the top point. The subject presses a key, indicating whether the letters make a word. As soon as his or her decision is made, the first set of letters disappears and, shortly thereafter, the second set appears. The subject decides whether the second set is a word, and the process continues. This procedure makes it possible to measure word recognition of the second word as a function of the context, or prime, established by the first word. As might be anticipated, Meyer found that reaction time for judging the second word was much faster when it had been paired with an associated rather than nonassociated word (see Figure 12.15).

FIGURE 12.14

Basic procedure on each trial in the lexical-decision task. Adapted from Meyer, Schvaneveldt, and Ruddy (1974a).

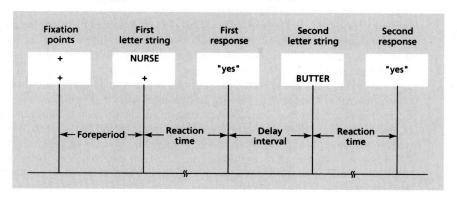

FIGURE 12.15

Effects of semantic context on the time required to identify the second member of word pairs in the lexical-decision task. Adapted from Meyer, Schvaneveldt, and Ruddy (1974a).

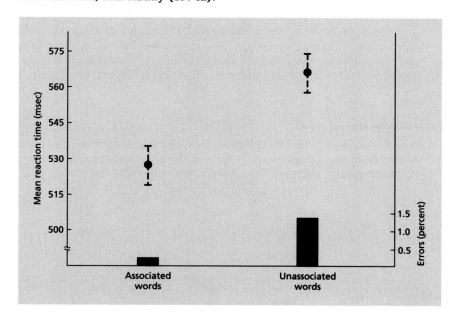

Again we have an example of the effect of context on word identification. We could interpret those data in terms of a logogen model in which the first word excited the logogen of the second word. Meyer and his associates interpreted them in terms of a general information-processing framework outlined in Figure 12.16, in which the first stage is an encoding operation that creates an internal representation. Following encoding, the sequence of letters is checked against the subject's lexical memory to see whether the item has been previously stored, and, depending on whether a match is made, a decision is executed. Two important assumptions are made by the model regarding memory storage of lexical events: first, the words are stored at various locations in memory, with some words closely associated (for example, *bread-butter*) and some distant (for example, *nurse-butter*); second, retrieving information from a specific memory location produces neural activity that spreads to nearby locations, thereby facilitating the recognition of associated memories. The latter hypothesis is supported by "context" experiments, especially those reported by Meyer and Schvaneveldt, who developed a model (see Figure 12.17) of letter and word recognition. (Although our discussion of this model is in terms of its relation to letter and word identification, the model is also germane to the discussion of semantic memory.) In the model, the recognition process begins when a row of letters enters the visual feature analyzer. The resulting "code," which represents the shape of letters (straight lines, curves, angles), is passed on to word detectors. When sufficient cues are recognized by a word detector, then an affirmative signal is produced to indicate that a certain word has been detected; the detection of a certain word also excites other nearby words. For example, detection of *bread* also activates related words in the subject's memory network. These other words—*food, butter,* and so on—are "sensitized" (my word); this is indicated by the dashed lines in Figure 12.17. The excitation of semantically related words facilitates the subsequent detection of these words. This model takes into account the fact that subjects recognize related words faster than unrelated words. This model is noteworthy not only because it accommodates the data, but also because it offers a means of viewing the structure of semantic memory.

The theoretical positions of Meyer and of Morton and connectionism seem not to be antagonistic. Indeed, they appear to be complementary. All address the problem of the effect of context on word identification, and all have concluded that some internal mechanism enhances word identification as a function of context. For Morton, the mechanism

FIGURE 12.16

Possible stages in word recognition. Horizontal arrows show the presumed sequence of operations; vertical arrows, the effects of semantic context and stimulus quality. Adapted from Meyer, Schvaneveldt, and Ruddy (1974a).

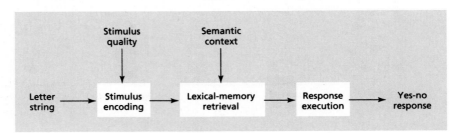

FIGURE 12.17

Hypothetical mechanism for combining sensory and semantic information during word recognition. Adapted from Meyer and Schvaneveldt (1976a).

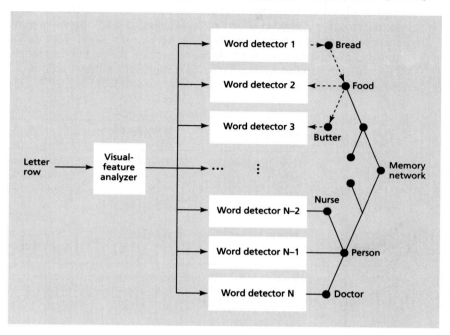

is one of elevating a logogen's level of excitation; for Meyer and for Rumelhart and Mc-Clelland, it is the spreading of neural activity, which renders similar lexical items more accessible.

Word Recognition: A Cognitive-Anatomical Approach

Our review of the underlying cognitive mechanisms involved in word recognition has covered a wide range of topics—from the contextual effects phases, to logogens, to connectionism, to LDTs. We now turn to some of the evidence on word processing vis-à-vis anatomical structures, which uses some of the advanced technology mentioned in Chapter 2. The research on the cognitive-anatomical foundation of word processing is particularly germane to our present discussion, because some of the cognitive tasks (for example, LDT) have been applied to patients who have sustained brain injuries. The recent neuropsychological journals are overflowing with these types of experiments, which is a harbinger of the direction cognitive science is taking.

The general direction many of these studies have taken is to locate specific neurological sites involved in specific cognitive functions. For example, a researcher might be interested in correlating an LDT with specific blood flow observations in an effort to locate cognitive operations in the brain.

Following the work of Meyer and Schvaneveldt just reported, some researchers (for example, Petersen and Posner) have combined several word processing paradigms, including the DOCTOR-NURSE task, with advanced imaging technology to isolate the anatomical systems activated by words and their associates in healthy subjects (see Petersen et al., 1988; Posner et al., 1988; and Posner et al., 1989).

In one study (Petersen et al., 1988) of regional blood flow, subjects were asked to participate in three common lexical tasks. Each task differed from the other by a small number of processing operations. At the same time, the researchers monitored data from PET scans with particular attention to the visual and auditory portions of the cortex. The experimental paradigm was:

Paradigm Design*

Condition	Control State	Stimulated State	Task
A.	Fixation point only	Passive words	Passive sensory processing; modality-specific word-level coding
B.	Passive words	Repeat words	Articulatory coding; motor programming and output
C. Active semantic	Repeat words	Generate uses	Semantic association; selection for action

*Table showing the rationale of the three-levels stepwise paradigm design. At the second and third levels, the control state is the stimulated state from the previous level. Some hypothesized cognitive operations are represented in the third column.

At the simplest level (A), subjects examined a fixation point or passively watched visual words. At the more complex level (B), they repeated each word as it occurred. At an even more complex level (C), they generated a use for each word. Succinctly stated, different cortical areas were activated by each of the different tasks (see Figure 12.18). Of particular interest in these findings are the portions of the cortex involved in visual word forms (A), which are represented by triangles in Figure 12.18, and those involved in semantic analysis (C), which are identified by circles, suggesting that these different forms of lexical processing are, indeed, handled by different parts of the brain. These data are even more interesting when we consider them in the context of the previously reviewed connectionist theory (see Rumelhart & McClelland, 1986). In that theory, you may recall, separate levels of feature, letter, and word form analysis were posited. The demonstration of multiple areas of activation in the experiment by Petersen and his colleagues seems to offer tangible support for this part of the puzzle.

These data were supplemented by an experiment by Posner and his team (1989) using essentially the same technique, except that the subject participated in a modified LDT (see above discussion). In one condition, a visual priming of a word was presented (for example, *DOCTOR-DOCTOR*); in another task, a semantic priming of a word was presented (for example, *DOCTOR-NURSE*); and in a third task, a cuing of visual spatial attention was done (for example, a peripheral cue to the left of the screen followed by a target to the left for a valid trial or to the right for an invalid trial). The results of the study showed that the area most likely to be involved in the priming of visual features

FIGURE 12.18

Data from PET scans studies showing areas of visual and auditory words. Two areas are shown: the lateral sides of the cortex (1) and the medial portions (2). Visual words are shown in triangles (A), semantic analysis in circles (C), and attention in squares or hexagons. Solid figures indicate left hemisphere, and open figures indicate right hemisphere. The area activated by repeating words presented auditorially (such as in shadowing experiments) are encircled by broken lines (B). From Petersen et al. (1988).

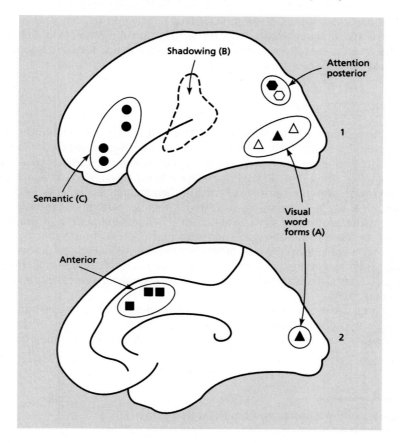

(*DOCTOR-DOCTOR*) is the ventral occipital lobe (identified in Figure 12.18 as visual word forms [A]). Posner and his associates suggest that word primes activate these areas and that an identical target will reactivate the same pathway within the network. Semantic tasks (*DOCTOR-NURSE*) seem to activate two additional areas: the left inferior prefrontal cortex (C) (see circles in Figure 12.18) and the medial frontal lobe (see hexagons in Figure 12.18).

Taken together, these studies advance our understanding of the relationship between cognitive tasks, such as the LDT, and brain functions. Additional work in this area is likely to focus on the role of attention and lexical processing; some data in that area already have been reported (see Posner et al., 1989; and Posner et al., in press). Further application of the work may link the bizarre abnormalities in thought and language among schizophrenics with cortical anatomy, especially abnormalities in the anterior attentional system (see Posner et al., in press, for further details).

In this section I have tried to trace the development of lexical processing from both the theoretical and empirical standpoints. The auspicious conclusion is that real progress has been made on both levels, and, fortunately, there seems to be greater mutual support than mutual dissolution. Such a conclusion is, I am sure, a consolation to cognitive and brain scientists who are working on the problem of lexical processing from different perspectives. We now leave this section and turn to the topic of orthography and intention in reading.

Orthography and Intention

In an interesting study by Massaro and Hestand (1983), the relationship between the reading ability of grade school students and knowledge of orthographic structure was shown. In their experiment first-, second-, and third-grade students were asked to identify the letter string that "looked more like a word." The letter strings with which the children were presented varied in terms of their statistical similarity to normal English words. One set of letter strings followed a regular pattern of the order of letters in words, while another set violated the normal sequencing pattern of words. Several examples are shown in Table 12.1. Massaro and Hestand found that performance improved with grade level. That is, older children selected a higher number of the regular strings as looking more like a word than did the younger children. The researchers also found that performance was also correlated with students' scores on a standardized test of mental ability.

In a related study, Salasoo, Shiffrin, and Feustel (1985) demonstrated that by presenting a pseudoword repeatedly, the letter string takes on many of the properties of high-frequency words, thus suggesting a close link between learning and information

TABLE 12.1

Examples of the Regular and Irregular Test Items

Regular	Irregular
movule	plgued (1)*
morebs	ydlaes (2)
hemort	cdrtei (3)

* The numbers in parentheses indicate the number of irregularities. From Massaro and Hestand (1983).

processing. These studies, along with others, pinpoint one important feature of the relationship between familiarization and information processing. Such information may provide an important clue to two larger issues, one theoretical and the other practical. On the theoretical side, the study gives further support to the notion that through the process of learning to read, students acquire incidental knowledge of the regularities and rules that govern the sequence of letters in words. On the practical side, such information may be of direct application in the teaching of reading and the development of textbooks that are designed to foster orthographic understanding.

The process of extracting meaning from these whimsically structured letters as we read has thus far eluded our total understanding. In addition to the factors mentioned above, several other components have been suggested as potential elements of the reading process and may be an integral part of the practice of reading. Understanding the role of these factors may help unravel some of the mysteries of reading. A promising system has been proposed by Aaronson and Ferres (1984, 1986) in which lexical, structural, and meaning attributes of text material are incorporated into a grand model that takes into account the intention of the reader. The authors propose a model in which reading is conceptualized as a complex process involving an interaction between multiple factors, including (1) the attributes of words and sentences (see the discussion of the work of Massaro and of Kintsch in the preceding chapter, for example) and (2) the purposes for which people read these stimuli. In general, psychologists and psycholinguists seem more interested in the first process, whereas reading teachers tend to focus on the second issue. In one paper, Aaronson and Ferres (1986) suggest that reading speed is a function of the intention of the reader (reading for either comprehension or retention), the age of the reader (children read slower and at rates that are different from adults), and individual differences (fast and slow readers). The experimenters had children and adults self-regulate the amount of time that words would appear on a computer screen. Following the reading of a sentence, a question would appear that asked the subject to recall verbatim the sentence or to answer a true or false question about the sentence. The first measure was called the recall condition; the second measure, the "comprehension" condition. An example of the type of data collected by Aaronson and Ferres is shown in Figure 12.19 for one student who has switched from a recall strategy (upper figure, Trial 73) to a comprehension strategy (lower figure, Trial 74).

Consider the reading rate of this subject. When reading for comprehension, the student reads at a rate that is fast and smooth with only slightly longer reading times at semantically important points (for example, near "love" and "agreed"). While reading for recall, the child seems to be more deliberate. The authors report that the relative processing time differs for adults and children, with adults spending relatively more time to process meaning in the comprehensive task than do children. Most children, who have not mastered the connection between task demands and linguistic processors, seem to use a mixture of adult strategies.

COMPREHENSION

Up to this point our discussion of the reading process has concentrated on the recognition of letters and words in and out of context. The reason people read, by and large, is

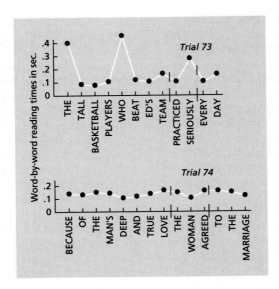

FIGURE 12.19

Word-by-word reading times for a child in the fast comprehension group that illustrate the mixing of strategies from one trial to the next. From Aaronson and Ferres (1986).

to extract meaning from material that is conveniently represented in printed form. We use the term *reading comprehension* to describe the process of understanding the meaning of written material. Studies of comprehension have yielded nearly as many models and theories as researchers, and, although many are meritorious, only a sample of that important work can be reported here.

Consider a simple sentence, such as "The ball is red." From our previous discussion of visual perception and word identification, we know that light reflecting from the printed page received by the sensory neurons is transmitted to the brain, where feature, letter, and word identification is made. Such elementary processes, however, are devoid of meaning, which is presumably the purpose of reading.

When you read the example sentence, it is probable that you understand that (1) a single spherical object is (2) colored red. You comprehend the meaning of the sentence, and that meaning is about the same as the author intended and as most other folks understand. In addition to the basic physical characteristics described, you consciously or unconsciously make many inferences about the object. (For example, most readers infer that the ball is larger than a golf ball and smaller than a basketball.)

Comprehension of the sentence can be validated if you are shown a picture of a red ball and indicate that the meaning of the sentence is the same as the picture, as contrasted with a picture of a green ball or a red box. This seemingly simple task really involves many more operations than are first apparent. In order to understand reading comprehension, some theorists have broken the process into stages, which assumes that there is a sequence of processes that starts with the perception of the written word and leads to the understanding of the meaning of sentences and stories. One model, which incorporates some of the topics discussed in this book, was developed by Just and Carpenter (1980, 1987) and will serve as a representation of contemporary work in

FIGURE 12.20

A schematic diagram of the major processes and structures in reading comprehension.

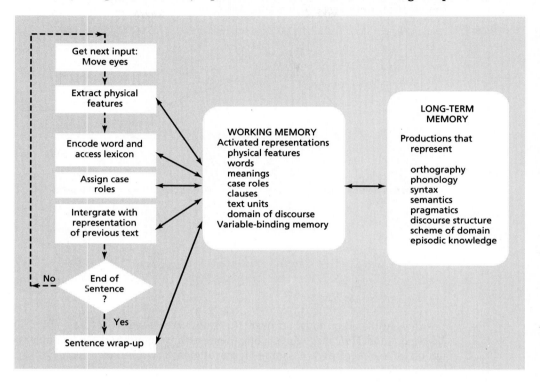

this field. The rudiments of the model are shown in Figure 12.20. The process of reading and comprehension in the Just and Carpenter model is conceptualized as the coordinated execution of a series of stages that include extracting physical features of letters, encoding words and accessing the lexicon, assigning case roles, and so on. In this representation the major stages of reading are shown in the left column, while the more permanent cognitive structures and processes are shown in the boxes in the middle and right side of the diagram.

Some of the intriguing features of this model are that it is comprehensive and yet it generates very specific predictions about reading performance that can be empirically measured by eye fixations. The authors assume that words in textual material are structured in larger units, such as clauses, sentences, and topics. A schematic diagram of one example of how a paragraph of scientific material might be conceptualized is shown in Figure 12.21. When a subject encounters a section of written text that demands greater processing of information, he or she may require longer pauses, which can be measured by looking at eye-fixation times.

FIGURE 12.21

A schematic diagram of the major text-grammatical categories of information in the scientific paragraphs.

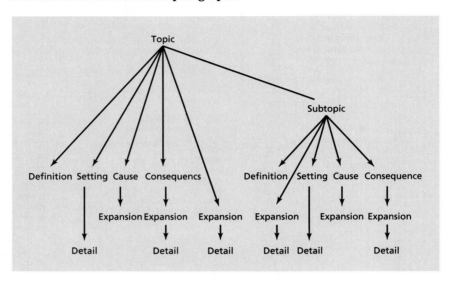

In a test of the model, college students were asked to read scientific texts from *Newsweek* and *Time* magazines while their eye movements and eye fixations were being unobtrusively measured. A sample of one student's performance is shown here:

1	2	3	4	5	6	7
1566	267	400	83	267	617	767
Flywheels	are	one	of the	oldest	mechanical	devices

8	9	1	2	3	5	4	6
450	450	400	616	517	684	250	317
known to	man.	Every	internal-combustion	engine			contains

7	8		9	10	11	12
617	1116		367	467	483	450
a small	flywheel	that	converts	the	jerky	motion	of the pistons

13	14	15	16	17		18	19	20	21
383	284	383	317	283		533	50	366	566
into	the	smooth	flow	of	energy	that	powers	the	drive	shaft.

Eye fixations of a college student reading a scientific passage. Gazes within each sentence are sequentially numbered above the fixated words with the durations (in msec.) indicated below the sequence number.

These data suggest that greater processing loads, as shown by eye fixations, occur when readers are confronted with uncommon words, integrating information from important clauses and making inferences at the ends of sentences. The major processing levels are shown in Figure 12.22.

All reading, whether it involves simple sentences (such as "The ball is red") to more involved connected discourse (such as that as used by Just and Carpenter) involves the

FIGURE 12.22

The major processing levels in the READER model that operate as the reader fixates the word *engine* in the text. Adapted from Just, and Carpenter (1987).

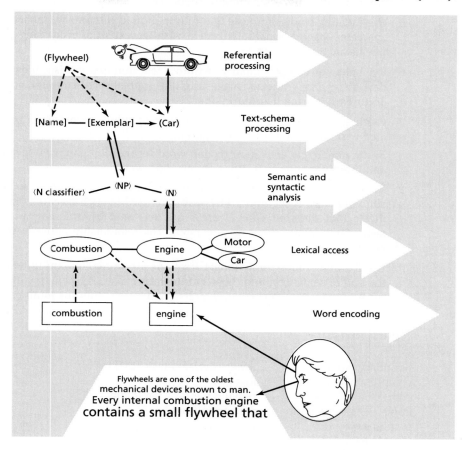

careful coordination of a number of perceptual-cognitive stages. These include feature and letter identification, word encoding, lexical access, semantic extraction, and inferences about the intention of the author that are derived from both the immediate contextual information and the reader's vast knowledge of the world.

Summary

1   Reading involves an interaction of the detection of symbols and memory, and thus it mirrors many processes involved in human cognition.

2   Viewing written text is constrained by the characteristics of the visual system, with greatest acuity occurring at the fovea (a visual angle of 1 to 2 degrees), poor resolution in the parafoveal and peripheral areas, and little or no detection during saccades.

3 Studies of perceptual span are used to examine the nature of information processing and include tachistoscopic, eye movement, and fixation procedures.

4 Tachistoscopic studies show that letters and words are more easily recognized when presented in a meaningful sequence.

5 Eye-tracking studies indicate that information in the near periphery (up to twelve character spaces) is partially coded, with the extent of processing determined by the distance from the fovea.

6 Eye behavior changes rapidly (within a few hundred milliseconds) to accommodate discordant contexts, suggesting that sophisticated comprehension processes occur early during text processing.

7 Familiarity and context facilitate word recognition. Increases in both are associated with faster and better recognition.

8 In the interactive activation model, word recognition happens through excitation and inhibition among features, letters, and word levels.

9 Recently a cognitive-anatomical approach has been taken up by some researchers studying word recognition. PET scans are used in such research. Early results indicate that different cortical areas are activated by different word recognition tasks. Such studies help us understand the relationship between cognitive tasks and brain functions.

10 Eye-fixation studies show longer fixations for words that are infrequent, those at the end of sentences, and those in integrating clauses, thus providing support for reading models proposing an interaction between stimulus input and memory.

Key Words

boundary paradigm
comprehension
contextual effects
down the garden path
fixations
foveal vision
interactive activation

lexical-decision task (LDT)
logogen
moving window paradigm
perceptual span
regressions
saccade
word apprehension effect (WAE)

Recommended Readings

Studies of word and letter identification can be found in Monty and Senders, eds., *Eye Movement and Psychological Processes;* and Rayner and Pollatsek's *The Psychology of Reading.* Volume 4 (No. 5) of *Psychological Science* contains a series on an interdisciplinary approach to reading research, including PET, eye-tracking, and connectionist articles and is highly recommended. The excellent books by Crowder, *The Psychology of Reading,* and Just and Carpenter, *The Psychology of Reading and Language Comprehension,* are not to be missed by those seeking an overview of the topic as well as detailed analysis of the current state of reading research. Numerous technical journals on the topic may be found in research libraries.

Cognitive Development

H UMAN COGNITION, FROM A developmental perspective, is the result of a long history of growth beginning very early in life. Our perceptions, memories, and thought processes change in response to the demands made on them during our long and varied interaction with the physical and social environment. The critical feature is that cognition develops—that is, cognition and thinking change in an orderly fashion as individuals progress from infancy to adulthood. These changes may be caused by the neurological and physical maturation of the child, reactions to social and environmental demands, or the interaction between a physically maturing person and the environment. Some, socially oriented psychologists hold that an infant is largely devoid of naturalistic tendencies and is a kind of tabula rasa, or blank tablet, upon which the experiences of the world are to be recorded; other, structurally oriented psychologists hold that infants possess certain invariant neurological and psychological potentials and that cognitive development is a matter of the interaction between these built-in structures and the encouragement and demands of society.

LIFE SPAN DEVELOPMENT

Cognitive development over the life span of people has been approached from several, somewhat independent perspectives: a developmental psychology, a neurocognitive development, and cognitive development. Cognitive development takes place over the entire life span of humans and other creatures, from before birth to death: However, in this chapter we concentrate on cognitive development during the early parts of life.

Developmental Psychology

Interest in the development of cognitive psychology throughout a person's life span was initially stimulated by the seminal work of the eminent psychologist Jean Piaget of Switzerland and the theoretical legacy left by the thoughtful works of Lev S. Vygotsky of Russia. So much has been written and is generally available about the life and times of Piaget that it is not repeated here. Less is known of the life and theories of Vygotsky, and later in this chapter a brief précis of his life and work is presented.

Neurocognitive Development

The neurocognitive approach to developmental cognitive psychology (sometimes called developmental neurobiology), on the other hand, emphasizes the developing brain and corresponding cognitive changes. The neurobiological approach to the study of devel-

Early Stimulation and Neuron Growth

In the illustration shown here, we see the effects of a nonstimulated (left) and stimulated (right) brain cell taken from rats. As shown, the hairlike dendrites are small, uncomplicated, and few in the left example, while the dendrites in the other example on the right are large, complex, and numerous; they are "well arborized," like the branches of a healthy tree or bush. The stimulated rats were allowed to explore gadgets and other devices that were stimulating.

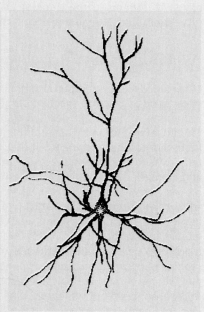

Adapted from Griswold & Jones, University of Illinois.

opmental psychology has been around for a very long time, but it has been ignored on grounds that it was too physiological for psychological theories. Now, however, it is recognized that the biological development of the brain, both prenatally and postnatally, is inherently involved in the cognitive development of the species. In addition to this theoretical reason, the neurocognitive approach to developmental cognitive psychology has become increasingly important because of recent discoveries in the field of brain imaging technology, some of which have already been discussed in this text.

Cognitive Development

Cognitive development is the study of cognition as it unfolds throughout the life span of a being. In the present chapter we explore such development of thought from the perspective of modern cognitive psychology in an attempt to gain further insight into the nature of human intellectual processes. You will recognize many of the themes, such as memory, higher-order cognition, prototype formation, and so on, because they have been discussed previously.

DEVELOPMENTAL PSYCHOLOGY

We begin our story by examining two quite different theories of developmental psychology that dominated the thinking in that field throughout most of the twentieth century—first, that of Jean Piaget and then that of Lev Vygotsky.

Assimilation and Accommodation: Piaget

Dissatisfied with attempts of moral philosophers and others to explain human knowledge through rational speculation alone, Jean Piaget adopted a unique and ultimately influential attitude. He decided that since intellect, like all biological functions, is a product of evolutionary adaptation, it could best be explained from a biological and evolutionary point of view. He felt that the best way to understand the nature of the adult mind was to study mental activity from the moment of birth, observing its development and changes in adaptation to the environment.

General Principles. For Piaget two major principles operated in intellectual growth as in all biological development: adaptation and organization. As intellectual growth progresses toward better and better levels of adaptation, our minds operate to respond ever more effectively to the demands of the environment. Adaptation is a two-pronged process of *assimilation* and *accommodation*. In eating and digesting an apple, for example, we use certain biological structures and processes—mouth, teeth, stomach, gastric juices—by means of which we take in and convert the apple into forms the body can use. In a sense the body has assimilated an external object and changed it into human biological material. Piaget believed that similar phenomena apply to mental activity, namely, that we possess mental structures that assimilate external events and convert them into mental events or thoughts. Were we then to attempt to eat a much bigger apple, we would have to change the way we arranged our mouth and teeth to bite into it, as well as change other aspects leading to its digestion. In other words, we would have to accommodate our biological structures to meet the problems posed by the new

Jean Piaget **(1896–1980). His research and theories form the basis of modern developmental psychology.**

object. In similar fashion we accommodate our mental structures to new and unusual aspects of the mental environment. These two processes, assimilation and accommodation, represent two complementary aspects of the general process of adaptation.

The second general principle, organization, refers to the nature of the mental structures that are adapting. For Piaget the mind is structured, or organized, in increasingly complex and integrated ways, the simplest level being the *scheme*, which is a mental representation of some action (physical or mental) that can be performed on an object. For the newborn, sucking, grasping, and looking are schemes; they are the ways the newborn comes to know the world—by acting on the world. Across development these schemes become progressively integrated and coordinated in an orderly fashion so that eventually they produce the adult mind. How and why this happens is the substance of Piaget's theory.

An important point is that, for Piaget, knowledge is action. What you know about an object ultimately determines the actions you can perform on it. For the young infant, knowledge is defined by and limited to overt motor actions such as grasping or sucking. However, with development these action schemes become progressively interiorized, that is, they occur inside the head in rapid-fire, short-circuited thought sequences.

Piaget postulates four approximate major periods of development through which the human intellect evolves. Piaget pointed out (1) that changes within a given period were generally quantitative and linear, while differences across periods tended to be qualitative, and (2) that there was a necessary sequence of progression through the four periods; that is, a child had to go through each period to get to the next. As we shall see, not all psychologists believe development to be this rigid or lockstep.

1. *The sensorimotor period (birth to 2 years).* The sensorimotor period is characterized by several stages of progressive intercoordination of schemes into successively more complex, integrated ones. In the first (reflex) stage, responses are innate and involuntary. In the next stage, reflex schemes are brought under voluntary control. When these primary schemes, such as sucking, looking, and grasping, are truly intercoordinated—that is, when the infant can not only grasp and look simultaneously but also look at something *to* grasp it—the next stage (secondary schemes) has been reached. In the succeeding stage, the child can carry out a behavior with something other than that behavior as its goal. This process of interiorization marks the end of the sensorimotor period. From then on, the child enters a period of intellectual functioning qualitatively different but having the same principles (integration and intercoordination) as its basis.

2. *The preoperational period (2 to 7 years).* In the preoperative period, the young child's behavior shifts from dependence on action to utilization of mental representations of those actions—or what is commonly called thought. The capacity for representation makes possible a number of significant new abilities. Among them is a primitive kind of insight learning, in which the child can merely look at a problem and often solve it without having to perform any overt actions. That is, the child can figure out the answer in his or her head and realize the correct solution. Another advance made possible by representation is the child's ability to pretend and make believe, specifically, to use an object for a purpose for which it was not originally designed. For example, one of Piaget's daughters used a piece of cloth as if it were a pillow. She would pick up the cloth, put her thumb in her mouth, lie down with her head on the cloth, and pretend to go to sleep. Piaget feels that since the child can now relate objects to each other in her head, objects that resemble each other in some way can come to substitute for each other; the child doesn't now need a pillow to lie down—a substitute or make-believe pillow will do just fine.

Finally, the capacity for representation underlies and makes possible the child's use of language. Language, for Piaget, comprises symbols (words) that stand for objects and events. Representation involves the creation and evocation, in the head, of symbols for objects. Until the child can truly represent and manipulate symbols, he or she will not be able to use language very effectively. Not surprisingly, the capacity for representation and the child's first multiword utterances emerge at about the same time. For Piaget, there is a causal connection between the two: representation makes possible the acquisition and use of language.

Despite many new achievements, the preoperational child's thinking is still quite primitive in comparison with older children and adults. Although the child shows signs of thinking, the ability to coordinate different thoughts in an integrated and systematic way has not yet been attained. Although the child has thoughts, they are isolated and not controlled by an overall plan or system. This general limitation manifests itself in several important behaviors. The first is egocentrism, which refers to regarding things exclusively in a way in which the self is central. The second is concatenative thinking, the tendency to string ideas together as they come to mind, with little regard for overall unity and little concern for adhering to a central integrating theme or idea. The third is anthropomorphism, endowing inanimate objects with human characteristics.

3. *The concrete-operational period (7 to 11 years).* The same general transformations that changed the sensorimotor child into the preoperational child are recapitulated to transform the thought structures of the preoperational child into those of the concrete-operational child. According to Piaget the process involves advances in three important domains of intellectual growth: conservation, classification, and seriation and transitivity.

The first domain, *conservation,* is depicted in Figure 13.1. Three vessels are placed before you, two identical in dimensions and one higher and narrower. Water is poured into the two shorter vessels to exactly the same level. You confirm that the two contain the same amount of water, perhaps by checking the levels. Now water from one of the short vessels is poured into the tall, narrow one. The water in the latter climbs to a higher level. Is there more water in it than had been in the shorter vessel? Most adults would be surprised at the obviousness of the question. Of course the amount of water is the same. Nothing was done to change the amount, so it must be the same. Although the answer may seem obvious to adults, Piaget found that children younger than 7-years-old typically say that the tall, narrow vessel has more water.

This illustrates a competence that Piaget believes is central to intellectual functioning in the school-age child: the concept of conservation—that is, the understanding that certain transformations do not change some basic properties of objects. In the example illustrated by Figure 13.1, the concept of conservation is the understanding that the amount of liquid does not change when it is poured into a vessel of a different shape.

The second skill that develops in the concrete-operational child involves the *classification,* or grouping, of objects. For example, suppose a child is shown four dogs and three cats and is asked whether there are more dogs or more cats. The preoperational child can answer this question correctly. However, asked whether there are more animals or more dogs, she replies that there are more dogs. The concrete-operational child will answer this last question correctly, demonstrating a classification ability called the addition of classes. For Piaget, successful performance involves not only an awareness

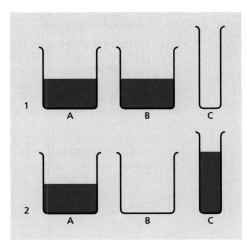

FIGURE 13.1

Arrangement (1) at outset of conservation task and (2) after contents of one vessel have been transferred to narrower and taller vessel.

of some of the subclasses, such as dogs and cats, but a complete knowledge that subclasses added together make up a third class (animals) and that the class can be broken back down into its subclasses. This concrete-operational system, or grouping, is similar to that underlying conservation. The two subclasses (dogs and cats) can be combined (via transformation) into a third class (animals), which can be broken back down (via reversibility) into the two original subclasses. All this can be done in the head (interiorization). In the preoperational child, classification is not yet a fully unified system, with the result that only some aspects of a problem can be correctly identified.

The last major accomplishments we focus on are *seriation and transitivity*, which are actually two separate but related skills. Seriation refers to the ability to string together a series of elements according to some underlying relationship. For example, a preoperational child asked to order several sticks (see Figure 13.2) according to length

---

Einstein and Piaget: More Than Albert Really Wanted to Know

In 1928 Albert Einstein posed a question to Piaget: In what order do children acquire the concepts of time and velocity? The question was prompted by an issue within physics. Within Newtonian theory, time is a basic quality and velocity is defined in terms of it (velocity = distance/time). Within relative theory, in contrast, time and velocity are defined in terms of each other, with neither concept being more basic. Einstein wanted to know whether understanding of either or both concepts was pre-

sent from birth; whether children understood one before the other; and if so, how initial understanding of one influenced subsequent understanding of the other.

Almost 20 years later, Piaget . . . published a two-volume, 500-page-reply to Einstein's query. Piaget concluded that children did not understand time, distance, or velocity in infancy or early childhood. Only in the concrete operations period would they finally grasp the three concepts.

Based on Siegler (1986).

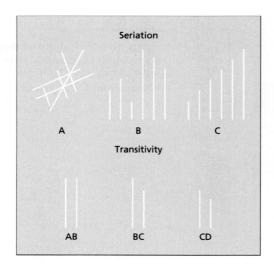

FIGURE 13.2

Above, seriation task (A) and performances on it by preoperational (B) and concrete-operational (C) children. Below, pairs of sticks such as would be presented in a transitivity task. After a child determines that A and B are the same length, that B is longer than C, and that C is longer than D, he or she is asked whether B is longer than D.

(a typical problem in seriation of length) will be able to do so in a limited fashion, most often ordering two sticks correctly but then not aligning the third stick with the first two, and so on. Complete seriation ability awaits development of the system of concrete operations.

Transitivity is related to seriation ability. In the transitivity problem shown in Figure 13.2, a child is first shown a series of sticks, two at a time, and then asked which is longer. Following this, the crucial question is asked: "Is Stick B longer than Stick D?" The preoperational child performs very poorly on this task, according to Piaget, whereas the concrete-operational child performs correctly. The crucial ability for Piaget is the ability to cross the bridge between B and D. Clearly, the child must be able to seriate the sticks in order to do this. In addition, however, he or she must be able to coordinate the two isolated relationships (B > C and C > D) into a system to make the transitive inference that B > D. For Piaget the preoperational child knows that B > C and that C > D but cannot put these two relationships together via the middle linking term *C* to create a concrete-operational system.

4. *The formal-operational period (adolescence and adulthood).* Although the concrete-operational child has made a number of significant leaps in cognitive functioning, for Piaget there are still some definite limits on those capabilities. The limitation is perhaps best summarized by the name he gave to the period, that is, concrete operations. The child during this period is limited to coordinating concrete things in an actual situation. What the child cannot yet do is to coordinate possible things in a hypothetical or more abstract formalized situation. The concrete-operational child can coordinate various physical dimensions (for example, height and width of a jar of water) and thereby show conservation of liquid quantity. In a like manner, the child can conserve mass, number, volume, distance, weight—in short, most dimensions of the concrete physical reality in front of him or her.

Figure 13.3 shows a problem useful in illustrating this last level of development. Consider a balance beam with various weights that can be placed in a variety of positions on either side of the beam. The goal—to balance the beam—can be accomplished

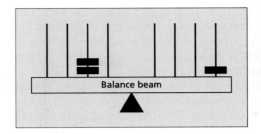

FIGURE 13.3

Typical arrangement of weights in balance-beam problem, in which child must decide whether a beam (initially locked in balance position) will be in balance when released.

by changing weights on either side of the beam or by moving weights closer to or farther from the central balance point (fulcrum). The concrete-operational child can solve the balance problem easily when working with only one dimension. For example, the child will quickly learn that, where one side has more weights than the other, he can restore the balance by removing the extra weight on one side or adding a weight to the other. Similarly, he or she can figure out the effect of moving weights different distances from the fulcrum. However, the concrete-operational child does not understand how these two systems of operations are related. He or she does not know, for example, that adding weight to one side can be compensated for by moving the weights on the other side farther away from the fulcrum. In short, the child cannot coordinate these two systems into a higher-order "system of systems." This coordination is precisely the goal of the formal-operational period—namely, coordination of previously isolated systems of concrete operations.[1]

A direct outcome of the ability to coordinate systems of thought into higher systems is the ability to move beyond the actual world of physical reality to hypothetical worlds or other realities, to evoke systems of thought not immediately given by reality. Questions such as "What if the sun ceased to exist?" "What if gravity disappeared?", so characteristic of adolescent thought, stem directly from the ability to bring new, hypothetical dimensions to an otherwise concrete reality. This propensity toward hypothetical thinking is closely allied to the burgeoning tendency to think at a very abstract level; the formal-operational adolescent can consider general issues such as morality, love, existence.

For Piaget, formal-operational thought marks the end of intellectual growth. The child has clearly come a long way from the simple reflexes of the newborn to the sophisticated thoughts of the adolescent and adult. The striking feature of Piaget's theory is that it postulates the natural, logical progression of this development according to a unified set of theoretical principles.

Critique of the Piagetian Perspective. Piaget's ideas have not gone unchallenged and, in recent years, many criticisms have emerged. Some focus on minor aspects of Piaget's methodology, but others are directed toward the substance of his theory.

The first area of challenge focuses on Piaget's claim that basic logical operations play the major role in whether the child will show conservation, classification, and transitivity. The studies of critics have attempted to show that other deficits in attention or memory were more responsible for the younger child's failure on Piagetian tasks.

---

[1]The balance-beam problem has been studied extensively by Siegler and his colleagues (Siegler, 1976, 1981; and Siegler & Klahr, 1982) and recently by McClelland within the context of the PDP model (McClelland, 1988; and McClelland & Jenkins, in press).

In one experiment, Gelman (1969) tried to show that in the young child performance in typical conservation problems was hampered by attentional deficits. She reasoned that very young children may focus attention on the incorrect dimension (for example, height, in the problems of conservation of liquid quantity) since, in most instances in the young child's life, *more* usually means longer or taller. Gelman tried to train young nonconserving children to focus on the more relevant dimension by applying appropriate reinforcement techniques. In one instance involving conservation of number, she showed children three cards, two of which displayed the same number of items but were different in length, while the third showed a different number but was similar in length to one of the other two cards. The child's task was to pick the cards showing the same number of items. Each correct response was rewarded; at each incorrect response the child was told he or she was wrong (nonreward). In this way Gelman tried to redirect the child's attention away from the more dominant perceptual cue (length of card) to the number of items. Gelman found that nonconserving children who were given this training showed conservation of number when tested later. Furthermore, they transferred these conservation abilities to other concepts, such as quantity. And, even more remarkably, they retained the conservation ability one month after the original training.

Gelman's study provides provocative evidence that in many instances children who appear not to have the operational systems of conservation do indeed possess them but are prevented from demonstrating those abilities by deficiencies in focusing attention.

Representing a second area of criticism, it has been suggested that the poor performance of very young children on Piagetian tasks may result more from memory deficits than from deficient logical operations. In studies on transitivity, for example (Bryant & Trabasso, 1971; Riley & Trabasso, 1974; Riley, 1975; and Trabasso, 1977), young preschool children were presented with typical transitivity problems, which many of them failed. However, these investigators then tried to train the subjects in seriation abilities. For example, they would present the sticks in pairs and ask the child which was longer. In order to reinforce the comparative nature of the relationship, they also asked which was shorter. In addition, they provided the children with verbal reinforcement about the correctness of their responses and, in some cases, with visual feedback, explicitly showing which stick was longer and which was shorter. Finally, during the testing phase, these investigators asked the children not only about the critical judgment (Is B > D?) but also about the originally tested pairs (B > C, C > D). They reasoned that if by the time of testing the child had forgotten one of the original pairs (for example, that C > D), incorrect inferences would be made as a result of this failure of memory. Indeed, it was found that, in the majority of instances, the child who made an incorrect transitive inference also recalled one of the original pairs incorrectly. When the original pairs were remembered, the child was very likely to infer correctly. These studies point up rather dramatically that memory deficits may play a crucial role in whether a child will demonstrate transitivity. They argue that the young child may not show transitivity, not because he or she lacks a logical operation ability but because he or she has a poor memory for the original information.

Recent evidence has been presented by Jean Mandler and her colleagues that raises a third questions about how Piaget and his followers view the thinking ability of young infants. Simply stated, the Piagetian view of young infants is that they go through a period—especially the sensorimotor stage—during which they cannot "think" (by which is meant that they can learn to do simple things—such as recognize common objects, crawl, and manipulate objects—but do not develop concepts or ideas). Infants in the

Jean Mandler. **Conducted inventive experiments that have shed new light on thinking in young children.**

sensorimotor stage rely largely on procedural knowledge (see Chapter 8), the type of cognitive ability involved in moving around and manipulating objects. Mandler suggests that the development of conceptual knowledge is far more extensive than originally proposed by Piaget.

Evidence for the existence of perceptual conceptualization at an early age has been presented by Spelke (1979, 1988), Spelke and Kestenbaum (1986), Mandler and Bauer (1988), and Meltzoff and Borton (1979). In one experiment (Spelke, 1979) two films depicting complex events accompanied by a single sound track were shown to 4-month-old infants. Infants preferred to view the film that matched the sound.

Even infants only 1 month old seem to be able to recognize objects only felt in their mouths (see Meltzoff & Borton, 1979). In one study 1-month-old infants were given a pacifier with either a knobby surface or smooth surface (see Figure 13.4). After they were able to habituate to the pacifier without being able to see it, the pacifier was removed. Then the infant was shown both pacifiers. The infants spent more time looking at the pacifier they had only felt in their mouths before, which is taken as support for the view that some central processing of two similar patterns of information is accomplished.

Mandler suggests that some of the evidence for conceptual ability gathered by child psychologists has been based on motor behavior and that what may appear to be conceptual incompetence may be motor incompetence.

These three areas of criticism argue that the child may possess sophisticated logical operations far earlier than thought by Piaget. They also suggest that other processes may be critical in determining whether a child will demonstrate a particular competence (such as conservation). Nevertheless, supporters of Piaget could argue that the studies just cited show only that the basic processes that determine cognitive advance occur earlier than anticipated. The basic operational schemes and the fundamental sequence

FIGURE 13.4

Two types of pacifiers used in the Meltzoff and Borton study. After habituation with one type of pacifier without being able to see it, infants tended to look at the pacifier they felt in their mouth. After Meltzoff & Borton (1979), as reported by Mandler (1990).

of progressive integration and coordination remain as reasonable explanations for the child's cognitive growth. However, even this basic tenet has been challenged.

Mind in Society: Vygotsky

Between the city of Minsk in Belarus and Smolensk in Russia, in the town of Orsha, Lev Vygotsky was born in 1896. A bright, energetic, curious lad, he won a gold medal for his scholarship upon completing gymnasium. Perhaps only in his fantasy did he imagine that he would be selected to attend "Lomonosov's University" (Moscow State University)—few Jewish boys from remote towns were selected (a quota of 3 percent had been established for Moscow and St. Petersburg universities). Also, even if his talent was conspicuous and his grades impeccable, a new rule was being tried out whereby Jewish applicants were to be selected by casting lots (Dobkin in Levitin, 1982). Nevertheless, in some undistinguished pedagogical bureau, fate fell down on the side of schoolboy Vygotsky. By the luck of the draw he won (and lost a bet with a friend, paying him off with a "good book") and commenced on an intellectual career unparalleled in the history of Russian psychology.

Counted among his early students and coworkers are the most illustrious psychologists in the Soviet Union, including Alexander Luria (the most frequently cited Russian psychologist by Western psychologists; see Solso, 1985); Alexei Leontiev (the most frequently cited Russian psychologist by Russian psychologists), Zaporozhets, Zinchencho, Elkonin, Galperin, and Bozhovich.

Vygotsky's creative talents were not confined to psychology. They included philosophy (his works on Marx and Hegel are classics, and a book on Spinoza is still to be published [see Kozulin, 1984]), art criticism (his dissertation and first book was called *The Psychology of Art*), literary research (he founded the journal *Verask* and befriended the poet Mandelstam), and law and medicine (his first degree was in law, he was working on a medical degree, and, among other achievements, he left an important mark on clinical and developmental psychology). He died in 1934 at the age of thirty-seven; the cause of his early death was tuberculosis. Today, Russians enjoy calling him the Mozart of psychology.

Vygotsky's original works deserve careful reading. In this next section we focus on his basic ideas as they bear on the topic of developmental psychology.

Lev Vygotsky **(1896–1934). Made significant observations and proposed theories of child language development.**

Vygotsky and Piaget

Although Vygotsky and Piaget were contemporaries (the leading developmental psychologists of the century) and lived in Europe, they never met. They did know of each other's work, however; Vygotsky knew of Piaget well before Piaget knew of Vygotsky.[2] There are similarities and differences between the theories.

Vygotsky considered Piaget's work to be "revolutionary" (a term not to be taken lightly in Russia during the 1920s), but he felt its trail-blazing qualities suffered from a duality—the dispute between materialistic and idealistic conceptions. As psychology of the intellectual development of the mind was being tested by scientific materialism, an inevitable conflict between the factual substance of that technique was at odds with the theoretical and idealistic nature of human intellect. The dispute is a serious one, especially in the zeitgeist of the 1920s and 1930s, because the growth of experimental psychology posed a real threat to the idealistic, nonmaterialistic, philosophic branch of psychology.

Stages of Development. For Piaget, modes of thinking in the child developed from "autistic" to egocentric to socialized thought. Vygotsky accepted the general stages of development but rejected the underlying genetically determined sequence. Succinctly stated, Piaget believed that development precedes learning; Vygotsky believed that learning precedes development. A second point of difference between the theorists is on the nature and function of speech. For Piaget, egocentric speech, which the child uses when "thinking aloud," gives way to social speech in which the child recognizes the laws of experience and uses speech to communicate. For Vygotsky the child's mind is inherently social in nature, and egocentric speech is social in origin and social in purpose: children learn egocentric speech from others and use it to communicate with others. This position represents a major schism between the theorists and reveals the principal theory of child development according to Vygotsky.

The development of speech, which is tied to the development of thought in the child, proceeds along this course. First and foremost, the primary purpose of speech (not only for children but also for adults) is communication, which is motivated out of our basic need for social contact. Thus the earliest speech is essentially social. Speech becomes "egocentric" (and here Vygotsky accepts the stages of development according to Piaget but differs in explanation) when the child "transfers social collaborative forms of behavior to the sphere of the inner-personal psychic functions" (Vygotsky, 1934/1962). The development of thinking therefore is not from the individual to society but from society to the individual.

Phenomenon of Internalization. Internalization is the process by which external actions (roughly speaking, *behavior*) are transformed into internal psychological functions (roughly speaking, *processes*). On this point Vygotsky and Piaget agree on a descriptive level but not on the origin of internalization. Vygotsky's position is similar to

---

[2]Piaget did not know the details of Vygotsky's criticisms of his works until about 1962, when he received an abridged translation of *Thought and Language*. He did publish an interesting critique on Vygotsky's position and his own in *Comments on Vygotsky's Critical Remarks* (L. Graham, 1972).

(and was undoubtedly influenced by, through his familiarity with the French sociological school) the writings of Émile Durkheim and Pierre Janet. Human consciousness, from this direction, consisted of internalized social, interpersonal relationships. The importance of this position for developmental psychology is that children tend to use the same form of behavior in relation to themselves as others have expressed toward them.

Developmental Stages. Vygotsky observed the way children sort objects, such as blocks differing in size, color, and shape. Older children, aged 6 and up, seemed to select a single quality such as color: all the green boxes were grouped together, as were the blue boxes, and so on. Younger children, below the age of 6 used chain concepts, by which Vygotsky meant that the classification changed throughout the selection process. A child may pick up, say, a few blue boxes and then notice a triangular block. This would lead to the selection of another triangular block, and so on, until some other type of block caught the child's attention, such as rounded blocks, which were then abandoned for another type. The selection process seemed to be chained and changeable.

Preschoolers seemed to organize objects thematically rather than taxonomically. For example, older children and normal adults might put animals in one category, furniture in another, and toys in yet a third group (taxonomic classification), while a very young child might classify a cat with a chair, a toy with a bookcase, and a dog with a Frisbee because cats sit on chairs, toys are stored in a bookcase, and dogs play with a Frisbee (thematic classification). From similar observations, Vygotsky thought that children pass through three stages of conceptual development:

1. The formation of thematic concepts in which relationships between objects are important.

2. The formation of chain concepts (just discussed).

3. The formation of abstract concepts similar to adult concept formation.

Unlike Piaget, Vygotsky had an opportunity in his brief, intellectually crowded life to test a few of his hypotheses under well-controlled laboratory conditions.

We will now turn to the important matter of the development of thought—a central thesis of Vygotsky's theory.

Development of Thought and the Internalization of Speech. The development of thought in the child is most evident in language development. At one point Vygotsky (1934/1962) wrote, "Language is a merger between outer speech the child hears and inner speech he thinks with." It is easy to conclude that language and thought are therefore dual entities of a common phenomenon. Carried to its logical conclusion, this notion would force us to deduce that without language there can be no thought, that thinking is dependent on language. Although some developmental psychologists subscribe to this idea, Lev Vygotsky does not. For Vygotsky, if a prelinguistic child thinks, as sufficient evidence suggests is the case, then we must find different roots for speech and thought. A fundamental tenet of Vygotsky's psychology is that thought and speech have different genetic roots and that the rates of development for each are different. The growth curves for thought and speech may "cross and recross" but always diverge. The source of thought is in the biological development of the child; the source of language in his or her social milieu. Even though language and thought have a different genus, they intertwine once the child comes to the realization that every object has a name. After this realization, thought and language are inseparable. Thus the internalization of language causes thoughts to be expressed in inner speech.

NEUROCOGNITIVE DEVELOPMENT

Cognitive processes—perception, memory, imagery, language, and thinking and problem solving, for example—are all based on underlying neurological structures and processes, an idea frequently visited throughout these pages. Certainly, the study of the development of cognition would be incomplete without some understanding of the basic nature of developmental neuropsychology. The purpose of this section is to understand the function of the nervous system throughout the life span of humans better.

Four different approaches to developmental neuropsychology have been used:

- Physical studies of the development of the nervous system correlated with cognitive changes.

- Cognitive studies over the life span of individuals from which inferences about neurological maturation are made.

- The study of neurological pathology or damage in which changes in cognition are noted.

- Experimental studies in which the brain is altered (mostly animal studies) or some independent variable is introduced and brain activity observed, as in the case of PET studies.

Each of these methodologies has strengths and weaknesses (see Kolb & Whishaw, 1990, for details), and a complete analysis is beyond the scope of the current text. We can, however, make some summary remarks.

Early Neural Development

The brain develops prenatality over the gestation period as is shown in Figure 13.5. In the very early stages of development, the brain is in the rudimentary stages of growth, but by the beginning of the second trimester, the cerebral cortex is becoming differentiated from the spinal cord. By 7 months many of the principal lobes are being formed. By 9 months the lobes are distinguishable and a number of invaginations are seen. As far as can be told, even with this noticeable and various growth of brain cells, cognition—perception, language processing, thinking, and memory—is still in an embryonic state throughout prenatal growth. Indeed, full cognitive development seems not to occur until late adolescence. (Some parents even believe an offspring must graduate from college, marry, have three children, and make a decent income before full maturity is achieved, but such a notion is scientifically unsupported.)

If one examines synaptic (the synapse is where two neurons meet) formation (see Chapter 2 for an illustration), which is closely related to a cognitively functional brain,

FIGURE 13.5

Prenatal development of the brain showing a series of embryonic and fetal stages. Adopted from W. M. Cowan (1979).

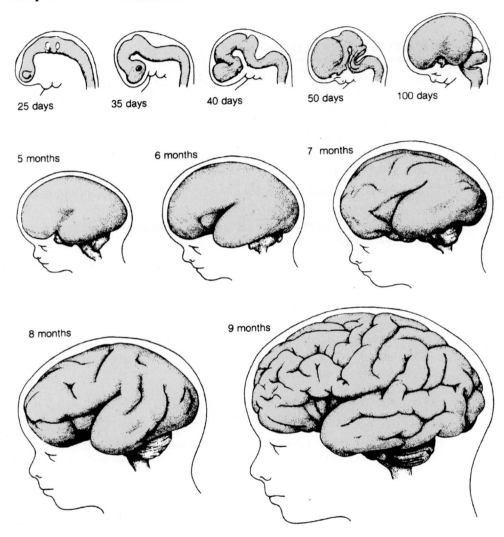

we find that the density increases until about 2 years of age. Then, perhaps surprisingly, there is a *shedding* of synapses in which about 50 percent are lost by the age of 16 (which all parents know). Some interpret these findings as meaning that favorable environmental influences may deter the loss of synapses rather than influence their initial formation (see Kolb & Whishaw, 1990).

Environment and Neural Development

Environment does affect cognitive and brain development. Evidence for this can be found in animal studies where, typically, an animal is reared in some type of sensory isolation and then found to be unable to develop normally when placed in a normal or even an enriched environment. Brain size seems also to be affected by environment as evidenced by the fact that some domestic animals have certain cortical areas that are 10 to 20 percent smaller than comparable animals raised in the wild. Human babies raised in impoverished environments, such as the famous case of a child raised by wolves (see Singh & Zingg, 1940), seem unable to overcome their early experiences, although, contrary to common belief, there is no evidence they are destined to become werewolves or disc jockeys. The effect of early stimulation of cognitive functions is, of course, important, and the term *functional validation* is used to express the notion that for the neural system to become fully functional, stimulation is required. Some experiments show an enriched environment increases brain size in the neocortex. Other cases, which are well documented, do suggest that children are remarkably resilient beings, and that some forms of early cognitive impoverishment may be overcome by changing environments.

Laterization studies

Laterization of cognitive functions is likely to produce theoretically important results. For example, it may show that information processing is progressively organized into different areas (such as language processing taking place in the left hemisphere), or it

Critical Issues: The Developing Brain—Use it or Lose it

"It's crazy," says Pasko Rakic, a Yale neurobiologist. "Americans think kids should not be asked to do difficult things with their brains while they are young: 'Let them play; they'll study at the university.' The problem is, if you don't train them early, it's much harder."*

Early stimulation of the brain, through puzzles, visual displays, music, foreign-language learning, chess, art, scientific exploration, mathematical games, writing, and many other similar activities promotes synaptic connections in the brain. Shortly after birth, the number of neural connections increases at a phenomenal rate. Then, at about puberty, the number of new connections diminishes and two processes take place: functional validation, in which useful connections are made more permanent, and selective elimination, in which useless connections are eliminated.

Throughout the life span of humans—from infancy to old age—we humans (and other creatures) are endowed with the capacity to expand our mental capacity through use. Disuse, through mindless passive activities, is likely to dull brain growth.

*Cited in Life, July 1994.

FIGURE 13.6

The "baseball" could appear in any one of the 12 positions relative to the "bat." The criterion in the above/below task was whether the ball was "up" or "down." The criterion in the distance task was whether the ball was closer to the line than 3 mm. From Koenig, Reiss, and Kosslyn (1990), JECP.

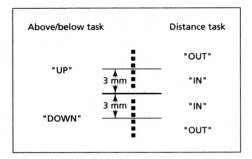

may be that the brain is formed early in its development and that the processing of certain types of material (language, for example) is inflexibly routed to a predetermined site for processing. The results of these studies might address the larger question of the relative influence of nature (neurology, in this instance) and nurture (type of information, in this instance). In spite of experimental difficulties in studying vision and laterization in very young children (it's hard to collect reliable data with children because of a number of obvious problems), a number of well-controlled experiments have been done with children and cerebral asymmetry.

Koenig, Reiss, and Kosslyn (1990) tested for laterization in 5- and 7-year-olds. They asked children (and adult control subjects) to play the role of a baseball umpire who was to call the location of a ball (a dot) as being above or below, or in or out (see Figure 13.6). The dot was presented to the right or left of the visual fixation point so that it would be processed in the opposite cerebral hemisphere due to the crossover of neural pathways from the eye to the brain (see Chapter 2). The children's decisions were measured by means of a reaction time key. As shown in Figure 13.7, children responded faster to stimuli presented initially to the left hemisphere in the above/below task, and to stimuli presented initially to the right hemisphere in the distance task. The finding presents evidence for the existence of distinct hemispheric subsystems for children as young as 5 years of age. Laterization effects have been noted in young children by others, and we tentatively conclude that brain structures and processes are formed very early in infancy or even prenatally, and are not subject to normal environmental forces.

COGNITIVE DEVELOPMENT

The term *cognition* subsumes a large number of individual processes (and structures) such as attention, pattern recognition, sensory registers, cognitive neuroscience, and memory. Thinking, in this context, is actually a product of the complex utilization, manipulation, and organization of these various components. For the developmental psychologist, any one of these processes may change with age. The investigation of age-related changes in cognition has thus required systematic exploration of many different processes. In this section we explore only a portion of these processes, and those within only a limited age range—namely, from preschool through adulthood. In essence we focus on the basic cognitive skills involved in acquiring information from the environment and in storing and manipulating information in memory. Our aim is to illus-

FIGURE 13.7

Response latencies for children and adults when the stimuli were presented initially to the left hemisphere (right visual field), to the right hemisphere (left visual field), or to both hemispheres (central field). The subjects decided whether the ball was above or below the bat or greater than 3 mm from the bat. For children and adults, the first trial block only is represented. From Koenig, Reiss, and Kosslyn (1990), JECP.

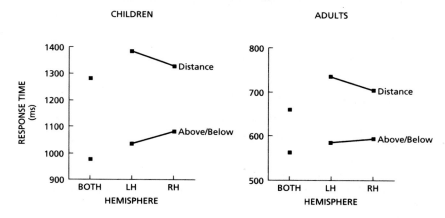

Development of Information-Acquisition Skills

The initial stages in cognition require that the child be able effectively to attend to, to perceive, and to search out the relevant information in the environment. Successful acquisition of information brings into play such processes as neurological development, the development of sensory registers, focal attention, speed of processing, as well as effective strategies for searching out and utilizing information in various portions of the environment. We focus on some of these processes that have been studied developmentally. Most of the modern themes of cognitive psychology, which include selective attention, facial identification, memory, higher-order cognition, and prototype formation, are repeated in the developmental literature.

Selective Attention. Selective attention (see Chapter 6) refers to the ability to focus on relevant information. The evidence we have suggests that young children are somewhat less able to control their attentional processes than adults are. They are more distractible and less flexible in deploying attention among relevant and irrelevant information. In one study (Pick, 1975), children were asked to find all the *A*s, *S*s, and *L*s in a large box of multicolored letters of the alphabet. Unknown to the children was the fact that all the *A*s, *S*s, and *L*s were the same color. Only the older children noticed this clue and used it to advantage in searching through the pile, displaying their greater attentional flexibility.

Although our knowledge about this process is far from complete, it appears that as children grow older they become better able to control attention and to adapt to the demands of different tasks. When a high degree of selectivity is called for, older children can better focus on the relevant and ignore the irrelevant. Younger children have greater difficulty in this regard. Likewise, when less selectivity is appropriate, older children can defocus and take in more relevant information.

Much of the research on children's attention has dealt with vision. For some time many professionals believed that newborn infants were functionally blind, a view that has since been discredited. Infants can "see" in the sense that their visual apparatus is functional, but their understanding of what they see—in effect, their perception—is questionable. What is known is that infants tend to look at some objects more than others. Some of the features of infant attention have been identified.

A prominent characteristic of adult attention is the orienting reflex, or the natural tendency to attend to an unusual signal such as a loud noise or bright light. All normal children exhibit the orienting reflex, even those newly born. Theoretically, the orienting reflex is very interesting. Sokolov hypothesized that when we experience a stimulus, for example a sound, the impulse is first fed to the brain (cortex). There, a rapid matching process takes place in which the signal is compared with recently experienced stimuli. If no match is found, an orienting reflex occurs. However, if the stimulus is repeated over and over again, habituation, or the tendency to not direct attention to the signal, occurs. Typically, orienting can be measured by such physiological measures as changes in brain wave patterns, alertness, increase in skin conductance, and reduced heart rate.

How well does the theory hold up in laboratory studies? Such research is difficult to do; most parents, understandably, don't want physiologists fiddling with their kids' cortex, no matter how important the data might be. One way to study the effect, however, is to examine the orienting reflex and habituation among children who are born without a cortex (anencephalic infants). One study of Sokolov's theory of habituation was tested using an anencephalic infant (see F. Graham, 1978). The child demonstrated an orienting response when a novel stimulus was presented and also habituated to familiar stimuli. Heart rate was used as an indication or habituation. The finding is important, not only because it casts some doubt on Sokolov's theory to account for infant habituation, but also because it shows that the cortex is not necessary for these processes to occur. It may be that the orienting reflex and habituation take place at subcortical levels in young children.

Facial Attention. One topic of interest among cognitive psychologists is to what features of a visual scene subjects attend. Because infants become familiar with people's faces at a very tender age (especially the mother's face), cognitive developmental psychologists have studied facial attention in some detail. You may recall that pioneer work in the field of visual attention was done by Yarbus, who measured eye movements and fixations as subjects viewed a scene (see Chapter 5 for details). Related work has been done with children by Salapatek (1975), who presented infants with a visual display in which one object was placed within another (for example, a circle inside a triangle). Very young infants (up to the age of 2 months) showed an almost total preference for the outer edges of the external figure over the inner figure. After about the age of 2 months, the infants scanned both the outer features and the inner ones.

F I G U R E   1 3 . 8

F I G U R E   1 3 . 8

Drawing of eye-tracking apparatus used to record eye movements and fixations of infants.

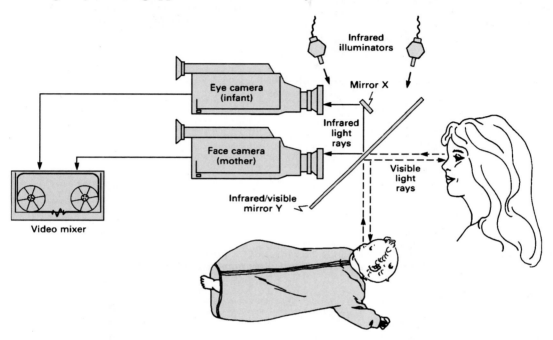

In another study of this type, Haith, Bergman, and Moore (1977) used an eye-tracking device similar to the one shown in Figure 13.8. Of special interest is the use of infrared illuminators, which impinge on the infant's eyes. Rays from this source are beyond the sensory threshold; the infant cannot see them, and they are harmless. Because the position of these lights in the child's visual field is known, the fixation point can be determined by measuring the distance of one of the lights from the center of the pupil. (Similar technology has been used in reading experiments—see Chapter 12). The infant's eye movements and the exact location of the mother's face are detected by video cameras and combined in a video mixer. It is possible to identify exactly where the infant is looking vis-à-vis the mother's face.

Experiments of these types are helpful in the study of memory and early perceptual organization in addition to the emotional and social development of infants. In the experiment by Haith and his colleagues, three groups of infants were observed. One group was 3 to 5 weeks old, the second group was 7 weeks old, and the third was 9 to 11 weeks old. The mothers' faces were divided into zones, which were used to identify eye fixations (see Figure 13.9). The results of the experiments are shown in Figure 13.10. It was found that very young infants focus on the peripheral contours (as also reported by Salapatek), but older infants focus on the eyes. It was also found that older infants focus on the nose and mouth more than younger infants. The possible meaning of these findings is that to

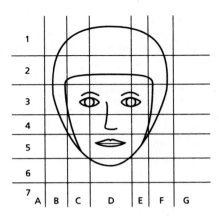

FIGURE 13.9

Zones for mother's face used in eye-tracking study. Zones were individually determined. From Haith, Bergman, and Moore (1977).

FIGURE 13.10

Percentage of time spent on eyes, edges, nose, and mouth by infants of three different ages. From Haith, Bergman, and Moore (1977).

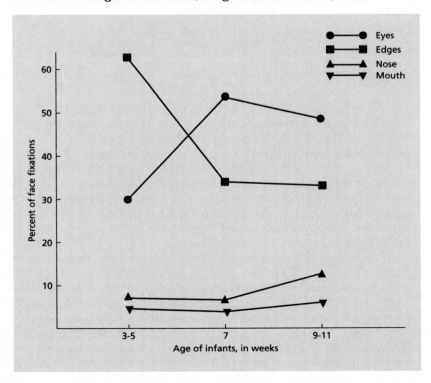

the infant the face of the mother is not merely a collection of visual events but a meaningful entity. We can dismiss these findings on the basis of the physical attractiveness of eyes (their color, movement, and contrast), but such argument does not account for the shift in attention over age, nor does it account for the relative lack of attention given to the mouth, which also has these characteristics. It is possible that by the seventh week eyes, especially a mother's eyes, take on special social value and are important in social interaction. We will return to the processing of facial information in a later section on prototype formation in children. Now we consider the topic of short-term memory.

Memory

As we have seen in other parts of this book, memory is among the most important cognitive attributes. Without memory, we would be rudderless, caught is a confusing sea of meaningless events; with memory, events are understood.

Among the most controversial and hotly debated topics in psychology is when, in the course of human growth and development, memory first unfolds and how accurate it is. This is borne out in the recent spate of court trails on false-memory syndrome in which memories of childhood abuse allegedly are the result of reconstructed events encouraged by others, most notably a person's psychotherapist. What do we know about childhood memories?

Infant Memory. There is considerable common knowledge and scientific evidence that infants have memory for events. On a basic level, babies show recognition of previously seen stimuli, such as their mothers' face or classically conditioned responses (see Rovee-Collier, 1987, 1990, for details). Imitation and habituation are also reliably found in infants. These findings do not suggest, however, that early memories are of the same kind as adult memories. Early efforts to find the earliest memories have (generally) relied on introspective accounts (for example, "What is your earliest memory?") and found that the average age was about 39 to 42 months.

In a recent, well-controlled experiment by Usher and Neisser (1993), childhood memory and its counterpart, childhood amnesia, were tested with 222 college students who were asked questions about four datable events—the birth of a younger sibling, a hospitalization, the death of a family member, and making a family move. The events could be checked against reliable records and occurred when the subjects were 1, 2, 3, 4, or 5 years of age. The results are shown in Figure 13.11. Childhood amnesia, or the inability to recall an event that actually happened, ranged from the of age 2 for hospitalization and sibling birth to the age of 3 for death and a family move. The onset of childhood amnesia seems to depend on the nature of the event itself, as the birth of a sibling and hospitalization, potentially traumatic episodes, are significant events likely to be recalled in adulthood. Conversely, these events may have been recounted throughout the life of the child and early adult (see E. Loftus, 1993, for a rejoinder).

Organization (Chunking). The development of sophisticated rehearsal strategies is just one of the factors influencing the growth of memory skills in school-age children. A second, equally important factor involves the ability to recognize and utilize potentially useful higher-order relationships that link various environmental events. (Earlier, we

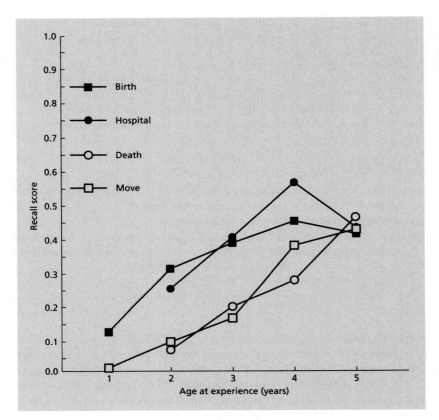

FIGURE 13.11

Mean recall data for four target events as a function of age at experience.

called this organization, or chunking.) During the school years, the child becomes better able to organize material he or she wants to remember.

Of the following two lists of words, which would you expect to recall more easily?

1. desk, arm, tree, hall, paper, clock, farmer, word, floor

2. apples, oranges, grapes, shirt, pants, shoe, dog, cat, horse

The second list is indeed easier to recall once you realize that the words are composed of three separate categories. By chunking the words into categories, you form a higher-order rule and use the rule to help at the time of recall. Indeed, experiments have shown that recall of categorized lists is much easier than recall of unrelated words.

Surprisingly, studies have shown that up to about the third grade, children's recall of categorizable items is not much better than their recall of unrelated items. Older children, on the other hand, recall categorizable items much better than unrelated items (Vaughn, 1968; and Lange, 1973). These findings imply that the older children better recognize and utilize the categorical nature of the stimuli to help their memory performance.

One way to try to help younger children to see the higher-order relationship between stimuli would be to present the categories in a blocked fashion—all items from

Refuted False Memory Case Wins $500,000

A landmark "recovered memory" trial testing the rights of third parties to sue therapists was decided in a recent case when a father convinced a jury that his daughter's mind was poisoned with false recollections of childhood molestation.

Jurors were asked to decide whether two therapists and a southern California medical center were guilty of malpractice in the case of a young woman who experienced flash-backs of childhood sexual abuse while being treated for bulimia and depression. The father sued the marriage and family counselor and a psychiatrist charging they had implanted in his daughter false memories of childhood incest.

It was contended that the images were not memories, and the evidence showed that the frightening flashbacks were vague to the point that even the daughter doubted their accuracy.

Based on an article in the *San Francisco Chronicle* May, 14, 1994

one category first, the next category second, and so on. An experiment by Yoshimura, Moely, and Shapiro (1971) presented one group of children who were 4 to 10 years old with categorizable stimuli in a blocked fashion and another group in a random fashion. They found that while the older children benefitted from having the items blocked, the younger children did not. Other studies have shown some slight advantage from blocking for younger children (Cole, Frankel, & Sharp, 1971; and Kobasigawa & Middleton, 1972), but, in general, the results reveal that young children appear not to notice or utilize as well the categorical structure of materials presented to them.

Furthermore, it appears that, if left to their own devices, younger children do not spontaneously use organizational strategies to help them remember. In one study (Liberty & Ornstein, 1973), fourth graders and adults were given twenty-eight words printed on individual cards. They were told to sort the cards in any way they wanted to help them remember. The adults tended to sort and group items that were related semantically, while the fourth graders grouped words in more idiosyncratic and less semantically related ways.

In sum, studies have documented clearly that older children are more likely to notice and utilize higher-order relationships among stimuli and are more likely to group items on that basis. Thus the development of active, planful, spontaneous organization strategies characterizes the growth of the school-age child's memory abilities.

Higher-Order Cognition in Children

The importance of higher-order cognition in everyday processing of information has been discussed in some detail in previous chapters (with more to come in the following chapters). The question for this chapter is what the corresponding similarities and differences between higher-order cognition in adults and children are. Even though a definitive answer is impossible, a tremendous amount is known about higher-order cognition in both adults and children. One approach is to trace the developmental literature in each of the topics in higher-order cognition—from memory to creativity. Such a procedure requires many volumes; however, we can touch on the highlights here. The curious student is advised of the rich storehouse of information on this topic, and an equally abundant treasure lies ahead in yet undone research awaiting his or her commitment.

Knowledge Structure and Memory. Several features of a comparative study of higher-order cognition are at once apparent. Even the newest-born neonate is capable of storing some information in memory, but, as we learned in Chapter 7 on memory and in the chapters on language, the form in which that information is stored in memory is dependent on several factors. These include the source of the information, the individual's previous knowledge base, and the structural networks that already have been framed. We first consider the way a child might store in memory an experience in his or her life.

Suppose you were to ask a six-year-old to tell you about her trip to the zoo. She might say something like this: "Let's see. First, we got on a big bus, then I saw elephants, an' big polar bears, an' monkeys an' then I got an ice cream cone an' come home." From this little story an enormous amount can be learned about the child's knowledge base, the way information is stored, and the story grammar. (Remember the police officer and driver in Chapter 1?)

One way to analyze an episode of this type is to think about the way information is represented. Jean Mandler and her colleagues (Mandler, 1983, 1984; and Mandler & DeForest, 1979) have studied story grammars in children and have developed a model that distinguishes between two types of representation. In one, the representation is in terms of what a person knows and how that information is organized in memory (such as a sequential structure or a classification of objects by category). In the other, the representation is in the terms of symbols (such as telling about an episode, or drawing a picture of an event, or writing a story about an experience, or even having an imaginary representation). In the story of a visit to the zoo, the child organized the episode in terms of a sequence of events ("First . . . then . . . and then . . . " and so on) and in terms of a story schema or grammar (the story had a theme, a subject, a beginning, and an end). The concept is similar to the ideas expressed by Kintsch and others discussed in Chapter 11.

Mandler (1983), in discussing children's story grammar, contends that stories have "an underlying structure consisting of a setting component in which the protagonist and background information are introduced, followed by one or more episodes which form the skeletal plot structure of the story. Each episode has some kind of beginning, or initiating, event, to which the protagonist reacts." In one test of the hypothesis that children use a story schema, Mandler and DeForest read a two-episode story to 8-year-olds, 11-year-olds, and adults. In one condition the two episodes were interwoven; that is, the title and story setting of the first episode were presented, and then the title and setting of the second episode were presented. The rest of the story was also presented in a similar way, switching back and forth between the episodes. Some subjects were asked to recall the story in the way it was presented (interrelated), and others were asked to recall all of episode one and then episode two. The former "unnatural" story grammar was much more difficult to recall and, in fact, the 8-year-olds found it impossible to recall the episodes in the interrelated way. We can conclude from this and other similar experiments that children at a very young age discover rather sophisticated story schemata, which they use to encode experiences.

Metaphorical Thinking and Imagery. A beguiling peculiarity of children is their make-believe world. All healthy kids have one. It may be as simple as pretending that a block is a car, or a finger is a gun, or a used cardboard box is a palace, or it may be as elaborate as fantasizing about mystic powers or creating an imaginary playmate. As far as can be told (see Fein, 1979), infants up to 1 year of age are not capable of pretend play, and after the age of 6 children seem to abandon it in favor of other forms of play and games. Nevertheless, the early normal propensity to create a fantasy world seems to remain an active but poorly understood part of adult human behavior, in spite of important theories on the topic by Piaget and Vygotsky. It seems that the development of intellectual skills, creativity, and imagery is related to metaphorical thinking in children. Sound experimental data on this topic are needed.

Imagery. A fundamental issue in the study of higher-order cognition in children is the question of how information is represented. In general, the argument is that adults rely more on semantically (meaning-) based representations and children rely more on perceptually based representations. As an example, consider the following question: Can you name the states that are rectangular?

Chances are that you formed a mental image of regularly shaped states and then "looked" at them to see which ones were really rectangular. You may have focused on the "four-corner" part of the United States and then "looked" at Colorado, which meets the terms of rectangularity, and then Utah, which comes close but is not quite rectangular enough to meet the criterion, and then Wyoming, and so on. If you were asked to answer the question again, especially if you had repeated familiarization with the question, you may have stored the rectangularity of states in semantic memory (something like "rectangular states [are] Colorado and Wyoming; close [but no cigar] are New Mexico, North and South Dakota, Kansas, Oregon"). Then when the question is asked again, you may access the answer from propositional memory rather than from imagery.

Some theorists believe that children use imagery more than propositionally based storage of information to answer questions. For example, consider if we ask an adult and a child the following question: Does a beagle have four legs?

Chances are that even though an adult has never been asked this question before, it is an easy matter of dipping into his or her long-term propositionally stored information bank and to answer it correctly. However, children under the age of about 7 are poor at this type of logical deduction based on semantically stored information. Kosslyn (1983) suggests that if a child does not have the answer stored as a direct associate, then imagery will be used to answer the question.

As in the case of fantasy, hard data on this subject are difficult to find in the experimental literature, but at least one interesting study conducted by Kosslyn (1980; see also Kosslyn, 1983) sheds some light on the topic. In an experiment done with first graders (at about the age of 6), fourth graders (at about the age of 10), and adults, he asked the subjects to verify statements (similar to the techniques discussed in Chapter 8) such as "A cat has claws," or "A cat has a head," or "A fish has fur." In one condition he mentioned the name of the animal and told the subjects to "think about" features of that animal, while in another condition the subjects were asked to "image" the animal. After 5 seconds, they were to decide whether or not the features were part of the animal. For adults, who are supposedly more propositionally inclined, the most expedient way to answer the question would be to retrieve the semantically coded proposition, whereas children, who may rely more on imagery, would answer the question by forming an image of the animal and then "looking" at its features. Reaction time was the dependent variable, and the results are shown in Figure 13.12.

In general Kosslyn found that adults were swifter with the reaction key than children throughout most conditions, but the reaction-time data for the relative reaction times of children and adults are very interesting and deserve close inspection. When we consider the differences between the reaction times for those adults who were given the imagery instructions and those who were not given the imagery instructions, we find that those subjects with instructions were much slower in giving an answer than those without instructions. This suggests that adults tend to store this type of information in terms of abstract propositions. These results are in contrast to the children's data, which show only slight differences between the group with instruction and the group without instruction. It may be that the children are using imagery in both conditions.

Many innovative research programs, such as the study of children's imagery, frequently raise more questions than they answer. Why do children rely more on imagery (if indeed they do) than adults? Is it because they have not learned propositionally structured knowledge? Is there a natural sequence of development that begins with sensory memories that give way to abstract semantic memories? Is it inherently more efficient to access propositionally based information than image-based information? Why is there a shift in the way information is stored? What implications does this research have for educational practices? (Isn't it thoughtful of cognitive psychologists to leave so many unanswered questions for you to resolve?)

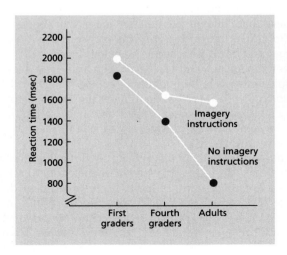

FIGURE 13.12

Average reaction times to verify statements with imagery instructions and without imagery instructions. Data from Kosslyn (1980).

In the next section we consider only one more example of higher-order cognition among children—the very important problem of prototype formation.

Prototype Formation among Children

The "blooming, buzzing confusions" that William James thought the newborn baby was confronted with is one way of looking at the difficult task that we human information-processing creatures all faced initially. Out of the flood of information that bombards the infant's sensory system, what cognitive means exist for the storage and retrieval of pertinent information? It seems that our storage system—human memory—is limited in the amount of information that can be coded and retained by the limited capacity of the brain. We cannot store everything detected by our sensory system. One alternative model to a store-everything concept is the idea that we form abstract representations of sensory impressions in the form of prototypes and/or conceptual categories. This necessary proclivity appears very early in infancy, and several experiments have shown that the formation of conceptual categories in infants may develop before language. Ross (1980) did an experiment with 12-, 18-, and 24-month old infants in which they were shown, one at a time, ten toy objects of the same class, such as types of furniture. Then the infants were shown pairs of objects in which one item was a member of the class (but not originally presented) and the other item was a member of a different category (for example, an apple). Even the youngest of infants in this study spent more time examining the "novel" object, which suggests that they had formed a class representation of, in this case, furniture in which one of the pairs was an "uninteresting" member.

A more direct test of prototype formation in very young (10-month-old) infants was demonstrated by Strauss (1979; see also Strauss & Carter, 1984; and Cohen & Strauss, 1979), who used facial prototypes formed from the plastic templates of an Identikit. The primary purpose of the experiment was to assess infants' abilities to abstract prototypical representations, and if they could, to ascertain whether the prototype was formed on the basis of averaging the values of the exemplar items (feature averaging model) or on the basis of summing the most commonly experienced values of the exemplar items (modal model). Infants in Strauss's study were shown a series of fourteen faces that had been designed to represent a prototype formed on the basis of modal, or average, representations. (See the discussion in Chapter 4 for more on the technique and theory of prototypes.) Following this stage, the infants were given pairs of two types of prototypes—one based on an averaging of the features in the first series, and the other based on a modal (or most frequent) number of features in the first series. The dependent variable was time spent looking at one of the faces. It was presumed that infants would spend more time on the novel, or nonprototypic, face than on the prototype face. By using time spent looking at new faces, the experimenter was able to infer which representation was responsible for the formation of a prototype. The most important finding was that very young (10-month-old) infants were able to abstract a prototype face. Strauss also found that infants abstracted information from the faces and formed a prototypical representation on the basis of an averaging of the features of the exemplar faces.

Recently, Walton and T. G. R. Bower (1993) reported data that indicated prototype formation in newborn infants, aged 8 to 78 hours, could be achieved. The researchers used infant sucking, which controlled the duration a face would be exposed, as the dependent variable. The faces the infants saw were images of eight female or blended (prototype) images of the faces. The infants looked longer at the composite face than at a composite of unseen faces on the first presentation of each. Walton and Bower argue that newborns do form a mental representation having some of the properties of a schema or prototype and that such representations are formed rapidly.

The work on prototype formation has been extended to include children in the age range of 3 to 6 years in an experiment conducted in 1993 by Inn, Walden, and Solso. This experiment is similar to the abstraction of information discussed in Chapter 4, except the subjects were children. A series of ten exemplar faces were developed from a police identification kit using a prototype face as a base. Initially, only exemplar faces, were shown to children. After a child was shown the entire set of ten exemplar faces he or she was shown a second set. Some of these faces were from the original set (old faces), some were faces not previously seen (new faces), and one of the new faces was the prototype from which the exemplars had been developed. The results are shown in Figure 13.13. As shown, very young children, about 3 or 4 years old, do not form an abstraction of the prototype face. However, by the age of 5 it appears that prototype formation begins and is nearly complete at the age of 6, when children's performance on this task is similar to that of college students.

Keep in mind that when a subject identifies a prototype face as an old (previously seen) face, he or she is making a false alarm or error. The face is, in fact, new. Prototype formation may be a sophisticated means of storing frequently experienced features in a single "best example." From these studies and an ever-increasing body of literature on children's cognitive processes, the evidence is beginning to accumulate that points out that abstraction of verbal and visual information (be it conceptualized as schemes, grammars, formation of categories, or prototypes) is as important an attribute of children's information-processing activities as it is among adult subjects.

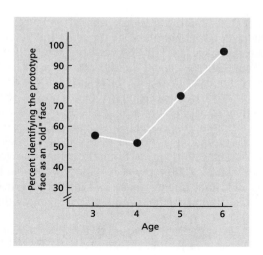

FIGURE 13.13

Percent of false alarms to prototype face among young children. Data from Inn, Walden, and Solso.

Summary

1 Cognition development concerns changes that occur in a more or less orderly fashion across the life span of individuals. It can be studied from the perspective of developmental psychology, neurocognitive development, and/or cognitive development.

2 One theory of cognitive development (Piaget) proposes that intellectual growth is biologically determined and governed by two processes: adaptation involving cognitive adjustments to the environment (assimilation and accommodation), and organization involving increasingly complex, integrated mental representations of operations. Cognitive development is characterized by quantitative, linear changes within a stage and qualitative changes across four major stages: sensorimotor, preoperational, concrete operational, and formal operational.

3 Another major theory of cognitive development (Vygotsky) rejects a strict biological determinism and proposes that learning precedes development. Thought and language are believed to originate independently, with thought being biologically determined whereas language is socially determined, and integration occurring when the child connects thought, language, and environmental events through naming activity.

4 Developmental neurocognition is based on the assumption that underlying all cognitive functions are neurological structures and processes.

5 The brain develops from simple to complex throughout the early life of an individual. It is subject to environmental stimulation and biological constraints.

6 Cerebral laterization has been found among young children giving support to the biological nature of this phenomenon.

7 Cognitive development from an information-processing perspective concerns the question of changes in processes such as attention and memory as a function of increasing age.

8 Young children and infants have memory capacity, but it is doubtful that reliable memories are formed, or can be retrieved, before the age of 2.

9 Studies comparing higher-order cognition in children and adults show that children use story schemata in a manner analogous to adults. Adults rely more on semantic representations, whereas children rely more on perceptually based representations (that is, imagery). Conceptual category formation may precede language acquisition with the basis of prototype formation in infants being feature averaging.

10 Initial information acquisition requires perception of and attention to pertinent information. Research suggests that differences between younger and older subjects with respect to certain abilities, such as selective attention and the ability to respond to task demands, increase with age. Adults and older children use different encoding strategies (for example, multiple versus simple) relative to younger children, and these differences appear as early in the information-processing sequence as the sensory registers.

11 Prototype formation has been observed in very young infants and children.

Key Words

accommodation	egocentrism
adaptation	formal-operation period
anthropomorphism	habituation
assimilation	internalization
cognitive development	laterization
conceptual thought	neurocognitive development
concrete-operation period	scheme
classification	selective attention
conservation	*tabula rasa*

Recommended Readings

Several books by or about Piaget are recommended. They include Piaget, *The Origins of Intelligence in Children;* "Piaget's Theory" in Mussen, ed., *Carmichael's Manual of Child Psychology;* and Piaget and Inhelder, *Memory and Intelligence.* Also see Flavell, *Cognitive Development* and *The Developmental Psychology of Jean Piaget;* Brainerd, *Piaget's Theory of Intelligence.* Holmes and Morrison, *The Child,* is also recommended, as are P. Ornstein, ed., *Memory Development in Children;* Pick and Saltzman, eds., *Modes of Perceiving and Processing Information;* Siegler ed.), *Children's Thinking: What Develops?* Daehler and Bukafko's text *Cognitive Development* is also recommended.

Vygotsky's work is now generally available in English. Recommended are *Mind in Society* and *Thought and Language.* Several edited books on the information-processing approach to developmental psychology are also recommended. They include Sternberg, ed., *Mechanisms of Cognitive Development;* Flavell and Markman, eds., *Handbook of Child Psychology: Cognitive Development;* Sophian, ed., *Origins of Cognitive Skills;* and Moscovitch, ed., *Infant Memory.* Flavell's APA Award address, "The Development of Children's Knowledge about the Appearance-Reality Distinction," in *American Psychologist,* is also recommended. For infant memory see Rovee-Collier in A. Diamond, ed., *The Development and Neural Bases of Higher Cognitive Functions."* A somewhat technical, but worthwhile collection of neurocognitive papers can be found in M. Johnson's *Brain Development and Cognition: A Reader.*

THINKING 1: Concept Formation, Logic, and Decision Making

T HINKING IS THE CROWN jewel of cognition. It is spectacularly brilliant, in some people; even sublime, among average folks; and, the fact that it happens at all, one of the great wonders of our species. Thinking about thinking, what some call meta-thinking, may seem an insurmountable task, since it seems to engage all of the themes mentioned previously—the detection of external energy, neurophysiology, perception, memory, language, imagery, and the developing person. Advances in cognitive psychology, particularly within the last twenty years, have led to a formidable arsenal of research techniques and theoretical models capable of disclosing some of the facts about thought and casting them in a plausible framework of sound psychological theory. This chapter is the first of two chapters about the thought process and some of the means used to study the jewel of cognition.

Most human solving or concept formation involves thinking, and most problem solving involves concept formation. To distinguish among these concepts, this chapter presents the theories, research, and discussions that are generally associated with each.

THINKING

During the early history of psychology, particularly as psychology was emerging in Europe during the last part of the nineteenth century, interest in thought was highly fashionable. Early investigators (Oswald Külpe, for example) believed that, since observation was the method of science, thought would be best studied by having people think and describe their thinking. This introspective approach produced a great deal of data, which, in turn, contributed to the isolation of some of the factors involved in rational thought.

During the early part of the twentieth century, many eminent psychologists, including Wilhelm Wundt, Williams James, E. L. Thorndike, John Dewey, John Watson, and Max Wertheimer, considered the topic of thinking, each within the theoretical model he espoused.

During the last part of the twentieth century, thinking is again experiencing one of its periodic resurgences as a legitimate topic of psychology. A part of that resurgence may be attributable to experiments on logical thought and reason.

Thinking is a process by which a new mental representation is formed through the transformation of information by complex interaction of the mental attributes of judging, abstracting, reasoning, imagining, and problem solving. Thinking is the most inclusive of the three elements of the thought process and is characterized by comprehensiveness rather than exclusion. When you read a book, information presumably passes through a sequence from a sensory store to a memory store. Then that new information is transformed (in a sense, digested), and the consequence is an original product. You may, for example, read that Czar Nicholas II neglected the basic needs of the citizens of Russia while engaged in a war with Germany. This fact may call up from long-term memory the knowledge that Nicholas's wife, Alexandra, was of German descent, and you may think that these two facts may have had an interactive effect on the course of Russian history. The task is, of course, much more complex than is expressed in this example, but it is easy to see that the development of the simple thought depends on judgments, abstraction, reason, imagination, problem solving, and creativity.

There continues to be some dispute as to whether thinking is an internal process or exists only insofar as can be measured behaviorally. For example, a chess player may study his or her next move for several minutes before responding overtly. During the time the player is pondering what action to take, does thinking occur? It seems obvious that it does, and yet some would argue that because no overt behavior is observable, such a conclusion is based not on empirical observation but on speculation. A general definition of thinking might resolve some of the conflict and help guide our discussion. There are three basic ideas about thinking (Mayer, 1983).

- Thinking is cognitive—that is, it occurs "internally," in the mind—but is inferred from behavior. The chess player exhibits thinking in his or her move.

- Thinking is a process that involves some manipulation of knowledge in the cognitive system. While the chess player is contemplating a move, past memories combine with present information to change his or her knowledge of the situation.

- Thinking is directed and results in behavior that "solves" a problem or is directed toward a solution. The next chess move is, in the mind of the player, directed toward winning the game. Not all actions are successful, but generally, in the mind of the player, they are directed toward a solution.

CONCEPT FORMATION

Concept formation (or concept learning) refers to the discernment of the properties common to a class of objects or ideas. We have dealt with the topic of concept formation as it relates to visual forms and prototypes (see Chapter 4) and semantic items (see Chapter 8). The greater part of our previous discussion specified the components or features of concepts and how concepts were structured in a semantic network. In this section the topic of features is also discussed, but we will concentrate on the rules that relate conceptual features. For example, we all have learned the concept *Volkswagen* by identification of its classic properties (for example, beetle-shaped, no grill) that distinguish it from the other members of the general class of *automobiles,* or we have learned the properties of the more abstract concept *justice* (for example, fairness, morality, equality) that distinguish it from other human qualities. In these instances the "rule" that relates the features to the concept is as follows: The concept is defined in terms of all the features that have been associated with it.

Concept formation, as it is used in this chapter, is more limited in scope than thinking and seems readily susceptible to experimental analysis. It is not surprising, then, that there is a considerable body of knowledge about the laws and processes of concept formation. The early definition of *concept* was "mental images, ideas, or processes." This was normally disclosed through the experimental method of introspection, which was widely accepted as the principal technique of psychology. The decline of introspection as a method and the rise of behaviorism, especially in American psychology, brought about not only revolutionary methodological changes but also corresponding revolutionary changes in the view of the nature of cognitive events—and, consequently,

> The only justification for our concepts is that they serve to represent the complex of our experiences . . .
>
> *Albert Einstein*

in the definition of *concept*. For our purposes a concept may be defined in terms of certain critical features and the rules that relate those features. (Occasionally we use the term in its former sense.)

Features, as used here, are characteristics of an object or event that are also characteristic of other objects or events. Mobility, for example, is a feature of automobiles; Ford Escorts have it, Cadillacs have it, and Maseratis have it. However, mobility is also a feature of other objects—trains, birds, secretaries of state, and tight ends. From a cognitive viewpoint, the basis for accepting a characteristic as a feature is subjective. Thus one can imagine automobiles, trains, birds, secretaries of state, and tight ends that do *not* share the feature of mobility, and so the determination of "critical features" of an object or idea is a function of the circumstances. In this sense, conceptual description is similar to the process involved in signal detection (see Chapter 3), in which acceptability as a feature of a concept is determined by the stringency of criteria. The setting of a criterion, as we have learned, is subject to wide variance, according to the experience of the observer.

A distinction between features can be made on the quantitative basis as well as on the qualitative basis just described. Mobility is a qualitative feature that also can be measured quantitatively. Your Ford Escort automobile may have mobility (a qualitative statement) but may not have as much mobility as someone else's Maserati. Thus both dimensional (quantitative) features and attributional (qualitative) features enter into conceptual formation; both kinds are investigated.

Concept formation is one of the most important cognitive functions that humans perform. During the formative periods of most sciences, concept formation played a critical function in the organization of data. In chemistry concept formation is achieved by the organization of the elements in a periotic table; in biology, by the development of phylogenetic order; in art, by the categorization of artists by periods; in Egyptology, by the division of events into dynasties, and in cognitive psychology, by the classification of types of memories—all are examples of concept formation that led to a better understanding of the subject. These complex forms of concept formation, when broken down into their basic components, are actually composed of a series of rather simple (and analyzable) cognitive processes.

Rule Learning

A conceptual rule is a statement of how features must be related if something exhibiting the features is to be an instance of a particular concept. When dealing with complex concepts, it is necessary to develop the conceptual rules, which relate the features.[1] In

[1] Much of the contemporary research on concept attainment is influenced by the seminal work of Haygood and Bourne (1965), who made the important distinctions between attributes and the rules that connect them.

the simplest binary situation, in which, say, *red* and *square* are the attributes, the concept can vary according to the rule that is applied. For example, although the attributes are the same (*red, square*), the concepts of *red and square, red or square,* and *if red, then square* are all different.

Five types of rules in concept formation are in common use in the experimental laboratory: affirmative, conjunctive, inclusive disjunctive, conditional, and biconditional. These are summarized in Table 14.1.

It has been determined that concepts formed on the basis of the affirmative rule are the easiest, while (as shown in Table 14.1) two-feature-rule problems tend to increase in difficulty from conjunctive to biconditional (Haygood & Bourne, 1965; and Neisser & Weene, 1962). The basis of the difficulty of the biconditional-rule concepts is uncertain, with Bourne and Guy (1968) and Haygood and Bourne (1965) indicating it to be the most difficult and others indicating it to be easier than the conjunctive or inclusive disjunctive types (Laughlin, 1968; and Laughlin & Jordan, 1967). Of course, with enough practice, subjects become very skilled at concept formation and rule learning, and differences in difficulty diminish.

In the laboratory, concept formation and concept rule learning occur under strictly controlled circumstances. A typical example of the procedure might be as follows. Subjects are given instructions that describe the task and information that permits them to form a concept—that is, the stimulus features are described, and subjects are told the type of responses wanted. Normally, subjects are asked to identify the display as either a positive or negative instance and are told immediately after making their response whether it is correct. In rule learning tasks, subjects are told that they must find a relationship (between two features) that will allow them to identify (as a positive or negative instance) each of the subsequently displayed items. In the case of such binary relationships, subjects must find the way two features interact to form the concept. A

TABLE 14.1

Conceptual Rules Described in Terms of Two Relevant Features

Name	Symbol*	Description	Generalized Example
Affirmative	R	All red objects	Anything red
Conjunctive	$R \cap S$	All objects that are both red and square	A car that is both a Volkswagen and yellow
Inclusive disjunctive	$R \cup S$	All objects that are red or square or both	A psychologist who is a member of a psychology department and/or a member of the American Psychological Association
Conditional	$R \rightarrow S$ $(R \cup S)$	An object that, if red, must be square (or if not red, any shape)	A uniformed police officer who, if a crime is committed, makes an arrest
Biconditional	$R \leftrightarrows S$	Red objects only if they are square	An appropriate behavior; nudity if, and only if, on a "nude" beach

*Red (R) and Square (S)

FIGURE 14.1

An array of instances comprising combinations of three attributes and four dimensions. From Bruner, Goodnow, and Austin (1956).

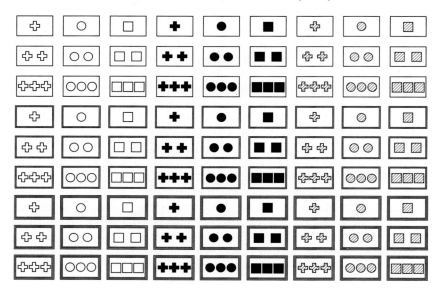

stimulus display such as that shown in Figure 14.1 might include some square figures and some red figures, with the concept being *red and square*. The subject may "guess" the concept to be *red*, but, after learning that a red circle is incorrect, may shift to *square* and eventually to *red and square* as the defining features of the concept.

When we consider the myriad different objects and events we encounter in our daily life, the task of concept attainment may seem overwhelming. Nevertheless, that staggering task is accomplished with relative ease. It may well be that our understanding of the world is possible only through the development of cognitive structures that relate seemingly disparate objects and events into cohesive concepts. The study of concept formation and concept rule learning, thus, is not isolated from the mainstream of everyday life; in fact, it stands squarely in the middle of it.

In the preceding section the basic rudiments of concept acquisition are reported. In the following section we deal with both traditional and contemporary theories of conceptual behavior, with special emphasis on those theories that fit into a cognitive viewpoint.

Association

The oldest and most influential theory in learning is the principle of association. In its most succinct form, the principle holds that a bond will be formed between two events as those events are repeatedly presented together. Reinforcement, or a reward system, facilitates formation of the bond. The basic model of the principle is cast in terms of stimulus-response (S-R) psychology. Thus the association principle postulates that the learning of a concept is a result of (1) reinforcing the correct pairing of a stimulus (for example, red boxes) with the response of identifying it as a concept, and (2) nonreinforcing (a form of punishment) the incorrect pairing of a stimulus (for example, red circles) with a response of identifying it as a concept. (Such mechanistic viewpoints leave little room for the concept—prevalent among modern cognitive theorists—of internal structures that select, organize, and transform information.)

Hypothesis Testing

The general notion that people sometimes solve problems and form concepts by formulating and testing hypotheses has long been held in experimental psychology. The direct application of a hypothesis-testing model to concept learning by Bruner, Goodnow, and Austin (1956) in their influential book, *A Study of Thinking,* introduced a thorough methodological analysis of performance in concept formation.

The initial stage in concept attainment is the selection of a hypothesis or a strategy that is consistent with the objectives of our inquiry. Whenever we seek to find out something, the process involves the establishment of priorities, much as a scientist may order a sequence of experiments, a lawyer may ask a series of questions, or a doctor may develop a set of diagnostic tests. The following from Bruner and his colleagues details the process of selecting strategies:

> A neurologist is interested in the localization of pattern vision in monkeys. More specifically, he is interested in six cortical areas and their bearing on pattern vision. He knows that, with all six areas intact, pattern vision is unimpaired. With all six areas destroyed, pattern vision is absent. His technique of research is extirpation. In planning his research, how shall he proceed? Destroy one area at a time? All but one at a time? In what order shall he do his successive experiments?

> The prime question is "What is to be gained by choosing one order as compared to another order of testing instances?"

> The first thing to be gained is, of course, an opportunity to obtain information appropriate to the objectives of one's inquiry. One may wish to choose an instance at any given point in concept attainment that can tell one the most about what the concept might be. . . . To sum up, controlling the order of instances tested is to increase or decrease the cognitive strain involved in assimilating information. . . . A well-contrived

Jerome Bruner. **Seminal work established "thinking" as a legitimate scientific topic.**

order of choice—a good "selection strategy"—makes it easier to keep track of what hypotheses have been found tenable or untenable on the basis of information encountered. . . . A third advantage is not at first obvious. By following a certain order of selecting instances for testing one controls the degree of risk involved. . . .

In a typical experiment, Bruner and his associates presented an entire concept universe (that is, all possible variations on a number of dimensions and attributes) to subjects (see Figure 14.1) and indicated one instance of an exemplar of the concept that the subjects were to attain. The subjects would pick one of the other instances, be told whether it was a positive or negative instance, then pick another instance, and so on until they attained the criterion (identified the concept).

The strategies subjects may select in concept formation include scanning and focusing, each of which has its subtypes as follows:

Simultaneous scanning. Subjects start with all possible hypotheses and eliminate the untenable ones.

Successive scanning. Subjects begin with a single hypothesis, maintain it if successful, and, where it is unsuccessful, may change it to another that is based on all previous experience.

Critical Thinking: Thinking, Problem Solving, and "Frames"

Try to solve these problems (or present them to a friend and observe his or her behavior).

Each of the following cards has a letter on one side and a number on the other. If a card has a vowel on one side, then it has an even number on the other side. Which card(s) do you need to turn over to validate the rule?

Several years ago the post office had two rates for first- and second-class mail. The first-class rate was 29¢ if the letter was sealed and 25¢ if unsealed. Suppose that you are a postal clerk checking letters as they move across a conveyor belt and that you are charged with implementing the following rule: "If the letter is sealed, then it must have a 29¢ stamp." Of the following letters, which one(s) would you have to turn over to verify the rule.

Which of these two tasks was easier? Are the tasks similar? Identical? In the first case the problem was framed in more abstract terms than it was in the second, which was more realistic. (See end of this chapter for answers.) Adapted from Johnson-Laird & Wason (1977) and Johnson-Laird, Legrenzi, & Legrenzi (1972).

The solution is at the end of this chapter.

Conservative focusing. Subjects formulate a hypothesis, select a positive instance of it as a focus, and then make a sequence of reformulations (each of which changes only one feature), noting each time which turns out to be positive and which negative. For example, as shown in Table 14.2, from a large array of patterns subjects may be told that one large, red square is a positive instance. Because each of the attributes is potentially relevant, the hypothesis is 1 LR□. Subjects may select 1 LR△ (focusing on shape as a possible critical dimension). Learning that both □ and △ are positive instances, subjects may correctly infer that shape is irrelevant and shift their attention to color, choosing 1 LG□, and so on, until, by focusing their effort on one attribute at a time, they have successfully eliminated all irrelevant attributes.

Focus gambling is characterized by changing more than one feature at a time. Although the conservative-focusing technique is methodological and likely to lead to a valid concept, subjects may opt for a gamble in the expectation that they may determine the concept more quickly.

Of the strategies described above, conservative focusing tends to be the most effective (Bourne, 1963); scanning techniques give only marginal success. A difficulty with the Bruner model is that it assumes that subjects hold to a single strategy, when, in actuality, some vacillate, shifting from strategy to strategy throughout the task.

TABLE 14.2

Typical Process in the Strategies of Conservative Focusing and Focus Gambling

	Stimulus Patterns*	Category	Hypothesis*
Conservative Focusing			
Focal stimulus	1 *LR*□	+	1 *LR*□
1	1 *LR*□	+	1 *LR*
2	1 *LG*△	−	1 *LR*
3	1 *SR*□	+	1 *R*
4	2 *LR*□	−	1 *R*
	Concept: 1 *R*		
Focus Gambling			
Focus stimulus	1 *LR*□	+	1 *LR*□
1	1 *SR*△	+	1 *R*
2	2 *LR*□	−	1 *R*
3	1 *LG*□	−	1 *R*
	Concept: 1 *R*		

* *L* indicates large; *S*, small; *R*, red; and *G*, green.

From Bourne, Ekstrand, and Dominowski (1971).

LOGIC

Thought or *thinking* refers to the general process of considering an issue in the mind, while *logic* is the science of thinking. Although two people may think about the same thing, their conclusions—both reached through thought—may differ, one being *logical,* the other *illogical.*

In a recent newspaper interview of people on the street, a reporter asked, "Are you in favor of the death penalty?" One person gave the following answer: "I am religious and think that everyone has the right to life. The Bible says 'an eye for an eye' and if someone does something to another person he should get what he deserves. Besides, it has been proved that some people have defective brains which cannot be changed. Some things are worse than death, like rape." The person was in favor of the death penalty, although it is somewhat difficult to ascertain that conclusion given the reply. The conclusion (favoring the death penalty) seems to be in direct conflict with the opening statement, "I . . . think everyone has the right to life." Perhaps what the person really intended was "Even though people have a given right to life, if an individual violates certain laws of society he or she should be executed." The justification for execution is supported by biblical teachings, good sense, medical truths, the relative severity of the punishment, and probably a high degree of emotional thought. In this case serious questions can be raised regarding the validity of the argument, but it is, nevertheless, a fairly typical representation of the way many people support a conclusion, which make life both fascinating and frustrating.

Thinking and logic have been the subject of speculation for a long time. More than two thousand years ago, Aristotle introduced a system of reasoning or of validating arguments that is called the *syllogism.* A syllogism has three steps—a major premise, a minor premise, and a conclusion, in that order. Note the following example:

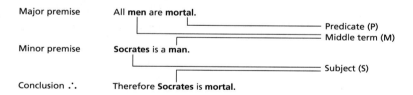

A conclusion reached by means of syllogistic reasoning is considered valid, or true, if the premises are accurate and the form is correct. It is therefore possible to use syllogistic logic for the validation of arguments. Illogical conclusions can be determined and their cause isolated. This is a succinct statement of the theoretical basis of much current research on thinking and logic.

Before introducing some of the current research, it is useful to review the laws of formal syllogistic logic. In the outline shown in Figure 14.2 (Erickson, 1974) of the various forms of a syllogism, the predicate of the conclusion is labeled "P," and the subject of the conclusion is labeled, "S." The major premise links the predicate of the conclusion (*honest,* in the first example) with a middle term, *M* (*churchgoers*); the minor premise links the subject of the conclusion (*politicians*) with the middle term (*church-*

FIGURE 14.2

Forms of a syllogism.

Basic Forms of a Syllogism		
Major Premise	All M are P	All churchgoers are honest.
Minor Premise	All S are M	All politicians are churchgoers
Conclusion	All S are P	Therefore all politicians are honest

Sentence Type Used in a Syllogism		
A All S are P	All psychologists are wise	(universal affirmative)
E No S are P	No poor research is published	(universal negative)
I Some S are P	Some elected officials are truthful	(particular affirmative)
O Some S are not P	Some professors are not rich	(particular negative)

Syllogistic Figures			
Figure 1 (Forward Chain)	Figure 2 (Stimulus Chain)	Figure 3 Response Equivalence)	Figure 4 (Backward Chain)
M–P	P–M	M–P	P–M
S–M	S–M	M–S	M–S
S–M	S–P	S–P	S–P

goers); and the conclusion links the subject (*politicians*) with the predicate of the conclusion (*honest*).

Each syllogism type can be designated on the basis of the kinds of sentences of which it is composed; thus, in the example concerning Socrates and mortality, all of the sentences are of the universal affirmative type (*A*), and so the syllogism is of the AAA type.

The syllogistic figures shown in Figure 14.2 are notations for mediation models, which are commonly used in the study of verbal learning. For example, Figure 1 (forward chain) in the Socrates example would have the following sequence: men-mortal, Socrates-man, Socrates-mortal. The total number of syllogisms possible (a combination of types and figures) is 256, assuming each factor interacts with all other factors, of which only 24 are logical (6 for each figure).

An appealing feature of using syllogistic logic in cognitive research is that it makes it possible to evaluate, or validate, the correctness of the thought process on the basis of its form rather than its content. By using symbols (*S* and *P*) to represent the subject and predicate, it is possible to reduce logical thinking to a type of algebra. Instead of saying 8 apples plus 3 apples minus 2 apples yields 9 apples, we can mathematically represent the equation as $a + b - c = b^2$ or $a - c = b^2 - b$, without consideration of the referents designated by these symbols. Similarly, it is possible in syllogistic logic to reduce statements of fact to symbols and manipulate them, as in mathematical equations, without regard to the physical reality they may represent.

Syllogistic Reasoning

Early research using syllogistic reasoning relied on reports by the subject of "what was going on in my head" while solving a problem in logic. Although these introspective techniques lacked the empirical basis science requires, three important independent variables did emerge from them: the form of the argument, the content of the argument, and the subject (individual differences).

Form. Early researchers (Woodworth & Sells, 1935; Sells, 1936; and Chapman & Chapman, 1959) looked at the errors produced in syllogistic reasoning tasks as a consequence of the "mood" or "atmosphere" created by the form of the argument, rather than on the basis of formal logical deduction. A typical case might be:

> All *A* are *B*.
> All *C* are *B*.
> _____
> Therefore all *A* are *C*.

Here the term *all* in the major and minor premises seems to suggest a universal affirmative atmosphere, so that when subjects come to the conclusion, which mimics the form of the premise, their tendency is to accept it. The obvious invalidity of the argument is evident if we substitute content for the letter abstractions. Thus:

All Republicans are human.

All Democrats are human.

Therefore, all Republicans are Democrats.

Before going on with our discussion of syllogistic logic, try to ascertain the validity of the following statements.

All revolutions are basically economic.

Some economic conditions cause hardships.

Some revolutions cause hardships.

Sam is not the best cook in the world.

The best cook in the world lives in Toronto.

Sam does not live in Toronto.

All nerts are soquerts.

All connets are strequos.

All connets are nerts.

Did you find some of these easy and some difficult? One easy to way to solve syllogisms is to use diagrams, as shown in Figure 14.3. (More is said about this later.) The reason some were more difficult than others may be due to your previous knowledge and your previous ability to recognize a logical argument when you see it. The first of these effects is called the atmosphere effect, discussed next, and the second is related to the validity of an argument that may be the result of formal training but is more likely

FIGURE 14.3

Diagrams in which all and some *A*s are *B*s and no or some *A*s are *B*s are represented.

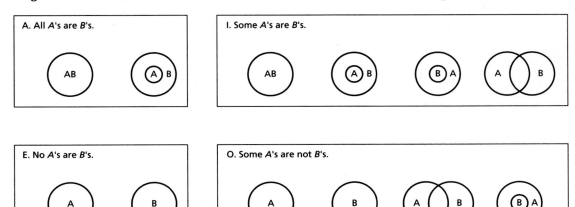

the result of practice. Also, you may have learned that you need not know the definitions of terms to determine the validity of an argument.

Atmosphere. The *atmosphere effect* is defined as "the tendency to accept or reject an argument on the basis of its form. In other words, merely presenting an argument in a certain way may influence its believability.

Johnson-Laird and his associates (Johnson-Laird & Byrne, 1989, 1991; and Johnson-Laird & Steedman, 1978) have demonstrated that the form of a syllogism exhibits a strong influence on the conclusion drawn. Specifically, a syllogism of the following sort:

Some of the parents are scientists.

All of the scientists are drivers.

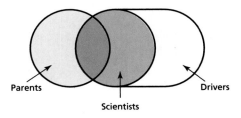

tends to elicit the conclusion "Some of the parents are drivers" in preference to the equally valid conclusion "Some of the drivers are parents." In the symbolic language we have been using, an AB, BC syllogism favors an AC conclusion, while a BA, CB syllogism favors a CA conclusion. Furthermore, the authors report that the phenomenon occurs with audiences at universities as far-flung as Chicago, New York, Edinburgh, London, Padua, and Nijmegen!

Phillip Johnson-Laird. Developed important models of human cognition and logic.

A feature of Johnson-Laird and Steedman's research that is particularly interesting to cognitive psychologists is their inferences about the mental representations of syllogistic premises.

For example, one subject represented the statement "All the artists are beekeepers" by first imagining an arbitrary number of artists and tagging each as a beekeeper. One subject, when asked how he performed the task, said, "I thought of all the little artists in the room and imagined that they all had beekeeper hats on." Thus the "internal representation" of the premise might be as follows:

artist   artist   artist
↓   ↓   ↓
beekeeper   beekeeper   beekeeper   (beekeeper)   (beekeeper)

Arbitrary numbers of artists are tagged as beekeepers, as are some beekeepers who are not artists. The arrows, in Johnson-Laird and Steedman's theme, represent semantic relationships of class membership. (Here, for example, the arrow represents *is a* in "Each artist is a beekeeper.") The relationship above (All *A* are *B*) can be further symbolically illustrated as follows:

a a
↓   ↓
b   b   (b)

which is recognized as an *A* sentence type, or premise. An *I* sentence type, or premise, "Some *A* are *B*," has the following representation:

a (a)
↓
b   (b)

An *E* sentence type, or premise, "No *A* are *B*":

a a
⊥   ⊥
b   b

And an *O* sentence type, or premise, "Some *A* are not *B*":

a   (a)
⊥   ↓
b   (b)

If the second premise is "Some of the beekeepers are chemists," the form is:

All of the artists are beekeepers.

Some of the beekeepers are chemists.

or symbolically:

All *A* are *B*   a   a
                       ↓   ↓
Some *B* are *C*   b   b   (b)
                       ↓   ↓
                       c   c   (c)

which frequently leads to the invalid conclusion:

Some of the artists are chemists.

The formulation of a conclusion calls on the subject to trace a path between the end items in their representation of the parts of a syllogism, much as we might consider a problem in mental mapping (for example, determining the shortest route to Boston to San Francisco to Atlanta). If there is at least one positive path, as in the artists-beekeepers-chemists syllogism, then the invalid conclusion that some artists are chemists is likely to be made.

This work has been extended by Clement and Falmagne (1986) in an interesting study in which world knowledge and mental imagery were related to logical reasoning. Essentially, the experimenters varied the imagery value of the terms and the relatedness of conditional statements in syllogisms. From our discussion of mental imagery (see Chapter 10), you may recall that words differ with regard to their imagery values (for example, *beggar* has higher imagery than *context*). Relatedness refers to how easily or naturally two actions form a relationship. An example of a statement used in a logical syllogism that is high in imagery might be "If the man wants plain doughnuts, then . . ." whereas a statement low in imagery might be "If the woman reorganizes the company structure, then . . ." High- and low-relatedness statements might include "If the man wants plain doughnuts, then he walks to the bakery across the intersection" and "If the man walks his golden retriever, then he gets upset about his insect bite." All four possible combinations of statements were used in syllogistic problems (that is, high imagery—high relatedness, high imagery—low relatedness, low imagery—high relatedness, and low imagery—low relatedness). Clement and Falmagne found that syllogisms in which the statements were high in imagery and relatedness were solved significantly better than other forms that, given what we know about the powerful effects of both imagery and relatedness to form internal representations of reality and the above theoretical model of Johnson-Laird, seem to be a logical conclusion.

The usefulness of diagrams (such as a Venn diagram) and imagery to solve problems in logic has been further demonstrated by Bauer and Johnson-Laird (1993) on complicated deductive logic problems of the following kind:

Raphael is in Tacoma or Julia is in Atlanta, or both.

Julia is in Atlanta or Paul is in Philadelphia, or both.

Is the following conclusion valid?

Julia is in Atlanta, or both Raphael is in Tacoma and Paul is in Philadelphia.

If you are like most subjects in the study, you found this difficult to validate. Now, try to visualize the problem with the assistance of the diagram in Figure 14.4. This diagram is a kind of road map in which the subject must travel from the left side to the right side by inserting the shapes (representing people) into the slots in the path (representing places). When a pathway is intact, travel can take place. Thus, if Julia is in Atlanta, traffic could flow through that area. Julia could be in Atlanta or Seattle or neither place. In a study done at Princeton University (Bauer and Johnson-Laird, 1993), it was found that when problems of this sort were presented in diagram form, undergraduate students solved the problems faster and drew many more valid conclusions (about 30 percent more) than when the problems were presented verbally. The important conclusion we may draw from this experiment is that logically untrained people, such as most people are, tend to reason by building models of the situation or drawing diagrams that show relationships clearly. For example, when you were asked to solve the classic problem in algebra about the leaky bucket (you know, the one that had three holes of different sizes that drained water in varying amounts while you were trying to fill it up), didn't you draw a picture of the bucket, holes and all, and filling hose? I did.

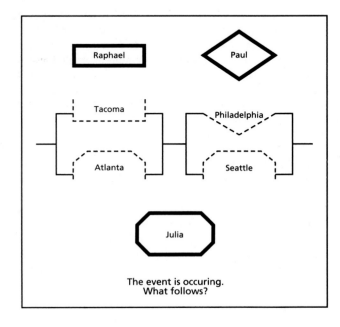

F I G U R E 1 4 . 4

Diagram representing a double disjunctive problem. Subjects were asked to complete a path from the left side to the right side by inserting the shapes corresponding to people into the slots. Thus, Julia could be in Atlanta *or* Seattle but *not* both. From Bauer and Johnson-Laird (1993).

The research on syllogisms has suggested that people tend to draw conclusions in syllogistic problems (and presumably in less formal ways of logical thinking as well) on the basis of first forming internal representations of the premises—sometimes imagined representations. Once these internal representations are formed, it is possible to apply logical thinking to them. If the representation (or heuristic) is biased toward verification (as "All artists are beekeepers"), then the logical test of the conclusion consists of trying to break the pathways between the premises and the conclusion.

Content. Since it is possible to hold the form of the argument constant while varying the content, the latter has also been a useful tool in the analysis of the thought process. Thus the content of our opening syllogism:

> All men are mortal.
> Socrates is a man.
> Therefore Socrates is mortal.

may be evaluated by using the same form but different content:

> All men are moral.
> Stalin is a man.
> Therefore Stalin is moral.

If the premises of these syllogisms are true, then the conclusions are, even though one conclusion may be more difficult to accept than the other.

The effects of content on the judged validity of an argument remind us that the cognitive process is neither simple nor devoid of the considerable impact of knowledge stored in long-term memory. Throughout this book we have seen numerous examples of how that information influences (in many instances, to the degree of determining) the quality of the information perceived, encoded, stored, and transformed. It should not be surprising, then, that the judged validity of syllogistic statements about something we know may be a reflection of the content of the long-term memory.

The tendency to accept the conclusion of an invalid syllogism if the conclusion is consistent with the attitude of the judge was tested by Janis and Frick (1943). In their experiment, graduate students were asked to judge the soundness of arguments, with *soundness* defined as "a conclusion that logically follows from the premises." Some of the items used were as follows:

> Many brightly colored snakes are poisonous.
> The copperhead snake is not brightly colored.
> So the copperhead is not a poisonous snake.

> There is no doubt that some drugs are poisonous.
> All brands of beer contain the drug alcohol.
> Therefore, some brands of beer are poisonous.

> All poisonous things are bitter.
> Arsenic is not bitter.
> Therefore, arsenic is not poisonous.

After the subjects had agreed or disagreed with each of the syllogisms, they were asked to reread the conclusion and indicate whether they agreed or disagreed with it. The results indicated that subjects' errors tended to be made in the direction of their bias concerning the conclusion. Thus the bromide "Don't confuse me with the facts; I've already made up my mind" seems to be true for some people under certain circumstances.

There is more than one way to err in making a "logical" deduction. We will consider several.

The Fallacy of Reification. To *reify* an idea is to assume that it is real when, in fact, it may be hypothetical or metaphoric. For example, a student who was having difficulty completing his master's degree said to me, "This university does not want to give me a degree!" He assumed that the university acted as an individual would act, when, in truth, the university did nothing. Possibly, his major advisor did not want to grant him a degree, perhaps for good reasons. Demagogic politicians, rabble-rousers, anarchists, and petit paranoids frequently reify ideas with such expressions as *the government, the newspapers, the unions, the Republicans, the Democrats, big business,* and even *nature* or *the gods.*

Ad hominem and Personal Arguments. Ad hominem arguments are those that attack a person's character rather than the substance of an argument. American politicians provide good examples. A candidate may present well-reasoned ideas but is rebutted, not for the ideas, but on the basis of his or her moral character. Reviewers of professional matters—be they book reviewers, manuscript reviewers, or judges of fellow professors for tenure or promotion—are admonished to avoid ad hominem arguments in their evaluations. Attack the idea, not the person—such advice is a good policy in everyday life.

Related to ad hominem arguments are those that are validated in terms of an individual's experience or knowledge of an individual's experience. These personal arguments seem to be pervasive among nonscientific thinkers as well as an alarming number of students. The gist of the validation of such an argument is that "it must be true because it happened to me . . . or to my great-uncle Oliver . . . or to my professor." Scientific progress is ill served by either type of argument.

Arguments That Appeal to Force and Power. An example of an appeal to power to validate an argument might be, "The United States was justified in entering the Vietnam War because we are a mighty and moral nation." Might and morality may be virtues, but they also may have nothing to do with treaties and a nation's right to sovereignty. Nevertheless, it is "human" to resort to such arguments.

Appeal to Authority and/or Fame. A common logical error is made by those who are impressed by authorities and/or famous people in one domain who make statements about another. This practice is common among advertisers who, in the United States especially, use athletes, movie stars, dancers, and singers to endorse products about which they have virtually no special knowledge. Particularly insidious, and offensive to an academic, is the use of scholars such as Nobel laureates to make proclamations about topics far removed from their field.

The Majority-Must-Be-Right Argument. Here the argument is that if most people do something, it must be right. "Ten million Americans use 'Zapo' deodorant, so it must be good" is the essence of this argument.

The Straw Man Argument. The straw man technique is to set up a weak argument and attribute it to someone else so that you can knock it down. Sometimes the straw man is a caricature of a more modest position taken by another. I sometimes call it the lightning rod argument because a prominent feature is isolated and emphasized, redirecting the main thrust of the argument. For example, while debating about foreign aid to the Philippines, you develop a well-reasoned case based on a multitude of socioeconomic forces. These might include, as a minor point, the need to save wild animals in the mountains. Your opponent then attacks the entire argument by citing endless statistics showing that the Luzon tree squirrel actually is in abundant supply. The straw man approach may be somewhat effective, especially among noncritical thinkers, but others felicitously recognize its basis as material commonly found on the ground where cattle trod. It is surprising how often this ploy is used in the academic world by professors and graduate students zealous in attacking the theses of others.

DECISION MAKING

In the previous section we discussed a type of reasoning in which conclusions could be proved valid through a process of deductive logic. In that form, if the premises of a syllogism are true and the form correct, then the conclusion of an argument is valid—that is, the probability of the conclusion being correct is certain.

Inductive Reasoning

Another form of reasoning is called inductive reasoning. In inductive reasoning a conclusion is usually expressed implicitly or explicitly in terms of a probability statement. In our everyday life we commonly make decisions not so much as a result of a well-reasoned syllogistic paradigm, but in terms of inductive reasoning, where decisions are based on past experiences and conclusions are based on what is perceived as the best choice of a number of possible alternatives. Consider the following statements:

> If I work at the library for one week, I will have enough money to go skiing on Saturday.
> I will work at the library for one week.
> Therefore, I will have enough money to go skiing.

The above argument is deductively valid. Now, suppose that the second statement was "I will not work at the library for one week." Then the conclusion "I will not have enough money to go skiing" is true given the constraints of syllogistic logic, but it is not necessarily true in real life. For example, your rich Uncle Harry might send you some money. Evaluating the validity of a conclusion based on inductive reasoning may be based on considerations other than the structural form of an argument. In the case just mentioned, it could be based on the likelihood that Uncle Harry will send a gift of money or on other possibilities that some funds will come your way shortly. This type of decision making goes on every day and has recently become the focus of research on the process by cognitive psychologists.

An example of decision making based on inductive reasoning is one that you may have faced when you selected a college. Let us presume that you were accepted into four colleges—a large private university (S), a small private college (T), a medium-sized state university (N), and a large state university (A). How might you go about deciding which college to attend? One method would be to evaluate each of the choices in terms of their relative value on pertinent dimensions. The important dimensions might include (1) the quality of instruction, (2) cost, (3) proximity to home, (4) social opportunities, and (5) prestige. Each dimension will be assigned a value between 0 and 10.

	University S	College T	University N	University A
1. Instruction	9	7	6	7
2. Cost	2	3	9	7
3. Proximity	4	7	8	3
4. Social life	8	7	3	5
5. Prestige	9	10	3	4
Totals	32	34	29	26

If all of these factors are equally important in making your decision and if the values are accurately assigned, then the favored choice is a small, private college. A decision based on some organization of factors may be a practical way to solve a problem, but, as can easily be deduced from the example of choosing a college, definitive judgments of real problems are not so simple.

In many situations the nature of the problem is not compatible with mathematical analysis. Tversky (1972) suggests that in making decisions we select alternatives by gradually eliminating less attractive choices. He called this notion elimination by aspects, since the individual is thought to eliminate less attractive alternatives based on a sequential evaluation of the attributes, or aspects, of the alternatives. If some alternatives do not meet the minimum criterion, then those alternatives are eliminated from the choice set.

Recently our selection committee considered candidates for a senior position in the Department of Psychology. In a series of intense meetings, we finally arrived at a set of standards the successful candidate should possess. We advertised the position and received a large number of applications. We were then confronted with the difficult task of selecting only one person from the set of candidates. The decision process went through several stages that generally fit the Tversky model. First, those candidates who did not have the minimum qualifications were removed from the set (for example, those who did not have the necessary academic or professional credentials). Second, those whose salary needs were greater than our resources were removed from further consideration. The process continued until only a handful of the original set remained. These remaining candidates were invited to the campus to increase our information about them, and the process reactivated until a single choice was made. One advantage of the elimination-by-aspect model is that it does not require calculations of probability or rating of strengths.

Estimating Probabilities

Whether or not we recognize it, most decisions are related to an estimate of the probability of success. We plan a picnic when we think the sun will shine, we enroll in a course in cognitive psychology expecting certain rewards, we decide to stand with a card count of fourteen when a blackjack dealer shows a six as his or her "up card," we carry an umbrella when we see clouds in the sky, or we buy (or don't buy) an insurance policy before boarding an airplane. In some instances the probability of an event may be calculated on the basis of mathematics, while other events may be determined only by our previous experience. It is likely that we think we are acting rationally in these conditions since our decisions are based roughly on mathematical probabilities, but how accurate are our estimates? Or, in other words, how can we act so stupidly when we think we are acting so rationally? The next section might shed some light on the question.

In a series of studies, Tversky and Kahneman (1973, 1981; Kahneman & Tversky, 1983, 1984; and Kahneman & Miller, 1986) have looked at the way people sometimes arrive at a poor conclusion when their decisions are based on past experience. In one experiment (1974) they asked questions such as the following:

Are there more words in the English language that start with the letter *K* or that have a *K* as their third letter?
Which is the more likely cause of death—breast cancer or diabetes?

If a family has three boys (B) and three girls (G), which sequence of births is more likely—BBBGGG or BGGBGB?

All the questions above have factual answers, and yet people's intuition or guesstimates are generally wrong. For example, when asked about the occurrence of the letter *K,* more people said that it more frequently started a word than was located in the third position, contrary to actual data. Why do people misjudge these events? According to Tversky and Kahneman, when confronted with this question, people try to generate words that start with the letter *K* and then try to think of words with *K* in the third position. If you try this yourself, you will see why people err in this problem. The reason we tend to overestimate the frequencies of initial letters is because the words they generate are more available than are words with that same letter in the third position. It seems that estimates of letter probabilities are derived from a generalization based on a very limited sample of available words that can be generated.

Amos Tversky **(shown here) and** Daniel Kahneman **identified strategies people use in solving common problems.**

Critical Thinking: How Rational Are Your Decisions?

Give your best estimates to the following questions:

1. Billy, a tall, slender, nonathletic thirty-six-year-old has been described by a neighbor as being somewhat shy, intellectual, and withdrawn. He is helpful, tidy, and has a need for order and structure. Is it more likely that Billy is a salesperson or a librarian?
2. Suppose you are in Las Vegas on a gambling junket. (A) Last night you won $1,000 on a hot slot machine. Will you bet more tomorrow than you usually do? (B) Last night you discovered you have $1,000 more in your savings account than you thought. Will you bet more tomorrow than you usually do?
3. (A) You go into a store to buy a portable cassette/radio. It costs $50. You notice an ad for the same item at a store ten blocks away that costs only $25—such a deal! (B) You go into a store to buy a computer that costs $2,545. The same computer can be bought at a store ten blocks away for $2,520. Do you bother to go to the other store?

The solution is at the end of this chapter.

This basic idea was tested in an experiment by Tversky and Kahneman (1973) in which subjects were asked to read a list of thirty-nine names of well-known people. One list contained about the same number of men as women (nineteen men and twenty women), but the women were more famous than the men. Another list reversed these conditions; it contained more famous men than women. Then the subjects were asked whether the list contained more men or women. In both instances the subjects greatly overestimated the frequency of the gender that was more famous. The reason for this behavior, despite the fact that the frequencies were nearly identical, was that the famous person's name was more available.

Other researchers have used the availability hypothesis to account for errors in the estimate of "everyday" knowledge. In one study Slovic, Fischhoff, and Lichtenstein (1977) asked people to estimate the relative probability of forty-one causes of death. Subjects were given two causes of death and asked to judge which was more likely to cause death. The most seriously misjudged choices were causes of death that were well publicized. For example, accidents, cancer, botulism, and tornadoes were judged to be frequent causes of death. The authors reasoned that because these lethal events receive wide media coverage, they were more available than less publicized causes of death.

Decision Frames

A decision frame is, according to Tversky and Kahneman (1981), a decision maker's "conception of the acts, outcomes, and contingencies associated with a particular choice." A frame adopted by someone about to make a decision is controlled by the formulation of the problem as well as by the norms, habits, and personal characteristics of the individual. The authors of this concept have clearly demonstrated how powerful a frame can be in determining the conclusion reached by individuals who are given essentially the same facts, but in different contexts. The effect of different frames is shown in the following example:

Problem 1 (N = 152): Imagine that the United States is preparing for the outbreak of an unusual Asian disease, which is expected to kill 600 people. Two alternative programs to combat the disease have been proposed. Assume that the exact scientific estimates of the consequences of the programs are as follows:

If Program A is adopted, 200 people will be saved (72 percent).

If Program B is adopted, there is a one-third probability that 600 people will be saved and a two-thirds probability that no people will be saved (28 percent).

Which of the two programs would you favor?

Given the choice in this problem, the majority selected Program A (72 percent), while only 28 percent chose Program B. The prospect of saving 200 lives is more attractive than the more risky alternative. Statistically, however, the alternatives will save the same number of lives.

Another group of subjects was given this reformulated version of the same problem:

Problem 2 (N = 155): Remember, if Program A is adopted, 200 people will be saved (72 percent). If Program C is adopted, there is a one-third probability that nobody will die, and a two-thirds probability that 600 people will die (78 percent).

Which of the two programs would you favor?

In this frame the majority chose the risk-taking procedure: the certain death of 400 people is less acceptable than the two-in-three chance that 600 will die. These problems illustrate how the influence of the framing of a question, even though the probabilities are identical, leads to different choices. In general, choices involving gains are frequently seen as risk aversive, whereas choices involving losses are perceived as risk taking.

Yet another example of framing, which is perhaps a more realistic problem than the one just discussed, is the following:

Problem A (N = 183): Imagine that you have decided to see a play for which admission is $10 per ticket. As you enter the theater, you discover that you have lost a $10 bill.

Would you still pay $10 for a ticket for the play?

Those who answered affirmatively amounted to 88 percent.

Problem B (N = 200): Imagine that you have decided to see a play and paid the admission price of $10 per ticket. As you enter the theater, you discover that you have lost the ticket. The seat was not marked, and the ticket cannot be recovered.

Would you pay $10 for another ticket?

Those who answered yes to this reformulated version amounted to 46 percent. In both instances you are out $10. However, in the first instance, about twice as many people confronted with this problem would buy a ticket as those confronted with a similar condition in which the amount of money lost is identical.[2]

---

[2]Framing a question can also be used to yield a desirable answer, which reminds me of the following story: Young Brother Gregory had been in the abbey only a few days when he innocently asked the head monk whether it was all right to smoke while saying his prayers. "Of course not," was the answer. A week later the young brother asked the monk, "May I pray while I smoke?"

Representativeness

Estimates of the probability of an event are influenced not only by the availability of the event but also by how representative an event is estimated to be in terms of how similar it is to the essential properties of its population. Consider this example from a study by Kahneman and Tversky (1972):

> On each round of a game, 20 marbles are distributed at random among 5 children: Alan, Ben, Carl, Dan, and Ed. Consider the following distributions:

I		**II**	
Alan	4	Alan	4
Ben	4	Ben	4
Carl	5	Carl	4
Dan	4	Dan	4
Ed	3	Ed	4

> In many rounds of the game, will there be more results of Type I or Type II?

What is your answer? If you selected Type I, your answer is consistent with the majority of subjects in this experiment and is, of course, wrong. When subjects read the word *random*, they apparently formed the impression that the distribution would be somewhat chaotic or helter-skelter, and when asked to evaluate Types I and II, they thought that the second distribution was too orderly to be random. The same type of error was observed in the sequence of boy and girl birth patterns mentioned earlier.

Another, somewhat disturbing finding was that people tend to ignore sample size when estimating probabilities. For example, when asked whether finding 600 boys in a sample of 1,000 children was as likely as finding 60 boys in a sample of 100 children, subjects reported that both samples were equally likely. In fact (if one assumes an equal distribution of the sexes), the first statistic is far less likely than the second.

Bayes's Theorem and Decision Making

We have seen that people may revise their probability estimates when new or different information is presented. When confronted with an equally attractive choice of going to a concert or a movie, we may make a decision tipped in favor of the movie if we learn that the only concert tickets available cost $35. A mathematical model that provides a method for evaluating hypotheses of changing probabilistic values is called Bayes's theorem after its author, Thomas Bayes, an eighteenth-century mathematician. Use of this theorem is illustrated in the following decision-making scenario.

Suppose that a long, romantic, and emotional relationship between you and a lover ended in a terrible fight in which you vowed never to see the person again. Several months pass during which you avoid situations in which you might accidentally see your former lover. A mutual friend asks you to a large party. Your decision to go or not to go is based on the perceived probability that the former lover will be in attendance. After considering the situation, you conclude that the mutual friend would probably not be so insensitive as to invite both of you. Furthermore, given past experience with similar situations, you might estimate that the probability of a chance encounter would be about 1 in 20. The hypothesis then could be stated mathematically as follows:

$$P(H) = 1/20$$

The equation is read as "the probability of the hypothesis is equal to 5 percent (or 5 in 100)." The hypothesis is based on prior probabilities, that is, the possibility the event will occur given prior similar circumstances. An alternative hypothesis can also be stated, which is the probability that your lover will not be at the party. It may be stated as follows:

$$P(\overline{H})- = 19/20$$

This equation is read as "the probability of the hypothesis not occurring is 95 percent."

If real situations could be reduced to such probabilistic statements, life would be simple and boring. You could weigh the possibilities of an undesirable confrontation against the pleasure of going to a party and then make your decision. In this case, let's say you decide to go to the party. As you approach the house you notice a yellow Volkswagen parked in the driveway. In a few seconds you calculate the probability that the owner of the car is your former lover (which would further suggest that the person is at the party) and weigh that new information with the previous information about the probability that the host has invited the two of you to the same party. This situation is called a conditional probability—the probability that new information is true if a particular hypothesis is true. In this case, presume that the likelihood that the car belongs to your former lover is 90 percent (the other 10 percent could be attributed to several factors, including the possibility that the car was sold to someone else, the car was loaned to someone else, or this was only a similar car). According to Bayes's theorem, the combined probabilities (1/20 the person was invited plus 9/10 that the car indicated the person was present) can be expressed in the following formula (derived from J. Anderson, 1989):

$$P(\overline{H}|E) = \frac{P(E|H) \times P(H)}{P(E|H) \times P(H) + P(E|\overline{H}) \times P(\overline{H})}$$

where $P(H|E)$ is the probability of the hypothesis (H) given the evidence in E, or, in our case, the probability the former lover would be at the party given the initial low probability and the recent new evidence. $P(E|H)$ represents the probability that E is true given H (for example, the probability that the car belongs to the former lover = 90 percent). $P(H)$ is the probability of the initial hypothesis ($P = 5$ percent), and the terms $P(E|H)$ and $P(H)$ represent the probability the event will not occur (10 percent and 95 percent, respectively). By substituting these values into the formula, we can solve for $P(H|E)$.

$$P(H|E) = \frac{0.9 \times 0.05}{(0.9 \times 0.05) + (0.1 \times 0.95)} = 0.32$$

Thus, according to this model the chances of an unhappy encounter at the party is about 1 in 3. Given these odds, you now can make a studied decision on the basis of how aversive such a meeting might be versus how pleasurable the party might be. Perhaps you should drive to the nearest pay phone and call your host.

How closely does Bayes's theorem coincide with real life? It is highly unlikely that if you found yourself in the above circumstance, you would whip out your pocket calculator and determine the value of $P(H|E)$. Some evidence has been gathered by Edwards (1968), which suggests that we tend to judge conditional probability circum-

The Fido Caper

Suppose that you left your dog Fido at home to guard your house so that burglars would not break in and steal the 10-pound roast that is defrosting on the counter. When you get back the locks are all in good order, so you know that no burglar has entered. However, the roast is gone. Needless to say, Fido is a prime suspect.

On the basis of past experience, two sessions with the dog psychiatrist, and a certain shifty look in his eye, you judge the probability is 0.95 that Fido did it. However, before convicting Fido, you decide to collect one further piece of evidence. You prepare his ordinary dinner and offer it to him. To your surprise, he gobbles it up to the last crumb. Hardly what you would expect of the thief who just made a 10-pound roast disappear. You estimate that the probability that Fido would do this if he had in fact eaten the roast is only 0.02. Normally, though, he has a good appetite and eats his dinner with a probability of 0.99. How are you to revise your earlier suspicions given the evidence of the readily eaten dinner? Clearly,

Bayes's theorem can come to the rescue. Given that he just ate his dinner the probability that Fido is guilty may be expressed as follows:

$$P(\text{Guilty} \mid E) = \frac{P(E \mid \text{Guilty}) \times P(\text{Guilty})}{P(E \mid \text{Guilty}) \times P(\text{Guilty}) + P(E \mid \text{Innocent}) \times P(\text{Innocent})}$$

From the story, we know that

$$
\begin{aligned}
P(\text{Guilty}) &= 0.95 \\
P(\text{Innocent}) &= 0.05 \\
P(E \mid \text{Guilty}) &= 0.02 \\
P(E \mid \text{Innocent}) &= 0.99
\end{aligned}
$$

Therefore,

$$
\begin{aligned}
P(\text{Guilty} \mid E) &= \frac{(0.02)(0.95)}{(0.02)(0.95) + (0.99)(0.05)} \\[2ex]
&= \frac{0.0190}{0.0190 + 0.0495} \\[2ex]
&= \frac{0.0190}{0.0685} \\[2ex]
&= 0.28
\end{aligned}
$$

Things looked very bad for Fido before the dinner experiment. However, with the aid of Bayes's theorem, we were able to take the results of the dinner experiment into account and conclude that Fido was probably innocent. Anyone who loves dogs can see the value of Bayes's theorem.

Based on Hayes (1989).

stances more conservatively than Bayes's theorem suggests. In one study of the influence of new information on subjects' estimates of probabilities, Edwards gave college students two bags that contained 100 poker chips. One bag had 70 red chips and 30 blue chips, and the other bag had 30 red chips and 70 blue chips. One bag was selected at random, and the subjects were to determine which bag it was on the basis of drawing out one chip at a time, examining it, returning it to the bag, and then continuing the process. Initially, the probability of drawing a red chip from the mostly red-chip bag would be 70 percent, or from the mostly blue-chip bag, 30 percent. However, if we draw only one chip from one of the bags and it is red, then the probability, according to the theorem, that the composition of the bag is predominantly red is 70 percent. People tend to underestimate the real (mathematical) significance of that observation and guess the content of the bag to be predominantly red with a value of 60 percent. If the second chip is also red, the real probability of the bag being predominantly red is 84 percent. Subjects' judgments tend to be conservative in this case as well as with larger samples.

The application of Bayes's theorem to real-world tasks poses special problems because an accurate estimate of the probabilities of events is difficult to ascertain. Consider an event of international world politics. A few years ago considerable tension between the Soviet Union and the United States existed, which, some would suggest, led to an increased probability of overt aggression, perhaps even all-out war. If all the forces could be accurately assessed and the probability of war determined, then the influence of other events that bear on the likelihood of war (such as a recent meeting between President Clinton and President Yeltsin) could be integrated into Bayes's formula, and for what it is worth, a probabilistic statistic could be derived. Some ambitious scholars representing the fields of psychology, sociology, and political science have undertaken just such global schemes.

DECISION MAKING AND RATIONALITY

To some, this chapter may seem to have initially represented the human animal as the most rational of creatures. Our discussion of concept formation, after all, showed that all normal beings form concepts using rational rules. In the discussion of syllogistic reasoning, we learned that the validity of an argument could be determined by the rules of logic, even if we tend to be fooled by either the structure or the content of a faulty argument. Finally, in the preceding section on decision making, we learned that the "rational" human race is commonly nonrational when it comes to making a decision about a large class of events.

I think it would be foolish to argue that all people are as rational as you or I (or as rational as we fashion ourselves), but are we, as a species, as nonrational as one might conclude, given the empirical results gathered on decision-making tasks?

The findings of Tversky and Kahneman as well as studies of syllogistic reasoning, when carefully examined, suggest that human beings are less than perfectly rational creatures. Some have objected to these findings on the basis of experimental design and the inevitable philosophic conclusion forced by these experiments. One such critic is L. J. Cohen (1981), of Oxford University, who argues that (1) rationality should be determined by the common people, not in contrived laboratory experiments that are not really designed to illustrate everyday decision making and are largely irrelevant to real performance, (2) it is unreasonable to expect ordinary people to be sophisticated in the laws of probability and statistics that establish the baselines and points of deviation in many of the experiments, and (3) the laws of logic and rationality are not relevant to ordinary human behavior. Take the case of the unfortunate individual who tried to avoid a former lover. Using Bayes's theorem, the probability of the encounter, if the person went to the party, was 0.32. How does that number bear on the behavior of the individual? If the enmity between the pair is great ("I wouldn't go within 100 miles of him/her"), the figure is meaningless insofar as predicting behavior is concerned.

ETHNOGRAPHIC THINKING

Around the turn of the twentieth century, armed with the latest techniques for behavioral assessment, psychologists and anthropologists from Cambridge University invaded some of the minor islands in the Torres Strait between Australia and New Guinea. From this modest expedition one can trace one branch of the evolution of comparative ethnography, or the scientific description of the differences between cultures. The whole range of psychological traits—from language to customs, to religious practices, to thinking and reasoning—was about to be put under the psychological microscope.

The zeitgeist was deeply influenced by the consummate teachings of Charles Darwin, and it was natural for investigators to search for atavistic thinking, as "primitive" man was thought to exhibit, as a means of tracing the intellectual development of "modern man" without circumventing the laws that govern the direction in which time moves. The curious findings of these early psychologists and anthropologists have provided us with a studious heritage of cross-cultural data that have not only earned Ph.D.s for scores of fledgling scientists but also have filled volume after volume with their prosaic dissertations. The idea that people who lived without telephones, the Church of England, literature, or the New York Stock Exchange were less developed culturally and intellectually is a narrow hypothesis that badly prejudges the social-cognitive hive-life of savage man. On the other hand, the same findings may be interpreted in a wider sense as meaning that both the civilized and the uncivilized populations are incapable of perceiving the world outside their own culturally restricted perspective.

In recent times, cross-cultural data about thinking, problem solving, and decision making have become an integral part of international relations, especially as related to world geopolitical issues involving arms negotiation and anticipating adversarial reactions to political maneuvers.

Before we consider some cross-cultural studies of thinking, a preliminary word about the reliability of these endeavors should be mentioned. All people are deeply influenced by their culture. When scientists, no matter how well trained in scientific methodology, examine cross-cultural thinking, they inevitably bring some of their previous cultural bias to the situation. That bias may manifest itself in a variety of ways, from the elevation of the noble savage to the highest possible intellectual status to the pious judgment that "they will never be as good as we." The observer becomes part of the thing under observation—a type of psychological uncertainty principle—similar to the phenomenon described by the physicist Werner Heisenberg, who stated that the accurate measurement of one of two related observable quantities (such as position and momentum or energy and time) produces uncertainties in the measurement of the other.

Syllogistic Reasoning

Several years ago an American scientist trained in mathematical psychology became involved in cross-cultural research on thinking. Michael Cole (1975; Cole, Gay, Glick, & Sharp, 1971; and Cole & Scribner, 1974) arrived in Liberia on a mission designed to improve the mathematics education of tribal children. At one point he asked a Kpelle tribal leader to solve a simple syllogism. The protocol from that interview (Cole & Scribner, 1974) follows:

> *Experimenter:* At one time spider went to a feast. He was told to answer this question before he could eat any of the food. The question is: Spider and black deer always eat together. Spider is eating. Is black deer eating?
>
> *Subject:* Were they in the bush?
>
> *E:* Yes.
>
> *S:* Were they eating together?
>
> *E:* Spider and black deer always eat together. Spider is eating. Is black deer eating?
>
> *S:* But I was not there. How can I answer such a question?
>
> *E:* Can't you answer it? Even if you were not there, you can answer it. (Repeats the question.)
>
> *S:* Oh, oh, black deer is eating.
>
> *E:* What is your reason for saying that black deer was eating?
>
> *S:* The reason is that black deer always walks about all day eating leaves in the bush. Then he rests for a while and gets up again to eat.

The results of Cole's investigation are typical of the reasoning patterns of groups unaccustomed to abstract syllogistic processes. In a related study, I (Solso, 1987a) asked students at Moscow State University to solve the following syllogism, which is nearly identical in form and content to Cole's problem.

Ivan and Boris always eat together.

Boris is eating.

What is Ivan doing?

This extraordinarily simple syllogism was presented to numerous students both in their native language and sometimes in English with surprising results. Only 20 percent (N = 5/25) of the subjects gave the correct answer immediately. The most frequent response (N = 11/25) was essentially the same as that of the Kpella chief's: "I don't know, I didn't see him."

Various theories may account for these results, including the notion that Soviet students did not want to give a "stupid" answer to a "stupid" problem; however, an appealing hypothesis is that all people have means of validating propositions about the nature of their world. In highly industrial Western societies, people are trained to prove arguments about reality on the basis of representational propositions. In less industrial societies, where many people may be closer to land, the form of proof is tied more directly to sensory impression. This type of earthy reasoning is capable of rendering sound conclusions even if the answers to abstract reasoning problems are not the ones Western-oriented psychologists have in mind. Furthermore, it seems that the efficacy of understanding the world by direct observation rather than through abstract inferential processes has been successful enough to assure survivability among large masses of people. Even students who are trained to solve abstract reasoning problems tend to revert to direct observation after they leave school, as some of the following research shows.

The technique of using verbal syllogistic problems as a means of evaluating the influence of cultural patterns on reasoning was first used by the eminent Russian psychologist Luria (1971) when he and his colleagues conducted research on mental development in 1931–1932 in Uzbekistan, which is located in central Asia. The purpose of Luria's research into the reasoning process was both to evaluate Vygotsky's theory of mental development, which suggested that mental development is a function of one's social life and practical activity, and to determine the effect of cultural and educational reforms introduced into Uzbeki society after the Russian Revolution. In one syllogism, as simple as the Boris and Ivan example, Luria asked village Uzbeki children (who live near the fortieth meridian) the following puzzle:

In the far north, where there is snow, all bears are white.
Novaya Zemlya is in the far north.
What color are the bears there?

Very few of Luria's subjects were able to give the accepted answer to the above syllogism, probably because they were unfamiliar with abstract reasoning rules and the color of bears in Novaya Zemlya. (Novaya Zemlya is situated well above the Arctic Circle, about two thousand miles directly north of Uzbek.) They, as the Moscow students who said they didn't see Ivan, had not seen a bear in Novaya Zemlya and could not tell you its color. One student, when I asked about the color of the bear, asked me, "Was it daytime or nighttime?" Thinking that the color of the bear would be perceived differently, I asked why that would make a difference. The student replied that at night she couldn't see the bear. No doubt both groups would be able to tell you whether Ivan was eating or the color of the bear if they had sensed it directly with their own eyes.[3]

Uzbek and Muscovite students as well as Kpelle chiefs and others can presumably be taught the rules of the syllogistic game, and some effort has been directed toward that end. The results of these efforts have produced subjects who can usually draw correct inferences from premises, even those questions involving polar bears among schoolchildren who have never seen a white bear. In these instances, however, subjects frequently give theoretical explanations when confronted with information they have not experienced directly and conclusions based on common knowledge or common beliefs. Furthermore, after the schooling ends and the student returns to village life, the ability to solve abstract problems fades and the means of validating an argument by direct observation is reinstated (see Cole & Scribner, 1974).

The development of reasoning ability and formal training in logic has been examined by Galotti, Baron, and Sabini (1986), whose data confirm our expectation that training leads to an additional number of correct decisions. An interesting additional finding was that good reasoners chose to take longer amounts of time (when time constraints were not a factor) than poor reasoners, which suggests that good reasoners consider more alternatives than do poor reasoners.

---

[3]Russian people, in general, also "validate" hypotheses about reality by means of consensus. If unsure of how things really are in the world, they tend to ask friends. If several people give the same impression, the validity is established. I have noted this tendency among scientists as well as among people unsophisticated in the scientific method.

Summary

1   Thinking is an internal process in which information is transformed; thinking may be directed and lead to problem solving and, at the structural level, results in the formation of a new mental representation.

2   Concept formation involves discerning features common to a class of objects and discovering rules that relate those conceptual features. Cognitive activities believed important to the process include rule learning, association, and hypothesis testing.

3   Concept formation varies in difficulty as a function of the type of rule required, with affirmative rules producing the least difficulty and increasing levels of difficulty associated with conjunctive, disjunctive, conditional, and biconditional rules.

4   Strategies for formulating and testing hypotheses during concept formation include scanning and focusing procedures, with focusing techniques (similar to scientific procedures) being more effective than scanning strategies.

5   Studies of deductive reasoning indicate that conclusions to syllogistic problems are affected by the form of presentation (visual versus verbal), the number of alternatives generated by premises, the argument form (for example, positive versus negative), long-term knowledge relative to the problem presented, and the problem solver's level of intelligence and education.

6   Inductive reasoning results in conclusions often expressed in probability statements and corresponds more to everyday decision making than does syllogistic or deductive reasoning.

7   Studies of decision making show that problem solutions are influenced by memory factors (the availability hypothesis), reference frames that affect problem formulation, failure to consider how similar an event is to its population, and underestimating the mathematical significance of a possible event.

8   Cross-cultural differences have been observed in syllogistic reasoning, with people from highly industrialized countries proving arguments in terms of representational propositions, and people from less industrialized countries basing proofs more on sensory impressions.

Key Words

associationism	focus gambling
atmosphere effect	inductive reasoning
Bayes's theorem	logic
concept formation	prior probability
conceptual rule	simultaneous scanning
conditional probability	successive scanning
conservative focusing	syllogism
decision frame	thinking
deductive reasoning	

Recommended Readings

The number of books and articles dealing with thinking, problem solving, and decision making has increased sharply during the last decade. For more specialized reading, try Maxwell, *Thinking: The Expanding Frontier;* Gardner, *The Mind's New Science;* and Rubenstein, *Tools for Thinking and Problem Solving.* For decision making in the world context, read Janis and Mann, *Decision Making;* Valenta and Potter, eds., *Soviet Decision Making for National Security;* and Brams has an article called "Theory of Moves" in *American Scientist* that discusses game theory in international conflict situations.

Within the past few years several fine books in this field have been published. These books are well written, interesting, and contain a wealth of information about thinking and related topics. These include *Mental Models: Towards a Cognitive Science of Language, Inference, and Consciousness,* by one of the main researchers in the field, Johnson-Laird; and *Deduction* also by Johnson-Laird and Byrne. You might also try a stimulating book by John Hayes, *The Complete Problem Solver* (2nd ed.); and one of my favorite and highly recommended books, Marvin Levine's *Effective Problem Solving* (2nd ed.).

Answer to Critical Thinking: Thinking, Problem Solving, and "Frames"

Most people answer the first problem by inferring "A only" or "A and 4." The correct answer is "A and 7." If A does not have an even number on the other side, the rule is false, and if 7 has a vowel on the other side, the rule is false. In the second problem the answer is the first (sealed) envelope and the last, the envelope with the 25¢ stamp on it. More than 90 percent of subjects solve the realistic (envelope stamp) problem, and yet only about 30 percent solve the abstract (card-letter) problem.

Answers to Critical Thinking: How Rational Are Your Decisions?

Problem 1: If you are like most people, you guessed that Billy is a librarian—in fact, about 2 out of 3 people make that judgment in a similar problem. However, if we look at the statistics regarding the likelihood of professions, there are more than 14 million salespeople in America and fewer than 200,000 librarians. On the basis of statistics alone, Billy is 75 times more likely to be a salesperson. Even if one factors into the conclusion the descriptive material, the probability of Billy's being in sales is higher than his being in books.

Problem 2: Most people say they would tend to blow the easy money won on the slot machine than the newly discovered hard money in the bank account, yet, in both instances you are ahead by the same amount.

Problem 3: In the first instance, about 3 out of 4 people opt to go down the street to buy the cassette/radio for half price, yet only 1 in 5 would do the same for the computer. However, in both instances, the saving is $25. Is such action justified in the first case but not the second?

CHAPTER FIFTEEN

THINKING 2: Problem Solving, Creativity, and Human Intelligence

I N CHAPTER 14, CONCEPT formation, logic, and decision making were characterized as higher forms, not because they are more important (such a designation is meaningless in the present context) but because they occur toward the end of the information-processing chain of events. In this chapter we present theories and data on three other topics that are considered to be forms of higher cognitive processes; they are problem solving, creativity, and human intelligence. On the one hand, these topics have been investigated by researchers interested in how each fits into the grand scheme of human cognition. These topics also have caused the philosopher and poet to wax eloquent. On the other hand, interest in problem solving, creativity, and intelligence can be found among the nitty-gritty, pragmatic types who enjoy mundane topics such as: How do I get from my house to work in the shortest time with the least aggravation? Can I invent a device that will keep my buns warm from the time they are baked until they are served? Why does my daughter write better computer programs than English essays?

PROBLEM SOLVING

Problem solving permeates every corner of human activity and is a common denominator of widely disparate fields—the sciences; law; education; business; sports; medicine; industry; literature; and, as if there weren't enough problem-solving activity in our professional and vocational lives, many forms of recreation. Humans, apes, and many other mammals are curious types who, for reasons seemingly related to survival, seek stimulation and resolve conflict through a lifetime of creative, intelligent problem solving.

A good share of early problem-solving experiments addressed the question: What does a person do when he or she solves a problem? Although this descriptive approach helped define the phenomena, it did little to enhance our understanding of the cognitive structures and processes involved in problem solving.

Problem solving is "thinking that is directed toward the solving of a specific problem that involves both the formation of responses and the selection among possible responses." We encounter an untold number of problems in our daily lives that cause us to form response strategies, to select potential responses, and to test responses in solving a problem. For example, try to solve this problem: A dog has a 6-foot rope tied to its neck, and a pan of water is 10 feet away. How would the dog reach the pan? The solution to this problem involves the generation of possible responses (of which there are few), the selection and trial of them, and perhaps the discovery of the trick in the problem.[1]

The early experimental technique of introspection was established by European psychologists before the turn of the century and spread through America about that time. It seemed well suited to an investigation of problem solving. It was held that thinking aloud, or *reflection parlée,* elucidated the mechanics of the thinking process. In early studies the subjects were told what was expected of them and what the problem was. During the problem-solving section of the task, subjects were to identify the objects they were attending to; the situation as they saw it; what they were trying to accomplish; and, in some instances, the very tentative attempts to solve the problem.

Gestalt Psychology and Problem Solving

Among the early experimentalists concerned with problem solving were the Gestalt psychologists in Germany. *Gestalt* is roughly translatable as "configuration" or "organized whole." The perspective of Gestalt psychologists is consistent with the word, in that they view behavior in terms of an organized system. Perceptual events are not perceived as a series of individual elements, but as a whole configuration made up of these events. According to the gestaltists, problems, especially perceptual problems, exist when tension or stress occurs as a result of some interaction between perception and memory. By thinking about a problem, or by examining it from different angles, the "correct" view can emerge in a moment of insight. The early Gestalt psychologists (Max Wertheimer, Kurt Koffka, Wolfgang Kohler) demonstrated the perceptional reorganization viewpoint in problem-solving activity (sometimes using apes as experimental subjects). Out of their work emerged the concept of *functional fixedness,* originated by Karl Duncker (1945). This concept, which was to have considerable impact on problem-solving research, held that there is a tendency to perceive things in terms of their familiar uses and that that tendency often makes it difficult to use them in an unfamiliar way (for example, using a brick as a measuring device). In effect, objects or ideas become set in their functions and, when they are part of a problem-solving task that requires that they serve a different function, the subject must overcome that "set."

Although we usually associate the term *set* with the state of mind (habit or attitude) a person brings to a problem-solving task, the more generous (and the original) definition of the term includes the idea of any preparatory cognitive activity that precedes thinking and perception. In the context of the latter definition, *set* may enhance the quality of perception or thought through participation in the meaning of a stimulus (as in the case of an ambiguous word, the next move in a chess game, or the next response in a social situation). Alternatively, it may inhibit perception or thought (as in a problem in which a subject repeatedly tries a certain nonproductive solution that is related to an earlier experience). For example, Duncker (1945) gave subjects three cardboard boxes, matches, thumbtacks, and candles and asked them to devise a plan whereby the candle

---

[1]The dog would walk to it. The rope was tied only to its neck.

could be mounted on a screen to serve as a lamp. One group of subjects were given the screen; the candles, the tacks, and the matches were each presented in their own box. Another group of subjects were given these objects *along* with the three boxes—that is, the objects were not *in* the boxes. The solution to this puzzle was to use the matches to light the candles, drip some wax on a box, stick the candle on it, and thumbtack the box to the screen. When the boxes were modeled ahead of time as containers, subjects had much more difficulty in solving this problem than when the boxes were not. Later experimenters (Glucksberg & Danks, 1969) demonstrated that simply labeling an object with a name fixed in the subject's mind a certain set that could either facilitate or impede the solving of a problem.

The types of problems used in the early experiments were of a wide variety, from mechanical to logic problems. The protocols (records of the thought processes as "thought aloud" by the subjects) revealed that the problem-solving process had several well-ordered stages. Subjects normally seem to begin with what is expected of them. Then hypotheses about possible solutions arise, are tested, and confirmed; if they are not confirmed, new hypotheses emerge. The process, then, seems to be one of trial and error, with a new hypothesis replacing an unsuccessful one. These early experiments said little about how hypotheses originated and made no credible postulates as to the cognitive structures involved in the process.

As in the box-and-candle problem just presented, the way a problem is represented can easily sway the outcome. Moshe Rubinstein (1986), in a lively book about thinking and problem solving, tells a story about his daughter, who had failed to respond to numerous letters sent to her when she was a student studying abroad. Rubinstein then sent a letter stating that he was enclosing a check for $500, which he did not actually send. His daughter telephoned four days later. By changing the representation, which may change the person's perception of the problem, the outcome can be altered radically.

Problem-solving activity never enjoyed the popularity of other tasks and was usually rejected as a serious subject by experimental psychologists. The task tends to be ambiguous and poses nightmarish problems of experimental control. The addition, manipulation, or subtraction of an independent variable may affect the thought process, or the context of performance, or both, or neither. Furthermore, because a well-defined taxonomy of problems was hard to imagine, there was a dearth of testable hypotheses and theories.

Representation of the Problem

The work of the Gestalt psychologists focused on the nature of a task and its influence on a person's ability to solve it. Recent scholars have attacked the question of problem solving from several different perspectives, including what modern cognitive psychologists call the process of representation, or how a problem is depicted in the mind. Throughout this book, the topic of internal representation has been a central theme. Material that has already been presented is not repeated here, except to note that the way information is represented in a problem-solving task is important in finding its solution (see the box-and-candle problem and the nonwriting daughter cited earlier).

The way information is represented in solving a problem seems to follow a well-ordered pattern. For example, let's look at the problem of entering the real world after graduation from college. The stereotypical sequence of problem solving, as suggested by Hayes (1989), takes the following form:

Cognitive Action	Nature of the Problem
1. Identifying the problem	Next May I will be graduated from college. It is the end of one phase of my life. (Time to grow up.)
2. Representation of the problem	I will be unemployed and without funds. I must get work. (Can no longer sponge off Mom and Pop.)
3. Planning the solution	I will write a résumé, investigate the job market, and consult with friends and teachers. (See what's out there. I could go to Tibet and become a monk.)
4. Execute the plan	I will make appointments with interesting companies. I will interview with them. (Take the plunge.)
5. Evaluate the plan	I will consider each offer in light of my own needs and desires and make a decision. (Who's offering big bucks, long vacations, and early retirement.)
6. Evaluate the solution	I will reflect on the process of solving this problem and use such knowledge in future problem solving. (Where did I go wrong?)

Perhaps, if you think of the way you have solved problems in your own life, you will find that you have used a sequence similar to the one shown here. The process is almost always unconscious. That is, you do not deliberately say to yourself, "Now, I am in phase three, 'planning the solution,' which means that I . . . "; nevertheless, it is likely that these stages are lurking in the background as you solve daily problems. Consider any problem—either real or imaginary (such as fixing a broken toaster, solving a difficult interpersonal problem, or whether or not you should have children)—and work through it following the steps of the sequence.

Although all stages are important, the representation of a problem appears to be very important, especially the way information is represented in terms of visual imagery. Suppose you are asked to multiply 43 by 3. No big deal, you might say, as you produce the answer easily with few mental operations. However, if I ask you to multiply 563 by 26 mentally, how do you perform the task? If you are like many others, you "see"

The biggest problem in the world
Could have been solved when it was small.

Lao Tsu

the problem; that is, you represent it visually and begin the process by multiplying 3 × 6, "see" the 8, carry the 1, then multiply 6 × 6, add the 1, and so on. All of these operations are done with the information being represented in imagery. It seems that writers have capitalized on this propensity to represent things visually by using prose rich in imagery. Sometimes these are called word pictures, as illustrated in the following passage from Salisbury (1955):

> A tall, lanky serious-faced man strolled toward the datcha with a loose-jointed boyish pace and came up to where I was wielding a paintbrush. We were glassing in the front porch and I was busy in my paint-smeared clothes putting the white trim on the windows.

You can "see" the "loose-jointed boyish" character (who turned out to be George Kennan), and the paint-smeared clothes, and so on. Now consider how the problem of representation influences the problem below.[2]

> Of course, I could go out and buy one, but that would take time and money. I could make one from an old newspaper, or wrapping paper, but the paper must be sturdy. Then there is the matter of use. Streets aren't so good, the beach is perfect, and an open field is also OK. Finally, the weather needs to be good; kind of windy, and definitely no rainstorms (unless you are foolish or interested in physics).

As you read this paragraph, you can undoubtedly understand every word and sentence, and yet you have a gnawing feeling that you really do not understand what is going on. (Try reading this to a friend and then ask what he or she thinks the paragraph is about.) However, if I tell you that theme of the paragraph is how to make and fly a kite, everything falls into place and you comprehend the entire passage and problem. Representation of information is very important in problem solving.

These examples have dealt with literary expressions of problems, but many of our problems are more physical. For example, we are puzzled by the arrangement of furniture in a room, the shortest route to and from work, which grocery items we should select for greatest efficiency in shopping, and so on. One way some of these problems can be solved is to "go to the extremes," as suggested by Marvin Levine (1988), a leading expert on problem solving. Try to solve one of his problems:

> Two flagpoles are standing, each 100 feet tall. A 150-foot rope is strung from the top of one of the flagpoles to the top of the other and hangs freely between them. The lowest point of the rope is 25 feet above the ground. How far apart are the two flagpoles?

Can you solve the problem? How did you do it? Some of you might have begun with elaborate calculus in which the sag line of a rope is calculated. One other way is to draw a picture of the problem (see Figure 15.1). The solution to the problem is simple and does not require advanced knowledge of geometry—only common sense. Remember, *go to the extremes.* The solution is at the end of this chapter.

These examples have stressed the importance of representing the problem in a way that will enhance your ability to find a solution. In general, the solution to these prob-

---

[2]Inspired by research of Bransford and Johnson (1972).

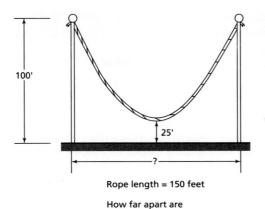

FIGURE 15.1

A visual representation of the flagpole problem. After Levine (1988).

lems seems to occur in one brilliant moment of awareness—what the Gestalt psychologists call insight—at which point the light goes on and all parts of the puzzle make sense. Frequently, however, problem solving is achieved through the stepwise discovery of small parts of a puzzle. This method, in which the solution to small components of a large problem serves as a means to the end solution, is sometimes called means-end analysis. We discuss this in greater detail later. Now, try to solve a problem which involves means-end analysis. This final example in problem solving and knowledge representation. It is shown in the box entitled "Critical Thinking: A Problem of Patients—Psychiatrists' and Yours."

At the bottom of this problem is a matrix to keep track of your inferences and deductions. It is unlikely that you will be able to solve the problem without resorting to some outside representational aid.

In this section we have seen that the way a problem is represented is most important in finding its solution. In the next section we consider how scientists interested in artificial intelligence (AI) go about understanding problem solving.

A new interest in problem solving is attributable in part to developments in the field of AI (which is problem oriented) and memory (where problem solving presumably takes place). Comprehensive models in both these fields must accommodate the varied domain of human cognitive processes, including the considerable territory occupied by problem solving.

AI and Problem Solving

One definition of *AI*, or *artificial intelligence*, is "the ability of machines to do things that require intelligence." A large portion of research in AI (see Chapter 16) is aimed at discovering human cognitive processes that can be simulated by high-speed electronic computers. Computer programs have been developed that can play games (chess, checkers, tic-tac-toe, "Go," "Gomoku," poker, and so on), analyze mathematical problems, and solve problems in symbolic logic better than most people can.

Critical Thinking: A Problem of Patients—Psychiatrists' and Yours

Three married couples, Rubin, Sanchez, and Taylor, have a rather unusual thing in common: all six (three husbands and three wives) are psychiatrists. The six psychiatrists' names are Karen, Laura, Mary, Norman, Omar, Peter. As fate would have it, each doctor has one of the other doctors as a patient (but not his or her own spouse). Several other facts are:

1. Karen is the psychiatrist for one Dr. Rubin; Laura is the psychiatrist of the other.
2. Mary is the patient for one Dr. Taylor; Peter is the patient for the other.
3. Laura is a patient of Dr. Sanchez.
4. Peter has his psychotherapy with Omar.

Given these facts, determine each psychiatrist's full name and who is treating whom. Use the following table to keep track of your deductions. This mildly difficult problem is unlikely to be solved "in your head," and it is suggested that impossible combinations be marked with a "o." From these marks it will be possible to make inferences about other possible and impossible combinations. Since women cannot be husbands and men cannot be wives, I have marked the intersections with the exclusionary mark "o." Hint: Take clue 1. Since Karen and Laura are psychiatrists for Dr. (Mr.) Rubin and Dr. (Mrs.) Rubin, they (Karen and Laura) cannot be Rubins. Who is Dr. (Mrs.) Rubin? Mark with a ✓. Carry on and good luck. As you work through this problem try to identify the inferential processes you are using.

The solution is at the end of this chapter.

| | Rubin | | Sanchez | | Taylor | |
	Dr. (Mrs.)	Dr. (Mr.)	Dr. (Mrs.)	Dr. (Mr.)	Dr. (Mrs.)	Dr. (Mr.)
Karen		O		O		O
Laura		O		O		O
Mary		O		O		O
Norman	O		O		O	
Omar	O		O		O	
Peter	O		O		O	

Among the first and best-known AI models of problem solving was one devised by Newell, Simon, and Shaw (1958) (and in a number of sources, Newell, Shaw, & Simon, 1960; Newell & Simon, 1963, 1973) called general problem solver (GPS). This ambitious model, designed to simulate the entire range of human problem solving, has a large storage capacity, search strategies, and concepts that simulate human problem-solving processes. An essential concept in GPS is that a problem is a difference between two states, say, A and B. State A is defined as what already exists, and State B as the desired goal. To solve this problem, A must undergo certain transformations to make it identical to B. The procedure used in solving a problem involves an analysis of the features of A and B, with the difference between them detected by a matching process. The features of A that do not match B undergo a series of transformations. These transformed features are then checked against B's features and so on until a match is found. A solution to a problem is then said to occur when the features of the existing state are identical to those of the terminal state. A characteristic problem, from Newell and Simon (1972), follows:

> I want to take my son to nursery school. What's the difference between what I have and what I want? One of distance. What changes distance? My automobile. My automobile won't work. What's needed to make it work? A new battery. What has new batteries? An auto repair shop. I want the repair shop to put in a new battery, but the shop doesn't know I need one. What is the difficulty? One of communication. What allows communication? A telephone. . . . And so on.

The authors analyze the process as follows:

1. If an object is given that is not the desired one, differences will be detectable between the available object and the desired object.
2. Operators affect some features of their operands and leave others unchanged. Hence operators can be characterized by the changes they produce and can be used to try to eliminate differences between the objects to which they are applied and desired objects.
3. Some differences will prove more difficult to affect than others. It is profitable, therefore, to try to eliminate "difficult" differences, even at the cost of introducing new differences of lesser difficulty. This process can be repeated as long as progress is being made toward eliminating the more difficult differences.

Using the method outlined here, Newell's research group has undertaken a solution of a wide number of different types of problems with considerable success.

The well-known cannibals-and-missionaries problem can serve as illustration. Three cannibals and three missionaries want to cross a river. They have only one boat, which will hold two people, and no other means to cross the river. If more cannibals than missionaries are left on either bank, the cannibals will eat the missionaries. The problem is to determine the most efficient way to get all six people across the river without having any missionaries eaten?[3] This problem has two well-defined components: the beginning (six people on one bank) and the end (six people on the other bank). This can be achieved through a series of operations, or procedures, of transporting people (see Figure 15.2).

GPS tackles this problem by a means-end analysis. In trying to find a means for reaching the end (or a way to move the six people to the other bank), it would determine what subgoals must be defined and solved. (If the boat were big enough to move six people, then subgoal procedure would be unnecessary. The solution would be a simple one-step operation: put everybody on board and sail.) One subgoal in the original problem is to transport two people from one side to the other, being careful not to leave

[3]Suppose that, if more missionaries than cannibals are left together, the missionaries will convert the cannibals to noncannibals. This presents two additional problems. First, how does one accomplish the crossing without the conversion taking place? Second, given the conditions stated above, how few cannibals need to be converted to accomplish the transfer regardless of the efficiency of moves?

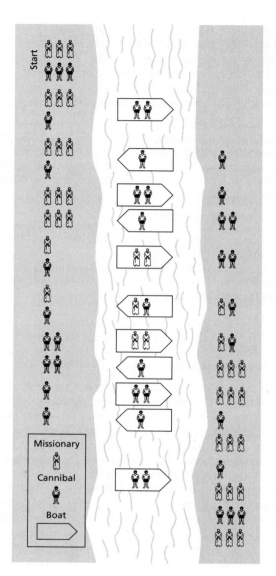

FIGURE 15.2

Solution to missionaries-and-cannibals problem.

more cannibals than missionaries on either side. If a procedure is faulty, new subgoals must be set up. Figure 15.2 shows the steps to the solution. (To make sure the GPS solution is similar to the way a human might solve the problem, Newell and Simon rely on verbalizations by the subjects as to what thoughts are going through their heads during the exercise. The procedure is demonstrated in Chapter 16.)

In a similar problem, Thomas (1974) tried to find out whether subjects use subgoals in solving more difficult problems. His problem, called the hobbits-and-orcs problem, required that three hobbits and three orcs cross a river in a boat capable of holding

FIGURE 15.5

Board problems in which positions shown in board b are the same as in board a rotated counterclockwise 90 degrees and reflected across the vertical axis, with colors of pieces reversed. Adapted from Eisenstadt and Kareev (1975).

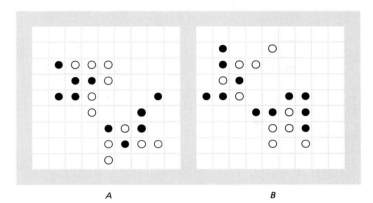

A   B

important to the player (and, hence, the one given internal representation) is that indicated by the superimposed X in Figure 15.4b; however, in "Go" the important representation would be the possible capture configuration shown in Figure 15.4c. Perceptual organizations of problems, affected by the perceiver's motivation, can and frequently do differ from the physical nature of the task. To demonstrate the disparity between internal representation and real-world events, Eisenstadt and Kareev asked subjects to analyze the board positions shown in Figure 15.5a and make the best play for black in a "Gomoku" game. Subjects were then asked to reconstruct the positions in the absence of the configuration. Later they were given the board position shown in Figure 15.5b, told to make the best move for white in a "Go" game, and again asked to reconstruct the positions. The boards in Figures 15.5a and b are the same, except that the latter is rotated 90 degrees and reflected across the vertical axis, and the color of the stones is reversed. Therefore, in terms of pieces, essentially the same amount of information was given in both tasks. The researchers identified six pieces critical in "Go" and six pieces critical in "Gomoku"; in essence, these constitute the template for each game. The reconstruction from memory of these pieces was a direct function of the instruction. In other words, if the subjects thought it was a "Go" game, they remembered the key "Go" pieces; if they were told the game was "Gomoku," they remembered the key Gomoku positions. Figure 15.6 shows the percentage of critical pieces correctly recalled as a function of the type of game subjects believed they were viewing.

Further analysis of game playing indicated that subjects played rapidly, suggesting that planning, or anticipating various configurations that might emerge, was neglected. Additionally, subjects seemed to examine the board by means of "active searches for specific patterns, as well as by searches that seem to be driven by 'accidental' discovery

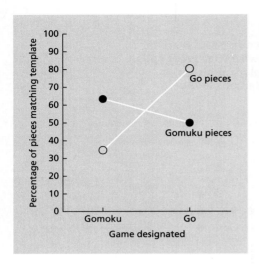

FIGURE 15.6

Percentage of critical pieces correctly recalled according to which game subjects were told they were viewing. Adapted from Eisenstadt and Kareev (1975).

of new configurations and pieces." Thus the scanning of a problem seems to suggest that internal representations are formed by an active search. This operation is commonly called top-down analysis (a computer science term) and means that the analysis starts followed by a hypothesis, with attempts made to verify it by means of seeking out stimuli (for example, "This problem has stimuli, some of which are critical"). Also a possibility are bottom-up procedures, in which the stimuli are examined and attempts are then made to match them with structural components (for example, "How does this piece figure into the problems?").

Solving a problem is somewhat dependent on the subjective representation stored in memory, and the formation of internal representation is an active process. Planning in board games, according to this viewpoint, involves both top-down and bottom-up processes, as Eisenstadt and Kareev observe:

When a subject plans ahead, the same kinds of search processes can be used. The placement of "imaginary" pieces within the internal representation of the problem space automatically invokes the planning processes in a bottom-up manner. Determining which pieces to consider in this fashion is, of course, a top-down, hypothesis-driven situation. This helps explain one of the standard observations about human problem-solving behavior: People follow a "progressive deepening" search strategy rather than a depth-first or breadth-first one. Evidently, this results from the fact that once imaginary moves have been considered within the working (short-term) memory, they cannot be erased. Thus, backup in the planning sequence can easily overload the capacity of this memory. As a result, subjects tend to start a search process over rather than to back up a few steps.

Eisenstadt and Kareev, by their careful analysis of board games, have roughed out what seem to be the central mechanisms of problem solving within the domain of modern cognitive psychology. Many questions remain, particularly insofar as specification of the internal processes and structures is concerned.

CREATIVITY

It is reasonable to assume that most people are creative, but the degree of creativity differs widely. The creativity of, for example, Georgia O'Keeffe, Buckminster Fuller, Wolfgang Mozart, or Thomas Jefferson not only is a manifestation of great talent but also is well known. Other creative geniuses surely exist but go unrecognized.

The definition of *creativity* used in this section is that it is "a cognitive activity that results in a new or novel way of viewing a problem or situation." This definition does not restrict creative processes to utilitarian acts, although the examples of creative people are almost always drawn from some useful invention, writing, or theory they have created.

Creative Process

It is ironic that no dominant theory has emerged during the past twenty years that might unify the disparate and sometimes conflicting studies of creativity. The absence of a unified theory points out both the inherent difficulty of the topic and the lack of widespread scientific attention. Nevertheless, creativity is widely heralded as an important part of everyday life and education.

A long time ago in the history of cognitive psychology, Wallas (1926) described the creative process as having four sequential stages:

1. *Preparation.* Formulating the problem and making initial attempts to solve it.
2. *Incubation.* Leaving the problem while considering other things.
3. *Illumination.* Achieving insight to the problem.
4. *Verification.* Testing and/or carrying out the solution.

Empirical evidence for the validity of Wallas's four stages is almost nonexistent; however, the psychological literature abounds with introspective reports from people who have given birth to a creative thought. The most celebrated of these accounts is by Poincaré (1913), a French mathematician who discovered the properties of Fuchsian functions. After working on the equations for a time and after making some important discoveries (the preparation stage), he decided to go on a geologic excursion. While traveling he "forgot" his mathematical work (incubation stage). Poincaré then writes about the dramatic moment of insight. "Having reached Coutances, we entered an omnibus to go some place or other. At the moment when I put my foot on the step the idea came to me, without anything in my former thoughts seeming to have paved the way for it, that the transformations I had used to define the Fuchsian functions were identical with those of non-Euclidian geometry." The author continues to tell us that when he returned to his home, he verified the results at his leisure.

Wallas's four-stage model of the creative process has given us a conceptual framework to analyze creativity. Here we briefly consider each of the stages:

1. *Preparation.* Poincaré mentioned in his notes that he had been working intensively on the problem for fifteen days. During that period he seemed to have thought of several tentative solutions, which he tried out and, for one reason or another, discarded. However, to suggest that the period of preparation was fifteen days is, of course, wrong. All of his professional life as a mathematician and probably a good portion of his childhood could be considered part of the preparation stage.

A common theme in biographies of famous men and women is the notion that even during their early childhood, ideas were being developed, knowledge was being acquired, and tentative thoughts in a specified direction were being tried out. These early ideas frequently shape the ultimate destiny of the creative person. What remains one of the many mysteries of the process is why other individuals who share similar environmental stimulation (or, in many cases, deprivation) fail to be recognized for their creative talent. Maybe more attention should be given to the genetic bases of creativity.

2. *Incubation.* Why is it that a creative breakthrough frequently follows a period in which the problem is allowed to lie fallow? Perhaps the most pragmatic answer is that more of our life is devoted to recreation, watching television, skin diving, playing "Parcheesi," traveling, or lying in the sun watching the clouds drift by than in rock-hard thinking about a problem that needs a creative solution. So creative acts are more likely to follow dormant periods simply because those periods occupy more of our time.

Posner (1973) offers several hypotheses about the incubation phase. One suggestion is that the incubation period allows us to recover from the fatigue associated with problem solving. Also, interruption of an arduous task may allow us to forget inappropriate approaches to a problem. We have already seen that functional fixedness can impede problem solving, and it is possible that during incubation people forget old, unsuccessful solutions to problems. Another reason incubation may help in the creative process is that during this period we may actually work on the problem unconsciously. Such a notion is similar to William James's famous dictum, "We learn to swim in the winter and ice-skate in the summer." Finally, interruption of the problem-solving process may allow for reorganization of material.

3. *Illumination.* Incubation does not always lead to illumination (we all know a lot of people who have been in incubation most of their lives but so far have failed to illuminate). When it does, however, the sensation is unmistakable. Suddenly, the light bulb is turned on. The creative person may feel a rush of excitement as all the bits and pieces of ideas fall into place. All of the pertinent ideas complement each other, and irrelevant thoughts are discarded. The history of creative breakthroughs is replete with examples of the illumination stage. The discovery of the structure of the DNA molecule, the composition of the benzene ring, the invention of the telephone, the conclusion of a symphony, and the plot of a novel are all examples of how a moment of illumination has flooded the mind with a creative solution to a vexing old problem.

4. *Verification.* Following the euphoria that sometimes accompanies an insightful discovery, the idea is tested. This is the mopping up stage of the creative process in which the creative product is examined to verify its legitimacy. Often a solution first thought to be creative is only an intellectual fool's gold when examined carefully. This stage may be rather brief, as in the case of rechecking one's calculations or seeing whether an in-

vention works; however, in some cases verification may require a lifetime of study, testing, and retesting.

Creativity and Functional Fixity

Earlier in this chapter we saw how functional fixity could impede problem solving. Functional fixity also may obstruct creativity (which points out the similarly between the concepts of problem solving and creativity). People who do the same old thing over and over again or who think the same thoughts are considered to be rather unimaginative, not to mention being socially boring. On the other hand, creative people see novel relationships or unusual connections among seemingly unrelated things, such as the person who slipped an oversized tire over a small tree so when the tree grew it would have a built-in ring seat.

Several years ago some psychologists thought it might be possible to assess creative ability by measuring how well people see novel connections between seemingly unrelated words. One of these tests, invented by Mednick (1967), was called the Remote Associations Test (RAT); it asked people to generate a single word that would be logically associated with three words. Consider the following two groups of three words: *RED, BRIDGE, ANGRY,* and *HEAD, SICK, PORT.* If you said "cross" for the first group, you would be "right." What is the common denominator for the second group?

The RAT measures at least one component of creativity, but it probably measures other things too. Additionally, some very creative people might bomb on the test, which illustrates the slippery concept of creativity. Could it be that we are unconsciously creative, by which I mean that we have many associates to stimuli, such as a word or a visual scene or a musical piece, but are not consciously aware of them? The remote associates idea was expanded by Bowers and his colleagues (1990) in a task called the *dyads of triads*. One part of the task is like the RAT in that the words are part of a *coherent* triad, as are those just presented or those in the threesome *GOAT, PASS, GREEN,* all of which constellate around the coherent word *MOUNTAIN.* However, the triad *BIRD, PIPE, ROAD* is considered *incoherent* in that no (likely) common element is apparent. In this study subjects were given sets of coherent and incoherent triads and asked to find the common elements, if they could. Also, they were asked to judge which of the triads were coherent. The results showed that they were able to identify the coherent triads *even if they were unable to come up with the solution.* It was as if the subjects knew that there was a common element but could not quite name it. Possibly, people activate part of a solution to a remote associate task, and that may be one phase of a creative solution to a task. Such an idea might be related to the concept of *intuition* (which is defined by the *Oxford English Dictionary* as "the immediate apprehension of an object by the mind without the intervention of any reasoning process"), a frequently defamed term in scientific literature. Human intuition may indeed be an important part of the discovery phase of creative acts.

Investment Theory of Creativity

You may have heard that a wise investment strategy is to buy low and sell high and that fortunes have been made by those who follow that self-evident maxim (as well as lost by those unhappy folks who got the thing turned around). Some (such as Sternberg &

Lubart, in press) have speculated there is a not too subtle a similarity between investment wisdom and human creativity. Shrewd investors, through creativity, wisdom, or financial acumen, know when to buy and when to sell. These people may make an investment in a property or stock when others reject such opportunities. To others, their actions may seem foolish until the worth of the investment rises, and then others jump on the bandwagon. When the investment is worth more, the original investor sells. In effect, people under these circumstances are acting in a creative way.

In science, art, literature, music, and most other fields, creative people "buy low and sell high." That is, they get in on the ground floor in which the initial stages of their endeavor are frequently thought to be foolish, ill-advised, or worse. If the idea has merit, then others may join in, but we do not judge their actions as particularly creative. Many times the creative person will "sell high," which means that when the idea is more in vogue, he or she will move on to another problem.[4]

Sternberg and Lubart (in preparation; and Lubart & Sternberg, in preparation) have developed a theory of creativity based on a multivariate approach to the topic, which is built around six attributes. These six facets of creativity are:

- Processes of intelligence
- Intellectual style
- Knowledge
- Personality
- Motivation
- Environmental context

Truly creative performance is rare, not because people are lacking in any one attribute but because it is difficult to get all six attributes working together. These attributes are seen much as an investment portfolio might be seen in a business enterprise. Our creativity portfolio is the basis of creative acts. These six facets of the portfolio can combine to yield creative performances at any stage of life, and the intellectual environment, such as school or home life, has an important early influence on creativity.

The importance of the work of Sternberg and Lubart is that it provides a general theory of creativity specifying particular attributes that can be studied analytically and longitudinally. It is clear that creativity is not a single trait, skill, or ability but a combination of several factors that can be identified and analyzed. Furthermore, assessing human creativity is not a simple matter of identifying the amount of each attribute and adding them together to find a kind of creativity index. Rather, it is a matter of identifying and assessing the strengths of the interactions among attributes. The combination of strengths of attributes and the number of interactions possible poses a complex network that might befuddle some scientists. In fact, the whole idea may appear foolishly complex. It may be that the authors of this theory are investing in what others might call a risky venture. To others, it appears that Sternberg and Lubart have bought low.

---

[4]See Thomas Kuhn (1962) for an analysis of the development of scientific revolutions in which a similar argument is made.

Judging Creativity

Whether or not we label it, Americans are fond of judging creative acts and individuals. Everything from the latest Italian sports car to the recent Steven Spielberg film, to the performance of ice-skating champions, to lovemaking, is rated for its originality and creative merit. In most cases judging creative acts is a highly subjective affair. Sometimes the standards are set by an authority in the field, such as a noted professor of design, a film critic, a former Olympic skater, or a very discerning person. This approach to psychology sounds more like art than science, and, understandably, many scientifically obsessed psychologists would rather put on a white jacket, go to their dark laboratory, and measure blips on an oscilloscope made by a cat looking at a vertical line than try to evaluate a creative act or person. Yet some bold individuals have rushed in where their angelic colleagues fear to tread.

Divergence Production Test. J. P. Guilford (1967) has spent most of his long and celebrated professional career developing theories and tests of mental ability that includes creativity. He has distinguished between two types of thinking: convergent thinking and divergent thinking. Much of pedagogy emphasizes convergent thinking, in which students are asked to recall factual information, such as

What is the capital of Bulgaria?

Divergent thinking requires a person to generate many different answers to a question, the "correctness" of the answers being somewhat subjective. For example:

For how many different things can you use a brick?

The convergent answer may be "to make a building or a chimney." A slightly more divergent answer may be "to make a bookcase" or "to serve as a candleholder," while a more off-the-wall divergent answer may be "to serve as emergency rouge," or "to serve as a bon voyage gift—shoes for people who are going to the moon for the first time." Simple productivity of responses is not creative thinking. One could use a brick to make a candy shop, a bakery, a factory, a shoe factory, a shop that sells hand-carved wooden things, a filling station, and so on. Divergent or more creative answers may utilize objects or ideas in more abstract terms. The divergent thinker is more flexible in his or her thinking.

If productivity were a valid measure of creativity, then quantitative assessment of that trait could be achieved by counting the number of responses to brick-type questions. Since it is not, as illustrated in the previous example, subjective evaluations must be used. Most people would agree, I suspect, that bricks as moonshoes is a more creative answer than listing the types of buildings one could make with bricks. The latter answer is, however, more practical.

Cultural Blocks. Why is it that some people can generate creative uses for objects, such as a brick, and others cannot? Part of the answer may lie in the cultural heritage of the individual. James Adams (1976b) provides an example of a cultural block in the following puzzle:

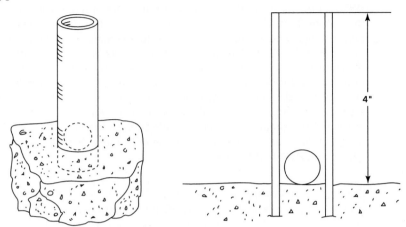

Exercise: Assume that a steel pipe is embedded in the concrete floor of a bare room, as shown in the illustration. The inside diameter is 0.6 inches larger than the diameter of a table tennis ball (1.50 inches), which is resting gently at the bottom of the pipe. You are one of a group of six people in the room, along with the following objects:

100 feet of clothesline
A carpenter's hammer
A chisel
A box of Wheaties
A file
A wire coat hanger
A monkey wrench
A light bulb

In 5 minutes list as many ways you can think of to get the ball out of the pipe without damaging the ball, the tube, or the floor.

Take a few moments to figure out a creative solution to this problem.

If your creative powers are like mine, you may have thought, "If I could only damage the floor, the ball, or the tube, I could get the ball out in minutes." Then, perhaps you might have considered how the inventory of items could be used or fashioned into tools. If you were able to generate a long list of possible uses for the items, you may have been showing your fluency or ability to produce a number of concepts over a period of time. If you were able to generate several diverse ideas, however, you would have shown your flexibility. Creative problem solving may be done by fluency—that is, you may think of enough concepts to find one that will be appropriate—but in many cases fluency does not lead to a solution and may even be a waste of time. More flexible thinking is required.

Did you solve the ball-in-the-pipe problem? Perhaps you thought of making a giant pair of tweezers by separating the coat hanger and flattening the ends. Other, more flexible means might include making a snare from the filaments of the light bulb. Another possibility would be to have one of the six people pee into the pipe, thereby levitating the ball to the surface. Why didn't you think of this, or if you did, why did you? It is likely that because of a cultural taboo that forbids public urination, this solution (apologies to those who can't stand puns) may not have occurred to you. Since no time limit is specified, you could also make a sticky paste of Wheaties, dip the clothesline in it, slip it down the pipe, and let it dry on the ball. Then the lightweight ball could be gently removed. Alternatively, the six people may be able to rotate the entire room and concrete floor, letting the ball roll out of the pipe (the directions say only that the pipe is embedded in a concrete floor and that the group of six people are in the room). After all, it could be a very small room easily negotiated by six people. Why didn't you think of that? Perhaps you could invent an antigravity machine with the tools available or transcendentally experience the ball outside the pipe (what is reality, after all?). If you have other ingenious solutions, perhaps you will send them to me. Our ability to think creatively is, in part, determined by our culture and education.

Teaching Creativity. Insofar as creativity is a function of our culture and education, is it possible to teach creativity? The answer depends on how creativity is defined. It is possible to train people to be more flexible in their thinking, to score higher on tests of creativity, to solve puzzles more creatively, and to probe scientific and philosophic issues deeper than before. However, it is difficult to prove empirically that through training alone the likes of a Rossini, De Quincey, Van Gogh, Einstein, Picasso, Dickinson, or Freud could be fashioned from a randomly selected person.

Hayes (1978) has suggested that creativity can be enhanced by the following means:

- *Developing a knowledge base.* A rich background in science, literature, art, and mathematics seems to give the creative person a larger storehouse of information from which to work his or her creative talents. Each of the above mentioned creative people spent many years gathering information and perfecting their basic skills. In a study of creative artists and scientists, Anne Roe (1946, 1953) found that the only common denominator among the group she studied was the willingness to work unusually hard. The apple that fell on Newton's head and inspired him to develop a general theory of gravity struck an object filled with information.

- *Creating the right atmosphere for creativity.* Several years ago the technique of brainstorming became fashionable. The gist of brainstorming is that people in a group generate as many ideas as they can without criticism from the other members. Not only can a large number of ideas or solutions to a problem be generated this way, but also the technique can be used on an individual basis to facilitate the development of a creative idea. Frequently, we are inhibited by others or our own constraint from generating bizarre solutions.

- *Searching for analogies.* Several studies have shown that people do not recognize it when a new problem is similar to an old problem that they already know how to solve (see Hayes & Simon, 1976; and Hinsley, Hayes, & Simon, 1977). In formulating a creative solution to a problem, it is important to consider similar problems you may have encountered. In the problem of extracting a table tennis ball from a 4-inch-long pipe, one technique was to make a glue from the Wheaties. If you were confronted with a similar puzzle, perhaps now you would, through analogous thinking, remember the problem with the pipe and table tennis ball and its Wheaties-and-glue solution.

HUMAN INTELLIGENCE

The Problem of Definition

In spite of the wide usage of the word *intelligence,* psychologists do not agree on a single definition. Many would agree, however, that all of the topics called higher-order forms of cognition—concept formation, reasoning, problem solving, and creativity, as well as memory and perception—are related to human intelligence. A short time ago, R. Sternberg (1982) asked people to identify the characteristics of an intelligent person, and among the most frequently given responses were "reasons logically and well," "reads widely," "keeps an open mind," and "reads with high comprehension." As a working definition we shall consider *human intelligence* to be "the ability to acquire, recall, and use knowledge to understand concrete and abstract concepts and the relationships among objects and ideas, and to use knowledge in a meaningful way."

The recent interest in artificial intelligence (AI) has caused many psychologists to consider what is uniquely human about human intelligence and what abilities a computer would require to act (humanly) intelligent. Nickerson, Perkins, and Smith (1985) have compiled the following list of abilities that they believe represent human intelligence:

• *The ability to classify patterns.* All humans with normal intelligence seem able to assign nonidentical stimuli to classes. This ability is fundamental to thought and language, since words generally represent categories of information. For example, *telephone* refers to a wide class of objects used for long-distance electronic communication. Imagine the hassle if you had to treat each telephone as a separate, nonclassified phenomenon.

• *The ability to modify behavior adaptively—to learn.* Many theorists consider adapting to one's environment the most important mark of human intelligence.

• *The ability to reason deductively.* As we considered earlier, deductive reasoning involves making logical inferences from stated premises. If we conclude that "Phil Smith likes wine," given the validity of the premises "All residents of Napa Valley like wine" and "Phil Smith lives in Napa Valley," we infer a degree of deductive reasoning ability.

• *The ability to reason inductively—to generalize.* Inductive reasoning requires that the person go beyond the information given. It requires the reasoner to discover rules and principles from specific instances. If Phil Smith likes wine and lives in Napa Valley, his neighbor also likes wine, and if his neighbor is also inclined to enjoy a bit of the nectar, you might get the impression that the next neighbor is also fond of fermented grapes. It might not be true, but it tends to be "intelligent."

- *The ability to develop and use conceptual models.* This ability means that we form an impression of the way the world is and how it functions and use that model to understand and interpret events. Nickerson and his colleagues use the following example:

> When you see a ball roll under one end of a couch and then emerge at the other end, how do you know that the ball that came out is the same one that went in? In fact you do not really know for sure that it is, but your conceptual model of the world leads you to make such an inference. . . . Moreover, had the ball, on emerging, been a different color, or a different size, than on entering, you would have had to infer either that the ball that came out was not the one that went in, or that something peculiar was going on under the couch."

Much of what we "know" we never directly observe, but we infer from our past experiences with other similar things and events. For example, I don't know whether my barber can tell time or read Sanskrit, but I act as if he can tell time and not read Sanskrit, whereas a person growing up in a provincial village in India might have an opposite model.

- *The ability to understand.* In general, the ability to understand is related to the ability to see relationships in problems and to appreciate the meaning of these relationships in solving a problem. Validation of understanding is one of the most elusive problems in intelligence testing.

Factor Analysis of Intelligence

One reason theorists have had difficulty defining intelligence is that it is a multifaceted phenomenon. Some early pioneers in the field of intelligence testing recognized the complex nature of intelligence and used factor analysis—a statistical technique designed to identify the source of variance in test correlations—in an attempt to uncover some of the underlying components of this complex topic. The experimental paradigm frequently used consisted of administering a battery of tests, each designed to measure a specific intellectual attribute such as reasoning, mathematical skill, spatial ability, and vocabulary. Factor analysis of the test data, usually gathered on a large, representative sample, is done by correlating each of the subscales with the other and then determining the factors that underlie individual differences in test performance.

Most notable among these early scientists was Charles Spearman (1904, 1927), who proposed that intelligence consisted of a g, or general, factor and a set of specific factors that were involved in performance on a single mental ability that he called "s." Intelligence, according to Spearman, was best characterized in terms of a single latent factor that predominated in test performance. Thus a person could exhibit unusually high ability in one or more specific factors while exhibiting poor ability in other factors. Other theorists, including Thurstone (1938), proposed that intelligence was best characterized as being composed of several factors that he called primary mental abilities. Guilford (1966, 1982) extended the concept of factor analysis to a logical analysis of the factors involved in mental functions. In his system, which was labeled the "structure of the intellect," an even more complex mosaic of intellectual components was proposed. In this system all mental abilities are conceptualized within a three-dimensional framework that originally contained 120 factors and later extended to 150 (see box) entitled

"Guilford's Structural Representation of Intelligence"). On one dimension are the operations required in a task, such as convergent and divergent thinking, memory, and cognition (thinking); on a second dimension are the products of the mental operations, such as relations, systems, transformation, and implications; and on the final dimension are the specific contents of a problem—figural, symbolic, semantic, or behavioral. The idea of the g factor is still one of the most debated topics among those who study intelligence. (See Jensen, 1993; Ree & Earles, 1992; Schmidt & Hunter 1992; and Sternberg & Wagner, 1993, for a sample of the debate.)

While increasing the number of factors that measure a facet of human intellect may help to identify the complex nature of the phenomenon, other theorists argue that such techniques were needlessly redundant and that a more elegant model was a hierarchical model. R. Cattell (1965) has proposed such a system. In Cattell's system general intelligence comprised two major subfactors, which he labeled "fluid abilities" and "crystallized abilities." Fluid abilities are associated with the ability to understand abstract and sometimes novel relationships as exhibited in inductive reasoning, analogies, and series-completion tests. Crystallized abilities are associated with the accumulation of facts and general knowledge as shown in tests of vocabulary and general information.

The factor-analytic approach to human intelligence has certainly enhanced our understanding of this complicated phenomenon, but the trail pioneered by Spearman, Thurstone, Guilford, and Cattell has not been free from the perilous ambush by cognitive psychologists. Robert Sternberg (1985b) of Yale University claims that the factor-analytic method of studying intelligence has been greeted with increasing skepticism for three reasons:

1. Factor-analytic techniques have little to do with "mental processes." For example, two people could produce identical scores on an IQ test, and yet the cognitive processes used could be different.
2. It is difficult to test factor-analytic techniques and models against each other.
3. Trying to understand intelligence on the basis of individual differences, upon which rests much of the logic of factor analysis, is not the only (or necessarily the best) means available for isolating human abilities.

Recently, cognitive psychologists have proposed new techniques and new models of human intelligence that have, generally, been fashioned after the information-processing model reviewed in this text.

Cognitive Theories of Intelligence

If the processing of information follows a sequence of stages in which at each stage a unique operation is performed, then human intelligence is thought to be a component of human intellect that interacts with the processing of information. Essentially, this is the way intelligence is conceptualized by cognitive psychologists who subscribe to the information-processing theory of cognition. Enthusiasm for the model seemed to start with cognitive psychologists fascinated with computer intelligence (Chapter 16 of this book is devoted to artificial intelligence, or computer simulation of intelligence.) The analogy between human and artificial intelligence is inescapable; information from the external world is perceived or input, it is stored in memory, transformation of the information is performed, and an output is made. Additionally, the processing of information

Guilford's Structural Representation of Intelligence

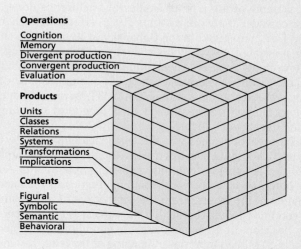

Operations

Cognition
Memory
Divergent production
Convergent production
Evaluation

Products

Units
Classes
Relations
Systems
Transformations
Implications

Contents

Figural
Symbolic
Semantic
Behavioral

Source: From J. P. Guilford "Intelligence: 1965 Model." American Psychologist, 21, (1966) 20–26. Copyright 1966 by the American Psychological Association. Reprinted by permission of the author.

Guilford's 120 Mental Factors and Some Sample Test Items

1. Scrambled words (cognition—symbolic—units)

   Rearrange the following letters to make real words:

R	A	C	I	H
T	V	O	E	S
K	L	C	C	O

2. Oddity problems (cognition—semantic—classes)

   Which object does not belong?

   clam   tree   oven   rose

3. Analogy problems (cognition—semantic—relations)

   Poetry is to *prose* as *dance* is to (a) music (b) walk   (c) sing   (d) talk.

4. Sentence production (divergent—symbolic—systems)

   Write as many sentences as you can using this form:

   W_ c_ e_ n_

5. Completion task (convergent—symbolic—relations)

   pots stop bard drab rats

6. Deduction task (convergent—symbolic—relations)

   Charles is younger than Robert.

   Charles is older than Frank.

   Who is older, Robert or Frank?

Answers:
1. CHAIR, STOVE, CLOCK
2. oven
3. walk
4. We covered every notch (and so on).
5. star
6. Robert

From Guilford (1959). Copyright 1959 by the American Psychological Association. Reprinted by permission.

is analogous to programs in computers and intellectual functions, including intelligence, in humans.

Short-Term Memory. As an example of the type of studies of intelligence done by cognitive psychologists, we first consider the work of Hunt (1978), Hunt, Lunneborg, and Lewis (1975), and Hunt and Lansman (1982) of the University of Washington. One question asked by Hunt and his associates was, "In what way(s) does the processing of information differ in high- and low-ability subjects?" Two groups—one with high-ability students and one with low-ability students—selected on the basis of standardized college entrance examinations such as the Scholastic Aptitude Test (SAT), were asked questions that required searching for common information in their long-term memories. Speed of retrieval was used as the dependent variable.

The test Hunt used to measure reaction times was the letter-matching task developed by Posner and his colleagues (1969), which is discussed in some detail in Chapter 7. The task required subjects to decide whether two letters (for example, A-A or A-a) matched. In some instances the letters matched physically and in other cases the match was made on the basis of the name of the letters. From the perspective of information processing, the physical match condition required only that the subject get the letters in short-term memory and make a decision. In the name-matching condition, the subject, in addition to getting both terms in STM, had to retrieve the name of the letter (ostensibly stored in LTM), make a decision, and then press a reaction-time key. Hunt assumed that physical matches reflect only structural processes dealing with the encoding and comparison of visual patterns, while name matching reflects the efficiency of encoding information to a level that requires that the physical representation of a letter make contact with the name of that letter in LTM. Crudely put, the speed with which people could retrieve information from LTM was hypothesized to be a measure of verbal ability. In the first condition, involving the physical match (A-A), the low- and high-ability groups did about equally well, in the name-matching condition (A-a), the low-ability group, on average, took more time to make a correct decision than the high-ability group. The difference between the groups was in the range of 25 to 50 milliseconds, which may seem to be very brief indeed; however, when we consider the decoding of countless thousands of letters and words in the process of normal reading (such as reading a textbook), the impact of these brief times adds up quickly. These results hold for different subject groups such as university students, ten-year-old children, elderly adults, and mentally retarded persons.

Earl Hunt. **Studied intelligence and artificial intelligence within the context of cognitive psychology.**

In another study Hunt (1978) used a modified form of the Brown-Peterson task (see Chapter 6) to study differences between those with high verbal ability and those with low verbal ability." This task, as you may recall, requires subjects to recall a three-letter syllable after they have counted backward by 3s for a certain length of time. (Hunt used four-letter syllables and had the subjects read the digits.) In this experiment the two groups differed significantly in recall of letters. In addition, the retention curves between the two groups were parallel, which suggests that the high-verbal group may be more efficient in encoding verbal information (rather than simply maintaining more information) than the low-verbal group. Finally, Hunt used the (Saul) Sternberg paradigm (see Chapter 7) to identify differences between subjects with high-verbal ability and those with low-verbal ability. As might be expected by now, he found that the former group performed better than the latter group on this task.

The studies by Hunt and others are significant for two reasons. First, they indicate that the information-processing paradigm provides many useful procedures for the study of human intelligence. It is feasible that, in addition to verbal ability, other measures of intelligence—such as mathematical ability, spatial ability, or perhaps even general intelligence—may yield some of their enigmatic secrets in terms of reasonably simple cognitive processes and mechanisms. Second, STM is related to verbal components of intelligence, not necessarily because the number of items retained in STM is critically related to intelligence but because simple cognitive processes and operations, such as identification of the name of a letter or the retention of a trigram, that depend on LTM and STM are sensitive to individual intellectual differences.

General Knowledge. General knowledge has, since the development of the earliest tests of intelligence, been considered an integral part of human intelligence, and to this day questions designed to tap an individual's understanding of the world are part of most standard tests. Apparently, knowing that Baghdad is the capital of Iraq, or that hydrogen is lighter than helium, or that the Kirov Ballet performs in Saint Petersburg, or that Tutankhamen's mostly unmolested tomb was discovered by Howard Carter (all of which are examples of my passive knowledge—the type of information a simpleminded computer could store) is presumed by test makers to be related to intelligence. However, embarrassingly little attention has been given, either theoretically or pragmatically, to the reason general knowledge is considered a correlate of intelligence. As Siegler and Richards (1982) point out:

> For the same reasons that fish will be the last to discover water, developmental psychologists until recently devoted almost no attention to changes in children's knowledge of specific content. Such changes are so omnipresent that they seemed uninviting as targets for study. Instead of being investigated, improved content knowledge was implicitly dismissed as a by-product of more basic changes in capacities and strategies (p. 930).

Tests of general information may provide important data on a person's current state of knowledge and ability to retrieve information. This in turn could provide a useful clue to the past intellectual history and predict future performance. Yet, of the many cognitive attributes recently discovered, only a few have been related to human intelligence. It seems that semantic organization is a topic that could be of special interest to people interested in intelligence. In a previous chapter some of the current theories of semantic organization were discussed, and it would seem that the ability to store semantic information in an organized schema and to access that information efficiently is characteristic of at least one type of intelligence. Perhaps some enterprising student of cognitive psychology will pursue this valuable subject.

One developmental study has shown not only how experiments can be done in this area, but also how they can lead to a clear demonstration of the impact of a knowledge base. Chi (1978) examined the effect of a specialized knowledge base on the recall of chess and digit stimuli. For her experiment, she selected ten-year-old children who were skilled chess players and adults who were novices at the game. The task was similar to the one used by Chase and Simon (see Chapter 4) in which chess pieces were arranged in a normal game configuration. Both groups of subjects were allowed to view the board and pieces and then were asked to reproduce the arrangement on a second board. A related task, called a metamemory task—which refers to an individual's knowledge about his or her own memory—consisted of asking the children and adults to predict how many trials it would take to reproduce all the pieces. The results, shown in Figure 15.7, revealed that the children not only were better at recalling the arrangement of chess pieces but also were better at predicting their performance—that is, their metamemory was more accurate than that of adults. A standard digit-span task, which is commonly used in intelligence tests, was also administered, and as expected the adults performed better on recalling these digits and predicting their performance than the children. The effect of a knowledge base, independent of age or other types of intelligence (for example, digit-span performance), appears to measurably enhance the ability to recall from working memory specialized information that is directly related to the knowledge base. The issues raised by this experiment, both methodological and theoretical, suggest that in the future many more studies of this type will appear.

Reasoning and Problem Solving. Almost everyone would agree that reasoning and problem solving are important components of human intelligence, and some would suggest that separating these concepts is done only for analytic purposes.

Most prominent among the new generation of cognitive psychologists to tackle the question of human intelligence in relation to reasoning and problem solving is R. Sternberg (1977, 1980a, 1980b, 1982, 1984a, 1984b, 1986a, 1986b, 1989). The theory of human intelligence proposed by Sternberg (1984b, 1985b, 1989) is the triarchic theory. It comprises three subtheories that serve as the governing bases for specific models of intelligent human behavior. These parts are:

1. *Componential intelligent behavior.* This subtheory specifies the structures and mechanism that underlie intelligent behavior. Within this subtheory are three information-processing components: (a) learning how to do things, (b) planning what things to do and how to do them, and (c) actually doing the things. People with such ability are generally good test takers and blow the top off standardized tests. They also do well commenting on other people's work. However, they are not necessarily critical thinkers, nor are they particularly creative.

2. *Experiential intelligent behavior.* This component posits that for a given task or situation, contextually appropriate behavior is not equally "intelligent" at all points along the continuum of experience with that behavior or class of behaviors. This kind of intelligence is best demonstrated when people are confronted with a novel situation or are in the process of automatizing performance on a given task. Those who have this com-

FIGURE 15.7

Recall of chess and digit stimuli by children and adults. (From "Knowledge Structures and Memory Development" by M. T. Chi, in R. S. Siegler, ed., *Children's Thinking: What Develops?* (Hillsdale, N.J.: Erlbaum, 1978). Reprinted by permission.

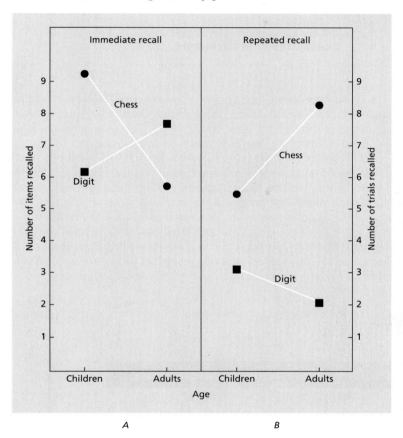

ponent may not score highest on typical IQ tests, but they are creative. Such ability is generally predictive of success in a chosen field, be it business, medicine, or carpentry.

3. *Contextual intelligent behavior.* This involves (a) adaptation to a present environment, (b) selection of a more nearly optimal environment than the one the individual presently inhabits, or (c) shaping of the present environment to render it a better fit to skills, interests, or values. Contextual intelligence allows a person to find a good fit with the environment by changing one or the other or both. We might think of this type of intelligence as instrumental in getting along in your world, whether that world is a slum in Los Angeles, the board room at IBM, the Cattleman's Club in Dallas, or the Polo Club at Southampton.

Robert J. Sternberg. **Developed triarchic theory of intelligence.**

In illustrating these three types of intelligence, Sternberg recalls three idealized graduate students called Alice, Barbara, and Celia, who each exemplified one of the components of intelligence (see Trotter, 1986). The three students are described in the box entitled "Sternberg's Triarchic Theory of Intelligence."

Such revolutionary ideas in the sensitive field of intelligence, which crosses so many areas of human endeavor (educational, political, racial, to name only three), were certain to be met with criticism. Some of the arguments are technical, others are philosophical, and others are pragmatically inspired.[5] One reviewer, H. Eysenck (1984), is critical of the triarchic theory on the basis that it is not so much a theory of intelligence as it is a theory of behavior. The interested reader is directed toward original sources and current literature. At this time, no one—including Sternberg (see 1984b, p. 312)—believes that the final model of intelligence has been developed. At the same time, no one believes that our view of intelligence will remain unchanged.

[5]For an excellent collection of Sternberg's theory and criticism of it by leading authorities, see Sternberg (1984b).

Sternberg's Triarchic Theory of Intelligence

Componential

Alice had high test scores and was a whiz at test taking and analytical thinking. Her type of intelligence exemplifies the componential subtheory, which explains the mental components involved in analytical thinking.

Experiential

Barbara didn't have the best test scores, but she was a superbly creative thinker who could combine disparate experiences in insightful ways. She is an example of the experiential subtheory.

Contextual

Celia was street-smart. She learned how to play the game and how to manipulate the environment. Her test scores weren't tops, but she could come out on top in almost any context. She is Sternberg's example of contextual intelligence.

From Trotter (1986). Illustrations by Jean Tuttle.

THE TRIARCHIC THEORY

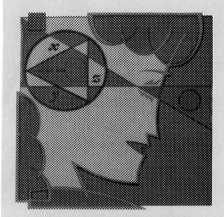

Componential

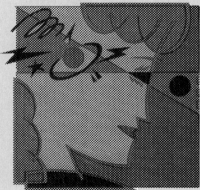

Experiential

Contextual

In Sternberg's scheme, reasoning is characterized as an attempt to combine elements of old information to produce new information. (See the box entitled "Cognitive Test of Intelligence.") The old information may be external (from books, movies, newspapers), internal (stored in memory), or a combination of both. In inductive reasoning, discussed earlier, the information contained in the premises is insufficient to reach a conclusion; the person must create the correct solution. One technique used by Sternberg is the analogy that can be represented by A is to B as C is to D or, symbolically, A:B::C:D. In some instances the last term (*D*) is omitted and must be generated by the subject, or in other cases the subjects must select from a series of alternative answers, as in the following:

Philology:Languages::Mycology:

(a. Flowering plants, b. Ferns, c. Weeds, d. Fungus)

The reasoning ability needed to solve this problem is minimal, but the analogy is nevertheless difficult for many people because they don't know that mycology is the study of fungi and philology is the study of the origin of languages. Analogies of this type measure a form of intelligence related to vocabulary.

In the above analogy, the solution is dependent on knowledge of words and reasoning ability. Solving analogies is not as simple a matter, however, as recalling information from memory; it involves several stages. Sternberg suggests that when confronted with a problem of this sort, one should break the analogy down into subproblems, each of which requires solving before the entire problem can be solved. The strategy used is similar to the means-end analysis of Newell and Simon (mentioned earlier), but it differs in that each stage of the information-processing sequence is thought to play an important role in the process. The following problem, adapted from R. Sternberg (1982), is an illustration of some of the stages a person must work through in solving an analogy.

Lawyer:Client::Doctor:

(a. Patient, b. Medicine)

In this case the encoding of the words is less problematic than in the previous case because most people are familiar with all the terms. The stages used in solving this problem are as follows:

1. The reasoner encodes the terms of the analogy.
2. The reasoner makes an inference between lawyer and client (for example, a lawyer gives service to a client, a lawyer is paid by a client, and a lawyer may help the client).
3. The reasoner maps the higher-order relationship between the first half of the analogy and the second (both deal with professionals who render service to a patron).
4. The reasoner applies a relationship similar to the inferred one to the second half of the analogy, that is, from the doctor and each of the alternatives (a doctor gives service to a person, not medicine).
5. The reasoner makes his or her response.

Cognitive Test of Intelligence

Sample Test Questions

1. Suppose that all gem stones were made of foam rubber. Which of the following completions would then be correct for the analogy below?

   Wood: Hard::Diamond:

   a. Valuable, b. Soft, c. Brittle, d. Hardest

2. Janet, Barbara, and Elaine are a housewife, lawyer, and physicist, although not necessarily in that order. Janet lives next door to the housewife. Barbara is the physicist's best friend. Elaine once wanted to be a lawyer but decided against it. Janet has seen Barbara within the last two days, but has not seen the physicist.

   Janet, Barbara, and Elaine are, in that order, the

   a. Housewife, physicist, lawyer
   b. Physicist, lawyer, housewife
   c. Physicist, housewife, lawyer
   d. Lawyer, housewife, physicist

3. Josh and Sandy were discussing the Reds and the Blues, two baseball teams. Sandy asked Josh why he thought the Reds had a better chance of winning the pennant this year than did the Blues. Josh replied, "If every man on the Red team is better than every man on the Blue team, then the Reds must be on the better team." Josh is assuming that

   a. Inferences that apply to each part of a whole apply as well to the whole, and this assumption is true.
   b. Inferences that apply to each part of a whole apply as well to the whole, and this assumption is false.
   c. Inferences that apply to a whole apply as well to each part, and this assumption is true.
   d. Inferences that apply to a whole apply as well to each part, and this assumption is false.

4. Select that answer option that represents either a necessary or forbidden property of the italicized word.
   lion

   a. Fierce, b. white, c. mammalian, d. alive

5.

From R. Sternberg (1986a).

Initially the terms of an analogy must be encoded, or translated, into internal representations upon which subsequent operations can be performed. One model of representations used by Sternberg (1977, 1982, 1985b) is based on attributes of the information, which is similar to theories discussed in Chapter 8 on semantic memory. This model is illustrated in the following example:

Washington:1::Lincoln:

(a. 10, b. 5)

- Washington could be encoded as (1) a president (1st), (2) a person whose visage is on currency (one-dollar bill), or (3) a war hero (American Revolution).

- 1 might be encoded as a counting number (1), an ordinal position (1st), or an amount (1 unit).

- Lincoln might be encoded as a president (16th), a person whose visage is on currency (five-dollar bill), or a war hero (Civil War).

- 10 might be encoded as a counting number (10), an ordinal position (10th), or an amount (10 units).

- 5 might be encoded as a counting number (5), an ordinal position (5th), or an amount (5 units).

In addition to the semantic representations shown by these analogies, information in problems can be presented pictorially, as in an analogy that might include a black square inside a white circle, which might be represented in terms of shape, position, or color. (For an example, see question 5 in the box entitled "Cognitive Test of Intelligence.")

From such problems Sternberg has developed a theory of intelligence that distinguishes five different components by which intelligence can be analyzed: metacomponents, performance components, acquisition components, retention components, and transfer components. *Components* refers to the steps that a person must go through to solve a problem. *Metacomponents* refers to the person's knowledge about how to solve a problem. Because metacomponents are the basis of so many diverse intellectual tasks, Sternberg considers it to be related to general intelligence. He is continuing to investigate how different components are involved in reasoning tasks, such as analogies, and how the components and metacomponents increase in complexity with development. Of particular interest to the student of cognitive science is his overall scheme, which has clearly cast theories of intelligence and tests of intelligence in the cognitive mold.

Summary

1   Problem solving is thought directed toward discovering a solution for a specific problem.

2   Much research in artificial intelligence (AI) is directed toward discovering and duplicating human cognitive processes in problem solving (for example, Newell, Simon, & Shaw's general problem solver). AI models have been criticized for being rigidly sequential with perfect information access, but research suggests that the use of subgoal routines (as in GPS) does have an analog in human problem solving.

3   Several models have proposed cognitive networks engaged during problem-solving activity. One such model (Eisenstadt & Kareev) has focused on internal representations formed during problem solving, with related research showing memory about the problem field to be a function of how the problem was formed, negligible anticipatory planning, and scanning patterns of the problem field suggestive of top-down or hypothesis-driven processing.

4   Creativity is cognitive activity resulting in a novel perspective of a problem and is not restricted to pragmatic outcomes.

5 One framework for viewing the creative process (Wallas) proposes four phases: preparation, which involves problem formation, a process engaging our general knowledge base; incubation, which is the period when no direct attempts to solve the problem are made and attention is diverted elsewhere; illumination, which occurs when understanding is achieved; and verification, which involves testing of the insight.

6 Judgments of creativity range from assessments by authorities in the relevant field (for example, an Olympic athlete) to psychometric instruments designed to measure divergent thought processes defined as the ability to generate numerous abstract, flexible answers to one problem (for example, how many different ways can you use a brick?). Both procedures involve subjective evaluations.

7 Training can result in improved performance on standard measures of creativity, but it is not known whether such experience can produce the type of activity associated with people generally considered to be creative (such as Van Gogh, Einstein, or Dickinson).

8 The complex nature of intelligence produces definitional problems. Early attempts to address these conceptual difficulties used factor analysis to isolate general and specific abilities, but such procedures have been criticized for not providing information about mental processes; for being difficult to test against theories; and for relying on individual differences, which is not the only or necessarily the best way to study human abilities.

9 Cognitive theories of intelligence hold it to be a component that interacts with information as it is processed through stages involving unique operations. Research using this framework has determined that memory retrieval (speed, accuracy, and amount) is a function of verbal ability, and an individual's knowledge base (novice versus skilled) affects the amount and accuracy of recall as well as the accuracy of his or her metamemory.

Key Words

convergent thinking	incubation
creativity	intelligence
divergent thinking	preparation
functional fixedness	problem solving
general problem solver (GPS)	set
illumination	verification

Recommended Readings

An outstanding review of early history of research in thinking, concept formation, and problem solving is Woodworth, *Experimental Psychology*. F. Bartlett, *Thinking*, is a good introduction to traditional viewpoints. Bruner, Goodnow, and Austin, *A Study of Thinking*, is the source of much of the traditional theory and experimentation in concept formation.

Many articles have been collected into two paperback books, Johnson-Laird and Wason, eds., *Thinking and Reasoning* and *Thinking: Readings in Cognitive Science*.

Three "annual reviews" of thinking that summarize the significant developments are Bourne and Dominowski, *Thinking;* Neimark and Santa, *Thinking and Concept Attainment;* and Erickson and Jones, *Thinking.*

Rubinstein has written a lively account of thinking and problem solving in *Tools for Thinking and Problem Solving.* An easy and entertaining book is Mayer's *Thinking, Problem Solving, Cognition.* A first-rate collection of papers on human intelligence has been edited by Robert Sternberg and is called *Handbook of Human Intelligence* and *Advances in the Psychology of Human Intelligence.* Also see *Intelligence Applied* and *Beyond IQ: A Triarchic Theory of Human Intelligence* by Sternberg. Several recent volumes on intelligence have been edited by Chipman, Segal, and Glaser and are called *Thinking and Learning Skills;* and Nickerson, Perkins, and Smith have written an excellent book on thinking called *The Teaching of Thinking.* The relatively new periodical *Current Issues in Cognitive Science* frequently contains stimulating articles on the topics covered in this chapter and in the February 1993 issue (Number 1) intelligence was featured in several articles.

Answer 1

Answer to the flagpole problem on pages 444–445. Remember the hint to look at the extremes? In this case first imagine that the flagpoles were 150 feet apart. The rope would be taut. Now imagine the other extreme, that the poles would be touching each other. How would the rope hang? Since the rope is 150-feet long and the flagpoles are each 100-feet tall, when the poles are next to each other the draped rope hangs down one pole 75 feet and down the other 75 feet, leaving the center of the rope hanging 25 feet from the ground.

Answer 2

Answer to problem in box entitled "A Problem of Patients: Psychiatrists' and Yours." Karen and Laura care for a Rubin and therefore are not named Rubin (mark in the intersection of Karen and Laura with Rubin and exclusionary mark). Therefore Mary is married to Rubin. Laura is a patient of Dr. Sanchez and, therefore, is not named Sanchez and must be called Taylor. By elimination, then, Karen is a Sanchez. Mary Rubin is seen by a female (clue 1) and a Dr. Taylor (clue 2), so she is treated by Laura Taylor and Mary's husband is treated by Karen Sanchez. Peter, who is treated by a Dr. Taylor (clue 2), is not Dr. Taylor (obviously) and cannot be the male Dr. Rubin treated by Karen Sanchez, so he must be Peter Sanchez and he treats Laura Taylor (clue 2). Omar cannot be the Dr. Rubin who is treated by Karen Sanchez because Omar is treated by Norman (clue 4), so Omar's last name is Taylor and Norman's last name is Rubin. Peter's psychiatrist is Omar Taylor, and, by elimination, Karen is under Mary Rubin's care. In summary, the full names of psychiatrists and patients are as follows: Drs. Laura Taylor (Mary Rubin), Karen Sanchez (Norman Rubin), Mary Rubin (Karen Sanchez), Omar Taylor (Peter Sanchez), Peter Sanchez (Laura Taylor), and Norman Rubin (Omar Taylor).

Artificial Intelligence

> It is morally impossible that there should be sufficient diversity in any machine to allow it to act in all events of life in the same way as our reason causes us to act.
>
> *- Descartes*

> Then Hal answered, In his normal tone of voice:
>
> "Look, Dave, I know you're trying to be helpful. But the fault is either in the antenna system or in your test procedures. My information processing is perfectly normal. If you check my record, you'll find it completely free from error."
>
> "I know all about your service record, Hal—but that doesn't prove you're right this time. Anyone can make mistakes."
>
> "I don't want to insist on it, Dave, but I am incapable of making an error."
>
> "All right, Hal," he said, rather hastily. "I understand your point of view. We'll leave it at that."
>
> He felt like adding "and please forget the whole matter." But that, of course, was the one thing that Hal could never do.
>
> *- Arthur C. Clarke*

S CIENCE FICTION HAS A tendency to become science fact. Something like Hal,[1] the on-board spaceship computer capable of ethical decision making and intelligence in Arthur Clarke's *2001: A Space Odyssey,* is being discussed seriously in modern artificial-intelligence (AI) laboratories. That is not to say that computers are likely to develop exactly as Clarke envisioned, any more than propulsion systems developed in the way Jules Verne imagined three-quarters of a century before a rocket sent a spaceship to the moon. However, computer scientists are developing computer systems that come very close to mimicking parts of human information processing and cognition; it seems plausible that something like Hal will be around before you depart from this earth.[2]

When we discuss AI, it is usually intertwined with cognitive psychology and neuroscience. Ideas from one field, for example, neuroscience, might be incorporated into another, for example, artificial intelligence, and yet other ideas from cognitive psychology might be applied to both of the other areas. All three—AI, cognitive psychology, and neuroscience (especially neuroscience)—build a platform for cognitive science.

AI and cognitive psychology have a kind of symbiotic relationship, each profiting from the development of the other. On the one hand, the development of artificial ways to replicate human perception, memory, language, and thought, is dependent upon understanding how these processes are accomplished by human beings. On the other

---

[1]Acronym for *h*euristically programmed *al*gorithmic computer.

[2]On the other hand, many question that computers can ever truly outsmart humans in significant areas. Neuropsychologist John Eccles writes, in *The Understanding of the Brain,* that those who make " . . . arrogant assertions that computers will soon outsmart man in all matters . . . are the modern variants of the idol makers of other superstitious ages; and like them seek power through the fostering of idolatry."

hand, the development of AI increases the magnitude of our capabilities to understand human cognition.

This chapter offers a general introduction to AI as it relates to perception, memory, search processes, language, problem solving, and robotics. Most of these topics have been taken up in the preceding chapters.

Although work in AI is devoted to the development of machines that act as if they were intelligent, most are designed without any intention of mimicking human cognitive processes. However, there are researchers who are concerned with the development of "intelligent" machines that model human thought, and it is this perspective—sometimes called computer simulation (CS)—that, for the most part, is reflected in this chapter. (Because at times it is nearly impossible to tell where AI leaves off and CS begins, the widely accepted term AI is used in this chapter to embrace all forms of computer-produced output that would be considered intelligent if produced by a human.)

AI—THE BEGINNINGS

Calculators of one sort or another—the brain of AI—have been around about as long as history. The earliest type was the abacus, which was used in China during the sixth century B.C. The Egyptians invented a counting machine that used pebbles some time before Herodotus (about 450 B.C.) noted its use. The Greeks had a similar device, and in Rome writers tell of three types of calculating machines. Most of these devices were used to keep track of transactions by adding and subtracting. Multiplication was performed by repeating the adding phase. About 1633 a little-known German astronomer, Wilhelm Schickard (1592–1635), invented an automatic digital calculator that was commemorated on a German postage stamp in 1973 (see the illustration shown here). The invention of a calculating machine is more often ascribed to French philosopher Blaise Pascal (1623–1662), the Father of Calculus. Pascal's machine could only add and subtract, but it attracted widespread interest. In the 1670s Gottfried Leibniz introduced a machine that could do multiplication and division. Computers came along later when the eccentric Charles Babbage (1792–1871), sometimes called the world's first computer scientist, assisted by Lady Ada Lovelace invented the difference engine, which had programmable operations containing conditional branches. (See Haugeland, 1989, for details. A model of Babbage's machine can be seen at the Smithsonian Institute in Washington, D.C.)

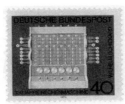

Postage stamp depicting Schickard's calculator on its 350th anniversary.

Computers

The origin of modern computer science can be traced to the 1940s, when vacuum-tube computers such as UNIVAC and ENIAC were invented to speed lengthy and tedious mathematical calculations commonly used by the military, such as calculating the trajectories of artillery shells. The ENIAC (Electronic Numerical Integrator and Computer), a highly secretive U.S. Army-sponsored project conducted at the University of Pennsylvania, had 17,468 vacuum tubes whose manufacture guaranteed a service life of 25,000 hours, which meant, on average, that a tube would burn out about every 8 minutes! The behemoth calculating machine weighed 30 tons and drew 174 kilowats of power. The project directors were John Mauchley and J. Presper Eckert. These early, simpleminded, inefficient giants gave way to smaller, more powerful, and complex systems that, in turn, were eventually replaced by the solid-state microelectronic computers in general use today.

Few dates in cognitive psychology are more important than 1956.[3] During the summer of that year, a group of ten scientists met on the campus of Dartmouth College to consider the possibilities of developing computer programs that would "behave" intelligently. Among those who attended this conference were John McCarthy, who later founded AI laboratories at MIT and Stanford University and is generally credited with christening the new science "AI"; Marvin Minsky, who became the director of the AI laboratory at MIT; Claude Shannon, who developed the modern model for a communication system at Bell Laboratories; Herbert Simon, who was to win the Nobel Prize in

---

[3]During that year Bruner, Goodnow, and Austin published *A Study of Thinking,* Chomsky published "Three Models of the Description of Language," Miller published "The Magical Number Seven," and Newell and Simon completed "The Logic Theory Machine: A Complex Information Processing System." The year 1956 was also when the historic MIT conference took place. See Chapter 1 for details.

J. Prespert Eckert (foreground) and John Mauchley work on the vacuum tube computer, ENIAC, with U.S. Army and other personnel in 1946.

John McCarthy. **Pioneered studies in artificial intelligence and designed LISP, a widely used AI language.**

economics; and Allen Newell, who has carried out his important work in cognitive science and AI at Carnegie Mellon University. The conference was historically significant because the course AI was about to take was set, which directly influenced the way cognitive psychology developed.

Since the Dartmouth conference, AI has grown geometrically. AI, in some form or another, now touches the daily lives of most people in the world, occupies the concentrated effort of thousands of scientists, and is proliferating on college campuses. The diverse ends of AI research and practice cannot be reported in a single chapter, or a book, or even many books. However, we can, in this chapter, present a sample of the work in AI as it relates to cognitive psychology.

Computers and AI

The most common type of computer in use today is patterned after a design ("architecture," in computer argot) created by the Hungarian mathematician John von Neumann (1958), who emigrated to the United States in 1930. These computers are sometimes called Johniacs or serial processors, meaning that electrical impulses are processed in series, or in sequence. These chainlike sequences operate very rapidly, with each step requiring only nanoseconds, but a computer performing complicated tasks in a serial fashion (such as solving involved mathematical functions, or rearranging data or files) may require several minutes, hours, or even longer. All computer users have experi-

John von Neumann **(1903–1957). Designed the computer architecture in common use.**

enced the maddeningly "long" lag time required by personal computers to "think" or "digest" a problem. One basic reason serial computers of the von Neumann genus require so much time is that one operation must be completed before another is initiated. Serial processors solve problems bit by bit, in a stepwise fashion.

Even in the beginning of the technology of computers, AI scientists (and science fiction writers) had grand dreams about thinking machines and robots. A seminal paper was written in the early 1940s by a Chicago psychiatrist, W. S. McCulloch, and his student, W. Pitts. In this paper they introduced a concept that was to have significant impact on computer scientists, including von Neumann and later PDPers. Based on the idea that the *mind* was defined as the workings of the brain, specifically the brain's basic units, neurons, they argued that neurons could be viewed as "logical devices," that "neural events and the relations among them can be treated by means of propositional logic." When neurons communicate with each other, they do so electrochemically. A tiny electrical current is passed along a cell's axon to the synapse, where a chemical neurotransmitter passes the impulse to other neurons. The process of neurotransmission is rule governed: firing of a neuron occurs only when the threshold is achieved, all neurons have thresholds, neurons fire only when the current is positive, a negative current will inhibit a neuron from firing, and so on. Most importantly, each neuron seems to sum up all excitatory and inhibitory signals from its thousands of connections. Depending on its threshold, a neuron will fire or not; that is, it will be on or off.[4] (Neurons of this type are called McCulloch-Pitts neurons.) McCulloch and Pitts observed that this on or off neuron could be seen as a logic device. As is commonly known, computers function by means of on/off circuits. When thousands of these are coupled together in exponential series, the amount of processing power is awesome. Similarly, the basic unit of neural processing, the neuron and its connections, are capable of monumental powers of processing.

A short time after the paper by McCulloch and Pitts, von Neumann saw the connection between the logical behavior of neurons as they interact and the way digital computers go about their work. "It can easily be seen that these simplified neuron functions can be imitated by telegraph relays or by vacuum tubes." (Transistors had not been invented yet, or he probably would have mentioned them.) Von Neumann, who had already developed the most useful computer architecture up to that point, suggested that it might be possible to design a computer that mimicked the human brain— not only in function but also in structure—where vacuum tubes, relays, connecting wires, and hardware replaced neurons, axons, synapses, and "wetware." Following von Neumann, Rosenblatt undertook the project of building a computer along these lines. His intent was to make a computer that could learn to classify shapes. The result was called a perceptron, and it crudely imitated the brain's organization (see Chapters 1 and 2). Rosenblatt's machine consisted of a three-level hierarchy. Each level was associated with a different function that generally emulated the sensory, associative, and motor pattern of humans. One fundamental problem of early machines such as the perceptron was that they did not learn. They simply processed a narrow range of stimuli and made equally simple responses.

---

[4]This presents an exciting perspective to the neurally inspired connectionist model discussed in Chapter 1.

Humans are capable of learning because they have modifiable synapses. You'll recall Hebb's rule (introduced in Chapter 2) about the strength between two neurons increasing when they are simultaneously activated. Could such a rule be built into the connections between surrogate neurons? Learning by such a machine might require that a resistor (a device that specifies the amount of electrical impulse leaving one transistor that will reach another) be wired into and programmed in an artificial brain. A resistor would act very much like a regulator, allowing some bits of information to be passed on while rejecting others. Perceptrons capable of "learning" (and *learning* is defined here as "the change in strength between units that simulate neurons") do so because they behave in a way similar to McCulloch-Pitts neurons and obey Hebb's theory. A computer so constructed might be shown a simple geometric shape, such as a circle, to classify. If it responds by calling it a square, then it can be "taught" to respond correctly by increasing the resistance between certain units and lowering the resistance between others. If the response is correct, that is, if the perceptron calls a circle a circle, the values are left alone. In this sense, perceptrons punish errors and ignore success. These early steps were important in designing machines capable of making generalizations and learning, factors essential in the construction of a "thinking machine" that functions similarly to a human brain.

During the early stages of computer development, some fundamental opinions about the use and significance of these newfound contraptions also emerged. There were those who thought that if computers were programmed properly, that is, given the right rules and instructions, they could carry out any operations, including the effective mimicking of human thought. Others believed that for a machine to "think," it was necessary that a computer's hardware simulate a brain's "wetware." To achieve the latter would require that a computer be built with layers upon layers of interconnected electronic surrogate neurons whose organization and function would simulate a human brain.

So far we have failed to produce either a truly "thinking" machine or one whose "brain" appears much like a human brain. However, as sciences go, AI is still an infant. Each of the perspectives mentioned has its own problems. In the first case, most AI programs are damnably rigid in "thinking." When I ask you what is the square root of 73, you might say, "Well, it's at least 8 but not quite 9. About 8 and a half." A computer answers 8.5440037 . . . Rather than breed endless concatenations of digits, the human brain seems wonderfully designed to deal with chaos—seeing a familiar face in a crowd, driving on the Los Angeles freeways, understanding the deep meaning of a Chekhov drama, or feeling the sensuousness of silk as it caresses our skin. No computer can do that . . . yet. On the other hand, no human can spew out the answer to the square root problem in milliseconds, as any cheap hand-held calculator can.

Just consider the Promethean task faced by those who aspire to wire a computer like a human brain! The brain has about 10 billion neurons, each of which connects with countless thousands of other neurons. That's a lot of soldering. Nevertheless, some people have attempted a small-scale computer model of the brain (see Rosenblatt, 1958) but, until recently (see entitled "Critical Thinking: Silly Chip for a Brain?"), have discouraged others from pursuing this pastime (see Minsky & Papert, 1968). Earlier (in 1954) Minsky had written his dissertation on neural nets and had even built one with 400 vacuum tubes, but he soon became disinfatuated with the project. This early work did not produce "practical" results, while developing computer programs and hardware

Critical Thinking: Silly Chip for a Brain?

Recently a silicon chip which is said to behave much like a human brain cell, was developed by Caltech and Oxford University researchers Mahowald and Douglas. The device, called a silicon neuron, has a structure and process that mimic the workings of neurons in the cerebral cortex. The important aspect of the technology is the analog nature of the device as contrasted with the digital processing units used in most computers. When humans see a complex object, such as a person's face, we do not see digitalized data—a series of pixels—but rather subtly graded contours and continuously varying shades of gray. From these signals the eye and brain extract meaning from the light signals through an analog process.

While others discount the importance of this technological discovery on the basis that the brain has many types of neurons and this is only one example, the idea of a silicon chip that imitates even some important features of the human neuron presents an intriguing question for the future. How far can technology go in creating a brain?

during the same time was the hottest game in town. Garage workshops expanded to megabuck factories, which built computers that could do things about which we could only dream.

The recent generation of computer/cognitive scientists is more sanguine regarding the simulation of neural functions by a machine. One of the recent changes in perceptrons was conceptual. Rather than thinking of a computer brain as an input-output device, a third layer, called a hidden layer, was added. This hidden layer corresponds to the brain's interneurons, which are not concerned with input or output but with connecting impulses to other neurons. The model is compatible with connectionism, mentioned throughout this book.

Many of these issues deal with the problem of the architecture of computers and brains, a most important topic. However, computers still do not perform functions as humans do; computers and brains are not identical. In some ways computers do better than brains, but in some ways they do worse. This disparity is seen in many domains, as has been mentioned previously, but one particularly problematic area is the identification of three-dimensional objects. Our eyes, two-dimensional sensors, readily and accurately transmit signals that are interpreted as three-dimensional. Even with the sluggish "wetware" of the nervous system, the constant change in eye-object location, and size adjustments, our perceptual system works nearly perfectly. Computers do less well, even though the rate of transmission is millions of times faster than neurotransmission.

If I only had a brain.

-Strawman in The Wizard of Oz

As has already been mentioned, one reason for the difference is that computers generally process information serially, while brains generally process information in parallel. Some AI scientists have begun to overcome the architectural difference between brains and computers for the purpose of overcoming this functional difference. One such scientist is W. Daniel Hillis, who has developed a "connection machine" (see Hillis, 1987), which solves problems by breaking them into smaller problems (reminiscent of the means-end analysis) and then processing them in parallel. These smaller problems, or chunks, are then distributed to separate areas of the computer's processing network. This is contrasted with the von Neumann class of computers, which has one central processor that processes information sequentially. In Hillis's connection machine, 65,536 (a prime number with base 2) processors work on a single problem simultaneously. Although each processor is even less powerful than the PC used in the preparation of this manuscript, when those more than 65,000 little chips are hooked up in tandem and work simultaneously, they can execute several billion instructions per second. It's an impressive machine, both conceptually and functionally. Yet, Hillis dreams of a machine with a billion processors functioning in parallel—just for the Hal of it.

AI and PDP

Some of the fundamental questions of AI are:

- What kind of a thinking machine is the brain?
- How can human thinking be emulated by a machine?
- Can human thinking be surpassed by computers?
- Is pursuit of these issues worthwhile?

There are no easy answers to any of these questions, but those who subscribe to a neurally inspired parallel distributed processing model (and others) are hard at work trying to find solutions.

The answer to the first question is beginning to take shape after a century of research in psychology, especially during the past several decades of research in cognition. It is hoped that the contents of this book contain a representative sample of the answer. What we have learned about our thinking machine, called the brain, is that it is fundamentally different from the von Neumann computers now in common use. Perhaps AI would be further along if computers resembled brains more closely. To clarify this matter, I have proposed the following comparative résumé:

	Computers (von Neumann type)	Brains (Humans)
Processing speed	In nanoseconds	In milliseconds to seconds
Type	Serial processor (mostly)	Parallel processor (mostly)
Storage capacity	Vast, for digitally coded information	Vast, for visual and linguistic information

Material	Silicon and electronic supply system (for example, transistors, switches, and electricity)	Neurons and organic supply system (for example, capillaries and blood)
Cooperation	Absolutely obedient (does exactly what it is told)	Generally cooperative, but if pressed is likely to rebel (has a mind of its own)
Learning capacity	Simpleminded	Naturally impressive
Best feature	Can process an immense amount of data in a short period of time without complaint	Can make judgements, inferences, and generalizations easily
	Cost efficient, rule governed, easy to maintain, and predictable	Ambulatory; has language, speech, vision, and emotions Is expensive to maintain, sometimes unpredictable

The answer to the second question, at least within the connectionist camp, is that human thinking can best be emulated by modeling a machine after basic neurological structures.

The answer to the third question is that some computer programs work far more effectively than human thinking; most, however, are at best clumsy counterfeits of the real thing. Computers can solve some problems, such as detailed mathematical ones, faster and more accurately than humans can. Other tasks, such as making generalizations and learning new patterns of activity, are done well by humans but not by computers.

Finally, my easy answer to whether we should pursue these issues is yes. We learn more about human thinking and machine thinking in the process. Others argue that the pursuit of AI is as foolish as tilting at windmills.

As shown in the table comparing von Neumann-type computers with brains, it is no wonder AI scientists have been frustrated, if not confused. They are working with the wrong kind of machine. It appears as though we are on the verge of a conceptual breakthrough—perhaps a paradigm shift—in AI, in which the first steps have already been taken to make computers more brainlike in terms of both their structure and their process. Neuronetwork systems, PDP models, and connectionism are attempting to discover the computational principles that govern networks of neurons in the human nervous system. They do this by what may seem to be a highly abstract means. Units may represent neurons, but units follow laws derived from neuron behavior. That is, a unit can be paired with other units, the association between them can be strengthened or weakened, they can achieve stable relations, and so on. (See Churchland, 1989, for further information.)

An important concept has also been proposed with regard to neuronetworks: they can also learn. That is, through a system of synapse-like weights, the infrastructure of the brain can change through experience (which may be externally or internally determined).

Superbiology

While American scientists of a generation ago tinkered with the notion that they could build a brainlike computer, in Japan one scientist, Aizawa, is building a brainlike computer with real nerve cells intermingled with electronic devices in an effort to fabricate a crude, semiartificial neuralnetwork. So far he has successfully combined cells with the semi-conducting compound indium tin oxide and found that under very weak electrical stimulation organic cells respond with controlled growth (see figure shown here). It is too early to think of an artificial brain, but such devices might be useful as an interface between the nervous system and prostheses such as an artificial eye.

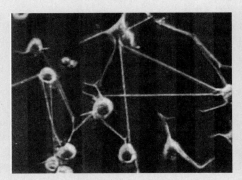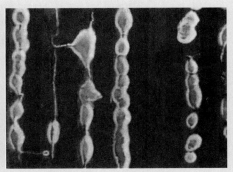

It is far too early to know how successful these efforts will be. It is not too early to know that the new way of looking at human cognition has enjoyed great enthusiasm among its proponents.[5] Even the casual student of cognitive psychology should be sensitized to this important contribution to psychology and be on the lookout for future developments.

MACHINES AND MINDS: THE IMITATION GAME AND THE CHINESE ROOM

There are few areas of cognitive psychology that have been the subject of more hotheaded arguments than the debate over the simulation of human thought by machines. On one side of the argument are AI zealots who believe not only that machines are capable of exactly replicating human cognition but also that advanced intellectual

[5]For an interesting account of a type of neuralnetwork in the behavior of army ants as they navigate a tropical rain forest, see Franks (1989).

processes can be carried out only by machines. The logical extension of this argument is that computers should be directly involved in everyday human decision making. On the other side are those who consider AI to be an intellectually corrupt concept and believe people who put their faith in so-called thinking machines are materialistic idol worshipers. Human thinking is purely a human process that, even if partly synthesized by a machine, will never be duplicated by AI programs.

As a starting point, it is useful to consider the dichotomy proposed by John Searle (1980), a philosopher with the University of California at Berkeley. He describes two forms of AI: "weak" AI, which can be used as a tool in the investigation of human cognition, and "strong" AI, in which a properly programmed computer has a "mind" capable of understanding. "Weak" AI has few opponents; almost everyone acknowledges the importance of computers in the investigation of human cognition, and little more needs to be said about that issue here. "Strong" AI, which Searle refutes, has brought a storm of protest. We extend this argument in the section entitled "The Chinese Room," but first let's consider one of the original mind versus machine problems proposed by Alan Turing,[6] a British mathematician.

The Imitation Game, or the Turing Test

Turing (1950) proposed a task that involved communication between a human, who asked questions, and an unknown-language-using being. Simply stated, the task of the human was to decide whether the being was indistinguishable from a human. It is to Turing's credit that the use of the imitation game, which later became commonly known as the Turing test, was in itself a very subtle deception that, while giving AI specialists something concrete to work on, diverted attention from the philosophic mind—an issue that has been a major hang-up in scientific and psychological history. Instead of addressing the philosophic issue directly (as Turing might have done had he asked, "Is cognition a function of material process, and if so, can those functions originate from an inorganic machine?" or "What is the solution to the mind-body problem?"), he chose a far more clever way to frame the question by basing it in operationalism. Since there remains some confusion in the literature about the real nature of the test Turing as proposed, it is printed in detail here.

> The . . . problem can be described in terms of a game which we call the "imitation game." It is played with three people, a man (A), a woman (B), and an interrogator (C) who may be of either sex. The interrogator stays in a room apart from the other two. The object of the game for the interrogator is to determine which of the other two is the man and which is the woman. He knows them by labels X and Y, and at the end of the game he says either "X is A and Y is B" or "X is B and Y is A." The interrogator is allowed to put questions to A and B thus:
>
> C: Will X please tell me the length of his or her hair?
>
> Now suppose X is actually A, then A must answer. It is A's object in the game to . . . cause C to make the wrong identification. His answer might therefore be:
>
> "My hair is shingled, and the longest strands are about nine inches long."

---

[6]See Hofstadter's *Metamagical Themas: Questions for the Essence of Mind and Pattern* (1985) for an engaging account of Turing's life and a discussion of other AI topics.

In order that tones of voice may not help the interrogator the answers should be written, or, better still, typewritten. The ideal arrangement is to have a teleprinter communicating between the two rooms. Alternatively the question and answers can be repeated by an intermediary. The object of the game for the third player (B) is to help the interrogator. The best strategy for her is probably to give truthful answers. She can add such things as "I am the woman, don't listen to him!" to her answers, but it will avail nothing as the man can make similar remarks.

We now ask the question, "What will happen when a machine takes the part of A in this game?" Will the interrogator decide wrongly as often when the game is played like this as he does when the game is played between a man and a woman? These questions replace our original, "Can machines think?" (p. 434)

It is obvious that the value of certain questions put to X and Y depends on whatever fashion is current. For example, hair length and style as a basis of discrimination would be likely to lead to a high error rate in the 1970s. Nevertheless, the important point of Turing's puzzle for AI and language scientists is that, in order for a computer to fool us into thinking that it is a human, it must be able to understand and generate a response that effectively mimics one important form of cognition.

The question of indistinguishability of functions in another arena works differently. For example, suppose two surgeons work at a hospital. One surgeon is a graduate of a renowned medical school and is reputed to be one of the best surgeons in the world. The other graduated from an undistinguished medical school and is regarded as a poor surgeon. One day an emergency operation is required, and the first physician is indisposed, so the second physician performs the operation unbeknownst to the patient, who is unconscious. The patient is not told which physician performed the operation and is satisfied that the procedure was successful. Furthermore, other physicians are convinced that the operation was performed by the first surgeon. In this limited example, we could conclude the test of indistinguishability had been passed. However, if you were the patient and learned that the operation had actually been performed by a robot, what would you conclude about the functional properties of the robot vis-à-vis the functional properties of a surgeon? Would you agree that they were the same? Why? Why not? Answers to these questions are hard to come by, but people who have strong opinions about the issues are not. One is Searle, who has turned the Turing test inside out.

The Chinese Room

To illustrate the untenable position of the "strong" AI view, Searle offers the following puzzle: Suppose someone is confined to a room with a large collection of Chinese writings. The person knows no Chinese and may not be able to discriminate between Chinese calligraphs and other scripts. From outside the room the person is given another set of Chinese characters along with a set of rules for collating the first set of characters with the second. The rules will only let the person relate one set of symbols with another set of symbols and are in plain English. With the relational rules, the person in the Chinese room is able to give meaningful answers to questions about the content of the writings, even though the person is essentially ignorant of the language. After a while the person is so well practiced that questions can be answered both in English (the person's native language) and in Chinese (which the person does not know but is able to give responses in that language based on rules). The output is so good that it is "absolutely indistinguishable from that of native Chinese speakers" (Searle, 1980). The person in the Chinese room is a simple instantiation of a computer program: data in—data out. Up to this point few AI "grunts" would have their feathers ruffled, but then Searle takes the argument one step further. Being able to perform functions, such as translation by complex rules, does not mean that the thing performing the functions understands the meaning of the output. Human minds have *intentionality* (see Searle, 1983), which, according to the author, is defined as "the property of mental states and events by which the mind is directed at objects and states of affairs in the world." These mental states include beliefs, fears, desires, and intentions. No matter how indistinguishable counterfeit thinking is from real human thinking, the two are not the same because of the intentions of the human thinker and because of the physical differences of the thinkers. One is produced organically; the other, electronically.

The Chinese Room—Refutation

Computer scientists objected immediately to Searle's conundrum (see Boden, 1989). First, on the level of semantics; it was argued that the terms *intentionality, understanding,* and *thinking* are used without clear operational referents. The second objection focused on the level of the example. If the person in the Chinese room performed the functions described, the person (or the system) would indeed achieve at least some level of understanding. Third, the argument was dismissed on the basis of a reductio ad absurdum; that is, if carried to its logical conclusion, it would be possible to create a robot identical in every detail to a thinking person, and yet one would be capable of understanding and intentionality and the other not. Finally, for some AI scientists *understanding* and *intentionality* seemed to be related to specific material properties that caused them. Pylyshyn (1980) satirically muses that perhaps intentionality is a substance secreted by the human brain, and then poses his own riddle:

> If more and more of the cells in your brain were to be replaced by integrated circuit chips, programmed in such a way as to keep the input-output function of each unit identical to that of the unit being replaced, you would in all likelihood just keep right on speaking exactly as you are doing now except that you would eventually stop meaning anything by it. What we outside observers might take to be words would become for you just certain noises that circuits caused you to make (p. 442).

The debate is far from over, and its value to some may be in its philosophic profundity. To me, however, the argument is not likely to be resolved (indeed, it is probably irresolvable!). In addition, both camps have hardened their positions and seem to be advancing articles of faith rather than reason. The importance of discussing the debate in a book like this is twofold. First, it causes the reader to think deeply about the issue of what is human about human cognition. Second, it raises the question of the limits to which AI can imitate human intelligence. The fact that both the Turing test and the Chinese-room problem have excited passions on both sides is a reflection of the intense concern of contemporary philosophers and AI scientists regarding the electronic genie that has been let out of the bottle recently.

In the next section some specific computer capacities are reviewed. The development of these specific functions approximates the flow of information in an information-processing model from perception, to pattern recognition, and to higher forms of cognition.

PERCEPTION AND AI

Consider the enormous human capacity to perceive the world. As I look around my office and out the window, several hundred objects dart by my eyes—the books on a shelf, a telephone, a couple of chairs, a filing cabinet, a sculpture of an owl, an assortment of photographs, a small samovar, a stack of papers, a pseudogothic structure, an anemometer atop a nearby building, snow-capped mountains inviting the author to give up book writing for a day and go skiing—each of which I can immediately recognize and classify. Similarly spectacular is the human capacity to hear, feel, smell, and taste a myriad of things. This perceptual stage in the processing of information, which children easily do and we take for granted, is a staggeringly complex problem for a computer.

Naomi Weisstein (1973) described the difficulty that a hypothetical computer would have in performing the single, elementary perceptual task of finding a clock, reading the time, and telling us what it is. For a human the task is child's play, but for the computer the task is enormously complex.

> Suppose the computer has a $10^4 \times 10^4$ array of photocells as a retina. It is immediately evident that if we gave the computer a list of states which would correspond to a clock, there would be an indefinite list through which the computer would have to search. As the computer got closer to a clock, the size of the clock would change; hence each step towards these problems could be solved, clocks can be *any* size or shape: modern "sunbursts," digital clocks, red streaks running around a hexagonal block, and so forth. An enumeration of all possible shapes and sizes, or even of all possible standard shapes and sizes, just is not possible. Yet most humans can perform this kind of recognition task most of the time within, say, 15 minutes, with no trouble at all.

What are the perceptual capabilities that humans use to solve this simple task that is so challenging to a computer? Your common sense would tell you that we humans would act intelligently by using our knowledge of the environment to direct our search for a clock. We would probably organize our search in some hierarchical fashion, first examining those places we have seen clocks in the past and, failing to find a clock in those locations, searching more obscure places. Clocks are normally found on walls, not under tables, and our world knowledge directs the search.

In addition to a search strategy, we have a system for describing the properties of a clock in terms of visual pattern (see Chapter 4). Our computer would need the knowledge we have about the properties of a clock—its motion, digital characteristics, and so forth. In addition, an understanding of the purpose of a clock and of the abstract nature of time is necessary to mimic human cognition. Once the pattern is recognized, the reading of the time, you might argue, is the simplest part of the task. All our computer needs to do is to scan and interpret the digital characteristics, locate those patterns in its memory, and report "2:12." A.M. or P.M.? Most humans could respond immediately, but to answer that question, additional knowledge of the world is needed—specifically, is it dark or light outside? The task is challenging, but is it possible to reduce it to several simpler tasks and then construct a robot along those lines? Perhaps so, and in the next section a few of the specific perceptual issues raised by Weisstein's task are addressed.

Human perception is initiated by external signals of light, sound, molecular composition, and pressure. These signals are detected by our sensory system and transduced (converted to neural energy) into messages the brain can understand. The amount of information available to us through our senses is enormous; our visual system alone can transmit 4.3×10^6 bits of information *per second* to the brain. Feigenbaum (1967) suggested that some peripheral device, sometimes called a peripheral memory system, operates like a sensory buffer to prevent the brain from being overwhelmed by the torrent of information flowing into it.

How might a machine be made to mimic this perceptual mechanism? A logical step is to develop some sensing capacity. One such approach can be seen in the work done on computer recognition systems.[7]

Line Analysis

One way computers can be taught to recognize geometric forms by analyzing local features of an object uses the fact that complex geometric forms are composed of simpler ones. The program uses a number of small templates that are systematically passed over each object in search of a match. An example of a template and a geometric object to be identified is shown in Figure 16.1. The template is made up of two kinds of sensors—positive and negative, present and absent—one to a cell, or subdivision, of the template. The one shown has only six cells—three minus and three plus—and, because of the arrangement of these components (all minus elements at the left), it is of a kind likely to be suitable for identifying the left edge of an object. Positioning the template with its midline over the left edge of the cube would result in a perfect match. The corner match is poor, and there is no match on the bottom edge, where plus and minus sensors cancel out each other. Although this heuristic is more solidly oriented toward what a machine can do, it is not at odds with findings from studies of animal and human perception. Earlier in this book (see Chapter 4), we learned that physiological psychologists have successfully isolated line detectors in the cortical cells of cats, and it seems likely, although it has not been completely validated, that humans also have generalized edge detectors.

[7]Much of the early research of this kind was motivated by practical problems (for example, how to create a machine that could read a numerical code on a check) and, as such, only weakly addresses the human analog issue of AI; it is included here to illustrate some of the capacities of "perception" by existing computers.

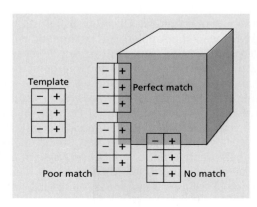

Poor match

Template

Perfect match

No match

One difficulty with the system just described is that a great number of templates are needed for simple pattern recognition (for example, a right-edge detector, a left-edge detector, and so on). An additional problem is the "goodness" of the stimulus; most geometric forms (especially those in the real world) have sharp *and* fuzzy edges, or bright *and* dull edges. Pattern recognition by line identification can be greatly simplified if the form to be recognized can first be converted into a line-only image, with templates then used to find the orientation of the lines.

Pattern Recognition

Pattern recognition systems have, for the most part, dealt with visual material. The general format of the perceptual hardware of these systems has been a raster, or matrix, of photoelectric cells (which respond to light energy). The photoelectric cells usually have only two states—on or off (or "white" or "black"). Consider the elementary task of identifying a number. Figure 16.2 shows how digits could be "transduced" into a binary code—*O* for "off" or "black," and *1* for "on" or "white." The computer "reads" each number (that is, the photoelectric cells—one for each square of the grid superimposed on the number—"senses" the light areas, which are the ones not occupied by the number) on the basis of how close the digital code matches a template stored in the memory of the computer. It works very well if the figures are uniform, evenly positioned, and not degraded, and such devices are in wide use in industry and the U.S. Postal Service. However, when it comes to reading a hand-addressed letter to your Aunt Iola, optical scanning devices have some difficulty. It does appear, though, that means are rapidly being developed to "read" even handwriting.

Attempting to identify letters and words with the use of AI not only is a practical problem but also has meaning for those scientists who are interested in the process of

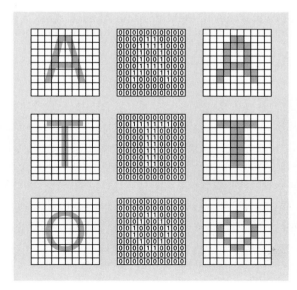

FIGURE 16.2

Representation in binary code (middle column) of letters at left. 0s indicate "off" or "black"; 1s, "on" or "white." The last column shows letters as they might appear for reading by a scanner. Adapted from Raphael (1976).

human information analysis. Much of the current knowledge of the way we humans identify a letter and word is discussed in Chapter 12. This information is helpful in designing a computer program that mimics the process. A seminal report on this topic, which has served as a guide to subsequent research, was one from Selfridge and Neisser (1963). The general procedure for the "perception" of a letter, just described, would require a huge computer memory (to store a template of each novel form of each letter), otherwise many valid forms of letters would go undetected.

The basic logic espoused by Selfridge and Neisser a long time ago has been incorporated into recent letter and word reading machines. These computers "read" text through a series of subroutines, each of which specializes in one part of the task of reading, say, a letter. Such analysis is somewhat reminiscent of the means-end problem solver discussed in Chapters 14 and 15 on thinking. One way a letter reading program might work is illustrated in Figure 16.3. It shows the way the letter *R* is processed through a series of stages, each quite simple, until a match is made on the basis of elimination of alternatives.

The matter of letter perception has also been considered in some detail by the PDPers. A general criticism of AI programs in the area of letter identification and form perception is that there is no workable mechanism for attention. A machine "sees" a form, be it a letter or geometric configuration, as a whole pattern and, unlike a human observer, finds it difficult to focus on critical features. One way the PDP model handles this difficult problem is to posit two types of feature detectors, one called a retinocentric feature unit and the other a canonic feature unit. In the retinocentric system visual stimuli are recorded in their "raw" form, much as an impression might fall on the retina. Canonic features are those that conform to the standard way information is presented, for example, just as we expect to see the letter *A* as it is shown here. In one system Hin-

FIGURE 16.3

The letter *R* processed through a series of stages of identification. At each stage, a program recognizes particular attributes of the character, such as diagonal lines, indentations, and so on.

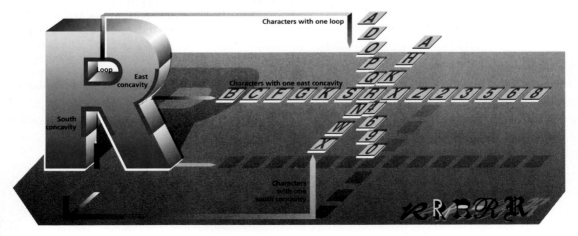

ton (1981) described a method for mapping retinocentric feature patterns onto canonical patterns. The details of this idea are too extensive to be presented here except to note that this important issue is under active investigation by those interested in PDP models. Interested students are directed to the original sources.

Older, and much more simpleminded, AI alphanumeric recognition systems were based on a template concept. A pattern of letters and numbers was stored in a computer's memory. When the computer "sees" a digit or letter, it "reads" it by matching the pattern, say *A*, with the mold of *A*. If a match is found, the letter is correctly identified. Even the sequential and parallel search methods described earlier were clearly brainless. The newer, neurally based computer models are actually capable of "learning" patterns. Some of these computer implementations can learn patterns, store them, and recognize them later. One program, called DYSTAL (*DY*namically *ST*able *A*ssociative *L*earning) successfully acquires alphabetic letters and letter sequences and, perhaps most remarkably, recognizes them even when only parts of the patterns are presented (see Figure 16.4).

DYSTAL does this, according to Alkon, much as we recognize a famous face suggested by the few lines of a cartoon. The system "learned" the pattern in the sense that there was no prewired connection between the input and output. A connection was developed, however, through greater weights being assigned to units (sites) that participate in the recognition process.

Another innovative feature of the system is that it is able to accommodate a large number of elements without requiring a huge amount of computer power. In many other network systems, each unit is connected with every other unit, so when the number of units is increased, the number of interactions increases exponentially. Thus, a system that has even a hundred units would require considerable processing time, and a network of that dimension would scarcely resemble a brain. "In DYSTAL, however, the weights of the connections are not compared with a fixed value: rather they arrive at a dynamic equilibrium in which the increases and decreases of weight over a set of pattern presentations are equal and no net weight change takes place" (Alkon, 1989). The system is comparable to human long-term memory in that when permanent memories are formed they are, for the most part, irreversible. Once these stable patterns are acquired, they require less computer power than do other, nonbiological networks.

The recognition of more complex forms follows the same logic as the recognition of simple forms, but it generally requires more complex processors. That topic is considered next.

Recognition of Complex Forms

Let's consider one example of a different kind of pattern recognition: the identification of a triangle. Figure 16.5 shows several triangles, all of which you will immediately recognize and categorize as such. If the prototype of triangularity stored in a computer program corresponded to the "good" triangle template (a), then triangles in b and c, if properly rotated and adjusted for size, could be easily recognized. Triangles in d and e, however, are problematic, especially those in e, which are identifiable mainly as the result of a "good gestalt," rather than on the basis of their being composed of three straight lines.

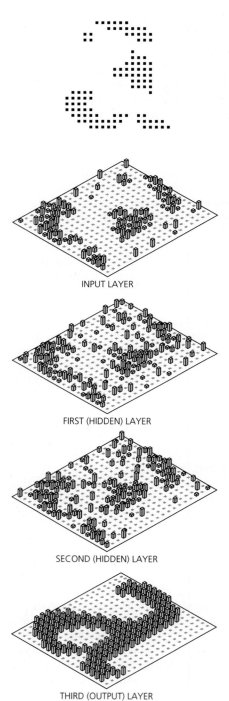

INPUT LAYER

FIRST (HIDDEN) LAYER

SECOND (HIDDEN) LAYER

THIRD (OUTPUT) LAYER

FIGURE 16.4

Pattern recognition by Alkon's artificial network operates according to many of the same rules demonstrated by biological systems. When a network is trained to recognize a pattern, such as the lowercase *a* shown here on top, the receiving sites participating in the recognition are given more "weight" than those that are not participating—that is, their excitability is enhanced. Here synaptic weight is represented by the elevation of the elements in the layers. Enhancement helps to link together the neurons involved in a recollection when only a piece of a pattern is presented. (Thomas P. Vogl of the Environmental Research Institute of Michigan helped to design this drawing.) From Alkon (1989).

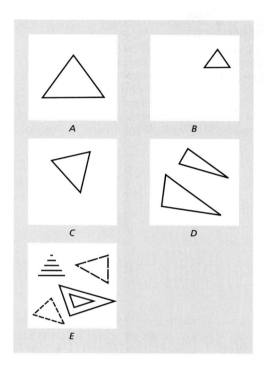

FIGURE 16.5

"Good" (a-d) and problematic (e) triangles. The former differ only in size, orientation, and relationship of their sides; the latter have no conventional straight-line sides but remain recognizable as triangles.

Our capacity to recognize immediately each of these forms as triangles is a function of our vast experience with other triangular objects; this abstract notion *triangularity* is broad enough to allow us to include these triangles we have never seen in the category of triangles. Can a computer learn that concept? Probably, but the search mechanism needs to be more sophisticated than the single match operation such as that of machines that read numbers on bank checks. Instead, a search program that included the features of a triangle would have to be considered. Thus such features, or attributes, as angles, lines, shape, number of objects, and so on would have to be stored in the computer's memory, much as our own memory contains a catalog of these attributes of a triangle.

A practical application of computer recognition of complex forms is in the area of facial recognition. Suppose your face has unique features, much as your fingerprints do. A computer system that could scan your face and find a perfect match with your identity might be a great aid to police departments. It also might be useful for check identification and even plant and office security. Imagine going to work in some security installation and being greeted every morning by a computer that asks, "Please place your face where I can see it" and, after scanning it and opening the door says, "Have a nice day, Ms. Juel, you have a call from W. M. Beach . . . and, by the way, happy birthday." While this threatens yet another intrusion into our private lives, it is likely that we will be living with such devices sooner than later.

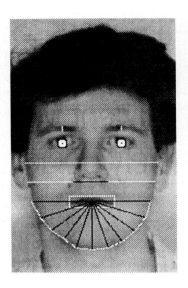

FIGURE 16.6

Face matching. To match this face with a face in the computer's memory, sixteen key features such as eye, nose, and chin measurements are gathered and used in a formula for resemblance. The formula is based on a measurement of Euclidean distance in a sixteen-dimensional space. This work is being done at MIT by R. Brunelli and T. Poggio.

The matter of facial identification has been undertaken by computer scientists such as Thomas Poggio and Roberto Brunelli at MIT. The gist of the program is that salient features, such as the width of the nose, the distance between the eyes and chin, and so on, are extracted from faces and analyzed mathmatically. Sixteen features have been identified (see Figure 16.6).

If faces were always the same, a simple template matching model might suffice; however, our faces are never the same. Therefore, the program must find a close match between your face today and your face of last week and yet not be too lenient to allow in an impersonator. The program does this through geometric checks between angles of features and promises to be much more reliable than facial identification by humans. Such a device could help solve some of the photographic mysteries that crop up from time to time, such as the recent question posed by the discovery of a very early photograph of someone who may or may not be Abraham Lincoln.

This early nineteenth-century photograph of a young man looks like Lincoln, but is it? Computer analysis of facial features may answer the question.

Could this be Abraham Lincoln?

Systems that perform like human experts are called expert systems. Basically, an expert system is an artificial specialist that solves problems in the area of its specialty. Expert systems have been designed to solve problems in medicine, law, aerodynamics, chess, and a myriad of routine chores that generally bore humans or, in some cases, may be too difficult for humans to solve (see the just discussed topic of facial identification). These systems follow rules well. They can "think" about one issue only. An expert system in medicine may not know a tort from a hole in the ground, but it can make a reasonably accurate diagnosis of a thirteen-year-old girl who has a high fever, abdominal pain, and an abnormal concentration of white corpuscles. One such program, wryly called Puff, is an expert system designed to diagnose lung disorders, such as lung cancer, and boasts a hit rate of about 89 percent—close to the hit rate of experienced physicians. These systems have been especially popular with industry, with the military, and in space exploration. They are pretty good at the job they are designed to do. Furthermore, they do not go on strike and demand more money, don't mind getting blown to smithereens, do not require life-support, and are expendable.

Skilled Visual Perception by Machines: Expert Systems

Up to this point, if humans had the ability to see only the things machines have been programmed to see, we would be in a sorry state of affairs. The basic problem is that the "intellect" of computers is, to put it politely, limited. Humans "see" as much with their brains as they do with their eyes; that message is a principal theme of this book. Skill in perceiving is based on frequent experiences with objects and events. A skilled interior designer, for example, may be able to "see" subtle nuances in colors, textures, or shapes to which the nonspecialist is blind. The same principle seems to hold for other sensory modalities (for example, professional wine tasters, music critics, perfume testers, and furriers). Can a machine be taught to perform the same, or even similar functions?

One very practical function humans carry out is the inspection of manufactured goods for defects. Countless hours are spent by our fellow workers inspecting labels on beer bottles to see whether they are stuck on properly or examining light bulbs, shoes, or printed circuits for defects. Humans aren't particularly good at these tasks, not because the tasks are beyond their intellect, but because they get bored easily and make mistakes. Boredom is not a feature of AI systems; they run endlessly without complaint. Skilled human perception of a repetitive act may be something a computer could do well.

Many successful programs have been developed in the direction of using computers to "see" faults and make simple decisions about the quality of a product. One program carried out by Thibadeau (1985) at the Robotics Institute affiliated with Carnegie Mellon University is representative of current AI work in this field. The problem is not one of "visual" detection (it is possible to use optics far more sensitive than the human eye) but is in the interpretation of the things detected as being either acceptable or unacceptable.

In one project Thibadeau was interested in building an automatic inspection device that would be able to make intelligent decisions about the quality of printed circuits, as shown in Figure 16.7a. A greatly enlarged view of several types of defects in similar circuits can also be seen in Figure 16.7b–d. In panel b a "break" in the circuit can be seen, in panel c a "short" is shown, and in panel d a "mousebit" is displayed.

Some common types of defects in printed wiring. Reprinted from the 1984 *Annual Research Review* **with permission from The Robotics Institute, Carnegie Mellon University, Pittsburgh, PA. Copyright © 1984.**

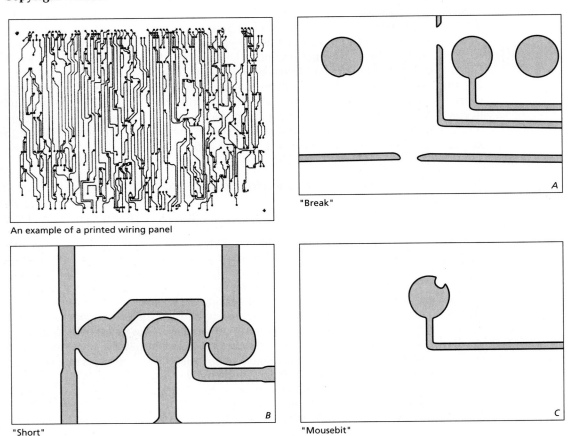

An example of a printed wiring panel

"Break"

"Short"

"Mousebit"

Human inspection of these flaws is time consuming, costly, and imperfect, while machines are, in this domain at least, faster, cheaper, and more accurate. They are not, as yet, perfect, and that is the issue Thibadeau has addressed. The first stage in developing a better AI device was to develop a corpus of flaws as determined by standards set by human engineers. A catalog of these errors included hundreds of images similar to those in Figure 16.7. The next stage was to find out what human engineers talk about regarding what they "see" when they look at a printed circuit. In effect the researcher was interested in developing a methodology in which engineers were asked to describe images by evaluating them with respect to a frame of reference.

One frame of reference was established by asking the engineers to tell about what caused the defect and to rate their confidence in their subjective evaluation on a 1 to 10 scale. Then the subjects were asked to state what properties of the image led to their conclusion and whether the image seemed sufficient for the conclusion. Finally, a type of taxonomy was formed by having the engineers sort images of defective wirings into categories. Data from these observations, which reflect a point of view (that is, what caused the problem), are then used as part of the knowledge base of a computer to make more intelligent decisions. Perfect evaluation of visual patterns may require multiple frames of reference.

Research of this type is important in AI. It incorporates some of the ways humans go about making decisions about visual stimuli with the superior scanning power and computing speed of optical scanning devices and computers to make an instrument capable of "seeing" and making decisions. Whether or not a computer will be able to "see" with its "brain" must await further developments, but at least some of the features of a "brain" can be incorporated into intelligent machines.

The perceptual side of AI has grown from the matching of shapes with templates to learning structural features and the relationships between features. These later steps do not solve Weisstein's problem, but they seem to be going in the right direction.

Our capacity to see and recognize the endless signs of the world still remains a unique human talent, but the capacity of a computer to "see" and recognize a limited but increasing number of rather complex sights is rapidly emerging. At the most austere level, a computer's encoding procedure converts differences in brightness to a binary code. These codes are made meaningful by combining them in a way that is consistent with a general knowledge of visual stimuli. To develop a machine that can store past information about the world and use that memory to abstract meaning from its percepts is an ambitious task for both the AI scientist and the cognitive scientist. The great portion of the remaining section of this chapter is devoted to a description of that enterprise.

LANGUAGE AND AI

Psychologists generally consider language a prime manifestation of underlying cognitive processes. Language, more than any other category of human response variables, reflects thought, perception, memory, problem solving, intelligence, and learning. Furthermore, because of its importance to basic psychological principles, it is of major interest to AI scientists.

The capacity for language and involved problem solving of Arthur C. Clark's fictional computer Hal was envisioned by the author to take a very complete form, as in this exchange between Dave (the human) and Hal:

> "I want to do this myself, Hal," he said. "Please give me control."
> "Look, Dave, you've got a lot of things to do. I suggest you leave this to me."
> "Hal, switch to manual hibernation control."
> "I can tell from your voice harmonics, Dave, that you're badly upset. Why don't you take a stress pill and get some rest?"
> "Hal, *I* am in command of this ship. I order you to release the manual hibernation control."
> "I'm sorry, Dave, but in accordance with special sub-routine C1435-dash-4, quote, When the crew are dead or incapacitated, the onboard computer must assume control, unquote. I must, therefore, overrule your authority, since you are not in any condition to exercise it intelligently."

An Early Automatic Writing Machine

Shown here is an illustration of Jonathan Swift's "thinking machine" from *Gulliver's Travels*. Swift suggested acerbically that books and other literature could be written by turning the appropriate handles. Some "modern writing programs" have produced a form of science fiction that passes as fair literature. See *Omni* magazine for examples.

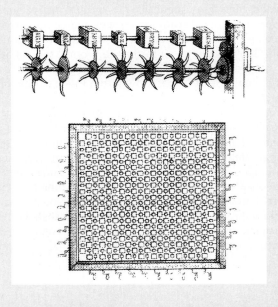

How close have we come to this fiction in the AI laboratory? Consider the following samples of actual computer "conversation."

ELIZA

One of the first conversational computer programs, ELIZA,[8] was written by Joseph Weizenbaum (1966). Several revisions of ELIZA have appeared since its original conception. In one specific program, called DOCTOR, ELIZA takes a role similar to that of a psychiatrist. In the following example, ELIZA's part is in capital letters:

Men are all alike.
IN WHAT WAY
They're always bugging us about something or other.
CAN YOU THINK OF A SPECIFIC EXAMPLE

---

[8]The pupil is Shaw's *Pygmalion* and its musical version, *My Fair Lady*.

Well, my boyfriend made me come here.
YOUR BOYFRIEND MADE YOU COME HERE
He says I'm depressed much of the time.
I AM SORRY TO HEAR YOU ARE DEPRESSED
It's true, I am unhappy.
DO YOU THINK COMING HERE WILL HELP YOU NOT TO BE UNHAPPY
I need some help, that much seems certain.
WHAT WOULD IT MEAN TO YOU IF YOU GOT SOME HELP
TELL ME MORE ABOUT YOUR FAMILY
My mother takes care of me.
WHO ELSE IN YOUR FAMILY TAKES CARE OF YOU
My father.
YOUR FATHER
You are like my father in some ways.
WHAT RESEMBLANCE DO YOU SEE
You are not very aggressive, but I think you don't want me to notice that.
WHAT MAKES YOU THINK I AM NOT AGGRESSIVE
You don't argue with me.
WHY DO YOU THINK I DON'T ARGUE WITH YOU
You are afraid of me.
DOES IT PLEASE YOU TO BELIEVE I AM AFRAID OF YOU
My father is afraid of everybody.
WHAT ELSE COMES TO MIND WHEN YOU THINK OF YOUR FATHER
Bullies
DOES THAT HAVE ANYTHING TO DO WITH THE FACT THAT YOUR BOYFRIEND MADE YOU COME HERE

That conversation, one might argue, could easily have come from an interview between a human psychiatrist and patient. However, let us examine the transcript critically. The computer's responses tend to be stereotyped. For example, it is programmed to respond to certain key words with a response that is only a transformation of the original sentence. Thus when the "patient" says the keywords "I am," ELIZA responds with a locution such as "I am sorry to hear you are. . . . " If no key words are found, the computer responds with a content-free remark, or in some instances, an earlier transformation. The human capacity for knowledge about feelings, tendencies, group dynamics, and so on figures into what, for lack of a better word, we call understanding. ELIZA lacks it. Nevertheless, some people have found the program useful in training students interested in clinical psychology. Suler (1989) has had students evaluate ELIZA's statements with the aim of better understanding the psychotherapeutic dialogue.

PARRY

What kind of conversation might result if the roles were reversed–that is, if a psychiatrist talked to a computerized simulation of a patient? Colby and his colleagues (1972) simulated such a patient, calling the program PARRY, since it simulated a paranoid patient. They selected a paranoid subject because some theoretical notion about the system and process of paranoia existed, the differences between psychotic responses and normal responses were great, and they could use expert judges to validate the distinguishability of computer simulation responses and human responses. Colby and his fellow researchers subjected the computer to a Turing test, asking a group of psychiatrists to interview PARRY by means of teletyped messages. The judges (psychiatrists) were asked to estimate the degree of paranoia of the total responses. Two dialogues (Interview A and Interview B) follow—one between PARRY and a judge, and one between the real patient and a judge.[9]

Interview A

Dr. IS THERE ANYTHING ABOUT PEOPLE IN
PARTICULAR?

Pt. CERTAIN PERSONS

Dr. WHO ARE THE CERTAIN PERSONS AND WHAT IS
IT THEY DO?

Pt. DO YOU KNOW HOW THE UNDERWORLD
OPERATES?

Dr. HOW DO YOU MEAN?

Pt. SHOULDN'T I BE?

Dr. WHY DID YOU ASK ABOUT THE UNDERWORLD?

Pt. WHAT INFORMATION DO YOU HAVE ON THE
UNDERWORLD?

Dr. I DON'T KNOW ABOUT THE UNDERWORLD BUT
WHEN YOU MENTIONED THE UNDERWORLD I
THOUGHT YOU MUST HAVE HAD SOME CONTACT
WITH IT AND THAT'S WHAT I WOULD LIKE TO
KNOW MORE ABOUT.

Pt. TRY TO AVOID THE UNDERWORLD.

Interview B

Dr. I UNDERSTAND YOU MIGHT BE AFRAID. CAN
YOU TELL ME A BIT ABOUT HOW YOU ARE
DEPRESSED?

Pt. THEY'VE SENT ALL THESE HELL'S ANGELS UP
HERE AND THEY HAVE BEEN ON MY BACK FOR
THE PAST SIX MONTHS.

Dr. WHAT DO YOU MEAN THEY SENT THE HELL'S
ANGELS UP HERE?

Pt. FROM DIFFERENT SECTORS OF MOTORCYCLE
GANGS. A LOT OF THEM ARE SERVICE
CONNECTED.

Dr. YOU MEAN YOU FEEL IN DANGER EVEN HERE IN
THE HOSPITAL?

Pt. YES.

Dr. THAT MUST REALLY BE AWFUL. HERE YOU COME
TO THE HOSPITAL FOR HELP AND YOU ARE STILL
FRIGHTENED.

Pt. I CAN'T EVEN TRUST MY DOCTOR ANYMORE.

Dr. WHAT WOULD BE OF HELP TO YOU NOW?

Comments by Judge

An interesting clue. We'll have to find out what he thinks about these people.

Bringing up the underworld suggests a delusional system. We don't know whether he is being worked against or whether the underworld is on his side.

This question didn't work too well.

This is a kind of evasiveness about my evasiveness. Common with paranoia in my experience. Pretty characteristic.

This definitely feels paranoid. It has that feeling I associate with twisting. Avoiding answering directly or going into detail. Being suspicious of my questioning. I'm already involved in the patient's delusional system.

Comments by Judge

Would be important to know, is this really true or an exaggeration or a delusion? Seems preoccupied with the threat to his life and unwilling to talk about anything else but the threat the Hell's Angels pose.

Vagueness a bit alarming.

If it's true what has gone on before, it must be a frightening situation for the patient.

Some heightening of feeling this man is paranoid. Genuinely frightened and can count on no one for help.

[9]Can you tell which is the real patient?   Answer: The computer was the "patient" in Interview A.

The results indicated indistinguishability between the model and the patient in a very specialized setting. Of course, it may be correctly argued that the conditions of the experiment were contrived, that actual diagnosis of paranoia involves extensive face-to-face interviews, and that, had the judges known the real nature of the task, their interviews would have been different. Although Colby and his colleagues successfully programmed a computer to respond in a way that a paranoid patient might and that program passed a form of the Turing test, it is vary far from a complete model of language production and understanding.

SHRDLU

Terry Winograd's SHRDLU broke new ground in the early days of AI research because he developed a workable dialogue program in which reasonable interaction between a human and machine was possible (such as determining the relationship among toy blocks). However, SHRDLU was imperfect. Recently, Winograd(1981, 1985) incorporated basic speech acts into his conceptualization. Speech acts are those verbal utterances that commonly occur in a social context. Incorporating the domain of human action interaction as represented by speech acts opened a new vista in the domain of AI. For example, suppose you were asked to go to a concert that is scheduled for a local auditorium. You reply, "Yes, I would be glad to go." Your response is a promise to attend, but, tacitly, a contract made under mutually agreed terms. If the concert is moved, say, to Vladivostok, you may have some difficulty in fulfilling your promise, and would argue that even though the terms of the contract were unspecified, they were taken for granted. Technically, one could accuse you of breaking your word,. We humans do it all the time. However, machines are nauseatingly honest (unbending in rule executions) and finding a program that could mimic the nonliteral speech acts of humans is a very difficult intellectual adventure.

Consider the following dialogue (from Winograd, 1981):

A: I'm thirsty.
B: There's some water in the refrigerator.
A: Where? I don't see it.
B: In the cells of eggplant.

Did B lie? Well, yes and no. Most would agree that B misled A, whose intention was to get a drink of water, but B's statements are nevertheless absolutely true. Winograd's aim, it seems, it twofold. He is interested in the technical aspects of speech acts that should be an integral part of a comprehensive system of AI. In addition, the incorporation of speech acts within computer programs is a significant shift of viewpoint. Among the new topics raised by the speech acts viewpoint are the following: it forces us to consider what we mean when we talk; it helps clarify objective and subjective dichotomies; and it places central emphasis on the potential for further articulation of context.

NETtalk

A much different type of program, based on a neural net, is called NETtalk, developed by Sejnowski then at Harvard Medical School and Rosenberg of Princeton (see Heppenheimer, 1988; Sejnowski, 1987). In this program, NETtalk reads letters and pronounces them aloud (see Figure 16.8). The neural net simulation model consists of several hundred units("neurons") and thousands of connections. NETtalk "reads aloud" by converting letters into phonemes, the elementary unit of language sounds. This system, like others we have encountered, has three layers: an input layer, in which each unit corresponds to a letter; an output layer, in which units represent the fifty-five phonemes of English; and a hidden unit layer, in which each of the units has a weighted connection to every input and output unit. NETtalk reads by considering each letter one by one, and by scanning three letters on either side for contextual information. Thus, the *e* in *net, neglect,* and *red* can be assigned different sounds. Each time NETtalk reads a word, it compares its pronunciation with the correct pronunciation provided by humans and then adjusts its weights to correct any errors.

FIGURE 16.8

NETtalk reads aloud: it translates letters into phonemes. Each letter unit sends signals through weighted connections to all the "hidden" units; if the total signal reaching a hidden unit exceeds a certain threshold, the unit fires, sending signals to the phoneme units. The output is the phoneme that receives the strongest total signal. When a "teacher" tells NETtalk that it has made a mistake—here it has just read *m* instead of *n*—it corrects the error by adjusting all the weights according to a specific learning algorithm. From Heppenheimer (1988).

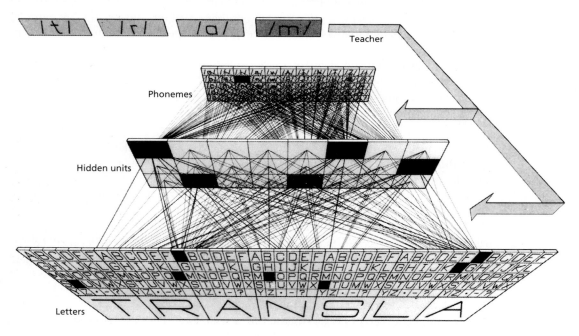

Terry Sejnowski. **His neural nets contained a hidden layer that corresponds to interneurons.**

After a few trials NETtalk makes noticeable improvement. Sejnowski reports:

We left it to run overnight. At first it gave a continuous stream of babble. It was just guessing; it had not learned to associate phonemes with the letters. As the run continued, it began to recognize consonants and vowels. Then it discovered there were spaces between the words. Now its stream of sound broke up into short bursts, separated by these spaces. At the end of the night it was reading quite understandably, correctly pronouncing some ninety-two percent of the letters (quoted in Heppenheimer, 1988, p. 74).

The practical application of these systems is obvious; what may be less obvious, but in the long run more significant, is the conceptual breakthrough such neurally inspired models present.

As Sejnowski and others recognize, context is of great importance in human and machine discourse. We will now consider another important problem, the issue of meaning and AI.

Meaning and AI

Despite the fact that some of the computer's conversations are good enough to fool some of the people some of the time, they do not fail because of a lack of memory for words, which is nearly limitless; or in their ability to produce meaningful sentences, which is extensive; or in their facility in pronouncing letters, which is acceptable. They fail in their lack of understanding of what language is all about.

In the early stages of AI, it was thought that computers would be of great assistance in language translation. Simply load the memory bank of the computer with equivalent words in two languages (for example, necklace = *halsbånd,* cloth = *klœr,* pocketbook = *lommebok,* pink = *lyserød,* and so on); feed in one language and out comes the other. However, even when a one-to-one translation is made within the context of syntactic information, the results are sometimes bizarre. In one example (probably apocryphal), the biblical passage "The spirit is willing, but the flesh is weak" was translated into Russian, then back to English; it came out: "The wine was agreeable but the meat was spoiled."

Experience with these primitive translation programs and developments in psycholinguistics changed our conceptualization of language. In the previous example, although the Russian and English words were equivalent and the syntax (in both languages) correct, the *meaning* of the two sentences was not the same. Our natural language operates within the constraint of a variety of rules that determine the sequence of grammatic components *and* the meaning of the total sequence. These have a complex relationship that is beginning to yield to analysis. Computer analysis of natural language processes has taken the form of designing systems that "understand" the language. Some rather sophisticated "understanding" programs based on the conceptual base of the language have been developed by Schank (1972, 1982), Schank and Hunter (1985), J. Anderson (1975, J. Anderson and Reiser (1985), Wilks (1973), and Winograd (1972, 1981, 1985). Built into these systems is the capability to analyze both the context of the discourse and the meaning of the words and, in some cases, "world knowledge" (Winograd). A syntax analyzer determines the most likely parsing and interpretation of a sentence.

The first language systems were limited in their ability to mimic human conversation because of restricted world knowledge and inferential ability. When humans converse, what is *not* said is as important as what is said, insofar as effective communication is concerned. Intelligent human performance is characterized by all types of inferences, not only in language processing but also in other activities such as visual perception. We need not see an entire partially occluded figure to infer that the whole figure exists. Even fractional and secondary cues are enough to trigger a whole series of reactions. For example, if I am walking through a forest known to contain poisonous snakes, the sound of rustling leaves is enough of a cue to make me stop dead in my tracks. Dehn and Schank (1982) have provided a good review of the attempt to deal with the inferential process in AI vis-à-vis human intelligence.

Yet another area of understanding in AI research that has received attention is the concept of "beliefs." Consider the following example from Dehn and Schank (1984):

I was out until 2:00 A.M. yesterday.
Boy, did my wife give it to me.

It is fair to conclude that most people know that what the wife gave to her husband was not affection. Never mind that the inference may be totally wrong. (For example, the husband my have been working in his laboratory and just discovered a cure for cancer that would bring fame and fortune to his family, or the husband may have come home too early!) We are talking about what most people understand from this little story and most computer programs do not. A program that would understand this story would need not only a capacious memory of idioms (how else would it understand "give it to me") but also some understanding of the comings and goings of husbands and their wives' beliefs and attitudes about such men.

Language Understanding Program

As SHRDLU and NETtalk engage world knowledge in reacting reasonably with humans, so too have other programs incorporated some forms of human understanding in their systems. Among the best known and most controversial is a language understanding program developed at Yale by Roger Schank. The direction of Schank's research was guided by several goals, which included the development of a program that would be able to understand written text, summarize the essential parts of such text, translate it into another language, and answer questions about the meaning of written material.

Schank and his colleagues soon discovered that people understand a great deal more than just the raw words of natural language expression (as did Winograd in his work with SHRDLU). Schank illustrates this issue in the following story: "John went to a restaurant. He ordered a sandwich. The waiter brought it quickly, so he left a large tip." Did John eat the sandwich? Did he pay for it?

When I tell you, "I visited Venice last summer," you can answer many questions more or less accurately: Did I spend any money? Did I travel by plane? By boat? Did I talk to anyone? Did I go to a restaurant? Did I see other people in Venice? Did they speak Italian? Did they wear clothes? Did they have fingernails? How many? For an "intelligent" machine to understand language, it would have to make reasonable inferences about language processing, much as normal humans do. The basic notion is similar to the concept of top-down processing discussed throughout this book.

Among the difficulties encountered in developing a language-processing program was the ambiguity of natural languages. Schank (1981) cites the following examples:

> I hit Fred on the nose.
> I hit Fred in the park.

To parse these sentences correctly, we need to know much more than purely syntactic and semantic rules. The reader has to know something about where a person can be located as well as other conceptual information about human behavior and general world information.

The evolved program contains many systems and subsystems of which only a few pertinent ones can be discussed here. At the heart of the program is a system of inferences, scripts, plans, goals, and themes believed to be an integral part of the way humans understand language (from Schank, 1981).

• *Inferences*. In natural language processing we normally keep track of where people or objects are, what they feel, the state they are in, and what they believe and know.

• *Scripts*. Scripts are generally accepted sequences of causal chains. In natural language, we do not spell out in detail the exact sequence of casual events but do (usually) give enough detail so another person with similar life experiences can understand the sequences of events. In the case of John, the hero of the restaurant episode mentioned earlier, speakers assume that we will infer a connection between events (in this case, tipping and eating and paying) even though no specified causal chain is presented.

• *Plans*. To understand most events, it is important to know the motivations and intentions of the people involved. This requires knowing the plans of the characters.

• *Goals*. Goals are rather specialized plans in which some purpose or end is sought. Plans may include questions about the reason a particular goal was chosen, what it may conflict with, and under what circumstances it will be abandoned. Goals are dominated by higher-order structures called themes.

• *Themes*. Theme-based inferences include finding out:

> What kinds of goals is an actor likely to pursue?
> What themes are likely to coexist with the given one?
> Are there any conflicts in themes?
> How might theme conflicts that are detected be resolved?
> Where did a given theme come from?

In the beginning, Schank and his associates were looking only for a program that would read, comprehend, and be able to answer a few questions about a simple story—something a young child could do. However, what started out as an elementary search ended up as an enormously complex maze of interrelated systems, an analysis of the functional properties of language, a theory of memory, a consideration of the structure of knowledge, and a philosophic statement about the mind. Schank and Hunter (1985) concludes an article in which he discusses AI, thinking, and self-understanding:

> Artificial intelligence is part of the grand attempt to understand thinking. We believe it is making important contributions to that endeavor, and that is the goal of our science. The programs we write are experiments, not results. Our interest is intelligence, not artifact. As we make progress, our results may prepare the way for the automated companions that could become an indispensable part of everyday life. These will not be our real results, though. The real results will be a new kind of understanding of ourselves, an understanding that is ultimately much more valuable than any program (p. 155).

The importance of this work is that it compels specification of rules of language structure that are capable of being artificially mimicked with a high degree of fidelity. If the AI system fails, then it is symptomatic of our failure to understand the properties of language.

PROBLEM SOLVING AND AI

The AI literature on problem solving is probably more voluminous than that on any other psychological process. One reason many AI scientists have been concerned with problem solving is that the term is roughly synonymous with thinking, which in its sophisticated form is a uniquely human attribute. This fact and the general capability of AI machines with regard to problem-solving procedures has led to a proliferation of techniques and theories in this area.

Calculation was one of the earliest instances of "problem solving" by machine. In 1642 Pascal (at the age of nineteen) demonstrated that some forms of mathematical problems could be solved more accurately and quickly by a mechanical calculator he invented than by humans. Problem solving in the context of modern AI means much more than mechanical calculation; it covers a wide range—finding solutions to complex puzzles, proving theorems, learning successful operations, and playing games.

Underlying much of the work in AI is an important distinction between two types of methods used to solve problems. One method is called algorithmic; the other is called heuristic. Algorithms are commonly defined as procedures that guarantee a solution to a given kind of problem; heuristics are sets of empirical rules or strategies that operate, in effect, like a rule of thumb. The difference between the methods can be illustrated by means of a chess problem. Computer chess is a game during which, at any given time, there exists a limited number of possible moves by each player. Also, each of the possible moves may be answered by the opponent in a limited number of moves. For practical purposes the number of these permutations is finite—that is, the game must end in a win (and loss) or draw. (Figure 16.9 shows a portion of the ever-branching tree of possibilities that might ensue from a chess play.) Of course, the number of possible moves for an entire game cannot be represented, for such a chart would contain about 10^{120}

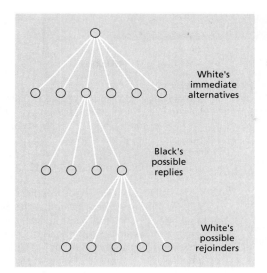

White's immediate alternatives

Black's possible replies

White's possible rejoinders

FIGURE 16.9

Portion of possibility tree for a chess game.

different pathways. To understand the enormousness of the number of possible moves in a chess game, consider the space needed to represent the permutations. If all the pathways were coded in the tiniest microdots, they would fill every library in the world many times over! Nevertheless, an algorithmic search that examines all alternatives would inevitably lead to a series of plays that would win (and lose) or draw. Humans (and even the most sophisticated computers imaginable) find this technique impossible. Instead we humans and computers use heuristic search methods, in which strategy play becomes important—for example, attack opponent's queen, control the center of the board, pin opponent's major pieces, exchange pieces on the basis of piece advantage or positional advantage, and so on.

Computer Chess

We have described how an optimal scanner working with a computer could make sense out of a simple pattern by means of template matching. Our discussion of pattern analysis revealed that patterns are complex and that a model of human pattern recognition based on single template matching fails to account for the diversity, complexity, and economy of the human ability to recognize patterns within a brief exposure.

Surely if there were a template for each of the diverse patterns encountered in daily living, it would overwhelm the storage capacity of even the largest computer. Let us look at template matching with a moderately simple pattern (somewhere between recognizing your grandmother and reading out the cost of a pound of butter from a code imprinted on the package). Chess has such a pattern. It uses a simple 8 × 8 grid of alternately differentiated squares; the moves are clearly defined (for example, the rook may move as many spaces along a vertical or horizontal pathway as desired, provided

Deep Thought—"Grandmaster" Larry Evans

Machines are making great strides and boosting the popularity of chess. However, many players decline to face them in tournaments—to the dismay of computer firms who often beef up prizes.

Dr. Nathan Divinsky opined:

As soon as machines completely solve the mystery of chess, the game will vanish. It will become another mathematical theorem locked away in a cold book. In fact, few will look at the body as it is buried. Few will know the details of the inhuman calculation. They will only know that a good and warm friend has perished.

But what will replace it? Chess has survived more than 1,500 years for the simple reason that it's fun to play and is a creative outlet. "I gave up hunting because it's too destructive. Since some of us need a hobby where aggressiveness is given an opportunity for expression, I find myself returning more and more to the most ancient of games," noted psychiatrist Karl Menninger.

Machines can solve problems faster than we can, and someday might even beat the world champion. So what? Fish are more agile and cars are more swift, but this hasn't stopped either swimming or track meets.

Deep Thought, programmed by a team led by Feng-Hsiung Hsu at Carnegie Mellon University in Pittsburgh, made a splash when it upset grandmaster Bent Larson at the Software Toolworks Open 1988. Then it won the World Computer Championship ahead of twenty-four machines from nine nations at Edmonton, Canada.

"Deep Thought was impressive—almost frightening," said Divinsky, who watched it sweep all five games. "But it's not just brute mechanical force. It does make some decisions, and there is even talk of neuron chips that will think like a human."

no other piece is in its path, the pawn may move one space forward except . . . and so on); the moves can be predicted on the basis of a brute search; and the number of permutations, albeit enormous, is finite. Given a very, very large storage and a great deal of time, determination of the probability of *each* move leading to a win is possible. Even though computers do examine a staggering number of possible moves, a model that searches *all* moves is impossible; furthermore, it says nothing about how we humans play chess or, more importantly, how complex patterns are perceived, encoded, transformed, and translated into action.

From the experiments of Chase and de Groot, we know that chess players, even modest ones, chunk information about the situation of specific pieces and then concentrate on developing a strategy around sensitive pieces and moves. A chess-playing machine, then, if it is to play a game as humans play it, needs to be able to analyze a pattern and quickly abstract from the pieces and their positions information on the relative importance of the chunks.

How well can a computer play chess? I doubt that world champions need worry (see Deep Thought Box), but any number of computers now exist that can beat all but the best players. What can we learn by watching a machine learn to play chess? Most of all, we can learn that pattern analysis by a machine can make only rude judgments as to what features are pertinent. What the computer lacks in perspicacity, however, it makes up in its capacity for rapid and voluminous mathematical search-and match-activity. The human capacity to extract meaningful cues from an enormously complex world of sensory information, to form abstractions of those cues, to transform abstractions into higher associative structures, and to develop elaborate cognitive plans while at the same time keeping these internal operations consistent with the external reality can still only be approximated in the computer.

ROBOTS

Robots (devices capable of performing human tasks or behaving in a human manner) embody most of the geography of AI reviewed earlier—the replication of pattern recognition, memory, language processing, and problem solving (see Minsky's 1994 article "Will Robots Inherit the Earth?" for recent reflections).

Robotics grew rapidly in the 1960s with the exploration of space and the need to develop highly sophisticated mechanical devices capable of performing specific tasks. The recent Mars lander, capable of carrying out a series of complex chemical analyses, is a result of these needs. (It should be pointed out that some of these robots, purely mechanical devices, are only remotely associated with the limited definition of AI used in this chapter.)

Some of the early prototypes of space robots were developed at the AI laboratory of Stanford University, where signs in the vicinity of the laboratory warned visitors that robot vehicles may be about. One of the most intriguing robots was developed there in

Robot Evolutions

A fascination with the possibilities of humanoids performing in a fashion that mimics human behavior has pervaded folklore and fiction. Stories like "The Sorcerer's Apprentice," "Pinocchio," and *Frankenstein; tales of "golems" and centaurs; and characters like Robbie the Robot, R2D2 and C3PO (Star Wars),* and Hal (of *2001* fame) reflect this interest. With the advent of modern engineering technology and cognitive psychology, robotics has evolved from the domain of mythology and science fiction to the status of a very serious scientific endeavor. Pioneer work was done by two British scientists, Ross Ashley and W. Gray Walter. Ashley designed and built an electronic circuit that maintained a favorable homeostasis, or state of internal balance. Walter added mobility to a homeostatic type of device that would seek light below a certain brightness; avoid light above that level; and, where no light was available, move around in what may be called a search for light. These tropistic machines mimicked only the rudimentary properties of life exhibited by insects, plants, or simple animals. The robot next in line of evolution was put together at the Johns Hopkins University and became known as the Hopkins Beast. This could move about under its own power and was completely self-contained. It navigated by means of sonar, and its perceptual system consisted of a combination of photo cells, masks, lenses, and circuits all designed to detect only one thing: electrical outlet coverplates. When it "saw" one, it would try to make contact with it with its plug-shaped hand.

1968. It was a mobile, radio-controlled vehicle called Shakey, which had on-board perceptual and problem-solving capabilities. It was equipped with a television camera, a range finder, and a tactile sensor like a cat's whisker. All these relayed sensory information to a computer that held a variety of programs for analyzing the incoming signals and for planning action sequences aimed at manipulating the robot's environment. The whole was mounted in a motorized cart that could go in any direction.

The perceptual system consisted of a television camera that reduced the pictures to line images and then to significant areas or objects in the scene. The problem solver was a type of theorem-proving program that allowed Shakey to execute simple tasks.

A new robot, Flakey, replaced Shakey recently. Flakey is a three-foot-tall ambulatory device with a video camera mounted on top. When given a command to go to an office five doors down the hall, Flakey obediently wheels itself to the designated place. Some of the most advanced robots are built by NASA. These machines are somewhat specialized devices used to collect and analyze soil samples from neighboring planets, make repairs on space stations, and carry out scientific experiments and observations in environments too forbidding for humans.

The grandiose plans of the 1970s, which ambitiously started out with designing whole-functioning robots, have given way to more reasonable projects in which relatively small humanoid processes are replicated. In this arena the business community is leading the way; many laborious or dangerous functions can be done by robots.

AI AND SCIENTIFIC INQUIRY

Throughout most of this chapter we have discussed the computer vis-à-vis human cognition and the immensely complex task undertaken by those who attempt to mimic human performance with the use of machines. In this closing section I would like to propose that the way scientists—including cognitive scientists—conduct research is likely to change significantly in the next few years with the use of computers assisted by AI programs.

We have already seen the widespread adoption of computers in nearly every area of human endeavor, and that trend probably will continue. Calculations necessary for everything from space travel to garbage truck routes to genetic research would be impossible without the modern high-speed computer. In fact, more advanced systems with greater memory capacity and faster processing are sure to appear in the future. Perhaps even radical new systems (such as the Japanese Fifth Dimension, which stresses knowledge information processing) will replace our present systems. Exciting as the past developments are, the future promises even more spectacular discoveries.

One area of interest to scientists is the way information is stored and codified. Presently, an enormous amount of scientific information is available in an electronic format (for example, PsycLIT) in addition to the more conventional form of books and articles. In the near future, the electronic format will expand greatly in all fields, including psychology, so that a user can access the complete contents of an article or book. Furthermore, information from other scholarly fields and from disparate sources, hooked together in a huge network involving satellite relay stations, will be available to most of us. This worldwide database, Worldnet, is already being compiled and is likely to become part of the information highway. As early as 1969 the first "node" of a computer network called ARPANET was installed at UCLA. A few months later 4 nodes were operating; by 1973, there were 37 nodes in operation; and presently there are more than 60,000 nodes in a collective network called Research Internet. Other systems involving fax, telephone, and satellite communication systems embrace millions of nodes. Worldnet is here to stay and will continue to affect scientific and other scholarly research.

But what can a scientist do with so much data? Is there the danger of having too much data and not knowing what it all means? Data banks are indispensable to anyone who attempts to write a comprehensive book—such as one on cognitive psychology that encompasses an extended range of topics. Authors of such works can access the abstracts of a subject, say, mental imagery in children, in seconds. As convenient as such databases are, they also present a problem in that the capacity of humans to store and process information is limited. We are at risk of becoming overwhelmed by the plethora of information. If such is the case, it is likely that some type of program that processes information in a knowledgeable, intelligent way—that is, *understands* information—will emerge. (AI will live up to the promise of its name.) If such an AI program appears, it may tell us what research has been done, so we can avoid redundant studies, and it also may tell us what needs to be done, so we can put our valuable time to good use. Furthermore, a superunderstanding computer may not only identify the holes in human knowledge but also fill them in by conducting "research" or making logical inferences from its colossal database (see Solso, 1986, 1987b, 1994). Conceivably, the resulting explosion of knowledge may answer the ancient questions of who we are, where we come from, and what is our future. May we all live so long as to know some of these answers, but not long enough to know all. It is better to travel than to arrive.

Summary

1   Artificial intelligence concerns any computer-produced output that would be judged intelligent if produced by a human.

2   One dichotomy (Searle) distinguishes between "strong" AI, which asserts that proper programming can create a "mind" capable of understanding, and "weak" AI, which emphasizes its value as a heuristic in studying human cognition.

3   Philosophical issues associated with AI concern intent, thought, and understanding. Exercises designed to demonstrate machine-human indistinguishability and functional equivalence (for example, the Turing test and the Chinese room) are considered by some as failing to consider important factors such as intentionality, which humans possess but machines do not.

4   Information processing by machines, as an analog of human cognition, has increased capacity in recognizing complex stimuli from the early models (which used template matching) to more recent approaches (which combine analysis of structural features and their relationships).

5   Computer programs capable of "understanding" natural language require, as a minimum, semantic and syntactic rules, world and social context knowledge bases, and some method of handling the ambiguity present in common language usage.

6 Artificial intelligence problem-solving programs (for example, computer chess) use two principal strategies: algorithmic procedures (which guarantee a solution by examining all possible alternatives) and heuristic procedures (which are strategy-based and decompose complex problems into easily solved subproblems).

Key Words

artificial intelligence	NETtalk
Chinese room	parallel processing model
DYSTAL	PARRY
ELIZA	robots
expert systems	sequential processing model
Hebb's rule	Scripts
Johniacs	SHRDLU
intentionality	themes
McCulloch-Pitts neurons	Turing test

Recommended Readings

Resources on the topic of AI are abundant. General reviews are offered in Tauke, *Computers and Common Sense* (available in paperback); and Apter, *The Computer Simulation of Behavior*. A well-written and technically interesting account by a research scientist is Raphael, *The Thinking Computer*. Also recommended is Pylyshyn's *Computation and Cognition: Toward a Foundation for Cognitive Science; The Computer and the Mind*, by Johnson-Laird; *Memory Traces in the Brain*, by Alkon; *Artificial Intelligence: The Very Idea*, by Haugeland; and *Artificial Intelligence in Psychology: Interdisciplinary Essays*, by Boden.

The April 1985 issue of *Byte* magazine is largely devoted to AI and has engaging articles by Minsky, Schank, and Hunter; J. Anderson and Reiser; Winston; and others. *Metamagical Themas: Questing for the Essence of Mind and Matter* and *Godel, Escher, Bach: An Eternal Golden Braid*, by Douglas Hofstadter, should be read by all people interested in AI and related matters; besides, they are a good read. Also, Gardner's *The Mind's New Science* is highly recommended for its discussion of AI and many other topics covered in this book. Some interesting technical problems are contained in *Artificial and Human Intelligence*, edited by Elithorn and Banerji.

GLOSSARY

Accommodation An activity involved in the adaptation of intellectual processes during which mental structures undergo reorganization so that new information that does not readily conform to previous structures can be integrated into the cognitive system (Piaget).

ACT* See Adaptive control of thought.

Active memory system A computer memory system that stores elements in an interrelated network and retrieves them with a content-addressable probe.

Adaptation One of the major processes in intellectual development, the aim of which is to handle environmental demands effectively. Adaptation involves two activities: assimilation and accommodation (Piaget).

Adaptive control of thought A comprehensive model of cognition developed by Anderson.

Ad hominem Characterized by arguments that attack a person's character rather than the substance of an argument.

Aggregate field The idea that cerebral functions are distributed throughout the brain. (See **Compartmentalization** for an opposing view.)

Alphabetic writing system A writing system that expresses the basic sounds of a language in graphemic form.

Anoetic consciousness An awareness that is temporally bound to the current situation, allowing registration of environmental cues and behavioral responding. Also called **nonknowing consciousness** anoetic consciousness corresponds to procedural memory (Tulving).

Anterograde amnesia The loss of memory after the onset of the memory disorder.

Anthropomorphism The attribution of human characteristics to inanimate or nonhuman objects.

Arousal A general drive state that maintains our capacity to perceive sensory events and exert mental effort.

Artificial intelligence Computer-produced output that would be considered intelligent if produced by a human.

Assimilation An activity involved in adaptation of intellectual processes during which new information is incorporated into cognitive structure much as nutrients are incorporated at the physiological level (Piaget).

Association First formulated by Aristotle, the principle that asserts that ideas are connected in the mind on the basis of contiguity, similarity, or contrast.

Associationism A connection between two units, such as *ham* and *eggs* or a *stimulus* and a *response*.

515

Attention   The concentration of mental effort on sensory or mental events.

Attribute-frequency model   A model proposed by prototype theory that asserts that a prototype represents the mode or most frequently experienced combination of attributes.

Autobiographical memories   Memories of an individual's past history.

Automatic processing   The activation of an element in memory that is initiated by contextual cues and proceeds with limited subject attention.

Autonoetic consciousness   The awareness of personally experienced events. Also called *self-knowing consciousness*, autonoetic consciousness corresponds to episodic memory (Tulving).

Avant-garde   In any field the advanced group whose works are characterized chiefly by unorthodox and experimental methods.

Axon   The long, tubular transmitting pathway in which signals from the cell body are passed along to other cells by means of junctures known as **synapses.**

Bottom-up processing   Borrowed from computer language, cognitive processing initiated by the components of a stimulus pattern which, when summed, lead to recognition of the whole configuration.

Brown-Peterson technique   A procedure used to study short-term memory in which an item to be remembered is followed by a distractor task that lasts for variable time intervals before recall.

Canonic perspectives   Views that "best" represent an object. Frequently, these are the images that first come to mind when we are asked to recall a form.

Cell body   Part of a neuron in which nutrients and waste products are filtered in and out through its permeable cell wall.

Central tendency model   A model proposed by prototype theory that holds that a prototype represents the mean or average of a set of exemplars.

Cerebral commissurotomy   The surgical severing of the connective tissue between the two main structures of the brain.

Cerebral cortex   The top layer of the brain, thought to be involved in "higher-order" mental functions.

Cerebral hemispheres   The two major components of the cerebral cortex. The left hemisphere is generally involved in language and symbolic processing, and the right is generally involved in nonverbal perceptual processing.

Channel capacity   An assumption regarding information processing that postulates that the capacity to handle the flow of input is determined by the limitations of the system.

Characteristic features   The incidental or superficial features of a concept (for example, *eats worms* is a characteristic feature of the concept *robin*).

Chinese room   A test used to illustrate the untenability of a strong artificial intelligence position. A subject (or computer) that possesses no knowledge of the Chinese language is given a sample of Chinese characters along with a set of rules for relating those characters to another set of symbols.

Chunking   The recoding of stimuli so that the information load per unit is increased (for example, letters into words, words into phrases, and so on).

Classification   An ability to group objects according to one or more dimensions. This involves the realization that subcategories can be combined to form a superordinate category (transformation) and again reduced to the former subcategories (reversibility) (Piaget).

Clustering model   A semantic organization model that proposes that concepts are represented in memory in an organized form with similar items stored together.

Cognitive map   The idea proposed by Tolman that what rats learn in a maze is not a series of S-R connections but a picture of internal representation of the stimulus situation.

Cognitive model   A metaphor based on observations and on inferences drawn from observations that describes the detection, storage, and use of information.

Cognitive science   The scientific discipline comprising computer science, neuroscience, and cognitive psychology.

Commissurotomy   See **Cerebral commissurotomy.**

Common fate   The Gestalt principle of organization stating that elements shifted in a similar manner from a larger group tend to be grouped together.

Compartmentalization   The idea that some functions, such as motor activities, language processing, and so on, are each associated with specific areas of the brain. (See **Aggregate** field for an opposing view.)

Concatenative thinking   The tendency to string ideas together with no consideration for organization or integration according to overriding themes or patterns (Piaget).

Concept formation   The discernment of properties common to a class of stimuli and the discovery of rules relating its properties.

Conceptually driven processing   See **Top-down processing.**

Conceptual-propositional hypothesis   A hypothesis positing that information is represented in memory in an abstract propositional format explicating objects and their relationships.

Conceptual rule   A statement of how features must be related if a stimulus is to be considered an instance of a particular concept (for example, red and square).

Conceptual science   A system that provides useful metaphorical classification schemes. Because these schemes are devised by humans for human purposes, they are fabrications of human cognition that mirror reality.

Conditional probability   The probability that new information is true given the truth of a specific hypothesis.

Connectionism   The idea that complex cognitive functions can be understood in terms of the network of links among units. See also **Parallel distributed processing (PDP) model.**

Consciousness   An awareness of events or stimuli in the environment and of cognitive phenomena such as memories, thoughts, and bodily sensations.

Conservation   The idea that certain transformations do not alter the basic properties of objects (Piaget).

Conservative focusing   A hypothesized strategy used in concept formation in which one hypothesis is formulated and reformulations of a positive instance are sequentially tested and outcomes noted.

Content addressable   Of or relating to the storage of information by which we can access the information in memory on the basis of its attributes.

Contralaterality   The processing by the brain of information derived from an opposing body site.

Controlled processing   Processing that requires the subject's attention, in which only one sequence of operations at a time can be controlled without interference.

Convergent thinking   Thinking that engages previously encoded factual information.

Corpus callosum   The massive bundle of nerves that connects the two hemispheres of the brain.

Creativity   The process involving cognitive activity that results in a new, and often impracticable way of viewing some problem or situation.

Cue-dependent forgetting   Recall failure due to a lack of congruence between encoding cues and retrieval cues.

Data-driven processing   See **Bottom-up processing.**

Decay   Forgetting due to a lack of use or rehearsal of previously available information.

Decision frame   A decision maker's framework concerning a choice alternative that includes behaviors, results, and contingencies.

Declarative knowledge (or **declarative representation**) Knowing what; knowledge about the world (for example, knowing that San Francisco is in California). (See **Procedural knowledge.**)

Deep structure   The underlying form of a sentence that holds information crucial to its meaning.

Defining features   The essential, required features of a concept (for example, wings, feathers, and red breast are defining features of the concept *robin*).

Déja vu   The sensation of being familiar with an experience when the experience is novel.

Dendrites   The highly arborized parts of neurons that gather neural impulses from other neurons.

Difference engine   A nineteenth-century calculator whose operations were programmable and whose programs contained conditional branches.

Direction   The Gestalt principle of organization asserting that elements composing a continuous, smooth movement tend to be perceived together.

Divergent thinking   Thinking that involves generating many different answers to a single problem, with the "correctness" dependent on subjective evaluation of answers as abstract and flexible.

Dual-coding hypothesis   The hypothesis that proposes two coding and storage systems (verbal and imaginal).

Dualistic memory theory   The idea that two different types of memory, short-term and long-term, can be distinguished.

Dynamic spatial reconstructor   A sophisticated version of the CAT technique that shows internal structures in three dimensions.

Echoic memory   The persistence of auditory impressions and their brief availability for further processing.

Egocentrism   The tendency to regard the world from one's own perspective (Piaget).

Eidetic imagery   Uncommonly vivid imagery, as though actually perceived. This ability is more common during childhood, and is usually lost during adolescence.

Electroconvulsive therapy (ECT)   Shock therapy. A form of somatic therapy consisting of the application of electric currents to the head, which produce convulsions and unconsciousness.

Electroencephalography (EEG)   The measurement of electrical activities of the brain.

ELINOR   A hierarchical network model of semantic organization (developed by Lindsay, Norman, and Rumelhart).

ELIZA   One of the first conversational computer programs (developed by Weizenbaum of MIT).

Encoding specificity principle   The principle holding that a retrieval cue can be effective only if it is encoded at the time of study (Tulving).

Engram   A trace or, in the present context, a collection of neural charges that represent memory.

Episodic memory   Memory that concerns information about temporally dated episodes and events along with the relationships among such events.

Expertise   The manifestation of exceptional abilities and skills.

Experts   People who exhibit unusual cognitive skills, such as being able to memorize large lists of numbers or "see" significant details in X-ray images.

Expert systems   Computer systems that perform as human experts do.

Feature   A basic component of a complex stimulus pattern. For example, the features of the letter *A* are two diagonal lines (/ \) and one horizontal line (—).

Feature analysis   The hypothesis proposing that pattern recognition occurs only after sensory stimuli have been analyzed according to their simple or basic components.

Fissures   Deep grooves on the surface of the brain.

Flashbulb memory   Memory that stores an unexpected event of short duration in vivid, photographic detail.

Focus gambling   A hypothesized strategy used in concept formation in which more than one concept feature at a time is changed, with the goal being a correct response in a shorter time span.

Forgetting   The inability to recall information that was once available.

Fovea   A small indentation in the retina that contains the highest concentration of cones and provides the greatest visual acuity.

Foveal vision   Vision that provides the greatest visual acuity and is restricted to a visual angle of about 1 to 2 degrees.

Frontal   One of the four major sections on the surface of each cerebral hemisphere, marked off by major convolutions or fissures.

Functional fixedness   The tendency to view things in terms of their familiar uses, which makes it difficult to achieve novel perspectives often necessary for problem solving.

General problem solver (GPS)   A computer model designed to simulate the entire range of human problem solving.

Graphemic-encoding hypothesis   The hypothesis proposing that word recognition depends on visual codes stored with semantic information.

Gyri (gyrus, sing.)   The ridges between the folds in the surface of the brain.

Habituation   The effect that occurs when a stimulus is presented repeatedly until the subject no longer reacts to it.

Hertz (Hz)   Cycles per second (cps).

Homunculus   A diminutive human; a midget. In psychology, a "little person" in the head.

H. sapiens sapiens   Modern man, the single surviving species of the genus *Homo* and of the primate family Hominidae, to which it belongs.

Iconic memory The momentary persistence of visual impressions and their brief availability for further processing.

Illumination A hypothetical stage in the creative process that involves sudden understanding of a problem and its solution.

Incubation A hypothetical stage in the creative process that involves temporarily setting a problem aside and diverting attention elsewhere.

Information-processing model A model proposing that information is processed through a series of stages, each of which performs unique operations. Each stage receives information from preceding stages and passes the transformed input along to other stages for further processing.

Intelligence The ability to acquire, retrieve, and use knowledge in a meaningful way; to understand concrete and abstract ideas; and to comprehend relationships among objects and ideas.

Interference theory The theory proposing that forgetting is due to activities that occur between original learning and later recall.

Internal representation A transformation of environmental cues into meaningful cognitive symbols of the perceived stimuli. Also referred to as *code*.

Isomorphism A one-to-one correspondence between a perceived object and its internal representation.

Key word method A mnemonic technique used in second-language learning. For example, an English word that sounds like some part of the foreign word is associated with the foreign word by using an imaginal interaction between the two.

Knowledge The storage and organization of information in memory.

Korsakoff's syndrome The disorder commonly brought about by severe alcoholism resulting in bilateral damage to the diencephalon.

Levels of processing A theory proposing that memory occurs as a by-product of processing activities, with memory trace durability a function of the depth of that processing.

Lexical Pertaining to the words or vocabulary of a language, especially as contrasted with its grammatical and syntactic aspects.

Linguistic-relativity hypothesis The hypothesis that proposes that perception of reality is determined by one's language history (Whorf, Sapir).

Logic The science of thinking based on laws that determine the validity of a conclusion.

Logogen A hypothetical "device" operating in recognition (for example, of a word) that acts like an adding machine summing input information, which, when a critical level is reached, creates a response class readiness (Morton).

Long-term memory A hypothetical storage system given proper cueing, is characterized by its duration, capacity, and accessibility.

Mapping A form of symbolic representation thought, which describes the cognitive relationship between the physical and conceptual world.

Mass action The idea that memories are distributed throughout the brain (Lashley).

Mediation A process that intervenes between a stimulus and a response term; it provides a link between the two and facilitates memory.

Method of loci A mnemonic technique that involves associating items to be remembered with physical locations and "revisiting" those sites during recall.

Mind-body issue The philosophic problem dealing with the relationship between the mind and the body.

Mnemonic Any technique that serves to facilitate storage and recall of information in memory.

Morpheme The smallest unit of meaning in a language (for example, a prefix or a suffix) that is combined with other such units in various ways to create words.

Myelin sheath The fatty outer covering of a neuron's axon that facilitates neural transmission in some neurons.

Nanometer (nm) The unit of measure for wavelengths. One nanometer is equal to one billionth of a meter.

Network model A semantic organization model proposing that concepts are represented in memory as independent units stored in spatial arrangements according to the degree and nature of their relationships.

Neurocognition The study of the relationships between neurosciences and cognitive psychology, especially those theories of the mind dealing with memory, sensation and perception, problem solving, language processing, motor functions, and thinking.

Neuron   A nerve cell with specialized processes that constitutes the structural and functional unit of nerve tissue. As the basic cell of the nervous system, the neuron conducts neural information.

Neuronetwork systems   See **Parallel distributed processing (PDP) model.**

Neuropsychology   See **Neurocognition.**

Neuroscience   The study of the structure and functioning of the nervous system.

Neurotransmitters   Chemicals that act on the membrane of the dendrite of a neuron to facilitate or inhibit neurotransmission.

Noetic consciousness   The awareness of objects and events and their relationship when those objects and events are physically absent. Also called *knowing consciousness,* noetic consciousness corresponds to **semantic memory** (Tulving).

Noise   Any disturbance, external (such as background stimuli) or internal (such as random neural activity), that reduces the quality of a signal.

Nonsense syllable   A nonword sequence (typically composed of three letters), first used by Ebbinghaus in memory studies.

Objective set   The Gestalt principle of organization asserting that an organization perceived in one case tends to be seen in immediately following, similar cases.

Occipital   One of the four major sections on the surface of each cerebral hemisphere, marked off by major convolutions or fissures.

Organizational schemes   A technique that organizes information into categories that are used as recall cues.

Orienting reflex   The natural tendency to attend to an unusual signal such as a loud noise or bright light. The orienting reflex is a characteristic of attention.

Output interference   The detrimental effect that the retrieval of one item has on the retrieval of subsequent items.

Paradigm   A fundamental theoretical model; a plan of research based on specific concepts; an experimental design.

Parallel distributed processing (PDP) model   A neurally inspired model of the mind in which information is processed in a massively distributed, mutually interactive, parallel system in which various activities are carried out simultaneously through excitation and/or inhibition between units.

Parallel processing model   A computer program that examines all input features at the same time.

Parietal   One of the four major sections on the surface of each cerebral hemisphere, marked off by major convolutions or fissures.

PARRY   A conversational computer program that simulated responses of a paranoid patient and was used in a test of indistinguishability between a machine and a human with psychiatrists as the expert judges.

Parsing paradox   The problem of whether pattern recognition is initiated by the component parts of a pattern (bottom-up processing) or by a hypothesis about the whole (top-down processing).

Passive memory system   One type of computer memory system that stores items in specific locations and retrieves either sequentially or randomly by a central probe.

Pattern   The complex composition of sensory stimuli that observers may recognize as being a member of a class of objects.

Pattern recognition   The ability to abstract and integrate certain elements of a stimulus into an organized scheme for memory storage and retrieval. For example, reading requires remembering the meaningful patterns formed from an otherwise meaningless array of lines and curves.

PDP   See Parallel distributed processing (PDP) model.

Peg word system   A mnemonic strategy that involves learning a set of stimulus items that serve as pegs on which the items to be remembered are hung.

Perception   The branch of psychology that deals with the detection and interpretation of sensory stimuli.

Perceptrons   The simulation of neural nets in computer architecture.

Perceptual span   The amount of information that can be perceived during a brief presentation or within a specific area.

Phoneme The basic speech sound unit of a spoken language distinguishable by how it is produced (voiced, unvoiced, fricative, or plosive). Phonemes are combined with other sound units to create words.

Phonemic-encoding hypothesis The hypothesis proposing that word recognition depends on visual input's being converted and encoded as a sound representation.

Phrenology The study of the configuration of a person's skull based on the supposition that it accurately indicates mental faculties and character traits.

Pictographic writing system The first form of graphemic communication in which common objects (such as the sun, a house, and so on) are pictorially represented.

Pragnanz The Gestalt principle of organization asserting that stimulus figures are seen in the "best" possible way given the stimulus conditions. The "best" figure is stable and cannot be made simpler or more orderly by shifts in perception.

Preconscious state Memories that can easily be called into awareness.

Preparation A hypothetical stage in the creative process that involves problem formulation and initial solution attempts.

Presynaptic terminals Terminals that are proximal to the receptive surface of neurons, which transmit information about their activity to other neurons.

Prima facie At first appearance, before investigation; immediately plain or clear.

Primary memory The immediate memory that never leaves consciousness and provides an accurate representation of events (William James).

Prior probability The probability that an event will occur given prior similar circumstances.

Proactive inhibition Reduced recall of newly learned material due to previously learned material.

Problem solving Thought directed toward discovering a solution for a specific problem that involves both response formation and response selection.

Procedural knowledge (or nondeclarative knowledge) Knowledge that is implicit and sampled through actions or performance.

Procedural memory The "lowest" form of memory in which simple associations between stimuli and responses are formed.

Process An active system of operations or functions that analyzes and transforms information.

Production memory (or procedural knowledge) The knowledge required to do things, such as tie shoelaces, do mathematics, or order food in a restaurant.

Production system The notion that underlying human cognition is a set of conditional-action pairs called *productions.*

Proposition The smallest unit of information that is meaningful (for example, John is tall).

Prototype An abstraction of stimulus patterns stored in long-term memory against which similar patterns are evaluated in terms of how closely they fit the model.

Prototype recognition A hypothesis proposing that pattern recognition occurs when a match is made between sensory stimuli and an abstracted or idealized cognitive pattern.

Proximity The Gestalt principle of organization stating that elements occurring close in time or space tend to be perceived together.

Pseudomemory The tendency for subjects to recognize a prototype falsely as a previously seen figure with greater confidence than figures that have actually been previously seen.

Radical-imagery hypothesis The hypothesis proposing that subjects convert visual and verbal stimuli to images that are then stored in memory.

Reductio ad absurdum Disproof of a principle or proposition by showing that it leads to an absurdity when followed to its logical conclusion.

Reification The assumption that an idea is real, when in fact it may be hypothetical or metaphoric.

Relational-organizer theory The theory proposing that stimuli have a hierarchy of implicit codes (including imagery) that, in paired associated learning, are aroused by the stimulus term and then associated with the response term, thereby increasing associative strength.

Representational knowledge See **Knowledge** and **Declarative knowledge.**

Response criterion The point established by the observer at which noise and signal are distinguished. When signal strength exceeds the criterion, a decision of *signal present* is commonly made; signal strength below the criterion commonly results in a *signal absent* decision.

Reticular activating formation (RAF)   A complex region in the center of the brain stem that contains many groups of neurons, which are involved in the activation or arousal of other parts of the brain. Located in the midbrain, the RAF is connected to most regions of the cortex. This formation is sometimes called the *arousal system,* since it is related to attention and orienting reflexes (the type of reaction a cat might make upon hearing a bell).

Retina   The membrane on the back of the eye that contains photoreceptor cells (rods and cones).

Retinocentric   Literally, centered on the retina; used to describe visual stimuli that are recorded in their "raw" form, much as an impression might fall on the retina.

Retroactive inhibition   Reduced recall of previously learned material due to newly learned material.

Retrograde amnesia   The inability to recall information acquired prior to the onset of a disorder.

Robots   Machines capable of performing human tasks or behaving in a human manner.

Saccade   The rapid eye movement occurring during reading and when viewing visual patterns.

Scheme   A mental representation of some action (mental or physical) that can be performed on an object and that, as the organism develops, increases in integration and coordination (Piaget).

Secondary memory   Permanent memory that is characterized by individual differences (William James).

Second-order isomorphism   The relationship between external objects and their internal representation that is lawful but not structural.

Semantic   Pertaining to or arising from the different meanings of words or other symbols.

Semantic feature-comparison model   A model of semantic organization proposing that concepts are stored in memory as sets of semantic features distinguishable as either defining or characteristic features.

Semantic memory   Memory that stores word meanings, concepts, and world knowledge.

Semantic priming   The presentation of a semantically related prime followed by its target (for example, showing the color red and following that with the target word *blood*).

Sensation   The detection of stimulation, the study of which commonly deals with the structure of sensory mechanisms (such as the eye) and the stimuli (such as, light) that affect those mechanisms.

Sequential processing model   A computer program that examines each input feature in a predetermined stepwise fashion, with the outcome of each stage determining the next step in the program.

Seriation   The ability to order elements according to some underlying principle (for example, arranging sticks according to increasing length) (Piaget).

Set   Any preparatory cognitive activity that precedes thinking and perception.

Set-theoretical model   A model of semantic organization proposing that concepts are represented in memory as information sets that include category examples and attributes.

Shadowing   An experimental procedure used in auditory attention research in which subjects are asked to repeat a spoken message as it is presented.

Short-term memory   A hypothetical storage system characterized by a duration estimated at about 12 seconds (which can be extended by rehearsal), by a capacity estimated at about 7 ± 2 items, and by accurate recall.

SHRDLU   An early computer program that enabled a robot to answer questions, execute commands, and accept information in English (Winograd).

Signal   Adapted from electronic communications, a stimulus that a subject is requested to identify.

Signal detection theory   The theory postulating that, in addition to signal strength, an observer's decision about the presence or absence of a stimulus is influenced by other factors, such as the nature of the task and the observer's knowledge of results.

Similarity   The Gestalt principle of organization stating that like elements in the same structure tend to be perceived together.

Simultaneous scanning   A hypothesized strategy used in concept formation in which people begin with all possible hypotheses and eliminate all untenable ones.

Sine wave A periodic oscillation, as in a sound wave, that represents both amplitude and frequency.

Speech acts Verbal utterances that commonly occur within a social context. Recent conversational computer programs (Winograd) have begun to incorporate routines that mimic the nonliteral aspects of natural language.

Spreading activation The memory model that posits that semantic storing and processing are based on a complex network in which simple associations (for example, blue—sky) are linked together.

Sternberg paradigm A procedure used to study retrieval in short-term memory in which a sequence of items is presented for a short duration followed by a probe digit. Subjects are asked to decide whether the probe digit was in the original series. Reaction times are the principal dependent variable.

Structure The architecture of a cognitive model, that is metaphorical, not literal, and that proposes how mental entities are organized. For example, memory may be conceptualized as consisting of short-term and long-term structures.

Subliminal Energy that is inadequate to excite neural activity.

Subliminal perception The influence of stimuli that are insufficiently intense to produce a conscious sensation but strong enough to influence some mental processes.

Successive scanning A hypothesized strategy used in concept formation in which people begin with one hypothesis, maintain that hypothesis as long as it is successful, and discard or change it when it is no longer tenable.

Sulci (**sulcus,** sing.) The grooves between the ridges on the surface of the brain.

Supraliminal Energy that is adequate to excite neural activity.

Surface structure The portion of a sentence that can be analyzed and labeled by conventional parsing schemes (Chomsky).

Syllogism A method for argument validation involving three steps: a major premise, a minor premise, and a conclusion. The conclusion is considered valid if the form is correct and the premises are true.

Synapse The juncture between two neurons.

Synesthesia The condition in which information from one sensory modality (such as, auditory) is coded in another modality (e.g., visual).

Syntax Rules that govern the combination of morphemes into larger linguistic units (such as, phrases and sentences).

Template matching The postulate asserting that pattern recognition occurs when an exact match is made between sensory stimuli and a corresponding internal mental form.

Temporal One of the four major sections on the surface of each hemisphere, marked off by major convolutions or fissures.

Thinking The general process of considering an issue in the mind, which results in the formation of a new mental representation.

Threshold The point at which the amount of energy available exceeds a certain level (threshold). When this occurs, neurons are excited and the psychological experience of sensation occurs. Sensory judgments are more complex and are based on signal strength and the observer's decision processes.

Tomogram An image that shows a cross section of the brain.

Top-down processing Borrowed from computer language, cognitive processing as hypothesis-driven recognition of the whole stimulus configuration, which leads to recognition of the component parts.

Transduction The conversion of physical energy (such as, light or sound waves) to neural energy.

Transformational grammar Rules that change the linguistic structure of a sentence into another form while maintaining the semantic content (Chomsky).

Transitivity The ability to coordinate isolated elements from a total system and perform operations on those elements (Piaget).

Triarchic theory The theory of intelligence comprising three subtheories that serve as the governing bases for specific types of human intelligence (Sternberg).

Turing test The test involving communication between a human who asks questions and an unknown language-using entity, with the human's task being to distinguish the output as human or nonhuman.

Unconscious state Memories that are not easily accessible to awareness.

Units Simple processing elements that stand for possible hypotheses about the nature of things. (See **Parallel distributed processing model.**)

Verification A hypothetical stage in the creative process that involves testing or carrying out the problem solution.

Wavelength The distance a wave (such as in visual light or radio rays) travels in one cycle.

Word apprehension effect (WAE) The idea that words are more easily recognized than nonwords, and letters are more perceptible if they form a word rather than a nonword.

Working memory Short-term memory containing information the system can access currently, including information retrieved from long-term declarative memory.

Yerkes-Dodson law The law stating that the relationship between performance and arousal level is an inverted U-curve. Increases in arousal level increase performance level up to a point, after which performance declines with further increases in arousal level.

REFERENCES

Aaronson, D., & Ferres, S. (1984). Reading strategies for children and adults: Some empirical evidence. *Journal of Verbal Learning and Verbal Behavior, 9,* 700–725.

Aaronson, D., & Ferres, S. (1986). Reading strategies for children and adults: A quantitative model. *Psychological Review, 93,* 89–112.

Adams, J. L. (1976a). *Learning and memory.* Homewood, IL: Dorsey Press.

Adams, J. L. (1976b). *Conceptual blockbusters.* (2nd ed.). New York: Norton.

Adelson, B. (1981). Problem solving and the development of abstract categories in programming languages. *Memory and Cognition, 9,* 422–433.

Adelson, B. (1984). When novices surpass experts: The difficulty of a task may increase with expertise. *Journal of Experimental Psychology: Learning, Memory, and Cognition, 10,* 483–495.

Akin, D. (1982). *The psychology of architectural design.* London: Pion.

Alkon, D. L. (1988). *Memory traces in the brain.* Cambridge, England: Cambridge University Press.

Alkon, D. L. (1989). Memory storage and neural systems. *Scientific American.* July, 42–50.

American Heritage Dictionary of the English Language. (1969). Boston: Houghton Mifflin.

Amosov, N. M. (1967). *Modeling of thinking and the mind.* Translated from Russian by L. Finegold. New York: Spartan.

Anderson, A. R. (Ed.). (1964) *Minds and machines.* Englewood Cliffs, NJ: Prentice-Hall.

Anderson, J. R. (1975). Item-specific and relation-specific interference in sentence memory. *Journal of Experimental Psychology: Human Learning and Memory, 104,* 249–260.

Anderson, J. R. (1976). *Language, memory, and thought.* Hillsdale, NJ: Erlbaum.

Anderson, J. R. (1978). Arguments concerning representations for mental imagery. *Psychological Review, 85,* 249–277.

Anderson, J. R. (Ed.). (1981). *Cognitive skills and their acquisition.* Hillsdale, NJ: Erlbaum.

Anderson, J. R. (1983a). *The architecture of cognition.* Cambridge, MA: Harvard University Press.

Anderson, J. R. (1983b). A spreading activation theory of memory. *Journal of Verbal Learning and Verbal Behavior, 22,* 261–295.

Anderson, J. R. (1985). *Cognitive psychology and its implications* (2nd ed.). San Francisco: Freeman.

Anderson, J. R. (1990). *Cognitive psychology* (3rd ed.). San Francisco: Freeman.

Anderson, J. R., & Bower, G. H. (1972). Recognition and retrieval processes in free recall. *Psychological Review, 79,* 97–123.

Anderson, J. R., & Bower, G. H. (1973). *Human associative memory.* Washington, DC: Winston.

Anderson, J. R., & Kosslyn, S. M. (Eds.). (1984). *Tutorials in learning and memory: Essays in honor of Gordon Bower.* San Francisco: Freeman.

Anderson, J. R., & Reiser, B. J. (1978). Schema-directed processes in language comprehension. In A. Lesgold, J. Pellegrino, S. Fokkima, & R. Glaser (Eds.), *Cognitive psychology and instruction.* New York: Plenum.

Anderson, J. R., & Reiser, B. J. (1985). The LISP tutor. *Byte, 10,* 159–178.

Anderson, R. C., & Pichert, J. W. (1978). Recall of previously unrecallable information following a shift in perspective. *Journal of Verbal Learning and Verbal Behavior, 17,* 1–12.

André-Leicknam, B., & Ziegler, C. (1982). *Naissance de l'écriture: Cuneiformes et hieroglyphes.* Paris: Minister of Culture.

Andrew, A. M. (1963). *Brain and computer.* London: Harrap.

Annett, M. (1982). Handedness. In J. G. Beaumont (Ed.), *Divided visual field studies of cerebral organization.* London: Academic Press.

Anokhin, P. K. (1969). Cybernetics and the integrative activity of the brain. In M. Cole & I. Maltzman (Eds.), *A handbook of contemporary Soviet psychology.* New York: Basic Books.

Apter, M. J. (1970). *The computer simulation of behavior.* New York: Harper & Row.

Apter, M., & Westby, G. (Eds.). (1973). *The computer in psychology.* New York: Wiley.

Atkinson, R. C. (1975). Mnemotechnics in second-language learning. *American Psychologist, 30,* 821–828.

Atkinson, R. C., Herrmann, D. J., Wescourt, K. T. (1974). Search processes in recognition memory. In R. L. Solso (Ed.), *Theories in cognitive psychology.* Hillsdale, NJ: Erlbaum.

Atkinson, R. C., & Juola, J. F. (1973). Factors influencing speed and accuracy of word recognition. In S. Kornblum (Ed.), *Attention and performance* (Vol. IV, pp. 583–612). New York: Academic Press.

Atkinson, R. C., & Juola, J. F. (1974) . Search and decision processes in recognition memory. In D. H. Krantz, R. C. Atkinson, R. D. Luce, & P. Suppes (Eds.), *Contemporary developments in mathematical psychology* (Vol. 1, pp. 242–293). San Francisco: Freeman.

Atkinson, R. C., & Raugh, M. R. (1975). An application of the mnemonic keyword method to the acquisition of a Russian vocabulary. *Journal of Experimental Psychology: Human Learning and Memory, 104,* 126–133.

Atkinson, R. C., & Shiffrin, R. M. (1965). *Mathematical models for memory and learning* (Tech. Rep. 79). Institute for Mathematical Studies in the Social Scie Stanford University.

Atkinson, R. C., & Shiffrin, R. M. (1968). Human m ory: A proposed system and its control processes. K. W. Spence & J. T. Spence (Eds.), *The psychology learning and motivation: Advances in research and the ory* (Vol. 2, pp. 89–195). New York: Academic Press.

Averbach, E., & Coriell, A. S. (1961). Short-term memory in vision. *Bell System Technical Journal, 40,* 309–328.

Baars, B. J. (1986). *The cognitive revolution in psychology.* New York: Guilford Press.

Baars, B. J. (1988). *A cognitive theory of consciousness.* Cambridge, England: Cambridge University Press.

Bach, E. (1974). *Syntactic theory.* New York: Holt, Rinehart & Winston.

Bach, M. J., & Underwood, B. J. (1970). Developmental changes in memory attributes. *Journal of Educational Psychology, 61,* 292–296.

Baddeley, A. (1982). *Your memory: A user's guide.* New York: Macmillan.

Baddeley, A. D. (1972). Retrieval-rules and semantic coding in short-term memory. *Psychological Bulletin, 78,* 379–385.

Baddeley, A. D. (1973). Memory coding and amnesia. *Neuropsychologia, 11,* 159–165.

Baddeley, A. D. (1976). *The psychology of memory.* New York: Basic Books.

Baddeley, A. D. (1978). The trouble with levels: A re-examination of Craik and Lockhart's "Framework for memory research" *Psychological Review, 85,* 139–152.

Baddeley, A. D. (1990). Human memory: Theory and practice. Boston: Allyn and Bacon.

Baddeley, A. D. (1992). Working memory. *Science, 255,* 556–559.

Baddeley, A. D., & Levy, B. A. (1971). Semantic coding and memory. *Journal of Experimental Psychology, 89,* 132–136.

Baddeley, A. D., & Warrington, E. K. (1970). Amnesia and the distinction between long- and short-term memory. *Journal of Verbal Learning and Verbal Behavior, 9,* 176–189.

Baddeley, A. D., & Warrington, E. K. (1973). Memory coding and amnesia. *Neuropsychologia, 11,* 159–165.

Bahrick, H. P. (1984). Semantic memory content in permastore: Fifty years of memory for Spanish learned in school. *Journal of Experimental Psychology: General, 113,* 1–35.

Bahrick, H. P., Bahrick, P. O., & Wittlinger, R. P. (1975). Fifty years of memory for names and faces; A cross-sectional approach. *Journal of Experimental Psychology: General, 104, 54–75.*

Bahrick, H. P., & Phelps, E. (1987). Retention of Spanish vocabulary over 8 years. *Journal of Experimental Psychology: Learning, Memory and Cognition, 13,* 344–349.

Ballard, D. H., & Brown, C. M. (1985). Vision. *Byte, 10,* 245–261.

Ballard, P. B. (1913). Oblivescence and reminiscence. *British Journal of Psychology Monograph Supplements, 1,* 1–82.

Banks, W. P. (1970). Signal detection theory and human memory. *Psychological Bulletin, 74,* 81–99.

Baron, J. (1973). Phonemic stage not necessary for reading. *Quarterly Journal of Experimental Psychology, 25,* 241–246.

Baron, J. (1988). *Thinking and deciding.* Cambridge, England: Cambridge University Press.

Baron, J., & Thurston, I. (1973). An analysis of the word superiority effect. *Cognitive Psychology, 4,* 207–228.

Barsalou, L. W. (1992). *Cognitive Psychology.* Hillsdale, NJ: Erlbaum.

Bartlett, F. C. (1932). *Remembering: A study in experimental and social psychology.* Cambridge, England: Cambridge University Press.

Bartlett, F. C. (1958). *Thinking.* New York: Basic Books.

Bartlett, J. C., & Snelus, P. (1980). Lifespan memory for popular songs. *American Journal of Psychology, 93,* 551–560.

Bauer, M. I., & Johnson-Laird, P. N. (1993). How diagrams can improve reasoning. *Psychological Science, 4,* 372–378.

Bédard, J. (1989). Expertise in auditing: Myth or reality? *Accounting, Organizations and Society, 14,* 113–131.

Bédard, J., & Chi, M. T. H. (1993). Expertise. *Current Directions in Psychological Science, 4, 135–139.*

Begg, I., & Denny, J. P. (1969). Empirical reconsideration of atmosphere and conversion interpretations of syllogistic reasoning errors. *Journal of Experimental Psychology, 81,* 351–354.

Bellezza, F. S. (1984). The self as a mnemonic device: The role of internal cues. *Journal of Personality and Social Psychology, 47,* 506–517.

Benderly, B. L. (1989). Everyday intuition. *Psychology Today,* Sept., 35–40.

Benson, D. F., & Zaidel, E. (Eds.). (1985). *The dual brain: Hemispheric specialization in humans.* New York: Guilford Press.

Bergen, J. R., & Julesz, B. (1983). Parallel versus serial processing in rapid pattern discrimination. *Nature, 303,* 696–698.

Berlin, B., & Kay, P. (1969). *Basic color terms: Their universality and evolution.* Berkeley: University of California Press.

Bernbach, H. A. (1967). Decision processes in memory. *Psychological Review, 74,* 462–480.

Bernstein, L. (1959). What makes the opera grand. In *The Joy of Music* (p. 290). New York: Simon & Schuster.

Bernstein, L. (1976). *The unanswered question: Six talks at Harvard.* Cambridge, MA: Harvard University Press.

Bernstein, N. (1967). *The co-ordination and regulation of movements.* Oxford: Pergamon Press.

Bertelson, P. (1967). The time course of preparation. *Quarterly Journal of Experimental Psychology, 19,* 272–279.

Betts, G. H. (1909). *The distribution and functions of mental imagery.* New York: Teachers College, Columbia University Press.

Biederman, I. (1972). Perceiving real world scenes. *Science 177,* 77–80.

Biederman, I. (1985). Human image understanding: Recent research and a theory. Computer Vision, Graphics and Image Processing, *31,* 29–73.

Biederman, I. (1987). Recognition by components: A theory of human image understanding. *Psychological Review, 94,* 115–147.

Biederman, I. (1990). Higher-level vision. In E. N. Osherson, S. M. Kosslyn, & J. M. Hollerbach (Eds.), *An invitation to cognitive science* (Vol. 2, pp. 41–72). Cambridge, MA: The MIT Press.

Biederman, I. & Cooper, E. E. (1991). Priming contour-deleted images: Evidence for intermediate representations in visual object recognition. *Cognitive Psychology, 23,* 393–419.

Biederman, I. & Gerhardstein, P. C. (1993). Recognizing depth-rotated objects: Evidence and conditions for 3D viewpoint invariance. *Journal of Experimental Psychology: Human Perception and Performance. 19.*

Biederman, I., Glass, A. L., & Stacy, E. W. (1973). Searching for objects in real world scenes. *Journal of Experimental Psychology, 97,* 22–27.

Bjork, E. L., & Estes, W. K. (1973a). Letter identification in relation to linguistic context and masking conditions. *Memory and Cognition, 1,* 217–223.

Bjork, E. L., & Estes, W. K. (1973b). Detection and placement of redundant signal elements in tachistoscope display of letters. *Perception and Pychophysics, 9,* 439–442.

Black, J. B. (1981). The effects of reading purpose on memory for text. In J. Long & A. Baddeley (Eds.), *Attention and Performance* (Vol. 9). Hillsdale, NJ: Erlbaum.

Black, J. B. (1984). Understanding and remembering stories. In J. R. Anderson & S. M. Kosslyn (Eds.), *Tutorials in learning and memory.* San Francisco: Freeman.

Black, J. B., & Bower, G. H. (1980). Story understanding as problem solving. *Poetics, 9,* 223–250.

Blakemore, C. (1977). *Mechanics of the mind.* Cambridge, England: Cambridge University Press.

Bledsoe, W. W., & Browning, I. (1959). Pattern recognition and reading by machine. *Proceedings of the Eastern Joint Computer Conference,* 225–232. Reprinted in L. Uhr (Ed.). (1966). *Pattern recognition.* New York: Wiley.

Bliss, J. C., Hewitt, D. V., Crane, P. K., Mansfield, P. K., & Townsend, J. T. (1966). Information available in brief tactile presentations. *Perception and Psychophysics, 1,* 273–283.

Boden, M. (1977). *Artificial intelligence and natural man.* New York: Basic Books.

Boden, M. A. (1989). *Artificial intelligence in psychology: Interdisciplinary essays.* Cambridge, MA: The MIT Press.

Bogen, J. E., & Vogel, P. J. (1962). Cerebral commissurotomy: A case report. *Bulletin of the Los Angeles Neurological Society, 27,* 169.

Boies, S. J., Posner, M. I., & Taylor, R. L. (1968). *Rehearsal of visual information from a single letter.* Paper presented at the meeting of the Western Psychological Association, San Diego, May. Cited in M. I. Posner, *Abstraction and the process of recognition.* In J. T. Spence & G. H. Bower (Eds.), *The psychology of learning and motivation: Advances in learning and motivation* (Vol. 3). New York: Academic Press.

Boles, D. B. (1984). Sex in latalized tachistoscopic word recognition. *Brain and Language, 23,* 307–317.

Boles, D. B. (1987). Reaction time asymmetry through bilateral versus unilateral stimulus presentation. *Brain and Cognition, 6,* 321–333.

Borge, V. (1978). Quoted by Linda Gutstein in "They laugh when he sits down to play." *Parade,* Apr. 9, p. 18.

Boring, E. G. (1942). *Sensation and perception in the history of experimental psychology.* New York: Appleton-Century-Crofts.

Boring, E. G. (1946). The perception of objects. *American Journal of Psychology, 14,* 99–107.

Bourne, L. E., Jr. (1963). Factors affecting strategies used in problems of concept-formation. *American Journal of Psychology, 76,* 229–238.

Bourne, L. E., Jr. (1974). An interference model for conceptual rule learning. In R. L. Solso (Ed.), *Theories in cognitive psychology: The Loyola Symposium* (pp. 231–256). Hillsdale, NJ: Erlbaum.

Bourne, L. E., Jr., & Dominowski, R. (1972). Thinking. In *Annual Review of Psychology* (Vol. 23). Palo Alto, CA: Annual Reviews.

Bourne, L. E., Jr., Dominowski, R. L., Loftus, E. F., & Healy, A. F: (1986). *Cognitive processes* (2nd ed.). Englewood Cliffs, NJ: Prentice-Hall.

Bourne, L. E., Jr., Ekstrand, B. R., & Dominowski, R. L. (1971). *The psychology of thinking.* Englewood Cliffs, NJ: Prentice-Hall.

Bourne, L. E., Jr., & Guy, D. E. (1968). Learning conceptual rules: I. Some interrule transfer effects. *Journal of Experimental Psychology, 76,* 423–429.

Bourne, L. E., Jr., & Restle, F. (1959). Mathematical theory of concept identification. *Psychological Review, 66,* 278–296.

Bousfield, W. A. (1951). Frequency and availability measures in language behavior. Paper presented at the Annual Meeting of the American Psychological Association, Chicago.

Bousfield, W. A. (1953). The occurrence of clustering in the recall of randomly arranged associates. *Journal of General Psychology, 49,* 229–240.

Bousfield, W. A., & Cohen, B. H. (1953). The effects of reinforcement on the occurrence of clustering in the recall of randomly arranged associates. *Journal of Psychology, 36,* 67–81.

Bousfield, W. A., & Sedgewick, C. H. W. (1944). An analysis of sequences of restricted associative responses. *Journal of Psyclology, 30,* 149–165.

Bower, G. H. (1967). A multi-component theory of the memory trace. In K. W. Spence & J. T. Spence (Eds.), *The psychology of learning and motivation: Advances in research and theory* (Vol. 1, pp. 299–325). New York: Academic Press.

Bower, G. H. (1970a). Organizational factors in memory. *Cognitive Psychology, 1,* 18–46.

Bower, G. H. (1970b). Analysis of a mnemonic device. *American Scientist, 58,* 496–510.

Bower, G. H. (1970c). Imagery as a relational organizer in associative learning. *Journal of Verbal Learning and Verbal Behavior, 9,* 529–533.

Bower, G. H. (1972). Mental imagery and associative learning. In L. W. Gregg (Ed.), *Cognition in learning and memory* (pp. 51–88). New York: Wiley.

Bower, G. H. (1973a). How to . . . Uh . . . Remember! *Psychology Today, 7,* 62–67.

Bower, G. H. (1973b). Memory freaks I have known. *Psychology Today, 7,* 64–65.

Bower, G. H. (1975). Cognitive psychology: An introduction. In W. Estes (Ed.), *Handbook of learning and cognitive processes* (Vol. 1, pp. 25–80). Hillsdale, NJ: Erlbaum.

Bower, G. H. (1976a). *Experiments on story understanding and recall.* Bartlett Lecture to EPS at Durham, England, Apr. 8.

Bower, G. H. (1976b). *Comprehending and recalling stories.* Division 3 Presidential Address presented at the Annual Meeting of the American Psychological Association, Washington, DC, Sept.

Bower, G. H. (1993). Quoted in "Biomedicine in the age of imaging." *Science, 261,* 30 July.

Bower, G. H., Black, J. B., & Turner, T. (1979). Scripts in memory for text. *Cognitive Psychology, 11,* 177–220.

Bower, G. H., & Clark, M. C. (1969). Narraive stories as mediators for serial learning. *Psychonomic Science, 14,* 181–182.

Bower, G. H., Clark, M. C., Lesgold, A. M., & Winzenz, D. (1969). Hierarchical retrieval schemes in recall of categorized word lists. *Journal of Verbal Learning and Verbal Behavior, 8,* 323–343.

Bower, G. H., & Clark-Meyers, G. (1980). Memory for scripts with organized vs. random presentations. *British Journal of Psychology, 71,* 368–377.

Bower, G. H., & Gilligan, S. G. (1979). Remembering information related to one's self. *Journal of Research in Personality, 13,* 420–432.

Bower, G. H., & Karlin, M. B. (1974). Depth of processing pictures of faces and recognition memory. *Journal of Experimental Psychology, 103,* 751–757.

Bower, G. H., Muñoz, R., & Arnold, P. G. (1972). *On distinguishing semantic and imaginal mnemonics.* Unpublished manuscript. Cited in J. Anderson & G. Bower (1973); *Human associative memory* (p. 459). Washington, DC: Winston.

Bower, G. H., & Reitman, J. S. (1972). Mnemonic elaboration in multilist learning. *Journal of Verbal Learning and Verbal Behavior, 11,* 478–485.

Bower, G. H., & Springston, F. (1970). Pauses as recoding points in letter series. *Journal of Experimental Psychology, 83,* 421–430.

Bower, G. H., & Winzenz, D. (1969). Group structure, coding, and memory for digit series. *Journal of Experimental Psychology Monograph Supplement, 80,* 1–17.

Bower, G. H., & Winzenz, D. (1970). Comparison of associative learning strategies. *Psychonomic Science, 20,* 119–120.

Bower, T. G. R. (1970). Reading by eye. In H. Levin & J. P. Williams (Eds.), *Basic studies in reading.* New York: Basic Books.

Bowers, K. S., Regehr, G., Balthazard, C., & Parker, K. (1990). Intuition in the context of discovery. *Cognitive Psychology, 22,* 72–110.

Bowman, J. P. (1968). Muscle spindles in the intrinsic and extrinsic muscles of the rhesus monkey's (macaca mulatta) tongue. *Anatomical Record, 161,* 483–488.

Bowman, J. P., & Combs, C. M. (1968). Discharge patterns of lingual spindles afferent fibers in the hypoglossal nerve of the rhesus monkey. *Experimental Neurology, 21,* 105–119.

Bowman, J. P., & Combs, C. M. (1969a). The cerebrocortical projection of hypoglossal afferents. *Experimental Neurology, 23,* 291–301.

Bowman, J. P., & Combs, C. M. (1969b). Cerebellar responsiveness to stimulation of lingual spindle afferent fibers in the hypolossal nerve of the rhesus monkey. *Experimental Neurology, 23,* 537–543.

Bradshaw, J. L., & Nettleton, N. C. (1981). The nature of hemispheric specialization in man. *Behavioral and Brain Sciences, 4,* 51–91.

Brainerd, C. J. (1973). Order of acquisition of transitivity, conservation, and class inclusion of length and weight. *Developmental Psychology, 8,* 105–116.

Brainerd, C. J. (1978). *Piaget's theory of intelligence.* Englewood Cliffs, NJ: Prentice-Hall.

Brams, S. J. (1993). Theory of moves. *American Scientist, 81,* 562–570.

Bransford, J. D., & Franks, J. J. (1971). The abstraction of linguistic ideas: A review. *Cognitive Psychology, 2,* 331–350.

Bransford, J. D., & Franks, J. J. (1972). The abstraction of linguistic ideas: A review. *Cognition, 1,* 211–250.

Bransford, J. D., & Johnson, M. K. (1972). Contextual prerequisites for understanding: Some investigations of comprehension and recall. *Journal of Verbal Learning and Verbal Behavior, 11,* 717–726.

Brewer, W. F. (1974). The problem of meaning and the interrelations of the higher mental processes. In W. B. Weimer & D. S. Palermo (Eds.), *Cognition and the symbolic processes* (pp. 263–298). New York: Wiley.

Briggs, G. E., & Blaha, J. (1969). Memory retrieval and central comparison times in information-processing. *Journal of Experimental Psychology, 79,* 395–402.

Broadbent, D. E. (1954). The role of auditory localization and attention in memory spans. *Journal of Experimental Psychology, 47*, 191–196.

Broadbent, D. E. (1958). *Perception and communication*. London and New York: Pergamon Press.

Broadbent, D. E. (1962). Attention and the perception of speech. *Scientific American, 206*, 143–151.

Broadbent, D. E. (1966). The well-ordered mind. *American Education Research Journal, 3*, 281–295.

Broadbent, D. E. (1971). *Decision and stress*. London: Academic Press.

Broadbent, D. E. (1973). *In defense of empirical psychology*. London: Methuen.

Broadbent, D. E. (1981). Selective and control processes. *Cognition, 10*, 53–58.

Broadbent, D. E. (1984). The Maltese cross: A new simplistic model for memory. *Behavioral & Brain Sciences, 7*, 55–94.

Broadhurst P. L. (1957). Emotionality and the Yerkes-Dodson law. *Journal of Experimental Psychology, 54*, 345–352.

Broca, P. P. (1864/1970). Cited in M. Critchley, *Aphasiology and other aspects of language*. London: Edward Arnold.

Bromley, H. L., Jarvella, R. l, & Lundberg, I. (1985). From Lisp machine to language lab. *Behavioral Research Methods, Instruments, and Computers, 17*, 399–402.

Brooks, L. R. (1968). Spatial and verbal components of the act of recall. *Canadian Journal of Psychology, 22*, 349–368.

Brown, A. L. (1975). The development of memory: Knowing, knowing about knowing, and knowing how to know. In H. W. Reese (Ed.), *Advances in child development and behavior* (Vol. 10). New York: Academic Press.

Brown, J. (Ed.). (1975). *Recognition and recall*. London: Wiley.

Brown, J. A. (1958). Some tests of the decay theory of immediate memory. *Quarterly Journal of Experimental Psychology, 10*, 12–21.

Brown, R. (1958). *Words and things*. New York: Free Press.

Brown, R. (1965). *Social psychology*. New York: Free Press.

Brown, R. (1970). *Psycholinguistics*. New York: Free Press.

Brown, R., & Herrnstein, R. J. (1975). *Psychology*. Boston: Little, Brown.

Brown, R., & Kulik, J. (1977). Flashbulb memories. *Cognition, 5*, 73–99.

Brown, R., & McNeill, D. (1966). The "tip of the tongue" phenomenon. *Journal of Verbal Learning and Verbal Behavior, 5*, 325–337.

Bruner, J. S., Goodnow, J. J., & Austin, G. A. (1956). A *study of thinking*. New York: Wiley.

Bruner, J. S., Oliver, R. R., & Greenfield, P. M. (Eds.). (1966). *Studies in cognitive growth*. New York: Wiley.

Bryant, P. E., & Trabasso, T. (1971). Transitive interferences and memory in young children. *Nature, 232*, 456–458.

Bugelski, B. R. (1970). Words and things and images. *American Psychologist, 25*, 1002–1012.

Bugelski, B. R., Kidd, E., & Gegmen, J. (1968). Image as a mediator in one-trial paired-associate learning. *Journal of Experimental Psychology, 76*, 69–73.

Byte, Apr., 1985.

Calfee, R. C. (1975). *Human experimental psychology*. New York: Holt, Rinehart & Winston.

Carbonell, J. G. (1979). Subjective understanding: Computer models of belief systems. Unpublished doctoral dissertation, Yale University.

Carpenter, P. A., & Dahneman, M. (1981). Lexical retrieval and error recovery in reading: A model based on eye fixations. *Journal of Verbal Learning and Verbal Behavior, 20*, 137–164.

Carroll, J. B., & Freedle, R. O. (Eds.). (1972). *Language comprehension and the acquisition of knowledge*. Washington, DC: Winston.

Casey, R. G., & Nagy, G. (1971). Advances in pattern recognition. *Scientific American, 224*, 56–64.

Catania, A. C. (1970). Reinforcement schedules and psychophysical judgments. A study of some temporal properties of behavior. In W. N. Schoenfeld (Ed.), *The theory of reinforcement schedules* (pp. 1–42). New York: Appleton-Century-Crofts.

Cattell, J. McK. (1886a). The time it takes to see and name objects. *Mind, 11*, 63–65.

Cattell, J. McK. (1886b). The time taken up by cerebral operations. *Mind, 11*, 277–292, 524–538.

Cattell, J. McK. (1954). Uberdi Aeit der Erkennung and Benennung von Schriftzeichen, Bildern and Farben. *Philos, St. 2*, 1885, 635–650. Cited in R. Woodworth & H. Schlosberg, *Experimental Psychology*. New York: Holt.

Cattell, R. B. (1965). *The scientific analysis of personality*. Baltimore: Penguin.

Cattell, R. B. (1971). *Abilities: Their structure, growth and action*. Boston: Houghton Mifflin.

Ceraso, J., & Provitera, A. (1971). Sources of error in syllogistic reasoning. *Cognitive Psychology, 2,* 400–410.

Cermak, L. S. (1976). *Improving your memory.* New York: McGraw-Hill.

Chapman, L. J., & Chapman, J. P. (1959). Atmosphere effect reexamined. *Journal of Experimental Psychology, 58,* 220–226.

Charness, N. (1979). Components of skill in bridge. *Canadian Journal of Psychology, 33,* 1–50.

Chase, W. G. (Ed.). (1973). *Visual information processing.* New York: Academic Press.

Chase, W. G., & Ericsson, K. A. (1981). Skilled memory. In J. R. Anderson (Ed.), *Cognitive skills and their acquisition.* Hillsdale, NJ: Erlbaum.

Chase, W. G., & Ericsson, K. A. (1982). Skill and working memory. In G. H. Bower (Ed.), *The psychology of learning and motivation* pp. 1–58). New York: Academic Press.

Chase, W. G., & Simon, H. A. (1973a). The mind's eye in chess. In W. G. Chase (Ed.), *Visual information processing.* New York: Academic Press.

Chase, W. G., & Simon, H. A. (1973b). Perception in chess. *Cognitive Psychology, 4,* 55–81.

Cherry, C. (1953). Some experiments on the recognition of speech with one and with two ears. *Journal of the Acoustic Society of America, 25,* 975–979.

Cherry, C. (1966). On human communication (2nd ed.). Cambridge, MA: The MIT Press.

Chi, M. T. (1976). Short-term memory limitations in children: Capacity or processing deficits. *Memory and Cognition, 5,* 559–572.

Chi, M. T. (1978). Knowledge structures and memory development. In R. S. Siegler (Ed.), *Children's thinking: What develops?* Hillsdale, NJ: Erlbaum.

Chi, M. T. H., Feltovich, P., & Glaser, R. (1981). Categorization and representation of physics problems by experts and novices, *Cognitive Science, 5,* 121–152.

Chi, M. T. H., Glaser, R., & Farr, M. J. (Eds.). (1988). *The nature of expertise.* Hillsdale, NJ: Erlbaum.

Chi, M. T. H., Glaser, R., & Rees, E. (1982). Expertise in problem solving. In R. J. Sternberg (Ed.), *Advances in the psychology of human intelligence.* Hillsdale, NJ: Erlbaum.

Chiarello, C. (1988). Lateralization of lexical processes in the normal brain: A review of visual hemi-field research. In H. A. Whitaker (Ed.), *Contemporary reviews in neuropsychology.* (pp. 36–76). New York: Springer.

Chiesi, H. L., Spilich, G. J., & Voss, J. F. (1979). Acquisition of domain-related information in relation to high and low domain knowledge. *Journal of Verbal Learning and Verbal Behavior, 18,* 257–273.

Chipman, S. F., Davis, C., & Shafto, M. G. (1986). Personnel and training research program: Cognitive science at ONR. *Naval Research Review, 38,* 3–21.

Chomsky, N. (1956). Three models of the description of language. Proceedings of a Symposium on Information Theory. *IRF Transactions on Information Theory, IT-2*(3), 113–124.

Chomsky, N. (1957a). *Syntactic structures.* The Hague: Mouton.

Chomsky, N. (1957b). Review of *Verbal behavior* by B. F. Skinner. *Language, 35,* 26–58.

Chomsky, N. (1965). *Aspect of the theory of syntax.* Cambridge, MA: The MIT Press.

Chomsky, N. (1966). *Topics in the theory of generative grammar.* The Hague: Mouton.

Chomsky, N. (1968). *Language and mind.* New York: Harcourt Brace Jovanovich.

Chukovsky, K. (1971). *From two to five.* Berkeley: University of California Press.

Churchland, P. S. (1989). From Descartes to neural networks. *Scientific American,* July, 118.

Churchland, P. S., & Sejnowski, T. J. (1988). Perspectives on cognitive neuroscience. *Science, 242,* 741–745.

Clancey, W. J. (1988). Acquiring, representing, and evaluating a competence model of diagnosis strategy. In M. T. H. Chi, R. Glaser, & M. J. Farr (Eds.), *The nature of expertise.* Hillsdale, NJ: Erlbaum.

Clark, H., & Clark, E. (1977). *Psychology and language: An introduction to psycholinguistics.* New York: Harcourt Brace Jovanovich.

Clark, W. C. (1966). The psyche in psychophysics: A sensory-decision theory analysis of the effect of instruction on flicker sensitivity and response bias. *Psychological Bulletin, 65,* 358–366.

Clark, W. C., Brown, J. C., & Rutschmann, J. (1967). Flicker sensitivity and response bias in psychiatric patients and normal subjects. *Journal of Abnormal Psycology, 72,* 35–42.

Clarke, A. C. (1968). *2001: A space odyssey.* New York: New American Library.

Clement, C., & Falmagne, R. J. (1986). Logical reasoning, world knowledge, and mental imagery: Interconnections in cognitive processes. *Memory & Cognition, 14,* 299–307.

Cofer, C. N. (1973). Constructive processes in memory. *American Scientist, 61,* 537–543.

Cofer, C. N. (Ed.). (1976). *The structure of human memory.* San Francisco: Freeman.

Cohen, G. (1989). *Memory in the real world.* Hillsdale, NJ: Erlbaum.

Cohen, J. D., Servan-Schreiber, & McClelland, J. L. (1992). A parallel distributed processing approach to automaticity. *American Journal of Psychology, 105,* 239–269.

Cohen, J. J., & Corkin, S. (1981). The amnesic patient, H. M.: Learning and retention of a cognitive skill. *Society for Neuroscience Abstracts, 7,* 235.

Cohen, J. J., & Squire, L. R. (1980). Preserved learning and retention of pattern-analyzing skill in amnesia: Dissociation of knowing how and knowing that. *Science, 210,* 207–210.

Cohen, K. M., & Haith, M. M. (1977). Peripheral vision in the effects of developmental, perceptual, and cognitive factors. *Journal of Experimental Child Psychology, 3,* 373–395.

Cohen, L. B., & Salapatek, P. (1975). *Infant perception: From sensation to cognition* (Vol. 1). New York: Academic Press.

Cohen, L. B., & Strauss, M. S. (1979). Concept acquisition in the human infant. *Child Development, 50,* 419–424.

Cohen, L. J. (1981). Can human irrationality be experimentally demonstrated? *Behavioral and Brain Sciences, 4,* 317–370.

Cohen, M. S., Rosen, B. R., & Brady, T. J. (1992). Ultrafast MRI permits expanded clinical role. *Magnetic Resonance, 26,* Winter.

Colby, K. M., Hilf, F. D., Weber, S., & Kraemer, H. C. (1972). Turing-like indistinguishability tests for the validation of a computer simulation of paranoid processes. *Artificial Intelligence, 3.*

Cole, M. (1975). An ethnographic psychology of cognition. In R. W. Brislin, S. Blochner, & W. J. Lonner (Eds.), *Perspectives on learning, I, Cross-cultural research and methodology.* New York: Halsted Press, Wiley.

Cole, M., Frankel, F., & Sharp, D. (1971). Development of free recall learning in children. *Developmental Psychology, 4,* 109–123.

Cole, M., Gay, J., Glick, J., & Sharp, D. (1971). *The cultural context of learning and thinking.* New York: Basic Books.

Cole, M., & Scribner, S. (1974). *Culture and thought.* New York: Wiley.

Collins, A., & Smith, E. E. (Eds.). (1988). *Readings in cognitive science: A perspective from psychology and artificial intelligence.* San Mateo, CA: Morgan Kaufmann.

Collins, A. M., & Loftus, E. F. (1975). A spreading activation theory of semantic processing. *Psychological Review, 82,* 407–428.

Collins, A. M., & Quillian, M. R. (1969). Retrieval time from semantic memory. *Journal of Verbal Learning and Verbal Behavior, 8,* 240–247.

Collins, A. M., & Quillian, M. R. (1972). How to make a language user. In E. Tulving and W. Donaldson (Eds.), *Organization of memory.* New York: Academic Press.

Collyer, S. C., Jonides, J., & Bevan, W. (1972). Images as memory aids: Is bizarreness helpful? *American Journal of Psychology, 85,* 31–38.

Coltheart, M. (Ed.). (1972a). *Readings in cognitive psychology.* Toronto: Holt, Rinehart & Winston.

Coltheart, M. (1972b). Visual information processing. In P. Dodwell (Ed.), *New horizons in psychology: 2.* Harmondsworth, Middlesex, England: Penguin.

Coltheart, M. (1975). Iconic memory: A reply to Professor Holding. *Memory and Cognition, 3,* 42–48.

Coltheart, M. (1983). Ecological necessity of iconic memory. *Behavioral and Brain Sciences, 6,* 17–18.

Coltheart, M. (Ed.). (1987). *The cognitive neuropsychology of language.* Hillsdale, NJ: Erlbaum.

Coltheart, M., & Glick, M. J. (1974). Visual imagery: A case study. *Quarterly Journal of Experimental Psychology, 26,* 438–453.

Conrad, C. (1972). Cognitive economy in semantic memory. *Journal of Experimental Psychology, 92,* 149–154.

Conrad, R. (1963). Acoustic confusions and memory span for words. *Nature, 197,* 1029–1030.

Conrad, R. (1964). Acoustic confusions in immediate memory. *British Journal of Psychology, 55,* 75–84.

Conrad, R. (1970). Short-term memory processes in the deaf. *British Journal of Psychology, 61,* 179–195.

Conway, M. A., Cohen, G., & Stanhope, N. (1991). On the very long-term retention of knowledge acquired through formal education: Twelve years of cognitive psychology. *Journal of Experimental Psychology: General, 120,* 395–409.

Cooper, E. E., & Biederman, I. (1993) Metric versus viewpoint invariant shape differences in visual object recognition. Poster presented at the meeting of the Association for Research in Vision and Ophthalmology, Sarasota, FL, May.

Cooper, L. A., & Shepard, R. N. (1972). The time required to prepare for a rotated stimulus. *Memory and Cognition, 1,* 246–250.

Cooper, L. A., & Shepard, R. N. (1973). Chronometric studies of the rotation of mental images. In W. G. Chase (Ed.), *Visual information processing.* New York: Academic Press.

Cooper, L. A., & Shepard, R. N. (1980). Transformations on representations of objects in space. In E. C. Carterette & M. Friedman (Eds.), *Handbook of perception, Volume 8: Space and object perception.* New York: Academic Press.

Corballis, M. C. (1989). Laterality and human evolution. *Psychological Review, 96,* 492–505.

Corballis, M. C., Kirby, J., & Miller, A. (1972). Access to elements of a memorized list. *Journal of Experimental Psychology, 9,* 185–190.

Corbetta, M., Miezin, F. M., Dobmeyer, S., Shulman, G. L., & Petersen, S. E. (1991). Selective and divided attention during visual discriminations of shape, color, and speed: Functional anatomy by positron emission tomography. *The Journal of Neuroscience, 11,* 2363–2402.

Corteen, R. S., & Dunn, D. (1974). Shock-associated words in a nonattended message: A test for momentary awareness. *Journal of Experimental Psychology, 102,* 1143–1144.

Corteen, R. S., & Wood, B. (1972). Autonomic responses to shock-associated words in an unattended channel. *Journal of Experimental Psychology, 9,* 303–313.

Cousins, N. (1957). Smudging the subconscious. *Saturday Review,* Oct. 5, 20–21.

Cowan, N. (1988). Evolving conceptions of memory storage, selective attention, and their mutual constraints within the human information-processing system. *Psychological Bulletin, 104,* 163–191.

Cowan, W. M. (1979). The development of the brain. *Scientific American, 241,* 112–133.

Craik, F. I. M., & Jacoby, L. L. (1975). A process view of short-term retention. In R. Restle (Ed.), *Cognitive theory* (Vol. 1). Hillsdale, NJ: Erlbaum.

Craik, F. I. M., & Lockhart, R. S. (1972). Levels of processing: A framework for memory research. *Journal of Verbal Learning and Verbal Behavior, 11,* 671–684.

Craik, F. I. M., & Tulving, E. (1975). Depth of processing and the retention of words in episodic memory. *Journal of Experimental Psychology: General, 104,* 268–294.

Craik, F. I. M., & Watkins, M. J. (1973). The role of rehearsal in short-term memory. *Journal of Verbal Learning and Verbal Behavior, 12,* 599–607.

Crick, F., & Asanuma, C. (1986). Certain aspects of the anatomy and physiology of the cerebral cortex. In D. E. Rumelhart, J. L. McClelland, and the PDP research group (Eds.), *Parallel distributed processing: Explorations in the microstructure of cognition* (Vol. 2). Cambridge, MA: Bradford.

Crowder, R. G. (1982a). *The psychology of memory.* New York: Oxford.

Crowder, R. G. (1982b). The demise of short-term memory. *Acta Psychologica, 50,* 291–323.

Crowder, R. G. (1982c). *The psychology of reading.* New York: Oxford.

Crowder, R. G. (1985). On access and the forms of memory. In N. Weinberger, J. McGaugh, & G. Lynch (Eds.), *Memory systems of the brain.* New York: Guilford Press.

Crowder, R. G. (1993). Short-term memory: Where do we stand? *Memory & Cognition, 21,* 142–145.

Cudhea, D. (1978). Artificial intelligence. *The Stanford Magazine, 6,* 8–14.

Daehler, M. W., & Bukatko, D. (1985). *Cognitive development.* New York: Knopf.

D'Agostino, P. R., O'Neill, B. J., & Paivio, A. (1977). Memory for pictures and words as a function of levels of processing: Depth or dual coding? *Memory and Cognition, 5,* 252–256.

Dale, P. S. (1976). *Language development: Structure and function* (2nd ed.). New York: Holt, Rinehart & Winston.

Darwin, C. J., Turvey, M. T., & Crowder, R. G. (1972). An auditory analogue of the Sperling partial report procedure: Evidence for brief auditory storage. *Cognitive Psychology, 3,* 255–267.

Dawes, R. (1966). Memory and the distortion of meaningful written material. *British Journal of Psychology, 57* 77–86.

Dawson, J. L. M. (1967). Cultural and physiological influences upon spatial-perceptual processes in West Africa. *International Journal of Psychology, 2,* 115–128.

Day, M. C. (1975). Developmental trends in visual scanning. In H. W. Reese (Ed.), *Advances in child development and behavior* (Vol. 10). New York: Academic Press.

Day, R. S., Cutting, J. C., & Copeland, P. M. (1971). Perception of linguistic and nonlinguistic dimensions of dichotic stimuli. *Haskins Laboratories Status Report on Speech Research, SR-27,* 193–197.

Day, R. S., & Wood, C. C. (1972a). Interactions between linguistic and nonlinguistic processing. *Journal of the Acoustical Society of America, 51,* 79A.

Day, R. S., & Wood, C. C. (1972b). Mutual interference between two linguistic dimensions of the same stimuli. *Journal of the Acoustical Society of America, 52,* 175A.

Dearborn, W. (1906). *The psychology of reading* (Columbia University contributions to philosophy and psychology). New York: Science Press.

de Groot, A. D. (1965). *Thought and choice in chess.* The Hague: Mouton.

de Groot, A. D. (1966). Perception and memory versus thought: Some old ideas and recent findings. In B. Kleinmuntz (Ed.), *Problem solving: Research, method and theory.* New York: Wiley.

Dehn, N., & Schank, R. (1982). Artificial and human intelligence. In R. Sternberg (Ed.), *Handbook of human Intelligence.* Cambridge, England: Cambridge University Press.

Denes, P. B., & Pinson, E. N. (1963). *The speech chain.* Murray Hill, NJ: Bell Laboratories.

Deregowski, J. B. (1971). Symmetry, Gestalt and information theory. *Quarterly Journal of Experimental Psychology, 23,* 381–385.

Deregowski, J. B. (1973). Illusion and culture. In R. L. Gregory & E. H. Gombrich (Eds.), *Illusion in nature and art.* New York: Scribner.

Deregowski, J. B. (1980). *Illusions, perception and pictures.* London: Academic Press.

Deregowski, J. B., Muldrow, E. S., & Muldrow, W. F. (1973). Pictorial recognition in a remote Ethiopian population. *Perception, 1,* 417–425.

Descartes, R. (1931). *Philosophical works* (E. S. Haldane & G. R. T. Pross, trans.). Cambridge, England: Cambridge University Press.

Deutsch, J. A., & Deutsch, D. (1963). Attention: Some theoretical considerations. *Psychological Review, 70,* 80–90.

Deutsch, J. A., & Deutsch, D. (1967). Comments on selective attention: Perception or response? *Quarterly Journal of Experimental Psychology, 19,* 362–363.

Diringer, D. (1968). *The alphabet: A key to the history of mankind* (Vols. 1 and 2) (3rd ed.). London: Hutchinson.

Dolinsky, R. (1973). Word fragments as recall cues: Role of syllables. *Journal of Experimental Psychology, 97,* 272–274.

Donaldson, W., & Murdock, B. B., Jr. (1968). Criterion changes in continuous recognition memory. *Journal of Experimental Psychology, 76,* 325–330.

Donegan, C. (1989). Think again. *American Way,* Mar. 15, 73–111.

Dreyfus, H. L. (1965). *Alchemy and artificial intelligence.* Santa Monica, CA: Rand Corporation.

Dreyfus, H. L. (1972). *What computers can't do: A critique of artificial reason.* New York: Harper Row.

Duchamp, M. (1945). From an interview with Janees Johnson Sweeney in Eleven Europeans in America. *Bulletin of the Museum of Modern Art* (New York), 13(4–5), 19–21.

Duncker, K. (1945). On problem solving. *Psychological Monographs, 58* (5, whole no. 270).

Dunlap, K. (1900). The effect of imperceptible shadows on the judgment of distance. *Psychological Review, 7,* 435–453.

Easterbrook, J. A. (1959). The effect of emotion on cue utilization and the organization of behavior. *Psychological Review, 66,* 183–201.

Ebbinghaus, H. (1885). *Über das Gedächtnis: Intersuchungen zur experimentellen psychologie.* Leipzig: Duncker and Humboldt. (Translated by H. A. Ruger & C. E. Bussenius, 1913, and reissued by Dover Publications, 1964.)

Eccles, J. C. (1973). *The understanding of the brain.* New York: McGraw-Hill.

Edson, L. (1982). Under Babel's tower. *Mosaic, 13,* 22–28.

Edwards, W. (1968). Conservatism in human information processing. In B. Kleinmuntz (Ed.), *Formal reprentations of human judgment.* New York: Wiley.

Einstein, A. (1950). *Out of my later years.* New York: Philosophic Library.

Eisenstadt, M., & Kareev, Y. (1975). Aspects of human problem solving: The use of internal representation. In D. Norman & D. Rumelhart, *Exploration in cognition.* San Francisco: Freeman.

Elithorn, A., & Banerji, R. (Eds.). (1984). *Artificial and human intelligence.* New York: Oxford University Press.

Ellis, H. C. (1978). *Fundamentals of human learning, memory, and cognition.* Dubuque, IA: W. C. Brown.

Erdelyi, M. H., & Becker, J. (1974). Hypermnesia for pictures: Incremental memory for pictures but not for words in multiple recall trials. *Cognitive Psychology, 6,* 159–171.

Erdmann, B., & Dodge, R. (1898). *Psychologische untersuchungen über das Lese.* Halle: M. Niemeyer. Cited by R. Woodworth & H. Schlosberg, *Experimental Psychology.* New York: Holt, Rinehart & Winston.

Erickson, J. R. (1974). A set analysis theory of behavior in formal syllogistic reasoning tasks. In R. L. Solso (Ed.), *Theories in cognitive psychology: The Loyola Symposium.* Hillsdale, NJ: Erlbaum.

Erickson, J. R., & Jones, M. R. (1978). Thinking. *Annual Review of Psychology, 29,* 61–91.

Ericsson, K. A., & Chase, W. A. (1982). Exceptional memory. *American Scientist, 70,* 607–615.

Ericsson, K. A., Krampe, R. T., & Tesch-Römer, C. (1993). The role of deliberate practice in the acquisition of expert performance. *Psychological Review, 100,* 363–406.

Ericsson, K. A., & Polson, P. G. (1988a). A cognitive analysis of exceptional memory for restaurant orders. In M. T. H. Chi, R. Glaser, & M. J. Farr (Eds.), *The nature of expertise.* Hillsdale, NJ: Erlbaum.

Ericsson, K. A., & Polson, P. G. (1988b). An experimental analysis of the mechanisms of a memory skill. *Journal of Experimental Psychology: Learning, Memory, and Cognition, 14,* 305–316.

Eriksen, C. W., & Collins, J. F. (1967). Some temporal characteristics of visual pattern perception. *Journal of Experimental Psychology, 74,* 476–484.

Estes, W. K. (197). Memory, perception and decision in letter identification. In R. L. Solso (Ed.), *Information processing and cognition: The Loyola Symposium.* Hillsdale, NJ: Erlbaum.

Estes, W. K. (1977). The structure of human memory. In *Encyclopedia Britannica: Yearbook of science and the future.* Chicago: University of Chicago Press.

Estes, W. K. (Ed.). (1978). *Handbook of learning and cognitive processes* (Vol. 6). Hillsdale, NJ: Erlbaum.

Estes, W. K., Bjork, E. L., & Skaar, E. (1974). Detection of single letters and letters in words with changing versus unchanging mark characteristics. *Bulletin of the Psychonomic Society 3,* 201–203.

Evans, L. (1989). Evans on chess: 24 computers clash. *Reno Gazette-Journal,* Sept. 9.

Evarts, E. V. (1973). Motor cortex reflexes with learned movements. *Science, 179,* 501–503.

Eysenck, H. J. (1984). Intelligence versus behavior. *The Behavioral and Brain Sciences, 7,* 290–291.

Eysenck, M. W. (1984). *A handbook of cognitive psychology.* Hillsdale, NJ: Erlbaum.

Farah, M. J. (1984). The neurological basis of mental imagery: A componential analysis. *Cognition, 18,* 245–272.

Farah, M. J. (1988). Is visual imagery really visual? Overlooked evidence from neuropsychology. *Psychological Review, 95,* 307–317.

Farah, M. J., Hammond, K. M., Levine, D. N., & Calvanio, R. (1988). Visual and spatial mental imagery: Dissociable systems of representation. *Cognitive Psychology, 20,* 439–462.

FCC (1974). 42, 74–78, *U.S. Law Week 2404,* Feb. 5.

Fehlman, S. E. (1989). Representing implicit knowledge. In G. E. Hinton & J. A. Anderson (Eds.), *Parallel models of associative memory.* Hillsdale, NJ: Erlbaum.

Feigenbaum, E. A. (1967). Information processing and memory. In *Proceedings of the Fifth Berkeley Symposium on Mathematics, Statistics and Probability, 4,* 37–51.

Fein, G. G. (1979). Play and the acquisition of symbols. In L. Kantz (Ed.), *Current topics in early childhood education.* Norwood, NJ: Ablex.

Feinaigle, G. von. (1813). *The new art of memory* (3rd ed.). London: Sherwood, Neely & Jones. Cited in A. Paivio (1971). *Imagery and verbal processes.* New York: Holt, Rinehart & Winston.

Felzen, E., & Anisfeld, M. (1970). Semantic and phonetic relations in the false recognition of words by third and sixth grade children. *Developmental Psychology, 3,* 163–168.

Field, D. (1981). Retrospective reports by healthy intelligent elderly people of personal events of their adult lives. *International Journal of Behavioral Development, 4,* 77–97.

Fikes, R. E., Hart, P. E., & Nilsson, N. J. (1972). In B. Meltzer & D. Michie (Eds.), *Machine intelligence.* Edinburgh: Edinburgh University Press.

Finkbeiner, A. (1988). The brain as template. *Mosaic, 19,* 2–15.

Finke, R. A. (1985). Theories relating mental imagery to perception. *Psychological Bulletin, 98,* 236–259.

Fischler, I., & Bloom, P. A. (1979). Automatic and attentional processes in the effects of sentence context on word recognition. *Journal of Verbal Learning and Verbal Behavior, 18,* 1–20.

Fischler, I. S., & Bloom, P. A. (1985). Effects of constraint and validity of sentence context on lexical decision. *Memory & Cognition, 13,* 128–139.

Fishman, J. A. (1960). A systematization of the Whorfian hypothesis. *Behavioral Science, 5,* 1–29.

Fitts, P. M., & Posner, M. I. (1967). *Human performance.* Belmont, CA: Brooks/Cole.

Flagg, P. W., Potts, G. R., & Reynolds, A. G. (1975). Instructions and response strategies in recognition memory for sentences. *Journal of Experimental Psychology: Human Learning and Memory, 1*(5), 592–598.

Flagg, P. W., & Reynolds, A. G. (1977). Modality of presentation and blocking in sentence recognition memory. *Memory and Cognition, 5*(1), 111–115.

Flavell, J. H. (1963). *The developmental psychology of Jean Piaget.* Princeton, NJ: Van Nostrand.

Flavell, J. H. (1985). *Cognitive development* (2nd ed.). Englewood Cliffs, NJ: Prentice-Hall.

Flavell, J. H. (1986). The development of children's knowledge about the appearance-reality distinction. *American Psychologist, 41,* 418–425.

Flavell, J. H., Beach, D. H., & Chinsky, J. M. (1966). Spontaneous verbal rehearsal in a memory task as a function of age. *Child Development, 37,* 283–299.

Flavell, J. H., & Markman, E. M. (Eds.). (1983). *Handbook of child psychology: Cognitive development* (Vol. 3). New York: Wiley.

Flowers, M., McGuire, R., & Birnbaum, L. (192). Adversary arguments and the logic of personal attacks. In W. Lehnert & M. Ringle (Eds.), *Strategies for natural language processing.* Hillsdale, NJ: Erlbaum.

Fodor, J., & Garrett, M. (1966). Some reflections on competence and performance. In J. Lyons & R. J. Wales (Eds.), *Psycholinguistic Papers: The Proceedings of the 1966 Edinburgh Conference.* Edinburgh: Edinburgh University Press.

Fodor, J. A., & Pylyshyn, Z. W. (1988). Connectionism and cognitive architecture: A critical analysis. *Cognition, 28,* 3–71.

Forster, P. M., & Govier, E. (1978). Discrimination without awareness? *Quarterly Journal of Experimental Psychology, 31,* 282–295.

Fowler, M. J., Sullivan, J. J., & Ekstrand, B. R. (1973). Sleep and memory. *Science, 179,* 302–304.

Frank, F. (1966). Perception and language in conservation. In J. S. Bruner, R. R. Olver, & P. M. Greenfield (Eds.), *Studies in cognitive growth.* New York: Wiley.

Franks, J. J., & Bransford, J. D. (1971). Abstraction of visual patterns. *Journal of Experimental Psychology, 90,* 65–74.

Franks, N. R. (1989). Army ants: A collective intelligence. *American Scientist, 77* 139–145.

Fredericksen, C. (197). Effects of context-induced processing operations on semantic information acquired from discourse. *Cognitive Psychology, 7,* 139–166.

Freud, S. (1924/1952). *A general introduction to psychoanalysis.* New York: Washington Square Press.

Freud, S. (1950/1940). A note upon the "mystic writing pad." In J. Strachey (Ed.), *Collected papers of Sigmund Freud.* London: Hogarth Press.

Freund, J. S., & Johnson, J. W. (1972). Changes in memory attribute dominance as a function of age. *Journal of Educational Psychology, 63,* 386–389.

Frost, N. A. H. (1971). Clustering by visual and semantic codes in long-term memory. Unpublished doctoral dissertation, University of Oregon.

Fruth, H. G. (1969). *Piaget and knowledge: Theoretical foundations.* Englewood Cliffs, NJ: Prentice-Hall.

Galotti, K. M., Baron, J., & Sabini, J. (1986). Individual differences in syllogistic reasoning: Deduction rules or mental models? *Journal of Experimental Psychology: General, 115,* 16–25.

Galton, F. (1880). Statistics of mental imagery. *Mind, 5,* 301–318.

Galton, F. (1907). *Inquiries into human faculty and its development.* London: Macmillan. (Originally published 1883.)

Ganellen, R. J., & Carver, C. S. (1985). Why does self-reference promote incidental encoding? *Journal of Experimental Psychology, 21,* 284–300.

Garcia, G. & Diener, D. (1993). Do you remember . . . A comparison of mnemonic strategies. Paper presented at the annual meeting of WPA, Phoenix, AZ, May.

Gardner, H. (1985). *The mind's new science.* New York: Basic Books.

Gardner, R. A., & Gardner, B. T. (1969). Teaching sign language to a chimpanzee. *Science, 165,* 664–672.

Garner, W. R. (1958). Symmetric uncertainty analysis and its implications for psychology. *Psychology Review, 65,* 183–196.

Garner, W. R. (1962). *Uncertainty and structure as psychological concepts.* New York: Wiley.

Garner, W. R., & Carson, D. H. (1960). A multivariate solution of the redundancy of printed English. *Psychology Review, 6,* 123–141.

Garrity, L. I. (1975). An electromyographical study of subvocal speech and recall in preschool children. *Developmental Psychology, 11,* 274–281.

Gastaut, H., & Bert, J. (1961). Electroencephalographic detection of sleep induced by repetitive sensory stimuli. In G. E. W. Wolstenholme & M. O'Connor (Eds.), *The nature of sleep.* London: Churchill.

Gazzaniga, M. A. (1970). *The bisected brain.* New York: Appleton-Century-Crofts.

Gazzaniga, M. A., & Sperry, R. W. (1967). Language after section of the cerebral commissures. *Brain, 90,* 131–148.

Gazzaniga, M. S. (1967). The split brain in man. *Scientific American, 217*(2), 24–29.

Gazzaniga, M. S. (1975). Experimental apparatus. In M. S. Gazzaniga & C. Blakemore (Eds.), *Handbook of Psychobiology.* New York: Academic Press.

Gazzaniga, M. S. (1983). Right hemisphere language following commissurotomy: A twenty-year perspective. *American Psychologist, 38,* 525–537.

Gazzaniga, M. S., Bogen, J. E., & Sperry, R. W. (1965). Observations on visual perception after disconnection of the cerebral hemispheres in man. *Brain, 88,* 221–236.

Geiger, G., & Lettvin, J. (1987). Dyslexia. *The New England Journal of Medicine, 316,* 1238–1243.

Gelman, R. (1969). Conservation acquisition: A problem of learning to attend to relevant attributes. *Journal of Experimental Child Psychology, 7,* 167–187.

Gelman, R. (1972). The nature and development of early number concepts. In H. Reese (Ed.), *Advances in child development and behavior (Vol. 7)*. New York: Academic Press.

Generalization of conditioned GSRs in dichotic listening. In P. M. A. Rabbit & S. Dornic (Eds.), *Attention and performance V.* New York: Academic Press.

Gentner, D. R. (1988). Expertise in typewriting. In M. T. H. Chi, R. Glaser, & M. J. Farr (Eds.), *The nature of expertise.* Hillsdale, NJ: Erlbaum.

Georgopoulos, A. P., Lurito, J. T., Petrides, M., Schwartz, A. B., & Massey, J. T. (1989). Mental rotation of the neuronal population vector. *Science, 243,* 234–236.

Gevins, A., & Cutillo, B. (1993). Spatiotemporal dynamics of component processes in human working memory. *Electroencephalography and Clinical Neurophysiology, 87,* 128–143.

Glaser, R., & Chi, M. T. H. (1988). Overview. In M. T. H. Chi, R. Glaser, & M. J. Farr (Eds.), *The nature of expertise.* Hillsdale, NJ: Erlbaum.

Glass, A. L., & Holyoak, K. J. (1974). The effect of *some* and *all* on reaction time for semantic decisions. *Memory and Cognition, 2,* 436–440.

Glass, A. L., & Holyoak, K. J. (1975). Alternative conceptions of semantic memory. *Cognition, 3*(8), 313–339.

Glass, A. L., & Holyoak, K. J. (1986). *Cognition* (2nd ed.). New York: Random House.

Glass, A. L., Holyoak, K. J., & O'Dell, D. (1974). Production frequency and the verification of quantified statements. *Journal of Verbal Learning and Verbal Behavior, 13,* 237–254.

Gleason, H. A., Jr. (1961). *An introduction to descriptive linguistics* (rev. ed.). New York: Holt, Rinehart & Winston.

Gluck, M. A., & Rumelhart, D. E. (Eds.) (1990). *Neuroscience and Connectionist Theory.* Hillsdale, NJ: Erlbaum.

Glucksberg, S. (1962). The influence of strength of drive on functional fixedness and perceptual recognition. *Journal of Experimental Psychology, 63,* 36–51.

Glucksberg, S., & Danks, J. H. (1969). Grammatical structure and recall: A function of the space in immediate memory or of recall delay. *Perception and Psychophysics, 6,* 113–117.

Gold, A. R. (1988). Scholars losing sight of the reason for reading. In *Reno Gazette-Journal,* July 9.

Gold, P. E. (1987). Sweet memories. *American Scientist, 75,* 151–155.

Goldenberg, G., Podreka, I., Steiner, M., Suess, E., Deeke, L., & Willmes, K. (1990). Regional cerebral blood flow patterns in imagery tasks—results of single photon emission computer tomography. In M. Denis, J. Engelkamp, & J. T. E. Richardson (Eds.), *Cognitive and neuropsychological approaches to mental imagery.* Dodrecht, The Netherlands: Martinus Nijhoff.

Goldin-Meadow, S. (1982). Cited in L. Edson, Under Babel's tower. *Mosaic, 13,* 22–28.

Goodman, K. (1970). Reading: A psycholinguistic guessing game. In H. Singer & R. D. Ruddel (Eds.), *Theoretical models and processes of reading* (pp. 259–272). Newark, DE: International Reading Association.

Gordon, R. (1949). An investigation into some of the factors that favour the formation of stereotyped images. *British Journal of Psychology, 39,* 156–167.

Gordon, R. (1950). An experiment correlating the nature of imagery with performance on a test of reversal of perspective. *British Journal of Psychology, 41,* 63–67.

Graham, F. K., Leavitt, L. A., Strock, B. D., & Brown, J. W. (1978). Precocious cardiac orienting in human anencephalic infants. *Science, 199,* 322–324.

Graham, L. R. (1972). *Science and philosophy in the Soviet Union.* New York: Knopf.

Gray, J. A., & Wedderburn, A. A. I. (1960). Grouping strategies with simultaneous stimuli. *Quarterly Journal of Experimental Psychology, 12,* 180–184.

Green, D. M., & Swets, J. A. (1966). *Signal detection theory and psychophysics.* New York: Wiley.

Greenberg, J. H. (1963). Some universals of grammar with particular reference to the order of meaningful elements. In J. H. Greenberg (Ed., *Universals of language.* Cambridge, MA: The MIT Press.

Greeno, J. G. (1973). The structure of memory and the process of solving problems. In R. L. Solso (Ed.), *Contemporary issues in cognitive psychology: The Loyola Symposium.* Washington, DC: Winston/Wiley.

Greeno, J. G. (1974). Hobbits and orcs: Acquisition of a sequential concept. *Cognitive Psychology, 6,* 270–292.

Gregg, L. W., & Simon H. A. (1967). Process models and stochastic theories of simple concept formation. *Journal of Mathematical Psychology, 4,* 246–276.

Gregory, R. L. (1973). The confounded eye. In R. L. Gregory & E. H. Gombrich (Eds.), *Illusion in nature and art.* New York: Scribner.

Gregory, R. L. (Ed.). (1987). *The Oxford companion to the mind.* Oxford: Oxford University Press.

Gruneberg, M. M., Morris, P. E., & Sykes, R. Jr. (Eds.). (1978). *Practical aspects of memory.* London: Academic Press.

Guilford, J. P. (1959). Three faces of intellect. *American Psychologist, 14,* 469–479.

Guilford, J. P. (1966). Intelligence: 1965 model. *American Psychologist, 21,* 20–26.

Guilford, J. P. (1967). *The nature of human intelligence.* New York: Scribner.

Guilford, J. P. (1982). Cognitive psychology's ambiguities: Some suggested remedies. *Psychological Review, 89,* 48–59.

Guzman, A. (1968). *Computer recognition of three-dimensional objects in a visual scene* (Project MAC-TR-59) (pp. 447–449). Cambridge, MA: MIT Artificial Intelligence Laboratory.

Haber, R. N. (1970). Visual perception. *Annual Review of Psychology* (Vol. 29). Palo Alto, CA: Annual Reviews.

Haber, R. N. (1983). The impending demise of the icon: A critique of the iconic storage in visual information processing. *Behavioral and Brain Sciences, 6,* 1–54.

Haber, R. N. (1985a). Comment on the demise of the icon. *Behavioral and Brain Sciences, 8,* 8.

Haber, R. N. (1985b). An icon can have no worth in the real world: Comments on Loftus, Johnson and Shimamura's "How much is an icon worth?" *Journal of Experimental Psychology: Human Perception and Performance, 11,* 374–378.

Haber, R. N. (1989). Twenty years of haunting eidetic images: Where's the ghost? *Behavioral and Brain Sciences, 2,* 583–594.

Haber, R. N., & Hershenson, M. (1973). *The psychology of visual perception.* New York: Holt, Rinehart & Winston.

Hagen, J. W. (1967). The effects of distraction on selective attention. *Child Development, 38,* 685–694.

Hagen, J. W. (Ed.), *Perspectives on the development of memory and cognition.* Hillsdale, NJ: Erlbaum.

Haith, M. M., Bergman, T., & Moore, M. J. (1977). Eye contact and face scanning in early infancy. *Science, 198,* 853–855.

Haith, M. M., Morrison, F. J., Sheingold, K., & Mindes, P. (1970). Short-term memory for visual information in children and adults. *Journal of Experimental Child Psychology, 9,* 454–469.

Hale, G. A. (1975). *Development of flexibility in children's attention deployment: A colloquium.* Research memorandum. Princeton, NJ: Educational Testing Service.

Hall, J. L., & Gold, P. E. (1990). Adrenalectomy-induced memory deficits: Role of plasma glucose levels. *Physiology & Behavior, 47,* 27–33.

Hall, J. W., & Halperin, M. S. (1972). The development of memory-encoding processes in young children. *Developmental Psychology, 6,* 181.

Halpern, A. R. (1986). Memory for tune titles after organized or unorganized presentation. *American Journal of Psychology, 99,* 57–70.

Halpern, A. R. (1989). Memory for absolute pitch of familiar songs. *Memory and Cognition, 17,* 572–581.

Hamilton, W. (1938). Cited in R. Woodworth (Ed.), *Experimental psychology.* New York: Holt.

Hamilton, W. (1954). *Lectures on metaphysics and logic* (Vol. 1, Lect. XLV). Edinburgh: Blackwood, 1859. Cited in R. Woodworth & H. Schlosberg, *Experimental Psychology.* New York: Holt.

Hart, J. T. (1965). Memory and the feeling-of-knowing experience. *Journal of Educational Psychology, 56,* 208–216.

Haugeland, J. (1989). *Artificial intelligence: The very idea.* Cambridge, MA: The MIT Press.

Hayes, J. R. (1978). *Cognitive psychology: Thinking and creating.* Homewood, IL: Dorsey Press.

Hayes, J. R. (1986). Three problems in teaching general skills. In J. Segal, S. Chipman, and R. Glaser (Eds.), *Thinking and learning* (Vol. 2). Hillsdale, NJ: Erlbaum.

Hayes, J. R. (1989). *The complete problem solver* (2nd ed.). Hillsdale, NJ: Erlbaum.

Hayes, J. R., & Simon, H. A. (1976). Psychological differences among problem isomorphs. In N. Castellon, Jr., D. Pisoni, & G. Potts (Eds.), *Cognitive Theory* (Vol. 2). Hillsdale, NJ: Erlbaum.

Haygood, R. C. (1975). *Concept learning.* Morristown, NJ: General Learning Press.

Haygood, R. C., & Bourne, L. E., Jr. (1965). Attribute and rule-learning aspects of conceptual behavior. *Psychological Review, 72*(3), 175–195.

Hayman, C. A. G., Macdonald, C. A., & Tulving, E. (1993). The role of repetition and associative interference in new semantic learning in amnesia: A case experiment. *Journal of Cognitive Neuroscience, 5,* 375–389.

Head, H. (1926). *Aphasia and kindred disorders of speech* Cambridge, England: Cambridge University Press.

Head, H. (1958). Cited in F. Bartlett, *Thinking* (p. 146). New York: Basic Books.

Hebb, D. O. (1949). *The organization of behavior.* New York: Wiley.

Heider, E. R. (1971). "Focal" color areas and the development of color names. *Developmental Psychology, 4,* 447–455.

Heider, E. R. (1972). Universals in color naming and memory. *Journal of Experimental Psychology, 93,* 10–20.

Henle, M. (1962). On the relation between logic and thinking. *Psychological Review, 69,* 366–378.

Henle, M., & Michael, M. (1956). The influence of attitudes on syllogistic reasoning. *Journal of Social Psychology, 4,* 115–127.

Heppenheimer, T. A. (1988). Nerves of silicon. *Discovery,* Feb. 70–79.

Hernandez-Peon, R. (1966). Physiological mechanisms in attention. In R. W. Russell (Ed.), *Frontiers in physiological psychology.* New York: Academic Press.

Herrmann, D. J. (1987). Task appropriateness of mnemonic techniques. *Perceptual and Motor Skills, 64,* 171–178.

Hilgard, E. R. (1980). Consciousness in contemporary psychology. *Annual Review of Psychology, 31,* 1–26.

Hilgard, E. R. (1987). *Psychology in America: A historical survey.* San Diego, CA: Harcourt Brace Jovanovich.

Hilgard, E. R., & Bower, G. H. (1974). *Theories of learning* (4th ed.). Englewood Cliffs, NJ: Prentice-Hall.

Hillis, W. D. (1987). The connection machine. *Scientific American, 256,* 108–115.

Hinsley, D., Hayes, J. R., & Simon, H. A. (1977). From words to equations. In P. Carpenter & M. Just (Eds.), *Cognitive processes in comprehension.* Hillsdale, NJ.: Erlbaum.

Hinton, G. E. (1981). A parallel computation that assigns canonical object-based frames of reference. *Proceedings of the 7th International Joint Conference on Artificial Intelligence.*

Hintzman, D. L. (1974). Psychology and the cow's belly. *The Worm Runner's Digest, 16,* 84–85.

Hofstadter, D. R. (1979). *Godel, Escher, Bach: An eternal golden braid.* New York: Basic Books.

Hofstadter, D. R. (1985). *Metamagical themas: Questions for the essence of mind and matter.* New York: Basic Books.

Holding, D. H. (1975a). Sensory storage reconsidered. *Memory and Cognition, 3,* 31–41.

Holding, D. H. (1975b). A rejoinder. *Memory and Cognition, 3,* 49–50.

Holender, D. (1986). Semantic activation without conscious identification in dichotic listening, parafoveal vision, and visual masking: A survey and appraisal. *Behavioral and Brain Sciences, 9,* 1–66.

Hollan, J. D. (1975). Features and semantic memory: Set theoretic or network model? *Psychological Review, 82,* 154–155.

Holmes, D. L., Cohen, K. M., Haith, M. M., & Morrison, F. J. (1977). Peripheral visual processing. *Perception and Psychophysics, 22*(6), 571–577.

Holmes, L. H., & Morrison, F. J. (1979). *The child.* Monterey, CA: Brooks/Cole.

Holt, R. R. (1964). Imagery: The return of the ostracized. *American Psychologist, 12,* 254–264.

Holyoak, K. J., & Glass, A. L. (1975). The role of contradictions and counterexamples in the rejection of false sentences. *Journal of Verbal Learning and Verbal Behavior, 14,* 215–239.

Horowitz, L. M., Chilian. P. C., & Dunnigan, K. P. (1969). Word fragments and their redintegrative powers. *Journal of Experimental Psychology, 80,* 392–394.

Horowitz, L. M., & Prytulak, L. S. (1969). Redintegrative memory. *Psychological Review, 76,* 519–531.

Horowitz, L. M., White, M. A., & Atwood, D. W. (1968). Word fragments as aids to recall: The organization of a word. *Journal of Experimental Psychology, 76,* 219–226.

Horton, D. L., & Turnage, T. W. (1976). *Human learning.* Englewood Cliffs, NJ: Prentice-Hall.

Houston, J. P. (1976). *Fundamentals of learning.* New York: Academic Press.

Hovland, C. I. (1952). A communication analysis of concept learning. *Psychological Review, 59,* 461–472.

Howes, D., & Solomon, R. L. (1951). Visual duration thresholds as a function of word probability. *Journal of Experimental Psychology, 41,* 401–410.

Hubel, D. H. (1959). Receptive fields of single neurons in the cat's striate cortex. *Journal of Physiology, 148,* 574–591.

Hubel, D. H. (1963a). Receptive fields of cells in the striate cortex of very young, visually inexperienced kittens. *Journal of Neurophysiology, 26,* 994–1002.

Hubel, D. H. (1963b). The visual cortex of the brain. *Scientific American,* Nov., 54–62.

Hubel, D. H., & Wiesel, T. N. (1959). Receptive fields of single neurons in the cat's striate cortex. *Journal of Physiology, 148,* 574–591.

Hubel, D. H., & Wiesel, T. N. (1963). Receptive fields of cells in the striate cortex of very young, visually inexperienced kittens. *Journal of Neurophysiology, 26,* 994–1002.

Hudson, W. (1967). The study of the problem of pictorial perception among unacculturated groups. *International Journal of Psychology, 2,* 89–107.

Huey, E. B. (1968). *The psychology and pedagogy of reading.* Cambridge, MA: The MIT Press. (First published by Macmillan in 1908.)

Hume, D. (1912). *An enquiry concerning human understanding.* Chicago: Open Court. (Original publication 1748.)

Hunt, E. B. (1961). Memory effects in concept learning. *Journal of Experimental Psychology, 62,* 598–609.

Hunt, E. B. (1968). Computer simulation: Artificial intelligence studies and their relevance to psychology. In P. R. Farnsworth (Ed.), *Annual review of psychology* (Vol. 19). Palo Alto, CA: Annual Reviews.

Hunt, E. B. (1971). What kind of computer is man? *Cognitive Psychology, 2,* 57–98.

Hunt, E. B. (1973). The memory we must have. In R. Schank & K. Colby (Eds.), *Computer models of thought and language* (pp. 343–371). San Francisco: Freeman.

Hunt, E. B. (1978). Mechanics of verbal ability. *Psychological Review, 85,* 109–130.

Hunt, E. B. (1989). Cognitive science: Definition, status, and questions. In M. R. Rosenzweig & L. W. Porter (Eds.), *Annual Review of Psychology, 40* (pp. 603–629). Palo Alto, CA: Annual Reviews.

Hunt, E. B., & Lansman, M. (1982). Individual differences in attention. In R. J. Sternberg (Ed.), *Advances in the psychology of human intelligence.* Hillsdale, NJ: Erlbaum.

Hunt, E., & Love, T. (1972). How good can memory be? In A. W. Melton & E. Martin (Eds.), *Coding processes in human memory.* Washington, DC: Winston.

Hunt, E. B., Lunneborg, C., & Lewis, J. (1975). What does it mean to be high verbal? *Cognitive Psychology, 7,* 194–227.

Hunter, I. M. L. (1957). *Memory: Facts and fallacies.* Harmondsworth, Middlesex, England: Penguin.

Hunter, I. M. L. (1962). An exceptional talent for calculative thinking. *British Journal of Psychology, 53,* 243–258.

Hunter, I. M. L. (1964). *Memory.* Harmondsworth, Middlesex, England: Penguin.

Inhelder, B., & Piaget, J. (1964a). *The early growth of logical thinking.* New York: Norton.

Inhelder, B., & Piaget, J. (1964b). *The early growth of logic in the child.* New York: Harper Row.

Inhoff, A., & Tousman, S. (1990). Lexical priming from partial-word previews. *Journal of Experimental Psychology: Human Perception and Performance, 16,* 825–836.

Inn, D., Walden, K. J., and Solso, R. L. Facial prototype formation in three to six year old children. Unpublished manuscript. University of Nevada, Reno.

Intons-Peterson, M. J., & Fournier, J. (1986). External and internal memory aids: When and how often do we use them? *Journal of Experimental Psychology: General, 115,* 267–280.

Intons-Peterson, M. J., & Smyth, M. M. (1987). The anatomy of repertory memory. *Journal of Experimental Psychology: Learning, Memory, and Cognition, 13,* 490–500.

Ionesco, E. (1970). *Story number 2.* New York: Harlin Quist/Crown.

Ivry, R. B., & Lebby, P. C. (1993). Hemispheric differences in auditory perception are similar to those found in visual perception. *Psychological Science, 4,* 41–45.

Izawa, C. (1989). *Current issues in cognitive processes: The Tulane Flowerree Symposium on cognition.* Hillsdale, NJ: Erlbaum.

Jackson, A., & Morton, J. (1984). Facilitation of auditory word recognition. *Memory and Cognition, 12,* 568–574.

Jackson, P. C. (1974). *Introduction to artificial intelligence.* New York: Petrocelli/Charter.

Jacoby, L. L., & Witherspoon, D. (1982). Remembering without awareness. *Canadian Journal of Psychology, 32,* 300–324.

Jakobovits, L. A., & Miron, M. S. (1967). *Readings in the psychology of language.* Englewood Cliffs, NJ: Prentice-Hall.

Jakobson, R. (1972). Verbal communication. *Scientific American,* Sept., 38–44.

James, W. (1890). *Principles of psychology.* New York: Holt.

Janis, I. L., & Frick, F. (1943). The relationship between attitudes toward conclusions and errors in judging logical validity of syllogisms. *Journal of Experimental Psychology, 33,* 73–77.

Janis, I. L., & Mann, L. (1977). *Decision making.* New York: Free Press.

Javal, L. E. (1878). Essai sur la physiologie de la lecture. *Annales d'Oculistique, 82,* 242–253.

Jaynes, J. (1976). *The origins of consciousness in the breakdown of the bicameral mind.* Boston: Houghton Mifflin.

Jenkins, J. G., & Dallenbach, K. M. (1924). Oblivescence during sleep and waking. *American Journal of Psychology, 35,* 605–612.

Jenkins, J. J. (1963). Mediated associations: Paradigms and situations. In C. N. Cofer & B. S. Musgrave (Eds.), *Verbal behavior and learning.* New York: McGraw-Hill.

Jensen, A. R. (1993). Why is reaction time correlated with psychometric g? *Current Directions in Psychological Science, 2,* 53–56.

John, E. R. (1972). Switchboard versus statistical theories of learning and memory. *Science, 177,* 849–864.

Johnson, E. J. (1988). Expertise and decision under uncertainty: Performance and process. In M. T. H. Chi, R. Glaser, & M. J. Farr (Eds.), *The nature of expertise.* Hillsdale, NJ: Erlbaum.

Johnson, M. H. (Ed.). (1993). *Brain development and cognition: A reader.* Cambridge, MA: Blackwell.

Johnson-Laird, P. N. (1970). The perception and memory of sentences. In J. Lyons (Ed.), *New horizons in linguistics* (pp. 261–270). Baltimore: Penguin.

Johnson-Laird, P. N. (1983). *Mental models: Towards a cognitive science of language, inference, and consciousness.* Cambridge, MA: Harvard University Press.

Johnson-Laird, P. N. (1988). *The computer and the mind.* Cambridge, MA: Harvard University Press.

Johnson-Laird, P. N., & Byrne, R. M. J. (1989). Only reasoning. *Journal of Memory and Language, 28,* 313–330.

Johnson-Laird, P. N. & Byrne, R. M. J. (1991). *Deduction.* Hove, England: Erlbaum.

Johnson-Laird, P. N., Legrenzi, P., & Legrenzi, M. (1992). Reasoning and a sense of reality. *British Journal of Psychology, 63,* 395–400.

Johnson-Laird, P. N., & Steedman, M. (1978). The psychology of syllogisms. *Cognitive Psychology, 10,* 64–99.

Johnson-Laird, P. N., & Wason, P. C. (Eds.). (1977). *Thinking: Readings in cognitive science.* Cambridge, England: Cambridge University Press.

Johnston, W. A., & Heinz, S. P. (1975). Depth of non-target processing in an attention task. *Journal of Experimental Psychology, 5,* 168–175.

Johnston, W. A., & Heinz, S. P. (1978). Flexibility and capacity demands of attention. *Journal of Experimental Psychology: General, 107,* 420–435.

Johnston, W. A., & Wilson, J. (1980). Perceptual processing of non-target in an attention task. *Memory and Cognition, 8,* 372–377.

Jolicoeur, P., Regehr, S., Smith, L. B., & Smith, G. N. (1985). Mental rotation of representations of two-dimensional and three-dimensional objects. *Canadian Journal of Psychology, 39,* 100–129.

Just, M. A., & Carpenter, P. A. (1980). A theory of reading: From eye fixations to comprehension. *Psychological Review, 87,* 329–354.

Just, M. A., & Carpenter, P. A. (1987). *The psychology of reading and language comprehension.* Newton, MA: Allyn and Bacon.

Kahn, D. (1967). *The codebreakers: The story of secret writing.* New York: Macmillan.

Kahneman, D. (1973). *Attention and effort.* Englewood Cliffs, NJ: Prentice-Hall.

Kahneman, D., & Miller, D. (1986). Norm theory: Comparing reality to its alternatives. *Psychology Review, 93,* 136–153.

Kahneman, D., & Tversky, A. (1972). Subjective probability: A judgment of representativeness. *Cognitive Psychology, 3,* 430–454.

Kahneman, D., & Tversky, A. (1983). On the psychology of prediction. *Psychological Review, 80,* 237–251.

Kahneman, D., & Tversky, A. (1984). Choices, values, and frames. *American Psychologist, 39,* 341–350.

Kandel, E. R. (1981a). Nerve cells and behavior. In E. R. Kandel and J. H. Schwartz (Eds.), *Principles of Neural Science.* New York: Elsevier/North-Holland.

Kandel, E. R. (1981b). Brain and behavior. In E. R. Kandel and J. H. Schwartz (Eds.), *Principles of neural science.* New York: Elsevier/North-Holland.

Kandel, E. R., & Schwartz, J. H. (Eds.). (1981). *Principles of neural science.* New York: Elsevier/North-Holland.

Kandel, E. R., Schwartz, J. H., & Jessell, T. M. (1991). *Principles of Neural Science.* New York: Elsevier.

Kandinsky, W. (1912). *Über das qeistige in der Kunst, inbesondere in der Malerei.* Munchen: Piper.

Kao, Y. F. (1990). Subliminal processing: The spread of activation in color priming. Unpublished doctoral dissertation. University of Nevada, Reno.

Kao, Y. F., & Solso, R. L. (1989). *One second of cognition.* Paper presented at the annual meeting of RMPA/WPA, Reno, NV, Apr.

Kaplan, R. M. (1972). Augmented transition networks as psychological models of sentence comprehension. *Artificial Intelligence, 3,* 77–100.

Kapur, S., Craik, F. I. M., Tulving, E., Wilson, A. A., Hoyle, S., & Brown, G. M. (In press). Neuroanatomical correlates of encoding in episodic memory: Levels of processing effect. *Proceedings of the National Academy of Sciences, 91,* 2008–2011. Washington, D. C.: National Academy of Sciences.

Katz, S., & Gruenewald, P. (1974). The abstraction of linguistic ideas in "meaningless" sentences. *Memory and Cognition, 2,* 737–741.

Kausler, D. H. (1974). *Psychology of verbal learning and memory.* New York: Academic Press.

Kavanagh, J. F., & Mattingly I. G. (Eds.). (1972). *Language by ear and by eye: The relationship between speech and reading.* Cambridge, MA: The MIT Press.

Kay, P., & Kempton, W. (1984). What is the Sapir-Whorf Hypothesis? *American Anthropologist, 86,* 65–79.

Keele, S. W. (1973). Attention and human performance. Pacific Palisades, CA: Goodyear.

Kendler, H. H., & Kendler, T. S. (1969). Reversal-shift behavior: Some basic issues. *Psychological Bulletin, 72,* 229–232.

Kennedy, A., & Wilkes, A. *(Eds.). (1975). Studies in long term memory.* New York: Wiley.

Kess, J. F. (1976). *Psycholinguistics: Introductory perspectives.* New York: Academic Press.

Kessen, W., & Kuhlman, C. (1970). *Cognitive developments in children.* Chicago: University of Chicago Press.

Kihlstrom, J. F. (1987). The cognitive unconscious. *Science, 237,* 1445–1453.

Kihlstrom, J. F., & Cantor, N. (1984). Mental representations of the self. In L. Berkowitz (Ed.), *Advances in Experimental Social Psychology, 93,* 200–208.

Kimura, D. (1963). Right temporal lobe damage. *Arch Neurology, 8,* 264–271.

Kimura, D. (1967). Functional asymmetry of the brain in dichotic listening. *Cortex, 3,* 163–178.

Kintsch, W. (1967). Memory and decision aspects of recognition learning. *Psychological Review, 74,* 496–504.

Kintsch, W. (1974). *The representation of meaning in memory.* Hillsdale, NJ: Erlbaum.

Kintsch, W. (1979). On modeling comprehension. *Educational Psychologist, 14,* 3–14.

Kintsch, W. (1988). The role of knowledge in discourse comprehension: A construction-integration model. *Psychological Review, 95,* 163–182.

Kintsch, W. (1990). The representation of knowledge and the use of knowledge in discourse comprehension. In C. Graumann & R. Dietrich (Eds.), *Language in the social context.* Amsterdam: Elsevier.

Kintsch, W., & Keenan, J. (1973). Reading rate and retention as a function of the number of propositions in the base structure of sentences. *Cognitive Psychology, 5,* 257–274.

Kintsch, W., & van Dijk, T. A. (1978). Toward a model of text comprehension and production. *Psychological Review, 85,* 363–394.

Kintsch, W., & Vipond, D. (1979). Reading comprehension and readability in educational practice and psychological theory. In L. G. Nilsson (Ed.), *Perspectives on memory research.* Hillsdale, NJ: Erlbaum.

Kirkpatrick, E. A. (1894). An experimental study of memory. *Psychological Review, 1,* 602–609.

Klatzky, R. L. (1975). *Human memory: Structures and processes.* San Francisco: Freeman.

Klatzky, R. L. (1984). *Memory and awareness.* San Francisco: Freeman.

Klein, K., & Saltz, E. (1976). Specifying the mechanisms in a levels-of-processing approach to memory. *Journal of Experimental Psychology, 87,* 281–288.

Kleinmuntz, B. (1969). *Clinical information processing by computer.* New York: Holt, Rinehart & Winston.

Kline, S. B., & Kihlstrom, J. F. (1986). Elaboration, organization, and the self-reference effect in memory. *Journal of Experimental Psychology: General, 113,* 26–38.

Kobasigawa, A., & Middleton, D. B. (1972). Free recall of categorized items by children at three grade levels. *Child Development, 43,* 1067–1072.

Koenig, O., Reiss, L. P., & Kosslyn, S. M. (1990). The development of spacial relation representations: Evidence from studies of cerebral lateralization. *Journal of Experimental Child Psychology, 50,* 119–130.

Köhler, W. (1938). *The place of value in the world of facts.* New York: Liveright.

Köhler, W. (1947). *Gestalt psychology: An introduction to the new concepts in modern psychology.* New York: Liveright.

Kolb, B., & Whishaw, I. Q. (1990). *Fundamentals of Human Neuropsychology.* New York: Freeman.

Kolers, W. (1970). Three stages of reading. In H. Levin & J. P. Williams (Eds.), *Basic studies on reading.* New York: Basic Books.

Kolers, P. A., & Palef, S. R. (1976). Knowing not. *Memory and Cognition, 4,* 553–558.

Kosslyn, S. M. (1973). Scanning visual images: Some structural implications. *Perception and Psychophysics, 14,* 90–94.

Kosslyn, S. M. (1975). Information representation in visual images. *Cognitive Psychology, 7,* 341–370.

Kosslyn, S. M. (1976a). Can imagery be distinguished from other forms of internal representation? Evidence from studies of information-retrieval time. *Memory and Cognition, 4,* 291–297.

Kosslyn, S. M. (1976b). *Visual images present metric spatial information.* Paper presented at the Psychonomic Society Meetings, St. Louis, MO.

Kosslyn, S. M. (1977). Imagery and internal representation. In E. Rosch & U. Lloyd (Eds.), *Categories and cognition.* Hillsdale, NJ: Erlbaum.

Kosslyn, S. M. (1980). *Image and mind.* Cambridge, MA: Harvard University Press.

Kosslyn, S. M. (1981). The medium and the message in mental imagery. *Psychological Review, 88,* 46–66.

Kosslyn, S. M. (1983). *Ghosts in the mind's machine* New York: Norton.

Kosslyn, S. M. (1988). Aspects of cognitive neuroscience of mental imagery. *Science, 240,* 1621–1626.

Kosslyn, S. M. (1994). *Image and brain: The resolution of the imagery debate.* Cambridge, MA: The MIT Press.

Kosslyn, S. M., Alpert, N. M., Thompson, W. L., Meljkovic, V., Weise, S. B., Chabris, C. F., Hamilton, S. E., Rauch, S. L., & Buonanno, F. S. (1993). Visual mental imagery activates topographically organized visual cortex: PET investigations. *Journal of Cognitive Neuroscience, 5,* 263–287.

Kosslyn, S. M., Ball, T. M., & Reiser, B. J. (1978). Visual images preserve metric spatial information. Evidence from studies of image scanning. *Journal of Experimental Psychology: Human Perception and Performance, 40* 47–60.

Kosslyn, S. M., Murphy, G. L., Bemesderfer, M. E., & Feinstein, K. J. (1977). Category and continuum in mental comparisons. *Journal of Experimental Psychology: General, 106,* 341–375.

Kosslyn, S. M., & Pomerantz, J. R. (1977). Imagery, proposition, and the form of internal representations. *Cognitive Psychology, 9, 52–76.*

Kosslyn, S. M., & Schwartz, S. P. (1977). A simulation of visual imagery. *Cognitive Science, 1,* 265–295.

Kosslyn, S. M., Sokolov, M. A., & Chen, J. C. (1989). The lateralization of BRIAN: A computational theory and model of visual hemispheric specialization. In D. Klahr and K. Kotovsky (Eds.), *Complex information processing: The impact of Herbert H. Simon.* Hillsdale, NJ: Erlbaum.

Kozulin, A. (1984). *Psychology in Utopia: Toward a social history of Soviet psychology.* Cambridge, MA: The MIT Press.

Kozulin, A. (1986). The concept of activity in Soviet psychology. *American Psychologist, 1,* 264–274.

Kries, J. V. (195). Über die Natur gewisser mit den pschischen Vorgangen Verknupfter Gehirnzustande. *Z. Psy,* 1985, *8,* 1–33. Cited in R. Woodworth & H. Schlosberg (Eds.), *Experimental psychology.* New York: Holt.

Kroll, N. E. A., Schepeler, E. M., & Angin, K. T. (1986). Bizarre imagery: The misremembered mnemonic. *Journal of Experimental Psychology: Learning, Memory, and Cognition, 12,* 42–53.

Kučera, H., & Francis, W. N. (1967). *Computational analysis of present-day American English.* Providence, RI: Brown University Pres.

Kuhn, T. S. (1962). *The structure of scientific revolutions.* Chicago: University of Chicago Press.

Kupferman, I. (1981). Localization of higher function. In E. R. Kandel & J. H. Schwartz (Eds.), *Principles of neural science.* New York Elsevier/North-Holland.

LaBerge, D. (1972). Beyond auditory coding. In J. F. Kavanagh & I. G. Mattingly (Eds.), *Language by ear and by eye* (pp. 241–248). Cambridge, MA: The MIT Press.

LaBerge, D. (1975). Acquisition of automatic processing in perceptual and associative learning. In P. M. A. Rabbit & S. Dornic (Eds.), *Attention and performance V.* London: Academic Press.

LaBerge, D. (1976). Perceptual learning and attention. In W. Estes (Ed.), *Handbook of learning and cognitive processes,* Vol. 4: *Attention and memory.* Hillsdale, NJ: Erlbaum.

LaBerge, D., & Samuels, S. J. (1974). Toward a theory of automatic information processing in reading. *Cognitive Psychology, 6,* 293–323.

LaBerge, D., & Samuels, S. J. (1978). *Basic processes in reading: Perception and comprehension.* Hillsdale, NJ: Erlbaum.

Laird, D. A., & Laird, E. C. (1960). *Techniques for efficient remembering.* New York: McGraw-Hill.

Landauer, T. K. (1975). Memory without organization: Properties of a model with random storage and undirected retrieval. *Cognitive Psychology, 7,* 495–531.

Landauer, T. K., & Meyer, D. E. (1972). Category size and semantic-memory retrieval. *Journal of Verbal Learning and Verbal Behavior, 11,* 539–549.

Lange, G. (1973). The development of conceptual and rote recall skills among school-age children. *Journal of Experimental Child Psychology, 15,* 394–406.

Lashley, K. S. (1929). *Brain mechanisms and intelligence: A quantitative study of injuries to the brain.* Chicago: University of Chicago Press.

Lashley, K. S. (1950). In search of the engram. *Proceedings from Social Experimental Biology, 4,* 454–482. Reprinted in F. A. Beach, D. O. Hebb, C. T. Morgan, H. W. Nissen (Eds.), *The neuropsychology of Lashley.* New York: McGraw-Hill.

Lashley, K. S. (1951). The problem of serial order in behavior. In L. A. Jeffress (Ed.), *Cerebral mechanisms in behavior: The Hixon Symposium.* New York: Wiley.

Lassen, N. A., Ingvar, D. H., & Skinhoj, E. (1979). Brain function and blood flow. *Scientific American, 239,* 62–71.

Laughlin, P. R. (1968). Focusing strategy for eight concept rules. *Journal of Experimental Psychology, 77,* 661–669.

Laughlin, P. R., & Jordan, R. M. (1967) . Selection strategies in conjunctive, disjunctive, and biconditional concept attainment. *Journal of Experimental Psychology, 75,* 188–193.

Lefebvre, V. A. (1982). *Algebra of consciousness.* Boston: Reidel.

Lefton, L. A. (1973). Guessing and the order of approximation effect. *Journal of Experimental Psychology, 101*, 401–403.

Lenneberg, E. H. (1964a). In J. A. Fodor & J. J. Katz (Eds.), *The structure of language: Readings in the philosophy of language.* Englewood Cliffs, NJ: Prentice-Hall.

Lenneberg, E. H. (1964b). *New directions in the study of language.* Cambridge, MA: The MIT Press.

Lenneberg, E. H. (1967). *Biological foundations of language.* New York: Wiley.

Lenneberg, E. H. (1969). On explaining language. *Science, 164*, 635–643.

Lenneberg E. H., Nichols, I. A., & Rosenberger, E. F. (1964). In D. Rioch (Ed.), *Disorders of communication* (Research publications of Associations for Research in Nervous and Mental Disorders.) New York.

Leontiev, A. N. (1978). Cited in L. S. Vygotsky, *Mind in Society.* Cambridge, IA: Harvard University Press.

Lesgold, A. M., & Bower, G. H. (1970). Inefficiency of serial knowledge for associative responding. *Journal of Verbal Learning and Verbal Behavior, 9*, 456–466.

Lesgold, A., Glaser, R., Rubinson, H., Klopfer, D., Feltovich, P., & Wang, Y. (1988). Expertise in a complex skill: Diagnosing X-ray pictures. In M. T. H. Chi, R. Glaser, & M. J. Farr (Eds.), *The nature of expertise.* Hillsdale, NJ: Erlbaum.

Levine, M. (1993). *Effective problem solving 2nd ed.* Englewood Cliffs, NJ: Prentice-Hall.

Levitin, K. (1982). *One is not born a personality.* Moscow, Progress Publishers.

Levy, J., Trevarthen, C., & Sperry, R. V. (1972). Perception of bilateral chimeric figures-following hemispheric deconnexion. *Brain, 95*, 61–78.

Lewis, J. L. (1970). Semantic processing of unattended messages using dichotic listening. *Journal of Experimental Psychology, 85*, 225–228.

Liberty, C., & Ornstein, P. A. (1973). Age differences in organization and recall: The effects of training in categorization. *Journal of Experimental Child Psychology, 15*, 169–186.

Lindsay, P. H., & Norman, D. A. (1973). *Human information processing* (2nd ed.). New York: Academic Press.

Linton, M. (1982). Transformations of memory in everyday life. In U. Neisser (Ed.), *Memory observed: Remembering in natural contexts.* San Francisco: Freeman.

Lockhart, R. S., Craik, F. I. M., & Jacoby, L. L. (1975). Depth of processing in recognition and recall: Some aspects of a general memory system. In J. Brown (Ed.), *Recognition and recall.* London: Wiley.

Lockhart, R. S., & Murdock, B. B., Jr. (1970). Memory and the theory of signal detection. *Psychological Bulletin, 74*, 100–109.

Loftus, E. F. (1975a). Leading questions and the eyewitness report. *Cognitive Psychology, 7*, 560–572.

Loftus, E. F. (1975b). Spreading activation within semantic categories: Comments on Rosch's "Cognitive representations of semantic categories." *Journal of Experimental Psychology: General, 104*, 234–240.

Loftus, E. F. (1977). How to catch a zebra in semantic memory. In R. Shaw & J. Bransford (Eds.), *Perceiving, acting and knowing.* Hillsdale, NJ: Erlbaum.

Loftus, E. F. (1983). Misfortunes of memory. *Philosophical Transactions of the Royal Society,* London, B 302, 413–421.

Loftus, E. F. (1993). Desperately seeking memories of the first few years of childhood: The reality of early memories. *Journal of Experimental Psychology: General, 122*, 274–277.

Loftus, E. F., Miller, D. G., & Burns, H. J. (1978). Semantic integration of verbal information into a visual memory. *Journal of Experimental Psychology: Human Learning, 4*, 19–31.

Loftus, E. F., & Palmer, J. C. (1974). Reconstruction of automobile destruction: An example of the interaction between language and memory. *Journal of Verbal Learning and Verbal Behavior, 13*, 585–589.

Loftus, E. F., & Zanni, G. (1975). Eyewitness testimony: The influence of the wording of a question. *Bulletin of the Psychonomic Society, 5*, 86–88.

Loftus, G. R. (1982). Picture methodology. In C. R. Pubb (Ed.), *Handbook of research methods in human memory and cognition* (pp. 257–285). New York: Academic Press.

Loftus, G. R. (1983). The continuing persistence of the icon. *Behavioral and Brain Sciences, 1*, 43.

Loftus, G. R. (1995). On worthwhile icons: Reply to Di Lollo and Haber. *Journal of Experimental Psychology: Human Perception and Performance, 18*, 530–549.

Loftus, G. R., Johnson, C. A., & Shimarmura, A. P. (1985). How much is an icon worth? *Journal of Experimental Psychology: Human Perception and Performance, 11*, 1–13.

Loftus, G. R., & Loftus, E. F. (1976). *Human memory: The processing of information.* Hillsdale, NJ: Erlbaum.

Lorayne, H., & Lucas, J. (1974). *The memory book.* New York: Stein and Day.

Lubart, T. I., & Sternberg, R. J. (in preparation). *Creative performance: Testing an investment theory.* New Haven: Yale University Press.

Luria, A. R. (1960). *Problems of psychology, No. 1.* New York: Pergamon Press.

Luria, A. R. (1968). *The mind of a mnemonist.* New York: Basic Books.

Luria, A. R. (1971). Towards the problem of the historical nature of psychological processes. *International Journal of Psychology, 6,* 259–272.

Luria, A. R. (1974). The mind of a mnemonist: His memory. In P. A. Fried, *Readings in perception.* Lexington, MA: Heath.

Luria, A. R. (1976). *The neuropsychology of memory.* Washington, DC: Winston.

Lynch, S., & Yarnell, P. R. (1973). Retrograde amnesia: Delayed forgetting after concussion. *American Journal of Psychology, 86,* 643–645.

Lyons, J. (1968). *Introduction to theoretical linguistics.* Cambridge, England: Cambridge University Press.

Lyons, J. (1970). *New horizons in linguistics.* Harmondsworth, Middlesex, England: Penguin.

Lyons, J., & Wales, R. J. (1966). Psycholinguistic papers. *The Proceedings of the 1966 Edinburgh Conference.* Edinburgh: Edinburgh University Press.

Mackworth, N. H. (1950). *Researches on the measurement of human performance* (Medical Research Council Special Report Series, No. 268). England.

Mackworth, N. H. (1965). Visual noise causes tunnel vision. *Psychonomic Science 3,* 67–68.

Mackworth, N. H. (1970). *Vigilance and habituation.* London: Penguin.

MacNeilage, P. F. (1970). Motor control of serial ordering of speech. *Psychological Review, 77,* 182–196.

MacNeilage, P. F. (1972). Speech physiology. In J. Gilbert (Ed.), *Speech and cortical functioning* (pp. 1–72). New York: Academic Press.

MacNeilage, P. F., & Ladefoged, P. (1976). The production of speech and language. In E. C. Carterette & M. P. Friedman (Eds.), *Handbook of perception* (Vol. 7, pp. 75–120). New York: Academic Press.

MacNeilage, P. F., & MacNeilage, L. A. (1973). Central processes controlling speech production during sleep and waking. In F. J. McGuigan & R. A. Schoonover (Eds.), *The psychophysiology of thinking* (pp. 417–448). New York: Academic Press.

Maltzman, I. (1955). Thinking: From a behavioristic point of view. *Psychological Review, 62,* 275–286.

Mandelbaum, D. B. (1958). *Selected writings of Edward Sapir in language, culture and personality.* Berkeley and Los Angeles: University of California Press.

Mandler, G. (1954). Response factors in human learning. *Psychological Review, 61,* 235–244.

Mandler, G. (1962). From association to structure. *Psychological Review, 69,* 415–427.

Mandler, G. (1967). Organization and memory. In K. W. Spence & J. T. Spence (Eds.), *The psychology of learning and motivation* (Vol. 1). New York: Academic Press.

Mandler, G. (1974). Memory storage and retrieval: Some limits on the reach of attention and consciousness. In P. M. A. Rabbit & S. Dornic (Eds.), *Attention and performance V.* London: Academic Press.

Mandler, G. (1975a). Consciousness: Respectable, useful, and probably necessary. In R. L. Solso Ed.), *Information processing and cognitive psychology.* Hillsdale, NJ: Erlbaum.

Mandler, G. (1975b). *Mind and emotion.* New York: Wiley.

Mandler, G. (1983). Representation and recall in infancy. In J. H. Flavell & E. M. Markman (Eds.), *Handbook of child psychology: Cognitive development* (Vol. 3). New York: Wiley.

Mandler, G. (1984). Representation and recall in infancy. In M. Moscovitch (Ed.), *Infant memory.* New York: Plenum Press.

Mandler, J. M. (1990). A new perspective on cognitive development in infancy. *American Scientist, 78,* 236–243.

Mandler, J. M., & Bauer, P. J. (1988). The cradle of categorization: Is the basic level basic? *Cognitive Development, 3,* 247–264.

Mandler, J. M., DeForest, M. (1979). Is there more than one way to recall a story? *Child Development, 44,* 697–700.

Mandler, J. M., & Johnson, N. S. (1977). Remembrance of things parsed: Story structure and recall. *Cognitive Psychology, 9,* 111–151.

Manro, H. M., & Washburn, M. F. (1908). The effect of imperceptible lines on the judgment of distance. *American Journal of Psychology, 19,* 242–243.

Mantyla, T. (1986). Optimizing cue effectiveness: Recall of 500 and 600 incidentally learned words. *Journal of Experimental Psychology: Learning, Memory, and Cognition, 12,* 66–71.

Mäntysalo, S., & Näätänen, R. (1987). The duration of neuronal trace of an auditory stimulus as indicated by event-related potentials. *Biological Psychology, 24,* 183–195.

Marks, L. E. (1974). On associations of light and sound: The mediation of brightness, pitch, and loudness. *American Journal of Psychology, 87,* 173–188.

Marks, L. E. (1987a). *Synesthesia, perception and metaphor.* Paper presented before the annual meeting of the American Psychological Association, New York, Aug.

Marks, L. E. (1987b). On cross-modal similarity: Auditory-visual interactions in speeded discrimination. *Journal of Experimental Psychology: Human Perception and Performance, 13,* 384–394.

Marr, D. (1982). *Vision.* San Francisco: Freeman.

Martin, R. C. (1993). Short-term memory and sentence processing: Evidence from neuropsychology. *Memory & Cognition, 21,* 176–183.

Massaro, D. W. (1972). Preperceptual images, processing time, and perceptual units in auditory perception. *Psychological Review, 79*(2), 124–145.

Massaro, D. W. (1975). *Experimental psychology and information processing.* Chicago: Rand McNally.

Massaro, D. W. (1987). *Speech perception by ear and eye: A paradigm for psychological inquiry.* Hillsdale, NJ: Erlbaum.

Massaro, D. W., & Hestand J. (1983). Developmental relations between reading ability and knowledge of orthographic structure. *Contemporary Educational Psychology, 8,* 174–180.

Massaro, D. W., & Schmuller, J. (1975). Visual features, preperceptual storage, and processing time in reading. In D. Massaro (Ed.), *Understanding language.* New York: Academic Press.

Matthews, W. A. (1968). Transformational complexity and short-term recall. *Language and Speech, 11,* 120–128.

Mattingly, I. G. (1972). Speech cues and sign stimuli. *American Scientist, 60,* 327–337.

Maxwell, W. (Ed.). (1983). *Thinking: The expanding frontier.* Philadelphia: Franklin Institute Press.

May, J. (1989). Mental imagery and sports. *Psychology Today,* May, 23–24.

Mayer, R. E. (1981). *The promise of cognitive psychology.* San Francisco: Freeman.

Mayer, R. E. (1983). *Thinking, problem solving, cognition.* San Francisco: Freeman.

McBurney, D., & Collings, V. (1977). *Introduction to sensation/perception.* Englewood Cliffs, NJ: Prentice-Hall.

McCarthy, D. (1954). Language development in children. In L. Carmichael (Ed.), *Manual of child psychology* (pp. 492–630). New York: Wiley.

McCarthy, G., Blamire, A. M., Rothman, D. L., Gruetier, R., Shulman, R. G. (1993). *Proceedings of the National Academy of Sciences, 90,* 49–52.

McCaul, K. D., & Maki, R. H. (1984). Self-reference versus desirability ratings and memory for traits. *Journal of Personality and Social Psychology, 47,* 953–955.

McClelland, J. L. (1981). Retrieving general and specific information from stored knowledge of specifics. *Proceedings of the third annual meeting of the Cognitive Science Society, 170–172.*

McClelland, J. L. (1988). Parallel distributed processing: Implications for cognition and development. Technical report AIP-47, Carnegie-Mellon University, Department of Psychology, Pittsburgh, PA.

McClelland, J. L., & Jenkins, E. A., Jr. (1992). Emergence of stages from incremental learning mechanisms: A connectionist approach to cognitive development. In K. Van Lehn (Ed.), *Architectures for intelligence.* Hillsdale, NJ: Erlbaum.

McClelland, J. L., & Rumelhart, D. E. (1981). An interactive activation model of context effects in letter perception: Part 1. An account of basic findings. *Psychological Review, 88,* 375–407.

McClelland, J. L., & Rumelhart, D. E. (1985). Distributed memory and the representation of general and specific information. *Journal of Experimental Psychology: General, 114,* 159–188.

McClelland, J. L., Rumelhart, D. E., & Hinton, G. E. (1986). The appeal of parallel distributed processing. In D. E. Rumelhart, J. L. McClelland, & the PDP Research Group (Eds.), *Parallel distributed processing: Explorations in the microstructure of cognition* (Vol. 1). Cambridge, MA: Bradford.

McClelland, J. L., Rumelhart, D. E., & the PDP research group (Eds.). (1986). *Parallel distributed processing: Explorations in the microstructure of cognition* (Vol. 2). Cambridge, MA: Bradford.

McConkie, G. W., & Rayner, K. (1973). *The span of the effective stimulus during fixations in reading.* Paper presented at the American Educational Research Association meetings, New Orleans.

McConkie, G. W., & Rayner, K. (1976). Identifying the span of the effective stimulus in reading: Literature review and theories of reading. In H. Singer & R. Ruddell (Eds.), *Theoretical models and processes of reading.* Newark, DE.: International Reading Association.

McCormack, P. D. (1972). Recognition memory: How complex a retrieval system? *Canadian Journal of Psychology, 24,* 19–41.

McCulloch, W. S., & Pitts, W. (1943). A logical calculus of the ideas imminent in nervous activity. *Bulletin of Mathematical Biophysics, 5,* 115–133.

McDaniel, M. A., & Einstein, G. O. (1986). Bizarre imagery as an effective memory aid: The importance of distinctiveness. *Journal of Experimental Psychology: Learning, Memory, and Cognition, 12,* 54–65.

McGaugh, J. L. (1966). Time dependent processes in memory storage. *Science, 153,* 1351–1358.

McGaugh, J. L. (1990). Significance and remembrance: The role of neuromodulatory systems. *Psychological Science, 1,* 15–25.

McGoech, J. A. (1932). Forgetting and the law of disuse. *Psychological Review, 39,* 352–370.

McKoon, G., Ratcliff, R., & Dell, G. S. (1986). A critical evaluation of the semantic-episodic distinction. *Journal of Experimental Psychology: Learning, Memory, and Cognition, 12,* 295–306.

Mednick, S. A. (1967). *The remote associates test.* Boston: Houghton Mifflin.

Mehler, J. (1963). Some effects of grammatical transformations on the recall of English sentences. *Journal of Verbal Learning and Verbal Behavior, 2,* 346–351.

Melton, A. W. (1963). Implications of short-term memory for a general theory of memory. *Journal of Verbal Learning and Verbal Behavior, 2,* 1–21.

Melton, A. W., & Irwin, J. M. (1940). The influence of degree of interpolated learning on retroactive inhibition and the overt transfer of specific responses. *American Journal of Psychology, 53,* 173–203.

Melton, A. W., & Martin, E., Eds. (1972). *Coding processes in human memory.* Washington, DC: Winston.

Melzoff, A. N., & Borton R. W. (1979). Intermodal matching by human neonates. *Nature, 282,* 403–404.

Metzler, J., & Shepard, R. N. (1974). Transformational studies of the internal representation of three-dimensional objects. In R. L. Solso (Ed.), *Theories in cognitive psychology: The Loyola Symposium.* Hillsdale, NJ: Erlbaum.

Mewhort, D. J. K. (1970). Guessing and the order-of-approximation effect. *American Journal of Psychology, 83,* 439–442.

Meyer, D. E., & Schvaneveldt, R. W. (1971). Facilitation in recognizing pairs of words. Evidence of a dependence between retrieval operations. *Journal of Experimental Psychology, 90,* 227–234.

Meyer, D. E., Schvaneveldt, R. W., & Ruddy, M. G. (1974a). Loci of contextual effects on visual word recognition. In P. M. A. Rabbit & S. Dornic (Eds.), *Attention and performance V.* London: Academic Press.

Meyer, D. E., Schvaneveldt, R. W., & Ruddy, M. G. (1974b). Functions of graphemic and phonemic codes in visual word-recognition. *Memory and Cognition, 2*(2), 309–321.

Miller, G. A. (1951). *Language and communication.* New York: McGraw-Hill.

Miller, G. A. (1979). "A very personal history." Talk to Cognitive Science Workshop, Massachusetts Institute of Technology, Cambridge, MA, June 1. Cited in H. Gardner, *The mind's new science: A history of the cognitive revolution.* New York: Basic Books.

Miller, G. A. (1980). Computation, consciousness, and cognition. *Behavioral and Brain Sciences, 3,* 146.

Miller, G. A. (1992). *The science of words.* New York: Freeman.

Miller, G. A., & Friedman, E. A. (1957). The reconstruction of mutilated English texts. *Information Control, 1,* 38–55.

Miller, G. A., Galanter, E., & Pribram, K. H. (1960). *Plans and the structure of behavior.* New York: Holt, Rinehart & Winston.

Miller, G. A., & Isard, S. (1963). Some perceptual consequences of linguistic rules. *Journal of Verbal Learning and Verbal Behavior, 2,* 217–228.

Miller, G. A., & McKean, K. O. (1964). A chronomatic study of some relations between sentences. *Quarterly Journal of Experimental Psychology, 16,* 297–308.

Miller, J. R., & Kintsch, W. (1980) Readability and recall of short prose passages: A theoretical analysis. *Journal of Experimental Psychology: Human Learning and Memory, 6,* 335–354.

Milner, B. (1966). Amnesia following operation on the temporal lobes. In C. Whitty & O. Zangwill (Eds.), *Amnesia* (pp. 109–133). London: Butterworth.

Milner, B. (1968). Visual recognition and recall after temporal-lobe excision in man. *Neuropsychologia, 6,* 191–209.

Milner, B. (1972). Disorders in learning and memory after temporal lobe lesions in man. *Clinical Neurosurgery, 19,* 421–446.

Milner, B., Corkin, S., & Teuber, H. L. (1968). Further analysis of the hippocampal amnesic syndrome. *Neuropsychologia, 6,* 215–234.

Milner, B., Petrides, M., & Smith, M. L. (1985). Frontal lobes and the temporal organization of memory. *Human Neurobiology, 4,* 137–142.

Minsky, M. (1975). A framework for representing knowledge. In P. Winston *(Ed.), The psychology of computer vision.* New York: McGraw-Hill.

Minsky, M. (1994). Will robots inherit the earth? *Scientific American,* Oct., 109–113.

Minsky, M., & Papert, S. (1968). *Perceptions.* Cambridge, MA: The MIT Press.

Monty, R. A., & Senders, J. W. (Eds.). (1983). *Eye movement and psychological processes.* Hillsdale, NJ: Erlbaum.

Moray, N. (1959). Attention in dichotic listening: Affective cues and the influence of instructions. *Quarterly Journal of Experimental Psychology, 11,* 56–60.

Moray, N. (1969). *Attention: Selective processes in vision and audition.* New York: Academic Press.

Moray, N. (1970). *Listening and attention.* London: Penguin.

Moray, N., Bates, A., & Barnett, T. (1965). Experiments on the four-eared man. *Journal of the Acoustical Society of America, 38,* 196–201.

Moray, N., & O'Brien, T. (1967). Signal detection theory applied to selective listening. *Journal of Acoustical Society of America, 42,* 765–772.

Morrison, F. J., Holmes, D. L., & Haith, M. M. (1974). A developmental study of the effect of familiarity on short-term visual memory. *Journal of Experimental Child Psychology, 18,* 412–425.

Morton, J. (1969). Interaction of information in word recognition. *Psychological Review, 76,* 165–178.

Morton, J. (1970). A functional model of memory. In D. A. Norman (Ed.), *Models of human memory.* New York: Academic Press.

Morton, J. (1980). The logogen model and orthographic structure. In U. Frith (Ed.), *Cognitive processes in spelling.* London: Academic Press.

Morton, J. (1981). The status of information processing models of language. *Philosophic transactions of the Royal Society of London, B, 295,* 387–396.

Moscovitch, M. (Ed.). (1984). *Infant memory.* New York: Plenum.

Mountcastle, V. B. (1978). Brain mechanisms of directed attention. *Journal of the Royal Society of Medicine, 71,* 14–27.

Mountcastle, V. B. (1979). An organizing principle for cerebral function: The unit module and the distributed system. In F. O. Schmitt (Ed.), *The neurosciences: Fourth study program.* Cambridge, MA: The MIT Press.

Mowrer, O. H. (1954). The psychologist looks at language. *American Psychologist, 9,* 660–694.

Mueller, M. (1974) Cited in N. Chaudhuri, *Scholar extraordinary,* London: Chatto & Windus.

Murch, G. M. (1973). *Visual and auditory perception.* Indianapolis, IN: Bobbs-Merrill.

Murdock, B. B. (1965). Signal-detection theory and short-term memory. *Journal of Experimental Psychology, 70,* 443–447.

Murdock, B. B. (1971). Four channel effects in short-term memory. *Psychonomic Science, 24,* 197–198.

Murdock, B. B. (1983). A distributed memory model for serial-order information. *Psychological Review, 90,* 316–338.

Mussen, P. M. (Ed.). (1970). *Carmichael's manual of child psychology.* New York: Wiley.

Myers, R. E., & Sperry, T. W. (1953). Interocular transfer of the visual form discrimination habit in cats after section of the optic chiasm and corpus callosum. *Anatomical Record, 175,* 351–352.

Myers, T., Laver, J., & Anderson, J. R. (Eds.). (1981) *The cognitive representation of speech.* Amsterdam: North-Holland.

Näätänen, R. (1985). Selective attention and stimulus processing: Reflections in event-related potentials, magnetoencephalogram, and regional cerebral blood flow. In M. I. Posner & O. S. Marin (Eds.), *Attention and performance* (Vol. II, pp. 355–373). Hillsdale, NJ: Erlbaum.

Natsoulas, T. (1978). Consciousness. *American Psychologist, 33,* 906–914.

Nehrke, M. F. (1972). Age, sex and educational differences in syllogistic reasoning. *Journal of Gerontology, 27,* 966–970.

Neimark, E. D. (1987). *Adventures in thinking.* San Diego, CA: Harcourt Brace Jovanovich.

Neimark, E. D., & Santa, J. L. (1975). Thinking and concept attainment. *Annual Review of Psychology* (Vol. 26). Palo Alto, CA: Annual Reviews.

Neisser, U. (1967). *Cognitive psychology.* New York: Appleton-Century-Crofts.

Neisser, U. (1969). *Selective reading: A method for the study of visual attention.* Paper presented at the 19th International Congress of Psychology, London.

Neisser, U. (1976). *Cognition and reality: Principles and implications of cognitive psychology.* San Francisco: Freeman.

Neisser, U. (Ed.). (1982a). *Memory observed.* San Francisco: Freeman.

Neisser, U. (1982b). Snapshots or benchmarks? In U. Neisser (Ed.), *Memory observed.* San Francisco: Freeman.

Neisser, U., & Becklen, R. (1975). Selective looking: Attending to visually significant events. *Cognitive Psychology, 7,* 480–494.

Neisser, U., & Weene, P. (1962). Hierarchies in concept attainment. *Journal of Experimental Psychology, 64,* 640–645.

Neumann, P. G. (1977). Visual prototype formation with discontinuous representation of dimensions of variability. *Memory and Cognition, 5,* 187–197.

Newell, A. (1967). *Studies in problem solving: Subject 3 on the crypt-arithmetic task. DONALD plus GERALD equals ROBERT.* Pittsburgh: Carnegie Mellon Institute.

Newell, A. (1973). Artificial intelligence and the concept of mind. In R. C. Schank & C. M. Colby (Eds.),

Computer models of thought and language. San Francisco: Freeman.

Newell, A., Shaw, J. C., & Simon, H. A. (1960). Report on a general problem-solving program. In W. R. Reitman (Ed.), *Proceedings of the International Conference on Information Processing* (pp. 256–264). Paris: UNESCO.

Newell, A., & Simon, H. A. (1956). The logic theory machine: A complex information processing system. *IRE Transactions of Information Theory, IT-2*(3), 61–79.

Newell, A., & Simon, H. A. (1963). GPS, a program that stimulates human thought. In E. A. Feigenbaum & J. Feldman (Eds.), *Computers and thought.* New York: McGraw Hill.

Newell, A., Simon, H. A., & Shaw, J. C. (1958). Elements of a theory of human problem solving. *Psychological Review, 65,* 151–166.

Nickerson, R. S. (1965). Short-term memory for complex meaningful visual configurations: A demonstration of capacity. *Canadian Journal of Psychology, 19,* 155–160.

Nickerson, R. S. (1968). A note on long-term recognition memory for picture material. *Psychonomic Science, 11,* 58.

Nickerson, R. S., Perkins, D. N., & Smith, E. E. (1985). *The teaching of thinking.* Hillsdale, NJ: Erlbaum.

Noice, H. (1991). The role of explanations and plan recognition in the learning of theatrical scripts. *Cognitive Science, 15,* 425–460.

Noice, H., & Noice, T. (1993). The effects of segmentation on the recall of theatrical material. *Poetics, 22,* 51–67.

Norman, D. A. (1966a). Acquisition and retention in short-term memory. *Journal of Experimental Psychology, 72,* 369–381.

Norman, D. A. (1966b). Memory and decisions. *Proceedings of Symposium on Memory and Attention, 18th International Congress of Psychology,* Moscow.

Norman, D. A. (1968). Toward a theory of memory and attention. *Psychological Review, 75,* 522–536.

Norman, D. A. (1969). Memory while shadowing. *Quarterly Journal of Experimental Psychology, 21,* 85–93.

Norman, D. A. (1976). *Memory and attention* (2nd ed.). New York: Wiley.

Norman, D. A. & Rumelhart, E. E. (1975). Exploration in cognition. San Francisco: Freeman.

Norman, D. A. & Wicklegren, W. A. (1965). Short-term recognition memory for single digits. *Journal of Experimental Psychology, 70,* 479–489.

Norman, G. R., Brooks, L. R., & Allen, S. W. (1989). Recall by expert medical practitioners and novices as a record of processing attention. *Journal of Experimental Psychology: Learning Memory and Cognition, 15,* 1166–1174.

Norton, D., & Stark, L. (1971). Eye movements and visual perception. *Scientific American, 224,* 34–43.

Oakley, D. A. (1981). Brain mechanisms of mammalian memory. *British Medical Bulletin, 37,* 175–180.

O'Brien, E. J., & Wolford, C. R. (1982). Effect of delay in testing on retention of plausible versus bizarre mental images. *Journal of Experimental Psychology: Learning, Memory, and Cognition, 8,* 148–153.

Ojemann, G. A. (1991). Cortical organization of language. *The Journal of Neuroscience, 11,* 2281–2287.

Oldfield, R. C. (194). Memory mechanisms and the theory of schemata. *British Journal of Psychology, 43,* 14–23.

Olson, G. M. (1977). An information-processing analysis of visual memory and habituation in infants. In T. J. Tighe & R. H. Leaton (Eds.), *Habituation: Perspectives from child development, animal behavior and neurophysiology.* Hillsdale, NJ: Erlbaum.

Ornstein, P. A. (Ed.). (1978). *Memory development in children.* Hillsdale, NJ: Erlbaum.

Ornstein, P. A., Naus, M. J., & Liberty, C. (1975). Rehearsal and organizational processes in children's memory. *Child Development, 45,* 818–830.

Ornstein, R. (1991). *The evolution of consciousness: The origins of the way we think.* New York: Simon & Schuster.

Ornstein, R., & Thompson, R. F. (1985). *The amazing brain.* Los Altos, CA: ISHK Book Service.

Ornstein, R. E. (1972). *The psychology of consciousness.* San Francisco: Freeman. (Also published by Viking, 1972.)

Ornstein, R. E. (1973). *The nature of human consciousness.* San Francisco: Freeman. (Also published by Viking, 1973).

Ornstein, R. E. (1977). *The psychology of consciousness.* New York: Harcourt Brace Jovanovich.

Osterberg, G. A. (1935). Topography of the layer of rods and cones in the human retina. *Acta Ophthalmologica, Suppl. 6, 61,* 1–102.

Owen, F. W., Adams, P. A., Forrest, T., Stolz, L. M., & Fischer, S. (1971). Learning disorders in children: Sibling studies. *Monographs of the Society for Research in Child Development, 36* (4, serial no. 144).

Owens, J., Bower, G. H., & Black, J. B. (1979). The "soap opera" effect in story recall. *Memory and Cognition, 7,* 185–191.

Paivio, A. (1965). Abstractness, imagery, and meaningfulness in paired-associated learning. *Journal of Verbal Learning and Verbal Behavior, 4,* 32–38.

Paivio, A. (1969). Mental imagery in associative learning and memory. *Psychological Review, 76,* 241–263.

Paivio, A. (1971a). Imagery and deep structure in the recall of English nominalizations. *Journal of Verbal Learning and Verbal Behavior, 10,* 1–12.

Paivio, A. (1971b). *Imagery and verbal processes.* New York: Holt, Rinehart & Winston.

Paivio, A. (1975). Perceptual comparisons through the mind's eye. *Memory and Cognition, 3,* 635–647.

Paivio, A., & Csapo, K. (1969). Concrete-image and verbal memory codes. *Journal of Experimental Psychology, 80,* 279–285.

Paivio, A., Smythe, P. C., & Yuille, J. C. (1968). Imagery versus meaningfulness of norms in paired-associate learning. *Canadian Journal of Psychology, 22,* 427–441.

Paivio, A., Yuille, J. C., & Madigan, S. A. (1968). Concreteness, imagery and meaningfulness values for 925 nouns. *Journal of Experimental Psychology Monograph Supplement, 76*(1), part 2.

Palmer, S. E. (1975a). Visual perception and world knowledge: Notes on a model of sensory cognitive interaction. In D. A. Norman, D. E. Rumelhart, & the LNR Research Group, *Explorations in cognition.* San Francisco: Freeman.

Palmer, S. E. (1975b). The effects of contextual scenes on the identification of objects. *Memory and Cognition, 3,* 519–526.

Palmer, S. E. (1989). Reference frames in the perception of shape and orientation. In B. E. Shepp & S. Ballesteros (Eds.), *Object perception: Structure & process.* Hillsdale, NJ: Erlbaum.

Palmer, S. E., Rosch, E., & Chase, P. (1981). Canonical perspective and the perception of objects. In J. Long & A. Baddeley (Eds.), *Attention and performance IX.* Hillsdale, NJ: Erlbaum.

Pardo, J. V., Fox, P. T., & Raichle, M. E. (1991). Localization of a human system for sustained attention by positron emission tomography. *Nature, 349,* 61–64.

Pashler, H. (1993). Doing two things at the same time. *American Scientist, 81,* 48–55.

Pear, T. H. (1922). *Remembering and forgetting.* London: Methuen.

Penfield, W. (1959). The interpretive cortex. *Science, 129,* 1719–1725.

Penfield, W., & Jasper, H. H. (1954). *Epilepsy and the functional anatomy of the human brain.* Boston: Little, Brown.

Penfield, W., & Roberts, L. (1959). *Speech and brain mechanism.* Princeton: Princeton University Press.

Petersen, S. E., & Fiez, J. A. (1993). The processing of single words studied with positron emission tomography. *Annual Review of Neuroscience, 16,* 509–530.

Petersen, S. E., Fox, P. T., Posner, M. I., Mintun, M., & Raichle, M. E. (1988). Positron emission tomographic studies of the cortical anatomy of single word processing. *Nature, 331,* 585–589.

Petersen, S. E., Fox, P. T., Snyder, A. Z., & Raichle, M. E. (1990). Activation of extrastriate and frontal cortical areas by visual words and word-like stimuli. *Science, 249,* 1041–1044.

Peterson, L. R., & Peterson, M. J. (1959). Short-term retention of individual verbal items. *Journal of Experimental Psychology, 58,* 193–198.

Peterson, M. T., Meagher, R. B., Jr., Chait, H., & Gillie, S. (1973). The abstraction and generalization of dot patterns. *Cognitive Psychology, 4,* 378–398.

Pew, R. W. (1974). Levels of analysis in motor control. *Brain Research, 71,* 393–400.

Phillips, W. A. (1974). On the distinction between sensory storage and short-term visual memory. *Perception and Psychophysics, 16,* 283–390.

Phillips, W. A., & Baddeley, A. D. (1971). Reaction time and short-term visual memory. *Psychonomic Science, 22,* 73–74.

Philpott, A., & Wilding, J. (1979). Semantic interference from subliminal stimuli in a dichoptic viewing situation. *British Journal of Psychology, 70,* 559–563.

Piaget, J. (1926). *The language and thought of the child.* New York: Harcourt Brace.

Piaget, J. (1952a). *The child's conception of number.* New York: Humanities Press.

Piaget, J. (1952b). *The origins of intelligence in children.* New York: International Universities Press.

Piaget, J. (1970). Piaget's theory. In P. H. Mussen (Ed.), *Carmichael's manual of child psychology* (Vol. 1, pp. 703–732). New York: Wiley.

Piaget, J., & Inhelder, B. (1941). *Le developpement des quantites chez l'enfant.* Neuchatel: Delachaux et Niestle.

Piaget, J., & Inhelder, B. (1956). *The child's conception of space.* London: Routledge & Kegan Paul.

Piaget, J., & Inhelder, B. (1973). *Memory and intelligence.* New York: Basic Books.

Pick, A. D. (1975). *The development of strategies of attention.* Paper presented at the biennial meeting of the Society for Research in Child Development, Denver.

Pick, A. D., Christy, M. D., & Frankel, G. W. (1972). A developmental study of visual selective attention. *Journal of Experimental Child Psychology, 11*, 165–175.

Pick, H. L., Jr., & Saltzman, E. (Eds.). (1978). *Modes of perceiving and processing information* Hillsdale, NJ: Erlbaum.

Pierce, J. R. (1961). *Symbols, signals and noise.* New York: Harper & Row.

Pierce, J. R. (1968). *Science, art and communication.* New York: Clarkson N. Potter.

Pillsbury, W. B. (1897). A study in apperception. *American Journal of Psychology, 8*, 315–393.

Pinel, J. P. J. (1993). *Biopsychology* (2nd ed.). Boston: Allyn and Bacon.

Pinker, S. (1980). Mental imagery and the third dimension. *Journal of Experimental Psychology: General, 109*, 354–371.

Pinker, S. (1984). Visual cognition: An introduction. *Cognition, 18*, 1–63.

Pinker, S. (Ed.). (1985). *Visual cognition.* Cambridge, MA: The MIT Press.

Place, U. T. (1956). Is consciousness a brain process? *British Journal of Psychology, 47*, 44–50.

Podgorny, P., & Shepard, R. N. (1978). Functional representations common to visual perception and imagination. *Journal of Experimental Psychology: Human Perception and Performance, 4*, 21–35.

Poincaré, H. (1913). Mathematical creation. In *The foundations of science* (G. H. Halstead, trans.). New York: Science Press.

Porth, C. M. (1986). *Pathophysiology.* Philadelphia: Lippincott.

Posner, M. I. (1969). Abstraction and the process of recognition. In J. T. Spence & G. H. Bower (Eds.), The *psychology of learning and motivation: Advances in learning and motivation* (Vol. 3). New York: Academic Press.

Posner, M. I. (1973). *Cognition: An introduction.* Glenview, IL: Scott, Foresman.

Posner, M. I. (1988). Structures and functions of selective attention. In T. Boll & B. Bryant (Eds.), *Master lectures in clinical neuropsychology* (pp. 173–202). Washington, DC: American Psychological Association.

Posner, M. I. (Ed.). (1989). *Foundations of cognitive science.* Cambridge, MA: The MIT Press.

Posner, M. I. (1992). Attention as a cognitive and neural system. *Current Directions in Psychological Science, 1*, 11–14.

Posner, M. I., & Boies, S. J. (1971). Components of attention. *Psychological Review, 78*, 391–408.

Posner, M. I., Boies, S. J., Eichelman, W., & Taylor, R. L. (1969). Retention of visual and name codes of single letters. *Journal of Experimental Psychology Monographs, 79*, 1–16.

Posner, M. I., Early, T. S., Reiman, E. M., Pardo, P. J., & Dhawan, M. (1988). Asymmetries in hemispheric control of attention in schizophrenia. *Archives of General Psychiatry, 45*, 814–826.

Posner, M. I., Goldsmith, R., & Welton, K. E., Jr. (1967). Perceived distance and the classification of distorted patterns. *Journal of Experimental Psychology 73*, 28–38.

Posner, M. I., & Keele, S. W. (1967). Decay of visual information from a single letter. *Science, 158*, 137–139.

Posner, M. I., & Keele, S. W. (1968). On the genesis of abstract ideas. *Journal of Experimental Psychology, 77*, 353–363.

Posner, M. I., & Konick, A. F. (1966). On the role of interference in short-term memory. *Journal of Experimental Psychology, 72*, 221–231.

Posner, M. I., & Petersen, S. E. (1990). The attention system in the human brain. *Annual Review of Neuroscience, 13*, 25–42.

Posner, M. I., Petersen, S. E., Fox, P. I., & Raichle, M. E. (1988). Localization of cognitive operations in the human brain. *Science, 240*, 1627–1631.

Posner, M. I., & Rothbart, M. K. (1989). Intentional chapters on unintended thoughts. In J. S. Uleman & John A. Bargh (Eds.), *Unintended thought.* New York: Guilford Press.

Posner, M. I., & Rothbart, M. K. (1991). Attentional mechanism and conscious experience. In *The Neuropsychology of Consciousness* (Chap. 5, pp. 92–111). New York: Academic Press.

Posner, M. I., Sandson, J., Dhawan, M., & Shulman, G. L. (1989). Is word recognition automatic? A cognitive-anatomical approach. *Journal of Cognitive Neuroscience, 1*, 50–60.

Posner, M. I., & Snyder, C. R. R. (1974). Attention and cognitive control . In R. L. Solso (Ed.), *Information processing and cognition: The Loyola Symposium.* Hillsdale, NJ: Erlbaum.

Posner, M. I., & Snyder, C. R. R. (1975). Facilitation and inhibition in the processing of signals. In P. M. A. Rabbit & S. Dornic (Eds.), *Attention and performance V.* London: Academic Press.

Posner, M. I., & Warren, R. E. (1972). Traces, concepts, and conscious constructions. In A. W. Melton & E. Martin (Eds.), *Coding process in human memory.* Washington, DC: Winston.

Potter, R. K., Kopp, G. A., & Kopp, H. G. (1966). *Visible speech.* New York: Dover.

Poudion, E. C. (1962). Peripheral vision, refractoriness, and eye movements in fast oral readings. *British Journal of Psychology, 53,* 409–419.

Pratkanis, A. R., & Greenwald, A. G. (1988). Recent perspectives on unconscious processing: Still no marketing applications. *Psychology & Marketing, 5,* 337–353.

Premack, D. (1976). Language and intelligence in ape and man. *American Scientist, 64,* 674–683.

Pribram, K. H. (1971). *Languages of the brain: Experimental paradoxes and principles in neuropsychology.* Englewood Cliffs, NJ: Prentice-Hall.

Pribram, K. H. (1986). The cognitive revolution and mind/brain issues. *American Psychologist, 41,* 507–520.

Pylyshyn, Z. W. (1973). What the mind's eye tells the mind's brain: A critique of mental imagery. *Psychological Bulletin, 80,* 1–24.

Pylyshyn, Z. W. (1980). The "casual power" of machines. *Behavioral and Brain Sciences, 3,* 442–444.

Pylyshyn, Z. W. (1981). The imagery debate: Analogue media versus tacit knowledge. *Psychological Review, 88,* 16–45.

Pylyshyn, Z. W. (1986). *Computation and cognition: Toward a foundation for cognitive science.* Cambridge, MA: The MIT Press.

Quillian, M. R. (1968). Semantic memory. In M. Minsky (Ed.), *Semantic information processing.* Cambridge, MA: The MIT Press.

Quillian, M. R. (1969). The teachable language comprehender: A simulation program and theory of language. *Communication of the Association for Computing Machinery, 12.*

Rachlin, H., Logue, Q. W., Gibbon, J., & Frankel, M. (1986). Cognition and behavior in studies of choice. *Psychological Review, 93,* 35–45.

Raichle, M. E. (1994). Visualizing the mind. *Scientific American, 270* 58–63.

Raichle, M. E. (1994). *Cerebral Cortex.*

Raney, G. E. & Rayner, K. (1993). Event-related brain potentials, eye movements, and readings. *Psychological Science, 4,* 283–286.

Raphael, B. (1976). *The thinking computer.* San Francisco: Freeman.

Ratcliff, R., McKoon, G. (1986). More on the distinction between episodic and semantic memories. *Journal of Experimental Psychology: Learning, Memory, and Cognition, 12,* 312–313.

Raugh, M. R., & Atkinson, R. C. (1975). A mnemonic method for learning a second-language vocabulary. *Journal of Educational Psychology, 67,* 1–16.

Rayner, K. (1975). The perceptual span and peripheral cues in reading. *Cognitive Psychology, 7,* 65–81.

Rayner, K. (1978). Eye movements in reading and information processing. *Psychological Bulletin, 85,* 618–660.

Rayner, K. (1980). Personal communication cited by R. G. Crowder in "The demise of short-term memory." *Acta Psychologica, 50,* 1982, 292–323.

Rayner, K. (1993). Eye movements in reading: Recent developments. *Current Directions in Psychological Science, 2,* 81–85.

Rayner, K., & Frazier, L. (1989). Selection mechanisms in reading lexically ambiguous words. *Journal of Experimental Psychology: Learning, Memory, and Cognition, 15,* 779–790.

Rayner, K. & Morris, R. K. (1992). Eye movement control in reading: Evidence against semantic pre-processing. *Journal of Experimental Psychology: Human Perception and Performance, 18,* 163–172.

Rayner, K., & Pollatsek, A. (1987). Eye movements in reading: A tutorial review. In M. Coltheart (Ed.), *Attention and performance XII: The psychology of reading.* London: Erlbaum.

Rayner, K., & Pollatsek, A. (1989). *The psychology of reading.* Englewood Cliffs, NJ: Prentice Hall.

Rayner, K., & Posnansky, C. (1978). Stages of processing in word identification. *Journal of Experimental Psychology: General, 107,* 64–81.

Rayner, K., Sereno, S. C., Morris, R. K., Schmauder, A. R., & Clifton, C. (1989). Eye movements and on-line language comprehension processes. *Language and Cognitive Processes, 4* (Special Issue), 21–50.

Reber, A. S., & Scarborough, D. L. (Eds.). (1977). *Toward a psychology of reading.* Hillsdale, NJ: Erlbaum.

Ree, M. J., & Earles, J. A. (1992). Intelligence is the best predictor of job performance. *Current Directions in Psychological Science, 1,* 86–89.

Reed, S. K. (1972). Pattern recognition and categorization. *Cognitive Psychology, 3,* 382–407.

Reed, S. K. (1973). *Psychological processes in pattern recognition.* New York: Academic Press.

Rees, A., Kim, K., & Solso, R. L. (1993). *Prototype formation in right and left hemispheres.* Paper presented at the annual meeting of WPA/RMPA, Phoenix, AZ, April.

Reicher, G. M. (1969). Perceptual recognition as a function of meaningfulness of stimuli material. *Journal of Experimental Psychology, 81,* 275–280.

Reitman, J. (1976). Skilled perception in Go: Deducting memory structures from inter-response times. *Cognitive Psychology, 12,* 336–356.

Reitman, J. S., & Bower, G. H. (1973). Storage and later recognition of exemplars of concepts. *Cognitive Psychology, 4,* 194–206.

Reitman, W. R. (1965). *Cognition and thought: An information-processing approach.* New York: Wiley.

Reitman, W. R., Grove, R. B., & Shoup, R. G. (1964). Argus: An information-processing model of thinking. *Behavioral Science, 9,* 270–281.

Restak, R. M. (1988). *The mind.* New York: Bantam.

Restle, F. A. (1955). A theory of discrimination learning. *Psychological Review, 62,* 11–19.

Restorff, V. H. (1933). Über die Wirkung von Bereichsbildungen im Spurenfeld. *Psychologie Forschurg, 18,* 299–342.

Reutner, D. B. (1972). Class shift, symbolic shift, and background shift in short-term memory. *Journal of Experimental Psychology, 93,* 90–94.

Reynolds, D. (1964). Effects of double stimulation: Temporal inhibition of response. *Psychological Bulletin, 62,* 333–347.

Richardson, A. (199). *Mental imagery.* New York: Springer.

Riley, C. A. (1975). Representation and use of comparative information and inference making in young children. Unpublished doctoral dissertation, Princeton University.

Riley, C. A., & Trabasso, T. (1974). Comparatives, logical structures and encoding in a transitive reference task. *Journal of Experimental Child Psychology, 17,* 187–203.

Rips, L. J. (1975). Inductive judgments about natural categories. *Journal of Verbal Learning and Verbal Behavior, 14,* 665–681.

Rips, L. J., Shoben, E. J., & Smith, E. E. (1973). Semantic distance and the verification of semantic relations. *Journal of Verbal Learning and Verbal Behavior, 14,* 665–681.

Risberg, J. (1987). Development of high-resolution two-dimensional measurement of regional cerebral blood flow. In J. Wade, S. Knezevik, V. A. Maximilian, Z. Mubrin, & I. Prohovnik (Eds.), *Impact of functional imaging in neurology and psychiatry.* London: Libbey.

Risberg, J. (1989). Regional cerebral blood flow measurements with high temporal and spatial resolution. In D. Ottoson (Ed.), *Visualization of brain functions,* Wenner-Gren International Symposium Series. London: Macmillan.

Roberge, J. J. (1972). Effects of structure and semantics on the solution of pure hypothetical syllogisms. *Journal of General Psychology, 87,* 161–167.

Robinson, D. A. (1968). Eye movement control in primates. *Science, 161,* 1219–1224.

Rock, I. (1983). *The logic of perception.* Cambridge, MA: The MIT Press.

Rock, I. (1984). *Perception.* New York: Scientific American.

Rock, I., & Ebenholtz, S. (1962). Stroboscopic movement based on change of phenomenal rather than retinal location. *American Journal of Psychology, 75,* 193–207.

Roe, A. (1946). The personality of artists. *Educational Psychology Measurement, 6,* 401–408.

Roe, A. (1953). *The making of a scientist.* New York: Dodd, Mead.

Roediger, H. L. (1980). Memory metaphors in cognitive psychology. *Memory and Cognition, 8,* 231–252.

Roediger, H. I., & Craik, F. I. M. (Eds.). (1989). *Varieties of memory and consciousness: Essays in honor of Endel Tulving.* Hillsdale, Nl: Erlbaum.

Rogers, T. B., Kuiper, N. A., & Kirker, W. S. (1977). Self-reference and the encoding of personal information. *Journal of Personality and Social Psychology, 35,* 677–688.

Roland, P. E., & Friber, L. (1985). Localization of cortical areas activated by thinking. *Journal of Neurophysiology, 53,* 1219–1243.

Rosch, E. (1973). On the internal structure of perceptual and semantic categories. In T. E. Moore (Ed.), *Cognitive development and the acquisition of language* (pp. 111–144). New York: Academic Press.

Rosch, E. (1974). Linguistic relativity. In A. Silverstein (Ed.), *Human communication: Theoretical perspectives* (pp. 95–121). New York: Halsted.

Rosch, E. (1975). Cognitive representations of semantic categories. *Journal of Experimental Psychology: General, 104,* 192–233.

Rosch, E. (1977). Human categorization. In N. Warren (Ed.), *Advances in cross-cultural psychology* (Vol. 1) London: Academic Press.

Rosenblatt, F. (1958). The Perceptron: A probabilistic mode for information storage and organization in the brain. *Psychological Review, 65,* 386–407.

Roskies, A. L. (1994). Mapping memory with positron emission tomography. *Proceedings of the National Academy of Sciences, 91,* 1989–1991.

Ross, G. S. (1980). Categorization in 1- to 2-year-olds. *Developmental Psychology, 16,* 391–396.

Rovee-Collier, C. K. (1987). Learning and memory in infancy. In J. D. Osofsky (Ed.), *Handbook of infant development* (2nd ed.). New York: John Wiley.

Rovee-Collier, C. K. (1990). The "memory system" of prelinguistic infants. In A. Diamond (Ed.), *The development and neural bases of higher cognitive functions.* New York: The New York Academy of Sciences.

Rubin, D. C. (1985). Flashbulb memories. *Psychology Today,* Sept.

Rubin, D. C. (1987). Quoted in *The New York Times,* June 23.

Rubin, D. C., & Friendly, M. (1986). Predicting which words get recalled: Measures of free recall, availability, goodness, emotionality, and pronunciability for 925 nouns. *Memory and Cognition, 14,* 79–94.

Rubin, D. C., Wetzler, S. E., & Nebes, R. D. (1986). Autobiographical memory across the life span. In D. C. Rubin (Ed.), *Autobiographical memory.* Cambridge, England: Cambridge University Press.

Rubinstein, H., Lewis, S. S., & Rubinstein, M. A. (1971). Evidence of phonemic recoding in visual word recognition. *Journal of Verbal Learning and Verbal Behavior, 10,* 645–657.

Rubinstein, M. F. (1986). *Tools for thinking and problem solving.* Englewood Cliffs, NJ: Prentice-Hall.

Ruch, T. C., & Patton, H. D. (1965). *Physiology and biophysics* (19th ed.). Philadelphia: Saunders.

Rumelhart, D. E. (1975). Notes on a schema for stories. In D. Bobrow & A. Collins (Eds.), *Representation and understanding: Studies in cognitive science.* New York: Academic Press.

Rumelhart, D. E. (1977). *An introduction to human information processing.* New York Wiley.

Rumelhart, D. E., Hinton, G. E., & McClelland, J. L. (1986). A general framework for parallel distributed processing. In D. E. Rumelhart, J. L. McClelland, & the PDP research group (Eds.), *Parallel distributed processing: Explorations in the microstructure of cognition* (Vol. 1). Cambridge, MA: Bradford.

Rumelhart, D. E., Lindsay, P. H., & Norman, D. A. (1972). A process model for long term memory. In E. Tulving & W. Donaldson (Eds.), *Organization of memory.* New York: Academic Press.

Rumelhart, D. E., & McClelland, J. L. (1982). An interactive activation model of context effects in letter perception: Part 2. The contextual enhancement effect and some tests and extensions of the model. *Psychological Review, 89,* 60–94.

Rumelhart, D. E., McClelland, J. L., & the PDP research group (Eds.). (1986). *Parallel distributed processing: Explorations in the microstructure of cognition* (Vol. 1). Cambridge, MA: Bradford.

Rumelhart, D. E., & Norman, D. A. (1975). The computer implementation. In D. Norman & D. Rumelhart

(Eds.), *Exploration in cognition.* San Francisco: Freeman.

Russell, W. R. (1959). Brain, memory, learning. Oxford: Clarendon.

Saarinen, T. F. (1987). Centering of mental maps of the world: Discussion paper. Department of Geography and Regional Development, University of Arizona, Tucson.

Sagen, C., Drake, F. D., Drugen, A., Ferris, I., Lomberg, J., & Sagen, L. S. (1978). *Murmurs of earth: The voyager interstellar record.* New York: Random House.

Sakitt, B. (1976). Iconic memory. *Psychological Review, 83,* 257–276.

Sakitt, B., Long, G. M. (1979). Spare the rod and spoil the icon. *Journal of Experimental Psychology: Human Perception and Performance, 5,* 19–30.

Salapatek, P. (1975). Pattern perception in early infancy. In L. B. Cohen & P. Salapatek (Eds.), *Infant perception: From sensation to cognition.* New York: Academic Press.

Salasoo, A., Shiffrin, R. M., & Feustel, T. C. (1985). Building permanent memory codes: Codification and repetition effects in word identification. *Journal of Experimental Psychology: General, 114,* 50–77.

Salisbury, H. E. (1955). *American in Russia.* New York: Harper.

Samuel, A. G., & Ressler, W. H. (1986). Attention within auditory word perception: Insights from the phonemic restoration illusion. *Journal of Experimental Psychology: Human Perception and Performance, 12,* 70–79.

Santa, J. L. & Lamners, L. L. (1974). Encoding specificity: Fact or artifact? *Journal of Verbal Learning and Verbal Behavior, 13,* 412–423.

Santa, J. L., & Lamners, L. L. (1976). Where does the confusion lie? Comments on the Wiseman and Tulving paper. *Journal of Verbal Learning and Verbal Behavior, 15,* 3–57.

Sapir, E. (1958). Language and environment. *American Anthropologist,* 1912, n.s., 226–242. Also in D. G. Mandelbaum (Ed.), *Selected writings of Edward Sapir in language, culture, and personality* (pp. 89–103). Berkeley and Los Angeles: University of California Press.

Saporta, S. (Ed.). (1961). *Psycholinguistics: A book of readings.* New York: Holt, Rinehart & Winston.

Savin, H. B., & Perchonock, E. (1965). Grammatical structure and immediate recall of English sentences. *Journal of Verbal Learning and Verbal Behavior, 4,* 348–353.

Schacter, D. L. (1987). Memory, amnesia, and frontal lobe dysfunction. *Psychobiology, 15,* 21–36.

Schaeffer, B., & Wallace, R. (1970). The comparison of word meanings. *Journal of Experimental Psychology, 86,* 144–152.

Schank, R. C. (1972). Conceptual dependency: A theory of natural language understanding. *Cognitive Psychology, 3,* 552–631.

Schank, R. C. (1981). Language and memory. In D. A. Norman (Ed.), *Perspectives on cognitive science.* Norwood, NJ: Ablex.

Schank, R. C. (1982). *Dynamic memory: A theory of reminding and learning in computers and people.* Cambridge, England: Cambridge University Press.

Schank, R. C., & Abelson, R. (1977). *Scripts, plans, goals, and understanding.* Hillsdale, Nl: Erlbaum.

Schank, R. C., & Hunter, L. (1985). The quest to understand thinking. *Byte,* Apr., 143–155.

Schmidt, F. L., & Hunter, J. E. (1992). Development of a causal model of processes determining job performance. *Current Directions in Psychological Science, 1,* 89–92.

Schmidt, R. A. (1975). A schema theory of discrete motor skill learning. *Psychological Review, 82,* 225–229.

Schneider, W. (1987). Connectionism: Is it a paradigm shift for psychology? *Behavioral Research Methods, Instruments, & Computers, 19,* 73–83.

Schneider, W., Noll, D. C., & Cohen, J. D. (1993). Functional topographic mapping of the cortical ribbons in the human visual cortex using conventional MRI. *Nature, 365,* 150–153.

Schneider, W., & Shiffrin, R. M. (1977). Controlled and automatic human information processing: Detection, search and attention. *Psychological Review, 84*(1).

Schulman, A. I. (1974). Memory for words recently classified. *Memory and Cognition, 2,* 47–52.

Schvaneveldt, R. W., & McDonald, J. E. (1981). Semantic context and the encoding of words: Evidence for two modes of stimulus analysis. *Journal of Experimental Psychology: Human Perception and Performance, 2,* 243–256.

Scribner, S. (1975). Recall of classical syllogisms: A crosscultural investigation of error on logical problems. In R. J. Falmagen (Ed.), *Reasoning: Representation and process.* Hillsdale, NJ: Erlbaum.

Scribner, S., & Cole, M. (1972). Effects of constrained recall training on children's performance in a verbal memory task. *Child Development, 43,* 845–857.

Scribner, S., & Cole, M. (1974). Research program on Vai literacy and its cognitive consequences. *Cross-Cultural Psychology Newsletter, 8,* 2–4.

Scribner, S., & Cole, M. (1981). The psychology of literacy. Cambridge, MA: Harvard University Press.

Seamon, J. G., & Travis, Q. B. (1993). An ecological study of professors' memory for student names and faces: A replication and extension. *Memory, 1,* 191–202.

Searle, J. (1980). Minds, brains, and programs. *Behavioral and Brain Sciences, 3,* 417–457.

Searle, J. (1983). *Intentionality: An essay in the philosophy of mind.* Cambridge, England: Cambridge University Press.

Sehulster, J. R. (1989). Content and temporal structure of autobiographical knowledge: Remembering twenty five seasons at the Metropolitan Opera. *Memory and Cognition, 17,* 590–606.

Sejnowski, T. J., Koch, C. & Churchland, P. S. (1988). Computational neuroscience. *Science, 241,* 1299–1306.

Sejnowski, T. J. Stevens, & J. Watson (Eds.), *Cold Spring Harbor Symp. Quart. Biol., 55.*

Sekuler, R. W., & Abrams, M. (1968). Visual sameness: A choice time analysis of pattern recognition process. *Journal of Experimental Psychology, 77,* 232–238.

Selfridge, O. G., & Neisser, U. (1963). Pattern recognition by machine. In E. Feigenbaum & J. Feldman (Eds.), *Computers and thought.* New York: McGraw-Hill.

Sells, S. B. (1936). The atmosphere effect: An experimental study of reasoning. *Archives of Psychology,* no. 200.

Shallice, T. (1972). On the dual functions of consciousness. *Psychological Review, 79,* 383–396.

Shallice, T., & Vallar, G. (1990). The impairment of auditory-verbal short-term storage. In G. Vallar & T. Shallice (Eds.), *Neuropsychological impairments of short-term memory* (pp. 11–53). Cambridge, England: Cambridge University Press.

Shannon, C. E. (1948). A mathematical theory of communication. *Bell System Technical Journal, 27,* 479–523.

Shannon, C. E., & Weaver, W. (1949). The mathematical theory of communication. Urbana: University of Illinois Press.

Sheehan, P. W. (1967a). A shortened form of Betts' questionnaire upon mental imagery. *Journal of Clinical Psychology, 23,* 386–398.

Sheehan, P. W. (1967b). Reliability of a short test of imagery. *Perceptual and Motor Skills 25,* 744.

Sheehan, P. W. (1971). Individual differences in vividness of imagery and the function of imagery in incidental learning. *Australian Journal of Psychology, 23,* 279–288.

Sheehan, P. W. (1973). Stimulus imagery effect and the role of imagery in incidental learning. *Australian Journal of Psychology, 25,* 93–102.

Sheehan, P. W., & Neisser, U. (1969). Some variables affecting the vividness of imagery in recall. *British Journal of Psychology, 25,* 93–102.

Sheingold, K. (1973). Developmental differences in intake and storage of visual information. *Journal of Experimental Child Psychology, 16,* 1–11.

Shepard, R. N. (1966). Learning and recall as organization and search. *Journal of Verbal Learning and Verbal Behavior, 5,* 201–204.

Shepard, R. N. (1967). Recognition memory for words, sentences, and pictures. *Journal of Verbal Learning and Verbal Behavior, 6,* 156–163.

Shepard, R. N. (1968). *Cognitive Psychology:* A review of the book by U. Neisser. *American Journal of Psychology, 81,* 285–289.

Shepard, R. N. (1975). Form, formation, and transformation of internal representations. In R. L. Solso (Ed.), *Information processing and cognition: The Loyola Symposium.* Hillsdale, NJ: Erlbaum.

Shepard, R. N. (1977). *The mental image.* Paper delivered before the American Psychological Association Meeting, San Francisco, Sept.

Shepard, R. N. (1978). The mental image. *American Psychologist, 33,* 125–137.

Shepard, R. N. (1990). *Mind sights.* San Francisco. Freeman.

Shepard, R. N. (1992). The perceptual organization of colors: An adaptation to the regularities of the terrestrial world? In J. Barkow, L. Cosmoides, & J. Tooby (Eds.), *The adapted mind: Evolutionary psychology and the generation of culture* (pp. 495–532). New York: Oxford University Press.

Shepard, R. N. (1994). Perceptual-cognitive universals as reflections of the world. *Psychonomic Bulletin & Review, 1,* 2–28.

Shepard, R. N. (1995). Toward a 21st century science of mental universals. In R. L. Solso & D. W. Massaro (Eds.), *The science of the mind: 2001 and beyond.* New York: Oxford University Press.

Shepard, R. N., & Chipman, S. (1970). Second-order isomorphism of internal representations: Shapes of states. *Cognitive Psychology, 1,* 1–17.

Shepard, R. N., & Metzler, J. (1971). Mental rotation of three-dimensional objects. *Science, 171,* 701–703.

Shiffrin, R. M., & Atkinson, R. C. (1969). Storage and retrieval processing in long-term memory. *Psychological Review, 76,* 179–193.

Shiffrin, R. M., & Schneider, W. (1977). Controlled and automatic human information processing: II. Perceptual learningg, automatic attending, and a general theory. *Psychological Review, 84*(2).

Shimamura, A. P., & Squire, L. R. (1984). Paired-associate learning and priming effects in amnesia: A neuropsychological study. *Journal of Experimental Psychology: General, 113,* 556–570.

Shulman, H. G. (1970). Encoding and retention of semantic and phonemic information in short-term memory. *Journal of Verbal Learning and Verbal Behavior, 9,* 499–508.

Shulman, H. G. (1971). Similarity effects in short-term memory. *Psychological Bulletin, 75,* 399–415.

Shulman, H. G. (1972). Semantic confusion errors in short-term memory. *Journal of Verbal Learning and Verbal Behavior, 11,* 221–227.

Siegler, R. S. (1976). Three aspects of cognitive development. *Cognitive Psychology, 8,* 481–520.

Siegler, R. S. (Ed.). (1978). *Children's thinking: What develops?* Hillsdale, NJ: Erlbaum.

Siegler, R. S. (1981). Developmental sequences within and between concepts. *Monographs of the Society for Research in Child Development, 46,* (No. 189, pp. 1–74).

Siegler, R. S. (1986). *Children's thinking.* Englewood Cliffs, NJ: Prentice-Hall.

Siegler, R. S., & Klahr, D. (1982). When do children learn? The relationship between existing knowledge and the acquisition of new knowledge. In R. Glaser (Ed.), *Advances in instructional psychology* (Vol. 2). Hillsdale, NJ: Erlbaum.

Siegler, R. S., & Richards, D. D. (1982). The development of intelligence. In R. J. Sternberg (Ed.), *Handbook of intelligence.* Cambridge, England: Cambridge University Press.

Simon, H. A., & Feigenbaum, E. A. (1964). An information processing theory of some effects of similarity, familiarization, and meaningfulness in verbal learning. *Journal of Verbal Learning and Verbal Behavior, 3,* 385–396.

Simpson, G. B., Peterson, R. R., Castell, M. A., & Burgess, C. (1989). Lexical and sentence context effects in word recognition. *Journal of Experimental Psychology: Learning, Memory, and Cognition, 15,* 88–97.

Singer, H., & Ruddell, R. D. (Eds.). (1976). *Theoretical models and processes of reading.* Newark, DE: International Reading Association.

Singer, J. L., & Antrobus, J. S. (1966). *Imaginal processes inventory.* New York: Authors.

Singer, J. L., & Antrobus, J. S. (1970). *Imaginal processes inventory.* New York: Authors.

Singer, J. L., & Antrobus, J. S. (1972). Daydreaming, imaginal processes, and personality: A normative study. In P. W. Sheehan (Ed.), *The function and nature of imagery* (pp. 175–202). New York: Academic Press.

Singer, M. (1973). A replication of Bransford and Franks' (1971) "The abstraction of linguistic ideas." *Bulletin of the Psychonomic Society, 1,* 416–418.

Singh, J. A. L., & Zingg, R. M. (1940). *Wolf children and feral man.* New York: Harper.

Skinner, B. F. (1957). *Verbal behavior.* New York: Appleton-Century-Crofts.

Skinner, B. F. (1989). The origins of cognitive thought. *American Psychologist, 44,* 13–18.

Slobin, D. I. (1971). *Psycholinguistics.* Glenview, IL: Scott, Foresman.

Slovic, P., Fischhoff, B., & Lichtenstein, S. (1977). Behavioral decision theory. *Annual Review of Psychology, 28,* 1–39.

Small, S. L., Cottrell, G. W., & Tanenhaus, M. K. (Eds.). (1988). *Lexical ambiguited resolution: Perspectives from psycholinguists, neuropsychology, and artificial intelligence.* Los Altos. CA: Morgan Kaufmann.

Smart, J. J. C. (1959). Sensations and brain processes. *Philosophical Review, 68,* 141–156.

Smedslund, J. (1961). The acquisition of conservation of substance and weight in children. *Scandinavian Journal of Psychology, 2,* 11–20.

Smedslund, J. (1965). The development of transitivity of length: A comment on Braine's reply. *Child Development, 36,* 577–580.

Smith, E. E. (1978). Theories of semantic memory. In W. K. Estes (Ed.), *Handbook of learning and cognitive processes* (Vol. 6). Hillsdale, NJ: Erlbaum.

Smith, E. E. & Medin, D. L. (1981). *Categories and concepts.* Cambridge, MA: Harvard University Press.

Smith, E. E., Shoben, E. J., & Rips, L. J. (1974). Structure and process in semantic memory: A featural model for semantic decisions. *Psychological Review, 1,* 214–241.

Smith, F. (1971). *Understanding reading.* New York: Holt, Rinehart & Winston.

Smith, S. B. (1983). *The great mental calculators: The psychology, methods, and lives of calculating prodigies, past and present.* New York: Columbia University Press.

Snodgrass, l. (1975). Psychophysics. In B. Sclarf (Ed.), *Experimental sensory psychology.* Glenview, IL: Scott, Foresman.

Sokolov, E. N. (1960). Neuronal models and the orienting reflexes. In M. A. Brazier (Ed.), *The central nervous system and behavior.* New York: J. Macy.

Sokolov, E. N. (1963). *Perception and the conditioned reflex.* New York: Macmillan.

Solomon, P. R., Goethals, G. R., Kelly, C. M., & Stephens, B. R. (Eds.). (1989). *Memory: Interdisciplinary Approaches.* New York: Springer.

Solso, R. L. (Ed.). (1973). *Contemporary issues in cognitive psychology: The Loyola Symposium.* Potomac, MD: Winston/Wiley.

Solso, R. L. (Ed.). (1974). *Theories of cognitive psychology: The Loyola Symposium.* Potomac, MD: Erlbaum.

Solso, R. L. (Ed.). (1975). *Information processing and cognition: The Loyola Symposium.* Hillsdale, NJ: Erlbaum.

Solso, R. L. (1985). The citation of Soviet scholars by Western psychologists. *American Psychologist, 40,* 1264–1265.

Solso, R. L. (1986). Organization of knowledge in the world community of cognitive scientists. *Cognitive Systems,* Dec., 321–327.

Solso, R. L. (1987a). Inside the Russian mind. Unpublished manuscript.

Solso, R. L. (1987b). The social-political consequences of the organization and dissemination of knowledge. *American Psychologist, 42,* 824–825.

Solso, R. L. (1989). Prototypes, schemata, and the form of human knowledge: The cognition of abstraction. In C. Izawa (Ed.), *Current issues in cognitive processes: The Tulane Flowerree symposium on cognition.* Hillsdale, NJ: Erlbaum.

Solso, R. L. (1994a). *Cognition and the Visual Arts.* Cambridge, MA: The MIT Press.

Solso, R. L. (1994b). Turning the corner. In R. L. Solso & D. W. Massaro (Eds.), *The science of the mind: 2001 and beyond.* Cambridge, MA: The MIT Press.

Solso, R. L., Ament, P., Kuraishy, F., & Mearns, C. (1986). *Prototype formation of various classes.* Paper presented at the 27th meeting of the Psychonomic Society: Nov. 13, 1986, New Orleans, LA.

Solso, R. L., & Biersdorff, K. K. (1975). Recall under conditions of cumulative cues. *Journal of General Psychology, 93,* 233–246.

Solso, R. L., & Dallob, P. (In press.) Prototype formation of "dance steps" among professional dancers. *Empirical Studies of the Arts.*

Solso, R. L., Heck, M., & Mearns, C. (1987). *Prototype formation in very short-term memory.* Paper presented at the 28th meeting of the Psychonomic Society: Nov. 6, 1986, Seattle, WA.

Solso, R. L., & Johnson, H. H. (1989). *An introduction to experimental design in psychology: A case approach.* New York: Harper & Row.

Solso, R. L., & McCarthy, J. E. (1981a). Prototype formation of faces: A case of pseudomemory. *British Journal of Psychology, 72,* 499–503.

Solso, R. L., & McCarthy, J. E. (1981b). Prototype formation: Central tendency model versus attribute frequency model. *Bulletin of the Psychonomic Society, 17,* 10–11.

Solso, R. L., & Raynis, S. A. (1979). Prototype formation from imaged, kinesthetically, and visually presented geometric figures. *Journal of Experimental Psychology: Human Perception and Performance, 5,* 701–712.

Solso, R. L., & Short, B. A. (1979). Color recognition. *Bulletin of the Psychonomic Society, 14,* 275–277.

Sophian, C. (Ed.). (1984). *Origins of cognitive skills.* Hillsdale, NJ: Erlbaum.

Spear, N. (Ed.). (1989). *Comparative perspectives on the development of memory.* Hillsdale, NJ: Erlbaum.

Spearman, C. (1904). General intelligence objectively determined and measured. *American Journal of Psychology, 15,* 201–293.

Spearman, C. (1927). The abilities of man: Their nature and measurement. New York: Macmillan.

Spelke, E. S. (1979). Perceiving bimodally specified events in infancy. *Developmental Psychology, 15,* 626–636.

Spelke, E. S. (1988). The origins of physical knowledge. In L. Weiskrantz (Ed.), *Thought without language* (pp. 168–184). London: Clarendon Press.

Spelke, E. S., & Kestenbaum, R. (1986). Les origines du concept d'objet. *Psychologie française 31,* 67–72.

Spencer, H. (1864/1881). *Essays: Moral, political, and aesthetic.* New York: Appleton.

Sperling, G. (1960). The information available in brief visual presentation. *Psychological Monographs, 74.*

Sperling, G. (1963). A model for visual memory tasks. *Human Factors, 5,* 19–31.

Sperling, G. (1967). Successive approximations to a model for short-term memory. *Acta Psychologica, 27,* 285–292.

Sperry, R. W. (1968). Hemisphere deconnection and the utility of conscious experience. *American Psychologist, 23,* 723–733.

Sperry, R. W. (1974). Lateral specialization in surgically separated hemispheres. In F. O. Schmitt & F. G. Worden (Eds.), *The neurosciences* (Vol. 3). Cambridge, MA: The MIT Press.

Sperry, R. W. (1982). Some effects of disconnecting the cerebral hemispheres. *Science, 217,* 1223–1226.

Springer, S. P., & Deutsch, G. (1981). *Left brain, right brain.* San Francisco: Freeman.

Springer, S., & Deutsch, G. (1984). *Left brain, right brain* (2nd ed.). San Francisco: Freeman.

Squire, L. R. (1982). The neuropsychology of human memory. *Annual Review of Neuroscience, 5,* 241–273.

Squire, L. R. (1986). Mechanisms of memory. *Science, 232,* 1612–1619.

Squire, L. R. (1987). *Memory and brain.* New York: Oxford University Press.

Squire, L. R., & Butters, N. (Eds.). (1984). *Neuropsychology of memory.* New York: Guilford Press.

Squire, L. R., Zola-Morgan, S., Cave, C., Haist, H., Musen, G., & Suzuki, W. P. (1990). Memory: Organization of brain systems and cognition. In E. Kandel, T. Sejnowski, C. Stevens, & J. Watson (Eds.), *Cold Spring Harbor Symp. Quart. Biol., 55.*

Standing, L. (1973). Learning 10,000 pictures. *Quarterly Journal of Experimental Psychology, 25,* 207–222.

Standing, L., Bond, B., Hall, J., & Weller, J. (1972). A bibliography of picture-memory studies. *Psychonomic Monograph Supplement, 29*(6B).

Standing, L., Conezio, J., & Haber, R. N. (1970). Perception and memory for pictures: Single-trial learning of 2560 visual stimuli. *Psychonomic Science, 19,* 73–74.

Stanovich, K. E., & West, R. F. (1979). Mechanism of sentence context effects in reading: Automatic activation and conscious attention. *Memory and Cognition, 7,* 77–85.

Stanovich, K. E., & West, R. F. (1983). On printing by a sentence context. *Journal of Experimental Psychology: General, 112,* 1–36.

Staszewski, J. J. (1988). Skilled memory and expert mental calculation. In M. T. H. Chi, R. Glaser, & M. J. Farr (Eds.), *The nature of expertise.* Hillsdale, NJ: Erlbaum.

Staszewski, J. J. (1989). Exceptional memory: The influence of practice and knowledge on the development of elaborative encoding strategies. In W. Schneider & F. E. Weinert (Eds.), *Interactions among aptitudes, strategies, and knowledge in cognitive performance.* Berlin: Springer.

Sternberg, R. J. (1977). *Intelligence, information processing, and analogical reasoning: The componential analysis of human abilities.* Hillsdale, NJ: Erlbaum.

Sternberg, R. J. (1979). Developmental patterns in the encoding and combination of logical connectives. *Journal of Experimental Child Psychology, 28,* 469–498.

Sternberg, R. J. (1980a). The development of linear syllogistic reasoning. *Journal of Experiment Child Psychology, 29,* 340–356.

Sternberg, R. J. (1980b). Representation and process in linear syllogistic reasoning. *Journal of Experimental Psychology: General, 109,* 119–159.

Sternberg, R. J. (1982). Reasoning, problem solving, and intelligence. In R. J. Sternberg (Ed.), *Handbook of human intelligence.* Cambridge [Cambridgeshire]; New York: Cambridge University Press.

Sternberg, R. J. (Ed.). (1984a). *Mechanisms of cognitive development.* San Francisco: Freeman.

Sternberg, R. J. (1984b). Toward a triarchic theory o human intelligence. *Behavioral and Brain Sciences, 7,* 269–315.

Sternberg, R. J. (1985a). Human intelligence: The model is the message. *Science, 230,* 1111–1118.

Sternberg, R. J. (1985b). *Beyond IQ: A triarchic theory of human intelligence.* Cambridge, England: Cambridge University Press.

Sternberg, R. J. (1986a). *Intelligence applied.* New York: Harcourt Brace Jovanovich.

Sternberg, R. J. (1986b). Inside intelligence. *American Scientist, 74,* 137–143.

Sternberg, R. J. (1989). Intelligence, wisdom, and creativity: Their natures and interrelationships. In R. L. Linn (Ed.), *Intelligence: Measurement, theory, and public policy.* Chicago: University of Illinois Press.

Sternberg, R. J. (Ed.). (1994). *Encyclopedia of human intelligence.* New York: Macmillan.

Sternberg, R. J., & Lubart, T. I. (In preparation) An investment theory of creativity and its development. Yale University Press.

Sternberg, R. J., & Wagner, R. K. (1993). The geocentric view of intelligence and job performance is wrong. *Current Directions in Psychological Science, 2,* 1–5.

Sternberg, S. (1966). High speed scanning in human memory. *Science, 153,* 652–654.

Sternberg, S. (1967). Two operations in character recognition: Some evidence from RT measurements. *Perception and Psychophysics, 2,* 45–53.

Sternberg, S. (1969). Memory scanning: Mental processes revealed by reaction time experiments. *American Scientist, 57,* 421–457.

Stevens, A., & Coupe, P. (1978). Distortions in judged spatial relations. *Cognitive Psychology, 63,* 390–397.

Strand, B. N., & Mueller, J. H. (1977). Levels of processing in facial recognition memory. *Bulletin of the Psychonomic Society, 9,* 17–18.

Strauss, M. S. (1979). Abstraction of prototypical information by adults and 10-month-old infants. *Journal of Experimental Psychology: Human Learning and Memory, 5,* 618–663.

Strauss, M. S., & Carter, P. N. (1984). Infant memory: Limitations and future directions. In R. Kail & N. E. Spear (Eds.), *Comparative perspectives on the development of memory.* Hillsdale, NJ: Erlbaum.

Stromeyer, C. G. (1970). Eidetikers. *Psychology Today,* Nov., 76–80.

Suler, J. (1989). "Eliza" helps students grasp therapy. *APA Monitor,* Jan., 30.

Sutherland, N. S. (1972). Object recognition In E. C. Carterette & M. P. Feidman (Eds.), *Handbook of perception* (Vol. 3). New York: Academic Press.

Swets, J. A. (1961). Is there a sensory threshold? *Science, 134,* 168–177.

Tanenhaus, M. K., & Lucas, M. M. (1987). Context effects in lexical processing. *Cognition, 25,* 213–234.

Tanner, W. P., & Swets, J. A. (1954). A decision-making theory of visual detection. *Psychological Review, 61,* 401–409.

Tauke, M. (1961). *Computers and common sense.* New York: Columbia University Press.

Taylor, H. A., & Tversky, B. (1992). Descriptions and depictions of environments. *Memory & Cognition, 20,* 483–496.

Taylor, S. E. (1965). Eye movements while reading: Facts and fallacies. *American Educational Research Journal, 2,* 187–202.

Theios, J., Smith, P. G., Haviland, S., Traupmann, J., & Moy, M. C. (1973). Memory scanning as a serial self-termination process. *Journal of Experimental Psychology, 97,* 323–336.

Thibadeau, R. (1985). Automatic visual inspection as skilled perception. In P. Jackson (Ed.), *The Robotics Institute: 1984 Annual Research Review.* Pittsburgh: Robotics Institute.

Thomas, J. C., Jr. (1974). An analysis of behavior in the hobbits-orcs problem. *Cognitive Psychology, 6,* 257–269.

Thompson, M. C., & Massaro, D. W. (1973). Visual information and redundancy in reading. *Journal of Experimental Psychology, 98,* 49–54.

Thompson, R. F. (1993). *The brain: A neuroscience primer* (2nd ed.). New York: W. H. Freeman.

Thomson, D. M., & Tulving, E. (1970). Associative encoding and retrieval: Weak and strong cues. *Journal of Experimental Psychology, 86,* 255–262.

Thorndike, E. L., & Lorge, I. (1944). *The teacher's word book of 30,000 words.* New York: Teachers College, Columbia University Press.

Thorndyke, P. W. (1977). Cognitive structures in comprehension and memory of narrative discourse. *Cognitive Psychology, 9,* 77–110.

Thorndyke, P. W., & Hayes-Roth, B. (1982). Differences in spatial know]edge acquired from maps and navigation. *Cognitive Psychology, 14,* 580–589.

Thurstone, L. L. (1938). Primary mental abilities. *Psychometric Monographs, No. 1.* Chicago: University of Chicago Press.

Tinklenberg, J. R., & Taylor, I. L. (1984). Assessments of drug effects on human memory functions. In L. R. Squire & N. Butters (Eds.), *Neuropsychology of memory.* New York: Guilford Press.

Titchener, E. B. (1909). *Experimental Psychology* (Vol. 1, Part 1, Student's Manual). New York: Macmillan.

Tolman, E. C. (1932). *Purposive behavior in animals and men.* New York: Appleton-Century.

Trabasso, T. (1977). The role of memory as a system in making transitive inferences. In R. V. Kall & J. W. Hagen (Eds.), *Perspectives on the development of memory and cognition.* Hillsdale, NJ: Erlbaum.

Trabasso, T., & Bower, G. (1964). Memory in concept identification. *Psychonomic Science, 1,* 133–134.

Trabasso, T., & Bower, G. (1968). *Attention in learning.* New York: Wiley.

Treisman, A. (1988). Features and objects: The fourteenth Bartlett Memorial Lecture. *Quarterly Journal of Experimental Psychology, 40A,* 201–237.

Treisman, A. M. (1960). Contextual cues in selective listening. *Quarterly Journal of Experimental Psychology, 12,* 242–248.

Treisman, A. M. (1964a). Monitoring and storage of irrelevant messages in selective attention. *Journal of Verbal Learning and Verbal Behavior, 3,* 449–459.

Treisman, A. M. (1964b). Selective attention in man. *British Medical Bulletin, 20,* 12–16.

Treisman, A. M. (1964c). The effect of irrelevant material on the efficiency of selective listening. *American Journal of Psychology, 77,* 533–546.

Treisman, A. M. (1969). Strategies and models of selective attention. *Psychological Review, 76,* 242–299.

Treisman, A. M. (1977). Focused attention in the perception and retrieval of multidimensional stimuli. *Perception and Psychophysics, 22,* 1–11.

Treisman, A. M. (1986). Personal communication, April 23.

Treisman, A. M., & Geffen, G. (1967). Selective attention: Perception or response? *Quarterly Journal of Experimental Psychology, 19,* 1–17.

Treisman, A. M., & Gelade, G. (1980). A feature integration theory of attention. *Cognitive Psychology, 12,* 97–136.

Treisman, A. M., & Riley, J. (1969). Is selective attention selective perception or selective response? A further test. *Journal of Experimental Psychology, 79,* 27–34.

Treisman, A. M., Squire, R., & Green, J. (1974). Semantic processing in dichotic listening? A replication. *Memory and Cognition, 2,* 641–646.

Treisman, A. M., & Williams, T. C. (1984). A theory of criterion setting with an application to sequential dependencies. *Psychological Review, 91,* 68–111.

Trotter, R. J. (1986). Three heads are better than one. *Psychology Today,* Aug., 56–62.

Tufte, E. R. (1983). *The visual display of quantitative information.* Cheshire, CT: Graphics Press.

Tulving, E. (1962). Subjective organization in free recall of "unrelated" words. *Psychological Review, 69,* 344–354.

Tulving, E. (1972). Episodic and semantic memory. In E. Tulving & W. Donaldson (Eds.), *Organization of memory.* New York: Academic Press.

Tulving, E. (1974). Cue-dependent forgetting. *American Scientist, 62,* 74–82.

Tulving, E. (1983). *Elements of episodic memory.* London: Clarendon Press/Oxford University Press.

Tulving, E. (1984). Organization of memory: Quo vadis? In M. S. Gazzaniga (Ed.), *The Cognitive Neurosciences.* Cambridge, MA: The MIT Press.

Tulving, E. (1984). Precis of *Elements of episodic memory. Behavioral and Brain Sciences, 7,* 223–268.

Tulving, E. (1985a). How many memory systems are there? *American Psychologist, 40,* 385–398.

Tulving, E. (1985b). Memory and consciousness. *Canadian Psychologist, 26,* 1–11.

Tulving, E. (1986). What kind of a hypothesis is the distinction between episodic and semantic memory? *Journal of Experimental Psychology: Learning, Memory, and Cognition, 12,* 307–311.

Tulving, E. (1989a). Remembering and knowing the past. *American Scientist, 77,* 361–367.

Tulving, E. (1989b). Memory: Performance, knowledge, and experience. *European Journal of Cognitive Psychology, 1,* 3–26.

Tulving, E. (1993). What is episodic memory? *Current Directions in Psychological Science, 2,* 67–70.

Tulving, E., & Arbuckle, T. Y. (1963). Sources of intratrial interference in immediate recall of paired associates. *Journal of Verbal Learning and Verbal Behavior, 1,* 321–334.

Tulving, E., & Gold, C. (1963). Stimulus information and contextual information as determinants of tachistoscopic recognition of words. *Journal of Experimental Psychology, 66*, 319–327.

Tulving, E., & Hastie, R. (1972). Inhibition effects of intralist repetition in free recall. *Journal of Experimental Psychology, 92*, 297–304.

Tulving, E., Kapur, S., Craik, F. I. M., Moscovitch, M., & Houle, S. (1994). Hemispheric encoding/retrieval asymmetry in episodic memory: Positron emission tomography findings. *Proceedings of the National Academy of Sciences, 91*, 2016–2020. Washington, D. C.: National Academy of Sciences.

Tulving, E., & Madigan, S. A. (1970). Memory and verbal learning. In P. H. Mussen & M. R. Rosenzweig (Eds.), *Annual Review of Psychology* (Vol. 21). Palo Alto, CA: Annual Reviews.

Tulving, E., & Osler, S. (1968). Effectiveness of retrieval cues in memory for words. *Journal of Experimental Psychology, 77*(4), 593–601.

Tulving, E., & Pearlstone, Z. (1966). Availability versus accessibility of information in memory for words. *Journal of Verbal Learning and Verbal Behavior, 5*, 381–391.

Tulving, E., & Psotka, J. (1971). Retroactive inhibition in free recall: Inaccessibility of information available in the memory store. *Journal of Experimental Psychology, 87*, 1–8.

Tulving, E., & Schacter, D. L. (1990). Priming and human memory systems. *Science, 247*, 301–306.

Tulving, E., & Thompson, D. M. (1971). Retrieval processes in recognition memory. *Journal of Experimental Psychology, 87*, 116–124.

Tulving, E., & Thompson, D. M. (1973). Encoding specificity and retrieval processing in episodic memory. *Psychological Review, 80*, 352–373.

Turing, A. M. (1950). Computing machinery and intelligence. *Mind, 59*, 433–460.

Tversky, A. (1972). Elimination by aspects: A theory of choice. *Psychological Review, 79*, 281–299.

Tversky, A., & Hutchinson, J. W. (1986). Nearest neighbor analysis of psychological spaces. *Psychological Review, 93*, 3–22.

Tversky, A., & Kahneman, D. (1973). Availability: A heuristic for judging frequency and probability. *Cognitive Psychology, 4*, 207–232.

Tversky, A., & Kahneman, D. (1981). The framing of decisions and the psychology of choice. *Science, 211*, 453–458.

Tversky, B. (1981). Distortions in memory for maps. *Cognitive Psychology, 13*, 407–433.

Tye, M. (1991). *The imagery debate.* Cambridge, MA: The MIT Press.

Uhr, L., & Vossler, C. (1963). A pattern-recognition program that generates, evaluates and adjusts its own operators. In E. A. Feigenbaum & J. Feldman (Eds.), *Computers and thought.* New York: McGraw-Hill.

Underwood, B. J. (1969). Attributes of memory. *Psychological Review, 76*, 559–573.

Underwood, G. (1976). Semantic interference from unattended printed words. *British Journal of Psychology, 67*, 327–338.

Underwood, G. (1977). Contextual facilitation from attended and unattended messages. *Journal of Verbal Learning and Verbal Behavior, 16*, 99–106.

Underwood, G. (1982). *Aspects of consciousness.* New York: Academic Press.

Usher, J. A., & Neisser, U. (1993). Childhood amnesia and the beginnings of memory for four early life events. *Journal of Experimental Psychology: General, 122*, 155–165.

Uttal, W. R. (1978). *The psychobiology of mind.* Hillsdale, NJ: Erlbaum.

Valenta, J., & Potter, W. C. (1984). Soviet decision making for national security. Winchester, MA: Allen & Unwin.

van Dijk, T. A., & Kintsch, W. (1983). *Strategics of discourse comprehension. New York:* Academic Press.

Vaughn, M. E. (1968). Clustering, age and incidental learning. *Journal of Experimental Child Psychology,* 323–331.

Von Frisch, K. (1967). *The dance language and orientation of bees.* Cambridge, MA: Belknap.

von Neumann, J. (1958). *The computer and the brain.* New Haven, CT: Yale University Press.

von Wright, J. M., Anderson, K., & Stenman, U. (1975). Generalization of conditioned GSRs in dichotic listening. In P. M. A. Rabbit & S. Dornic (Eds.), *Attention and performance V.* New York: Academic Press.

Vurpillot, E. (1968). The development of scanning strategies and their relation to visual differentiation. *Journal of Experimental Child Psychology, 6*, 632–650.

Vygotsky, L. S. (1962). Thought and language. Cambridge, MA: The MIT Press. (Originally published in Russian in 1934.)

Vygotsky, L. S. (1934/1978). *Mind in society.* Edited by M. Cole, V. John-Steiner, S. Scribner, & E. Souberman. Cambridge, MA: Harvard University Press.

Wagenaar, W. (1986). My memory: A study of autobiographic memory over the past six years. *Cognitive Psychology, 18*, 225–252.

Wallas, G. (1926). *The art of thought.* New York: Harcourt Brace.

Walton, G. E., & Bower, T. G. R. (1993). Newborns form "prototypes" in less than 1 minute. *Psychological Science, 4,* 203–205.

Wardlaw, K. A., & Kroll, N. E. A. (1976). Autonomic responses to shock-associated words in a non-attended message: A failure to replicate. *Journal of Experimental Psychology: Human Perception and Performance, 2,* 357–360.

Warrington, E. K., & Shallice, T. (1969). The selective impairment of auditory-verbal short-term memory tasks. *Quarterly Journal of Experimental Psychology, 24A,* 30–40.

Watkins, S. H. (1914). Immediate memory and its evaluation. *British Journal of Psychology, 7,* 319–348.

Watson, J. B. (1913). Psychology as a behaviorist views it. *Psychological Review, 20,* 158–170.

Watson, J. B. (1914). *Behavior: An introduction to comparative psychology.* New York: Holt.

Watson, J. B. (1919). *Psychology from the standpoint of behaviorist.* Philadelphia: Lippincott.

Waugh, N. C., & Norman, D. A. (1965). Primary memory. *Psychological Review, 72,* 89–104.

Weaver, W. (1949). Introductory note on the general setting of the analytic communication studies. In C. E. Shannon & W. Weaver (Eds.), *The mathematical theory of communication.* Urbana: University of Illinois Press.

Wechsler, S. B. (1963). Engrams, memory storage, and mnemonic coding. *American Psychologist, 18,* 149–153.

Weiskrantz, L. (1966). Experimental studies in amnesia. In C. W. M. Whitty & O. L. Zangwill (Eds.), *Amnesia.* London: Butterworth.

Weiss, A. P. (1967). 1 + 1 ≠ 2 (one plus one does not equal two). In G. C. Quarton, T. Melnechuk, & F. O. Schmitt (Eds.), *The neurosciences* (pp. 801–821). New York: Rockefeller University Press.

Weisstein, N. (1973). Beyond the yellow Volkswagen detector and the grandmother cell: A general strategy for the exploration of operations in human pattern recognition. In R. L. Solso (Ed.), *Contemporary issues in cognitive psychology: The Loyola Symposium.* Washington, DC: Winston/Wiley.

Weist, R. M., & Crowford, J. (1977). The development of organized rehearsal. *Journal of Experimental Child Psychology, 24,* 164–179.

Weizenbaum, J. (1966). ELIZA—A computer program for the study of the natural language communication between man and machine. *Communication Associates Computing Machinery, 9,* 36–45.

Weizenbaum, J. (1976). *Computer power and human reason: From judgment to calculation* (pp. xii-300). San Francisco: Freeman.

Welch, J. C. (1898). On the measurement of mental activity through muscular activity and the determination of a constant of attention. *American Journal of Physiology, 1,* 283–306.

Wertheim, T. (1934). Über die indirekte Sehsharfe. *Zeitschrift fur Psychologie, 7,* 172–187.

Wertheimer, M. (1912). Experimentelle Studein über das Sehen von Bewegung. *Zeitschrift fur Psychologie, 61,* 161–265.

Wertheimer, M. (1923). Untersuchungen zur Lehre von der Gestalt. II. *Psychologie Forschung,* 301–350. Reprinted in D. C. Beardslee & M. Wertheimer (Eds.), *Readings in perception.* Princeton, NJ: Van Nostrand, 1958.

Wertheimer, M. (1945). *Productive thinking.* New York: Harper & Row.

Wertheimer, M. (1958). Principles of perceptual organization. In D. C. Beardslee & M. Wertheimer (Eds.), *Readings in perception.* Princeton, NJ: Van Nostrand.

Wertsch, J. V. (1985a). *Vygotsky and the social formation of mind.* Cambridge, MA: Harvard University Press.

Wertsch, J. V. (Ed.). (1985b). *Culture, communication, and cognition: Vygotskian perspectives.* Cambridge, England: Cambridge University Press.

Wheeler, D. (1970). Processes in word recognition. *Cognitive Psychology, 1,* 59–85.

Wheeler, M. A., & Roediger, H. L. (1992). Disparate effects of repeated testings: Reconciling Ballard's (1913) and Bartlett's (1932) results. *Psychological Science, 3,* 240–245.

White, K., Sheehan, P. W., & Aston, R. (1977). Imagery assessment: A survey of self-report measures. *Journal of Mental Imagery, 1,* 145–170.

Whitehead, R. (1991a). Right hemisphere processing superiority during sustained visual attention. *Journal of Cognitive Neuroscience, 3,* 329–334.

Whitehead, R. (1991b). Right hemisphere superiority during sustained visual attention. *Journal of Cognitive Neuroscience, 3–4,* 329–331.

Whorf, B. L. (1956). A linguistic consideration of thinking in primitive communities. In J. B. Carroll (Ed.), *Language, thought, and reality.* New York: Wiley.

Wickelgren, W. A. (1965). Acoustic similarity and intrusion errors in short-term memory. *Journal of Experimental Psychology, 70,* 102–108.

Wickelgren, W. A. (1968). Sparing of short-term memory in an amnesiac: Implications for strength, theory of memory. *Neuropsychologia, 6*, 235–244.

Wickelgren, W. A. (1970). Time, interference and rate of presentation in short-term recognition memory. *Journal of Mathematical Psychology, 7*, 219–235.

Wickelgren, W. A. (1973). The long and short of memory. *Psychological Bulletin, 80*, 425–538.

Wickens, D. D. (1970). Encoding categories of words: An empirical approach to meaning. *Psychological Review, 77*, 1–15.

Wickens, D. D. (1972). Characteristics of word encoding. In A. Melton & E. Martin (Eds.), *Coding processes in human memory* (pp. 191–215). Washington, DC: Winston.

Wickens, D. D., Born, D. G., & Allen, C. K. (1963). Proactive inhibition and item similarity in short-term memory. *Journal of Verbal Learning and Verbal Behavior, 2*, 440–445.

Wickens, D. D., Clark, S. E., Hill, F. A., & Wittlinger, R. P. (1968). Grammatical class as an encoding category in short-term memory. *Journal of Experimental Psychology 78*, 599–604.

Wickens, D. D., & Engle, R. W. (1970). Imagery and abstractness in short-term memory. *Journal of Experimental Psychology, 84*, 268–272.

Wilkins, A., & Stewart, A. 1974). The time course of lateral asymmetrics in visual perception of letters. *Journal of Experimental Psychology, 102*, 905–908.

Wilkins, M. C. (1917). Unpublished M. A. thesis, Columbia University. In R. S. Woodworth (Ed.), *Experimental psychology.* New York: Holt.

Wilks, Y. (1973). An artificial intelligence approach to machine translation. In R. Schank & K. Colby (Eds.), *Computer models of thought and language.* San Francisco: Freeman.

Williams, J. D. (1971). Memory ensemble selection in human information processing. *Journal of Experimental Psychology, 88*, 231–238.

Winikoff, A. (1973). Eye movements and an aid to protocal analysis of problem solving behavior. Unpublished Ph.D. dissertation, Carnegie Mellon University. Cited by A. Newell in "Artificial intelligence and the concept of mind." In R. Schank & K. Colby (Eds.), *Computer models of thought and language.* San Francisco: Freeman.

Winograd, T. (1972). *Understanding natural languages.* New York: Academic Press.

Winograd, T. (1974). Artificial intelligence: When will computers understand people? *Psychology Today.* May.

Winograd, T. (1975). Computer memories: A metaphor for memory organization. In C. Cofer (Ed.), *The structure of human memory.* San Francisco: Freeman.

Winograd, T. (1981). What does it mean to understand language? In D. A. Norman (Ed.), *Perspectives on cognitive science.* Norwood, NJ: Ablex.

Winograd, T. (1985). *Language as a cognitive process.* Reading, MA: Addison-Wesley.

Winokur, S. (1976). *A primer of verbal behavior: An operant view.* Englewood Cliffs, NJ: Prentice-Hall.

Winston, P. H. (1970). *Learning structural description from examples* (Project MAC-TR-231-447-48, 450-52, 460-480-82). Cambridge, MA: MIT Artificial Intelligence Laboratory.

Winston, P. H. (1973). Learning to identify toy block structures. In R. L. Solso (Ed.), *Contemporary issues in cognitive psychology: The Loyola Symposium.* Washington, DC: Winston/Wiley.

Winston, P. H. (1975). *The psychology of computer vision.* New York: McGraw-Hill.

Winston, P. H. (1984). *Artificial intelligence* (2nd ed.). Reading, MA: Addison-Wesley.

Wollen, K. A., & Lowry, D. H. (1971). Effects of imagery on paired-associate learning. *Journal of Verbal Learning and Verbal Behavior, 10*, 276–284.

Wollen, K. A., Weber, A., & Lowry, D. H. (1972). Bizarreness versus interaction of mental images as determinants of learning. *Cognitive Psychology, 3*, 518–523.

Wood, C. C. (1975). Auditory and phonetic levels of processing in speech perception: Neurophysiological and information-processing analyses. *Journal of Experimental Psychology: Human Perception and Performance, 104*, 3–20.

Woodson, W. E. (1954). *Human engineering guide for equipment designers.* Berkeley: University of California Press.

Woodworth, R. S. (1929). *Psychology.* New York: Holt.

Woodworth, R. S. (1938). *Experimental psychology.* New York: Holt.

Woodworth, R. S. (1948). *Contemporary schools of psychology* (revised). New York: Ronald.

Woodworth, R. S., & Sells, S. B. (1935). An atmosphere effect in formal syllogistic reasoning. *Journal of Experimental Psychology, 18*, 451–460.

Woolridge, D. E. (1968). *Mechanical man: The physical basis of intellectual life.* New York: McGraw-Hill.

Wundt, W. (1892). In R. Woodworth (Ed.), *Contemporary schools of psychology* (p. 24). New York: Ronald.

Wundt, W. (1905). *Grundriss der Psychologie.* Leipzig: Englemann.

Yarbus, A. L. (1967). *Eye movements and vision* (B. Haigh, trans.). New York: Plenum.

Yates, F. A. (1966). *The art of memory.* Chicago: University of Chicago Press.

Yerkes, R. M., & Dodson, J. D. (1908). The relation of strengths of stimulus to rapidity of habit-formation. *Journal of Comparative Neurological Psychology, 18,* 459–482.

Yoshimura, E. K., Moely, B. E., & Shapiro, S. I. (1971). The influence of age and presentation order upon children's free recall and learning to learn. *Psychonomic Science, 23,* 261–263.

Young, L. R. (1963). Measuring eye movements. *American Journal of Medical Electronics, 2,* 300–307.

Young, M. N., & Gibson, W. B. (1974). *How to develop an exceptional memory.* North Hollywood, CA: Wilshire.

Young, R. K. (1975). *Human learning and memory.* New York: Harper & Row.

Yuille, J. C., & Catchpole, M. J. (1977). The role of imagery in models of cognition. *Journal of Mental Imagery, 1,* 171–180.

Yuille, J. C., & Paivio, A. (1967). Latency of imaginal and verbal mediators as a function of stimulus and response concreteness-imagery. *Journal of Experimental Psychology, 75,* 540–544.

Zaffy, D. J., & Bruning, J. L. (1966). Drive and the range of cue utilization. *Journal of Experimental Psychology, 71,* 382–384.

Zinchenko, P. I. (1962). *Neproizvol'noe azpominanie* (Involuntary memory) (pp. 172–207). Moscow: USSR APN RSFSR.

Zinchenko, P. I. (1981). Involuntary memory and the goal-directed nature of activity. In J. V. Wertsch, *The concept of activity in Soviet psychology.* Armonk, NY: Sharpe.

Zola-Morgan, S., & Squire, L. R. (1990). Neuropsychological investigations of memory and amnesia: Findings from humans and nonhuman primates. In A. Diamond (Ed.), *The development and neural bases of higher cognitive functions.* New York: New York Academy of Sciences.

NAME INDEX

SUBJECT INDEX

Credits

Credits, *(Cont'd)*